DOMESDAY BOOK

Norfolk

History from the Sources

DOMESDAY BOOK

A Survey of the Counties of England

LIBER DE WINTONIA

Compiled by direction of

KING WILLIAM I

Winchester
1086

DOMESDAY BOOK

general editor
JOHN MORRIS

33

Norfolk

edited by
Philippa Brown

from a draft translation prepared by
Marian Hepplestone, Janet Mothersill and Margaret Newman

(Part Two)

PHILLIMORE
Chichester
1984

1984
Published by
PHILLIMORE & CO. LTD.
London and Chichester
Head Office: Shopwyke Hall,
Chichester, Sussex, England

© Mrs. Susan Morris, 1984

ISBN 0 85033 478 0 (case)
ISBN 0 85033 479 9 (limp)

Printed in Great Britain by
Biddles Ltd., King's Lynn, Norfolk

NORFOLK

(Part One)
Introduction

The Domesday Survey of Norfolk
(to Landholder XI, Bishop Osbern)

(Part Two)

The Domesday Survey of Norfolk
(Landholder XII, Godric the steward to
LXVI, Annexations)

Notes
Index of Persons
Index of Places
Maps and Map Keys
Systems of Reference
Technical Terms

H*vnd*. *de* G*renehov*.T*erræ*. GOdrici dapiferi. .XII.

Godeſtuna . ten& . Oſgotus libe . Semp . xii . uiłł . 7 . xvi . borđ.

★ Tc̄ . iiii . ſeruꝰ p̄ 7 modo . i . Semp in dn̄io . ii . car̊ . & . hom̊ . v . 7 . x.

202 b

libi homines manebant ibi . quos rex . W . dedit Ro . comiti . & p̄ea
. G . in quoꝛ . ii . bꝫ habebat Stigandus . Archi . eps̄ . com̄atione . Semp
int̄ eos . iii . car̊ . Silua . ad xx . porc̊ . Tc̄ . iii . molin̄ . modo . v . & . i.
piſcar̊ . & . iiii . ac̊ . p̄ti . Inuen̄ . G . vii . an̄ . modo . ſimilit̄ modo
iii . runc̊ . Tc̄ . li . ou̅s . modo . c . 7 h̄t . i . lḡ in longo . & dim̊ in lato.
& de gelto redđ . xiii . đ . Tc̄ uał . l . ſoł . 7 p̄ . c . ſoł . m̄ . vi . lib̄.

⁊ In acr . tenuit qđā lib̄ ho̅ oſwart . terra ad . ii . boů . modo . G.
& uał . xv . đ.

⁊ In oxenburch . jacent . lx . ac̄ . q̄ ten̄ . i . lib̄ ho̅ . & . i . uiłł . & p̄tin&
in godeſtuna . ap̄ptiate ſt̄.

⁊ F*eorhov* . H̄ W*aranpli*n̄c*ham* . xlv . ac̄ . terræ
tenuit Eduinus lib̄ ho̅ . t . r . e . ſemp ii . uiłł . & . vi . borđ . & . iiii . ac̄
p̄ti . & dim̊ moli . & . iii . car̊ . Tc̄ uał . xx . ſoł modo . xl.

⁊ In toketorp ten̄ Galfus . i . ſocꝰ . edrici . xx . ac̊ terræ & dim̊ . car̊.
& dim̊ molin̊ . 7 uał . v . ſoł . & totū Waranplicham . h̄t dim̊ lḡ in lōgo.
& dim̊ in lato . & . ix . đ . de gelto.

⁊ W*alessam* . H̄ . In opetune . ten& Rađ . iii . libi hoes . & . i.
in Waleſſā . de . l . ac̄ . terræ x . ac̄ p̄ti . ſemp . i . car̊ . Tc̄ uał . x . ſoł . m̄ . xxi . s.
& ſt̄ in ſoca regis

LANDS OF GODRIC THE STEWARD

The Hundred of (South) GREENHOE
1 Osgot held GOODERSTONE freely.
   Always 12 villagers; 16 smallholders. Then 4 slaves, later and now 1.
   Always 2 ploughs in lordship; 5 men's [ploughs].
   Also 10 free men dwelt there whom King W(illiam) gave to Earl R(alph) and later to G(odric), in 2 of whom Archbishop Stigand had the patronage. 202 b
   Always 3 ploughs between them.
   Woodland for 20 pigs. Then 3 mills, now 5. 1 fishery; meadow, 4 acres. G(odric) found 7 head of cattle, now the same. Now 3 cobs. Then 51 sheep, now 100.
   It has 1 league in length and ½ in width, it pays tax of 13d.
   Value then 50s; later 100s; now £6.

2 In (South) ACRE a certain free man, Osward, held; land for 2 oxen. Now G(odric holds).
   Value 15d.

3 In OXBOROUGH appertain 60 acres which 1 free man held.
   1 villager.
   It belongs in Gooderstone. They are assessed (there).

FOREHOE Hundred
4 Ralph (holds) WRAMPLINGHAM, 45 acres of land. Edwin, a free man, held before 1066.
   Always 2 villagers; 6 smallholders.
   Meadow, 4 acres; ½ mill; 3 ploughs.
   Value then 20s; now 40.

5 In *TOKETORP* Walter holds; 1 Freeman of Edric's, 20 acres of land.
   ½ plough; ½ mill.
   Value 5s.
   The whole of Wramplingham has ½ league in length and ½ in width, tax of 9d.

WALSHAM Hundred
6 In UPTON Ralph holds; 3 free men and 1 in (South) WALSHAM, at 50 acres of land;
   meadow, 10 acres.
   Always 1 plough.
   Value then 10s; now 21s.
   They are in the King's jurisdiction.

Adhuc in WALESSā ten̄& gert.1.libum hom̄ femi
nā touū de.1.car̄ terre. Sēp.111.bord̄.& dim̄.car̄. 7 xx.ac̄ p̄ti.
Silua.vii.porc̄.dim̄ salin̄.& ibi adhuc xvii.soc̄.de.1.car̄.terræ.
semp.1.car̄.& dim̄.xii.ac̄ p̄ti. Tc̄ ual.x.sol.modo.xx.com̄s h̄t
socā.De istis.111.in optune.7.1.lib̄ hō in Walessam.1.fuit com̄d
touū.11.abbis de holmo.tercius retgari.

203 a

HEINESTEDE. H̃. In stoke ten̄ id.1.lib̄ hō.&.1.soc̄.Edwini
de.L.1111.ac̄ terræ.&.111.ac̄ p̄ti.& sub eis.1.uill̄. Semp.1.car̄ & d̄.
In porrikelanda.1.lib̄ hō.eduini.t.r.e.de xii.ac̄.&.1.bord̄.&
d̄ ac̄.p̄ti.Semp.dim̄.car̄.
In framingahā.1.lib̄ hō eduini com̄.de.xx.ac̄ terræ.&.11.bord̄.
semp 7.1.ac̄.7 dim̄ p̄ti.Semp.dim̄.car̄.7 sub eo integri.111.libi
hoēs 7.111.dim̄ int̄ oēs.x.ac̄.terræ Semp int̄ om̄s.dim̄.car̄.
In ailuertuna.11.libi hoēs edwini.de xiii.ac̄.7 dim̄.Tc̄.dim̄.car̄.
Modo nichil.
In holuestuna.1111.integri libi hoēs 7 1111.& dim̄ eduuini.
de xL.ac̄ terræ.7.111.ac̄.p̄ti.&.1.bord̄. Semp 1.car̄ & dim̄.
In ead̄.11.soc̄.11.ac̄ terræ. In rokelund.vi.integri libi hoēs
Edwini.&.11.dim̄.Lx.ac̄.Semp.1.car̄ & dim̄.
In brambretuna.11.libi hoēs Eduuini.d̄.xi.ac̄. Sēp dim̄.car̄.7.
.1.ac̄.& dim̄.p̄ti.
In sutherlingahā.11.integri libi hoēs edwini.& 1111.d̄.xL.ac̄
terræ.7.111.ac̄ p̄ti.&.1111.bord̄. Semp.1.car̄.

Further in (South) WALSHAM Gyrth holds 1 free man, the woman Tofa, at 1 c. of land.
> Always 3 smallholders.
> ½ plough; meadow, 20 acres; woodland, 7 pigs; ½ salt-house.
> Further 17 free men there, at 1 c. of land.
>> Always 1½ ploughs; meadow, 12 acres.

Value then 10s; now 20.
> The Earl has the jurisdiction.
> Of these 3 in Upton and 1 free man in (South) Walsham, 1 was under the patronage of Tovi, 2 of the Abbot of Holme, and the third of Redger.

HENSTEAD Hundred 203 a

7 In STOKE (Holy Cross) he also holds; 1 free man and 1 Freeman of Edwin's, at 54 acres of land;
> meadow, 3 acres.
> Under them 1 villager.
> Always 1½ ploughs.

8 In PORINGLAND 1 free man of Edwin's before 1066, at 12 acres.
> 1 smallholder.
> Meadow, ½ acre; always ½ plough.

9 In FRAMINGHAM 1 free man under the patronage of Edwin, at 20 acres of land.
> Always 2 smallholders.
> Meadow, 1½ acres. Always ½ plough.
> Also under him 3 whole free men and 3 halves(-a-free-man).

Between them all 10 acres of land.
> Always between them all ½ plough.

10 In YELVERTON 2 free men of Edwin's, at 13½ acres.
> Then ½ plough, now nothing.

11 In HOLVERSTON 4 whole free men and 4 and a half of Edwin's, at 40 acres of land;
> meadow, 3 acres.
> 1 smallholder.
> Always 1½ ploughs.

In the same 2 Freemen; 2 acres of land.

12 In ROCKLAND (St. Mary) 6 whole free men of Edwin's and 2 halves(-a-free-man); 60 acres. Always 1½ ploughs.

13 In BRAMERTON 2 free men of Edwin's, at 11 acres.
> Always ½ plough; meadow, 1½ acres.

14 In SURLINGHAM 2 whole free men of Edwin's and 4 halves(-a-free-man), 40 acres of land;
> meadow, 3 acres.
> 4 smallholders.
> Always 1 plough.

202 b, 203 a

In kerkebei . I . lib hō edwini . d̃ . vi . ac̃ . trae . & ſub eo . iii . libi
de . xi . ac̃ terrae . Int̃ oēs . dim.car.

In Rokelund . iiii . libi hoēs haſlec . viii . ac̃ terrae . & . d̃ ac̃ . p̃ti.
& . iii . bord. & iſte edwin fuit tein dñic . R . e . Tc̃ oēs ual . xl.
ſol M̃ . lx . Et de oib3 his libis ſoca in hund.

Appletuna ten . edwin . t . r . e . p . ii . car̃ terrae . Semp . viii.
bord . & . i . ſeru . Semp in dñio . i . car̃ . 7 dim car̃ hom . & . vi.

203 b

ac̃ p̃ti . Silua ad . xii . porc̃ . 7 . iiii . uas . apū . Semp . i . eq̃ . &.
. v . an . 7 lx . ous . 7 . viii . por . 7 . viii . ſoc . 7 dim . de . xl . ac̃ . terrae.
7 . i . car̃ & dim . & . ii . libi hoēs . eduini ante godrici . de . xl . ac̃.
& . i . ac̃ . & p̃ti . ſemp . i . car̃ . Tc̃ ual . xl . ſol . m̃ . iii . lib . 7 . x . ſol.

LOTHNINGA . H̃ . Halgatuna ten Radulfus quā tenu-
er . iii . libi hoēs . ii . edwini . i . gert . comd . t . r . e . ii . car̃ terrae . Sub
eis . ſemp xii . bord . Semp int oēs . iii . car̃ . 7 dim . In ead uilla . xii.
hoēs . vi . quorū erant in ſoca falde . & alii . vi . erant libi . Int oēs
. xl . ac̃ terrae . Sep . ii . car̃.

In d̃ Aſcebei . vi . libi hoēs integri . 7 vi . dim . Aſlac . 7 Lefrici comd
de xx . ac̃ terrae . Semp . i . car̃ . & dim.

In clakeſtona . ii . libi hoēs aſlac & Lefrici . comd . 7 . vi . d̃ hoēs Int
oms . xvi . ac̃ . terrae . Semp dim . car̃ . Int oēs . xvi . ac̃ p̃ti . & h fuit
libatū . Go . p . i . man . Tc̃ . i . equs . modo . ii . & . ii . an . m̃ . cc . ous . Tc̃
v . porc . m̃ . xl . Tc̃ totū ual . xl . ſol . M̃ . iiii . lib . Rex 7 coms ſoca & ſacā.
Halgatona ht . iiii . qr in longo . 7 . iii . in lato . & de gelto . iiii . d̃.

15 In KIRBY (Bedon) 1 free man of Edwin's, at 6 acres of land.
Under him 3 free (men), at 11 acres of land.
Between them all ½ plough.

16 -In ROCKLAND (St. Mary) 4 free men of Aslac's; 8 acres of land;
meadow, ½ acre.
3 smallholders.
This Edwin was a lord's thane of King Edward's.
Value of all then 40s; now 60.
The jurisdiction of all these free men (is) in the Hundred.

17 Edwin held ALPINGTON before 1066, as 2 c. of land.
Always 8 smallholders; 1 slave.
Always 1 plough in lordship; ½ men's plough; meadow, 6 acres; woodland for 12 pigs; 4 beehives. Always 1 horse; 5 head of cattle; 60 sheep; 8 pigs. 203 b
Also 8 Freemen and a half, at 40 acres of land.
1½ ploughs.
Also 2 free men of Edwin's, the predecessor of Godric, at 40 acres;
meadow, 1 acre. Always 1 plough.
Value then 40s; now £3 10s.

LODDON Hundred

18 Ralph holds HELLINGTON which 3 free men held, 2 under the patronage of Edwin, 1 of Gyrth before 1066; 2 c. of land.
Under them always 12 smallholders.
Always between them all 3½ ploughs.
In the same village 12 men, 6 of whom were in fold-rights and the other 6 were free. Among them all 40 acres of land.
Always 2 ploughs.

19 In half ASHBY (St. Mary) 6 whole free men and 6 halves(-a-free-man) under the patronage of Aslac and Leofric, at 20 acres of land. Always 1½ ploughs.

20 In CLAXTON 2 free men under the patronage of Aslac and Leofric, and 6 halves-a-(free-)man. Between them all 16 acres of land.
Always ½ plough.
Meadow between them all, 16 acres. This was delivered to Godric as 1 manor.
Then 1 horse, now 2. 2 head of cattle. Now 200 sheep. Then 5 pigs, now 40.
Value of the whole then 40s; now £4.
The King and Earl (have) the full jurisdiction.
Hellington has 4 furlongs in length and 3 in width, tax of 4d.

In nortuna . 1 . libā femina . xvi . ac̄ . trāē . & ptin& in halgatona.

In Clareſtona . v . libi hoēs . & dim̄ eduini com̄ . xxx . 1111 . ac̄ terræ . Sēp
d̄ car̄ int̄ oēs . 1 . ac̄ p̄ti . Socā in hund̄ . In Aſebei . 1 . lib̄ & dim̄ . v . ac̄.

In Karlentona . 1111 . libi hoīes . ejd̄ eduini . xxx . ac̄ . Semp dim̄.
car̄ . & . 11 . ac̄ p̄ti . Socā in hund̄ . In lotna . 11 . libi hoēs ejd̄e.
de . xx1111 . ac̄ . Tc̄ & p̄ . 1 . car̄ . m̄ dim̄.

★ In Waſinga ford . 1 . lib̄ hō ejd̄ē . dim̄ xxx . ac̄ . & . 11 . bord̄ . socā in hund̄
& . ſub eo . v1 . libi ejd̄ . xvi . ac̄ . Semp . 11 . car̄ . 1111 . ac̄ p̄ti . & . 1 . mol̄.

204 a

In Siſlanda . 1 . lib̄ hō ejd̄ . de . 111 . ac̄ . In alcmuntona . 111 . libi hoēs
ejd̄e . de . v111 . ac̄ terræ . Semp arant . cū . 111 . bobʒ Socā in hund̄ . &
oēs iſti libi redd̄ . xx . ſol̄ . Altmuntona h̄t . vi qr̄ in longo . 7 . 111 . in
lato . quicūq̢ ibi ten& . & . vi . den̄ de gelto . Torp h̄t . 1 . lḡ in longo
& dim̄ in lato . & de gelto . 1111 . d̄ . & obolū q̇cūq̢ ibi teneat.

HVNDRET DE ENSFORDA. Sparham ten& Edwin
. 1 . lib̄ hō . t . r . e . modo . G . de rege . 11 . car̄ . terræ . ſemp . 11 . uilli . 7
xvi . bord̄ . Tc̄ & . p̄ . 11 . ſer̄ . modo . 1 . Tc̄ & p̄ . 11 . car̄ in dominio . m̄ . 111.
Tc̄ . 1111 . car̄ . hom̄ . p̄ . 7 . modo . 11 . & . vi . ac̄ . p̄ti . 7 . dim̄ . molin̄.
ſilua . c . porc̄ . Qn̄ recep̄ . 11 . runc̄ . modo . 111 . ſemp . v11 . an̄.
& . xx . 111 . porc̄ . Tc̄ . lx . ous̄ . modo . lxxx . modo . x . uaſa apū.
Et lib̄ hō xxx . ac̄ terræ . 1 . ac̄ p̄ti . ſemp . dim̄ . car̄ . 1 . æccl̄ia
xl . ac̄ . & . vi . ac̄ . ſiluæ . Tc̄ & p̄ ual̄ . lx . ſol̄ . modo . c . ſol̄ . & h̄t
. 1 . lḡ in longo . & . x . qr̄ . in lato . 7 reddit . v111 . d̄ . & obolū de gelto.

21 In NORTON (Subcourse) 1 free woman, 16 acres of land. She belongs in Hellington.

22 In CLAXTON 5 free men and a half under the patronage of Edwin, 34 acres of land.
    Always ½ plough among them all.
    Meadow, 1 acre.
    The jurisdiction (is) in the Hundred.
In ASHBY (St. Mary) 1 free (man) and a half, 5 acres.

23 In CARLETON (St. Peter) 4 free men of the same Edwin's, 30 acres.
    Always ½ plough;
    meadow, 2 acres.
    The jurisdiction (is) in the Hundred.
In LODDON 2 free men of the same man's, at 24 acres.
    Then and later 1 plough, now ½.

24 In WASHINGFORD 1 free man of the same man's, half of 30 acres.
    2 smallholders.
    The jurisdiction is in the Hundred.
    Also under him 6 free (men) of the same man's, 16 acres.
        Always 2 ploughs; meadow, 4 acres; 1 mill.

25 In SISLAND 1 free man of the same man's, at 3 acres. In ALCMUNTONA 3 free men of the same man's, at 8 acres of land.
    They have always ploughed with 3 oxen.
    The jurisdiction (is) in the Hundred. All those free (men) pay 20s.

26 ALCMUNTONA has 6 furlongs in length and 3 in width, whoever holds there; tax of 6d.
    TORP has 1 league in length and ½ in width, tax of 4½d, whoever holds there.

The Hundred of EYNSFORD

27 Edwin, 1 free man, held SPARHAM before 1066, now G(odric) from the King; 2 c. of land.
    Always 2 villagers; 16 smallholders. Then and later 2 slaves, now 1.
    Then and later 2 ploughs in lordship, now 3. Then 4 men's ploughs, later and now 2.
    Meadow, 6 acres; ½ mill; woodland, 100 pigs. When he acquired it 2 cobs, now 3. Always 7 head of cattle; 23 pigs. Then 60 sheep, now 80. Now 10 beehives.
    Also a free man, 30 acres of land; meadow, 1 acre. Always ½ plough.
    1 church, 40 acres.
    Woodland, 6 acres.
Value then and later 60s; now 100s.
    It has 1 league in length and 10 furlongs in width; it pays tax of 8½d.

⁊In binétre.ıı.libi hões.xx.aç.terræ.&.ıı.aç.p̄ti.semp.ı.car.
&.ual&.ııı.sol.

HVND.DE TAVRESHAM. In besetuna.ı.lib̄ hō
xxx.aç.dim.car.&.ıı.aç p̄ti.&.ual.ıı.sol.Rex & cōms socā

HVND.DE HVMILIART. Meltuna ten Eduuin⁹
tein t.r.e.ıı.car.terræ.semp.ıx.uill.&.v.bord &.ıııı.
ser.Tc.ıı.car in dominio.P.ı.modo.ıı.Tc.ııı.car hom.
P 7 m.ıı.silu.Lx.porc.xx.aç p̄ti. Semper.ı.molin
Tc.ı.runc.modo.ıı.semp.x.an.7.xııı.porc.modo
xL.ous.ııı.uasa apu.7.ıx.libi hões soca falde & comd tantu.

204 b
.L.aç semp.ıı.car.&.ııı.aç p̄ti Rex & cōms. Rex & cōms socā.& ual.vııı.
sol.& man ual.Tc.vı.lib̄.Post.c.sol.modo.vıı.lib.& ıııı.libi hões
comd tant.xxx.aç terræ.semp.ı.car.&.ı.aç.& dim p̄ti.& ual.v.sol.
⁊In hederseta.ıx.libi homines.xL.ııı.aç.comd tantū & soca falde
semp.ı.car.&.ıı.aç p̄ti.& ual.v.sol.
⁊Paruā Meltunā.ten Eduuin⁹.t.r.e.de sc̄o benedicto.&.ita qd eā
abbati.concesserat post morte suā.semp.ıı.car terræ.&.ııı.bord.&
.ı.seru.&.ıı.car in dominio.ııı.aç p̄ti.semp.ı.runc.&.v.an.modo
xv.porc.7 Lxxxx.ous.Tc ual.xL.sol.p̄ Lx.modo.ıııı.lib.huic manerio adjacent semp.xıı.libi homines com tantu.& soca falde.
dim.car terre.7.ııı.aç.semp.ııı.car.7.ııı.aç p̄ti.& ual.xx.
sol. In his duabz meltunis.ı.car terræ ten quida lib̄ hō teinn⁹
&iā.t.r.e.pro manerio.Tc.ııı.uill.&.ı.car in dn̄io.& dim
★ car hom.hoc ten& Godric⁹.& tenebat qn.R.fecit 7 ē in p̄tio de
duobz maneriis.

28 In BINTREE 2 free men, 20 acres of land; meadow, 2 acres.
    Always 1 plough.
Value 3s.

The Hundred of TAVERHAM
29 In BEESTON (St. Andrew) 1 free man, 30 acres.
    ½ plough; meadow, 2 acres.
Value 2s.
    The King and the Earl (have) the jurisdiction.

The Hundred of HUMBLEYARD
30 Edwin, a thane, held (Great) MELTON before 1066, 2 c. of land.
    Always 9 villagers; 5 smallholders; 4 slaves.
    Then 2 ploughs in lordship, later 1, now 2. Then 3 men's
      ploughs, later and now 2.
    Woodland, 60 pigs; meadow, 20 acres; always 1 mill. Then 1
      cob, now 2. Always 10 head of cattle; 13 pigs. Now 40
      sheep; 3 beehives.
    Also 9 free men in fold-rights and patronage only, 50 acres.   204 b
    Always 2 ploughs; meadow, 3 acres.
    The King and the Earl (have) the jurisdiction.
Value 8s. Value of the manor then £6; later 100s; now £7.
    Also 4 free men in patronage only, 30 acres of land.
    Always 1 plough; meadow, 1½ acres.
Value 5s.

31 In HETHERSETT 9 free men, 43 acres, in patronage only and in
    fold-rights. Always 1 plough; meadow, 2 acres.
Value 5s.

32 Edwin held LITTLE MELTON before 1066 from St. Benedict in such
    a way that he had granted it to the Abbot after his death; always
    2 c. of land.
    3 smallholders; 1 slave.
    2 ploughs in lordship; meadow, 3 acres. Always 1 cob; 5 head
      of cattle. Now 15 pigs; 90 sheep.
Value then 40s; later 60; now £4.
    12 free men have always been attached to this manor in
    patronage only and in fold-rights; ½ c. of land and 3 acres.
    Always 3 ploughs; meadow, 3 acres.
Value 20s.
    In these two Meltons a certain free man, (who was) also a
    thane, held 1 c. of land before 1066 as a manor.
        Then 3 villagers.
        1 plough in lordship; ½ men's plough.
    Godric holds this and held it when R(alph) forfeited. It is in
    the valuation of the 2 manors.

In Meltuna . ix . libi hões comd tantũ . c . x . ac . semp . ii . bord . Tc
. iii . car . 7 dim . modo . iiii . v . ac . & dim pti . silua . iiii . porc . Tc
ual . xxiii . sol . modo . xxx . & . viii . d . & parua Maltuna ht . x . qr
in longo . & . v . in lat . & . viii . d . 7 . i . ferdinc . de gelto.

In coleneia ten Walt xviii . libi hões . com tantũ 7 xxx ac . i . car
terræ & dim . & . ii . bord . Tc . v . car . m . iiii . & . vii . ac . pti . & . i . mol.
7 . i . lib hõ . sub ante Rogi . bigot . comdatione . tantũ . & ten&
dim ac . terræ q mercatus e . pq rad forisfecit de terra rogeri.

Tc ual . xxx . sol . modo . xl . 7 ht . viii . qr in longo . & . viii . in lato.

& . viii . d . & . i . ferding de gelto.

In hedeRseta ten ide . iiii . libi homines comd tantũ . lx . ac
semp . i . car & dim . & . v . ac pti . 7 ual . x . sol . & . viii . d . Rex & coms soc.
In ead ten . id . xvi . libi homines comd tantũ . xxxiii . ac . sep . i . car & dim.
& ual . iii . sol . & . iiii . d . Coms . Alanus soca.

In dunestun . vii . libi hões 7 dim . comd tantũ . c . xi . ac . & . i . bord
semp . i . car & dim . & . i . molin . & . ii . ac pti . 7 ual . xiii . sol . & ht
dim lg in longo . & . iii . qr in lato . 7 vi . d . & obolũ de gelto.

In Suerdest . vii . xl . ii . ac . ii . libi hões . 7 d comd tant . & . i . bord.
semp . i . car . & . i . ac pti . & ual . vi . sol.

In florenduna . iii . libi hões . xviiii . ac træ . t . r . e . semp dim car
& ual . ii . sol . & . viii . d . duos ex his tenuit antec . Ro . bigot comd
tantũ . & de tercio ./ antec . Godrici similit . modo totũ ten& Go-
-dric

33 In (Great) MELTON 9 free men in patronage only; 110 acres.
Always 2 smallholders.
Then 3½ ploughs, now 4. Meadow, 5½ acres; woodland, 4 pigs.
Value then 23s; now 30(s) 8d.
Little Melton has 10 furlongs in length and 5 in width, tax of 8¼d.

34 In COLNEY Walter holds; 18 free men in patronage only; 30 acres, 1½ c. of land.
2 smallholders.
Then 5 ploughs, now 4. Meadow, 7 acres; 1 mill.
Also 1 free man under the patronage only of the predecessor of Roger Bigot. He holds ½ acre of land which he bought, after Ralph forfeited, from Roger's land.
Value then 30s; now 40.
It has 8 furlongs in length and 8 in width, tax of 8¼d. 205 a

35 In HETHERSETT he also holds; 4 free men in patronage only, 60 acres. Always 1½ ploughs; meadow, 5 acres.
Value 10s 8d.
The King and Earl (have) the jurisdiction.

In the same he also holds; 16 free men in patronage only, 33 acres.
Always 1½ ploughs.
Value 3s 4d.
Count Alan (has) the jurisdiction.

36 In DUNSTON 7 free men and a half in patronage only, 111 acres.
1 smallholder.
Always 1½ ploughs; 1 mill; meadow, 2 acres.
Value 13s.
It has ½ league in length and 3 furlongs in width, tax of 6½d.

37 In SWARDESTON 7 [free men], 42 acres; 2 free men and a half in patronage only.
1 smallholder.
Always 1 plough; meadow, 1 acre.
Value 6s.

38 In FLORDON 3 free men, 19 acres of land before 1066.
Always ½ plough.
Value 2s 8d.
Two of these Roger Bigot's predecessor held in patronage only, and Godric's predecessor the third likewise. Now Godric holds the whole.

⁊In Kenincham ten̄ Ancholfus̨.ɪ.foc̷.xxx.ac̄.femper dim̄⁊.car⁊.&.ual.v.fol.
⁊In fueineftorp.ɪɪ.foc̷⁊.xxx.v.ac̷⁊.femp dim̄⁊.car⁊.7.ɪ.bord̄.&.ɪ.ac̷⁊ p̄ti.7 ual.ɪɪ.fol.&.vɪɪɪ.d̄.
⁊In Kefewic.ɪ.hȏ.x.ac̷⁊.7 ual xvɪ.d̄.Rex & cōms fup ōīns focā.
⁊CLAVELINGA.H̃.Hechinchā.tenuit hagana de ftigand t.r̃.ē.ɪɪɪɪ.car⁊.terræ.femp.vɪ.uilli.&.vɪ.bord̄.&.ɪ.feru⁊.Tc̄.ɪ.car⁊ in dominio.m̄.ɪɪ.Tc̄.ɪɪ.car⁊ hom̃.modo.ɪ.&.ɪɪ.car⁊ poffent fieri.x.ac̄ p̄ti.filua.ɪɪɪɪ porc̷.femp.ɪ.molin.Marefc.ʟx.oūs. Tc̄.ɪ.runc̷.modo.ɪɪ.modo.ɪɪɪɪ.añ.7 xx.porc̷.&.ɪ.æcclia .vɪɪɪ.ac̷⁊.Ex h̃.xxx.ac̷⁊.terræ.calūpniat⁊.R.bigot ad feud̄

205 b   ⁊Aleftani.
7 xvɪɪ libi homines.ɪ.car⁊.ɪ.car⁊ terræ.com̃d⁊ tantū.Tc̄.ɪɪɪɪ.car⁊ m̄.ɪɪɪ.7.ɪɪɪ.ac̄ p̄ti.huic manerio addidit.cōms.R.vɪɪɪ.libos.hoēs t.r.Wilłmi.&.hnt.ɪ.car⁊ terræ.&.ɪɪ.bord̄.&.vɪ.libi hoēs⁊ fub illis .xɪɪ.ac̷.Tc̄ & p̄⁹.ɪɪɪɪ.car⁊.modo.ɪɪɪ.vɪɪ.ac̄ p̄ti.Maneriū ual.Tc̄ xx fol⁒ modo ʟx.7 libi homines.xxx.fol.Tota ĥt.ɪ.lḡ in longo.&.vɪɪɪ. qr̃ in lato.7 xɪɪ.d̄.de gelto.
⁊In hals dim̄ lib ȟȏ.ɪ.ac̷⁊ & dim̄.&.ual.ɪɪɪ.d̄.
⁊In nortuna.ɪɪɪ.libi hoēs⁊ sc̃i benedicti.xxxvɪɪ.ac̷.&.dim̄⁊.femp.ɪ.car⁊. &.ual.v.fol.⁊In Sudwda.ɪ.lib ȟȏ.ɪ.ac̷ terræ de q̨⁊ habuit ante ceffor Rog̃ filii Rainart.com̃d⁊.t.r.e.&.ual.ɪɪ.d̄.
Hunc tenebat godric⁹ qn̄.R.forisfecit.

39 In KENNINGHAM Ansculf holds; 1 Freeman, 30 acres.
Always ½ plough.
Value 5s.

40 In SWAINSTHORPE 2 Freemen, 35 acres.
Always ½ plough.
1 smallholder.
Meadow, 1 acre.
Value 2s 8d.

41 In KESWICK 1 man, 10 acres.
Value 16d.
The King and Earl (have) the jurisdiction over all.

CLAVERING Hundred

42 Hagni held HECKINGHAM from Stigand before 1066, 4 c. of land.
Always 6 villagers; 6 smallholders; 1 slave.
Then 1 plough in lordship, now 2. Then 2 men's ploughs, now 1, 2 could be there.
Meadow, 10 acres; woodland, 4 pigs. Always 1 mill; marsh, 60 sheep. Then 1 cob, now 2. Now 4 head of cattle; 20 pigs.
Also 1 church, 8 acres.
From this R(oger) Bigot claims 30 acres of land as part of Alstan's Holding.   205 b
Also 17 free men, 1 c. of land in patronage only.
Then 4 ploughs, now 3. Meadow, 3 acres.
To this manor Earl R(alph) added 8 free men after 1066; they have 1 c. of land.
2 smallholders and 6 free men under them, 12 acres.
Then and later 4 ploughs, now 3. Meadow, 7 acres.
Value of the manor then 20s; now 60; the free men, 30s.
The whole has 1 league in length and 8 furlongs in width, tax of 12d.

43 In HALES a half-a-free-man, 1½ acres.
Value 3d.

44 In NORTON (Subcourse) 3 free men of St. Benedict's; 37½ acres.
Always 1 plough.
Value 5s.

45 In SOUTHWOOD 1 free man, 1 acre of land. The predecessor of Roger son of Rainard had the patronage of him before 1066.
Value 2d.
Godric held this when R(alph) forfeited.

XIII.

TERRÆ HERMERI. H̄. DE CLACHESLofa.

In marſam . xx . āc tenuit Turchetel ad ſochã ſc̄e Adelđ . Semp
ii . uiłłi . q̃ tc̄ habebant . iii . boues . m̄ . ii . & . i . āc . p̄ti . Semp uał .
. iii . ſoł . iiii . đ . min̂ . h̄ tr̄a m̄ſurata ē in breui . S̃ ᴀdel.

¶ In Phinchã . iii . uiłłi . 7 . xv . borđ . 7 vii . ſeru . 7 . iii . car̂ in dominio.
7 xiii . āc p̄ti . Tc̄ . iiii . runc̄ . modo . i . Tc̄ . xii . an̂ . modo . ix . Tc̄ . xxx.
porc̄ . modo xxvi . Tc̄ . cc . lx . oūs . m̄ . clxxv . Semp uał . viii . liƀ.
^{quarta pars eccliæ}
huic manerio adjac& dim̃ l̄g ſilue . & . i . qr̂ . in longo . & . i . qr̂ . in lato.

¶ In b̄tuna ten̄ Wiłł . ii . car̂ terræ . quã tenuit Turchetel lib̄ hõ . S̃ep
. v . uiłł . 7 . iii . borđ . Tc̄ . iii . ſeru . modo . i . Semp . iiii . āc . ſilũ . & . xx.
āc p̄ti . Semp . ii . car̂ in dominio . Tc̄ . ii . car̂ hominũ . modo . i.
Semp . iii . an̂ . modo . iiii . runc̄ . Tc̄ . xxx . oūs . modo . lxi . i . æccłia

206 a

xii . āc . Tc̄ . v . porc̄ . m̄ . xv . Semp uał . lx . ſoł . ʜuic man̂ ſemp
jacent . vii . libi hões ad ſocã de falda ⋮ & com̄datione tantũ ; q̃ h̄t . xxx.
āc terræ . Semp . i . car̂ & dim̃.

¶ Wermegai ten̄ Turchetel . p̄ man̄ . i . car̂ terræ . Semp . viii . uiłłi . & .
. ii . ſeru . & . viii . āc p̄ti . 7 i . car̂ in d̄nio . i . car̂ . hom̂ . quarta pars molin̂
& . iii . piſcar̂ . Semp . iii . uac̄ . 7 xviii . porc̄ . modo . lx . oūs . Tc̄ . iiii . uaſa ap̄ũ .
m̄ . ii . Semp lx . ſoł . & . h̄t . v . qr̂ in longo . 7 . ii . in lato . & . reddit . ii . đ . de -
^{7 . i . æcclia}
gelto regis . de . xx . ſoł.

LANDS OF HERMER

The Hundred of CLACKCLOSE

1 In MARHAM Thorketel held 20 acres as part of the jurisdiction of St. Etheldreda.
   Always 2 villagers who then had
   3 oxen, now 2. Meadow, 1 acre.
   Value always 3s less 4d.
   This land is measured in the return of St. Etheldreda.

2 In FINCHAM
   3 villagers; 15 smallholders; 7 slaves.
   3 ploughs in lordship;
      meadow, 13 acres. Then 4 cobs, now 1. Then 12 head of cattle, now 9. Then 30 pigs, now 26. Then 260 sheep, now 175. ¼ of a church.
   Value always £8.
   To this manor is attached ½ league of woodland. (It has) 1 furlong in length and 1 furlong in width.

3 In BARTON (Bendish) William holds 2 c. of land, which Thorketel, a free man, held.
   Always 5 villagers; 3 smallholders. Then 3 slaves, now 1.
   Always woodland, 4 acres; meadow, 20 acres.
   Always 2 ploughs in lordship. Then 2 men's ploughs, now 1.
   Always 3 head of cattle. Now 4 cobs. Then 30 sheep, now 61. 1 church, 12 acres. Then 5 pigs, now 15.
   Value always 60s.
   7 free men have always appertained to this manor, in foldrights and patronage only, who have 30 acres of land. Always 1½ ploughs.

   206 a

4 Thorketel held WORMEGAY as a manor, 1 c. of land.
   Always 8 villagers; 2 slaves.
   Meadow, 8 acres;
   1 plough in lordship; 1 men's plough;
   A ¼ of a mill; 3 fisheries. Always 3 cows; 18 pigs. Now 60 sheep. Then 4 beehives, now 2. Also 1 church.
   [Value] always 60s.
   It has 5 furlongs in length and 2 in width, of a 20s King's tax it pays 2d.

Wesbruge . II . car terræ . teñ idē . tchetel . t . r . e . Semp . IX . uill . & . VII . bord . 7 . IIII . seru . & . II . car in dnio . dim car hom . & VI . ac pti . 7 dim ac . siluæ . 7 . I . molin . Tc . II . runc . m . I . Tc . x . an . modo . XIII . Sep . VI . porc . Tc . c . xx . ous . modo . LX . Semp ual . LX . sol . H uilla ht in long v . qr . & . in lat . III . & reddit . II . d . de gelto de xx . sol.

Torpelanda teñ bordin . I . car terræ . quā tenuit turchetel . t . r . æ. Semp . v . uill . II . bord . xx . ac pti . Semp . I . car in dnio . Tc . I . car hom . modo . II . bous . Semp . IIII . an . Tc . XXIIII . ous . m . LXXX . Tc . IX . porc . modo . x . I . æcclia . VI . ac . Tc ual . xxx . sol . modo . xx . hæc tra ht . I . lg in longo . & . IIII . qr . in lato . & reddit . VIII . d . de gelto regis . de xx . sol. Stou ten& . idē t . r . e . III . car terræ . Tc & p . VII . uill . modo . II . Semp . xv . bord . & . VIII . seru . 7 . xl . ac pti . 7 . I . siluæ . Semp . III . car in dominio . & . I . piscar . Tc . v . runc . m . II . 7 xxvI . eque siluestr . Tc VII . uaccæ . modo . I . xLIIII . porc . Tc . cc . xl . ous . modo c . lx . Tc II . uasa apū . modo . xIIII . Adjacent huic man . v . libi hoes de ōi consuetudin . 7 ad socā Adjacent etiā xvII . libi hoes consueti ad faldā . & comdati de xxIIII . ac . 7 soca eoz sci bened . & herm . hoc totū ual Tc & p vIII . lib . modo . VII . I . æcclia . L . III . ac terræ 7 ual . III . sol.

Winebotesha 7 Stou . he uille hnt . I . lg in longo & dim in lato . & reddt . xvI . d . de gelto regis . de . xx . sol.

5   WEST BRIGGS, 2 c. of land. Thorketel also held before 1066.
	Always 9 villagers; 7 smallholders; 4 slaves.
	2 ploughs in lordship; ½ men's plough;
		meadow, 6 acres; woodland, ½ acre; 1 mill. Then 2 cobs, now 1. Then 10 head of cattle, now 13. Always 6 pigs. 1 church, at 5 acres. Then 120 sheep, now 60.
    Value always 60s.
    This village has 5 furlongs in length and 3 in width, of a 20s tax it pays 2d.

6   Bordin holds THORPLAND 1 c. of land, which Thorketel held before 1066.
	Always 5 villagers; 2 smallholders.
	Meadow, 20 acres.
	Always 1 plough in lordship. Then 1 men's plough, now 2 oxen. Always 4 head of cattle. Then 24 sheep, now 80. Then 9 pigs, now 10. 1 church, 6 acres.
    Value then 30s; now 20.
    This land has 1 league in length and 4 furlongs in width, of a 20s King's tax it pays 8d.

7   He also held STOW (Bardolph) before 1066; 3 c. of land.
	Then and later 7 villagers, now 2. Always 15 smallholders; 8 slaves.
	Meadow, 40 acres; woodland, 1 [acre].
	Always 3 ploughs in lordship;
	1 fishery. Then 5 cobs, now 2. 26 wild mares. Then 7 cows, now 1. 44 pigs. Then 240 sheep, now 160. Then 2 beehives, now 14.
    5 free men are attached to this manor with all customary dues and at jurisdiction. 17 free men are also bound to the fold and in patronage, at 24 acres. Their jurisdiction (is) St. Benedict's and Hermer's.   206 b
    Value of all this then and later £8; now 7.
	1 church, 53 acres of land;
	value 3s.

8   WIMBOTSHAM and STOW (Bardolph). These villages have 1 league in length and ½ in width, of a 20s King's tax they pay 16d.

Ristuna ten̄. helmerus. I. car̄ terræ quā tenuit Ketel. I. lib̄ hō
t. r. e. semp. vii. uiłł. &. i. bord̄. &. ii. serui. & car̄ in dominio. Tc̄ dim
car̄ hom̄. 7 m̄. &. viii. ac̄ p̄ti. dim̄ piscar̄. semp. I. runc̄. Tc̄. v. uac.
modo. iiii. Tc̄. vi. porc̄. modo. xix. 7 c.viii. ou͞s. Tc̄ ual. xx. soł. p̄
& modo. xx. In ead. vii. soc̄. de. xx.i. ac̄ terræ. &. iii. ac̄ p̄ti. semp
. I. car̄. & ual&. v. soł. Totū ħt. iiii. q̄r in longo. &. iii. in lato. & redd̄
iiii. d̄. de gelto. de. xx. soł.

Stratesetā ten̄ Fulb̄tus. ii. car̄ terræ quās tenuit. Suartinc lib̄ hō
t. r. e. Semp. vi. uiłł. &. ii. bord̄. &. i. seru. &. viii. ac̄ p̄ti. & dim̄ pisc̄.
&. ii. car̄ in dominio. Viłł. ii. boues. semp. I. runc̄. &. ii. an. &. viii. porc̄.
Tc̄. c.xl. ou͞s. modo lxxx. In eadē. xiii. lib̄i hōes. cc. x. ac̄. 7. I. ecc̄lia
de. xxx. ac̄. semp. ii. car̄. &. vii. ac̄ p̄ti. ħ fuit lib̄atū p̄. I. car̄. ad p
ficiendū. I. man̄. ħ totū ual&. iiii. lib̄. 7 xv. soł. com̄datio illoꝝ
duoꝝ hom̄. fuit antē baignardi. H uilla ħt. vii. q̄r in longo. &. iiii
in lato. 7 reddit. viii. d̄. de gelto de xx. soł.

In Wella. vi. bord̄. & s̄ p̄ciati hund̄ & d̄ de fredebruge. Tilinghetuna. I. car̄ terræ. ten̄ Turchetel lib̄ hō. t. r. e. semp. vii. uiłł.
7. vii. bord̄. Tc̄. ii. seru. modo. I. &. xxiiii. ac̄ p̄ti. semp. I. car̄ in
d̄nio. &. I. car̄ hom̄. 7. vii. salinæ. Tc̄. I. runc̄. modo nuł. semp
vi. an. Tc̄. xvi. porc̄. m̄. vii. Tc̄. ccc. x. ou͞s. modo. ccc. xv. sēp
uał. lx. soł. huic jac&. I. soc̄. vi. ac̄ terræ. & uał. xii. d̄.

9   A(e)lmer holds RYSTON, 1 c. of land, which 1 free man, Ketel, held before 1066.
   Always 7 villagers; 1 smallholder; 2 slaves.
   A plough in lordship; then and now ½ men's plough.
   Meadow, 8 acres; ½ fishery; always 1 cob. Then 5 cows, now 4. Then 6 pigs, now 19. 108 sheep.
Value then 20s; later and now 20.
   In the same 7 Freemen, at 21 acres of land; meadow, 3 acres.
   Always 1 plough.
Value 5s.
   The whole has 4 furlongs in length and 3 in width, of a 20s tax it pays 4d.

10 Fulbert holds STRADSETT, 2 c. of land, which Swarting, a free man, held before 1066.
   Always 6 villagers; 2 smallholders; 1 slave.
   Meadow, 8 acres; ½ fishery;
   2 ploughs in lordship; 2 oxen of the villagers.
   Always 1 cob; 2 head of cattle; 8 pigs.
      1 church, 30 acres. Then 140 sheep, now 80.
In the same 13 free men, 210 acres.
   Also 1 church, at 30 acres.
   Always 2 ploughs; meadow, 7 acres.
   This was delivered for 1 c. [of land] to make up 1 manor.
Value of all this £4 15s.
   The patronage of those 2 men was of Baynard's predecessor.
   This village has 7 furlongs in length and 4 in width, of a 20s tax it pays 8d.

11 In UPWELL 6 smallholders. They have been assessed.

The Hundred and a Half of FREEBRIDGE

12 TERRINGTON. Thorketel, a free man, held 1 c. of land before 1066.
   Always 7 villagers; 7 smallholders. Then 2 slaves, now 1.
   Meadow, 24 acres.
   Always 1 plough in lordship; 1 men's plough.
      7 salt-houses. Then 1 cob, now none; always 6 head of cattle. Then 16 pigs, now 7. Then 310 sheep, now 315.
Value always 60s.   207 a
   1 Freeman appertains here; 6 acres of land.
Value 12d.

↲In isingetuna ten& semp. turchetel. I. car & dim̄ terræ semp
IIII. uilt. & XI. bord. Tc. II. car in dn̄io. modo. I. semp dim̄ car hom̄.
7 x. ac p̄ti. I. æcclia. II. ac. & dim̄ salina. semp. IIII. an̄. Tc. xx.
porc. modo. III. Tc. c. xx. oūs. m̄. c. semp ual. LX. sol. huic man̄
jac. t. r. e. 7 m̄. xv. libi hoēs de. xxx. ac. semp. I. car. &. IIII. ac. p̄ti.
Tc. ual. xv. sol. m̄. x. de h̄ hab suus ant com̄datus. & possent recede
si darent. II. sol. Stigandus habuit soca.

↲In Rynghetona. II. car terræ ten̄ turchetel lib hō. t. r. e. semp
XI. uilli. &. VII. bord. &. II. seru. xxx. ac p̄ti. semp. II. car in dominio.
&. I. car hom̄. 7. I. molin̄. & dim̄. silua. de. xx. porc. &. IIII.
salin̄. & qn̄tæ tercia pars. semp. I. runc. &. IIII. an̄. 7 xxvII. porc.
. I. æcclia xxx. ac.
c. oūs. huic man jacent. xIII. soc. xxx. vII. ac. semp. I. car. semp ual.
vI. lib. &. IIII. sol. Tota ht. I. lḡ in longo 7 in lato. & reddit xII. d
de xx. sol. de geto regis. & in ead mensura c̄ eswinic.

↲S^cREPEHAM. HV̄NDRET. Helincham ten̄ Wari-
boldus quā tenuit Turchetel lib hō. t. r. e. III. car terræ. semp
III. uilt. &. II. bord. &. v. ser. silua. de. c. porc. xxx. ac. p̄ti.
semp. III. car in domin̄. semp. IIII. runc. &. vIII. an̄. & vI. eque cū pull.
Tc. xx. porc. m̄. xxvII. Tc. cxx. oūs. m̄. c. I. æcclia. xx. ac.
. 7 xxvIII. soc. LX ac. &. vI. ac p̄ti. semp. III. car. Tc & p ual
IIII. lib. modo. c. sol. 7 totū ht. I. lḡ in longo. & dim̄ in lato.
7. xIx. d. de gelto. quicūq ibi habeat.

13 In ISLINGTON Thorketel has always held 1½ c. of land.
Always 4 villagers; 11 smallholders.
Then 2 ploughs in lordship, now 1. Always ½ men's plough; meadow, 10 acres. 1 church, 2 acres. ½ salt-house, always 4 head of cattle. Then 20 pigs, now 3. Then 120 sheep, now 100.
Value always 60s.
15 free men appertained to this manor before 1066 and now, at 30 acres. Always 1 plough; meadow, 4 acres.
Value then 15s; now 10.
Of these his predecessor had the patronage, and they could withdraw if they gave 2s. Stigand had the jurisdiction.

14 In (North) RUNCTON Thorketel, a free man, held 2 c. of land before 1066.
Always 11 villagers; 7 smallholders; 2 slaves.
Meadow, 30 acres.
Always 2 ploughs in lordship; 1 men's plough;
1½ mills; woodland at 20 pigs; 4 salt-houses and one-third of a fifth. Always 1 cob; 4 head of cattle; 27 pigs; 100 sheep. 1 church, 30 acres.
13 Freemen appertain to this manor, 37 acres.
Always 1 plough.
Value always £6 4s.
The whole has 1 league in length and in width, of a 20s King's tax it pays 12d. West Winch is in this measurement.

SHROPHAM Hundred

15 Warenbold holds (Great) ELLINGHAM which Thorketel, a free man, held before 1066; 3 c. of land.
Always 3 villagers; 2 smallholders; 5 slaves.
Woodland at 100 pigs; meadow, 30 acres.
Always 3 ploughs in lordship.
Always 4 cobs; 8 head of cattle; 6 mares with foals. Then 20 pigs, now 27. Then 120 sheep, now 100. 1 church, 20 acres.
Also 28 Freemen, 60 acres; meadow, 6 acres. Always 3 ploughs.
Value then and later £4; now 100s.
The whole has 1 league in length and ½ in width, tax of 19d, whoever is in possession.

⁊ *LAWENDIC. HVND*. Lechā ten̄ turchetel lib̃ hō
207 b
t.r.e.III.car̃ terræ.ꝑ man̄ Tc̃ & p̃.IIII.uiłł m̃.III.Tc̃ & p̃.IIII.borđ
m̃.III.Tc̃ p̊.IIII.feru̅.modo.VIII.ac̃ p̃ti.femp.II.car̃ in dn̄io.&.I.
car̃ hom̃.filua.VII.por.femp.I.molin̄.&.III.foc̃.IIII.ac̃.terræ
⁊.I.uirgata.Tc̃.II.runc̃.Tc̃.IX.an̊.modo.III.femp.XXVII.
porc̃.Tc̃.cc.ou̅s.m̃.cc.xx.dim̃ æcclia.IIII.ac̃.Huic
manerio jac&.dim̃ car̃ terræ.femp.II.borđ.⁊ quarta pars uni̊
mercati.m̃ ten̄ Wiłł.Tc̃.I.car̃.m̃ dim̃ car̃.&.II.ac̃ prati.femp
xx.v.ou̅s.&.II.porc̃.hoc eft in torp.Tc̃ & p̊ uał xL.foł.⁊ m̃
.L.⁊ fup eu̅.x.foł.

⁊ In Ruhhā ten̄ fulbtus.I.car̃ terræ.tenuit id.t.r.e.Tc̃.I.borđ
Tc̃.I.car̃.modo.dim̃.⁊ dim̃ poteft reftaurari.& uał.x.foł.
Soca regis in muleham. ⁊ Totu̅ fup̃i Leccham.VIII.qr̊.in long̊
&.VI.in lato.qui cu̅q̣ ibi teneat.&.VII.đ.&.I.obolu̅ de gelto.

⁊ *HVND*.⁷ᵃ *DE MITTEFORT*.Winebga.tenuit Tur
chetel lib̃ hō.t.r.e.III.car̃.terræ.⁊.I.ac̃.⁊ dim̃.Tc̃ IX.uiłł.modo.
XIII.Tc̃.VIII.borđ.modo.XII.femp.VIII.feru̅.&.IIII.
car̃.in dn̄io.Tc̃ &.p̊.III.car̃ hom̃.modo.IIII.Tc̃.filua.c.L.porc̃.
modo.c.⁊.x.⁊.xvI.ac̊ p̃ti.Tc̃.I.molin̄.modo.II.femp.II.runc̃.
&.VIII.an̊.⁊ xL.vII.porc̃.modo.c.ou̅s.II.min̊.Tc̃ Lx.cap̃.I.æcclia
vI.ac̃.&.I..berewita.Gerolfeftuna.I.car̃.terræ.femp.I.uiłł.⁊.I.
borđ.&.I.car̃.⁊.IIII.ac̃ p̃ti.⁊.I.runc̃.⁊.III.an̊.&.xL.IIII.
ou̅s.Tc̃ uał.vI.łib.modo.vII.I.æcclia.vII.ac̃.

LAUNDITCH Hundred

16 Thorketel, a free man, held LITCHAM before 1066, 3 c. of land,   207 b
as a manor.
    Then and later 4 villagers, now 3. Then and later 4 smallholders,
        now 3. Then and later 4 slaves, now [ ].
    Meadow, 8 acres.
    Always 2 ploughs in lordship; 1 men's plough;
    woodland, 7 pigs; always 1 mill.
    Also 3 Freemen; 4 acres of land and 1 rood.
    Then 2 cobs. Then 9 head of cattle, now 3; always 27 pigs.
        Then 200 sheep, now 220. ½ church, 4 acres.
½ c. of land appertains to this manor.
    Always 2 smallholders.
    ¼ of 1 market. Now William holds.
    Then 1 plough, now ½ plough.
    Meadow, 2 acres. Always 25 sheep; 2 pigs.
    This is in (the lands of Gayton) Thorpe.
Value then and later 40s; now 50; and above that 10s.

17 In ROUGHAM Fulbert holds 1 c. of land; he also held it before
1066.
    Then 1 smallholder.
    Then 1 plough, now ½, ½ could be restored.
Value 10s.
    The King's jurisdiction (is) in Mileham.

18 The whole of the above LITCHAM (has) 8 furlongs in length and 6
in width, whoever holds there, tax of 7½d.

The Hundred and a Half of MITFORD

19 Thorketel, a free man, held WHINBURGH before 1066, 3 c. of land
and 1½ acres.
    Then 9 villagers, now 13. Then 8 smallholders, now 12; always
        8 slaves.
    4 ploughs in lordship. Then and later 3 men's ploughs, now 4.
    Then woodland, 150 pigs, now 110. Meadow, 16 acres. Then 1
        mill, now 2. Always 2 cobs; 8 head of cattle; 47 pigs. Now
        100 sheep, less 2. Then 60 goats. 1 church, 6 acres.
    Also 1 outlier, GARVESTON, 1 c. of land.
        Always 1 villager; 1 smallholder.
    1 plough;
        meadow, 4 acres; 1 cob; 3 head of cattle; 44 sheep.
    Value then £6; now 7.
        1 church, 7 acres.

In eadē Girolfeſtuna . xix . libi homines . c . ac̔ . terræ . iiii . car̔ .
& . ix . ac̔ . p̄ti . Tc̄ ual . xx . ſot . m̄ . L.v . 7 . iiii . d̄ . de his ten Bordin̔
208 a
xxiiii . ac . 7 ual . in eod p̄tio . iiii . ſot . Ex his teſtatur hund̄
qd̄ ſuus antec̄ nullā habuit conſuetudine̔ . p̄t comdati
one̔ . & ex h̄ offert judiciū . & quidā homo hermeri offert
juditiū qd̄ ſuus ante c̄ habuit omne̔ conſuetudine̔ . t . r . e .
p̄t ſocā ſce̔ Adeldrede 7 qd̄ poterat terrā ſuā uende . Ex hoc
deder̔ uades . Totū h̄t . i . l̄g in longo . 7 . i . leuga in lato . 7 . iii . d̄ .
7 . i . obolū de gelto . 7 Girofeſtuna . v . qr̔ in longo . & . iiii . in lato .
7 xiii . d̄ de gelto .

In Scippedana Adelelm̄ ten̄ . i . ſoc̔ . xvi . ac̔ . terræ . & ual .
iiii . ſot .

In Winebga . i . ſoc̔ . xxx . ac̔ . & ii . ac̔ p̄ti . Tc̄ . i . car̔ . m̄ . dim̄ .
Tc̄ ual . xvi . ſot . modo viii . Hundret teſtatur qd n̄ poterat uendere ſuā terrā ſed uicecom̄s h̄ c̄tradicit qd̄ poterat uende
ſine licencia dn̄i ſui ;

In Jakeſham . iiii . ſoc̔ . ſui antec̔ . xx . ac̔ terræ . t . r̔ . e . Tc̄ . i . car̔ .
modo dim̄ . & . i . ac̔ p̄ti . Tc̄ ual& . iiii . ſot . M̄ . ii . Toddenham
tenuit turchetel . t . r . e . lxvi . ac̔ terræ . p̄ man̔ ſemp̄ . iii .
ſeru̔ . & . ii . uitt . & . i . car in dominio . & . i . ac̔ p̄ti . & dim molin̄ .
& . i . an̄ . Tc̄ . c . xl . ous̄ . m̄ . c . lx . 7 xxxviii . porc̔ . Tc̄ ual xvi .
ſot . modo . xx . & h̄t . vii . qr̔ in longo . & . vi . in lato . quicūq ibi
teneat . 7 xxii . d̄ 7 . i . obolū de gelto . Om̄s æccliæ de tota terra
Hermeri . ſt app̄tiatæ cū maneriis ;

In the same GARVESTON 19 free men, 100 acres of land.
4 ploughs; meadow, 9 acres.
Value then 20s; now 55(s) 4d.
Of these Bordin holds 24 acres.
Value 4s in the same valuation.

208 a

Of these the Hundred testifies that his predecessor had no customary dues except patronage; of this it offers judicial ordeal. A certain man of Hermer's offers judicial ordeal that his predecessor had every customary due before 1066 except the jurisdiction of St. Etheldreda, and that he could sell his land. They have given pledges of this.

The whole has 1 league in length and 1 league in width, tax of 3½d. Garveston (has) 5 furlongs in length and 4 in width, tax of 13d.

20 In SHIPDAM Adelhelm holds; 1 Freeman, 16 acres of land.
Value 4s.

21 In WHINBURGH 1 Freeman, 30 acres; meadow, 2 acres. Then 1 plough, now ½.
Value then 16s; now 8.
The Hundred testifies that he could not sell his land but the sheriff counters this (saying) he could sell without the permission of his lord.

22 In YAXHAM 4 Freemen of his predecessor's, 20 acres of land before 1066. Then 1 plough, now ½. Meadow, 1 acre.
Value then 4s; now 2.

23 Thorketel held (East) TUDDENHAM before 1066, 66 acres of land as a manor.
Always 3 slaves; 2 villagers.
1 plough in lordship;
meadow, 1 acre; ½ mill; 1 head of cattle. Then 140 sheep, now 160. 38 pigs. 1 church, 20 acres.
Value then 16s; now 20.
It has 7 furlongs in length and 6 in width, whoever holds there, tax of 22½d.
All the churches of all Hermer's land are assessed with the manors.

HVMILIART . *H̃* . Vrnincham ten& Vaganus
. III . car terræ . & . XII . ac . quas tenuit Leuolt . teinnus

208 b

t . r . e . III . car terræ 7 . XII . ac . Tc̄ . IIII . uilł . P . II . modo
modo null . Semp . XIIII . borđ . Tc̄ . III . seru . modo . I . semp
III . car in dominio . Tc̄ . I . car & dim hom . modo . I . XVI . ac p̄ti.
Silua . VI . porc . semp . II . runc , Tc̄ . II . an . m̊ . IX . Tc̄
. I . æcclia . de . x . ac.
II . porc . modo . XIII . Tc̄ LX . ou̅s . m̊ . L . Tc̄ & p9 ualł LX.
soł . modo . LXXX . & h̄t . I . lg in longo . & dim in lato . & . x . đ
de gelto . & huic id terræ jacent . VIII . lib̄i homines
soca faldæ . & comdatione tantū XX . VIII . ac . sēp
. I . car . & . ual& . IIII . soł . Rex & coms de hoc
& de manerio socā.

209 a

TERRA Abb̄is de Sc̄o Eadmundo. .XIIII.

Hunđ de Clacheslosa . In Phincham . XVI . ac . træ . 7 . IIII . ac . p̄ti . 7 . ualł
. II . soł . 7 . VIII . đ . In Runghetuna tenuit Sc̄s . E . t . r . e . II . car . tre . Sēp
. V . uilł . 7 . IIII . bor . 7 . II . ser . XII . ac . p̄ti . XVI . ac . siluæ . I . moł . I . piscina.
7 . II . car . in dn̄io . tc̄ . I . car . hom . m̄ . II . bou . Sēp . I . runc . VIII . an . XXX . por.
XV . ou . huic man̄ . jacent . XXVII . lib̄i . hoēs . s; soca remanebat . Sc̄o . E.
hn̄tes . I . car . træ . Sēp . III . car . II . bor . Iacent &iam huic man̄ . dim . car.
træ . Sēp . IIII . bor . 7 . I . ser . 7 . I . car in dn̄io . 7 adhuc jacent . XXX . ac . 7 . I . uilł
7 . II . bor . Sēp ualł . VII . lib̄ . 7 . IIII . soł . HUIC manerio jac& . I . berewita quæ
uocat Isinghetuna . 7 ē in alio hunđ . Totū hoc maneriū h̄t . I . leu in lon̄ . 7 . V . qr.
in lat . 7 reddit . VIII . đ . qn̄ totū hunđ reddit . XX . soł . de . gelto.

HUMBLEYARD Hundred

24 Wagen holds WRENINGHAM, 3 c. of land and 12 acres; which
Leofwold, a thane, held before 1066; 3 c. of land and 12 acres. 208 b
Then 4 villagers, later 2, now none; always 14 smallholders.
Then 3 slaves, now 1.
Always 3 ploughs in lordship. Then, the men, 1½ ploughs, now 1.
Meadow, 16 acres; woodland, 6 pigs; always 2 cobs. Then 2 head of cattle, now 9. Then 2 pigs, now 13. Then 60 sheep, now 50. 1 church, at 10 acres.
Value then and later 60s; now 80.
It has 1 league in length and ½ in width, tax of 10d.
Also 8 free men appertain to this land in fold-rights and patronage only; 28 acres. Always 1 plough.
Value 4s.
The King and the Earl (have) the jurisdiction of this and of the manor.

14 LAND OF THE ABBOT OF ST. EDMUND'S 209 a

The Hundred of CLACKCLOSE

1 In FINCHAM 16 acres of land;
meadow, 4 acres.
Value 2s 8d.
In RUNCTON St. E(dmund) held before 1066 2 c. of land.
Always 5 villagers; 4 smallholders; 2 slaves.
Meadow, 12 acres; woodland, 16 acres; 1 mill; 1 fish pond; 2 ploughs in lordship. Then 1 men's plough, now 2 oxen.
Always 1 cob; 8 head of cattle; 30 pigs; 15 sheep.
27 free men appertain to this manor, but the jurisdiction remained with St. E(dmund), who have 1 c. of land.
Always 3 ploughs.
2 smallholders.
There also appertains to this manor, ½ c. of land.
Always 4 smallholders; 1 slave.
1 plough in lordship.
A further 30 acres appertain there;
1 villager; 2 smallholders.
Value always £7 4s.
1 outlier appertains to this manor, which is called ISLINGTON; it is in another Hundred.
All this manor has 1 league in length and 5 furlongs in width, it pays 8d when the whole Hundred pays tax of 20s.

꜄Sutreiam . ıı ; cař . trǣ . Sep̄ . xıııı ; uiłł ; 7 . vıı . bor 7 . v . ſer . xxıııı . ac̃ . p̃ti ; tc̄
. ıı . cař . in dñio . m̃ . ııı . Tc̄ . ıı . cař . hom̃ . m̃ . ııı . ı ; piſc̃ . ıııı . runc̃ . xxxı . anim̃;
xı . por . ʟxxx . oũ . xı . equæ ſiluaticæ ; tc̄ . uał . xxxıı . soł ; m̃ . ıııı . lib̃ . h̃t . dim
leu in long . 7 ; ıııı ; q̃r in lať . 7 . ııı . d̃ . de g.

꜄In hidlingeia . ʟvııı . ac̃ . trǣ . ııı ; uiłł . ı . cař . ıııı ; ac̃ p̃ti . ap̃p̃tiat ē ſup̃ . In ead̃
. ıı . bor . ı ; ac̃ ; 7 jacent in Runghetuna ; In Derhā . ı . ſoc̃ . vı ; ac̃ . uał . vı . d̃ . In Torp . ı . lib̃
ho̅ . ıııı . ac̃ co̅m̃d . tant̄ . 7 . sc̄s benedict̃ ſocā . uał . vııı . d̃ .

꜄Fredebruge Hund̃ . 7 dim̃ ; In Ilſinghetuna tenẽ . Sc̄s . E . ı ; cař . tre.
Sep̄ . xxv . uiłł . ı . cař ; in dñio . ı ; cař . hom̃ . xx . ac̃ ; p̃ti . ıııı . an̄ . ʟxxx . oũ . nuic
manerio jacent . vı . ſoc̃ . in Lena . xxvı . ac̃ . trǣ . Sep̄ . ı . cař . 7 . ı . sał . uał . xʟ . soł
In Middeltuna . tenẽ . Ricuard̃ de abbẽ ; ı . cař . trǣ . qm̃ tenuit . S . e̅ . t . r . e̅ .
; ıııı . uiłł . 7 . ıı ; bor . ı . ſer ; ı . cař . in dñio . xx . ac̃ . p̃ti . ıı . sał . ııı . uac̃ . xxıııı . oũ;
; ıııı . porc̃ . ı ; ſoc̃ . de . v . ac̃ . uał . xx . soł.

꜄Scerpham Hund ; In Buccham ; tenuit . S . e̅ . ı . cař ; trǣ . t . r . e̅ . tc̄ . ıııı .
uiłł . m̃ . v . Sep̄ . vııı ; bor . Tc̄ . ıııı ; ſer . m̃ . ıı ; x . ac̃ . p̃ti . tc̄ . ı . mol . m̃ null

Sep̄ . ı . cař . in dñio . 7 . ı . cař . hom̃ . ı . runc̃ . vıı . an̄ ; vı . porc̃ . xxvııı . oũ .
. vıı . ſoc̃ . dim̃ . cař . trǣ . Sep̄ . ıı . cař . ııı . ac̃ . p̃ti . ııı . bor . Silu . v . por . uał . xʟ . soł.

2   SOUTHERY, 2 c. of land.
    Always 13 villagers; 7 smallholders; 5 slaves.
    Meadow, 24 acres. Then 2 ploughs in lordship, now 3. Then 2 men's ploughs, now 3. 1 fishery; 4 cobs; 31 head of cattle; 11 pigs; 80 sheep; 11 wild mares.
    Value then 32s; now £4.
    It has ½ league in length and 4 furlongs in width; tax of 3d.

3   In HILGAY 58 acres of land.
    3 villagers.
    1 plough; meadow, 4 acres.
    It is assessed above.
    In the same 2 smallholders, 1 acre. (Their lands) appertain in Runcton.
    In (West) DEREHAM 1 Freeman, 6 acres.
    Value 6d.
    In THORPLAND 1 free man, 4 acres, in patronage only.
    St. Benedict (has) the jurisdiction.
    Value 8d.

FREEBRIDGE Hundred and a Half

4   In ISLINGTON St. E(dmund) holds 1 c. of land.
    Always 25 villagers.
    1 plough in lordship; 1 men's plough; meadow, 20 acres; 4 head of cattle, 80 sheep.
    6 Freemen appertain to this manor in Lynn, 26 acres of land.
    Always 1 plough; 1 salt-house.
    Value 40s.

5   In MIDDLETON Richard holds from the Abbot 1 c. of land which St. E(dmund) held before 1066.
    3 villagers; 2 smallholders; 1 slave.
    1 plough in lordship; meadow, 20 acres; 2 salt-houses; 3 cows; 24 sheep; 4 pigs.
    1 Freeman, at 5 acres.
    Value 20s.

SHROPHAM Hundred

6   In BUCKENHAM St. E(dmund) held 1 c. of land before 1066.
    Then 4 villagers, now 5; always 8 smallholders. Then 4 slaves, now 2.
    Meadow, 10 acres. Then 1 mill, now none. Always 1 plough in lordship; 1 men's plough; 1 cob; 7 head of cattle; 6 pigs; 28 sheep.
    7 Freemen, ½ c. of land. Always 2 ploughs; meadow, 3 acres.
    3 smallholders. Woodland, 5 pigs.
    Value 40s.

⁊Gildecros Hund̄. Guidenham ten& ⋮ Goscelin⁹ de abb̄e q̇d tenuit
.S̄. E . p̄. dim̄. car̄.trǣ c̄ soca. Sēp. II. uil̄t ⁙ I ⋮ bor III . ac̄. p̄ti. dim̄ car̄ in dn̄io. ⁊
. II . bou. hom̄. tc̄ . I . mol. val ⋮ x . sol.

⁊In Nortunā ten&. Idē ⋮ I . car̄. trǣ. q̇d tēn ⋮ I . soc̄ ⋮ S̄. Ē ⋮ Sēp. v. uil̄t . ⁊. III bor̄. m̄. v.
. I . ac̄. p̄ti. Sēp. II . car̄. in dn̄io ⁊ . dim̄. car̄. hom̄. Silu. x . por̄. I . mol. ⁊ . I . soc̄. dim̄ ac̄⋮
m̄. III . runc. XII. an. x . por. XLV . ou. VI . uasa ap̄. Val. xxx . sol. ht . I . leu. in lon.
⁊ . dim̄ in lat. q̇oq̄. ibi teneat . ⁊ . VIII . d. ⁊ . ob de . g. ⁊ . I . ferding. Ecclīǣ. v ⋮ ac̄. val.

⁊In Gadesthorp ten lib̄ ho t . r . e . xxx ⋮ ac̄. M q̇dā Anglic de abb̄e ⋮ m̄. I . bor.
. III . ac̄. p̄ti. tc̄. dim̄. car̄. m̄. I . tc̄. ual. v . sol. m̄. x ⋮ de hoc habuit abbas cōm̄d.
t . r . e . Soca in Cheninghala . reḡ.

⁊In Snareshul ten& Fulcher de abb̄e . xxx ⋮ ac̄. q̇d tenuit . I . soc̄. Sēp. I . bor̄⋮
dim̄. car̄. val. II . sol.

⁊In Herlinga. Ricaiard . I . car̄. trǣ de abb̄e. q̇d tenuit . S̄. E . t . r . e . Sēp. IIII ⋮ uil̄t.
⋮ III . bor. I . ser. III . ac̄. p̄ti. tc̄ . I . car̄. in dn̄io ⋮ m̄. II . Sēp. II . car̄. hom̄. I . runc̄. VIII . an.
. III . por. tc̄ . cxx . ou. m̄. CLXXX . Tc̄ ual. xx . sol. m̄ ⋮ XL.

⁊Lawendic. Huhd. Wenlingā ten& Idē ⋮ R . de abb̄e q̇d ten. S̄. E . p̄.
. I . car̄. trǣ. II . uil̄t. VI ⋮ bor. VI . ac̄. p̄ti. I ⋮ car̄. in dn̄io. ⁊ . I . car̄. ⁊ . dim̄. hom̄.

GUILTCROSS Hundred

7   Jocelyn holds QUIDENHAM from the Abbot which St. E(dmund) held as ½ c. of land with the jurisdiction.
    Always 2 villagers; 1 smallholder.
    Meadow, 3 acres; ½ plough in lordship; the men, 2 oxen.
        Then 1 mill.
    Value 10s.

8   In (Blo) NORTON he also holds 1 c. of land which 1 Freeman of St. E(dmund's) held.
    Always 5 villagers. Then 3 smallholders, now 5.
    Meadow, 1 acre. Always 2 ploughs in lordship; ½ men's plough; woodland, 10 pigs; 1 mill.
    Also 1 Freeman, ½ acre.
    Now 3 cobs; 12 head of cattle; 10 pigs; 45 sheep; 6 beehives.
    Value 30s.
    It has 1 league in length and ½ in width, whoever holds there, tax of 8¾d.
    (Belonging) to the church, 5 acres;
    value 10d.

9   In GASTHORPE a free man held before 1066, 30 acres; now a certain Englishman (holds) from the Abbot.
    Now 1 smallholder.
    Meadow, 3 acres. Then ½ plough, now 1.
    Value then 5s; now 10.
    The Abbot had the patronage of this before 1066. The jurisdiction is in the King's (manor of) Kenninghall.

10 In (Great) SNAREHILL Fulcher holds 30 acres from the Abbot which 1 Freeman held.
    Always 1 smallholder.
    ½ plough.
    Value 2s.

11 In HARLING Richard (holds) 1 c. of land from the Abbot which St. E(dmund) held before 1066.
    Always 4 villagers; 3 smallholders; 1 slave.
    Meadow, 3 acres. Then 1 plough in lordship, now 2. Always 2 men's ploughs; 1 cob; 8 head of cattle; 3 pigs. Then 120 sheep, now 180.
    Value then 20s; now 40.

LAUNDITCH Hundred

12 R(ichard) also holds WENDLING from the Abbot which St. E(dmund) held as 1 c. of land.
    2 villagers; 6 smallholders.
    Meadow, 6 acres; 1 plough in lordship; 1½ men's ploughs;

Silu̅ . c . porc̃ . 7 . i . foc̃ . xii . ac̃ . Sep̅ . i . bor . tc̃ . i . car̃ . m̃ . dim̃ . Sep̅ . i . mol . xix . porc̃ .
tc̃ . ual . xx . fol . m̃ . xxx . ht̃ . ix . q̃r . in lon̅g̃ . 7 . vi . in lat̃ . 7 . ii . d̃ . 7 . ob̃ . de . g̃ .

⁋ Feorhou Hun̅d . Marthinghefordā . tenuit . S . E . t . r . e . Sep̅ . iiii .
uill . 7 . i . fer . Tc̃ . i . car̃ . m̃ . ii , 7 . i . car̃ . 7 . dim̃ . hom̃ . Silu̅ . viii . porc̃ . vi . ac̃ . p̃ti .
Sep̅ . ii . mol . ii . runc̃ . xxii . an̅ . viii . potc̃ . cxxx . ou̅ . ix . cap̃ . 7 . iii . foc̃ .
Sep̅ ual . xl . fol . ht̃ . i . leu̅ in lon̅ . 7 . iii . q̃r . 7 . dim̃ . in lat̃ . 7 . vi . d̃ . 7 . ob̃ de . g̃ .
alii ibi tenent .

⁋ Blafelda Hun̅d . Buchanaham ten& Rog̃ de . abb̃ . q̃d tenuit.

210 a

. S . E . ad uictu̅ . t . r . e . m̃ ten& Rog̃ bigot a fco̅ . E . p . i . car̃ . trae . Sep̅ . viii . bor .
7 . i . car̃ . in dn̅io . tc̃ . 7 . p̃ . ii . car̃ . hom̃ . m̃ . dim̃ . ix . ac̃ . p̃ti . tc̃ . ii . runc̃ . m̃ . i . tc̃ . ii .
an̅ . m̃ . nich̃ . m̃ . vi . porc̃ . xxi . ou̅ . tc̃ . 7 p̃ ual . xxx . fol . m̃ . xx . 7 . xi . q̃r in
lon̅g̃ . 7 . vi . in lat̃ . 7 . xx . d̃ . de . g̃ . q̃cq̃ ibi teneat . 7 huic manerio adjacent
. x . libi hoes . com̃d . de lx . ac̃ . vi . ac̃ . p̃ti . tc̃ . 7 p̃ . v . car̃ . m̃ . ii . 7 . dim̃ . tc̃ . 7 p̃ ual
x . fol . m̃ . xx .

⁋ Heinefteda Hun̅d . Caftru̅ ten& Sep̅ . S . E . p man̅ . 7 . p . iii . car̃ . tre
Sep̅ . x . uill . 7 . vii . bor . 7 . ii . car̃ . in dn̅io . 7 . iiii . car̃ . hom̃ . vi . ac̃ . p̃ti . dim̃ . mol .
m̃ . iii . runc̃ . v . an . xxx . porc̃ . xl . ou̅ . 7 . iiii . foc̃ . de . xxv . ac̃ . trae . conceffu
regis c̅ o̅i c̅fuet 7 ptinent in man̅ ifto . tefte hun̅d . Tc̃ ual . xl . fol . m̃ . c .
ht̃ . vi . q̃r in lon̅g . 7 . iiii . in lat̃ . 7 . xvi . d̃ . de . g̃ . 7 plures ibi tenent .
Ecclie . xi . ac̃ . ual . xvi . d̃ .

woodland, 100 pigs.
Also 1 Freeman; 12 acres.
Always 1 smallholder.
Then 1 plough, now ½. Always 1 mill; 19 pigs.
Value then 20s; now 30. It has 9 furlongs in length and 6 in width, tax of 2½d.

FOREHOE Hundred

13 St. E(dmund) held MARLINGFORD before 1066.
Always 4 villagers; 1 slave.
Then 1 plough, now 2. 1½ men's ploughs; woodland, 8 pigs; meadow, 6 acres. Always 2 mills; 2 cobs; 22 head of cattle; 8 pigs; 130 sheep; 9 goats.
Also 3 Freemen.
Value always 40s.
It has 1 league in length and 3½ furlongs in width, tax of 6½d.
Others hold there.

BLOFIELD Hundred

14 Roger holds BUCKENHAM from the Abbot which St. E(dmund) 210 a
held before 1066 for supplies. Now Roger Bigot holds from St. E(dmund) as 1 c. of land.
Always 8 smallholders.
1 plough in lordship. Then and later 2 men's ploughs, now ½. Meadow, 9 acres. Then 2 cobs, now 1. Then 2 head of cattle, now nothing. Now 6 pigs; 21 sheep.
Value then and later 30s; now 20.
(It has) 11 furlongs in length and 6 in width, tax of 20d, whoever holds there.
To this manor are attached 10 free men in patronage, at 60 acres; meadow, 6 acres. Then and later 5 ploughs, now 2½.
Value then and later 10s; now 20.

HENSTEAD Hundred

15 St. E(dmund) has always held CAISTOR (St. Edmunds) as a manor and as 3 c. of land.
Always 10 villagers; 7 smallholders.
2 ploughs in lordship; 4 men's ploughs; meadow, 6 acres; ½ mill. Now 3 cobs; 5 head of cattle; 30 pigs; 40 sheep.
Also 4 Freemen, at 25 acres of land by grant of the king, with all customary dues, and they belong in that manor, as the Hundred testifies.
Value then 40s; now 100.
It has 6 furlongs in length and 4 in width, tax of 16d.
More hold there.
(Belonging) to the church, 11 acres; value 16d.

Broc tenuit Comes gurt . t . r . e . 7 . rex . W . dedit scō . E . qn pmū uenit
ad scm̄ . E . ; IIII . car tr̄æ . Tc . xxxIII . uill . m̄ . xxxvIII . Sep . III . ser . m̄
. III . car . in dn̄io . 7 . vI . hom̄ . Silu . xxx . por . Ix . ac . p̄ti . m̄ . v . runc . xIIII .
an . xL . porc . m̄ . Lxv . ou . 7 . xx . cap . 7 . xLvII . soc . I . car . 7 . dim . tr̄æ . 7 . sep
Ix . car . int hōes . In Scotessa . xvI . libi hōes hōes guert . cm̄d . de . I . car tr̄æ .
ptinent in broc . 7 sub eis . vII . bor . 7 . IIII . ac . p̄ti . 7 . III . car . 7 q̄rta pars ecc̄liæ .
Ex hoc ten& berenger . xx . ac.

In Hou . I . lib hō | ptinens in broc. guert . de . I . car . tr̄æ . qd ten& berenger . Sep . v . uill . 7 . vI . bor .
7 . II . car . in dn̄io . Tc . 7 p . III . car . hom̄ . m̄ . II . Silu . xL . porc . Ecc̄liæ . xv . ac .
ual . II . sol .

In Porringelant . I . lib hō guert cm̄d ptinens in broc . xxx . ac . 7 . I . bor .
de . dim . ac . sep . I . car . Sup om̄s istos libos hōes habuit . Rex . E . soca
7 . sac . 7 post ea guert accepit p uim . sed rex . W . dedit c man . soca . 7 sac .
de om̄ibʒ libis guert . sic ipse tenebat . hoc reclamant monachi.

210 b

Tc 7 p ual . x . lib . m̄ . xv . Broc ht . I . leu . in lon . 7 . IIII . qr . & . I . leu in lato .
7 . de gelto . xvII . d . 7 . obol . Alii ibi ten .

Hersam dim . Hund . Thorp ten . S . E . t . r . e . p man . 7 . p . II . car . tr̄æ . tc .
. vIII . uill . m̄ . Ix . 7 . vIII . bor . Sep . II . car . in dn̄io . 7 . vI . car . hom̄ . tc silu . Lx . por . m̄ . xL .
. xII . ac . p̄ti . Tc . I . mol . m̄ . non . Sep . IIII . runc . x . anim . xI . por . x . ou . xx . cap .
7 In brodise . II . soc . ptinentes isti man . de . I . car . tr̄æ 7 . II . uill . 7 . II . bor . Tc ual
. IIII . lib . m̄ . c . sol . ht . vII . qr . in lon 7 . vI . in lat . 7 . de . g . IIII . d . Ecc̄liæ . xII .
ac . ual . II . sol .

16 Earl Gyrth held BROOKE before 1066. King William granted it to St. E(dmund) when first he came to St. E(dmund's); 4 c. of land.
Then 33 villagers, now 38; always 3 slaves.
Now 3 ploughs in lordship; 6 men's [ploughs]; woodland, 30 pigs; meadow, 9 acres. Now 5 cobs; 14 head of cattle; 40 pigs. Now 65 sheep; 20 goats.
Also 47 Freemen, 1½ c. of land; always 9 ploughs between the men.
In SHOTESHAM 16 free men under the patronage of Gyrth, at 1 c. of land. They belong in Brooke. Also under them 7 smallholders.
Meadow, 4 acres; 3 ploughs; ¼ of a church.
Berenger holds 20 acres of this.
In HOWE 1 free man of Gyrth's who belongs in Brooke, at 1 c. of land which Berenger holds.
Always 5 villagers; 6 smallholders.
2 ploughs in lordship. Then and later 3 men's ploughs, now 2. Woodland, 40 pigs.
(Belonging) to the church, 15 acres;
value 2s.

17 In PORINGLAND 1 free man under the patronage of Gyrth who belongs in Brooke; 30 acres.
1 smallholder, at ½ acre.
Always 1 plough.
King Edward had the full jurisdiction over all those free men; later Gyrth acquired it by force, but King William granted with the manor the full jurisdiction of all Gyrth's free men just as he held it himself. The monks claim this.
Value then and later £10; now 15. 210 b
Brooke has 1 league in length and 4 furlongs and 1 league in width, tax of 17½d. Others hold there.

EARSHAM Half-Hundred
18 St. E(dmund) held THORPE (Abbots) before 1066 as a manor and as 2 c. of land.
Then 8 villagers, now 9; 8 smallholders.
Always 2 ploughs in lordship; 6 men's ploughs. Then woodland, 60 pigs, now 40. Meadow, 12 acres. Then 1 mill, not now.
Always 4 cobs; 10 head of cattle; 11 pigs; 10 sheep; 20 goats.
Also in BROCKDISH 2 Freemen who belong to that manor, at 1 c. of land. 2 villagers; 2 smallholders.
Value then £4; now 100s.
It has 7 furlongs in length and 6 in width, tax of 4d.
(Belonging) to the church, 12 acres;
value 2s.

In Menhan tenet Frodo de abbe . I . car trae . 7 . xxx . ac . qd ten . II . foc . 7 . fub
eis . IX . uilt . 7 . VII . bor . tc int ons . v . car . m . VII . Silu . LII . por . XII . ac pti.
apptiatu e in Menham. Tc . I . mol . m . null . ht . II . leu . 7 . v . qr . in long.
7 . VII . in lat . 7 . de . g . VII . d.
In Heroluestuna . I . lib ho sci . E . comd . 7 . foca Stigandi . in hersa . XII . ac . trae
val . sep . xx . d.
In Sterestuna . I . lib ho . sci . E . cmd . f; foca Stingandi in hersa . v . ac . trae.
Val . x . d . hoc e in dnio.
Sterestuna ten& . Rog bigot de abbe . qd tenuit brictflet liba femina sci e.
comd . p . II . car . trae . tc . III . uilt . m . II . Sep . III . fer . Tc . II . car . in dnio . m null.
. VI . ac . pti . tc . 7 p . XL . fol . m . xx . ht . I . leu 7 . v . qr . in lon . 7 . v . qr . in lat 7
. XIII . d de . g . qcq ibi teneat.
In Heroluestuna ten& Frodo . I . uilt . 7 . dim . de . XIII . ac . 7 ptinet in Mha.
Dice dim Hund . Teueteshala ten& sep . scs . E . p . III . car . trae.
Sep . XVIII . uilt . 7 . xv . bor . 7 . II . fer . 7 . III . car . in dnio . 7 . XII . car . hom.
Silu LXXX . porc . x . ac . pti . Sep . v . runc . xxIIII . anim . xxxv . porc . XL . ou.
xxIIII . cap . 7 . v . foc in ead de . Lx . ac . Sep . II . car . In ead . I . lib ho sci . E.
dim . car . trae . I . uilt . 7 . dim . II . bor . Sep . I . car . Silu . xv . porc . Duae ecctiae
211 a
de . XL . ac . val . VII . fol . 7 . VI . d . Isti manerio adjac& . I . buuita Geffinga
de . I . car . 7 . II . uilt . 7 . II . bor . Sep . I . car . in dnio . 7 . II . car . hom . Silu . xv . por . 7

19 In MENDHAM Frodo holds 1 c. of land and 30 acres from the
Abbot which 2 Freemen held. Also under them
9 villagers and 7 smallholders.
Then between them all 5 ploughs, now 7. Woodland, 52 pigs;
meadow, 12 acres.
It is assessed in Mendham.
Then 1 mill, now none.
It has 2 leagues and 5 furlongs in length and 7 in width, tax
of 7d.

20 In HARLESTON 1 free man under the patronage of St. E(dmund)
and in the jurisdiction of Stigand in EARSHAM; 12 acres of land.
Value always 20d.

21 In STARSTON 1 free man under the patronage of St. E(dmund) but
in the jurisdiction of Stigand in Earsham; 5 acres of land.
Value 10d.
This is in lordship.

Roger Bigot holds STARSTON from the Abbot which Beorhtflaed,
a free woman under the patronage of St. Edmund, held as 2 c.
of land.
Then 3 villagers, now 2; always 3 slaves.
Then 2 ploughs in lordship, now none. Meadow, 6 acres.
[Value] then and later 40s; now 20.
It has 1 league and 5 furlongs in length and 5 furlongs in width,
tax of 13d, whoever holds there.

22 In HARLESTON Frodo holds;
1 villager and a half, at 13 acres.
It belongs in Mendham.

DISS Half-Hundred
23 St. E(dmund) has always held TIVETSHALL, as 3 c. of land.
Always 18 villagers; 15 smallholders; 2 slaves.
3 ploughs in lordship; 12 men's ploughs; woodland, 80 pigs;
meadow, 10 acres. Always 5 cobs; 24 head of cattle; 35
pigs; 40 sheep; 24 goats.
Also 5 Freemen in the same, at 60 acres; always 2 ploughs.
In the same 1 free man of St. E(dmund's), ½ c. of land.
1 villager and a half; 2 smallholders.
Always 1 plough; woodland, 15 pigs.   211 a
2 churches, at 40 acres;
value 7s 6d.
To this manor is attached 1 outlier, GISSING, at 1 c. [of land].
2 villagers; 2 smallholders.
Always 1 plough in lordship; 2 men's ploughs; woodland,
15 pigs.

xvIII. foc. de. LXXXX. ac. Fulcherus. ten&. xxII. ac. Sep. III. bor. 7. v. car.
7. II. ac. pti. tc. ual. vII. lib. m. IX. 7. xv. fol. Tiueteffala. ht. I. leu. 7
. IIII. qr. in long. 7. dim. leu. in lat. 7. de. g. xvII. d.
In Simplinga. vI. foc. ptinent ifti man. de. xxxII. ac. 7. I. bor. 7. II. ac. pti.
sep. int. oms. I. car. apptiat st fupi.

⁊ In Ead. lib ho. xL. ac. qd ten&. Fulc. 7. II. bor. Sep. I. car. 7. II. ac. pti. Silu.
. IIII. porc. Val. x. fol.

⁊ Brefingham ten& S. E. sep. p. man. 7. p. II. car. træ. Sep. vI. uill. xvI. bor.
7. II. car. in dnio. 7. II. car. hom. Silu. xx. por. xII. ac. pti. m. II. an. xI. por.
7. xII. foc. de. Lx. ac. 7 n poſant dare l uendere tra fua Sep. II. car. 7. dim.
Silu. vI. porc. IIII. ac. pti. tc ual. xL. fol. m. Lx. Ecclię. xv. ac. ual. II. fol
ht. vIII. qr. in long. 7. vI. in lat. 7. xII. d. de. g.

⁊ In Brefingham tenuit Almar a sco Edm. t. r. e. I. car. træ. m ten&. Rog
bigot a sco. Sep. I. uill. 7. IIII. bor. Tc. II. car. in dnio. Poft 7 m. I. 7. dim.
Tc 7 p. II. car. hom. m. I. Silu. vI. por. vI. ac. pti. Tc. III. runc. m. I.
Tc. IIII. an. m. III. tc. xx. por. m. vIII. m. Lx. ou. 7. I. foc. de. I. ac. 7. dim.
Sep. ual. xx. fol.

⁊ In Ragheduna ten& Fulcher de dnio. I. car. træ qd ten. S. E. Sep. II. uill.
7. vII. bor. 7. I. car. in dnio. 7. II. car. hom. 7. II. ac. pti. 7. v. foc. de. xxI. ac. pti.
Sep. II. car. 7. I. runc. 7. II. an. 7. v. por. 7. xII. ou. Val. xx. fol

Also 18 Freemen, at 90 acres.
Fulcher holds 22 acres.
   Always 3 smallholders;
   5 ploughs; meadow, 2 acres.
Value then £7; now (£)9 15s.
   Tivetshall has 1 league and 4 furlongs in length and ½ league in width, tax of 17d.
In SHIMPLING 6 Freemen belong to this manor, at 32 acres.
   1 smallholder; meadow, 2 acres; always 1 plough between them all. They are assessed above.
In the same a free man, 40 acres, which Fulcher holds.
   2 smallholders.
   Always 1 plough; meadow, 2 acres; woodland, 4 pigs.
Value 10s.

24 St. E(dmund) has always held BRESSINGHAM as a manor and as 2 c. of land.
   Always 6 villagers; 16 smallholders.
   2 ploughs in lordship; 2 men's ploughs; woodland, 20 pigs;
      meadow, 12 acres. Now 2 head of cattle; 11 pigs.
   Also 12 Freemen, at 60 acres; they could not grant or sell their land.
   Always 2½ ploughs; woodland, 6 pigs; meadow, 4 acres.
Value then 40s; now 60.
   (Belonging) to the church, 15 acres;
value 2s.
   It has 8 furlongs in length and 6 in width, tax of 12d.

25 In BRESSINGHAM A(e)lmer held 1 c. of land from St. Edmund before 1066; now Roger Bigot holds from the Saint.
   Always 1 villager; 4 smallholders.
   Then 2 ploughs in lordship, later and now 1½. Then and later 2 men's ploughs, now 1. Woodland, 6 pigs; meadow, 6 acres. Then 3 cobs, now 1. Then 4 head of cattle, now 3. Then 20 pigs, now 8. Now 60 sheep.
   Also 1 Freeman, at 1½ acres.
Value always 20s.

26 In ROYDON Fulcher holds in lordship 1 c. of land which St. E(dmund) held.
   Always 2 villagers; 7 smallholders.
   1 plough in lordship; 2 men's ploughs; meadow, 2 acres.
   Also 5 Freemen, at 21 acres of meadow.
      Always 2 ploughs; 1 cob, 2 head of cattle; 5 pigs; 12 sheep.
Value 20s.

↟In Sceluagrā . ıı . foc . dim . car̃ . tr̃æ . 7 . vı . ac̃ . 7 . fub eó . vıı . bor̃ . 7 . ı . car̃.
Silu . xıı . por̃ . ıı . ac̃ . p̃ti . Vat . xı . fot . ↟ In Frenfe . ıı . foc̃ . s̃cı . E . de . xvı . ac̃.
Sẽp . dim̃ . car̃ . vat . ıı . fot.
↟Dicclefburc tenuit sẽp . s̃cs . E . p man̄ . 7 . p̃ . ıı . car̃ . tr̃e . m̃ tenent . ıı . p̃brı
de . ab̃b̃e . Sẽp . ııı . uitt . 7 . xıı . bor̃ . 7 . ıı . car̃ . in dñıo . 7 . ııı . car̃ hom̃.

211 b

Silu . xvı . porc̃ . vı . ac̃ . p̃ti . 7 . ıııı . foc̃ . xx . ac̃ . Sẽp . ı . car̃ . ı . ac̃ . p̃ti . vat xl . fot.
ħt . v . q̃r̃ . in lon̄ . 7 . ııı . in lat . 7 . vı . d̃ . de . g̃ . Ecctie . xxx . ac̃ . uat . ııı . fot.
↟Semere tenet sẽp . s̃cs . E . p man̄ . de . ıı . car̃ . tr̃æ . Sẽp . xıı . bor̃ . 7 . ıı . car̃.
in dñıo . 7 . ıı . car̃ . hom̃ . Silu . xıı . por . ııı . ac̃ . p̃ti . 7 . ı . foc̃ . de . x . ac̃ . Sẽp . ar̃
c̃ . ıı . bou . vat . xl . fot . ħt . v . q̃r̃ . in lon̄ . 7 . v . in lat . 7 . vı . d̃ . de . g̃.
In Ead ten& Fulcher . ı . foc̃ s̃cı . E . de . xx . ac̃ . 7 . ıı . bor̃ . 7 . d̃ . car̃ . 7 . ı . ac̃ . p̃ti.
vat . v . fot.
↟In Geffinga . ı . lib̃ hõ . 7 . dim̃ . de . xxxııı . ac̃ . 7 . ıı . bor̃ . Tc̃ . ı . car̃ . m̃ . dim̃ . Tc̃ uat
ııı . fot . m̃ . x . hoc inuafit Rog̃ hõ . R . malet.
↟In Sceluagrā . ı . lib̃ hõ . fcı . E . xıı . ac̃ . 7 . ıı . bou . vat . xvı . d̃ . Ecctiæ . xvı . ac̃.
uat . ıı . fot . 7 . vı . d̃ . Quando Rad comes fuit poteftatiuus 7 fui 7 tr̃æ fuæ.
feruientes ej̃ cambier̃ c̃ feruientib; s̃cı . E . ııı . hões . de borftuna . p aliis . ııı.
in Geffinga . qd comes habuit . ııı . 7 . Ab̃b̃ . ııı.

27 In SHELFANGER 2 Freemen, ½ c. of land and 6 acres.
       Under him 7 smallholders.
       1 plough; woodland, 12 pigs; meadow, 2 acres.
    Value 11s.

28 In FRENZE 2 Freemen of St. E(dmund's), at 16 acres.
       Always ½ plough.
    Value 2s.

29 St. E(dmund) has always held DICKLEBURGH as a manor and as 2 c.
    of land; now 2 priests hold from the Abbot.
       Always 4 villagers; 12 smallholders.
       2 ploughs in lordship; 4 men's ploughs; woodland, 16 pigs;   211 b
          meadow, 6 acres.
       Also 4 Freemen, 20 acres.
          Always 1 plough; meadow, 1 acre.
    Value 40s.
       It has 5 furlongs in length and 4 in width, tax of 6d.
       (Belonging) to the church, 30 acres;
    value 3s.

30 St. E(dmund) has always held SEMERE as a manor, at 2 c. of land.
       Always 12 smallholders.
       2 ploughs in lordship; 2 men's ploughs; woodland, 12 pigs;
          meadow, 3 acres.
       Also 1 Freeman, at 10 acres. He has always ploughed with
          2 oxen.
    Value 40s.
       It has 5 furlongs in length and 5 in width; tax of 6d.
    In the same Fulcher holds; 1 Freeman of St. E(dmund's) at 20
    acres.
       2 smallholders;
       ½ plough; meadow, 1 acre.
    Value 5s.

31 In GISSING 1 free man and a half, at 33 acres.
       2 smallholders.
       Then 1 plough, now ½.
    Value then 4s; now 10.
       Roger, R(obert) Malet's man, annexed this.

32 In SHELFANGER 1 free man of St. E(dmund's), 12 acres.
       2 oxen.
    Value 16d.
       (Belonging) to the church, 16 acres,
    value 2s 6d.
       When Earl Ralph was influential and his (men) and his lands,
    his servants exchanged with the servants of St. E(dmund) 4 men
    of Burston for another 4 in Gissing, so that the Earl had 4 and
    the Abbot 4.

In Siplinga . I . lib hō . 7 . dim̄ . de . xiiii . ac̄ . Sēp . dim̄ . car̄ . 7 . I . ac̄ . p̄ti . Val . xxviii . d.
In Regadona . iiii . foc . de . v . ac̄ . ap̄ptiati st in brefinghā .

⁊ Loddinga Hund . Lodnā tenð Frodo de abbe qd ten . S . E . t . r . e.
p . iii . car . trǣ . 7 . x . ac̄ . Sēp . iii . uilt . tē . viii . . bor . m̄ . xvi . Tc . ii . car . in
dn̄io . m̄ . iii . Tc . iii . car . hom . m̄ . i . Silu . lx . por . viii . ac̄ . p̄ti . m̄ . i . mol . Sēp
Ecclīæ . ix . ac̄. iiii . ac̄ . p̄ti . val . v . fol.
. I . runc̄ . m̄ . xii . an̄ . 7 . xxx . por . 7 lxxx . oū . ii . uafa . ap . 7 ibi st . xi . foc .
ad omnē confuet . xx . ac . Sēp . ii . car . Tc ual . xl . fol . m̄ . lxxx . ht . xiiii .
qr . in long . 7 . ix . in lat . 7 . de g . xvi . d . qcq; ibi teneat . Scs . E . foca .
In brō tenð Ide . i . car . trē . qd ten . Toli uicecomes . 7 . dedit fēg . Edm̄ .
t . r . e . 7 . p ea tenuit ab eo p firmā . ii . dierū . Sēp . i . car . in dn̄io . 7 . iiii . ac̄ .
p̄ti . 7 . i . runc . 7 . iiii . foc . de . v . ac . Sēp . dim̄ . car . val xx . fol . S . E . foca .

⁊ In Mundhalā tenð Gofelin . I . foc . de . xxx . ac̄ . fēp . i . uilt . 7 . i . bor . 7 . dim̄ .
car . val . xxxii . d . ⁊ n Topecroft tenet berengari de abbe . ii . car . trē
qd tenuer . ii . p̄rs . t . r . e . Sēp . iiii . uilt . 7 . x . bor . tē . ii . fer . m̄ . i . Sēp . ii . car
in dn̄io . 7 . iii . car . hom . Silu . iii . porc . iii . ac̄ . p̄ti . 7 . i . foc . de . ii . ac̄ . Tc . ual .
xxx . fol . m̄ . xl . Scs . E . foca .

33   In SHIMPLING 1 free man and a half, at 14 acres.
    Always ½ plough; meadow, 1 acre.
    Value 28d.

34   In ROYDON 4 Freemen, at 5 acres. They are assessed in Bressingham.

   LODDON Hundred
35   Frodo holds LODDON from the Abbot which St. E(dmund) held before 1066, as 3 c. of land and 10 acres.
    Always 3 villagers. Then 8 smallholders, now 16.
    Then 2 ploughs in lordship, now 3. Then 2 men's ploughs, now 1. Woodland, 60 pigs; meadow, 8 acres. Now 1 mill; always 1 cob.
    (Belonging) to the church, 60 acres; meadow, 4 acres;
   value 5s.
    Now 12 head of cattle; 30 pigs; 80 sheep; 2 beehives.
    There are 11 Freemen (bound) to all customary dues, 20 acres.
    Always 2 ploughs.
   Value then 40s; now 80.
    It has 14 furlongs in length and 9 in width, tax of 16d, whoever holds there. St. E(dmund has) the jurisdiction.
   He also holds 1 c. of land in BROOME which Toli the Sheriff held and granted to St. Edmund before 1066. Later he held it from them at the revenue of 2 days' allowance.
    Always 1 plough in lordship; meadow, 4 acres; 1 cob.
    Also 4 Freemen, at 5 acres.
    Always ½ plough.
   Value 20s. St. E(dmund has) the jurisdiction.

36   In MUNDHAM Jocelyn holds; 1 Freeman, at 30 acres.
    Always 1 villager; 1 smallholder.
    ½ plough.
   Value 32d.

37   In TOPCROFT Berenger holds from the Abbot 2 c. of land, which 2 priests held before 1066.
    Always 4 villagers; 10 smallholders. Then 2 slaves, now 1.
    Always 2 ploughs in lordship; 3 men's ploughs; woodland, 3 pigs; meadow, 3 acres.
    Also 1 Freeman, at 2 acres.
   Value then 30s; now 40. St. E(dmund has) the jurisdiction.

In Langahala . 7 . In ᴋercheſtuna xxvii.

ſoc̈ . ii . caŕ . 7 . dim̈ . tr̃æ . 7 . ii . uiƚƚ . 7 . xi . bor . Sēṕ . vi . caŕ . viii . ac̈ . p̃ti . app̃ciati
ſt in broc . Eccliæ . xii . ac̈ . vaƚ . xvi . đ . Langhala . ħt . i . leu̇ . in loń .
7 . dim̈ . in laṫ . 7 . de gelto . xvi . đ . q̄c̄q̨ . ibi teneat.

⁊ Depwade Hund . Tibham tenuit S . E . t . r . e . ṕ . ii . caŕ . tr̃æ . 7 . ʟx . ac̈ .
m̂ ten& Ricuard́ . Sēṕ . v . uiƚƚ . 7 . ix . bor . 7 . i . ſer . 7 . ii . caŕ . in dn̄io . 7 . i . caŕ
hom̂ . v . ac̈ . p̃ti . vi . añ . xʟ . cap . Tc̄ uaƚ . xʟ . ſoƚ . m̂ . ʟx . 7 ħt . i . leu̇ 7 . dim̈ .
in loń . 7 . i . leu̇ in laṫ . 7 . xviii . đ . de . gelto.

⁊ Torp ten& Rob́ de uaƚs qđ teń . S . Ė . p man . 7 . ṕ . i . caŕ . tr̃æ . Sēṕ . vii .
uiƚƚ . 7 . iii . bor . 7 . i . ſer . 7 . i caŕ . in dn̄io . 7 . i . caŕ . hom̂ . ii . ac̈ . p̃ti . 7 . i . moƚ .
7 . ii . anim̂ . 7 . iiii . por . xvi . ou̇ . 7 . iii . ſoc̈ . xxx . ac̈ . sēṕ . caŕ . Ecłæ . xii . ac̈ .
Tc̄ . uaƚ . xx . ſoƚ . m̂ . xxx 7 . i . lib̃ hō de q́ abuit abbas dim̈ cōm̄d . t . r . ė .
de . i . caŕ . tr̃æ . qđ ten& Idē . 7 . ix . lib̃i hōes . 7 . dim̈ . ſub ſe . c̄m̄d . tanṫ . xxx . ac̈ .
★ 7 . i . uiƚƚ . 7 . i . bor . Tc̄ . inẗ eos . iii . caŕ . 7 . dim̈ . m̂ . iii . ii . ac̈ . p̃ti . In Frichetuna
ten& Idē . ii . lib̃os . hōes de . xxiii . ac̈ . 7 . i . uiƚƚ . 7 . iii . bor . 7 . i . caŕ . In Stratuna
. i . lib̃ hō . xv . ac̈ . 7 . dim̈ . caŕ . In Torp . ii . lib̃i hōes . xii . ac̈ . 7 . dim̈ . caŕ . Tc̄ uaƚ . xxx .
ſoƚ . m̂ . ʟ . ʜoc ten& Idē . R . Torp ħt . i . leu̇ in loń . 7 . iii . q̇r in laṫ . 7 . i . đ . 7 . iii .
ferd́ . de . ḡ . In Frietuna . i . lib̃ hō reḡ . de . xv . ac̈ 7 . ii . bor . 7 uaƚ . v̈ . ſoƚ . hoc ten& Idē . R .

38 In LANGHALE and in KIRSTEAD 27 Freemen, 2½ c. of land and 10 acres.
   2 villagers; 11 smallholders.
   Always 6 ploughs; meadow, 8 acres.
   They are assessed in Brooke.
   (Belonging) to the church, 12 acres;
   value 16d.
   Langhale has 1 league in length and ½ in width, tax of 16d, whoever holds there.

DEPWADE Hundred
39 St. E(dmund) held TIBENHAM before 1066, as 2 c. of land and 60 acres. Now Richard holds.
   Always 5 villagers; 9 smallholders; 1 slave.
   2 ploughs in lordship; 1 men's plough; meadow, 5 acres; 6 head of cattle; 40 goats.
   Value then 40s; now 60.
   It has 1½ leagues in length and 1 league in width, tax of 18d.

40 Robert of Vaux holds (Morning) THORPE which St. E(dmund) held as a manor and as 1 c. of land.
   Always 7 villagers; 3 smallholders; 1 slave.
   1 plough in lordship; 1 men's plough; meadow, 2 acres; 1 mill; 2 head of cattle; 4 pigs; 16 sheep.
   Also 3 Freemen, 30 acres; always 1 plough.
   (Belonging) to the church, 12 acres.
   Value then 20s; now 30.
   Also 1 free man of whom the Abbot had half the patronage before 1066, at 1 c. of land. He also holds this. Also 9 free men
   Also 9 free men and a half under himself in patronage only; 30 acres.
   1 villager; 1 smallholder.
   Then between them 3½ ploughs, now 3. Meadow, 2 acres.
In FRITTON he also holds 2 free men, at 23 acres.
   1 villager; 3 smallholders;
   1 plough.
In STRATTON 1 free man, 15 acres; ½ plough.
In (Morning) THORPE 2 free men, 12 acres; ½ plough.
Value then 30s; now 50. R(obert) also holds this.
   (Morning) Thorpe has 1 league in length and 3 furlongs in width, tax of 1¾d.
In Fritton 1 free man of the King's, at 15 acres; 2 smallholders.
Value 3s. R(obert) also holds this.

⁋Clauelinga Hund Kercheby ten& Rasrid de abbe. qd tenuit. S. E. t. r. e. p. ii. car. trae. Sep. i. uilt. 7. xi. bor. tc. ii. car. in dnio. m. iii. Sep. v. car. hom. xiiii. ac. pti. Silu. vi. porc. tc. dim. mot. m. i. 7. dim. Ecclie. xx. ac. in elemosina. 7. ii. part. uni ecclie. de. xiiii. ac. In dnio. iiii. runc. iiii. an. xv. porc. c. ou. 7. iii. libi. hoes. iii. car. trae 7. iiii. car. 7. dim. 7. iii. ac. pti. Tc. ual. xl. sol. m. vi. lib. Ecclie. xx. ac. ual. xx. d. ht. ix. qr in long. 7. v. in lat. 7. de. g. x. d. 7. ob.

⁋Hals tenuer. ix. hoes. de. lx. ac. iiii. erant. soc. 7. vii. soca 7 cmd tantu Sep. ii. bor 7. v. libi hoes. vi. ac. ho est in ptio de Lodnes. 7 Frodo ten& de abbe In Nortuna. i. lib ho cmd. xxx. ac. Sep. i. car. 7. i. ac. pti. 7. ix. libi hoes sub eo. de. xx. ac. qd ten& Gosselin. Sep. dim. car. ual. v. sol. Sup hos. ix. rex. 7. comes soca. Ecclie. xx. ac. libe trae. In Ead lib ho cmd t. r. e. viii. ac. 7. ii. bou. ual. xii. d.

⁋In Kechinga. i. lib ho simil. viii. ac. qd ten& abb in dnio. 7. ual. viii. d. In Hals. ii. libi hoes. i. ac. ual. iiii. d. hoc ten& Ide. F

CLAVERING Hundred

41 Radfrid holds KIRBY (Cane) from the Abbot which St. E(dmund) held before 1066, as 2 c. of land.
Always 1 villager; 11 smallholders.
Then 2 ploughs in lordship, now 3. Always 5 men's ploughs; meadow, 14 acres; woodland, 6 pigs. Then ½ mill, now 1½. (Belonging) to the church, 20 acres in alms. Also two-thirds of 1 church, at 14 acres. In lordship 4 cobs; 4 head of cattle; 15 pigs; 100 sheep.
Also 3 free men, 3 c. of land; 4½ ploughs; meadow, 3 acres.
Value then 40s; now £6.
(Belonging) to the church, 20 acres;
value 20d.
It has 9 furlongs in length and 5 in width, tax of 10½d.

42 9 men held HALES, at 64 acres. 2 were Freemen and 7 in jurisdiction and patronage only.
Always 2 smallholders; also 5 free men; 6 acres.   212 b
This is in the valuation of Loddon. Frodo holds from the Abbot.
In NORTON (Subcourse) 1 free man in patronage, 30 acres.
Always 1 plough; meadow, 1 acre.
Also 9 free men under him, at 20 acres. Jocelyn holds this.
Always ½ plough.
Value 5s.
The King and the Earl (have) the jurisdiction over these 9.
(Belonging) to the church, 20 acres of free land.
In the same a free man in patronage before 1066, 8 acres; 2 oxen.
Value 12d.

43 In HECKINGHAM 1 free man likewise, 8 acres, which the Abbot holds in lordship.
Value 8d.
In HALES 2 free men, 1 acre.
Value 4d. F(rodo) also holds this.

.XV. **TERRA SCE** Adeldredæ Hund 7 Dim̃. de Clakeflofa. de . x.
leitis. Mareham tenuit Sc̃a . A . t . r . e . Tc . IIII . car . in dn̄io . m̃ . III . Tc . vI .
car . hom . m̃ . III . Sẽp xIx . uiłł . 7 . xIII . bor . tc . vII . ſer . m̃ . v . xxvI . ac . p̃ti , 7
. I . moł . tc . x . runc . m̃ . IIII . tc . I . uac . m̃ . vI . tc . cxxxI . ou . m̃ . ccc . tc . xxIIII
por . m̃ . xxIII . нec tr̃a ħt . I . leu in long . 7 . c . perc ; 7 dim leu . in lat . 7 . I .
qr . 7 in Mareſc neſcit m̃ſurā . Sẽp . uał . x . łib . huic manerio adjacebant . t . r . e .
xxvII . ſoc . c̃ õi conſuetudine . ſ; poſtq̃ rex . Witł . aduenit ; habuit eos hugo de
montfort p̃t unū . 7 . W . de uuar . I . ſoc . de . vI . ac . de . ecc̃lia . hec tota tr̃a redd
. xIIII . d . de . g . q̃n hund . 7 . d . reddebat . geltum de . xx . ſoł . m̃ ſimił
In becheſuuella . I . car . tr̃æ . 7 . I . car . in dn̄io . 7 . I . car . hom . vII . uiłł . I . ſer .
. x . ac . p̃ti . vał . xx . ſoł .
In Phincham ten . S . A . t . r . e . xxx . ac . tr̃æ . Sẽp . III . bor . 7 . I . car . x . ac . p̃ti .

213 a

Vał . x . ſoł . In нidlingeia . IIII . bor . II . ac . 7 . uał . vI . d .
In Photeſtorp . I . car . tr̃æ . 7 . III . uiłł . 7 . II . bor . Sẽp . I . car . in dn̄io . 7 . dim .
car . hom . 7 . II . ac . p̃ti . 7 . Lxxx . ou . vIII . por . Vał . xx . ſoł . ħt . IIII .
qrant . in lon . 7 . III . in lat . 7 . IIII . d . de g . hanc tr̃a caluм̃pniat eſſe libam
Vlchetel ħo hermeri . q̃cq̃; m̃ judicet . t́ bello t́ juditio . 7 ali e p̃ſto pbare
eo m̃ . qd jacuit ad ecc̃liam die q̃ rex . E . obiit . S; totus hund teſtat́ .
eā fuiſſæ t . r . e ad ſcam adeld .

In Forham . III . bor . xII . ac . vał . II . ſoł . In Dunhā . II . uiłł . xII . ac .
7 . I . ac . p̃ti . vał . xII . d . Totū Dunham ħt . III . qr in long . 7 . II .
in lat . 7 . IIII . d . de . g . q̃cq̃; ibi teneat .

LAND OF ST. ETHELDREDA

Hundred and a Half of CLACKCLOSE of 10 leets

1 St. E(theldreda) held MARHAM before 1066.
> Then 4 ploughs in lordship, now 3. Then 6 men's ploughs, now 3.
> Always 19 villagers; 13 smallholders. Then 7 slaves, now 5.
> Meadow, 26 acres; 1 mill. Then 10 cobs, now 4. Then 1 cow, now 6. Then 131 sheep, now 300. Then 24 pigs, now 23.
>
> This land has 1 league and 100 perches in length and ½ league and 1 furlong in width. In Marshland the measurement is unknown. Value always £10.
>
> 27 Freemen were attached to this manor before 1066 with all customary dues, but after King William arrived Hugh of Montfort had them except for 1; W(illiam) of Warenne (has) 1 Freeman, at 6 acres from the church.
>
> All this land paid tax of 14d when the Hundred and Half paid tax of 20s; now likewise.

2 In BEXWELL 1 c. of land.
> 1 plough in lordship; 1 men's plough.
> 7 villagers; 1 slave.
> Meadow, 10 acres.
> Value 20s.
>
> In FINCHAM St. E(theldreda) held 30 acres of land before 1066.
> Always 3 smallholders,
> 1 plough; meadow, 10 acres.
> Value 10s.   213 a
>
> In HILGAY 4 smallholders; 2 acres.
> Value 6d.
>
> In FODDERSTONE 1 c. of land.
> 3 villagers; 2 smallholders.
> Always 1 plough in lordship; ½ men's plough; meadow, 2 acres; 80 sheep; 8 pigs.
> Value 20s.
> It has 4 furlongs in length and 3 in width; tax of 4d.
>
> Ulfketel, Hermer's man, claims this land to be free, in whatever way it be adjudged, either by battle or judicial ordeal. And another is ready to prove in the same way that it lay with the church on the day King Edward died. But the whole Hundred testifies that it belonged to St. Etheldreda before 1066.

3 In FORDHAM 3 smallholders, 12 acres.
> Value 2s.
>
> In DOWNHAM (Market) 2 villagers, 12 acres; meadow, 1 acre.
> Value 12d.
>
> The whole of Downham (Market) has 3 furlongs in length and 2 in width, tax of 4d, whoever holds there.

Ḣund̂. 7. dim̃. de Fredebruge Waltunā tenuit. Scā. Aeld̂.
. t. r. e. ꝑ. IIII. car̃. tr̃æ. Sẽp. xx. uiłł. xl. bor. Tc̃. xvii. ſer̃. m̃. xiii.
. c. ac̃. ꝑti. I. piſc̃. Sẽp. v. car̃. in dnio. 7. III. car̃. hom̃. tc̃. xxii. ſał.
m̃. xxiiii. Sẽp. vi. runc̃. tc̃. xviii. añ. m̃. xvi. tc̃. xxii. por. m̃.
xxiii. Sẽp. Ⓜ ccc. ou. hic jacent. xlvii. ac̃. tr̃e in Eſingatuna.
q̇d̃ ſẽp. tenent. II. uiłł. 7. vii. ſoc̃. de. I. car̃. tr̃æ. 7. xi. bor. 7. III. ſer̃.
Sẽp. II. car̃. Sẽp uał. xv. łib. ⸗In Acra. dim̃. car̃ tr̃æ. teñ. Ṡ. A.
t. r. e. II. bor. I. ſer̃. I. ac̃. ꝑti. Sẽp. dim̃. car̃. xxx. ou. vał. III. ſoł.
⸗In Eſingatuna teñ. Ṡ. A. I. car̃. tr̃æ. t. r. e. tc̃. I. car̃. m̃. dim̃. II. uiłł
. III. bor. xx. ac̃. ꝑti. II. ſał. huic manerio jacent. xviii. ſoc̃. de
xvii. ac̃. 7. dim̃. Totũ uał. xvi. ſoł.

⸗Ḣund̂ de Grimeſhou. Feltuuełłā. ten& ſep. ſcā. A. ꝑ. vi. car̃
tr̃æ. tc̃. xl. uiłł. m̃. xxviii. tc̃. v. bor. m̃. x. tc̃. xiiii. ſer̃. m̃. xii.
Tc̃. v. car̃. in dn̄io. m̃. IIII. tc̃. viii. car̃. hom̃. m̃. vii. xxx. ac̃ ꝑti.
Sẽp. II. runc̃. xi. añ. cxl. ou. Tc̃. xxxiii. por. m̃. xxii. I. moł.
. 7. II. piſc̃. Sẽp uał. xii. łib. ƕt. I. leŭ. 7. dim̃. in łoñ. 7. I. leug̃
in łat̃. 7. xxx. d̃. 7 oboł de. g̃.

Huic manerio jacebant. t. r. e. xxviiii. ſoc̃. ſoc̃. c̃ omĩ conſuet̃ q̃s m̃
ten&. W. de gar̃. 7. vi. libos hoēs ſoca 7. cõm̃d tantũ. Totũ ƕt. Idẽ. W.
⸗Nort walde. ten& ſẽp. Ṡ. A. ꝑ. vi. car̃. tr̃æ. Sẽp. viii. uiłł. xviiii. bor
. IIII. ſer̃. tc̃. III. car̃ in dn̄io. m̃. IIII. tc̃. v. car̃. hom̃. m̃. III. xvi. ac̃. ꝑti. II. moł.
. II. piſc̃. II. runc̃. xi. añ. cxxx. ou. tc̃. xxxi. por. m̃. xxii. tc̃ uał. viii. łib. m̃. ix.
hic jacebant. t. r. e. III. ſoc̃. c̃ omĩ conſuet̃. 7. IIII. libi hoēs ſoca 7. cõm̃d tantũ. Totũ ten&
. W. de uuar̃. ƕt. I. leŭ in łoñ. 7. dim̃ in łat̃. 7. xxx. d̃. 7 ob̃ de. g̃. Alii ibi tenent.

The Hundred and a Half of FREEBRIDGE

4   St. Etheldreda held (West) WALTON before 1066, as 4 c. of land.
    Always 20 villagers; 40 smallholders. Then 17 slaves, now 13.
    Meadow, 100 acres; 1 fishery. Always 5 ploughs in lordship;
       3 men's ploughs. Then 22 salt-houses, now 24; always 6
       cobs. Then 18 head of cattle, now 16. Then 22 pigs, now 23;
       always 1,300 sheep.
    Here appertain 47 acres of land in (the lands of) Islington
    which 2 villagers have always held.
       Also 7 Freemen, at 1 c. of land. 11 smallholders, 3 slaves.
          Always 2 ploughs.
    Value always £15.

5   In ACRE St. E(theldreda) held ½ c. of land before 1066.
       2 smallholders; 1 slave.
       Meadow, 1 acre. Always ½ plough; 30 sheep.
    Value 3s.

6   In ISLINGTON St. E(theldreda) held 1 c. of land before 1066.
       Then 1 plough, now ½.
       2 villagers; 3 smallholders.
       Meadow, 20 acres; 2 salt-houses.
       18 Freemen appertain to this manor, at 17½ acres.
    Value of the whole 16s.

The Hundred of GRIMSHOE

7   St. E(theldreda) has always held FELTWELL, as 6 c. of land.
       Then 40 villagers, now 28. Then 5 smallholders, now 10. Then
          14 slaves, now 12.
       Then 5 ploughs in lordship, now 4. Then 8 men's ploughs,
          now 7. Meadow, 30 acres. Always 2 cobs; 11 head of cattle;
          140 sheep. Then 33 pigs, now 22. 1 mill; 2 fisheries.
    Value always £12.
       It has 1½ leagues in length and 1 league in width, tax of 30½d.
       34 Freemen appertained to this manor before 1066 with all   213 b
    customary dues, whom now W(illiam) of Warenne holds and 6
    free men in jurisdiction and patronage only. W(illiam) also has
    the whole.

8   St. E(theldreda) has always held NORTHWOLD, as 6 c. of land.
       Always 8 villagers; 19 smallholders; 3 slaves.
       Then 3 ploughs in lordship, now 4. Then 5 men's ploughs, now
          3. Meadow, 16 acres; 2 mills; 2 fisheries; 2 cobs; 11 head of
          cattle; 130 sheep. Then 31 pigs, now 22.
    Value then £8; now 9.
       3 Freemen appertained here before 1066 with all customary
    dues. Also 4 free men in jurisdiction and patronage only.
    W(illiam) of Warenne holds the whole.
       It has 1 league in length and ½ in width, tax of 30½d. Others
    hold there.

213 a, b

℣ Mondefort tenet sep̃ . S̃ . A . III . car . tr̃æ . tc̃ . xIIII . uill̃ . m̃ . x . tc̃ . IIII . bor . m̃ . VIII .
tc̃ . IIII . ſer . m̃ . II . Sep̃ . II . car in dñio . tc̃ . III . car . hom . m̃ . II . xvI . ac̃ .
p̃ti . Sep̃ . dim . mol̃ . v . añ . xxxIII . ou . tc̃ . II . ſer . m̃ . III . Val̃ xL . ſol .
huic man̄ . adjacent . vII . ſoc̃ . ē om̃i conſuet . q̃s m̃ ten& . W . h̃t . I . leũ .
in lon̄ . 7 . dim . in lat . 7 . xI . ð . de . g̃ .
℣ Scerpham . Hund Brugã ten& . sep̃ . sc̃a . A . IIII . car . tr̃æ . Sep̃ .
xII . uill . tc̃ . x . bor . m̃ . xvII . Sep̃ . IIII . ſer . III . car . in dñio . III . car . hom̄ .
. IIII . ac̃ . p̃ti . Silũ xv . porc̃ . II . mol . II . runc̃ . v . añ . tc̃ . cc . ou . m̃ . cLxxx .
xxv . por . huic manerio ptinent . xxx . ac̃ . in dñio . que st̃ in breham
7 . xxx . ac̃ . in Rudham . tc̃ ual̃ . vI . lib̃ . m̃ . vIII . Totũ h̃t . I . leũ . in lon̄ .
7 . III . qr̃ . in lat . 7 . xII . ð . de . g̃ . huic manerio jac̃ . I . pbr̃ . 7 ual̃ . II . ſol .
7 . ñ pot̃at uend̃e . tr̃a ſuã . 7 . I . ſoc̃ . dim . car . tr̃æ . 7 . dim . car . 7 . ual̃ . II . ſol
iſte fuit de lib̃is hominib3 Rõgi bigot . ſ; abbas eũ derationauit . 7 . ten&
℣ Gildecros Hund . In Benhã . I . ſoc̃ . II . car . tr̃æ . ten . S̃ . A . t . r . c̃ .
tc̃ . 7 p̃ . x . uill . m̃ . IIII . Sep̃ . vI . bor . Tc̃ . IIII . ſer . xxIIII . ac̃ . p̃ti . Silũ . c . por
tc̃ . II . car . in dñio . P . ð . m̃ . I . 7 . I . car pot̃ reſtaurari . Tc̃ . 7 . p̃ . II . car
hom . m̃ . I . 7 . alia pot̃ rest . tc̃ . IIII . añ . m̃ . II . tc̃ . xvI . por . m̃ . II .
hoc man̄ ten& . W . de Scohies . de abbia . Et . III . ſoc̃ . xx . ac̃ . tr̃e
Sep̃ . dim . car . II . ac̃ . p̃ti . Tc̃ . ual̃ . Lx . ſol . m̃ . xL . In ead̃ . III . lib̃i hões
. ð . car . tr̃æ . 7 . v . ac̃ . de qb3 ñ habuit . n c̃m̃d . Soca in Keninchala reg̃

9   St. E(theldreda) has always held MUNDFORD, 3 c. of land.
   Then 14 villagers, now 10. Then 4 smallholders, now 8. Then
      4 slaves, now 2.
   Always 2 ploughs in lordship. Then 3 men's ploughs, now 2.
      Meadow, 16 acres. Always ½ mill; 5 head of cattle, 33 sheep.
      Then 2 slaves, now 3.
Value 40s.
   To this manor are attached 7 Freemen with all customary dues,
whom W(illiam) now holds.
   It has 1 league in length and ½ in width, tax of 11d.

   SHROPHAM Hundred
10 St. E(theldreda) has always held BRIDGHAM, 4 c. of land.
   Always 12 villagers. Then 10 smallholders, now 17; always 4
      slaves.
   3 ploughs in lordship; 3 men's ploughs; meadow, 4 acres;
      woodland, 15 pigs; 2 mills; 2 cobs, 5 head of cattle. Then
      200 sheep, now 180. 25 pigs.
   To this manor belong 30 acres in lordship which are in
BRETTENHAM and 30 acres in ROUDHAM.
Value then £6; now 8.
   The whole has 1 league in length and 3 furlongs in width; tax
of 12d.
   1 priest appertains to this manor.
Value 2s. He could not sell his land.
   Also 1 Freeman, ½ c. land; ½ plough.
Value 2s.
He was among the free men of Roger Bigot, but the Abbot proved
(his claim to) him, and he holds.

   GUILTCROSS Hundred
11 In BANHAM 1 Freeman, 2 c. of land. St. E(theldreda) held before
1066.
   Then and later 10 villagers, now 4; always 6 smallholders. Then
      4 slaves.
   Meadow, 24 acres; woodland, 100 pigs.
   Then 2 ploughs in lordship; later ½, now 1, 1 plough could be
      restored. Then and later 2 men's ploughs, now 1, another
      could be restored.
   Then 4 head of cattle, now 2. Then 16 pigs, now 2.
W(illiam) of Écouis holds this manor from the Abbey.
   Also 3 Freemen, 20 acres of land. Always ½ plough; meadow,
      2 acres.
Value then 60s; now 40.
   In the same 3 free men, ½ c. of land and 5 acres. (The Abbot)
had nothing except the patronage of them. The jurisdiction (is)
in the King's (manor of) Kenninghall.

vi . ac̷ . p̷ti . tc̄ . ı . car̷ . 7 . dim̄ . m̄ . ı . val̷ . x . fol . Hos lib̄bos hoēs tenuit Rafrid . Poſt
. W . de fcohies . 7 abbas faifiuit eos ppt̄ c̄m̄d fuā.

⫶ In Rifeurda . ı . car̷ . trǣ . 7 . dim̄ . ten̄ . S̄ . A . ſēp . ııı . uilł . ı . ſer̷ . vııı . ac̷ . p̷ti . Tc̄ . ıı . car̷ .
m̄ . nult . f; poſst reſt . Tc̄ . dim̄ car̷ . hom̄ . m̄ . ı . bou̷ . 7 . ı . foc̷ . ıı . ac̷ . Tc̄ . ual̷ . xx .
fol . m̄ . vııı . hoc ten& Joh̄s nepos Walerami.

In Rifeurda . Vluric̷ lib̄ hō . lx . ac̷ . t . r . e . ııı . ac̷ . p̷ti . tc̄ . ı . car̷ . Socam
Keninghala . tc̄ . ual̷ ; x . fol . m̄ . v . Hic uluric̷ forisfact̷ fuit erga reḡ . W .
de . vııı . lib̄ . 7 . ido remanfit in manu reḡ . hoc &iam ten& Idē de ab̄b̄e.

⫶ In Nortuna . ı . foc̷ . lxxx . ac̷ . 7 . ı . ac̷ . p̷ti . 7 . ı . uilł . 7 . vıı . bor . 7 . ı . car̷ . val̷
xv . fol . Iſte fuit de libis hōib; . R . bigot f; ab̄b̄ de rationaū.

⫶⫶ Lauuendic . Hund . Offuic ten& ſēp . S̄ . A . ı . car̷ . trǣ . ſēp . ıııı . bor .
7 . ııı . foc̷ . vı . ac̷ . Sēp . ı . car̷ . in dn̄io . tc̄ . ıı . car̷ . hom̄ . m̄ . dim̄ . 7 . dim̄ . car̷
pot reſt . ıı . ac̷ . p̷ti . filu̷ . xxıııı . porc̷ . Val̷ xx . fol . Rainald fili̷ iuonis
ten& de ab̄b̄e f; p̄ tenuit de rege.

⫶ In hou ten& ſēp . ı . car̷ . trǣ . Sēp . vııı . uilł . x . bor . vııı . ac̷ . p̷ti . ııı . car̷ .
Silu̷ . c . por . ı . mol . hoc jac& in Derhā . c̄ om̄i confuet̷ . 7 . in p̄tio . Soca
in Mulehā . reḡ de . ıı . foc̷ . q̄ ſīnt xxııı . ac̷ . 7 . ııı . ac̷ . p̷ti . filu̷ . ııı . porc̷ .
dim̄ . car̷ . val̷ . ııı . fol . Ab̄b̄ habuit c̄m̄d . 7 focā faldæ.

Meadow, 6 acres. Then 1½ ploughs, now 1. 214 a
Value 10s.
Radfrid held these free men, later W(illiam) of Écouis; the Abbot took possession of them because of his patronage.

12 In RUSHFORD St. E(theldreda) held 1½ c. of land.
Always 3 villagers; 1 slave.
Meadow, 8 acres. Then 2 ploughs, now none, but they could be restored. Then ½ men's plough, now 1 ox.
Also 1 Freeman, 2 acres.
Value then 20s; now 8.
John, Waleran's nephew, holds this.
In Rushford Wulfric, a free man (held) 60 acres before 1066; meadow, 4 acres. Then 1 plough. The jurisdiction (is) in Kenninghall.
Value then 10s; now 5.
This Wulfric incurred a forfeiture of £8 to King William and thus it was in the King's hand. (John) also holds this from the Abbot.

13 In (Blo) NORTON 1 Freeman, 80 acres;
meadow, 1 acre.
1 villager; 7 smallholders.
1 plough.
Value 15s.
He was among R(oger) Bigot's free men, but the Abbot proved (his claim to him).

LAUNDITCH Hundred

14 St. E(theldreda) has always held OXWICK, 1 c. of land.
Always 4 smallholders. Also 3 Freemen, 6 acres.
Always 1 plough in lordship. Then 2 men's ploughs, now ½; ½ plough could be restored. Meadow, 2 acres; woodland, 24 pigs.
Value 20s.
Reynold, son of Ivo, holds from the Abbot, but formerly he held from the King.

15 In HOE (the Saint) has always held 1 c. of land.
Always 8 villagers; 10 smallholders.
Meadow, 8 acres; 3 ploughs; woodland, 100 pigs; 1 mill.
This appertains in (East) Dereham, with all customary dues and in (its) valuation. The jurisdiction is in the King's (manor of) Mileham as to 2 Freemen who have 24 acres.
Meadow, 4 acres; woodland, 4 pigs; ½ plough.
Value 4s.
The Abbot had the patronage and the fold-rights.

Mittefort Hund 7 . dim. Derham ten& sep . S . A . v . car . trae
tc . xx . uilt . m̃ . xvi . tc . xx . bor . m̃ . xxv . 7 . ii . fer . Tc . ii . car . in dñio
m̃ . iii . tc . viii . car . hom . m̃ . vii . Tc filu . dc . por . m̃ . ccc . sep . iii . mol
. iiii . runc . xii . añ . xx . porc . c . ou . vii . foc . xxx . ac . ii . ac . pti . iiii . ac.
filuae . Tc ual . x . lib . m̃ . xiii . ht . i . leu . in lon . 7 . dim . in lat . 7 . xv . d.
de . g . Tota foca ifti hund 7 . dimidii . jacebat ad scam . A . t . r . e . 7 ual
. ix . fol.

Torp ten& sep . S . A . iii . car . trae . sep . x . uilt . xx . bor . m̃ . iiii . fer.
Tc . i . car . in dñio . m̃ . ii . Sep . vii . car . 7 . dim . hom . Tc filu . dccc . por . m̃ . dc.

214 b

. viii . ac . pti . Sep . i . mol . ii . runc . xi . añ . xxvii . porc . lxxxxvii . ou . xxxviii.
cap . 7 . xii . foc . xl . ac . sep . v . car . xii . ac . pti . Silu . xii . porc . tc ual . lx . fol . m̃ . xi.
lib . 7 . ht . i . leu . in lon . 7 . i . leu . in lat . 7 . xv . d . de . g . 7 . fup oms foc
de iftis . ii . maner . xv . d.

Cauelea . ten& bner de abbe . qd ten . fca . A . t . r . e . i . car . tre . sep . iiii . uilt.
xi . bor . i . car in dñio . dim . car hom . 7 tota pot fieri . Silu . xx . porc . xx . ac pti
m̃ . i . runc . iiii . añ . v . por . v . foc . xx . ac . ual . xx . fol . ht . iiii . qr in lon . 7 . iiii.
in lat . 7 . v . d . de . g . hanc tra . calupniat Godric ad feudu . R . comitis.
qd eam tenuit anteq forisfac& . 7 hoc teftat . hund.

In Dodenham . i . foc . fcae . A . ii . car . trae . vii . bor . i . mol . iii . ac . pti.
S . p . i . car . 7 . dim . Tc ual . xx . fol . m̃ . xii . Rad de bella fago ten& de abbe.

In Mateshala . viii . foc . xxx . ac . Tc . ii . car . m̃ . i . viii . ac . pti . Tc . ual . xx.
fol . m̃ . xiii . 7 viii . d.

MITFORD Hundred and a Half

16 St. E(theldreda) has always held (East) DEREHAM, 5 c. of land.
    Then 20 villagers, now 16. Then 20 smallholders, now 25.
      2 slaves.
    Then 2 ploughs in lordship, now 3. Then 8 men's ploughs,
      now 7. Then woodland, 600 pigs, now 300. Always 3 mills;
      3 cobs, 12 head of cattle; 20 pigs; 100 sheep.
    Also 7 Freemen, 30 acres. Meadow, 2 acres; woodland, 3 acres.
  Value then £10; now 13.
  It has 1 league in length and ½ in width, tax of 15d.
  Before 1066 the whole jurisdiction of this Hundred and a Half
appertained to St. E(theldreda).
Value 60s.

17 St. E(theldreda) has always held THORPE, 3 c. of land.
    Always 10 villagers; 20 smallholders. Now 4 slaves.
    Then 1 plough in lordship, now 2. Always 7½ men's ploughs.
    Then woodland, 800 pigs, now 600. Meadow, 8 acres.   214 b
      Always 1 mill; 2 cobs; 11 head of cattle; 27 pigs; 97 sheep;
      38 goats.
    Also 12 Freemen, 40 acres. Always 5 ploughs; meadow, 12
      acres; woodland, 12 pigs.
  Value then 60s; now £11.
  It has 1 league in length and 1 league in width, tax of 15d. On
all the Freemen of these 2 manors (is charged) 15d.

18 Berner holds CALVELY from the Abbot, which St. E(theldreda)
held before 1066; 1 c. of land.
    Always 4 villagers; 11 smallholders.
    1 plough in lordship; ½ men's plough, and the whole could be
      there. Woodland, 20 pigs; meadow, 20 acres. Now 1 cob;
      4 head of cattle; 5 pigs.
    5 Freemen, 20 acres.
  Value 20s.
  It has 4 furlongs in length and 4 in width, tax of 5d.
  Godric claims this land as part of Earl R(alph's) Holding
because he held it before he forfeited. This the Hundred testifies.

19 In (North) TUDDENHAM 1 Freeman of St. E(theldreda)'s, 2 c. of land.
    7 smallholders.
    1 mill; meadow, 3 acres; always 1½ ploughs.
  Value then 20s; now 12.
  Ralph of Beaufour holds from the Abbot.

20 In MATTISHALL 8 Freemen, 30 acres.
    Then 2 ploughs, now 1. Meadow, 8 acres.
  Value then 20s; now 13(s) 8d.

⁊In Torp.7.In Turſtuna.7.In Jacheſhā.v.foc̄⁊.ſc̄e.A.L.ac̄⁊.sēp⁊.I.car̄⁊.
val.VIII.fol.⁊In Jacheſham.XIIII.foc̄⁊.LXXXX.ac̄⁊.sēp.II⁊.car̄.IIII.ac̄⁊.p̄ti
val.XX.fol.Roḡ bigot ten& de ab͡be.ſ; p̄ tenuit de rege

★ ⁊Hund̄ de brodeſcros.In Bruneſtor.I.foc̄⁊.7 car̄.t̄ræ.Sēp.VIII.bor.
★ 7.I.car̄.in d̄nio.7.I.car̄.hom̄⁊.III.ac̄⁊.p̄ti.I.mol.val.LX.fol.
★ ⁊Heineſteda Hund̄.dim̄⁊;⁊Pullaham tenuit.S.A.t.r.e.
p.XV.car̄.t̄ræ.Sēp LX.uill.XXV.bor.VII.ſer⁊.III.car̄ in d̄nio.
Tc̄.XX.car̄.hom̄.m̄.XVI.XVI.ac̄⁊.p̄ti.Tc̄.ſilu.DC.por.m̄.CCC.
7.I.mol.III.runc̄⁊.XI⁊.XL.por.L.ou.XL.cap.IIII.uaſa apū⁊.
Tc̄ ual.VIII.lib̄.m̄.XV.h̄t.II.leū⁊.in lon⁊.7.I.leū⁊.in lat⁊ 7.de
g⁊.XXX.d.

⁊In Pleſtuna tenuit lib̄ hō ſub ſc̄a.A.t⁊.r⁊.e⁊.I.car̄.t̄ræ.m̄ ten&
Roḡ de Ramis de ab͡be.Sēp.V.bor.7.I.ſer⁊.Tc̄.7 p̄.II.car̄ in d̄nio
m̄.III.Sēp.dim̄⁊.car̄.hom̄.Silu⁊.XVI.por.VIII.ac̄⁊.p̄ti.Tc̄.7 p̄

ual XX.fol.m̄.X.h̄t.V.qrant⁊.in lon⁊.7.V.in lat⁊ 7.de.g⁊.IIII.d.plures ibi
tenent
⁊Dice.dim̄⁊ Hund̄.Teluetunā ten& sēp.ſc̄a.A.p.II.car̄.t̄ræ.Sēp
VI.uill.7.I.bor.tc̄.II.car̄.in d̄nio.m̄.null.Sēp.I.car̄ hom̄.IIII.ac̄⁊.p̄ti.
Tc̄.ſilu⁊.LX.por.m̄.XXX.Val.XX.fol.h̄t.I.leū⁊.in long.7.dim̄⁊.in lat⁊.
7.de g⁊.VII.d.
⁊In Teueteſhala.II.foc̄⁊.dim̄⁊.car̄;t̄ræ.7.II.ac̄⁊.7.II.uill⁊.7.dim̄⁊.7.II.bor
7.I.car̄.ſilu⁊.XV.porc̄.I.ac̄;7.dim̄⁊.p̄ti.val.X.fol

21 In THORPE, *THUR(E)STUNA* and YAXHAM 5 Freemen of St. E(theldreda's), 50 acres. Always 1 plough.
Value 8s.

22 In YAXHAM 14 Freemen, 90 acres. Always 2 ploughs; meadow, 4 acres.
Value 20s.
Roger Bigot holds from the Abbot, but formerly he held from the King.

Hundred of BROTHERCROSS
23 In BROOMSTHORPE 1 Freeman, [ ] c. of land.
Always 8 smallholders.
1 plough in lordship; 1 men's plough; meadow, 3 acres; 1 mill.
Value of the half, 10s.

HENSTEAD Half Hundred
24 St. E(theldreda) held PULHAM before 1066, as 15 c. of land.
Always 60 villagers; 25 smallholders; 7 slaves.
3 ploughs in lordship. Then 20 men's ploughs, now 16. Meadow, 16 acres. Woodland, then 600 pigs, now 300. 1 mill; 3 cobs; 11 head of cattle; 40 pigs; 50 sheep; 40 goats; 4 beehives.
Value then £8; now 15.
It has 2 leagues in length and 1 league in width, tax of 30d.

25 In BILLINGFORD a free man held under St. E(theldreda) 1 c. of land before 1066. Now Roger of Raismes holds from the Abbot.
Always 5 smallholders; 1 slave.
Then and later 2 ploughs in lordship, now 3. Always ½ men's plough; woodland, 16 pigs; meadow, 8 acres.
Value then and later 20s; now 10.   215 a
It has 5 furlongs in length and 5 in width, tax of 4d.
More hold there.

DISS Half-Hundred
26 St. E(theldreda) has always held THELVETON, as 2 c. of land.
Always 6 villagers; 1 smallholder.
Then 2 ploughs in lordship, now none. Always 1 men's plough, meadow, 4 acres. Woodland, then 60 pigs, now 30.
Value 20s.
It has 1 league in length and ½ in width; tax of 7d.

27 In TIVETSHALL 2 Freemen, ½ c. of land and 2 acres.
2 villagers and a half; 2 smallholders.
1 plough; woodland, 15 pigs; meadow, 1½ acres.
Value 10s.

⨏ Lodinga Hund̅. In Tortuna. vi. soc̅. q̅s ten&. Godric̅ dapifer. de. xx.
ac̅. Sep̅. i. car̅. 7 in Torp. vi. soc̅. de. xiii. ac̅. 7 ħnt. i. car̅. 7. viii. bor.
7. ptinet in berc ⸝ c̅ o̅i consuet. 7. ibi ap̅p̅tiati st̅.

⨏ Depwade Hund̅ In Stratuna tenuit. i. soc̅. xii. ac̅. t. r. e. val
xii. d̅. In Herdeuuic. i. soc̅. xv. ac̅. 7. dim̅. car̅. ual. ii. sol. Rex. 7. comes.
socam.

★ TERRA SC̅I benedicti de Rameseio. Hund̅ de Clacheslosa   . XVI.
Hidlingeiam. ten& Scs benedict. ii. car̅. tr̅æ. Sep̅. viii. uilt. 7. xi. bor.
. v. ser. viii. ac̅. p̅ti. ii. car̅. in d̅n̅io. 7. ii. bou. hom. iii. runc. v. anim. x. por
lxx. ou. tc̅ ual. lxxx. sol. m̅. lxx. De hoc man. tulit   Willt de Warenna.
viii. hoes. consuetudinarios ad hoc maneriu̅. de. xliiii. ac̅ tr̅æ. ut hund̅
testat. hoc Man. ht. v. q̅r. in long. 7. iiii. 7. d̅. in lat. 7. reddit. viii. d̅
de gelto de. xx. sol

215 b
Winebotesham ten&. S. b. ii. car̅. tr̅æ. sep̅. xiii. bor. 7. ii. car̅ in d̅n̅io. 7
. xii. ac̅. p̅ti. Past. de. xviii. d̅. iiii. por. xvi. ou. Tc̅. ual. iiii. lib. m̅. iii.

⨏ In Snora. dim̅. car̅ tr̅æ. val. x. sol.
In Derham. iii. soc̅. t. r. e. vi. ac̅. tr̅æ. 7. dim̅. car̅. val. xii. d̅. In Phorham. xxiiii.
ac̅. 7 ual. ii. sol. 7. viii. d̅. In ead̅. lib ho̅. xxiiii. ac̅. val. iii. sol. In Wtuuella.
xvi. bor. ual. v. sol. De soca hundreti 7. dimidii. ht. S. B. lxx. sol.

LODDON Hundred

28 In THURTON 6 Freemen whom Godric the Steward holds, at 20 acres.
Always 1 plough.
Also in TORP 6 Freemen, at 13 acres. They have 1 plough; 8 smallholders.
It belongs in BERGH (Apton) with all customary dues. They are assessed there.

DEPWADE Hundred

29 In STRATTON 1 Freeman held 12 acres before 1066.
Value 12d.
In HARDWICK 1 Freeman, 15 acres; ½ plough.
Value 2s.
The King and the Earl (have) the jurisdiction.

16 LAND OF ST. BENEDICT OF RAMSEY

The Hundred of CLACKCLOSE

1 St. Benedict holds HILGAY, 2 c. of land.
Always 8 villagers; 11 smallholders; 5 slaves.
Meadow, 8 acres; 2 ploughs in lordship; the men, 2 oxen; 3 cobs; 5 head of cattle; 10 pigs; 70 sheep.
Value then 80s; now 70.
William of Warenne took from this manor 8 men bound by customary dues to this manor, at 44 acres of land, as the Hundred testifies. This manor has 5 furlongs in length and 4½ in width, of a 20s tax it pays 8d.
St. B(enedict) holds WIMBOTSHAM, 2 c. of land. 215 b
Always 13 smallholders.
2 ploughs in lordship; meadow, 12 acres; pasture at 18½; 4 pigs; 16 sheep.
Value then £4, now 3.

2 In SNORE ½ c. of land.
Value 10s.
In (West) DEREHAM 3 Freemen before 1066, 6 acres of land; ½ plough.
Value 12d.
In FORDHAM 24 acres.
Value 2s 8d.
In the same a free man, 24 acres.
Value 3s.
In OUTWELL 16 smallholders.
Value 5s.
Of the jurisdiction of the Hundred and a Half St. B(enedict) has 70s.

Hunđ 7 . dim̃ . de Fredebruge . Walſocā ten . S̃ . B̃ . sẽp . 1 . car̃ . tr̃æ . Sẽp . xi . uiłł . 7 . vi . bor . xii . ac̃ . p̃ti . 1 . car̃ . in dñio . dim̃ . car̃ hom̃ . 1 . piſc̃ . vii . añ . huic maner̃ jac̃ sẽp . vii . ſoc̃ . de . xiii . ac̃ . Val̃ . xx . ſot̃.

Hunđ de Dochinga . Brõceſtrã tenđ . sẽp . S̃ . B̃ . iii . car̃ . in dñio . 7 . vii . car̃ hom̃ . xxv . uiłł . xvi . bor . v . ſer̃ . ii . ac̃ . p̃ti . i . mot̃ . v . bor . vi . ac̃ . 7 lx . ac̃ tr̃æ quæ sẽp ſt in dñio . ii . runc̃ . vi . animat̃ . xxiiii . porc̃ . đc . ou . Totũ ual̃ . x . liƀ . Totũ h̃t . i . leũ . iñ lon̂ . 7 . đim̃ . in lat̃ . 7 . xxviii . đ . de . g̃ .

Hunđ de Smetheduna . Rinc̃teda . tenđ sẽp . S . B . ii . car̃ . in dñio . xxi . uiłł . v . bor . iii . ſer̃ . k̃ntes . iii . car̃ . v . ac̃ . p̃ti . i . runc̃ xxiiii . porc̃ . c . ou . 7 . xxii . ſoc̃ . i . car̃ . tr̃æ . 7 . iii . car̃ . 7 . in hoc manerio poſſ̃t reſtaurari . ii . car̃ . tc̃ ual̃ . vi . liƀ m̃ . v . 7 . x . ſot̃ . h̃t . i . leũ . 7 . đim̃ . in long̃ . 7 . i . leũ . in lat̃ . 7 . xlii . đ . de . g̃ . Scs . B . ſocã . De hoc manerio ablati ſt̃ . xxxi . ſoc̃ . q̃ ibi jacebant . t̃ . r̃ . ẽ . De his habuit Raſrid . ix . 7 m̃ tenet eos . W . de Scohies 7 . W . de uuar̃ . vii . 7 In Flicesuuella man̂ . reg̃ . iii . 7 . W . de Noiers . iiii . Rog̃ bigot . v . 7 In Huntaneſtuna regis . i . de . ii . ac̃ .

Hunđ de brodeſcros . In bruneham ten̂ . S̃ . B̃ . t̃ . r̃ . ẽ . i . liƀm hom̃ . de dim̃ . car̃ . tr̃æ Sẽp . xviii . bor . tc̃ . dim̃ . car̃ . m̃ . nich̃ . Sẽp . ii . car̃ . hom̃ . Sẽp ual̃ . x . ſot̃ hoc tenđ Rog̃ bigot de aƀƀ .

The Hundred and a Half of FREEBRIDGE

3   St. B(enedict) has always held WALSOKEN, 1 c. of land.
    Always 11 villagers; 6 smallholders.
    Meadow, 12 acres; 1 plough in lordship; ½ men's plough;
       1 fishery; 7 head of cattle.
    7 free men have always appertained to this manor, at 13 acres.
    Value 20s.

The Hundred of DOCKING

4   St. B(enedict) has always held BRANCASTER.
    3 ploughs in lordship; 7 men's ploughs.
    25 villagers; 16 smallholders; 5 slaves.
    Meadow, 2 acres; 1 mill.
    5 smallholders, 6 acres.
    Also 60 acres of land which have always been in lordship; 2
       cobs; 6 head of cattle; 24 pigs; 600 sheep.
    Value of the whole £10.
    The whole has 1 league in length and ½ in width, tax of 28d.

The Hundred of SMETHDON

5   St. B(enedict) has always held RINGSTEAD.
    2 ploughs in lordship.
    21 villagers; 5 smallholders; 3 slaves, who have 3 ploughs.
    Meadow, 5 acres; 1 cob; 24 pigs; 100 sheep.
    Also 22 Freemen, 1 c. of land.
       3 ploughs and in this manor 2 ploughs could be restored.
    Value then £6; now (£)5 10s.
      It has 1½ leagues in length and 1 league in width, tax of 42d.
    St. B(enedict) has the jurisdiction.
      31 free men were taken from this manor who appertained there
    before 1066. Of these Radfrid had 9 and he has them now;
    W(illiam) of Écouis and W(illiam) of Warenne (have) 7; in
    TITCHWELL (the King's) manor (are) 3; W(illiam) of Noyers (has)
    4 and Roger Bigot 5; in HUNSTANTON the King's (manor) 1, at
    2 acres.

The Hundred of BROTHERCROSS

6   In BURNHAM St. B(enedict) held 1 free man before 1066, at ½ c.
    of land.
    Always 18 smallholders.
    Then ½ plough, now nothing. Always 2 men's ploughs.
    Value always 10s.
    Roger Bigot holds this from the Abbot.

TERRA Sci benedicti de holmo ad uictũ monacoȝ .XVII.
Walefham H Walefham ten&. S.B. p̄. II. car̋ɫ. trǣ. t. r. e. Sēp [R. comes habuit foca̋...]
. VIII. bor. tc̃. I. car̋. in dn̄io. m̃. II. 7. I. car̋. 7. dim̋. hom̋. XXII. ac̋. p̋ti. II. faɫ. ȋ.
runc̋. VII. por. CC. ou̇. 7. IIII. foc̋. de. XXXII. ac̋. 7. I. ac̋. p̋ti. Sēp. dim̋ car̋.
In Fifcele. XXIIII. ac̋. trǣ. 7. II. bor. Sēp uaɫ. totũ. XL. foɫ. Adhuc in Walsā
dim̋. car̋. 7. VI. bor. 7. VI. ac̋. p̋ti. 7. v. foc̋. Sēp; I. car̋. Vaɫ. X. foɫ.
In Vptuna. v. ac̋. trǣ. in eod p̄tio. / In baftuuic t̋. r̋. e. I. car̋. trǣ. 7. XX. ac̋.
Sēp. IX. uiɫɫ. 7. I. fer̋. 7. I. car̋. in dn̄io. 7. I. car̋. hom̋. XIIII. ac̋. p̋ti. Sēp. I. runc̋. XX. ou̇.
7. IX. foc̋. de. XLVI. ac̋. 7. III. ac̋. p̋ti. 7. I. car̋. vaɫ. XX. foɫ. tc̃ ⸵ m̃. XL.
/ In Redeham tenuit S̋. b. t̋. r̋. e. I. car̋. trǣ. Sēp. II. uiɫɫ. v. bor. I. car̋. in dn̄io. 7. I.
car̋. hom̋. XX. ac̋. p̋ti. VI. an̋. m̃. VI. por. XX. ou̇. 7. I. foc̋. III. ac̋. tc̃. uaɫ. X. foɫ. m̃.
XX. 7. baftuuic. ht̋. dim̋ leu̇; in long̃. 7. dim̋. in lat̋. 7. de. g̋. XVI. đ. De redehā
habebat abbas foc̋ fup hos q̃ fequebant̋ faldā. 7. de aliis foca in hund̃
/ Feorhou. Hund̃. IN Carletuna tenuit S̋. B. LX. ac̋. t̋. r̋. e. Sēp. v. uiɫɫ. 7.
. II. bor. 7. I. car̋. hom̋. III. ac̋. p̋ti. vaɫ. v. foɫ. In berefort. XXX. ac̋. ten. S̋. B.

LAND OF ST. BENEDICT OF HOLME
FOR THE SUPPLIES OF THE MONKS

WALSHAM Hundred

1 St. B(enedict) held (South) WALSHAM, as 2 c. of land before 1066. Earl R(alph) had the jurisdiction before 1066.
    Always 8 smallholders.
    Then 1 plough in lordship, now 2. 1½ men's ploughs; meadow, 22 acres; 2 salt-houses; 1 cob; 7 pigs; 200 sheep.
    Also 4 Freemen, at 32 acres; meadow, 1 acre; always ½ plough.
In FISHLEY 24 acres of land.
    2 smallholders.
Value of the whole always 40s.
    Further, in (South) Walsham ½ plough.
        6 smallholders;
        meadow, 6 acres.
    Also 5 Freemen; always 1 plough.
Value 10s.
In UPTON 5 acres of land in the same valuation.

2 In (Wood)BASTWICK before 1066 1 c. of land and 20 acres.
    Always 9 villagers; 1 slave.
    1 plough in lordship; 1 men's plough; meadow, 14 acres.
        Always 1 cob; 20 sheep.
    Also 9 Freemen, at 46 acres; meadow, 3 acres; 1 plough.
Value then 20s; now 40.

3 In REEDHAM St. B(enedict) held before 1066 1 c. of land.
    Always 2 villagers; 5 smallholders.
    1 plough in lordship; 1 men's plough; meadow, 20 acres; 6 head of cattle. Now 6 pigs; 20 sheep.
    Also 1 Freeman, 3 acres.
Value then 10s; now 20.
    (Wood)bastwick has ½ league in length and ½ in width; tax of 16d.
    Of Reedham the Abbot had the jurisdiction over those who sought the fold; of the others the jurisdiction (was) in the Hundred.

FOREHOE Hundred

4 In CARLETON (Forehoe) St. B(enedict) held 60 acres before 1066.
    Always 5 villagers; 2 smallholders.
    1 men's plough; meadow, 3 acres.
    Value 5s.
In BARFORD St. B(enedict) holds 30 acres.

⁅Erpingaham Nord Hund. Turgartunā ten&. sep̃. Sc̃s. B. ıı. car̃. tr̃æ.
Sep̃. ıııı. uiƚƚ. 7. ıııı. bor. 7. ıı. car̃ in dñio. 7. ı. car̃. hom̃. ıııı. ac̃. p̃ti. siƚu. xx. por.
. ı. moƚ Tc̃. ı. runc̃. 7. ıı. añ. m̃. ııı. tc̃. ıx. por. m̃. xı. tc̃. xxx. cap̃. m̃. xvııı.
7. xlıx. foc̃. de. ı. car̃. tr̃æ. Sep̃. v. car̃. ıı. ac̃. p̃ti. 7. dim̃. Tc̃. uaƚ. ııııı. lib̃. m̃. vı.
ħt. xııı. qr̃. in long̃. 7. vı. in lat̃. 7. de. g̃. xvı. d̃. 7. ob̃. 7. foca hab̃ sc̃s. bened̃.
⁅In Scipedana. dim̃. car̃. tr̃æ de uic̃tu monachoᵹ. ı. uiƚƚ. ııı. bor. Sep̃. ı. car̃
in dñio. 7. dim̃. car̃. hom̃. 7. ı. ac̃. p̃ti. Vaƚ. x. foƚ. 7. vııı. d̃.
⁅In Repes dim̃. car̃. tr̃æ. ı. uiƚƚ. v. bor. ı. car̃. in dñio. Tc̃. ı. car̃. hom̃. m̃. dim̃.
vaƚ. x. foƚ.
⁅In Attinga. ıı. car̃. tr̃æ Sep̃. ıı. uiƚƚ. 7. vııı. bor. ıı. car̃. in dñio. ıı. car̃. hom̃.
Siƚu. ıııı. porc̃. ıı. ac̃. p̃ti. ıı. runc̃. ııı. añ. v. por. lx. ou. 7. ııı. lib̃i hoẽs q̃ pot̃.

216 b

tr̃am fuam dare & uende. dim̃. car̃. tr̃e. 7. ıı. ac̃. p̃ti. Sep̃. ı. car̃. Tc̃. uaƚ. xxx.
foƚ. m̃. xl. ħt. vııı. qr̃. in long̃. 7. v. 7. dim̃. in lat̃. 7. xııı. d̃. 7. ob̃ de. g̃.
⁅Flecweſt Hund. Wintretunā ten&. S̃. B. sep̃; p̃. ı. car̃. tr̃æ. v. bor.
7. ı. car̃. in dñio. dim̃. car̃. hom̃. vı. porc̃. 7. ibi ſt. v. lib̃i hoẽs sc̃i. B. cõmd̃ tantū.
de. xlv. ac̃. dim̃. ac̃. p̃ti. Sep̃. ı. car̃. 7. ı. foc̃. de. c. ac̃. 7. ita ẽ in monaſtio
qd̃ nec uende nec forisfacere pot̃ ext̃ ecc̃lia. ſ; foca ẽ in hund̃. vı. ac̃. p̃ti. Sep̃
ıx. bor. ı. car̃. in dñio. 7. ı. car̃. hom̃. 7. fub eo ſt. ıııı. lib̃i hoẽs cõmd̃ tant̃. ıx. ac̃.
Vaƚ xxıııı. foƚ. 7. v. lib̃i hoẽs. xxıııı. d̃. ħt. ıx. qr̃. in long̃. 7. vııı. in
lat̃. 7. xxx. d̃. de. g̃.

NORTH ERPINGHAM Hundred
5 St. B(enedict) has always held THURGARTON, 2 c. of land.
Always 4 villagers; 4 smallholders.
2 ploughs in lordship; and 1 men's plough; meadow, 4 acres; woodland, 20 pigs; 1 mill. Then 1 cob; 2 head of cattle, now 3. Then 9 pigs, now 11. Then 30 goats, now 18.
Also 49 Freemen, at 1 c. of land.
Always 5 ploughs; meadow, 2½ acres.
Value then £4; now 6.
It has 13 furlongs in length and 6 in width, tax of 16½d.
St. Benedict has the jurisdiction.

6 In SHIPDEN ½ c. of land for the supplies of the monks.
1 villager; 3 smallholders.
Always 1 plough in lordship; ½ men's plough; meadow, 1 acre.
Value 10s 8d.

7 In REPPS ½ c. of land.
1 villager; 5 smallholders.
1 plough in lordship. Then 1 men's plough, now ½.
Value 10s.

8 In ANTINGHAM 2 c. of land.
Always 2 villagers; 8 smallholders.
2 ploughs in lordship; 2 men's ploughs; woodland, 4 pigs; meadow, 2 acres; 2 cobs; 3 head of cattle; 5 pigs; 60 sheep.
Also 3 free men who could grant and sell their land; ½ c. of   216 b
land; meadow, 1 acre; always 1 plough.
Value then 30s; now 40.
It has 8 furlongs in length and 5½ in width; tax of 13½d.

WEST FLEGG Hundred
9 St. B(enedict) has always held WINTERTON, as 1 c. of land.
5 smallholders.
1 plough in lordship; ½ men's plough; 6 pigs.
Also there are 5 free men under the patronage only of St. B(enedict), at 45 acres;
meadow, ½ acre; always 1 plough.
Also 1 Freeman, at 100 acres; he is (bound) to the monastery to such an extent that he can neither sell nor forfeit (his land) outside the church, but (his) jurisdiction is in the Hundred.
Meadow, 6 acres.
Always 9 smallholders.
1 plough in lordship; 1 men's plough.
Also under him are 4 free men in patronage only, 9 acres.
Value 24s; the 5 free men, 24d.
It has 9 furlongs in length and 8 in width, tax of 30d.

216 a, b

In Rotholfuesby. ten. S. B. t. r. e. 1. car. trae. Sep. vi. uill. 7. 1. car. in dnio. 7. dim. car. hom. vii. porc. viii. ac. pti. 7. xi. libi hoes. sci. ben. comd. tant. de. xliiii. ac. trae. 7. 1. ac. pti. 7. dim. sal. Sep. ii. car. Silu. iii. por. Tc ual. xx. sol. m. xxvi. 7. viii. d. Ad huc ptinent isti manerio xx. ac. trae. ht. x. qr. in lon. 7. ix. in lat. 7. xxv. den. de. g. 7. iii. ferding

Asseby ten& sep scs. b. ii. car. trae. Sep. vii. bor. i. car. in dnio. 7. dim. car. hom. . x. ac. pti. silu. vi. por. 7. xiii. soc. e soca 7. saca lxii. ac. v. ac. pti. Sep. . ii. car. Tc ual. xx. sol. m reddit. xxvi. sol. 7. viii. d. 7. ht. viii. qr. in long. 7. iiii. 7. dim. in lat. 7. xv. d. de. g. qcq ibi teneat.

Tna ten& sep. S. B. 1. car. trae. Sep. vi. bor. viii. ac. pti. i. car. in dnio 7. dim. car. hom. ii. runc. vi. porc. x. soc. xl. v. ac. vi. ac. 7. dim. pti. . ii. car. tc ual. xx. sol. m. xxvi. 7. viii. d. ht. in lon. v. qr. 7. iiii. in lat. 7. ix. d. de. g. alii ibi ten.

Orbi ten& sep. S. B. 1. car. 7. dim. trae. Sep. ii. uill. x. ac. pti. ii. car In dnio. 7. ii. bou. hom. iii. runc. ii. an. vi. por. Tc ual. xx. sol. m. xxx. ht. vi. qr in long. 7. iii. in lat. 7. de. g. ix. d. qcq ibi ten. Isti maner ptinent. x. libi hoes. sci. benedicti. cmd. de lxxxiiii. ac. 7. xiiii. ac. pti. Sep. ii. bor. ii. car. val vi. sol.

Burc 7 Bithlakebei ten. S. B. sep. 1. car. trae. Tc. 1. car. in dnio. m. dim. v. ac. pti.

10 In ROLLESBY St. B(enedict) held before 1066, 1 c. of land.
Always 6 villagers.
1 plough in lordship; ½ men's plough; 7 pigs; meadow, 8 acres.
Also 11 free men under the patronage only of St. Benedict, at 44 acres of land;
meadow, 1 acre. ½ salt-house. Always 2 ploughs; woodland, 3 pigs.
Value then 20s; now 26(s) 8d.
Further, there belong to this manor 20 acres of land.
It has 10 furlongs in length and 9 in width; tax of 25¾d.

11 St. B(enedict) has always held ASHBY, 2 c. of land.
Always 7 smallholders.
1 plough in lordship; ½ men's plough; meadow, 10 acres; woodland, 6 pigs.
Also 13 Freemen with full jurisdiction, 62 acres; meadow, 5 acres; always 2 ploughs.
Value then 20s; now it pays 26s 8d.
It has 8 furlongs in length and 4½ in width; tax of 15d, whoever holds there.

12 St. B(enedict) has always held THURNE, 1 c. of land.
Always 6 smallholders.
Meadow, 8 acres; 1 plough in lordship; ½ men's plough; 2 cobs, 6 pigs.
10 Freemen, 45 acres; meadow, 6½ acres; 2 ploughs.
Value then 20s; now 26(s) 8d.
It has 5 furlongs in length and 4 in width; tax of 9d.
Others hold there.

13 St. B(enedict) has always held OBY, 1½ c. of land.
Always 2 villagers.
Meadow, 10 acres; 2 ploughs in lordship; the men, 2 oxen; 3 cobs; 2 head of cattle; 6 pigs.
Value then 20s; now 30.
It has 6 furlongs in length and 3 in width; tax of 9d, whoever holds there.
To this manor belong 10 free men under the patronage of St. Benedict, at 84 acres; meadow, 14 acres. Always 2 smallholders; 2 ploughs.
Value 6s.

14 St. B(enedict) has always held BURGH (St. Margaret) and BILLOCKBY, 1 c. of land. 217 a
Then 1 plough in lordship, now ½. Meadow, 5 acres.

7 . vi . libi hões . S̄ . B . cm̄d . tantū . xliiii . ac̷ . vii . ac̷ . p̄ti . Sēp . ii . bor . val . xviii . sol . 7
hii libi hões . tc̄ . ual . xvi . đ . m̄ . ii . sol . In burc . ten . S . b . xxx . ac̷ . 7 . iiii . ac̷.
p̄ti . iii . bor . i . car̷ . in dn̄io . val . iii . sol.

⸿ In Martham . iii . soc̷ . x . ac̷ . val . xii . đ . In bastuuic . i . lib̃ hō . S . b . cm̄d . ii .
ac̷ . 7 . dim̷ . val . iiii . đ . In Repes . vi . libi hões . xxxvi . ac̷ . ii . ac̷ 7 . dim̷ . 7 . dim̷ .
car̷ . Tc̄ . ual . ii . sol . m̄ . iii . In Martham . lib̃ hō . s . b . vi . ac̷ . 7 . iii . ac̷ . q̷ ten& cec̷ .
7 . dim̷ . ac̷ . p̄ti . Val . xii . đ . In Clipesby . i . lib̃ hō . In hovby . i . lib̃ hō . de . xxiii .
ac̷ . Sēp . i . car̷ . vi . ac̷ . p̄ti . Val . xxx . đ . In Thoroluesby . lib̃ hō . v . ac̷ . val . iiii . đ.
Bastuuic h̃t . vi . q̷r̷ . in long . 7 . iii . in lat . 7 . de̷ . g̷ . iii . đ.

⸿ Heinesteda Hund In Scotesham ten . s . b . sēp . iii . car̷ . træ . Tc̄ . xi .
uill . m̄ . v . Tc̄ . xii . bor . m̄ . x . Sēp . i . ser̷ . 7 . ii . car̷ . in dn̄io . Tc̄ . v . car̷ . hom .
m̄ . iii . silu . xx . por . viii . ac̷ . p̄ti . i . mol . i . runc̷ . i . an . m̄ . viii . por̷ . xxii . ou.
7 . v . soc̷ . in ead . lviii . ac̷ . 7 . i . ac̷ . 7 . dim̷ . p̄ti . 7 . i . car̷ . 7 . dim̷ . int̷ oms . Tc̄ ual
. iii . lib . m̄ . iii . h̃t . i . leu . 7 . dim̷ . in long . 7 . de g̷ . ii . sol xvi . đ . Alii ibi ten.
In Grenesuill . ten& sēp . s . b . i . car̷ . træ . tc̄ . ii . uill . m̄ . i . Sēp . vi . bor . tc̄ . ii . ser̷.
tc̄ . i . car̷ . 7 . dim̷ . in dn̄io . m̄ . ii . tc̄ . i . car̷ . hom . m̄ . dim̷ . i . mol . i . runc̷.
Sēp . xii . porc̷ . xii . ou . i . uasa . ap . Tc̄ ual . xx . sol . m̄ . xxx . h̃t . i . leu . in lon̷.
7 . dim̷ . in lat . 7 . ii . sol . de . g̷ . s; plures ibi ten.

Also 6 free men under the patronage only of St. B(enedict), 44
acres; meadow, 7 acres; always 2 smallholders.
Value 18s. Value of these free men then 16d; now 2s.
In Burgh (St. Margaret) St. B(enedict) holds 30 acres;
meadow, 4 acres.
3 smallholders.
1 plough in lordship.
Value 3s.

15 In MARTHAM 3 Freemen, 10 acres.
Value 12d.
In BASTWICK 1 free man under the patronage of St. B(enedict),
2½ acres.
Value 4d.
In REPPS 6 free men, 36 acres. [Meadow], 2½ acres; ½ plough.
Value then 2s; now 3.
In MARTHAM a free man of St. B(enedict's), 6 acres; and 3 acres
which a blind man holds; meadow, ½ acre.
Value 12d.
In CLIPPESBY 1 free man.
In OBY 1 free man, at 23 acres. Always 1 plough; meadow, 6 acres.
Value 30d.
In ROLLESBY a free man, 5 acres.
Value 4d.
Bastwick has 6 furlongs in length and 3 in width, tax of 3d.

HENSTEAD Hundred
16 In SHOTESHAM St. B(enedict) has always held 3 c. of land.
Then 11 villagers, now 5. Then 12 smallholders, now 10.
Always 1 slave.
2 ploughs in lordship. Then 5 men's ploughs, now 3. Woodland,
20 pigs; meadow, 8 acres; 1 mill; 1 cob; 1 head of cattle.
Now 8 pigs; 22 sheep.
Also 5 Freemen in the same, 58 acres; meadow, 1½ acres. 1½
ploughs between them all.
Value then £3; now 3.
It has 1½ leagues in length, tax of 16d.
Others hold there.

17 In GRENSVILL St. B(enedict) has always held 1 c. of land.
Then 2 villagers, now 1. Always 6 smallholders. Then 2 slaves.
Then 1½ ploughs in lordship, now 2. Then 1 men's plough,
now ½. 1 mill; 1 cob. Always 12 pigs; 12 sheep; 1 beehive.
Value then 20s; now 30.
It has 1 league in length and ½ in width, tax of 2s. But more
hold there.

⪙In Saiffelingham tenuit Edric lib hō Stigandi. I. car̄. trǣ. 7. dim̄.
ſub eo. t. r. e. c̄ ſoca 7. ſaca. p̄q̄ rex uenit in Angliā ut auꝑ ſe redimer̃ſ̃
a captione Walerami inuadauit eam Idē Edric. ꝑ. I. marca auri. 7
ꝑ. VII. lib. in ſc̄o benedicto. m̄ ten& Joh̃s nepos p̄dicti Walerami.
de ſc̄o benedicto in feudo. Tc̄. XI. bor. m̄. IX. 7. dim̄. Sēp. I. ſer.

217 b

Tc̄. II. car̄. in dn̄io. Poſt nult. m̄. I. Tc̄. II. car̄ hom̄. m̄. I. m̄. I. runc in dn̄io.
7. t. r. e. IX. ſoc. m̄. v. de. XXX. ac̄. 7. IIII. ac̄. p̃ti. Tc̄. II. car̄. m̄. dim̄. 7. I. mol̄.
Tc̄ ual. XL. ſol. p̄ 7 m̄. XXX. h̄t. II. leu. in lon. 7. dim̄. in lat. 7 XVI. d̄. de. g.
ſ; plures ibi ten.

In Ead. jacent. X. ac̄. trē in dn̄io. ſ. b. 7. p̄ſtauit. Edrico. teſte hund̄

⪙LOTNINGA Hund̄. Hardale ten& ſēp. ſ. b. ꝑ. II. car̄. trǣ. Sēp. v. bor.
Tc̄. II. car̄. in dn̄io. m̄. I. m̄. II. bou hom̄. Silu. III. por. VIII. ac̄. p̃ti. 7. I. runc.
. IIII. an. XXIIII. por. M. CL. ou. 7. IIII. ſoc. de. VII ac. Sēp. dim̄. car̄. Tc̄. ual
m̄. XXX. h̄t. VIII. qr̄ in lon. 7. VII. in lat. 7. de. g. XI. d̄. alii. ibi ten.

⪙Hund̄ de Enſfort. In Wicinghahā dim̄. car̄. trǣ. I. bor. I. car̄.
. II. ac̄. p̃ti. Val. X. ſol. Soca. in Folſā reḡ.

⪙Hund̄ de Taureham. In Vrocheſham tenuit Rad̄ Stalra. IIII.
ſoc. de. I. car̄. trǣ 7. jacent in houetuna. q̄m Idē. R. dedit ſc̄o. B. t. r. Willi.
Sēp. I. car̄. VIII. ac̄. p̃ti. val. VI. ſol.

⪙In Racheia. lib hō. XXX. ac̄. t. r. e. Tc̄. I. car̄. m̄. d̄. II. ac̄. p̃ti. val. XVI. d̄.
hec trā foriſfacta ē. t. r. Willi. ſ; q̄da monach dedit dim̄ marcā auri ꝑ
foriſfactura. p̄poſitis. ſcil Aluni de Coleceſtra. 7. ſic habuit trā abſq̃ licentia
regis.

18 In SAXLINGHAM Edric, a free man of Stigand's, held; 1½ c. of land under him before 1066 with full jurisdiction. After the King came into England so that he might however redeem himself from capture by Waleran this Edric pledged it for 1 mark of gold and for £7 to St. Benedict. Now John, nephew of the said Waleran holds from St. Benedict's as a Holding.
   Then 11 smallholders, now 9 and a half; always 1 slave.
   Then 2 ploughs in lordship, later none, now 1. Then 2 men's   217 b
      ploughs, now 1. Now 1 cob in lordship.
   Also before 1066, 9 Freemen, now 5, at 30 acres; meadow, 4
      acres. Then 2 ploughs, now ½. 1 mill.
   Value then 40s; later and now 30.
   It has 2 leagues in length and ½ in width, tax of 16d. But more hold there.
   In the same appertain 10 acres of land in the lordship of St. B(enedict). (St. Benedict) leased them to Edric as the Hundred testifies.

   LODDON Hundred
19 St B(enedict) has always held HARDLEY, as 2 c. of land.
   Always 5 smallholders.
   Then 2 ploughs in lordship, now 1. Now, the men, 2 oxen;
      woodland, 3 pigs; meadow, 8 acres; 1 cob; 4 head of cattle;
      24 pigs. Now 150 sheep.
   Also 4 Freemen, at 7 acres; always ½ plough.
   Value then [   ]; now 30.
   It has 8 furlongs in length and 7 in width, tax of 11d. Others hold there.

   The Hundred of EYNSFORD
20 In WITCHINGHAM ½ c. of land.
   1 smallholder.
   1 plough; meadow, 2 acres.
   Value 10s.
   The jurisdiction (is) in the King's (manor of) Foulsham.

   The Hundred of TAVERHAM
21 In WROXHAM Ralph the Constable held 4 Freemen, at 1 c. of land. (Their lands) appertain in Hoveton (St. John). This (the same) R(alph) granted to St. B(enedict) after 1066.
   Always 1 plough; meadow, 8 acres.
   Value 6s.

22 In RACKHEATH a free man, 30 acres before 1066.
   Then 1 plough, now ½. Meadow, 2 acres.
   Value 16d.
   This land was forfeited after 1066, but a certain monk gave ½ mark of gold for the forfeiture to the reeves, namely to A(i)lwy of Colchester. Thus he had the land without permission of the King.

Erpincham Nord Hund̄ Scotohou ten̛& sep̄ . ſ . b . p̄ . III.
car̛ . tr̄ǣ . Tc̄ . XIIII . uiłł . m̄ . IX . Sep̄ . III . bor̛ . II . car̛ . in dn̄io . tc̄ . VI . car̛.
hom̛ . m̄ . I . 7 . dim̛ . X . ac̛ . p̄ti . Silư . XX . por̛ . tc̄ . I . mol̛ . Sep̄ . II . runc̛.
III . an̄ . XI . porc̛ . 7 . IX . foc̛ . dim̛ . car̛ tr̄ǣ . Sep̄ . III . car̛ . 7 . dim̛ . tc̄ uał
XL . ſoł . m̄ . LX . ħt . I . leư . in lon̄ . 7 . đ . in lat̄ . 7 . XX . ~~porc~~ pc̛ . 7 . XVI . đ
de . g̛ . In Eſtuna ten̛ . Rađ ſtalra . t . r̄ . e . I . car̛ . tr̄ǣ . 7 . dedit eam
ecclīa . XIIII . ac̛.

218 a

t . r̄ . Willi . c̄ uxore ſua ad ab̄biam . conceſſione reḡ . Sep̄ . II . bor̛ . 7 . I . car̛ . 7
. I . ac̛ . 7 . dim̛ . p̄ti . In Ead̛ tenuit . ſ . b . dim̛ . car̛ tr̄ǣ . 7 . II . bor̛ . 7 ē in p̄tio de houetuna

Suanetunā ten̛& sep̄ . ſ . b . p̄ . III . car̛ . tr̄ǣ . sep̄ . XV . uiłł . 7 . V . bor̛ . tc̄ . II . ſer̛.
Sep̄ . II . car̛ . in dn̄io . IIII . car̛ . hom̛ . XII . ac̛ . p̄ti . Silư . C . porc̛ . II . runc̛ . XI . porc̛.
XXV . cap̛ . 7 . I . foc̛ . XXX . ac̛ . Tc̄ . dim̛ . car̛ . Sep̄ . uał . LX . ſoł . ħt . I . leư . in lon̄g.
7 . I . leư . in lat̄ . 7 . IIII . đ . de . g̛ . Eccłie . VII . ac̛.

Caletorp ten̛& sep̄ . ſ . b . I . car̛ . tr̄ǣ . 7 . dim̛ . tc̄ . VI . uiłł . m̄ . VII . sep̄ . III . bor̛.
. I . car̛ . in dn̄io . 7 . III . car̛ . hom̛ . IIII . ac̛ . p̄ti . Silư . XV . por̛ . I . mol̛ . 7 . tcia pars
alti . Sep̄ . X . an̄ . V . por̛ . 7 . III . foc̛ . XX . ac̛ . 7 . I . car̛ . 7 . I . ac̛ . p̄ti . tc̄ . uał . XX.
ſoł . m̄ . XXX . In Ead̛ . I . car̛ . tr̄ǣ ten̛ . ſ . b . t . r̄ . e . sep̄ . III . uiłł . 7 . IIII . bor̛.
7 . I . car̛ . 7 . dim̛ . I . ac̛ . p̄ti . Silư . XV . por̛ . tcia pars moł . vał . XV . ſoł . Eccła
ſine tr̄a . Totū ħt . IX . qr̛ . in lon̄g . 7 . VI . in lat̄ . 7 . V . đ . de . g̛.

NORTH ERPINGHAM Hundred

23 St. B(enedict) has always held SCOTTOW, as 3 c. of land.
Then 14 villagers, now 9; always 3 smallholders.
2 ploughs in lordship. Then 6 men's ploughs, now 1½. Meadow, 10 acres; woodland, 20 pigs. Then 1 mill. Always 2 cobs; 3 head of cattle; 11 pigs.
Also 9 Freemen, ½ c. of land; always 3½ ploughs.
Value then 40s; now 60.
(Belonging) to the church, 14 acres.
It has 1 league in length and ½ (league) and 20 perches in width, tax of 16d.

24 In EASTON Ralph the Constable held before 1066, 1 c. of land and he gave it after 1066 with his wife to the Abbey, by the King's grant.   218 a
Always 2 smallholders.
1 plough; meadow, 1½ acres.
In the same St. B(enedict) held ½ c. of land.
2 smallholders.
It is in the valuation of Hoveton (St. John).

25 St. B(enedict) has always held SWANTON (Abbot), as 3 c. of land.
Always 15 villagers; 5 smallholders. Then 2 slaves.
Always 2 ploughs in lordship; 4 men's ploughs; meadow, 12 acres; woodland, 100 pigs; 2 cobs; 11 pigs; 25 goats.
Also 1 Freeman, 30 acres. Then ½ plough.
Value always 60s.
It has 1 league in length and 1 league in width, tax of 4d.
(Belonging) to the church, 7 acres.

26 St. B(enedict) has always held CALTHORPE; 1½ c. of land.
Then 6 villagers, now 7; always 3 smallholders.
1 plough in lordship; 3 men's ploughs; meadow, 4 acres; woodland, 15 pigs; 1 mill and one-third of another. Always 10 head of cattle; 5 pigs.
Also 3 Freemen, 20 acres; 1 plough; meadow, 1 acre.
Value then 20s; now 30.
In the same St. B(enedict) held 1 c. of land before 1066.
Always 3 villagers; 4 smallholders.
1½ ploughs; meadow, 1 acre; woodland, 15 pigs; one-third of a mill.
Value 15s.
A church without land.
The whole has 9 furlongs in length and 6 in width, tax of 5d.

⁊In Tuit ten& sep̃.ſ.b.ıı.caŕ.tr̃æ.sep̃.ııı.uilł.xıı.bor.Tc̃.ı.caŕ in dñio
m̃.ı.⁊.dim̃.Tc̃.ııı.caŕ.hom̃.m̃.ıı.⁊.d̃.ı.ać.p̃ti.Silũ.ʟ.por͞e.ı.moł.m̃.ı.⁊.d̃.
.ııı.an̨.xııı.por.Tc̃ uał.xxx.soł.m̃.xʟ.ht̃ dim̃ leu̇ in lon̨.⁊.d̃.i̇ lat̃.
⁊.v.d̃.de.g̨.ı.ob̃ min̨.Ecclæ.vı.ać.

⁊In Hobuiſſe.ı.caŕ tr̃æ.ten̨.ſ.b.Sep̃.ıı.bor.⁊.ı.caŕ.ıı.ać.p̃ti.Silũ.xx.por.
dim̃.moł.Tc̃.uał.x.soł.m̃.xvı.

In Erpincham.ı.caŕ.tr̃æ.ten̨ Idẽ.sep̃.ııı.uilł.ııı.bor.ıı.caŕ.ı.ać.p̃ti.
uał.x.soł.

In Tutincghetuna.ı.caŕ.tr̃æ.ten̨.ſ.b.t̃.r̃.ẽ.sep̃.ı.uilł.⁊.ıı.bor.⁊.ı.caŕ.
.ıı.ać.p̃ti.ı.moł.Vał.x.soł.De dimidia hac tr̃a erat saiſit̃.R.comes
qn̄ forisfecit̃.⁊ de c̃omdatione uni̊ feminæ que eā tenebat.

In banincham.xxx.ać.tr̃æ.ten̨ sep̃.ſ.b.sep̃.dim̃.caŕ.vał.v.soł.

218 b

⁊In Vlſtuna.ı.caŕ.tr̃æ.ten̨.ſ.ben̨.t̃.r̃.ẽ.sep̃.ııı.bor.⁊.ı.caŕ.⁊.dim̃.
.ı.ać.p̃ti.Tc̃ uał.xvı.soł.m̃.xx.ht̃.vı.qŕ.in long̨.⁊.v.in lat̃.⁊.ıı.d̃.
⁊.ob̃ de.g̨.Dim̃ ecclı̃æ.ıııı.ać.

⁊In belaga.ı.soć.ııı.ać.Vał.vı.d̃.Dim̃.ecclı̃æ.ııı.ać.In Ead̃.x.soć.
⁊.d̃.ten̨.Rad̃ ſtalra.t̃.r̃.ẽ.ʟxııı.ać.ıı.ać.p̃ti.Sep̃.ıı.caŕ.In Ead̃.ı.soć.
sc̃ı ben̨.xxx.sep̃.ıı.uilł.⁊.ı.bor.⁊.ı.caŕ.hoc ẽ in p̃tio de houetuna.

27 In THWAITE St. B(enedict) has always held 2 c. of land.
Always 3 villagers; 12 smallholders.
Then 1 plough in lordship, now 1½. Then 3 men's ploughs, now 2½. Meadow, 1 acre; woodland, 50 pigs. Then 1 mill, now 1½. 3 head of cattle; 13 pigs.
Value then 30s; now 40.
It has ½ league in length and ½ in width, tax of 5d less ½d.
(Belonging) to the church, 6 acres.

28 In HAUTBOIS St. B(enedict) holds 1 c. of land.
Always 2 smallholders.
1 plough; meadow, 2 acres; woodland, 20 pigs; ½ mill.
Value then 10s; now 16.

29 In ERPINGHAM (the Saint) also holds 1 c. of land.
Always 4 villagers; 3 smallholders.
2 ploughs; meadow, 1 acre.
Value 10s.

30 In TUTTINGTON St. B(enedict) held 1 c. of land before 1066.
Always 1 villager; 2 smallholders.
1 plough; meadow, 2 acres; 1 mill.
Value 10s.
Earl R(alph) had possession of half this land when he forfeited and of the patronage of one woman who held it.

31 In BANNINGHAM St. B(enedict) has always held 30 acres of land.
Always ½ plough.
Value 5s.

32 In WOLTERTON St. Benedict held 1 c. of land before 1066. 218 b
Always 4 smallholders.
1½ ploughs; meadow, 1 acre.
Value then 16s; now 20.
It has 6 furlongs in length and 5 in width; tax of 2½d.
(Belonging) to ½ of a church, 4 acres.

33 In BELAUGH 1 Freeman, 3 acres.
Value 6d.
(Belonging) to ½ of a church, 3 acres.
In the same Ralph the Constable held 10 Freemen and a half before 1066, 63 acres;
meadow, 2 acres; always 2 ploughs.
In the same 1 Freeman of St. Benedict's, 30 [acres].
Always 2 villagers; 1 smallholder.
1 plough.
This is in the valuation of Hoveton (St. John).

In Wic mera . xii . ac̛ . t̄re . ten̄ ⁷. f . b . t̛ . r̛ ⸱e̛ . Val̛ . xvi . d̛.

/ HEC SEDES AB̄B̄I̛Æ.

/ Tunefteda Hund . *HORNINGAM* . ten& sēp ⁷. S̛ . B.
ꝑ . iii . car̛ . t̄ræ . Sēp . xviii . uilt̛ . xi . bor . Tc̄ . ii . fer̛ ⁷. m̄ nult̛ ⁷. Sēp . ii . car̛ . in dn̄io . 7 . vi . car̛ . hom̄ 7 . c . ac̛ . p̄ti . Silu ⁷. c . porc̛ . Sēp . i . mol̛ . i . runc̛.
. iiii . an̛ ⁷. x . porc̛ . ccclx . oư . Sēp ual̛ . iiii . lib̄ . h̄t . i . leư ⁷. 7 . dim̄ . in long ⁷.
7 . i . leư . in lat̛ ⁷. 7 . vi . d̛ . de ⸱ g ⁷.

/ Snatefhirdā . v . car̛ . t̄ræ . ten& sēp . Idē ⁷. v . car̛ . t̄ræ . Sēp . v . uilt̛.
xvi . bor . i . car̛ . in dn̄io . vi . car̛ . hom̄ . iiii . an̛ ⁷. v . por . 7 ⸱ xxvii . foc̛.
in ead t̄ra . Sēp . viii . car̛ . val̛ . iiii . lib̄ . h̄t . i . leư ⁷. 7 . dim̄ in lon̄ ⁷. 7 . i . leư.
in lat̛ ⁷. 7 . xxviii . d̛ . de . G̛ . Eccl̄ie . x . ac̛.

/ Houetunā ten̄ . Rad̛ . ftalra . t ⁷. r̛ ⁷. e̛ ⁷. vi . car̛ . t̄ræ . Sēp . iiii . uilt̛ . vi . bor.
7 . ii . car̛ . in dn̄io . 7 . iii . car̛ . hom̄ . Silu ⁷. xvi . por . x . ac̛ . p̄ti . 7 . iiii . foc̛.
. i . car̛ . t̄ræ 7 . d̛ . 7 . xxx . ac̛ . Sēp . v . uilt̛ . xi . bor . v . car̛ . 7 dim̄ . x . ac̛ . p̄ti.
7 . i . foc̛ . xxviii . ac̛ . 7 . vii . foc̛ . cx . ac̛ . Sēp . v . car̛ . 7 . d̛ . Tc̄ ual̛ . vii . lib̄.
m̄ . c . fol̛ . h̄t . i . leư ⁷. 7 . ii . q̄r in lon̄ ⁷. 7 . i . leư in lat̛ ⁷. 7 . xviii . d̛ . de ⸱ g ⁷.
. ii . eccl̄iis . xvi . ac̛.

34 In WICKMERE St. B(enedict) held 12 acres of land before 1066. Value 16d.

THIS (IS) THE SITE OF THE ABBEY

TUNSTEAD Hundred

35 St. B(enedict) has always held HORNING, as 3 c. of land.
    Always 18 villagers; 11 smallholders. Then 2 slaves, now none.
    Always 2 ploughs in lordship; 6 men's ploughs; meadow, 100 acres; woodland, 100 pigs. Always 1 mill; 1 cob, 4 head of cattle; 10 pigs; 360 sheep.
Value always £4.
    It has 1 league and a half in length and 1 league in width; tax of 6d.

36 NEATISHEAD, 5 c. of land. The same has always held 5 c. of land.
    Always 5 villagers; 16 smallholders.
    1 plough in lordship; 6 men's ploughs; 4 head of cattle; 5 pigs.
    Also 27 Freemen on this land.
        Always 8 ploughs.
Value £4.
    It has 1½ leagues in length and 1 league in width; tax of 28d.
    (Belonging) to the church, 10 acres.

37 Ralph the Constable held HOVETON (St. John) before 1066, 6 c. of land.
    Always 4 villagers; 6 smallholders.
    2 ploughs in lordship; 3 men's ploughs; woodland, 16 pigs; meadow, 10 acres.
    Also 4 Freemen, 1½ c. of land and 30 acres.
        Always 5 villagers; 11 smallholders.
    5½ ploughs; meadow, 10 acres.
    Also 1 Freeman, 28 acres.
    Also 7 Freemen, 110 acres. Always 5½ ploughs.
Value then £7; now 100s.
    It has 1 league and 2 furlongs in length and 1 league in width; tax of 18d.
    (Belonging) to 2 churches, 16 acres.

⁊ Walsam ten̄& sēp. s̄cs. b. iii. caṛ. tr̄æ. 7. dim̄. Sēp. xii. uiƚƚ. 7.

219 a

. v̇. bor. ii. caṛ. in dn̄io. 7. ii. caṛ. 7. dim̄. hom̄. viii. ac̣. p̄ti. Silu̇. c. por. . i. moƚ. i. runc̣. i. an̄. viii. porc̣. xxxi. foc̣. iii. caṛ. tr̄æ 7. l. ac̣. 7. i. uiƚƚ. 7. i. uiƚƚ. 7. i. bor. Sēp. xv. caṛ. Silu̇. xvi. por. iiii. ac̣. p̄ti. Vaƚ. c. foƚ. ħt. . i. leu̇. 7. dim̄. in long. 7. i. leu̇. in lat̄. 7. vi. pc̣. 7. xviii. d. de. ġ. Eccƚiæ xxx. ac̣.

⁊ Felmincham ten̄. sēp. f. b. lxxvii. ac̣. Sēp. v. bor. i. caṛ. in dn̄io. 7. dim̄. caṛ. hom̄. i. ac̣. p̄ti. 7. iiii. foc̣. l. ac̣. i. caṛ. i. ac̄⁊. p̄ti. Vaƚ. xxi. foƚ. ⁊ eccƚie. ii. ac̣.

⁊ Paftun̄a ten̄. Idē. t̄. r. e. i. caṛ. tr̄æ. ii. uiƚƚ. ii. bor. i. caṛ. in dn̄io. dim̄. caṛ. hom̄. m̄. i. moƚ. vaƚ. x. foƚ. ħt. i. leu̇. in long. 7. iiii. in lat̄. 7. xv. d̄. alii. ibi ten̄.

In Widituna. i. caṛ. tr̄æ. ten̄&. f. b. sēp. ii. uiƚƚ. 7. ii. bor 7. i. caṛ in dn̄io. 7. dim̄. caṛ. hom̄. vaƚ. viii. foƚ.

In b̄tuna ten̄&. sēp. f. b. dim̄. caṛ tr̄æ. sēp. i. bor. 7. i. caṛ. 7. i. ac̣. p̄ti. vaƚ. v. foƚ. 7. iiii. d̄. In Ead̄. i. foc̣. xxx. ac̣. v. bor. i. caṛ. i. ac̣. p̄ti. vaƚ. x. foƚ.

⁊ Wrdefted̄a ten̄& sēp. f. b. t̄. r. e. ii. caṛ. tr̄æ. 7. d̄. sēp. viii. uiƚƚ. xxx. bor. ii. caṛ. in dn̄io. 7. iii. caṛ. hom̄. viii. ac̣. p̄ti. filu̇. xvi. por. sēp. i. moƚ. 7. iii. foc̣. in ead̄ tr̄a. t̄c uaƚ. lx. foƚ. m̄. iiii. liƀ.

38 St. B(enedict) has always held (North) WALSHAM, 3½ c. of land.
     Always 12 villagers; 5 smallholders.
     2 ploughs in lordship; 2½ men's ploughs; meadow, 8 acres;
       woodland, 100 pigs; 1 mill; 1 cob, 1 head of cattle, 8 pigs.
     31 Freemen, 3 c. of land and 50 acres.
       1 villager; 1 smallholder.
       Always 15 ploughs; woodland, 16 pigs; meadow, 4 acres.
   Value 100s.
     It has 1½ leagues in length and 1 league and 6 perches in width, tax of 18d.
     (Belonging) to the church, 30 acres.

219 a

39 St. B(enedict) has always held FELMINGHAM, 77 acres.
     Always 5 smallholders.
     1 plough in lordship; ½ men's plough; meadow, 1 acre.
     Also 4 Freemen, 50 acres.
       1 plough; meadow, 1 acre.
     (Belonging) to the church, 2 acres.
   Value 21s.

40 (The Saint) also held PASTON before 1066, 1 c. of land.
     2 villagers; 2 smallholders.
     1 plough in lordship; ½ men's plough. Now 1 mill.
   Value 10s.
     It has 1 league in length and 4 in width, [tax of] 15d. Others hold there.

41 In WITTON St. B(enedict) holds 1 c. of land.
     Always 2 villagers; 2 smallholders.
     1 plough in lordship; ½ men's plough.
   Value 8s.

42 In BARTON (Turf) St. B(enedict) has always held ½ c. of land.
     Always 1 smallholder.
     1 plough; meadow, 1 acre.
   Value 5s 4d.
   In the same 1 Freeman, 30 acres.
     5 smallholders.
     1 plough; meadow, 1 acre.
   Value 10s.

43 St. B(enedict) has always held WORSTEAD. Before 1066 2½ c. of land.
     Always 8 villagers; 30 smallholders.
     2 ploughs in lordship; 3 men's ploughs; meadow, 8 acres;
       woodland, 16 pigs; always 1 mill.
     Also 3 Freemen on this land.
   Value then 60s; now £4.

218 b, 219 a

.II. eccliis. xxviii. ac. in eod ptio. hec tra erat de uicto monachoz. t.r.e. m ea ht. Rob balistari de abbe. ht. I. leu. in long. 7. dim. in lat. 7. de. g. 7. xviii. d. de. g. In Ead. ten& sep scs. b. I. car. tre. t. r. e. sep. II. uilt. x. bor. 7. I. car. in dnio. 7. II. car hom. II. ac. pti. silu. vi. por. val. xl. sol.

219 b

In besetuna. I. soc. sci. b. xxx. ac. IIII. bor. II. ac. pti. val v. sol 7. IIII. d. Oms ecclie. st in ptio c maneriis.

In Ristuna. III. soc. f. b. lx. ac. Sep. dim. car. In ptio de Scotohou

In btuna. III. soc. xxxIII. ac. Sep. III. bor. I. car. val. vII. sol.

In dilham. I. soc. xxx. ac. I. bor. I. car. val. vi. sol. 7. vIII. d.

In Saleia. I. soc. xvi. ac. val. xvi. d. In Ead. xx. ac. 7. jacent in estuna 7. in ptio.

In Smalbga. I. soc sci. b. q tenebat. I. car libæ træ. 7. eam dedit sco. b. t. r. e. 7 adhuc ten& de abbe. Sep. II. uilt. 7. I. car. 7. dim. 7 .II. ac. pti. ual. xx. sol. In Ead xxvIII. soc. I. car. træ. Sep. IIII. car. I. ac. pti. val. xx. sol. Totu ht. x. qr in long. 7. xII. pc. 7. vi. qr in lat. 7. vIII. d. de. g.

(Belonging) to 2 churches, 28 acres in the same valuation. This land was for the supplies of the monks before 1066; now Robert the Crossbowman has it from the Abbot.

It has 1 league in length and ½ (a league) and 1 perch in width, tax of 18d.

In the same St. B(enedict) has always held 1 c. of land (as) before 1066.

Always 2 villagers; 10 smallholders.
1 plough in lordship; 2 men's ploughs; meadow, 2 acres; woodland, 6 pigs.
Value 40s.

44 In BEESTON (St. Lawrence) 1 Freeman of St. B(enedict's), 30 acres.   219 b
4 smallholders.
Meadow, 2 acres.
Value 5s 4d.
All the churches are in the valuation with the manors.

45 In (Sco) RUSTON 3 Freemen of St. B(enedict's), 60 acres; always ½ plough.
In the valuation of Scottow.

In BARTON (Turf) 3 Freemen, 33 acres.
Always 3 smallholders.
1 plough.
Value 7s.

In DILHAM 1 Freeman, 30 acres.
1 smallholder.
1 plough.
Value 6s 8d.

48 In SLOLEY 1 Freeman, 16 acres.
Value 16d.
In the same 20 acres; they appertain in Easton and (are) in the valuation.

49 In SMALLBURGH 1 Freeman of St. B(enedict's) who held 1 c. of free land. He gave it to St. B(enedict) before 1066, and still holds from the Abbot.
Always 2 villagers.
1½ ploughs; meadow, 2 acres.
Value 20s.
In the same 28 Freemen, 1 c. of land. Always 4 ploughs; meadow, 1 acre.
Value 20s.
The whole has 10 furlongs and 12 perches in length and 6 furlongs in width, tax of 8d.

⌠In b̄tuna.i.foc̄.Sc̄i.B. 7 Rad comitis.t.r.e.xvi.ac.val.xvi.d.7.
.ii.eccl̄e xxxiii.ac.Val.xv.d.

⌠In Haninga.ii.car tr̄æ.ten.S.b.t.r.e. 7.edric de eo.ita q̄d abb̄
ei ded̄at dimidiā de suo dn̄io. 7 ille concesserat abb̄i aliā medietatē
de suo feudo. 7 totū ita tenebat de abb̄e 7. deseruiebat; In hac tr̄a s̄t
sēp.xiii.bor. 7.ii.car.in dn̄io. 7.iii.car.hom̄.xxv.ac.pti.Silu.viii.por.
.i.mol.ii.runc.iiii.an.xii.por.xl ou.xxx.cap. 7.viii.foc.xli.
ac.sēp.ii.car.v.ac.pti.val totū xl.fol.h̄t.i.leu.in long. 7.x.q̄r.
in lat. 7 x.d de g.q̄cq̄ ibi teneat. hoc ten& Rob̄ malet. 7
Rob̄ de g'auilt de eo.

⌠In Walsā.iiii.sochem.lvii.ac.Sēp.i.car.i.ac.pti.val.v.fol

7.viii.d.de duob; ex his habuit.W.malet cōmd tantū.
In Ead.x.bor.vii.ac. 7.val.x.d.

⌠Hund de Hapinga.Lodham ten& sēp.S.B.p.v.car.tr̄æ.
Sēp.xv.uill. 7.xiii.bor.ii.ser.iii.car.in dn̄io.ii.car 7 dim.
hom̄.Silu.xvi.por.c.ac.pti.iii.runc.xvi.por iii.uasa apū. 7 cxv.
foc̄. 7.dim.iii.car.tr̄æ. 7.xv.ac.Sēp.x.car.xv.pti. 7.iiii.libi hōēs
7.dim.i.car.tr̄æ. 7.xv.ac.Sēp.iii.bor.ii.car.v.ac.pti. Ex his habuit
Abbas cōmd tantū. Rex. 7. comes focā. Tc ual. totū.c.fol.m̄.vi.lib.
7.h̄t.ii.leu 7.dim. 7.xv.pc.in lon. 7.i.leu. 7.dim.in lat. 7.lxx.pc.
7.v.fol.de.g.q̄cq̄ ibi teneat.

50 In BARTON (Turf) 1 Freeman of St. B(enedict's) and of Earl Ralph's before 1066, 16 acres.
Value 16d.
   Also 2 churches, 33 acres; value 15d.

51 In HONING St. B(enedict) held 2 c. of land before 1066, and Edric from him, on the terms that the Abbot had given him half of his lordship and he had granted the other moiety of his Holding to the Abbot, so he held the whole from the Abbot and did (him) service.
   There have always been 13 smallholders on this land.
   2 ploughs in lordship; 3 men's ploughs; meadow, 25 acres; woodland, 8 pigs; 1 mill; 2 cobs; 4 head of cattle; 12 pigs; 40 sheep; 30 goats.
   Also 8 Freemen, 41 acres. Always 2 ploughs; meadow, 5 acres. Value of the whole 40s.
   It has 1 league in length and 10 furlongs in width; tax of 10d, whoever holds there. Robert Malet holds this and Robert of Glanville from him.

52 In (North) WALSHAM 4 Freemen, 57 acres. Always 1 plough; meadow, 1 acre.
Value 5s 8d.
   W(illiam) Malet had the patronage only of 2 of these.
   In the same 10 smallholders, 7 acres.
Value 10d.

220 a

The Hundred of HAPPING

53 St. B(enedict) has always held LUDHAM, as 5 c. of land.
   Always 15 villagers; 13 smallholders; 2 slaves.
   3 ploughs in lordship; 2½ men's ploughs; woodland, 16 pigs; meadow, 100 acres; 3 cobs; 16 pigs; 3 beehives.
   Also 115 Freemen and a half, 3 c. of land and 15 acres. Always 10 ploughs; meadow, 15 acres.
   Also 4 free men and a half, 1 c. of land and 15 acres. Always 3 smallholders. 2 ploughs; meadow, 5 acres.
   Of these the Abbot had the patronage only, the King and the Earl the jurisdiction.
Value of the whole then 100s; now £6.
   It has 2½ leagues and 15 perches in length and 1½ leagues and 70 perches in width; tax of 5s, whoever holds there.

Waſtaneſham. ten& sep̃. s̃c̃s. b. p̃. II. caŕ. t̃r̃æ. 7. VIII. ac̃.
Sep̃. III. bor. 7. I. caŕ. in dn̄io. 7. dim̃. caŕ. hom̃. LX. ac̃. p̃ti. II. runc̃.
. VI. porc̃. VIII. ou. 7. XXV. ſoc̃. 7. dim̃. CLX. ac̃. Tc̃. III. caŕ. 7. dim̃
m̃. III. XII. ac̃. p̃ti. 7. II. lib̃i hoēs cōm̃d tantū. xx. ac̃. 7. I. caŕ. Ex his
. II. bʒ rex. 7. comes h̃nt ſocā. 7. de alio toto. s̃c̃s. ben̄. Totū sep̃
ual. IIII. lib̃. 7. lib̃i hoes. XXXFIII. d̃. 7 h̃t. I. leu. 7. dim̃. 7. I. qŕ
in lon̄. 7. I. leu in lat̃. 7. XXX. d̃. qcq̓ ibi teneat.

H Wimpwella ten&. sep̃. s̃c̃s. b. p̃. I. eaŕ. t̃r̃æ. 7. dim̃. Sep̃. v.
uiłł. 7. II. bor. 7. I. caŕ. in dn̄io. 7. I. caŕ hom̃. IIII. ac̃ p̃ti. 7. I.
. runc̃. IIII. por̃. 7. I. lib̃ hõ c̃m̃d tantū. IX. ac̃ 7. dim̃
caŕ. val. XII. d̃. R. 7. C. ſocā. Totū maneriū
ual. xxx. ſol. S; Godric reddebat. IIII. lib̃
qn̄ eū tenebat ad feudū comitis.

220 b

Stalham ten& sep̃. S̃c̃s. B. I. caŕ. t̃re. Sep̃. II. uiłł. 7. I. bor
7. I. caŕ. in dn̄io. 7. I. caŕ. hom̃ Silu. III. porc̃. IIII. ac̃. p̃ti. I. runc̃.
. VI. porc̃. 7. I. hõ. XXIX. ac̃. tenens t̃r̃a ſuā de s̃c̃o ben̄. t. r. e. Sep̃
dim̃. caŕ. II. ac̃. p̃ti. Rex. 7. C. ſocā. 7. IX. lib̃i hoēs. LXXV. ac̃. Tc̃. II.
caŕ. m̃. I. 7. dim̃. Ex his habuit ab̃b̃ cōm̃d. tant. 7. R. 7. C. ſocā. Totū
man. ual sep̃. xx. ſol. 7. lib̃i hoēs. II. ſol. 7. h̃t. I. leu. 7. III. qŕ. in
lon̄. 7. V. qŕ in lat̃. 7. XVII. d̃. & ob̃ de. g.

In Hincham. xxx. ac̃. t̃re ten&. sep̃. s̃c̃s. b. sep̃. dim̃. caŕ.
7. I. ac̃. p̃ti. Val. VI. ſol. 7. VIII. d̃.

In Heccles. I. lib̃ hõ. xv. ac̃. qd̃ ten. S̃. b. c̃ om̃i conſuetudine. ſ;
rex. 7. comes ſocā. 7. val. xv. D̃.

In Ludham. I. ſoc̃. ĩ. b̃. xxx ac̃. IIII. bor. III. ac̃. p̃ti. dim̃. caŕ
7 val. II. ſol.

54 St. B(enedict) has always held WAXHAM, as 2 c. of land and 8 acres.
Always 3 smallholders.
1 plough in lordship; ½ men's plough; meadow, 60 acres;
2 cobs; 6 pigs; 8 sheep.
Also 25 Freemen and a half, 160 acres. Then 3½ ploughs, now 3. Meadow, 12 acres.
Also 2 free men in patronage only, 20 acres; 1 plough.
Of these 2 the King and Earl have the jurisdiction, and of all the rest St. Benedict.
Value of the whole always £4; the free men, 34d.
It has 1½ leagues and 1 furlong in length and 1 league in width, [tax of] 30d, whoever holds there.

55 St. B(enedict) has always held WHIMPWELL, as 1½ c. of land.
Always 5 villagers; 2 smallholders.
1 plough in lordship; 1 men's plough; meadow, 4 acres; 1 cob; 4 pigs.
Also 1 free man in patronage only, 9 acres; ½ plough.
Value 12d.
The King and Earl (have) the jurisdiction.
Value of the whole manor 30s, but Godric paid £4 when he held it as part of the Earl's Holding.

56 St. B(enedict) has always held STALHAM, 1 c. of land.   220 b
Always 2 villagers; 1 smallholder.
1 plough in lordship; *1 men's plough*; woodland, 3 pigs;
meadow, 4 acres; 1 cob; 6 pigs.
Also 1 man, 29 acres, who held his land from St. Benedict before 1066.
Always ½ plough; meadow, 2 acres.
The King and Earl (have) the jurisdiction.
Also 9 free men, 75 acres. Then 2 ploughs, now 1½. Of these the Abbot had the patronage only, and the King and Earl the jurisdiction.
Value of the whole manor always at 20s; the free men, 2s.
It has 1 league and 3 furlongs in length and 5 furlongs in width, tax of 17½d.

57 In INGHAM St. B(enedict) has always held 30 acres of land.
Always ½ plough; meadow, 1 acre.
Value 6s 8d.

58 In ECCLES 1 free man, 15 acres, which St. B(enedict) holds with all customary dues, but the King and Earl (have) the jurisdiction.
Value 15d.

59 In LUDHAM 1 Freeman of St. B(enedict's), 30 acres.
4 smallholders.
Meadow, 3 acres; ½ plough.
Value 2s.

⁊In H Wimpwella . I . lib hō . XII . ac̠ . Val . XXXII . đ.
⁊Eastflec Hund . In Phileby . ten⁊ sep̄ s̄c̄s . b.
. I . car̠ . trē ⁊ . XX . ac̠ . Sep̄ . IIII . bor . ⁊ . I . car̠ . in dn̄io . ⁊ . III.
ac̠ . p̠ti . ⁊ . I . sal . m̄ . I . runc̠ . ⁊ . III . libi hōes . cōmd tantū.
. XLII . ac̠ . sep̄ . I . uill . ⁊ . I . car̠ . ⁊ . dim̄ . ⁊ . I . ac̠ . ⁊ . dim̄ . p̠ti.
val . III . sol.

⁊In Scroteby . CIX . ac̠ . ten⁊ sep̄ Sep̄ . S . b.
Sep̄ . III . bor . Tc̄ . I . car̠ . in dn̄io . Sep̄.
dim̄ . car̠ . hom̄ . II . ac̠ . p̠ti . Val . X . sol

⁊ ht . I . leu . in lon . ⁊ . V . qr̠ . in lat̠ . ⁊ . XX . đ . de g.
⁊In Castro . I . car̠ . trǣ . ten⁊ sep̄ . Sc̄s . b . Sep̄ . IIII . bor . ⁊ . I . car̠
in dn̄io . ⁊ . dim̄ . car̠ . hom̄ . VII . ac̠ . ⁊ . dim̄ . p̠ti . VI . sal . ⁊ . XIIII . libi
hōes sub abbē c̄md̄at tantū . I . car̠ . trǣ . ⁊ . I . bor . Tc̄ . II . car̠ hom̄.
m̄ . IIII . Tc̄ ual . XX . sol . m̄ . V . ⁊ . XIIII . libi hōes . sub abbē c̄md̄
tant . q̄s abbas de rationauit sup̄ Godricū . val . XL . sol.
⁊Humiliart Hund Hecham ten⁊ sep̄ . S . B . III . car̠ . trǣ
sep̄ . III . uill . V . bor . II . car̠ . in dn̄io . tc̄ . I . car̠ . hom̄ . m̄ . dim̄ . ⁊
una car̠ . ⁊ . dim̄ poss⁊ restaur̄ . XX . ac̠ . p̠ti . II . mol . I . runc̠ . VII . porc̠.
XII . ou . ⁊ . VI . soc̠ . de . dim̄ . car̠ . trǣ . sep̄ . II . car̠ . Tc̄ ual . IIII . lib . m̄
. C . sol . huic manerio ē lib hō sub abbē c̄md̄ . tant . ⁊ . ht . XXX . ac̠.
⁊ . dim̄ . car̠ . III . ac̠ . p̠ti . Val . II . sol . ht . X . qr̠ . in lon . ⁊ . VII.
in lat̠ . ⁊ . II . đ . ⁊ . III . ferđ . de . g.
⁊Depwade Hund . Tipham ten⁊ sep̄ . S . B . I . car̠ . trǣ . ⁊ . dim̄.
⁊ . XV . ac̠ . sep̄ . IIII . uill . V . bor . I . car̠ . in dn̄io tc̄ . I . car̠ . ⁊ . dim̄.
hom̄ . m̄ . I . ⁊ . III . ac̠ . p̠ti . silu . X . porc̠ . VI . por . Val . XXV . sol

60 In WHIMPWELL 1 free man, 12 acres.
Value 32d.

EAST FLEGG Hundred

61 In FILBY St. B(enedict) has always held 1 c. of land and 20 acres.
Always 4 smallholders.
1 plough in lordship; meadow, 3 acres; 1 salt-house. Now 1 cob.
Also 3 free men in patronage only, 42 acres. Always 1 villager.
1½ ploughs; meadow, 1½ acres.
Value 3s.

62 In SCRATBY St. Benedict has always held 109 acres.
Always 3 smallholders.
Then 1 plough in lordship. Always ½ men's plough; meadow, 2 acres.
Value 10s.
It has 1 league in length and 5 furlongs in width, tax of 20d. 221 a

63 In CAISTER St. B(enedict) has always held 1 c. of land.
Always 4 smallholders.
1 plough in lordship; ½ men's plough; meadow, 7½ acres; 6 salt-houses.
Also 14 free men under the Abbot in patronage only, 1 c. of land. 1 smallholder. Then 2 men's ploughs, now 4.
Value then 20s, now 25.
Also 14 free men *under the Abbot in patronage only* whom the Abbot proved (to be his) against Godric.
Value 40s.

HUMBLEYARD Hundred

64 St. B(enedict) has always held HEIGHAM, 3 c. of land.
Always 3 villagers; 5 smallholders.
2 ploughs in lordship. Then 1 men's plough, now ½; 1½ ploughs could be restored. Meadow, 20 acres; 2 mills; 1 cob; 7 pigs; 12 sheep.
Also 6 Freemen, at ½ c. of land; always 2 ploughs.
Value then £4; now 100s.
In this manor is a free man under the Abbot in patronage only. He has 30 acres; ½ plough; meadow, 3 acres.
Value 2s.
It has 10 furlongs in length and 7 in width, tax of 2¾d.

DEPWADE Hundred

65 St. B(enedict) has always held TIBENHAM, 1½ c. of land and 15 acres.
Always 4 villagers; 5 smallholders.
1 plough in lordship. Then 1½ men's ploughs, now 1. Meadow, 3 acres; woodland, 10 pigs; 6 pigs.
Value 25s.

220 b, 221 a

.XVIII. **TERRA** Sci Stephani de Cadomo.

/Hund 7 Dim de Fredebruge.   Wellā tenuit Stigand
.t.r.e. Sep.x.uill.7.II.car.tre.7.VI.bor.7.I.fer.xxx.ac.pti.
tc.II.car.in dnio.P.v.bou.m.II.car.I.car.hom.II.mol.huic
man jacent.xIIII.foc.de.xxvIII.ac.tre.Tc.I.car.m.v.an.
Sep.vII.por.tc.xv.ou.m.Lx.Tc.7.p.ual.Ix.lib.m.x.
Wella.7 Gaituna ht.I.leu.7.dim.in long.7.dim in lat.7
reddit.xvi.d.de.g.qcq, ibi teneat. In Wella.jac& adhuc
.v.qr pasturæ in long.7.IIII. in lat.7 e in eod ptio.

.XIX. **TERRA** Willi de Scohies.

/Hund 7.dim de Fredebruge. Ilfinghetunā tenuit Scula lib hō
t.r.e.p man.7.p.II.car.træ m ten&.W.in dnio Sep.III.uill.
.vII.bor.Tc.II.car.in dnio.Post 7.m.I.x.ac.pti.c.ou.Tc.xxx.
por.m.xvI.hic jacent.vII.foc.xII.ac.Tc.ual.xL.fol.m.Lx.
/In Ecleuuartuna ten& Ricard de.W.xL.ac.7 ual.vI.fol.
hanc tra tenuit Rafrid.7 comes Rad.derationauit dimidia.
7.tenuit ea die q forisfecit. M eam ten& Vruoi hō Rafridi ad
feudū Willi de Scohies 7.reuocat rege ad tutore.

In Ilfinghetuna.tenuit Tchill lib hō.t.r.e.dim.car.træ.
m.W.in dnio.sep.III.bor.tc.dim.car.m.II.bou.xL.ac.pti.7
dim.sal.tc.ual.x.fol.m.xx.Tota Ilfinghetuna ht.I.leu.
in long.7.dim;7.dim.leu.in lat.7.reddit.xII.d.de.xx.fol
de.g.
Mideltuna tenuit Tchill p man.7.p.II.car træ.m.W.i dnio.
Sep.IIII.uill.7.vI.bor.7.IIII.fer.xxx.ac.pti.II.car.in dnio.tc
.I.car.hom.m.dim.I.mol.I.pifc.vIII.sal.Sep.I.rune.tc.II.uac
tc.xvI.por.m.x.tc.Lxxx.ou.m.Lxx.Tc ual.c.fol.m.vII.lib

18   LAND OF ST. STEPHEN OF CAEN

The Hundred and a Half of FREEBRIDGE

1 Stigand held WELL before 1066.
    Always 10 villagers, 2 c. of land; 6 smallholders; 1 slave.
    Meadow, 30 acres. Then 2 ploughs in lordship, later 5 oxen,
       now 2 ploughs. 1 men's plough; 2 mills.
    14 free men appertain to this manor, at 28 acres of land.
      Then 1 plough. Now 5 head of cattle; always 7 pigs. Then
       15 sheep, now 60.
Value then and later £9; now 10.
Well and Gayton have 1½ leagues in length and ½ in width, it pays tax of 16d, whoever holds there. In Well there appertains further, pasture 5 furlongs in length and 4 in width; it is in the same valuation.

19   THE LAND OF WILLIAM OF ÉCOUIS

The Hundred and a Half of FREEBRIDGE

1 Skuli, a free man, held ISLINGTON before 1066 as a manor, as 2 c. of land. Now W(illiam) holds in lordship.
    Always 3 villagers; 7 smallholders.
    Then 2 ploughs in lordship, later and now 1. Meadow, 10 acres;
       100 sheep. Then 30 pigs, now 16.
    Here appertain 7 Freemen, 12 acres.
Value then 40s; now 60.

2 In CLENCHWARTON *Richard holds from W(illiam)* 40 acres.
Value 6s.
    Radfrid held this land and Earl Ralph proved half (to be his). He held it on the day he forfeited; now Wulfwy, Radfrid's man, holds it as part of the Holding of William of Écouis; he vouches the King as warrantor.

3 In ISLINGTON Thorkell, a free man, held ½ c. of land before 1066; now W(illiam holds) in lordship.
    Always 3 smallholders.
    Then ½ plough; now 2 oxen. Meadow, 40 acres; ½ salt-house.
Value then 10s; now 20.
    The whole of Islington has 1½ leagues in length and ½ league in width; of a 20s tax it pays 12d.

4 Thorkell held MIDDLETON as a manor, as 2 c. of land. Now W(illiam holds) in lordship.
    Always 4 villagers; 6 smallholders; 4 slaves.
    Meadow, 30 acres; 2 ploughs in lordship. Then 1 men's plough,
       now ½. 1 mill; 1 fishery; 8 salt-houses; always 1 cob. Then 2
       cows. Then 16 pigs, now 10. Then 80 sheep, now 70.
Value then 100s; now £7.

Runghetunā tenuit Idē . t̃ . r̃ . ẽ . p̃ man̄ . 7 . p . I . car̃ . tr̃æ m̂ . W . i dn̄io
Sēp . II . bor . xx . ać . p̃ti . I . car̃ . in dn̄io . dim̃ . car̃ . hom̃ . huic maner̃
jać . VII . foć . t̃ . r̃ . ẽ . de . LX . ać . tc̃ . II . car̃ . m̂ . I . VIII . ać . p̃ti . Totū
ual̃ . LX . fol̃ . In Mideltuna ten& . W . in đ . VI . libos . hōes de . I . car̃
tr̃æ . sẽp . I . car̃ . filū . c . porc̃ . Val̃ . XXIIII . fol̃ . 7 . VIII . đ . de . II b; habuit
Stigand̃ focā . 7 fuit liƀata Rafrido . p . I . car̃ . tr̃æ.

Gaitunā ten& Vluoĩ . I . car̃ . tr̃æ . qđ ten Tchill̃ . t̃ . r̃ . ẽ . Tc̃ . VIII .
bor . m̂ . VI . XII . ać . p̃ti . sẽp . I . car̃ in dn̄io . Tc̃ . 7 . p̃ . dim̃ . car̃
hom̃ . m̂ . II . 7 Val̃ . xx . fol̃.

Mafincham ten& Rađ fili herluini . qđ tenuit Goduin̄.
liƀ hõ . t̃ . r̃ . ẽ . Sēp . VI . uitl̃ . Tc̃ . I . car̃ . in dn̄io . Tc̃ . ual̃ . x . fol̃.
m̂ . v . De hoc habuit anteć . Witl̃i . de Warenna
c̃m̃d tant̃ . 7 foca in Mafinchā regis.

Dochinga Hund . BRECham ten

bern . fub eduardo rege . I . car̃ tr̃æ . m̂ tenet . R . de ebrois
Tc̃ I . car̃ . p̃ . nulla . m̂ . I . sẽp . I . uitl̃s . 7 . II . bor . dim̃ car̃ hoūm.
7 ual̃ . x . fol̃ . I . ecćla . IIII . ać . In eadē tẽn . liƀ . hõ . Tor . t.
e r . Sub Stigando . IIII . car̃ tr̃æ . Tc̃ . II . car̃ in dn̄io 7 m̂
Tc̃ 7 p̃ . II . car̃ hoūm . m̂ . I . Tc̃ 7 p̃ . XIIII . uitl̃i . m̂ . II . femp.
I . bor . Tc̃ ual̃ . XL . fol̃ . m̂ . IIII . liƀ . Stigandus habuit focā

5 He also held (North) RUNCTON before 1066 as a manor, as 1 c. of land. Now W(illiam holds) in lordship.
  Always 2 smallholders.
  Meadow, 20 acres; 1 plough in lordship; ½ men's plough.
  7 Freemen appertained to this manor before 1066, at 60 acres.
    Then 2 ploughs, now 1. Meadow, 8 acres.
  Value of the whole 60s.

6 In MIDDLETON W(illiam) holds in lordship 6 free men, at 1 c. of land. Always 1 plough; woodland, 100 pigs.
  Value 24s 8d.
    Stigand had the jurisdiction over 2 and it was delivered to Radfrid for 1 c. of land.

7 Wulfwy holds GAYTON, 1 c. of land which Thorkell held before 1066.
  Then 8 smallholders, now 6.
  Meadow, 12 acres; always 1 plough in lordship. Then and later ½ men's plough, now 2.
  Value 20s.

8 Ralph son of Herlwin holds MASSINGHAM, which Godwin, a free man, held before 1066; 1 c. of land.
  Always 6 villagers.
  Then 1 plough in lordship.
  Value then 10s; now 5.
    William of Warenne's predecessor had the patronage only over this; the jurisdiction (is) in the King's (manor of) Massingham.

DOCKING Hundred

9 Bernard held (Great) BIRCHAM under King Edward; 1 c. of land. 222 b
  Now R(oger) of Evreux holds.
    Then 1 plough, later none, now 1.
    Always 1 villager; 2 smallholders.
    ½ men's plough.
  Value 10s.
    1 church, 4 acres.
  In the same a free man, Thor, held 4 c. of land under Stigand before 1066.
    Then 2 ploughs in lordship, and now. Then and later 2 men's ploughs, now 1.
    Then and later 14 villagers, now 2; always 1 smallholder.
  Value then 40s; now £4.
    Stigand had the jurisdiction.

Et . III . libi hoes ; LXXXV . ac tre . t . r . e . Tc . II . car 7 p
7 m . I . Tc . II . bor . 7 . I . lib . ho xxx . ac tre brunardus ten&
semp . II . boues . Totum . ual . XII . sol . Rafrid tenuit
hos hoes . 7 m . st . in manu regis quia non fuit q rationarat
Tota ht . I . leug . int . 7 . I . leug in lat . quicumq ibi te
neat . 7 reddit XXVII . d . de . XX . sol . de gelto .

H̃ . de Smetheduna . In Rincteda . tenet Ro
gerus . II . libos hoes . I . car terre . Et in holm . II . libo hoes
XL . ac . 7 III . bor . semp . I . ca 7 dim . 7 st in ptio de brecha
In eade tenet ide . I . lib dim car tre Tc . I . ca p dim .
m . II . bou . semp ual v . sol .

H̃ . SCREPHA . In Wilgeby . II . car tre . tenuit
Fader . t . r . e . Tc . x . uilli . p 7 m . VI . semp . IX bor . Tc
IIII . s . m . I . 7 XIIII . ac pti Tc . I . car 7 dim . in dnio
p . I . m . II . Tc . I . car 7 dim houm p . 7 m . I .
filu . x . por . Tc . I . r . m . III . semp . v .
an . 7 IX . por . Tc . XL . ou . m . LII . 7 . XII .
soc . XL . ac . Tc . I . car 7 dim . p . 7 m . I . Tc 7 p . ual . XL . sol
m . LX . 7 ht dim . leug . in long . 7 dim . in lato . quicumq ibi
teneat . 7 xv . d . de gelto . I . eccla . x ac 7 ual . III . sol .

In Bucham . tenet Rogerus . I . car terre . semp . IIII . bor .
7 IIII . ac . pti . 7 . I . car in dnio . silua LX . por . Tc XXIIII . ou . m .
XXX . Tc 7 p . ual . XII . m . XX . tc . VI . por . m . XI .

Also 3 free men (whom) the same holds, 85 acres of land before 1066.
>Then 2 ploughs, later and now 1.
>Then 2 smallholders.

Also 1 free man, Brunard, holds 30 acres of land; always 2 oxen. Value of the whole 12s.

Radfrid held these men. Now they are in the hand of the King because there was no-one to claim them.

The whole has 1 league in length and 1 league in width, whoever holds there, of a 20s tax it pays 27d.

The Hundred of SMETHDON

10 In (Little) RINGSTEAD Roger holds 2 free men, 1 c. of land; and in HOLME (Next The Sea) 2 free men, 40 acres. 3 smallholders.
>3 smallholders.
>Always 1½ ploughs.

They are in the valuation of (Great) Bircham.

In the same he also holds 1 free (man), ½ c. of land. Then 1 plough, later ½, now 2 oxen.

Value always 5s.

SHROPHAM Hundred

11 In WILBY Fathir held 2 c. of land before 1066.
>Then 10 villagers, later and now 6; always 9 smallholders.
>Then 4 slaves, now 1.
>Meadow, 14 acres. Then 1½ ploughs in lordship, later 1, now 2. Then 1½ men's ploughs, later and now 1. Woodland, 10 pigs. Then 1 cob, now 3. Always 5 head of cattle; 9 pigs. Then 40 sheep, now 52.

Also 12 Freemen, 40 acres. Then 1½ ploughs, later and now 1.   223 a
Value then and later 40s; now 60.

It has ½ league in length and ½ in width, whoever holds there, tax of 15d.

1 church, 10 acres;
value 3s.

12 In BUCKENHAM Roger holds 1 c. of land.
>Always 4 smallholders.
>Meadow, 4 acres; 1 plough in lordship; woodland, 60 pigs.
>Then 24 sheep, now 30.

Value then and later 12[s?]; now 20.
>Then 6 pigs, now 11.

H̃. GILLECROS. In Benham . II . cā tr̃e ̦p mañ . tenuit
Fader . liber hõ . t . e . r . ſemp v . uiłt . 7 vi . bor . 7 i . ſer . 7 xx.
ac̃ p̃ti . ſilu̧ . c . por . ſẽp i . cā . in dñio . 7 . i . car̃ houm . ſẽp . i . r.
7 . II . añ 7 tc̃ vIII . por . Tc̃ xxx . ou̧ 7 xvi . ſoc̃ . xxIIII . ac̃ tr̃e.
Tc̃ 7 p̃ . II . car̃ . m̃ . I . car̃ 7 dim̃ . 7 I . cā . poſſet reſtaurari.
I . eccl̃a . xxx . ac̃ . 7 ual . xxII . ſol . Tc̃ 7 p̃ . ual xL . m̃ . L.
de hoc mañ . tenet . odarus . I . car̃ . tr̃e . 7 II . bor . 7 I . car̃
ſẽp . ual . xx . ſol.

In Cheiunchala ſoca de . vi . foris facturis.

In Herlinga tenuit Ketel . lib̃ hõ t̃ . r . e . II . car̃ tr̃e
̦p mañ . modo tenet ingulfus . ſemp . v . uiłt . 7 . IIII . bor.
Tc̃ . I . ſer . 7 IIII . ac̃ p̃ti . ſẽp I . car̃ in dñio 7 . I . car̃ houm.
ſilu̧ . xvI . por . 7 . I . car̃ . poſſet reſtaurari . ſẽp . I . mol . 7 II.
ſoç . xx . ac̃ tr̃e . 7 III . ac̃ p̃ti ſẽp . dim̃ . car̃ . m̃ . I . r . ſẽp.
III añ . m̃ . vIII . por . 7 xx . ou̧ . 7 . I . uas ap̃u . I . eccl̃a IIII ac̃.
Tc̃ . ual . xxx . ſol . m̃ . xL . Totum h̃t . I . leũg . in long 7
I . leũg . in lat̃ . 7 xvII . d̃ . 7 . I . ferding . q̃cumq̧ ibi teneat.
7 vII . ac̃ 7 dimidia tr̃e jacet huic tr̃e 7 ſilũ . xII . por.

223 b

H̃ Mittefort . In Letetuna . I . lib̃ hõ . xxvII . ac̃ . 7 . I.
ac̃ 7 dim̃ . p̃ti . 7 . I . bor . 7 dim̃ car̃ 7 ual . xxxII . d̃.

H̃ . GALGOV . I Creic tenuit . Turchilł t . e . r . I . car̃
tr̃e . modo Turſtinus . Sẽp . I . uiłłs . 7 . xII . bor . Tc̃ . I . ſer.
Sẽp . II . car̃ in dñio . 7 . I . car̃ houm . III . ac̃r p̃ti . I . mol.
Tc̃ Lx . ou̧ . m̃ . nulł . 7 . II . ſoc̃ . de . II . ac̃ . Tc̃ 7 p̃ . ual . xL.
ſol . m̃ . xxx.

GUILTCROSS Hundred

13 In BANHAM Fathir, a free man, held 2 c. of land as a manor before 1066.
    Always 5 villagers; 6 smallholders; 1 slave.
    Meadow, 20 acres; woodland, 100 pigs. Always 1 plough in lordship; 1 men's plough. Always 1 cob; 2 head of cattle. Then 8 pigs; then 30 sheep.
    Also 16 Freemen, 24 acres of land.
    Then and later 2 ploughs, now 1½ ploughs; 1 plough could be restored.
    1 church, 30 acres.
Value 22s.
Value then and later 40[s?]; now 50.
    Oder holds 1 c. of land from this manor.
    2 smallholders; 1 plough.
Value always 20s.

14 In KENNINGHALL the jurisdiction of the 6 forfeitures.

15 In HARLING Ketel, a free man, held 2 c. of land before 1066 as a manor. Now Ingulf holds.
    Always 5 villagers; 4 smallholders. Then 1 slave.
    Meadow, 4 acres. Always 1 plough in lordship; 1 men's plough; woodland, 16 pigs; 1 plough could be restored. Always 1 mill.
    Also 2 Freemen, 20 acres of land.
    Meadow, 3 acres; always ½ plough. Now 1 cob. Always 3 head of cattle. Now 8 pigs; 20 sheep; 1 beehive. 1 church, 4 acres.
Value then 30s; now 40.
    The whole has 1 league in length and 1 league in width; [tax of] 17¼d, whoever holds there.
    7½ acres of land appertain to this land; woodland, 12 pigs.

MITFORD Hundred

16 In LETTON 1 free man, 27 acres.
    Meadow, 1½ acres.
    1 smallholder.
    ½ plough.
    Value 32d.

GALLOW Hundred

17 Thorkell held 1 c. of land before 1066 in CREAKE, now Thurstan.
    Always 1 villager; 12 smallholders. Then 1 slave.
    Always 2 ploughs in lordship; 1 men's plough; meadow, 3 acres; 1 mill. Then 60 sheep, now none.
    Also 2 Freemen, at 2 acres.
Value then and later 40s; now 30.

H. ERPINGAHĀ NORTH.

Silingeham teñ seiardus bar . t . r . e . iii . car tre . Sep
x uilli . 7 xii . bor . Tc vi . p 7 m . v . tc . iii . car in dnio . p 7 m .
ii . tc iiii . car . hou . p 7 m . ii . Tc silu . ad . c . lx . por m . ad
. c . iiii . acr pti . Semp . i . r . 7 . ii . añ . Tc v . por . m . xv Tc
lx . cap . m . l . 7 . i . soc de xii . ac . tre . Sep . ual . iiii . lib . 7 .
ht i . leug in long . 7 i . in lato . 7 de gelto . xi . d . 7 obolu .

Salthus teñ seiar bar . t . e . r . iii . car tre . sep . iiii uilt .
x . bor . tc . iii . i dnio 7 p . dim . m . i . sep . ii . car houm . Silu
ad . c . por . tc 7 sep ual . xl . sol . Et ille habet socam . 7 saca
et in siling ē mensurata .

In repes teñ gert . t r . e . i . libū hoēm . 7 arduinus teñ
qndo Radulf se foris fecit . m tenet . quintinus . de Wil .
7 reuocat libatore . Rotb . blundū xxx . ac tre . Sep
. i . uills . 7 . i . bor . 7 i . ac pti . 7 . i . car . tc ual . ii . sol
7 m . x .

In besentuna teñ . Turkil haco . t . r . e . i . car tre .

m tenet ingulfus Sep iii . uill . 7 xv . bor Tc 7 p . i . car .
in dnio . m . i . 7 dim . Sep i . car . 7 dim . hou . Silu ad . xx . por
i . ac pti . Sep . i . r . 7 . ii . añ . Tc vii . por . m . ii . Tc . xxii .
cap . Tc 7 p . ual . xx . sol . 7 . m . xl . 7 ht . i . leug in long 7 v .
qr . in lato . 7 de gelto xi . d . 7 obolū

In ru Netune tenet ide . i . car tre Sep . x . bor . 7 . i . car in
dnio . 7 . i . car houm . Silu ad . x . por . m . vii . por . m . lx . ou
7 v . soc de xv . ac tre . sep dim . car . Tc ual . xx . sol . m . xl .
i . eccla vi . ac 7 ē msurata in besetuna .

NORTH ERPINGHAM Hundred

18 Siward Bairn held SHERINGHAM before 1066, 3 c. of land.
 Always 10 villagers; 12 smallholders. Then 6 slaves, later and now 5.
 Then 3 ploughs in lordship, later and now 2. Then 4 men's ploughs, later and now 2. Then woodland for 160 pigs, now for 100. Meadow, 4 acres. Always 1 cob; 2 head of cattle. Then 5 pigs, now 15. Then 60 goats, now 50.
 Also 1 Freeman, at 12 acres of land.
 Value always £4.
 1 church, 15 acres;
 value 4s.
 It has 1 league in length and 1 in width, tax of 11½d.

19 Siward Bairn held SALTHOUSE before 1066, 3 c. of land.
 Always 4 villagers; 10 smallholders.
 Then 3 [ploughs] in lordship, later ½, now 1. Always 2 men's ploughs; woodland for 100 pigs.
 Value then and always 40s.
 He has the full jurisdiction. It is measured in Sheringham.

20 In REPPS Gyrth held 1 free man before 1066 and Hardwin held when (Earl) Ralph forfeited; now Quintin holds from William and calls to witness Robert Blunt who gave him possession; 30 acres of land.
 Always 1 villager; 1 smallholder.
 Meadow, 1 acre; 1 plough.
 Value then 2s; now 10.

21 In BEESTON (Regis) Thorkell Hako held 1 c. of land before 1066. Now Ingulf holds.
 Always 3 villagers; 15 smallholders.
 Then and later 1 plough in lordship, now 1½. Always 1½ men's ploughs; woodland for 20 pigs; meadow, 1 acre. Always 1 cob, 2 head of cattle. Then 7 pigs, now 2. Then 22 goats.
 Value then and later 20s; now 40.
 It has 1 league in length and 5 furlongs in width, tax of 11½d.

224 a

22 In RUNTON he also holds 1 c. of land.
 Always 10 smallholders.
 1 plough in lordship; 1 men's plough; woodland for 10 pigs. Now 7 pigs; now 60 sheep.
 Also 5 Freemen, at 15 acres of land; always ½ plough.
 Value then 20s; now 40.
 1 church, 6 acres. It is measured in Beeston (Regis).

H̃. WALES'AM. In b̃ningehā ten̄. Eaduin̉ b̃uitā
1 . lib̃ hō. t̃ r . e . XL . ac̃r terre . III . bor. Tc̃ . 1 . car̉ . p̃ dim̄.
m̂ . 1 . 7 . 11 . ac̄ p̃ti . xxx . oũ . Ap̃tiatia ē in ftoches.

⁋ In redtchā ten̄ . bricric̉ . t . r . e . 11 . car̉ . terre . m̂ tenet
Ricard̉ . p̃ man̄. Sēp XI . bor. Tc̃ . III . fer̉ . p̃ . 7 m̂ . 1 . Tc̃ . 1 . car̉
7 dim̄ . in dn̄io . m̂ . 1 . Sēp . 1 . car̉ . 7 dim̄ . hoūm . XX . ac̄ p̃ti.
Tc̃ ual . XL . m̂ . LX . fol . ħt . 1 . leug̃ . in long̃ . 7 . III . qr̉ .
7 dim̄ . 1 . leug̃ . in lat̃ . 7 de gelto XVI . d̃ . qcumq̧ ibi teat
1 . eccla . XL . ac̃r 7 . ual VI . fol . 7 . VIII . d̃ . Hic calumpniat̃
abbas de holmo . 1 . foc̄ . XL . ac̄ tr̃e . 7 ħ . teftatur . 7 adhuc
calũp̄n , 1 . bor . 7 . 1 . ac̃r tr̃e . teftim̄ hund̃.

⁋ In pankesforda ten̄ . Goduin̉ . 1 . lib̃ hō t̃ . r . e . xxx .
ac̃r tr̃æ . m̂ tenet . hugo . IIII . bor tc̃ . 1 . car̉ . VI . ac̄ p̃ti.
sēp . dim̄ car̉ hoūm . 1 . eccla . VIII . ac̄ 7 ual XII . d̃ . Tc̃ ual
x . fol m̂ . xx . Sed . R . com̄ . habuit focam.

224 b

⁋ In fifcele tenet id̃e . 1 . dim̄ . hm̄ . 11 ac̄ . de XII . d̃ .

H̃. BLAFELDA. In linpeho ten̄ Harduinus . 11 de cōnd̃
tantū . m̂ . odarus . XXXIIII . ac̃r . tr̃æ . 7 . 1 . bor . V . ac̃r p̃ti . Sēp.
1 . car̉ Tc̃ ual . x . fol m̂ . XXIII . fol.

⁋ Et in plumeftede . 11 . lib̃i hoēs Harduini t . e . r . VIII . ac̄ tr̃e
Quod tenet Hugo . sēp arat̉ cũ . 11 . bouib̃ . Sēp . ual . 11 fol.
In b̃ningeham . tenet id̃e . xx . ac̃r . tr̃e . in dn̄io . 7 jacent
in ftokesbei.

⁋ In futhuide . tenet . id̃e XXIX ac̄ tr̃e . 7 . ī ea . 1 . bor . 7
dim̄ . 7 . III . ac̃r . p̃ti . 7 dim̄ . car̉ . sēp . Sēp . ual . XXXII . d̃ .

WALSHAM Hundred

23 In (North) BURLINGHAM Edwin, 1 free man, held an outlier before 1066, 40 acres of land.
    3 smallholders.
    Then 1 plough, later ½, now 1. Meadow, 2 acres; 30 sheep.
It is assessed in Stokesby.

24 In REEDHAM Brictric held 2 c. of land before 1066; now Richard holds it as a manor.
    Always 11 smallholders. Then 3 slaves, later and now 1.
    Then 1½ ploughs in lordship, now 1. Always 1½ men's ploughs; meadow, 20 acres.
Value then 40; now 60s.
    It has 1 league and 3 furlongs in length and ½ league in width, tax of 16d, whoever holds there.
    1 church, 40 acres;
value 6s 8d.
    Here the Abbot of Holme claims 1 Freeman, 40 acres of land; (this) the Hundred testifies. Further he claims 1 smallholder and 1 acre of land; by witness of the Hundred.

25 In PANXWORTH Godwin, 1 free man, held before 1066, 30 acres of land. Now Hugh holds.
    4 smallholders.
    Then 1 plough; meadow, 6 acres; always ½ men's plough.
        1 church, 8 acres;
value 12d.
Value then 10s; now 20.
    But Earl R(alph) had the jurisdiction.

26 In FISHLEY he also holds 1 half a man, 2 acres, at 12d.   224 b

BLOFIELD Hundred

27 In LIMPENHOE Hardwin held 2 free men by patronage only, now Oder (holds); 34 acres of land.
    1 smallholder.
    Meadow, 5 acres; always 1 plough.
Value then 10s; now 23s.

28 Also in PLUMSTEAD 2 free men of Hardwin's before 1066, 8 acres of land. This Hugh holds. It has always been ploughed with 2 oxen.
Value always 2s.
    In (North) Burlingham he also holds 20 acres of land in lordship. They appertain in Stokesby.

29 In SOUTHWOOD he also holds 29 acres of land.
    1½ smallholders on it.
    Meadow, 3 acres; always ½ plough.
Value always 32d.

FLEWEST H̄. In Wintretona . tenet idē . 1 . lib̃ hoɱ
7 in repes . 1 . In afchebei . 1 . f; 7 duo 7 dim̃ . s̄ci . beñ . de Holmo
cōmđ tantũ de xlvi . ac̄ terre . Sep̃ . 1 . car̂ 7 s̃ in p̄tio fto -
- kefbei.

H̄. LOTNINGA. In brant tñ alvinus . lib̃ homo
fub ftigando t̄ . r . e . modo tenet Odar . l . arc̄ terre.
7̂ . 1 . bor . Tc̄ . 1 . car̂ p̂ . 7 m̃ . nichil 7 ual̃ . x . fol̃ . Soca ĩ hunđ.

H̄. DE ENSFORDA. Witciñ ham teñ . Hardewi
nus . 1 . lib̃ hō t̄ . r . e . iii . car̂ tr̃e . Tc̄ . xvi . bor . 7 p̂ . 7 m̃.
xiii . sep̃ . iiii . f . sep̃ . ii . car̂ in dñio . 7 . 1 . car̂ hoūm . 7 viii.
ac̄ p̃ti . filu . v . por . sep̃ . ii . mol̃ . m̃ . 1 . r . 7 . iiii . an̂ . Tc̄
xii . por . m̃ . xvi . Tc̄ . lxxx . ou . m̃ . c . Tc̄ xxx cap̃.
m̃ . x . Et . xii . foc̄ . lxxx . ac̄ tr̃e . sep̃ . v . car̂ 7 ii.
ac̄ p̃ti . 1 . eccla . fine tr̃a.

225 a
In Weftuna . beruita . 1 car̂ . tr̃e 7 sep̃ . 1 . uill̃ . 7 xii . bor . 7̂ 1 . fer fep̃
1 . car̂ in dñio . 7 . 1 . car̂ hoūm . 7 ii . ac̄ p̃ti . 7 . x . foc̄ . lxxx . ac̄ tr̃e
tc̄ 7 p̂ . viii . car̂ m̃ . vii . 7 . poteft fieri . 7 ii . ac̄ p̃ti . 1 . eccla xii.
ac̄ . 7 ual̃ . iiii . đ . Totum Val̃ . tc̄ . vii . lib̃ . p̂ . viii . lib̃ . x fol̃.
m̃ . fimil̃ . Et . ii . libi hoēs quintin . dim̃ car̂ tr̃e . 7 . ii . bor.
sep̃ . 1 . car̂ . 7 dim̃ . 7 . ual̃ . xxx . fol̃ de his duob₇ Soca in folfam
regis . f₇ W . tenet . 7 h̃t . 1 . leug̃ . in long̃ 7 in lat̃ 7 redd̃ . xxx
xx đ . in geltum quicumq₇ ibi teneat.

H̄. DE TAVERHAM. In Atlebruge . xxxv . ac̄ teræ
ii . libi hoēs . sep̃ . ii . bor 7 dim̃ . car̂ . 7 . ii . ac̄ p̃ti . 7 s̃t in p̄tio dē
Witcinchaɱ . Rex 7 comes focam.

WEST FLEGG Hundred

30 In WINTERTON he also holds 1 free man and in Repps 1, in Ashby 1, but also 2 and a half under the patronage only of St. Benedict of Holme, at 46 acres of land.
Always 1 plough.
They are in the valuation of Stokesby.

LODDON Hundred

31 A(i)lwin, a free man, held in BRANT before 1066 under Stigand, now Oder holds; 50 acres of land.
1 smallholder.
Then 1 plough, later and now nothing.
Value 10s.
The jurisdiction (is) in the Hundred.

The Hundred of EYNSFORD

32 Hardwin, 1 free man, held WITCHINGHAM before 1066, 3 c. of land.
Then 16 smallholders, later and now 13; always 4 slaves.
Always 2 ploughs in lordship; 1 men's plough; meadow, 8 acres; woodland, 5 pigs. Always 2 mills. Now 1 cob; 4 head of cattle. Then 12 pigs, now 16. Then 80 sheep, now 100. Then 30 goats, now 40.
Also 12 Freemen, 80 acres of land. Always 5 ploughs; meadow, 2 acres.
1 church without land.

An outlier in WESTON (Longville), 1 c. of land.   225 a
Always 1 villager; 12 smallholders; 1 slave.
Always 1 plough in lordship; 1 men's plough; meadow, 2 acres.
Also 10 Freemen, 80 acres of land. Then and later 8 ploughs, now 7; 1 could be there. Meadow, 2 acres.
1 church, 12 acres;
value 4d.
Value of the whole then £7; later £8 10s; now likewise.
Also 2 free men of Quintin's, ½ c. of land.
2 smallholders;
always 1½ ploughs.
Value 30s from these 2.
The jurisdiction is in the King's (manor of) Foulsham, but W(illiam) holds.
It has 1 league in length and in width, it pays 20d in tax, whoever holds there.

The Hundred of TAVERHAM

33 In ATTLEBRIDGE 35 acres of land; 2 free men.
Always 2 smallholders.
½ plough; meadow, 2 acres.
They are in the valuation of Witchingham. The King and Earl (have) the jurisdiction.

224 b, 225 a

H̄. DE ERPINGAHĀ SVD. In Corpeſtig . I . Vilɫ . ptinet
in Witcingeham . xxxx . ac̄ tr̄e 7 . II . bor . sēp . I . car̄ 7 ual
vi . ſoɫ . tres : partes de I . ecclā . IX . ac̄ 7 uaɫ . vI . d . 7 . I . ſoc̄
iiii . ac̄ In tortuna . 7 Vaɫ . vIII . d.

H̄. Stuɴetada . In Paſtuna . I . lib̄ ho̅ Edrici c̄om̄d .
tantū xx . ac̄ tr̄e . sēp . I . bor 7 uaɫ . xII . d . In Suauelda
vi . ac̄ lib̄ . ho̅ . 7 uaɫ . vI . d . Sc̄s benedictus . ſocam .

H̄. Eaſt de Flec . Stokesbey ten̄ . Eduinus lib̄ ho̅
Guerd . III . car̄ . tr̄e . sēp xv uilli ; 7 vI . bor . 7 IIII . ſer Tc̄
II . car̄ 7 dim̄ . in dn̄io . p . 7 m̄ . III . 7 sēp . I . car̄ hoūm . xx .
ac̄ p̄ti . 7 II . ſal 7 II . ſaɫ . 7 . II . r . Tc̄ . IIII . an̄ . m̄ . vI . semp
x . por . Tc̄ cxx . oū . m̄ . cLxxx . 7 I . eccla xxIII . ac̄ tr̄e . 7
III p̄ti 7 ual . xvI . d . & xxI hoēs Lxxx . ac̄ tr̄e . jacent

sēp huic manerio . Rex 7 comes ſoca . de toto . sēp . v . car̄ 7 IIII . ac̄
p̄ti . 7 . III lib̄ hoēs . quos addidit harduinus . t̄ . r . e . Willi . 7 ht
c . ac̄ tr̄e . ex h̄ habuit ſuus . anteceſſor t̄ . r . e . c̄om̄d . sēp . IX . bor
7 III . car̄ . 7 vIII . ac̄ p̄ti . 7 . I . ſal . Tc̄ uaɫ x . ſoɫ . m̄ . xvI . 7 . M̄ . uaɫ .
tc̄ . c . ſoɫ . m̄ . x . lib̄ . 7 tam̄ reddidit duob; annis unoq̄q̄; anno
xv . lib̄ . 7 . IIII . ſoɫ . 7 ht . I . leug̃ in long . 7 . I . leug̃ . in laɫ . 7 . II ſoɫ .
de g . In Trikebei . tenet . hugo . x . libo hoēs . 7 in mal
tebei . II . 7 dim̄ . 7 in Filebey . I . car̄ tr̄æ 7 dim̄ . 7 . xIII . ac̄ . sēp . II . bor .
7 dim̄ . 7 . II . car̄ 7 dim̄ . 7 . xIII . ac̄ p̄ti . v . ſaɫ . I . eccla . v . ac̄ . 7 uaɫ . vI . d .
Tc̄ uaɫ . xL . ſoɫ . m̄ . Lxxx . R . 7 . C . ſocam .

The Hundred of SOUTH ERPINGHAM

34 In CORPUSTY 1 villager belongs in Witchingham, 40 acres of land.
    2 smallholders.
    Always 1 plough.
    Value 6s.
    ¾ of 1 church, 9 acres;
value 6d.
    Also 1 Freeman, 4 acres, in THURTON.
    Value 8d.

TUNSTEAD Hundred

35 In PASTON 1 free man under the patronage only of Edric, 20 acres of land.
    Always 1 smallholder.
    Value 12d.
    In SWAFIELD 6 acres; a free man.
    Value 6d.
    St. Benedict (has) the jurisdiction.

The Hundred of EAST FLEGG

36 Edwin, a free man of Gyrth's, held STOKESBY, 3 c. of land.
    Always 15 villagers; 6 smallholders; 4 slaves.
    Then 2½ ploughs in lordship, later and now 3. Always 1 men's plough; meadow, 20 acres; 2 salt-houses; 2 cobs. Then 4 head of cattle, now 6. Always 10 pigs. Then 120 sheep, now 180.
    1 church, 23 acres of land; meadow, [acres].
Value 16d.
Also 21 men, 80 acres of land, have always appertained to this manor. The King and Earl (have) the jurisdiction of the whole.
    Always 5 ploughs; meadow, 4 acres.
Also 3 free men of William's whom Hardwin added before 1066. They have 100 acres of land. Of these his predecessor had the patronage before 1066.
    Always 9 smallholders.
    3 ploughs; meadow, 8 acres; 1 salt-house.
Value then 10s; now 16.
Value of the manor then 100s; now £10; and yet for 2 years it has paid £15 4s each year.
    It has 1 league in length and 1 league in width, tax of 2s.

37 In THRIGBY Hugh holds 10 free men, in MAUTBY 2 and a half, in FILBY 1, ½ c. of land and 13 acres.
    Always 2 smallholders and a half.
    2½ ploughs; meadow, 13 acres; 5 salt-houses.
    1 church, 5 acres;
value 6d.
Value then 40s; now 80.
    The King and Earl (have) the jurisdiction.

H̃. de humiliart. In Coleneia. tenet Robt̃. de uals. I. lib h̃m
xxx. ãc. t̃re. 7 III. ãc p̃ti. Tc̃ dim̃. cař. 7 ual. II sol.

H̃. DE DEPWADA. In Taseburch tenet. Almař. de
stigando xxx. ãc t̃re. modo tenet Rog̃ de ebrois. IIII. ãc
p̃ti tc̃. I. cař m̃ dim̃. 7 tc̃ia pars mol. 7 ual. xv. sol.

H̃. CLAVELINGA. In Thuruertuna tenet Odař. VII.
libi hões. 7 dim. de qbz antec̃ Rad de bolla fago. habuit
c̃om̃d tantũ t. r. e. xLv. ãc tc̃. I. cař 7 dim̃. m̃ d. 7 ual. x. sol.

.XX. TERRA. R. DE BELLO FAGO.

H̃ de DOCHINGE. Niwetuna tenuit. t̃. r. e. Toue lib
homo. II. cař t̃re. sep̃ IIII. uilli. 7 III. bor. Tc̃. III. ser. p̃. 7 m̃. I.
Tc̃. I. cař. in dñio. p̃. II. m̃. III. Tc̃ 7 p̃. IIII. cař houm. m̃. II. 7
dim̃. Sep̃. II. r. 7. x. por. Tc̃. cc. xx. ou m̃. ỡxL. Hic jacent
. xI. libi hões. I. cař t̃re. 7 dim̃. 7 xI. ãc 7 dim̃. Tc̃. IIII. cař Houm.

m̃. II. 7 dim̃. I. eccla. xx. ãc. ual. xvI. d. Hos libos Hões.
habuit. Eudo suus ant̃. Stigandus. socam. Tc̃ ual Lx. sol
p̃ 7 m̃. c. Totum ht̃ dim̃. leug̃ in long̃. 7 dim̃ in lat̃. 7 reddit
xv. d. de. xx. sol de gelto.

In Brecham teñ. Fradre tein regis. e.. III. cař. terre. sep̃.
v. uill. 7 IIII. bor. Tc̃. II. cař in dñio p̃ 7 m̃. nihil. semp. II. cař 7
dim̃ houm. 7. II. libi. II. ãc tc̃ ual. L. sol. m̃. xx. 7 ht̃. I. leug̃
in long̃. 7 I. leug̃ in lat̃. qc̃q ibi teneat. 7 reddit. xxvII. d de gelto.

The Hundred of HUMBLEYARD

38 In COLNEY Robert of Vaux holds 1 free man, 30 acres of land; meadow, 3 acres. Then ½ plough.
Value 2s.

The Hundred of DEPWADE

39 In TASBURGH A(e)lmer held 30 acres of land from Stigand; now Roger of Evreux holds.
Meadow, 4 acres. Then 1 plough, now ½; one-third of a mill.
Value 15s.

CLAVERING Hundred

40 In THURLTON Oder holds; 7 free men and a half of whom his predecessor, Ralph of Beaufour, had the patronage only before 1066; 45 acres.
Then 1½ ploughs, now ½. ½ of a church, 12 acres.
Value 10s.

20 LAND OF R(ALPH) OF BEAUFOUR

The Hundred of DOCKING

1 Tovi, a free man, held (Bircham) NEWTON before 1066, 2 c. of land.
Always 4 villagers; 3 smallholders. Then 3 slaves, later and now 1.
Then 1 plough in lordship, later 2, now 3. Then and later 4 men's ploughs, now 2½. Always 2 cobs; 10 pigs. Then 220 sheep, now 540.
Here appertain 11 free men, 1½ c. of land and 11½ acres.
Then 4 men's ploughs, now 2½. 1 church, 20 acres; value 16d. 226 a
Eudo, his predecessor, had these free men; Stigand (had) the jurisdiction.
Value then 60s; later and now 100.
The whole has ½ league in length and ½ in width, of a 20s tax it pays 15d.

2 In (Great) BIRCHAM Fathir, a thane of King Edward's, held, 3 c. of land.
Always 5 villagers; 4 smallholders.
Then 2 ploughs in lordship, later and now nothing. Always 2½ men's ploughs.
Also 2 free (men), 2 acres.
Value then 50s; now 20.
It has 1 league in length and 1 league in width, whoever holds there, it pays tax of 27d.

H̃. Smetheduna. Rincteda ten̄ i. lib̃ hō t.r.e. dim̄
car tr̄e; Semp. ii uill. 7 dim̄ car 7 ual. iii. fol. Sc̄s benedict͛ facā

H̃ de *FRIDREBRUGE*. In Waltuna ten̄. Bunde lib̃ homo
t̄.r.e. i. car tr̄e. m̂ tenet Odar̓. 7 iiii. uilli. 7 viii. bor.
7. iiii. ac̄ p̃ti. femp. i. car in dn̄io. 7 i. car houm. 7. i. lib̃ hō. viii.
ac̄ tr̄e. 7 ual. xx. fol.

H̃ *SCEREPHAM*. In Elincham. ii. libi hoēs. xlviiii. ac̄
ii. bor. 7. ii. libi hoēs. xxii. ac̄ tr̄e. 7 vi. ac̄ 7 dim̄. p̃ti. filu̇
viii. por. sēp dim̄. car̓. 7 ii. bou̇. Tc̄ ual. x. fol. m̂. xx. Soca
in bucham. In Herkeham. tenet Caurinc̄. iii. car.
tr̄e. quo tenuit Vlf. i. lib̃ homo t̄ r.e. Tc̄ 7 p̃. ii. uill.
m̂. i. femp. ii. bor. Tc̄ 7 p̃. ii. fer̓. xii ac̄ p̃ti. Tc̄. i. car. p̃.
ii. hou̇. m̂. i. car 7 dim̄. Tc̄. ii. car. houm. p. i. m̂. i.
7 dim̄ 7. x. foc̄. viii. ac̄. tr̄e. femp. ii. r̓. m̂. ii. uac̄.
Tc̄ vi. por. m̂. iii. Tc̄ xliiii. ou̇. m̂. xxviii. Tc̄ ual
xx. f. m̂. xxx. Totum ht̄ dim̄ leug̃ in long̃ 7 dim̄.

in lato 7 vi. d̄. 7. i. obolum. 7. i. ferding̃. de. g̓.

H̃. *LAW*endic. Suanetua ten̄. Goduinus. lib̃ homo.
t̄.r.e. viii. car̓. tr̄æ. sēp. xxiiii. uill. Tc̄ 7 p̃. xxxviiii. bor
m̂. liiii. Tc̄. 7 p̃. vi. x. ac̄ p̃ti. Tc̄. iiii. car in dn̄io. p̃. iii.
m̂. v Tc̄ 7 p̃. xiii. car houm. m̂. xviii. filu̇. b. por. sēp. iii.
mol. 7. i. pisc̄. sēp. i. r. Tc̄. ii. an. Tc̄ xxxviiii. por. m̂. xlviii
Tc̄. lx. ou̇. m̂. lxxxv. huic manerio jacent. vii foc̄ c̄ omi con
fuetudine. 7 ht̄. xi. bor. 7. ii. ac̄ p̃ti. sēp. ii. car. 7. i. lib̃ hō.
xii. ac̄ tr̄e 7. ii. ac̄ p̃ti tunc dim̄. car. m̂ nichil. de q̓ fuus ante

SMETHDON Hundred

3   1 free man held RINGSTEAD before 1066, ½ c. of land. Now Richard holds.
   Always 2 villagers.
   ½ plough.
   Value 3s.
   St. Benedict's (had) the jurisdiction.

The Hundred of FREEBRIDGE

4   In (West) WALTON Bondi, a free man, held 1 c. of land before 1066; now Oder holds.
   4 villagers; 8 smallholders.
   Meadow, 4 acres. Always 1 plough in lordship; 1 men's plough.
   Also 1 free man, 8 acres of land.
   Value 20s.

SHROPHAM Hundred

5   In (Great) ELLINGHAM 2 free men, 49 acres. 2 smallholders.
   Also 2 free men, 22 acres of land; meadow, 6½ acres. Woodland, 8 pigs. Always ½ plough; 2 oxen.
   Value then 10s; now 20.
   The jurisdiction (is) in Buckenham.

6   In HARGHAM Waring holds 3 c. of land where Ulf, 1 free man, held before 1066.
   Then and later 2 villagers, now 1. Always 2 smallholders. Then and later 2 slaves.
   Meadow, 12 acres. Then 1 men's plough, later 2 oxen, now 1½ ploughs. Then 2 men's ploughs, later 1, now 1½.
   Also 10 Freemen, 8 acres of land. Always 2 cobs. Now 2 cows. Then 6 pigs, now 3. Then 44 sheep, now 28.
   Value then 20s; now 30.
   The whole has ½ league in length and ½ in width, tax of 6¾d.   226 b

LAUNDITCH Hundred

7   Godwin, a free man, held SWANTON (Morley) before 1066, 8 c. of land.
   Always 24 villagers. Then and later 39 smallholders, now 54. Then and later 6 slaves.
   Meadow, 10 acres. Then 4 ploughs in lordship, later 3, now 5. Then and later 13 men's ploughs, now 18. Woodland, 500 pigs. Always 3 mills; 1 fishery; always 1 cob. Then 2 head of cattle. Then 39 pigs, now 48. Then 60 sheep, now 85.
   7 Freemen appertain to this manor with all customary dues. They have 11 smallholders.
   Meadow, 2 acres; always 2 ploughs.
   Also 1 free man, 12 acres of land; meadow, 2 acres. Then ½ plough, now nothing. Of whom his predecessor had the patronage

cessor habuit . t . r . e . cōmdatione tantū . Soca in mullā
7 eudo eum . tenuit 7 Rad . tenet dono regis . I . eccla . I . aç
7 dim̄ . ual . II . d . Tc̄ 7 p̊ ual . VIII . lib̄ . m̂ . XII . s; p̄q̊ habuit de
dit ad firmam . XXV . lib̄ . 7 ht̄ I . leug̃ . 7 dim̄ . in long . 7 . I . leug̃
in lato . 7 X . d . de gelto.

⁊ In *LECESH*am tenuit . Fader . t . r . e . III . car̉ tr̄e 7 dim̄ .
m̂ tenet ricard . Tc̄ . IX . uilti . post . VIII . m̂ . V . semp . VII .
bor . Tc̄ . III ser . VI . aç p̄ti . tc̄ 7 p̊ . II . car in dn̄io . m̂ . I . 7
alia post restaurari . semp . I . car 7 dim̄ . hom̄ . siluā . XXX .
por . sēp . I . mol . Tc̄ I . pisc̄ . 7 q̇rta pars . saline . semp . I . r .
Tc̄ . VII . animal . Tc̄ . XXIIII . por m̂ . V . Tc̄ . LXXX . ou . m̂ .
cc . X . IIII . uasa apum . 7 . VI . soc̄ . dim̄ . car̉ tr̄e . 7 . II . aç p̄ti .
Semp . I . car . Tc̄ ual . XL . sol . p̊ 7 m̂ . LX . 7 I . lib homo . LX .
aç tr̄e sub heroldo . 7 . II . bor . 7 . I . aç 7 dim̄ . p̄ti . Tc̄ dim̄ car̉
sed posset fieri . Tc̄ . ual . V . sol . m̂ . IIII . Soca in mulcham.

1 . eccla XXX acr̄ 7 ual . XVI . d . Totum ht̄ . I . leug̃ . in long 7 dim̄
in lato . 7 VII . d . 7 . I . obolū de gelto.

⁊ In Derham . II . car terre ten̄ . Herold sub stigando m̂ tenet
Odarus . sēp . IIII . uilli . 7 . XV . bor . Tc̄ . II . s . VI . aç p̄ti . tc̄ . II .
car in dn̄io . p̊ 7 m̂ . I . 7 alia . posset restaurari . semp . II . car̉ .
hoūm . silū . XXX . por . sēp . I . mol . 7 V . soc̄ . XLIII . aç tr̄e .
7 II . aç p̄ti . Tc̄ 7 p̊ . I . car . m̂ dim̄ . 7 tota posset restaurari
Tc̄ . I . r . Tc̄ IIII . an . Tc̄ VII . por . m̂ . II . Tc̄ VII . cap̂ . m̂ . VIII .
tc̄ ual . XX . sol . m̂ . XL . totum ht̄ . I . leug̃ 7 V . q̇r in long
7 dim̄ . 7 III . q̇r in lato . 7 de gelto . X d . qui cumq̇ ibi teneat
Tota soca in mulham.

only before 1066. The jurisdiction (is) in Mileham. Eudo held him, and Ralph holds of the King's gift.

1 church, 1½ acres;
value 2d.

Value then and later £8; now 12s. After he had it he granted it at revenue (for) £25.

It has 1½ leagues in length and 1 league in width; tax of 10d.

8 In LEXHAM Fathir held before 1066 3½ c. of land; now Richard holds.

Then 9 villagers, later 8, now 5. Always 7 smallholders. Then 3 slaves.

Meadow, 6 acres. Then and later 2 ploughs in lordship, now 1; another could be restored. Always 1½ men's ploughs; woodland, 30 pigs; always 1 mill. Then 1 fishery; ¼ of a salt-house. Always 1 cob. Then 7 head of cattle. Then 24 pigs, now 5. Then 80 sheep, now 210. 4 beehives.

Also 6 Freemen, ½ c. of land.

Meadow, 2 acres; always 1 plough.

Value then 40s; later and now 60.

Also 1 free man, 60 acres of land under Harold.

2 smallholders.

Meadow, 1½ acres. Then ½ plough but there could be (a whole one).

Value then 5s; now 4.

The jurisdiction (is) in Mileham.

1 church, 30 acres;
value 16d.

227 a

The whole has 1 league in length and ½ in width; tax of 7½d.

9 In (East) DEREHAM Harold held 2 c. of land under Stigand; now Oder holds.

Always 4 villagers; 15 smallholders. Then 2 slaves.

Meadow, 6 acres. Then 2 ploughs in lordship, later and now 1; another could be restored. Always 2 men's ploughs; woodland, 30 pigs; always 1 mill.

Also 5 Freemen, 43 acres of land;

meadow, 2 acres. Then and later 1 plough, now ½; the whole could be restored. Then 1 cob; then 4 head of cattle. Then 7 pigs, now 2. Then 7 goats, now 8.

Value then 20s; now 40.

The whole has 1 league and 5 furlongs in length and ½ (league) and 3 furlongs in width; tax of 10d, whoever holds there.

The whole jurisdiction (is) in Mileham.

H̃ FEORHOV . & dim̃ . Diepham tenuit Leuinus
lib̃ hō t . r . e . i . car tr̃e ; ⁷ˡˣˣˣ ᵃᶜ͞ʳ modo tenet idem . ſemp . ix .
uilli . tc̃ x . bor . m̃ . ix . Tc̃ ⁷ pō . ii . ſer . m̃ nulł . ſēp . iii .
car in dn̄io . 7 . i . car ⁷ 7 dim̃ . hoūm . filū . xii . por . 7 x .
ac̃ p̃ti . ſemp . i . r̃ . 7 x . añ . 7 xvii . por . xxxii . cap̃
huic manerio jacent . ſemp . xxv . ſoc̃ 7 . i . car ⁷ terre
7 xxvi . ac̃ ſemp vi . car ⁷ 7 dim̃ . Et p̃t hoc . vi . liberi
hōes additi ſt̃ huic manerio . t̃ r . W . quos tenuit
eudo . 7 ħt . cxx . acr̃ . tr̃æ . 7 xx . bor . 7 iiii . car ⁷ .
7 vi . ac̃ p̃ti . Tc̃ ual . iiii . lib̃ . caput manerii . 7
Rađ . dedit totum ad firmā . ,p . xii . lib̃ . ſ; m̃ tam̃
ñ reddit n . vi . lib̃ . 7 . vi . libi hōes ual . lv ſol . hoc
teſtatur . Hundret . hoƺ . iii . fuere ſochemanni

227 b

Stigandi 7 ſocā in hincham . regis 7 ħt . x . q̃r . in longo . 7 vi . in
lato . 7 xvii . đ . 7 . iii . ferđ .

Morlea tenuit Leuuinus lib̃ homo . t̃ . r . e . i . car terre .
,p man̄ . modo tenet Hugo . ſēp . ix . uilł . Tc̃ . i . car ⁷ 7 dim̃ . m̃ . ii .
7 dim̃ ⁷ car hoūm . 7 iii . ac̃ p̃ti . ſēp i . ŗ . Tc̃ . i . añ . m̃ . ii . Tc̃
viii . por . m̃ . xlvii . 7 v . libi hōes . t . e . r . Soca illoƺ . in Hinc-
-ham regis . Sēp ual . xl . ſol . Huic manerio additi ſt̃ . xiiii .
libi hōes . lx . ac̃ tr̃e . 7 . ii . car ⁷ . 7 . iii ac̃ p̃ti . 7 ual . xl . ſol .
iſti fuerunt hōes . Stigandi . Soca in hincham . 7 P̃q̃ hoc
ſt̃ additi . ii . libi hōes . t̃ . ẹ . r . Wilł . xxx . ac̃ . 7 ual . xxii .
ſol . un fuit hō Stigandi . 7 alt regis . Soca eoƺ in hinhā
7 ħt dim̃ leug̃ in longo 7 dim̃ in lato . 7 xiiii . đ . 7 . iii . feorđ .
in gelto .

FOREHOE Hundred and a Half

10 Leofwin, a free man, held DEOPHAM before 1066, 1 c. of land and 80 acres; now (Ralph) also holds.
>Always 9 villagers. Then 10 smallholders, now 9. Then and later 2 slaves, now none.
>Always 3 ploughs in lordship; 1½ men's ploughs; woodland, 12 pigs; meadow, 10 acres. Always 1 cob; 10 head of cattle; 17 pigs; 32 goats.
>25 Freemen have always appertained to this manor, 1 c. of land and 26 acres. Always 6½ ploughs.

Besides this 6 free men were added to this manor after 1066, whom Eudo held. They have 120 acres of land.
>20 smallholders;
>5 ploughs; meadow, 6 acres.

Value of the capital messuage, then £4.

Ralph granted the whole at revenue for £12, and yet now it only pays £6.
>Also 6 free men.

Value 55s.
>This the Hundred testifies. Of these 3 were Stigand's Freemen.

The jurisdiction is in the King's (manor of) Hingham. 227 b
>It has 10 furlongs in length and 6 in width, [tax of] 17¾d.

11 Leofwin, a free man, held MORLEY before 1066, 1 c. of land as a manor. Now Hugh holds.
>Always 9 villagers.
>Then 1½ ploughs, now 2½ men's ploughs. Meadow, 3 acres. Always 1 cob. Then 1 head of cattle, now 2. Then 8 pigs, now 47.

Also 5 free men before 1066; the jurisdiction of them is in the King's (manor of) Hingham.

Value always 40s.
>To this manor were added 14 free men, 60 acres of land.
>2 ploughs; meadow, 3 acres.

Value 40s.
>Those were Stigand's men; the jurisdiction (is) in Hingham.

Besides this 2 free men were added after 1066, 30 acres.

Value 22s.
>1 was Stigand's man, the other the King's; the jurisdiction of them (is) in Hingham.
>It has ½ league in length and ½ in width, 14¾d in tax.

Bereforda tenuit Stigand ad ſocam . t̄ . e . r .
xxx . acr̄ tr̄e . modo tene Ricard . ſemp . vIII . uiłłi . 7 . I . car̄
in dn̄io 7 I . car̄ hom̄ . III ac̄ p̄ti . 7 ual . xx . ſol . In eadē . xxx .
acr̄ tenuit lib̄ hō t̄ . r . e . ſub ſtigando . Soca in hinchā
regis 7 ual . v . ſol .

In Cronkethor tenet idē . xxx . ac̄r tr̄e quo ten . Coleman . lib̄ homo ſub ſtigando ſoca 7 cōm̄d ; ſemp . vI . bor .
7 dim̄ car̄ . 7 . I . mol . 7 . v . ac̄ p̄ti . 7 ual . xxx . ſol . ex hoc
calumpniat̄ . Rad . baig . unū . dim̄ hominē de . III . acr̄
7 ht III . qr̄ . in long . 7 II . in lato . 7 vII . d . 7 . I . feording d g

H̄ 7 dim̄ . Mitteforde   Hokelinka ten . Sigar̄
lib̄ hō . t . r . e . IIII . car̄ tr̄e . 7 ſemp . III . uiłłi . 7 xxIII .

bor . 7 IIII . ſer . Tc̄ . IIII . car . in dn̄io . m̄ . v . tc̄ vII . car̄ hoūm .
m̄ . v . Silua . cc . por . 7 xv . ac̄ p̄ti . 7 I . mol . 7 dim̄ . ſep . Ix an .
7 xxxIII ; por . tc̄ Lxxx . où . m̄ . cxIII . 7 tc̄ III . ſoc̄ . m̄ . vII .
Lx . ac̄ . terre . Tc̄ ual . IIII . lib̄ . m̄ . c . ſol . Huic manerio jacent
x ; libi . hoēs 7 dim̄ . II . car̄ . tr̄e .
In Toddencham . tenet Ricard . xI . bor ſēp . v . car̄ 7 x . ac̄r .
p̄ti . ſemp . II . mol . ſemp ual . IIII . lib̄ . Tota hoc helinga ht
dim̄ leūg . in long . 7 dim̄ in lat̄ 7 v . d . 7 . I . obolū de gelto .
Et Totdenham . v . qr̄ . in long . 7 IIII . in lat̄ . 7 de gelto . xxI .
rī . eccla xx . ac̄ 7 ual xvī d̄ .
d . 7 I . obolum . qcq, ibi teneat . In mateſhala . xIIII . libi
hoēs . II . car̄ tr̄æ . 7 dim̄ . 7 xx . ac̄ . 7 xII . uiłł . 7 v . car̄ . 7 vI . ac̄
p̄ti . I . eccla . xx . ac̄ 7 ual . xvI . d . Tc̄ ual . Lx ſol . m̄ . xLIII .
7 ht . vII . qr̄ in long . 7 vI . in lat̄ . 7 xxxvI . d . 7 . obolū . de gelto .
In caſttudenham . vI . lib̄ hoēs dim̄ . car̄ terre 7 . III . ac̄ . un .
ht . IIII . bor . ſēp . I . car̄ 7 dim̄ . 7 . II . ac̄ p̄ti . 7 ual . xIIII . ſol .
7 vIII . d . Totum . hoc fuit ſibi lib̄atum . p̄ tr̄am 7 ſuo antec̄ .

12 Stigand held BARFORD at jurisdiction before 1066, 30 acres of land. Now Richard holds.
    Always 8 villagers.
    1 plough in lordship; 1 men's plough; meadow, 3 acres.
  Value 20s.
    In the same a free man held 30 acres before 1066 under Stigand. The jurisdiction is in the King's (manor of) Hingham.
  Value 5s.

13 In CROWNTHORPE he also holds 30 acres of land where Coleman, a free man, held under Stigand in jurisdiction and patronage.
    Always 6 smallholders.
    ½ plough; 1 mill; meadow, 5 acres.
  Value 30s.
    Of this Ralph Baynard claims 1 half a man, at 3 acres.
    It has 3 furlongs in length and 2 in width, tax of 7¼d.

  MITFORD Hundred and a Half

14 Sigar, a free man, held HOCKERING before 1066, 4 c. of land.
    Always 3 villagers; 23 smallholders; 4 slaves.   228 a
    Then 4 ploughs in lordship, now 5. Then 7 men's ploughs, now 5. Woodland, 200 pigs; meadow, 15 acres; 1½ mills.
    Always 9 head of cattle; 33 pigs. Then 80 sheep, now 113.
    Then 3 Freemen, now 7; 60 acres of land.
  Value then £4; now 100s.
    10 free men and a half appertain to this manor, 2 c. of land.

15 In (North) TUDDENHAM Richard holds.
    11 smallholders.
    Always 5 ploughs; meadow, 10 acres; always 2 mills.
  Value always £4.
    The whole of Hockering has ½ league in length and ½ in width, tax of 5½d. (North) Tuddenham (has) 5 furlongs in length and 4 in width, tax of 21½d, whoever holds there.
    2 churches, 20 acres;
  value 16d.

16 In MATTISHALL 14 free men, 2½ c. of land and 20 acres.
    12 villagers.
    5 ploughs; meadow, 6 acres. 1 church, 20 acres;
  value 16d.
  Value then 60s; now 43.
    It has 7 furlongs in length and 6 in width, tax of 36½d.

17 In EAST TUDDENHAM 6 free men, ½ c. of land and 3 acres. 1 has 4 smallholders.
    Always 1½ ploughs; meadow, 2 acres.
  Value 14s 8d.
    All this was delivered to him for the land and to his predecessor.

⊽In mateshala. iiiii. libi hoēs. t̄ r. e. ii. car̄ tr̄e. Semp
iiii. bor. Tc̄ iiii. car̄ m̄. ii. x. acr̄ p̄ti. 7 ual tc̄. xx. s̄.
m̄. xxxii. 7 iiii. d. Socā suā hab de abb.

H̃ WALESSĀ. In bastuic ten̄. Godricus. i. lib
hō. t̄. r. e. iiii. soc̄. ptinentes in grofsā. vii. ac̄ terre
7. i. uill. de xv. ac̄ tr̄e.
Tunestalle tnuit idem Godric. t̄ r. e. p man̄.
modo tenet turold. lx. Tc̄. iii. bor. m̄. v 7 viii. ac̄ p̄ti

228 b
Semp. i. car̄. inter se 7 hoēs. Sēp. ual. x. s̄. 7 soca regis.
In bastuic ten̄. ulketel. 7 Withri. hoēs heroldi. iiii. soc̄ 7 dim̄
7 vi. bor. xi. ac̄ tr̄e. i. ac̄ p̄ti. Sep dim̄. car̄. 7 st̄ ī p̄tio groffahā
In eadem uilla tenet ulketel. xl. ac̄ tr̄e. iiii. ac̄ p̄ti apptiatū ē

H̃. BLAFELDA. In plūmesteda. i. bor. de. ix. ac̄ tr̄e
Sēp. arat cū. ii. bouib; Ap̄p̄tiati st̄ in Wrofsam.
⊽In blafelda. ii. bor. d. xii. ac̄ tr̄e. i. ac̄ p̄ti. Ap̄p̄tiati st̄ in
Wrofsham.

H̃. HEINESTEDE. In castra. v. libi. hoēs. 7 dim̄. Goduuini. de xlii. ac̄ tr̄e. 7 dim̄. 7. ii. ac̄ p̄ti. Sēp. dim̄ car̄
7 ptinet in merkeshalle. In castra adhuc ÷ i. car̄ tr̄e.
in dn̄io dim̄ mol. 7 ē in p̄tio m̄keffale.

H̃. Dicē dim̄ Regedona ten̄ Lefriz filius bose tegn
regis. p man̄. modo tenet Hugo. Tc̄ 7 p. ix. uill. m̄. v. Tc̄
7 p. xii. bor. m̄. xi. Sēp. i. ser. Sēp. ii. car̄ in dn̄io. 7. ii.
car̄ hoūm Silu. xxx. por. 7 iiii. ac̄ p̄ti. Sēp. ii. eq ī aula

18 In MATTISHALL 5 free men before 1066, 2 c. of land.
    Always 4 smallholders.
    Then 4 ploughs, now 2; meadow, 10 acres.
    Value then 20s; now 32(s) 4d.
    They have their jurisdiction from the Abbot.

WALSHAM Hundred

19 In (Wood)BASTWICK Godric, 1 free man, held before 1066.
    4 Freemen belonging in Wroxham, 7 acres of land. 1 villager,
      at 15 acres of land.
Godric also held TUNSTALL before 1066 as a manor, now Thorold
holds; 60 [acres].
    Then 3 smallholders, now 5.
    Meadow, 8 acres; always 1 plough between him and the men.   228 b
Value always 10s.
    The jurisdiction is the King's
In (Wood)bastwick Ulfketel and Withri, Harold's men, held.
    4 Freemen and a half and 6 smallholders, 11 acres of land.
    Meadow, 1 acre; always ½ plough.
They are in the valuation of Wroxham.
    In the same village Ulfketel held 40 acres of land.
    Meadow, 4 acres.
It is assessed.

BLOFIELD Hundred

20 In PLUMSTEAD 1 smallholder, Godric's man, at 9 acres of land. He
has always ploughed with 2 oxen.
They are assessed in Wroxham.

21 In BLOFIELD 2 smallholders, at 12 acres of land; meadow, 1 acre.
They are assessed in Wroxham.

HENSTEAD Hundred

22 In CAISTOR (St. Edmunds) 5 free men and a half of Godwin's, at
42½ acres of land;
    meadow, 2 acres. Always ½ plough. It belongs in Markshall.
    In Caistor (St. Edmunds) a further 1 c. of land; ½ mill in
lordship.
    It is assessed in Markshall.

DISS Half-Hundred

23 Leofric son of Bose, a King's thane, held ROYDON as a manor; now
Hugh holds.
    Then and later 9 villagers, now 5. Then and later 12 smallholders,
      now 11. Always 1 slave.
    Always 2 ploughs in lordship; 2 men's ploughs; woodland, 30
      pigs; meadow, 4 acres. Always 2 horses at the hall;

Sep̃.vi añ.Tc̃.xl.por.m̃.xxx.Tc̃.lx.oũ.m̃.xxii.
cap̃.7 vi.soc̃ de xxiiii.ac̃.tr̃e.Tc̃.7 p̃.i.car̃.m̃ dim̃.
Sep̃ ual xl.sol.x.q̃r̃.in long̃ 7 viii.in lato.7 de
gelto.ix.d̃.

H̄ de Tauresh̃ã.   Vrocsh̃ã tenuit Stigand.
t̃.r.e.ii.car̃ tr̃e.Tc̃.ix.uill.p̃ 7 m̃.v.bor.7 ii.
car̃ in dñio.tc̃.i.car̃ 7 dim̃.hoũm.m̃.i.7 xx.ac̃ p̃ti.
7 iiii.añ.7 xx.por.Silu.c.por.c.oũ.7 xiii.soc̃.

229 a

xl.ac̃ tr̃e.7 ii.ac̃ p̃ti tc̃.ii.car̃.m̃.i.7 dim̃.Rex 7 comes:
soc̃a.7 vii.lib̃i hõẽs.cc.x.ac̃.Tc̃.iii.car̃ 7 dim̃.p̃ 7 m̃.ii.
7 xv.ac̃ p̃ti.silu.xii.por.7 .i.car̃ 7 dim̃ posset restaurari.
Tc̃ ual.manerium.iii lib̃.m̃.iiii.7 vii.lib̃i hõẽs xxxviii.sol.

In eadẽ.iii.lib̃i hõẽs; (heroldi) i.car̃ tr̃e 7 xxx ac̃.sep̃.ii.uill.7 vi.bor
Tc̃.iii.car̃.p̃.7 m̃.ii.7 tcia.posset restaurari.7 .x.ac̃ p̃ti.
Silua.xx.por.7 in edẽ.iii.lib̃i hom̃ones.xx.ac̃.i.car̃.

ii.ecclesias xxxiii.ac̃ tr̃e 7 ual iii.sol.
In Racheia.iii.lib̃i hõẽs.xx.ac̃.7 iii.bor.Tc̃.i.car̃.p̃.
7 m̃.dim̃.In besetuna.i lib̃ homo.xxx.ac̃ tr̃æ.tc̃.i.car̃.p̃.7
m̃ dim̃.7 .ii.ac̃ p̃ti.dim̃i eccla.7 ual.xii.d̃.
In Crotuuit.vi.lib̃i hõẽs dim̃ car̃.tr̃e.7 iii.bor.Tc̃.ii.car̃
p̃ 7 m̃.i.Tc̃ totũ ual.xxx.sol m̃ xlv.7 iiii d̃.Rex 7 comes
soc̃a.sed.Rad̃ eam tenuit.Totũ Vrosch̃am.i.leug̃ 7 dim̃
in long.7 i.leug̃ in lato.7 xxx.d̃.de gelto q̃c̃q̨ ibi teneat.

always 6 head of cattle. Then 40 pigs, now 30. Then 60 sheep, now 22 goats.

Also 6 Freemen, at 24 acres of land. Then and later 1 plough, now ½.

Value always 40s.

(It has) 10 furlongs in length and 8 in width, tax of 9d.

The Hundred of TAVERHAM

24 Stigand held WROXHAM before 1066, 2 c. of land.

Then 9 villagers; later and now 5 smallholders.

2 ploughs in lordship. Then 1½ men's ploughs, now 1. Meadow, 20 acres; 4 head of cattle; 20 pigs; woodland, 100 pigs; 100 sheep.

Also 13 Freemen, 40 acres of land; meadow, 2 acres. Then 2 ploughs, now 1½. The King and the Earl (have) the jurisdiction.

229 a

Also 7 free men, 210 acres. Then 3½ ploughs, later and now 2. Meadow, 15 acres; woodland, 12 pigs; 1 plough; ½ could be restored.

Value of the manor then £3; now 4; and the 7 free men, 38s.

In the same 3 free men of Harold's, 1 c. of land and 30 acres.

Always 2 villagers; 6 smallholders.

Then 3 ploughs, later and now 2; a third could be restored. Meadow, 10 acres; woodland, 20 pigs.

In the same 3 free men, 20 acres;

1 plough. .... 2 churches, 33 acres of land;

value 3s.

25 In RACKHEATH 3 free men, 20 acres.

3 smallholders.

Then 1 plough, later and now ½.

In BEESTON (St. Andrew) 1 free man, 30 acres of land.

Then 1 plough, later and now ½. Meadow, 2 acres. ½ church; value 12d.

In CROSTWICK 6 free men, ½ c. of land.

3 smallholders.

Then 2 ploughs, later and now 1.

Value of the whole then 30s; now 45(s) 4d.

The King and the Earl (have) the jurisdiction, but Ralph held it.

The whole of Wroxham (has) 1½ leagues in length and 1 league in width, tax of 30d, whoever holds there.

Draituna tenuit. Aldulf lib hō. t r. e. ii. car tře. m̃ tenet
odarus. sēp. vii. uilli. 7. viii. bor. Tc. iii. ser. sep. i. car.
in dñio. 7. iii. car hoūm. 7. i. car posset restaurari. 7 x. ac
p̃ti. Silua. iii. por. 7. i. r. 7 ii. añ. xiiii. por. Tc. clxxx.
ou. m̃. lx. Tc. lx. cap̃. 7. ii. soc. xxii. ac tře. Tc dim̃.
car. i. eccla. viii. ac 7 ual. xvi. đ. Tc ual. xl. sol. m̃. l.
7 ħt. i. leug in long. 7 dim̃. in lato. 7 viii. đ. 7. iii. ferdingos
de gelto. Rex 7 comes socam. In felethor. tenet ricardus.
iii. libos hoēs. xliii. ac tře. 7 ual. ii. sol. Rex 7 comes socā.

In Tauresham tenet idem. i. car tře quā tenuit Olfus.
t r. e. sēp iiii. uilli. 7. iii. bor. sēp. i. car in dñio. 7. i. car.
hoūm. 7. x. ac p̃ti. silu. v. por. 7 quarta pars mol. 7. v.
soc. xiii. ac tře. sēp. i. car. in dñio. ii. r. 7. i. añ. m̃. xii. por
7 lx. ou. Tc 7 p. ual. xx sol. m̃. xxx. quarta pars. i.
eccla xv. ac. 7 ual. xvi. đ.

H̃ DE ENSFORDA. In salla tenet Odarus. i. lib hō t. e. r.
xxx. ac tře. semp viii. bor. 7. i. car 7 dim̃. 7 i. ac p̃ti. silu
v. por 7 quarta pars mol. 7 ual. x. sol.

H̃. ERPINCHĀ SVD. In bukestuna. v. libi hoēs; vii. car
terre. Vn ex ħ fribz fuit com̃d ancesc malet 7 non fuit
inde saisitus. Tc. xx. uilli. p̃. 7. m̃. xii. m̃. xvii. bor. Tc viii.
car in dñio. p̃. iiii. m̃. iiii. Tc viii. car hoūm. p̃. iii. m̃. iii.
7 dim̃. xii. p̃ti. Tc silu. m. por. m̃. cc. sēp. i. mol. 7. iii. r.
Tc. iii. añ. Tc xxxii. por. m̃. xviii. 7. i. eccla de xxx. ac.
in elemosina 7 ual iii. sol. 7 ual c. 7 ħt. i. leug in long.

vi. qr 7 dim̃ in lato. 7 x. đ. de gelto.

26 Aldwulf, a free men, held DRAYTON before 1066, 2 c. of land. Now Oder holds.
 Always 7 villagers; 8 smallholders. Then 3 slaves.
 Always 1 plough in lordship; 3 men's ploughs; 1 plough could be restored. Meadow, 10 acres; woodland, 3 pigs; 1 cob; 2 head of cattle; 14 pigs. Then 180 sheep, now 60. Then 60 goats.
 Also 2 Freemen, 22 acres of land.
 Then ½ plough. 1 church, 8 acres;
value 16d.
Value then 40s; now 50.
 It has 1 league in length and ½ in width, tax of 8¾d.
 The King and the Earl (have) the jurisdiction.
In FELTHORPE Richard holds 3 free men, 43 acres of land.
Value 2s.
 The King and Earl (have) the jurisdiction.

27 In TAVERHAM he also holds 1 c. of land which Ulf held before 1066.
 Always 4 villagers; 3 smallholders.
 Always 1 plough in lordship; 1 men's plough; meadow, 10 acres; woodland, 5 pigs; ¼ of a mill.
 Also 5 Freemen, 13 acres of land.
 Always 1 plough in lordship; 2 cobs; 1 head of cattle. Now 12 pigs; 60 sheep.
Value then and later 20s; now 30.
¼ of 1 church, 15 acres;
value 16d.

The Hundred of EYNSFORD

28 Oder holds in SALL; 1 free man before 1066; 30 acres of land.
 Always 8 smallholders.
 1½ ploughs; meadow, 1 acre; woodland, 5 pigs; ¼ of a mill.
Value 10s.

SOUTH ERPINGHAM Hundred

29 In BUXTON 5 free men, brothers, 7 c. of land. 1 of these brothers was under the patronage of the predecessor of Malet. Malet and he did not have possession of him.
 Then 20 villagers, later and now 12. Now 17 smallholders.
 Then 8 ploughs in lordship, later 4, now 4. Then 8 men's ploughs, later 3, now 3½. Meadow, 12 [acres]. Woodland, then 1000 pigs, now 200. Always 1 mill; 3 cobs. Then 3 head of cattle. Then 32 pigs, now 18. 1 church, at 30 acres in alms;
value 3s.
Value 100[s].
 It has 1 league and 6½ furlongs in width, tax of 10d.

229 b

In brantuna xxv 7 dim̃ . foc̃.

I . cacr̃ . 7 xxx . ac̃ . tc̃ vII . car̃ . p̃ . v . m̃ . III . Tc̃ ual . xx . fol . m̃.
xL . Soca in marsã.

In Scotohou . I . car̃ tr̃e . 7 vIII . ac̃ . teñ . I . foc̃ s̃ci benedicti
de holmo . sẽp . II . uilli . 7 IIII . bor . Tc̃ . II . car̃ . m̃ . I . 7 dim̃ . 7 . III
acr̃ p̃ti . 7 . I foc̃ . III . ac̃ tr̃e . Tc̃ ual . x . fol . modo vIII.
& Brantuna ht̃ . vI . q̃r̃ in lon̄g . 7 v . in lat̃ . 7 v . đ . 7 obolum.
de gelto . In Belaga . I . lib̃ homo Heroldi . I . car̃ . tr̃e . 7 xI . acr̃.
tc̃ I . car̃ m̃ . dim̃ 7 III . ac̃ p̃ti . In edẽ . I . foc̃ . Rad̃ . Stalr̃a . t̃ . r . e.
xv . ac̃ 7 ual II . fol . In houetuna . hoc dedit idẽ Rad̃ . Sc̃o benedic̃to
7 eudo eum tulit . modo ht̃ . Rad̃ . de belfago . In Belaga xxII . ac̃
tr̃e . vII . foc̃ . Tc̃ . II . car̃ p̃ 7 m̃ . I . 7 ual . vIII . fol . Rad̃ . Stalr̃a 7 Stigand
focam . 7 Radulfus dedit fuam partem s̃co benedicto . Tota belaga
ht̃ . Ix . q̃r̃ . in lon̄g . 7 III . 7 dim̃ . in lat̃ . 7 vI . đ . de ḡ . In Sc̃egutuna
xI . ac̃ 7 dim̃ . I . foc̃ s̃ci benedicti . 7 ual . xvII . đ . hunc tulit Radboda
p̃pofitus Rad̃ . de abbatia fub evdone anteceffore . Radulfi.
In ohbouueffa dim̃ . car̃ tr̃e . I . foc̃ . s̃ci . benẽ . sẽp . IIII . bor.
7 I . car̃ . 7 . II . ac̃ p̃ti . filua . xx . por 7 dim̃ . mol . Tc̃ ual . x . fol.
m̃ . xII . hanc tr̃am habuit eudo delibatione ut Rad̃ . dicit
Obuueffa . ht̃ . vI . q̃r̃ . in lon̄g . 7 . IIII . in lat̃ 7 . II . đ de ḡ.
In Lamers . xx . ac̃ . tr̃e . I . lib̃ hõ . fem̃ . sẽp . I . bor . 7 . ẽ in p̃tio de buc
heftuna . In Vlẽtuna tenet Turold . I . lib̃ hõ . xxx . ac̃ tr̃e . t . e . r.
sẽp . III . bor . 7 . I . car̃ . 7 ual . x . fol . Rex 7 comes focã . In Scotohov.
III . libi hõs . s̃ci . beñ . xxx . ac . femp đ . car̃ . 7 ual . III . fol.

30 In BRAMPTON 25 Freemen and a half, 1 c. and 30 acres.
Then 7 ploughs, later 5, now 3.
Value then 20s; now 40.
The jurisdiction (is) in Marsham.

31 In SCOTTOW 1 Freeman of St. Benedict's of Holme holds 1 c. of land and 8 acres.
Always 2 villagers; 4 smallholders.
Then 2 ploughs, now 1½. Meadow, 3 acres.
Also 1 Freeman, 3 acres of land.
Value then 10s; now 8.
Brampton has 6 furlongs in length and 5 in width; tax of 5½d.
In BELAUGH 1 free man of Harold's, 1 c. of land and 11 acres.
Then 1 plough, now ½. Meadow, 3 acres.
In the same 1 Freeman of Ralph the Constable's before 1066, 15 acres.
Value 2s. (He is included) in Hoveton.
The same Ralph gave this to St. Benedict and Eudo took him away, now Ralph of Beaufour has him.
In Belaugh 22 acres of land; 7 Freemen.
Then 2 ploughs, later and now 1.
Value 8s.
Ralph the Constable and Stigand had the jurisdiction; Ralph gave his part to St. Benedict.
The whole of Belaugh has 9 furlongs in length and 3½ in width; tax of 6d.
In SKEYTON 11½ acres; 1 Freeman of St. Benedict's.
Value 17d.
Radbod, Ralph's reeve, took him from the Abbey under Eudo, Ralph's predecessor.

32 In HAUTBOIS ½ c. of land; 1 Freeman of St. Benedict's.
Always 4 smallholders.
1 plough; meadow, 2 acres; woodland, 20 pigs; ½ mill.
Value then 10s; now 12.
Eudo had this land by livery, as Ralph says.
Hautbois has 6 furlongs in length and 4 in width; tax of 2d.
In LAMAS 20 acres of land; 1 free woman; always 1 smallholder.
It is in the valuation of Buxton.
Thorold, 1 free man, held in WOLTERTON, 30 acres of land before 1066.
Always 3 smallholders.
1 plough.
Value 10s.
The King and the Earl (have) the jurisdiction.
In SCOTTOW 3 free men of St. Benedict's, 30 acres; always ½ plough.
Value 3s.

H̃. Tunesteda . In Slaleia . i . socaman͛ sc̃i beneditus.
i . car . tr̃e . sep̃ . xii . uilt . 7 viii . bor . 7 . ii . car . 7 dim̃ 7 vi . ac̃ p̃ti
Silua . vi . por . 7 . iiii . soc̃ . xvi . ac̃ . semp dim̃ . car . 7 ual . xl . sol
7 ht̃ . vi . qr̃ in long̃ . 7 v . qr̃ in lat̃ . 7 . iiii . d . 7 obolum . de g̃.
i . eccla . i . ac̃ . 7 ual . ii . d.

H̃. Humiliart . Molkebtuna . tenet . Ricard͛ . quam ten̄.
Ordinc . tegn͛ . t . r . e . ii . car . tr̃e . Tc̃ 7 p͛ . x . uilti . m̂ . vii . Tc̃ . vii.
bor . m̂ . xvi . tc̃ . ii . ser . m̂ . i . sep̃ . ii . car in dñio . 7 . ii . car . hoūm.
x . ac̃r p̃ti . Silu . xvi . por . sep̃ . i . mol . m̂ . i . r . tc̃ i . an͛ . m̂ . vi por.
7 vi . soc̃ lx . ac̃ . sep̃ . i . car . 7 dim̃ . & in Carletuna tenet idẽ
iiii . libi . hoẽs . 7 in Suerdestuna tenet idẽ vii . int̃ totum . lvi.
ac̃ sep̃ . i . car . 7 dim̃ . 7 . ii . ac̃ p̃ti . Tc̃ 7 p͛ . ual . lx . sol . m̂ . c . 7 libi
hoẽs hoẽs ual . vi . sol . 7 ht̃ vi . qua . in long̃ . 7 . v . in lat̃ . 7 vi . d.
de g̃ . i . eccla . xv . 7 ual . ii . sol . In . Molkebtuna tenet idẽ
i . lib̃ hõ sub stigando com̃d . tantum . xxx . ac̃ tc̃ . ii . car 7.
i . ac̃ p̃ti . sep̃ . ual . xx . sol.

230 a

Markeshalla ten̄ . Goduin͛ . lib̃ hõ . Stigandi . ii . car tr̃e.
Tc̃ xii . uilsti . p͛ 7 m̂ . xi . tc̃ viii . bor . p͛ . 7 m̂ . vii . tc̃ 7 p͛ . ii . ser.
m̂ . i . tc̃ . ii . car in dñio . p͛ . i . m̂ . ii . sep̃ . v . car . hoūm . xvi . ac̃ p̃ti.
7 sep̃ . ii . mol . 7 dim̃ . modo . ii . r . 7 iiii . an̄ . 7 xx . por . tc̃ . iiii . ou
m̂ . xxiiii . 7 . i . lib̃ . hõ . viii . ac̃ tr̃e . 7 dim̃ sep̃ . dim̃ car . Tc̃
ual c . sol . p͛ . viii . lib̃ . m̂ . xi . lib̃ . i . eccla . vi . ac̃ . 7 ual . xii . d.
7 ht̃ vi . qr̃ . in long̃ . 7 . v . in lato . 7 vi . d . 7 . obolum . de g̃.
Rex 7 comes . soca de libis hõib . In dunestuna . i . lib̃ hõ
vi . ac̃ . 7 . ẽ in p̃tio de merkeshla

TUNSTEAD Hundred

33 In SLOLEY 1 Freeman of St. Benedict's, 1 c. of land.
    Always 12 villagers; 8 smallholders.
    2½ ploughs; meadow, 6 acres; woodland, 120 pigs.
    Also 3 Freemen, 16 acres; always ½ plough.
Value 40s.
    It has 6 furlongs in length and 5 furlongs in width; tax of 4½d.
    1 church, 1 acre;
value 2d.

HUMBLEYARD Hundred

34 Richard holds MULBARTON which Ording, a thane, held before 1066, 2 c. of land.
    Then and later 10 villagers, now 7. Then 7 smallholders, now 16. Then 2 slaves, now 1.
    Always 2 ploughs in lordship; 2 men's ploughs; meadow, 10 acres; woodland, 16 pigs; always 1 mill. Now 1 cob. Then 1 head of cattle. Now 6 pigs.
    Also 6 Freemen, 60 acres; always 1½ ploughs.
He also holds in (East) CARLETON; 4 free men.
In SWARDESTON he also holds 7. Among the whole 56 acres.
    Always 1½ ploughs; meadow, 2 acres.
Value then and later 60s; now 100. Value of the free men 6s.
    It has 6 furlongs in length and 5 in width; tax of 6d.
    1 church, 15 [acres];
value 2s.
He also holds in MULBARTON; 1 free man under Stigand in patronage only, 30 acres.
    Then 2 ploughs; meadow, 1 acre.
Value always 20s.

35 Godwin, a free man of Stigand's, held MARKSHALL, 2 c. of land.   230 a
    Then 12 villagers, later and now 11. Then 8 smallholders, later and now 7. Then and later 2 slaves, now 1.
    Then 2 ploughs in lordship, later 1, now 2. Always 5 men's ploughs; meadow, 16 acres; always 2½ mills. Now 2 cobs; 4 head of cattle; 20 pigs. Then 4 sheep, now 24.
    Also 1 free man, 8½ acres of land; always ½ plough.
Value then 100s; later £8; now £11.
    1 church, 6 acres;
value 12d.
    It has 6 furlongs in length and 5 in width; tax of 6½d.
    The King and the Earl (have) the jurisdiction of the free men.
    In DUNSTON 1 free man, 6 acres.
It is in the valuation of Markshall.

H̄. CLAVELINGA. Thurketeliart ten̄ . t . lib̄ hō
Stigandi . II . car tr̄e . semp . III . uill̄ . 7 . XII . bor 7 III . ser̃
7 . II . car in dn̄io . Tc̄ . II . car̃ hoūm . m̄ . I . x . I . xv . ac̄ p̃ti .
m̄ . I . mol . Sēp . I . r . m̄ . VIII . an̄ . tc̄ . VII . por . modo . XXXVI .
Tc̄ . c . xx . ou . m̄ . cc . v . uasa apū . 7 . I . eccla . xx . ac̄ . 7 ual
XL . d̃ . & xv . libi . hões falde 7 com̄dc XL . ac̄ . sēp . vi . car̃ .
7 vi . ac̄ p̃ti . Tc̄ ual . IIII . lib̄ . 7 m̄ . similit̄ . Aldebvrý . ten̄ .
I . lib̄ homo . Stigandi . II . car̃ . tr̄e . sēp . I . uills . 7 v . bor . tc̄
III . ser . m̄ . II . 7 sēp . II . car in dn̄io Tc̄ . I . car hoūm . xv . ac̄ p̃ti .
silu . xx . por . 7 sēp . I . r . 7 xv . libi . hões . soca falde . 7 com̄d .
XL . ac̄ . tc̄ . III . car . m̄ . II . 7 . II . ac̄ p̃ti . 7 ual . XL . sol . I . eccla .
XII . ac̄ . 7 ual . II . sol . Huic manerio . jacent . XI . libi hões
II . car . tr̄e 7 dim̄ . 7 xxx . ac̄ . de VII . habuit suus anteces.
com̄d . t̄ r . ē . 7 de IIII . Stigandus 7 fuit suo antecessori.
libatum . p̃ tr̄a . semp . XII . bor . 7 v . car̃ 7 dim̄ . 7 XXIIII . ac̄
p̃ti . Silu . vi . por . Tc̄ ual . xxxIII . sol . m̄ . vi . lib̄ . 7 x . sol .
Totum h̄t . I . leug̃ in long̃ 7 dim̄ . in lato . 7 . II . sol . 7 . III .
obol . de g̃ . qcq̧ . . teneat   In Nortuna . II . libi hões
com̄d . t̄ . r . e . XXIII . ac̄ . Tc̄ . I . car̃ . 7 . I . ac̄ p̃ti . 7 ual .
II . sol . In Rauincham . I . soc̄ . I . ac̄ . 7 ual , II . d̃ .
In Tost . I . soc̄ . x . ac̄ 7 dim̄ . 7 ual . XII . d̃ .

TERRE Rainaldi filii iuonis H̄ . de cla   . XXI .
chelosa . In pincham ten̄ . I . lib̄ hō t . e . r . xvi . ac̄ tr̄e .
7 . I . ac̄ p̃ti . Semp . II b . 7 ual . II . sol . Hanc tr̄am inuasit
Wihenoc .

CLAVERING Hundred

36 1 free man of Stigand's held *THURKETELIART*, 2 c. of land.
    Always 3 villagers; 12 smallholders; 3 slaves.
    2 ploughs in lordship. Then 2 men's ploughs, now 1. ....
        Meadow, 15 acres. Now 1 mill; always 1 cob. Now 8 head of
        cattle. Then 7 pigs, now 36. Then 120 sheep, now 200.
        5 beehives. 1 church, 20 acres;
    value 40d.
        Also 15 free men in fold[-rights] and patronage, 40 acres.
        Always 6 ploughs; meadow, 6 acres.
    Value then £4; now the same.
    1 free man of Stigand's held ALDEBY, 2 c. of land.
        Always 1 villager; 5 smallholders. Then 3 slaves, now 2.
        Always 2 ploughs in lordship. Then 1 men's plough; meadow,
            15 acres; woodland, 20 pigs; always 1 cob.
        Also 15 free men in fold-rights and patronage, 40 acres.
        Then 3 ploughs, now 2. Meadow, 2 acres.
    Value 40s.
        1 church, 12 acres;
    value 2s.
        11 free men appertain to this manor, 2½ c. of land and 30 acres.
    His predecessor had the patronage of 7 before 1066, and
    Stigand of 4. It was delivered to his predecessor for land.
        Always 12 smallholders.
        5½ ploughs; meadow, 24 acres; woodland, 6 pigs.
    Value then 33s; now £6 10s.
        The whole has 1 league in length and ½ in width, tax of 2s and
        3 halfpence, whoever holds.
    In NORTON (Subcourse) 2 free men in patronage before 1066,
    23 acres. Then 1 plough; meadow, 1 acre.
    Value 2s.
    In RAVENINGHAM 1 Freeman, 1 acre.
    Value 2d.
    In TOFT (Monks) 1 Freeman, 10½ acres.
    Value 12d.

21   LAND OF REYNOLD SON OF IVO

The Hundred of CLACKCLOSE
1 In FINCHAM 1 free man held 16 acres of land before 1066.
    Meadow, 1 acre; always 2 oxen.
    Value 2s.
    Wihenoc annexed this land.

In b̄tuna vi. car tr̄e. toli. i. lib̄ hō. t̄. r. e. Tc̄
vi. uiƚƚi. 7 p̊. m̂. vii. Sēp v. bor. Tc̄ v. f. m̂. ii. xii. ac̄ p̄ti.
Sēp. ii. car̊. in dn̄io. tc̄ 7 p̊. i. car̊. hoūm m̂. dim̄. Huic
manerio jacent. v. lib̄i hoēs ad focam tantū com̄d. 7 ii. de
om̄i confuetudine illi. v. hab̄. i. car̊. 7 xii. ac̄ p̄ti. 7
iiłłi. ii. vi. ac̄ tr̄e in dn̄io qn̄. rec̄. lx. oues 7 m̂. tc̄ xi. por.

230 b

m̂. xv. Tc̄ totum uaƚ. lxxx. foƚ. p̊. 7 m̂. lx. 7. v. Hoēs uaƚ.
x. foƚ. In eadem uilla. iii. car̊ tr̄æ tēn turchillus. i. lib̄.
hō. t̄. r. e. Sēp. vi. uiƚƚi 7 v. bor. Tc̄ 7 p̊. v. f. m̂. ii. xx
ac̄ p̄ti. Tc̄ iii. car̊ in dn̄io. p̊. nulla m̂. ii. Semp. i. car̊ hoūm
7. lx. oues. 7 vii. p. Iacent huic man̄. iiii. lib̄i hoēs ad focam
tanť 7 hab̄. xxx. ac̄ tr̄e. Tc̄. i. car̊. m̂. dim̄. 7 viii. ac̄ p̄ti.
7 iiii. ac̄ filue. Tc̄ totum. uaƚ. x. lib̄ p̊. lx. foƚ. m̂. lxxxv.
7. v. lib̄i hoēs. xlii. foƚ. 7 viii. d̄. In b̄tuna tēn. chetel. lib̄.
homo t. r. e. i. car̊ tr̄e. Sēp. iiii. uiƚƚ. 7. ii. b. 7 xx.
ac̄ p̄ti. Tc̄. ii. car̊ in dn̄io. P̊. nulla. m̂. i. femp car̊ hoūm
★ Tc̄ uaƚ. lx. foƚ. P̊. 7 m̂. xxx. Totum hoc manerio ħt. i.
leuḡ. in lonḡ In lato dim̄ leuḡ. 7. iii. q̊rdran. Quando totū
hundret. reddit. xx. foƚ. de gelto. 7 tota hec uilla xvi. d̄.
In crepelefham. tēn. alia lib̄a fēm. t. e. r. ii. car̊ tr̄e. Sēp
viii. uiƚƚi. 7. iiii. bor. 7 vii. fer̊. 7 viii. ac̄. p̄ti. Tc̄ in dn̄io. iii.
car̊. p̊. iii. m̂. iiii. Sēp. i. pifc̄. 7. i. r. ii. an̄. Tc̄. ii. por. Tc̄

2   In BARTON (Bendish) 1 free man, Toli, 6 c. of land before 1066.
    Then 6 villagers, later and now 7. Always 5 smallholders. Then
        5 slaves, now 2.
    Meadow, 12 acres. Always 2 ploughs in lordship. Then and
        later 1 men's plough, now ½.
    5 free men appertain to this manor at jurisdiction in patronage
only, and 2 with all customary dues. The 5 have 1 plough; meadow,
12 acres. The 2 (had) 6 acres of land in lordship when he acquired
them, and 60 sheep and now. Then 11 pigs, now 15.   230 b
Value of the whole then 80s, later and now 60. Value of the 5
men, 10s.
In the same village 1 free man, Thorkell, held 3 c. of land
before 1066.
    Always 6 villagers; 5 smallholders. Then and later 5 slaves, now 2.
    Meadow, 20 acres. Then 3 ploughs in lordship, later none, now
        2. Always 1 men's plough; 60 sheep; 7 pigs.
    5 free men appertain to this manor at jurisdiction only. They
        have 30 acres of land.
    Then 1 plough, now ½. Meadow, 8 acres; woodland, 4 acres.
Value of the whole, then £10, later 60s, now 85; of the 5 free
men, 42s 8d.
In BARTON (Bendish) Ketel, a free man, held 1 c. of land before
1066.
    Always 4 villagers; 2 smallholders.
    Meadow, 20 acres. Then 2 ploughs in lordship, later none, now 1.
        Always a men's plough.
Value then 40s; later and now 30.
    The whole of this in the manor has 1 league in length (and) ½
league and 3 furlongs in width, when the whole Hundred pays
tax of 20s the whole of this village also (pays) 16d.

3   In CRIMPLESHAM another free woman held 2 c. of land before 1066.
    Always 8 villagers; 4 smallholders; 7 slaves.
    Meadow, 8 acres. Then 3 ploughs in lordship, later 3, now 4.
        Always 1 fishery; 1 cob; 2 head of cattle. Then 2 pigs. Then

cc.xl.ou͘.m̄.ccc.Huic man̄ jacent.xx.libi hoēs.
ad focam.7 com̄d.de.lx ac̄.Tc̄ 1.car̋ 7 dim̄.m̄.1.In eadē
uitta.Tchillus tenet.1.car̋ trǣ.femp.1.bor.7.1.f.7 viii.
ac̄ p̄ti.7 dim̄ pifc̄.Tc̄.1.car̋ jacent &iam.v.libi hoēs
de iiii.ac̄ ad focā 7 com̄d tantum.Hoc tum ual femp
viii.lib̄.In creplefham.iii.lib̄.hoēs.d.1.car̋ trē.femp
iiii.bor.7 xii.ac̋ p̄ti de iftis h̄t com̄d 7 ꝯfuetudinē.
Tc̄ ual.xvi.fol.m̄.viii.In toimere iii.lib̄.ad focā falde
7 com̄d.alii focā fc̄i.b.femp ual.xiiii.d̄.1.lib̄.hō.xl.
ac̄.7 ual.ii.fol.Totum creplefham h̄t.1.leuḡ.in lonḡ
7 dim̄ in lato.7 reddit.viii.d̄.de.xx.fol.de gelto.regis.
d̄cq̋ ibi teneat.Wigreham.ii.car̋ trē.ten̄ toli.lib̄ hō
t̄ r.e.Tc̄.xv uitti.p̋ 7 m̄.xi.fēp.viii.bor.tc̄.vi.fer
m̄.iiii.7 xx.ac̄ p̄ti.Siluā.xii.por.femp.ii.car̋ in dn̄io.
tc̄.i.car̋.7 dim̄.houm.m̄.i.femp.dim̄.mol.7.i.pifc̄.
Sēp.i.r̄.7 xxviii.equǣ.7 xxv.pulli.7.ii.an̄.tc̄.xv.
por.m̄.vii.tc̄.lxxxx.oues.m̄.cclx.7.ual.c.fol.
f; reddidit.viii.lib̄.ad omnē confuetud̄.Huic man̄
jacent.iiii.libi hoēs de.xii.acr̋.In ftokes.iiii.libi hoēs
com̄d.7 om̄i c̄fuetudine de.xii.ac̋.7.i.lib̄ hō de.ii acr̋.
In eadē tenent.Rogerus 7 Hugo.ii.foc̄ de lxxiiii.ac̄.sēp
i.7 dim̄.7.x.ac̄ p̄ti.Hoc totum ual.xx.fol.Totum.Wigrehā
h̄t dim̄ leuḡ in lonḡ 7 in lato.7 reddit.vi.d̄.7.i.obolum.de
xx.fol.de gelto.regis.

240 sheep, now 300.
20 free men appertain to this manor at jurisdiction and in patronage only, at 60 acres.
Then 1½ ploughs, now 1.
In the same village Thorkell holds 1 c. of land.
Always 1 smallholder; 1 slave.
Meadow, 8 acres; ½ fishery. Then 1 plough.
5 free men also appertain, at 4 acres, at jurisdiction and in patronage only.
Value of all this always £8.
In Crimplesham 3 free men, at 1 c. of land.
Always 4 smallholders.
Meadow, 12 acres.
Of these he has the patronage and the customary dues.
Value then 16s; now 8.
In TOOMBERS 3 free (men) at fold-rights and in patronage; the others (are of the) jurisdiction of St. B(enedict).
Value always 14d.
1 free man, 40 acres.
Value 2s.
The whole of Crimplesham has 1 league in length and ½ in width; of a 20s King's tax it pays 8d, whoever holds there.

4 WEREHAM, 2 c. of land; Toli, a free man, held before 1066.
Then 15 villagers, later and now 11. Always 8 smallholders.
Then 6 slaves, now 4.
Meadow, 20 acres; woodland, 12 pigs; always 2 ploughs in lordship. Then 1½ men's ploughs, now 1. Always ½ mill; 1 fishery. Always 1 cob; 28 mares; 25 foals; 2 head of cattle. Then 15 pigs, now 7. Then 90 sheep, now 260.
Value 100s, but it paid £8 for all customary dues.
4 free men appertain to this manor, at 12 acres.
In STOKE (Ferry) 4 free men in patronage and with all customary dues, at 12 acres. Also 1 free man, at 2 acres.
In the same Roger and Hugh hold 2 Freemen, at 74 acres.
Always 1½ [ploughs].
Meadow, 10 acres.
Value of all this 20s.
The whole of Wereham has ½ league in length and in width; of a 20s King's tax it pays 6½d.

Wella ten̄.toli.lib hō.t̄.r.e.car tr̄æ.

231 a

semp.VIIII.uilli.7 v.bor.Tc̄.VI.f.p̄ 7 m̄.II.7.VIII.ac p̃ti.semp
II.car.in dn̄io.Tc̄.II.car houm.p̄ 7 modo.I.7.I.pisc̄.sēp.I.r.7.II.
an̄.Tc̄.XII.por.m̄.VII.tc̄ LXXX.oues.m̄.CLX.Semp ual.VI.
lib.f; reddidit.VIII.lib.huic man̄.jac̄.XVII.libi hōes.de LXIIII.
ac.terre.Tc̄.I.car 7 dim̄.m̄.I.7 ual.XIII.fol.7 IIII.d̄.
Istos inuasit uiuibenoc. Tota uuella.ht.I.leug in long.
7 in lat 7 reddit.II.fol.de XX.fol.de gelto.regis.

Buchetuna tenuit t̄chillus.t̄ r.ē.m̄.tenet.Ranulfus
sēp.car tr̄e.7 XXIIII.ac.7 v.uill.Tc̄.II.f.sēp.X.ac p̄ 7.
I.car in dn̄io sēp.I.r.7 IIII.an̄.7.VIII.por.CXXVI.oues.
Huic man.jacent.v.fochem̄.d.XII.ac.7 tenet idem
Tunc ual.XL.fol.m̄.LXII.7.VI.di.Tota buchetuna ht
v.q̄r.in lat.7.IIII.in lat.7 reddit.VIII.d.de XX.fol.de gel
regis. Sculdeham ten̄ idē turchill.t̄ r.e.I.car.tr̄e.7 VI.ac.
modo tenet.Ranul..Tc̄.III.uill.m̄.v.Tc̄.VII.b.m̄.VII.
sēp.III.f.Tc̄ 7 p̄.II.car.in dn̄io.m̄.I.m̄.dim̄ car houm.
silu.XX.por.VI.ac p̃ti.tc̄.I.r.tc̄.IIII.an̄.m̄.VI.tc̄
XVI.por.m̄.III.tc̄.CXX.oues.m̄.CXXVI.7.III.uafa
apū.7 dim̄ pisc̄.huic man jacent.II.fochem̄.de.X.
ac.tc̄ ual.LX.fol.m̄.XL.7 VI.d̄.Huic etiam jacent
X.libi homines.t̄ r.e.de.XXX.ac.com̄datione tantū
7 tenet idē.sēp dim̄.car.7.II.ac p̃ti.Tunc ual.VI.fol.
m̄.XVI.Hos nuasit uuihenoc.

5 Toli, a free man, held UPWELL before 1066; a c. of land.
    Always 9 villagers; 5 smallholders. Then 6 slaves, later and   231 a
      now 2.
    Meadow, 8 acres; always 2 ploughs in lordship. Then 2 men's
      ploughs, later and now 1. 1 fishery. Always 1 cob; 2 head of
      cattle. Then 12 pigs, now 7. Then 80 sheep, now 160.
  Value always £6, but it paid £8.
  17 free men appertain to this manor, at 64 acres of land.
    Then 1½ ploughs, now 1.
  Value 13s 4d.
    Wihenoc annexed these.
    The whole of Upwell has 1 league in length and in width, of a
  20s King's tax it pays 2s.

6 Thorkell held BOUGHTON before 1066, now Ranulf holds; always
  1 c. of land and 24 acres.
    5 villagers. Then 2 slaves.
    Meadow, always 10 acres; 1 plough in lordship. Always 1 cob;
      4 head of cattle; 8 pigs; 126 sheep.
    5 Freemen appertain to this manor, at 12 acres. He also holds.
  Value then 40s; now 62(s) 6d.
    The whole of Boughton has 5 furlongs in length and 4 in width;
  of a 20s King's tax it pays 8d.

7 Thorkell also held SHOULDHAM before 1066, 1 c. of land and 6
  acres; now Ranulf holds.
    Then 3 villagers, now 5. Then 7 smallholders, now 7. Always 3
      slaves.
    Then and later 2 ploughs in lordship, now 1. Now ½ men's
      plough; woodland, 20 pigs; meadow, 6 acres. Then 1 cob.
      Then 4 head of cattle, now 6. Then 16 pigs, now 3. Then
      120 sheep, now 126. 3 beehives; ½ fishery.
    2 Freemen appertain to this manor, at 10 acres.
  Value then 60s; now 40(s) 6d.
    10 free men also appertained to this before 1066 at 30 acres
  and in patronage only. He also holds.
    Always ½ plough; meadow, 2 acres.
  Value then 6s; now 16.
    Wihenoc annexed these.

In bicham. xxIIII . ac
tre . ten . I . lib hō . hunc inuaſit uuihenoc . & antec.

231 b

hermen . habuit com̄d . tantum . 7 reddit . v . fol . In forteſthorp.
dim̄ . car tre . t . r . e . m̄ tenet Ran̄ . sep̄ . dim̄ . car . 7 I . bor . 7 ual.
x . fol . hoc inuaſit . Wihenoc . In Wella . I . bor . In thorp . I . foc.
. II . ac . 7 ual III . d.

H̄ . 7 dim̄ . de FREDREBRUGE . In Weſuuinic . II . car . tre.
ten . Goduuinus . lib hō . t r . e . m̄ tenet ide sep̄ . xIIII . uiℓti . 7 vI.
bor . Tc IIII . fer . m̄ . I . 7 xx . ac p̄ti . sep̄ . II . car . in dn̄io . 7 dim̄ . hoūm
7 . II . fat . sep̄ . x . an̄ . 7 xvIIII . por . Lxxx . ou . huic man̄ . jacent . 7 . tenet
ide . xxIII . foc . xxxvI . ac tre . sep̄ . dim̄ . car . 7 . IIII . ac p̄ti . Tc ual.
III . lib . p c . fol . m̄ . x . lib . Wiche ten . Leuricus lib hō . II . car
terre . t . r . e . modo tenet Roḡ . Tc xII . uiℓti . m̄ . vII . Sep̄ . III.
bor . 7 . II . f . 7 . xx . ac p̄ti . Tc . II . car in dn̄io . m̄ . I . Tc . I . car hoūm.
m̄ . dim̄ . Hic jacent . vII . foc . xII . ac terre . 7 tenet . ide . 7 II . ac
p̄ti . sep̄ . dim̄ . car . Tc . v . an̄i . Tc . vII . por . m̄ . v . Tc . cc . ou
m̄ . xxx . Tc dim̄ . fat . Tc ual . IIII . lib . m̄ . xL . fol . 7 . I . car
poteſt reſtaurari . Tota ℏt . vI . q̄r . in lonḡ . 7 . III . in lato.
7 reddit . vI . d . de xx . fol . de gelto . q̄cq̄ ibi teneat.

In maſinicham . Lx . ac tere . ten . Vlmarus . lib hō t . e . r.
m̄ tenet . Radulfus . sep̄ . IIII . uiℓti . Tc . I . car . m̄ . dim̄ . 7 ual
xIII . fol . 7 . IIII . d.

8   In BEECHAMWELL 1 free man held 24 acres of land. Wihenoc annexed him. Herman, his predecessor, had the patronage only. He pays 5s.   231 b
   In FODDERSTONE ½ c. of land before 1066; now Ranulf holds.
      Always ½ plough.
      1 smallholder.
   Value 10s.
      Wihenoc annexed this.
   In UPWELL 1 smallholder; in (Shouldham) THORPE 1 Freeman, 2 acres.
   Value 3d.

   The Hundred and a Half of FREEBRIDGE

9 In WEST WINCH Godwin, a free man, held 2 c. of land before 1066; now (Ranulf) also holds.
      Always 14 villagers; 6 smallholders. Then 4 slaves, now 1.
      Meadow, 20 acres. Always 2 ploughs in lordship; ½ men's [plough]; 2 salt-houses. Always 10 head of cattle; 19 pigs; 80 sheep.
      23 Freemen appertain to this manor; he also holds; 36 acres of land. Always ½ plough; meadow, 4 acres.
   Value then £3; later 100s; now £10.

10 Leofric, a free man, held (Ash)WICKEN before 1066, 2 c. of land. Now Roger holds.
      Then 12 villagers, now 7. Always 3 smallholders; 2 slaves.
      Meadow, 20 acres. Then 2 ploughs in lordship, now 1. Then 1 men's plough, now ½.
      7 Freemen appertain here, 12 acres of land. He also holds. Meadow, 2 acres; always ½ plough. Then 5 head of cattle. Then 7 pigs, now 5. Then 200 sheep, now 30. Then ½ salt-house.
   Value then £4; now 40s.
      1 plough could be restored.
      The whole has 6 furlongs in length and 3 in width; of a 20s tax it pays 6d, whoever holds there.

11 In MASSINGHAM Wulfmer, a free man, held 60 acres of land before 1066; now Ralph holds.
      Always 4 villagers.
      Then 1 plough, now ½.
   Value 13s 4d.

H̃. de Grimeſhou. In eſtarforda. teñ. II. libi hōes
xIIII. ac̰ t̃re 7 fueř libati. Wihenoc. m̃. tenet Radulfus
ſemp̰ dim̃ car̰. 7 ual. II. ſol. 7 vIII. d̃.

H̃. de GRENEHOV. In caldanchota teñ q̃dam lib hō
232 a
dim̃ ca t̃re. t̃ r̃. e. Tc̃. II. uitti. 7. I. lib hō. de. v. ac̰r. ſub ipſo. Tc̃. 7. sēp dim̃
car̰. 7. I. ac̰ p̃ti & dim̃. 7. I. mol. Tc̃. ual. III. s̃. m̃. v. s̃ 7 hanc t̃ram. teñ. q̃dā lib hō
ſ; p̰q̃ rex ueñ ĩ hanc t̃ram. Wihenoc occupant eam. ideoq̃ teñ. R. 7 ſocā 7 ſac̃
hab& rex. Inneadē uilla. III. libos hōes tenentes. L. ac̰r. 7. hab. d̃. car̰. 7 ual.
III. s̃. 7 eodē m̃. teñ iſtos. ∫ Cleietorpa. teñ. Toli. t̃. r. e. m̃ tenet. Ernald.
Tc̃ 7 p̰. vI. uitt. m̃. I. 7. II. bor. Sēp. III. ſer. Tc̃ 7 p̰. II. car̰. m̃. I. Tc̃ hōum
I. car̰. 7 p̰. m̃. d̃. Silua ad. xvI. por. II. p̃tĩ. Qñ rec̃. I. r̃. m̃. xv. eque ſiluatic̣e.
Tc̃ xx. por. m̃. xI. Tc̃. c. oues. m̃. ccc. 7. III. ſochem̃ tene idē. xx.
ac̰. 7 sēp dim̃. car̰. 7 De his. III. hab& rex. ſoc̣a. Tc̃ ual. Lx. s̃. m̃. xL.
★ Quidā. lib hō. In pinkenhā teñ idē. xxx. ac̰ t̃rc̣e. 7 p̰. q̃ rex uenit in iſtam
patriā teñ. iſta t̃ram. Comes. R. S; unus hō. Wihenoc. amauit q̃ndā.
fem̃. fem̃. ĩ illa t̃ra. 7 dux̃ eam.. 7 p̰ea. teñ. ille. iſta t̃ram. ad fedũ. W.
ſine dono. r. 7 ſine libatione. 7 ſucceſſoribʒ ſuis. Sēp dim̃. car̰. 7. I. bor.
7. I. ac̰. ſilue. 7. II. ac̰. 7 dim̃. p̃ti. sēp. ual. III. ſol. ∫ In Houtuna. I.
                                                      tenet Herluin'.
lib hō. de xvI. ac̰. 7 ual. xvI. d̃. nunc inuaſit Wihenoc. In pikenham.
xv. ac̰. inuaſit. Wihenoc. 7 ual. xvI. d̃. hoc calūpniat̃. Rad. de toeni.
hund. teſt.

The Hundred of GRIMSHOE
12 In STANFORD 2 free men held 14 acres of land; they were delivered to Wihenoc; now Ralph holds.
Always ½ plough.
Value 2s 8d.

The Hundred of (South) GREENOE
13 In CALDECOTE a certain free man held ½ c. of land before 1066.   232 a
Then 2 villagers and 1 free man, at 5 acres, under him.
Then and always ½ plough; meadow, 1½ acres; 1 mill.
Value then 3s, now 5s.
A certain free man held this land, but after the King came into this land Wihenoc appropriated it; therefore R(eynold) holds, and the King has the full jurisdiction.
In the same village (he holds) 3 free men holding 50 acres. They have ½ plough.
Value 3s.
He holds them in the same way.

14 Toli held CLEYTHORPE before 1066, now Arnold holds.
Then and later 6 villagers, now 1. 2 smallholders; always 3 slaves. Then and later 2 ploughs, now 1. Then 1 men's plough, later and now ½. Woodland for 16 pigs; meadow, 2 [acres]. When he acquired it 1 cob, now 15 wild mares. Then 20 pigs, now 11. Then 100 sheep, now 300.
He also holds 3 Freemen, 20 acres; always ½ plough. Of these 3 the King has the jurisdiction.
Value then 60s; now 40.
A certain free man. In PICKENHAM he also holds 30 acres of land. After the King came into that district Earl R(alph) held that land. But 1 man of Wihenoc's loved a certain woman on that land and took her (as his wife). Later he held that land as part of W(ihenoc)'s Holding, without the King's gift, and without livery, and (it passed) to his successors.
Always ½ plough.
1 smallholder.
Woodland, 1 acre; meadow, 2½ acres.
Value always 3s.

15 In HOUGHTON (ON THE HILL) Herlwin holds; 1 free man, at 16 acres.
Value 16d.
Wihenoc annexed him.
In PICKENHAM Wihenoc annexed 15 acres.
Value 16d.
Ralph of Tosny claims this; the Hundred testifies (to it).

H̄. WAINELVND. Pennewrde teñ Herold. t̄. r. e. i. car̄ 7 dim̄.
m̄ tenet idē. Tc̄ 7 p̄. vi. uilli. m̄; viii. bor. Tc̄ 7 p̄. iiii. s. m̄. ii. x.
ac̄ p̄ti. sēp. ii. car̄ in dñio. 7 dim̄. car̄ hōum. silu. c̄. por. 7. i. r.
m̄. ii. sēp. vi. añ. Tc̄. xxxv. por. m̄. xxii. Tc̄. xxvii. oū.
m̄. lx. 7. iii. uasa. apū. 7. vii. soc̄ dim̄
car̄. 7 xvi. ac̄. Sēp. i. car̄ 7 dim̄.
Sēp. ual. xl. sol.

232 b

In Essalai. tenet idē. xv. soc̄ regis. e. in saba. i. car̄. t̄re. 7 viii. ac̄.
sēp. iii. uill. 7. iii. bor. t̄c. i. s̄. 7 vi. ac̄ p̄ti. Sēp vi. car̄ 7 dim̄. sib̄.
c̄. por. Sēp. ual. xxx. sol. Totū ħt dim̄. leug̃. in long̃ 7 dim̄. in lat̄
7 de gelto. xv. d. In Trectuna. viii. libi hōes. iii. car̄ terre.
7 xxviii. ac̄. t̄. r. e. m̄ tenet Ranulfus. 7 ii. bor. xx. ac̄ p̄ti.
Tc̄. vi. car̄. p̄. iiii. m̄. ii. 7 dim̄. 7. iii. car̄. possent. ee. hoc libatē
ē. p una car̄ t̄re. Tc̄ ual. iiii. libi. 7 x. sol. m̄. ual. lx. sol.

H̄. Lawendic. Svttuna tenuit Olova. q̄dā fem̄.
t̄. r. e. p man̄. ii. car̄. terre. m̄ tenet Uotericus. Tc̄ 7 p̄.
xvi. uill. m̄. x. semp. ii. ser. 7. x. ac̄. p̄ti. Tc̄ silua. xc. por. m̄. c.
Tc̄ i. car̄ in dñio. Post dim̄. i. car̄ 7 dim̄. tc̄. iii. car̄ hōum. p̄. 7 m̄.
i. 7 dim̄ car̄. possēt restaurari. Tc̄. v. por. m̄ simil. tc̄ cxx. m̄. c.
Hoc teñ. Stigand in mulesha. Tc̄ ual xl. sol. m̄. lxxx. 7 ħt
dim̄ leug̃ in long̃. 7 v. q̄r in lat̄. 7 v. d. de gelto.

H̄. Mittefordam. Iachesham teñ. Ailid. t̄. r. e. iiii. ac̄
de silua. 7. i. ac̄. de p̄ti. 7 ual. xii. d.

WAYLAND Hundred

16 Harold held PANWORTH before 1066; 1½ ploughs. Now (Reynold) also holds.
 Then and later 6 villagers, now 5. Always 8 smallholders. Then and later 4 slaves, now 2.
 Meadow, 10 acres. Always 2 ploughs in lordship; ½ men's plough; woodland, 100 pigs. 1 cob, now 2. Always 6 head of cattle. Then 35 pigs, now 22. Then 27 sheep, now 60. 3 beehives.
 Also 7 Freemen; ½ c. [of land] and 16 acres; always 1½ ploughs.
Value always 40s.

17 He also holds in ASHILL; 15 [Freemen]; the jurisdiction is the King's in Saham (Toney); 1 c. of land and 8 acres.   232 b
 Always 3 villagers; 3 smallholders. Then 1 slave.
 Meadow, 6 acres. Always 6½ ploughs; woodland, 100 pigs.
Value always 30s.
 The whole has ½ league in length and ½ in width, tax of 15d.

18 In THREXTON 8 free men, 3 c. of land and 28 acres before 1066; now Ranulf holds.
 2 smallholders.
 Meadow, 20 acres. Then 6 ploughs, later 4, now 2½; 3 ploughs could be there.
 This was delivered for 1 c. of land.
Value then £4 10s; value now 60s.

LAUNDITCH Hundred

19 A certain woman, Olova, held SUTTON before 1066 as a manor, 2 c. of land; now Boteric holds.
 Then and later 16 villagers, now 10. Always 2 slaves.
 Meadow, 10 acres. Then woodland, 200 pigs, now 100. Then 1 plough in lordship, later ½; [now] 1½ ploughs. Then 3 men's ploughs, later and now 1; ½ plough could be restored. Then 5 pigs, now the same. Then 120 [sheep], now 100.
 Stigand held this in Mileham.
Value then 40s; now 80.
 It has ½ league in length and 5 furlongs in width, tax of 5d.

MITFORD Hundred

20 Aethelgyth held in YAXHAM before 1066; 4 acres of woodland; 1 acre of meadow.
Value 12d.

H̃. De GALGOV. Peneſtorpa ten̄. Sclula t̃.r.e.ıı.car̰
tr̃e m̃ tenet. Ran̄. Sep̃. xııı. bor. 7. ıı. ſer. Sep̃ in dn̄io
.ıı.car̰.m̃.ı. Silu̧.xıı.por.ııı.aç p̃ti.ı.mot̃. Tc̃.ı.r̄.
m̃ ſimil̃. Semp.ıııı.an̄. Tc̃.xx.por.m̃.lx. Sep̃.
 cc.7 xl.ou̧.m̃.ıııı.uas ap̃. Tc̃ uat̃.xl.ſot
 m̃.ſimilit̃. 7 hab̃.ıııı.q̃r.in long̃.
 7.ııı.in lat̃.7.vı.d̃.t̃ gelto.

233 a

H̃. DE BRODERCROS. In reineh̃a t.e.r. ten̄. Bond.
ııı.lib̃ı ho̧es m̃ tenet boteric̰. 7 herold.ı.m̃. Renald. de dim̃ car̰
tr̃e. Sep̃.ı.car̰.ııı.aç p̃ti.tc̃ uat̃.x.s̃.m̃.v.7 he̯. heroldi calup̰niat̰
uicemos in fagenham eȩȩ. 7 hund̃ teſtat̰.

H̃. DE HOLT. In Wiuetuna ten̄. Turchetes̃.t.e r.ıı.car̰
tr̃e modo idȩ. Sep̃ vıı. uiłł. 7 xxvıı. bor. Sep̃ in dn̄io.ıı.car̰.tc̃
ho̧um.v.car̰.m̃.ııı.7 d̃.ıııı.aç p̃ti.ı.mot̃. 7 d̃.m̃.ııı.an̄.tc̃
xv.por.m̃.xxvııı.tc̃.cvıı ou̧.m̃.lxxx. Tc̃ 7 p̰.xl.ſot.m̃.vı.
lib̃. 7 h̃t ı̧ long̃.ı.liug̃. 7 in lat̃.7.xvıı.d̃.7 obolu̧ in gelto.

H̃. GRENEHOV. Walſingah̃a. ten̄. ketel.ı.lib̃ ho̧.t.e r.
sep̃.xvıııı.bor.ı.car̰.ıı.car̰ tr̃e.tc̃.ıı.s.m̃.ı.ıı.aç p̃ti.
Tc̃ 7 p̰.ıı.car̰. in dn̄io.m̃.ııı. ſilu̧.vııı.por.ııı.eq̃.qn̄ rec̃.ıı an̄
m̃.ı.tc̃.xv₉p̰.m̃.xvıııı. ſep̃.çxx.ou̧.xxıııı.ſoc̃a. jacent huic.
ville.lx. 7.x.aç tr̃e.ıı.bor. 7 d̃.mot̃. tc̃.ııı.car̰.7 qn̄ rec̃. 7 m̃.
ı.car̰. 7 d̃.tc̃ vat̃ vı.lib̃.m̃.ſmilı̧. 7 h̃t.d̃.leug̃ longi. 7 d lati.
7.xvııı.d̃.de gelto. Et alia. Walſingah̃a tn̄. ketel.t̃.r.e.ıı.
car̰ tr̃e. sep̃.ıııı. uiłł.tc̃.xxı.bor.xvııı. sep̃.ıı.s.tc̃.ıı.car̰ in dn̄io
7 qn̄ rec̃.ı.m̃.ıı.car̰.ho̧um. 7 p̰.ı.m̃.ı.car̰ ſilu̧.vı.p̰.ı.aç p̃ti.ı.mot̃

The Hundred of GALLOW

21 Skuli held PENSTHORPE before 1066, 2 c. of land. Ranulf now holds.
   Always 13 smallholders; 2 slaves.
   Always 2 ploughs in lordship, now 1. Woodland, 12 pigs; meadow, 3 acres; 1 mill. Then 1 cob, now the same. Always 4 head of cattle. Then 20 pigs, now 60. Always 240 sheep. Now 4 beehives.
   Value then 40s; now the same.
   It has 4 furlongs in length and 3 in width; tax of 6d.

The Hundred of BROTHERCROSS   233 a

22 Bondi held in RAYNHAM before 1066; 4 free men. Boteric now holds. Harold (held) 1; now Reynold (holds) at ½ c. of land.
   Always 1 plough; meadow, 3 acres.
   Value then 10s; now 5.
   The sheriff claims that Harold's man is in (the lands of) Fakenham, and the Hundred testifies (to it).

The Hundred of HOLT

23 Thorketel held in WIVETON before 1066, 2 c. of land; now (Reynold) also (holds).
   Always 7 villagers; 27 smallholders.
   Always in lordship 2 ploughs. Then 5 men's ploughs, now 3½. Meadow, 4 acres; 1½ mills. Now 3 head of cattle. Then 15 pigs, now 28. Then 107 sheep, now 80.
   [Value] then and later 40s; now £6.
   It has in length 1 league and in width; 17½d in tax.

(North) GREENHOE Hundred

24 Ketel, 1 free man, held WALSINGHAM before 1066.
   Always 19 smallholders; 1 plough; 2 c. of land. Then 2 slaves, now 1.
   Meadow, 2 acres. Then and later 2 ploughs in lordship, now 3. Woodland, 8 pigs; 3 horses. When he acquired it, 2 head of cattle, now 1. Then 15 pigs, now 19. Always 120 sheep.
   24 Freemen appertain to this village; 60 and 10 acres of land. 2 smallholders. ½ mill. Then 3 ploughs. When he acquired it and now 1½ ploughs.
   Value then £6; now the same.
   It has ½ league in length and ½ in width, tax of 18d.
   Ketel held the other WALSINGHAM before 1066, 2 c. of land.
   Always 4 villagers. Then 21 smallholders, [now] 18. Always 2 slaves.
   Then 2 ploughs in lordship, when he acquired it 1, now 2. [Now 2] men's ploughs, later 1, now 1 plough. Woodland, 6 pigs; meadow, 1 acre; 1 mill.

v . foke . xiiii . aĉ . tre . i . mol . tc . d . car 7 m̂ . qn̄ . recē . 7 . v . eq.
m̂ . iiii . sēp . v . tc . xii . p̄ . m̂ . xiiii . lxxx . ou sēp . tc . vi . uafa ap
m̂ . ii . tc . iiii . lib . m̂ . c . fol . 7 ht . i . leug longi . 7 d . lati . xxiiii.
d de gelto . quicq, ibi teat . ∫Stiuecai ten . Ketel . t . r . e.
ii . car tre m̂ tenet Ran . sēp xvi . bor . tc . iii . i . s . m̂ . iii.
iii . aĉ pti . tc ii . car in dn̄io . 7 sēp . i . car hoūm . ii . mol . tc . m̂ . i.

233 b

qn̄ . rec . iii . eq . m̂ . iiii . 7 . m̂ . v . an̄ . qn̄ . rec . xxx . p̄ . 7 . m̂ . xii 7 qn̄ . req.
c . lxxx . ou . 7 . m̂ . cc . xl . vi . foche jacent huic uille . v . aĉ . tre.
sēp . d . car tre . Huic man̄ . addiditi . st . iiii . focem . tenet ide p libacio
ne regis . i . car . terre . 7 dim . vii . bor . sēp . iii . car . ii . aĉ . pti . 7 . i.
mol 7 d . Tc . ual . ista uilla . iiii . lib 7 hi . iiii . hōes . redd . xl . fol . . 7.
m̂ . similit 7 ht . d . leug . longi . 7 d . lati . 7 xxiiii . d . de gelto.
i . eccla . xxx . aĉ 7 ual . ii . fol.

H̄ . LOTHNINGA . Karlentona . ten alficus lib hō sub

rege . e . p . xxx aĉ . tre . Tc . vii . bor . p̄ . vi . m̂ . iiii . Sēp . i . car
7 dim . Tc . ii . car . hoūm . p̄ . i . 7 dim . m̂ . i . tc . xiiii . por . m̂ . iii.
m̂ . lx . ou . 7 xiiii . libi hōes ulfi com̄d . libati . ad pficiendum . hoc
man . de . lx . aĉ . tc . ii . car . p̄ . 7 . m̂ . i . 7 . v . aĉ pti . 7 hic . ē liba tra.
de eccla . lxxx . aĉ . Tunc ual . xx . fol . m̂ . xl . ht . i . leug . in long
iv . qr̄ . in lato . 7 de gelto . viii . d.

5 Freemen, 14 acres of land.
  1 mill. Then ½ plough, and now. When he acquired them also 5 horses, now 4; always 5 [.....]. Then 12 pigs, now 14.
  Always 80 sheep. Then 6 beehives, now 2.
[Value] then £4; now 100s.
  It has 1 league in length and ½ in width; tax of 24d, whoever holds there.

25 Ketel held STIFFKEY before 1066, 2 c. of land. Now Ranulf holds.
  Always 16 smallholders. Then 3, [later] 1 slaves, now 3.
  Meadow, 3 acres. Then 2 ploughs in lordship; always 1 men's plough. Then 2 mills, now 1. When he acquired it 3 horses, now 4. Now 5 head of cattle. When he acquired it 30 pigs, now 12. When he acquired it 180 sheep, now 240.
  6 Freemen also appertain to this village; he also (holds); 5 acres of land, always ½ c. of land.
  To this manor were added 4 Freemen. He also holds by the King's livery; 1½ c. of land. 7 smallholders. Always 3 ploughs; meadow, 2 acres; 1½ mills.
Value then of that village £4, and these 4 men paid 40s; now the same.
  It has ½ league in length and ½ in width; tax of 24d.
  1 church, 30 acres;
value 2s.

LODDON Hundred

26 Aelfric, a free man, held CARLETON (St. Peter) under King Edward, as 30 acres of land.
  Then 7 smallholders, later 6, now 4.
  Always 1½ ploughs. Then 2 men's ploughs, later 1½, now 1.
  Then 14 pigs, now 3. Now 60 sheep.
  Also 14 free men under the patronage of Wulfsi who were delivered to make up this manor, at 60 acres.
  Then 2 ploughs, later and now 1. Meadow, 5 acres.
  Here there is free land of the church, 80 acres.
Value then 20s; now 40.
  It has 1 league in length and 4 furlongs in width, tax of 8d.

233 b

H̃. DE ENSFORDA. Witewellā teñ . Ketel 1 . lib hō t̃ r . e.
11 . car tr̃e 7 xv . ac̃ . p mā . Tc̃ 7 p̊ . viii . Uilt . m̂ . vii . sēp . xvii . bor.
Tc̃ 7 p̊ . iiii . s . m̂ . ii . sēp . ii . car in dn̄io . Tc̃ p̊ vi . car hoūm p̊ 7 m̂ . iiii.
7 xiiii . ac̃ . p̃ti . silu . lxxx . por . iii . mol . m̂ . ii . 7 dim̃ . pisc̃ . qn̄ . rec̃e
it . r̃ . m̂ . i . sēp . vi . añ . tc̃ lxxx . por m̂ . xxxiiii . tc̃ . l . ou . m̂ . lx.
sēp . xx . cap̃ . tc̃ vi . uasa apū . m̂ . xii . 7 ii . libi hões . dim̃ . car tr̃æ.
tc̃ 7 p̊ . i . car̃ . 7 dim̃ . m̂ . i . 7 . iii . ac̃ p̃ti . 7 . ii . libi hões dim̃ . car̃ . tr̃e.
sēp . i . car̃ . 7 ii . ac̃ p̃ti . silu . v . por . Tc̃ Val . iiii . lib m̂ . vi . lib 7 xvi . đ.
Isti . ii . libi hões . Val . vi . sol . 7 ht . i . leug iñ long 7 dim̃ . in lat
7 redd . v . d . in geltū de hundret . de . xx . s̃t . ⫻ In Witeingeham

234 a
teñ . ketel . i . lib hō t . r . e . dim̃ car tr̃e 7 . iii . ac̃.
m̂ tenet . Boter . sēp . i . uilts . 7 . x . bor . sēp . i . cã in dn̄io . 7 . i . car̃ hoūm
7 . iii . ac̃ p̃ti . sēp . i . mol . sēp . iiii . añ . 7 vi; por . tc̃ 7 . p̊ . val . xx . sol.
7 m̂ . xxx . s̃t ⫻ Heueringalanda . teñ . Goduuinus ; i . lib hōmo t . e r.
i , car tr̃e . tc̃ p̊ . iii . uilt . m̂ . ii . sēp . iii . bor ; m̂ . iii . s . sēp . ii . car in dn̄io.
tc̃ . i . car̃ hoūm . 7 p̊ 7 m̂ dim̃ . 7 viii . ac̃ p̃ti . silua . xxx . por . 7 dim̃ pisc̃e.
sēp . ii . r̃ . 7 . v . añ . Tc̃ . xxx . por . m̂ . xx . tc̃ . xl . ou m̂ . lxxx . sēp . cap̃.
7 xx . uasa . apū . 7 iii . soc̃ . v . ac̃ tr̃e . sēp . Ual . lx . sol . i . ecclã . x . ac̃.
⫻ In eadē . teñ . Goduuinus . t . r . e . e . ac̃ tr̃e . sēp . ii . Uilt . Tc̃ 7 p̊ . iii . bor
m̂ nult tc̃ . i . cã . in dn̄io p̊ . 7 m̂ nill . sēp . i . car hoūm . 7 viii . ac̃ p̃ti . silu . xx . por.

The Hundred of EYNSFORD

27 Ketel, 1 free man, held WHITWELL before 1066, 2 c. of land and 15 acres as a manor.
    Then and later 8 villagers, now 7. Always 17 smallholders. Then and later 4 slaves, now 2.
    Always 2 ploughs in lordship.
    Then and later 6 men's ploughs, later and now 4. Meadow, 14 acres; woodland, 80 pigs. 3 mills, now 2. ½ fishery. When he acquired it 2 cobs, now 1. Always 6 head of cattle. Then 80 pigs, now 34. Then 50 sheep, now 60. Always 20 goats. Then 6 beehives, now 12.
    Also 2 free men, ½ c. of land. Then and later 1½ ploughs, now 1. Meadow, 3 acres.
    Also 2 free men, ½ c. of land. Always 1 plough; meadow, 2 acres; woodland, 5 pigs.
Value then £4; now £6 16d.
Value of those 2 free men, 6s.
It has 1 league in length and ½ in width; it pays 5d towards tax of the Hundred of 20s.

28 In WITCHINGHAM 1 free man, Ketel, held before 1066, ½ c. of land and 3 acres. Now Boteric holds.
    Always 1 villager; 10 smallholders.
    Always 1 plough in lordship; 1 men's plough; meadow, 3 acres; always 1 mill. Always 4 head of cattle; 6 pigs.
Value then and later 20s; now 30s.

29 Godwin, 1 free man, held HAVERINGLAND before 1066, 1 c. of land.
    Then and later 3 villagers, now 2. Always 3 smallholders. Now 3 slaves.
    Always 2 ploughs in lordship. Then 1 men's plough, later and now ½. Meadow, 8 acres; woodland, 30 pigs; ½ fishery. Always 2 cobs, 5 head of cattle. Then 30 pigs, now 20. Then 40 sheep, now 80. Always goats; 20 beehives.
    Also 3 Freemen, 5 acres of land.
Value always 60s.
    1 church, 10 acres.
In the same Godwin held before 1066, 100 acres of land.
    Always 2 villagers. Then and later 3 smallholders, now none.
    Then 1 plough in lordship, later and now none. Always 1 men's plough; meadow, 8 acres; woodland, 20 pigs.

Et . I . foc̃ . XI . ac̃ . tr̃e . sẽp . Val . xx . fol . ⁋ In eadẽ tẽn . Edric̹ . I . lib̃ hõ t . e . r.
c . ac̃ tr̃e . m̃ tenet herluin . sẽp . III . bor . tc̃ . I . s . tc̃ : I . cã . in dñio . p̹ nullꝯ
m̃ . I . 7 . II . foc̃ . XVI . ac̃ tr̃e . 7 XVI . ac̹ p̃ti . fenp dim̃ cã . filu . xx . por . m̃ .
IIII r̃ . 7 VII . añ . 7 . VIII . por . 7 LXXXV . ou . sẽp . val xx . fol . ⁋ In eadẽ tẽn
Vlketel . t̃ . r . e . dim̃ car tr̃e . m̃ tene . Rañ . tc̃ . IIII . bor . p̹ 7 . m̃ . III . tc̃
I . car̃ in dñio p̹ 7 m̃ . dim̃ . 7 vr̃ . ac̹ . p̃ti . filu . XL . por . 7 ual . xx . fol . 7 h̃t . I .
leug̃ in long̃ . 7 in lato . 7 reddit . VII . d̃ . in geldum . regis . ⁋ In Nortuna
tẽn . Sc̃s Edmund̹ . t . r . e . II . car̃ tr̃e . sẽp . VIII . vill . tc̃ . VIII . bor .
m̃ . XVI . femp̹ I . car̃ in dñio . Tc̃ 7 p̹ . III . car̃ hoũm . m̃ . II . 7 VIII . ac̹ p̃ti .
filu . xxx . por . sẽp . VI . añ . 7 . VI . por . 7 XII . cap̃ . tc̃ 7 p̹ . val . xx . fol .

m̃ xxx.   H̃ . DE TAUERHÃ . In Faltorp . tẽn . Goduinus
xx . ac̹ . sẽp . I . uills . 7 VIII . bor . sẽp . dim̃ . car̃ 7 II . ac̹ p̃ti . 7 ual . x . fol . hoc
jacet in hauinkelanda.

H̃ DE SVD ERPINCHAM . Scotohu tẽn . ketel . t̃ . r . e . II . car̃ .

234 b

tr̃e 7 dim̃ . m̃ tenet Rog̃ , sẽp . VIII . bor .
7 . II . car̃ . in dñio tc̃ . I . car̃ hoũm . 7 m̃ . fim̃ilit̃ 7 VI ac̹ . p̃ti .
Silua . V . por . 7 tc̃ tc̃ia pars . mol . tc̃ . III . por . m̃ . IIII .
7 xx . ou . 7 . III . uafa apũ 7 . VI . foc̃ . XLII . ac̃ tr̃e . sẽp . III . car̃ .
Tc̃ ual . xx . fol . m̃ . XL . Huic . manerio addidit Wiehnoc . II . foc̃
sc̃i benedic̃ti . de XVIII . ac̃ terre . quos idẽ tenet . Tc̃ . I . car̃ .
modo dim̃ . 7 s̃t in eodẽm p̃tio .

Also 1 Freeman, 11 acres of land.
Value always 20s.
In the same Edric, 1 free man, held before 1066, 100 acres of land. Now Herlwin holds.
> Always 3 smallholders. Then 1 slave.
> Then 1 plough in lordship, later none, now 1.
> Also 2 Freemen, 16 acres of land.
>> Meadow, 16 acres. Always ½ plough; woodland, 20 pigs. Now 4 cobs; 7 head of cattle; 8 pigs; 85 sheep.

Value always 20s.
In the same Ulfketel held before 1066, ½ c. of land. Now Ranulf holds.
> Then 4 smallholders, later and now 3.
> Then 1 plough in lordship, later and now ½. Meadow, 6 acres; woodland, 40 pigs.

Value 20s.
> It has 1 league in length and in width; it pays 7d towards the King's tax.

30 In (Wood) NORTON St. Edmund held before 1066, 2 c. of land.
> Always 8 villagers. Then 8 smallholders, now 16.
> Always 1 plough in lordship. Then and later 3 men's ploughs, now 2. Meadow, 8 acres; woodland, 30 pigs. Always 6 head of cattle; 6 pigs; 12 goats.

Value then and later 20s; now 30.

The Hundred of TAVERHAM

31 Godwin holds 20 acres in FELTHORPE.
> Always 1 villager; 8 smallholders.
> Always ½ plough; meadow, 2 acres.

Value 10s.
This appertains in Haveringland.

The Hundred of SOUTH ERPINGHAM

32 Ketel held SCOTTOW before 1066, 2½ c. of land. Roger now holds.   234 b
> Always 8 smallholders.
> 2 ploughs in lordship. Then 1 men's plough, now the same.
>> Meadow, 6 acres; woodland, 5 pigs. Then one-third of a mill.
>> Then 3 pigs, now 4. 20 sheep; 3 beehives.
> Also 6 Freemen, 42 acres of land; always 3 ploughs.

Value then 20s; now 40.
To this manor Wihenoc added 2 Freemen of St. Benedict's, at 18 acres of land, whom he also holds. Then 1 plough, now ½. It is in the same valuation.

In inghewurda . I . lib hō
heroldi dim̄ car̄ tr̄e q̇s idē tenet . sēp vi . bor . 7 . i . car̄ in dn̄io.
7 . I . car̄ hoūm . 7 . II . foc̄ . IIII . ac̄ . 7 . II . ac̄ p̄ti . filu . v . por . 7 dim̄
mol . 7 xxx . ou̇ . 7 ual . xv . fol . 7 ht̄ . x . q̇r̄ . in lonḡ . 7 viii.
in . lato . 7 xiii . đ . de gelto.
In Tortuna tenet Herluuiṅ . dim̄ car̄ tr̄e . sēp . v . bor.
7 . I . fer̄ . 7 . I . cā . in dn̄io 7 dim̄ . hoūm . IIII . ac̄ p̄ti . 7 ual . x . fol.
In eadē idē . II . foc̄ Heroldi de cauftuna . lx . ac̄ tr̄e . 7 . II . bor.
sēp . I . car̄ . 7 . III . p̄ti . 7 ual xii . fol . 7 ht̄ dim̄ leuḡ, 7 dim̄.
in lato . 7 vii . đ . de ḡ . In BANINCHĀ tenet Roger . I.
uill̄s . de cauftuna . xvi . ac̄ . II . fol . ual . hoc inuafit . Wihenoc
7 reddebat . v . fol . in cauftuna ⸵ idē . uill̄s ⸵

H̄ Tonefteda . In Slaleia . tenet idē . xx . ac̄ quas teñ
Scheit in dn̄io . de fcotohou . femp . I . uill̄s 7 ē in p̄tio de
Scothou . In Vrdeftada tenet idē . III . ac̄ 7 in eadē p̄tio.
Om̄s eccl̄e funt in p̄tio c̄ maneriis.

H̄ . de NORWIC . Ewicman teñ . t̄ . e . r . I . car̄, 7 dim̄ . Sub
ftigando 7 xvi . ac̄ p̄aftura 7 vii . ac̄ p̄ti . m̄ Raipnaldus fili iuonis.
tc̄ 7 p̄ . I . car̄ . m̄ . II . 7 . c . ou̇ . sēp . ual . xxx . fol.

33 In INGWORTH 1 free man of Harold's, ½ c. of land which he also holds.
>   Always 6 smallholders.
>   1 plough in lordship; 1 men's plough.
>   Also 2 Freemen, 4 acres; meadow, 2 acres. Woodland, 5 pigs; ½ mill; 30 sheep.
>   Value 15s.
>   It has 10 furlongs in length and 8 in width, tax of 13d.

34 Herlwin holds in THURTON, ½ c. of land.
>   Always 5 smallholders; 1 slave.
>   1 plough in lordship; ½ men's [plough]; meadow, 4 acres.
>   Value 10s.
>   In the same he also (holds); 2 Freemen of Harold's from Cawston, 60 acres of land.
>   2 smallholders.
>   Always 1 plough; meadow, 3 acres.
>   Value 12s.
>   It has ½ league in length and ½ in width, tax of 7d.

35 In BANNINGHAM Roger holds.
>   1 villager from Cawston, 16 acres.
>   Value 2s.
>   Wihenoc annexed this. The villager also paid 5s in Cawston.

TUNSTEAD Hundred

36 In SLOLEY he also holds 20 acres which Skeet held in the lordship of Scottow.
>   Always 1 villager.
>   It is in the valuation of Scottow.
>   In WORSTEAD he also holds 3 acres.
>   In the same valuation.
>   All the churches are in the valuation with the manors.

The Hundred of NORWICH

37 Ewicman held 1½ c. of land before 1066, under Stigand.
>   Pasture, 16 acres; meadow, 7 acres.
>   Now Reynold son of Ivo (holds).
>   Then and later 1 plough, now 2. 100 sheep.
>   Value always 30s.

TRA Radulfi . detoenie . H̃ de grenehou . Nechetuña teñ -
Radulfus quā tenuit herold . t . r . e . Tc̄ & semp . xxxii . uilt . & xi .
bor̃ . & vi . ser̃ . & iiii . car̃ . ĩ dñio . & x . hoūm . Silua ad . ⊙ . por̃ .
xx . ac̃ . p̃ti . 7 i . mol . 7 i . salina . Qn̄ rec̄ . iiii . r̃ . & m̃ . xix . añ . 7 c .
por̃ . 7 c . oues & . v . 7 lxxx . cap̃ . i . eccła De . xxxvi . ac̃ & ual &
xxxvi . đ . 7 v . socheɱ . ibi manent . habent̃ . v . car̃ . 7 hab . ĩ
lungo . i . m̃ . & đ . ĩ lato . 7 redđ . ĩ gelt . ix . đ . qn̄ . h̃ . scotat . xx . s̄ .
7 i . socheɱ . ĩ bradenhā . Semp . đ . car . trãe . 7 i . car . 7 sub ipso .
viii . socheɱ tentes . đ . car̃ . trẽ . 7 Semp . i . car . Silua ad . xx .
por̃ . iiii . ac̃ . p̃ti . ⫽ 7 ĩ pichenhā . i . beruita . ii . car̃ . ĩ dñio . Tc̄
& p̃t . viii . uilt . m̃ . v . m̃ . ii . bor̃ . Tc̄ & p̃t . hoūm . i . car̃ . m̃ . đ .
7 vi . soc̄ . sup . xx . ac̃ . habent . i . car̃ . Silua ad . xx . por̃ . iiii .
★ ac̃ . p̃ti . Qn̄ rec̄ . iueñ . ii . r̃ . & xviii . p̃ . 7 xxxvi . oues . & m̃ .
  .i. eccła de xvii . acr'. Sił-ad xvii. đ.
★ ⫽ 7 al . beruita . q̃ uocant cressingahā . Tc̄ & sẽp . v . uilt .
& i . bor̃ . & ii . ser . i . car . in dñio . 7 ii . soc̄ . it . omes . ii . car .
Siua . viii . por̃ . iii . ac̃r . p̃ti . i . mol . i . pisc̄ . Sẽp . i . r̃ . 7 ii .
   . i . eccła de xv . acr'. Val . xv . đ.
añ . lx . oues . ii . min⁹ . ⫽ 7 in paruo Cressingaham . al beruita .
Sẽp . xx . uilt . 7 vii . bor̃ . iiii . ser̃ . ii . car̃ . ĩ dñio semp .
7 houm . vi . car̃ . 7 vi . soc̄ . tenuerunt . ii . car̃ & tenent .
x . ac̃r . p̃ti . i . mol . Qn̄ rec̄ . ii . r̃ . & m̃ . xxxi . p̃ . xxxii . oues .
vi . añ . 7 hab . in longo . i . m̃ . & đ . ĩ lato . 7 redđ ĩ gel . iii . đ .

LAND OF RALPH OF TOSNY

The Hundred of (South) GREENHOE

1 Ralph holds NECTON which Harold held before 1066.
Then and always 32 villagers, 11 smallholders; and 6 slaves.
4 ploughs in lordship; 10 men's [ploughs].
Woodland for 1,000 pigs; meadow, 20 acres; 1 mill; 1 salt-house.
When he acquired it and now 4 cobs. Now 19 head of cattle;
100 pigs; 105 sheep; and 80 goats.
1 church, at 36 acres;
value 36d.
Also 5 Freemen dwell there; they have 5 ploughs.
It has 1 mile in length and ½ in width; it pays 9d in tax when the Hundred pays 20s scot-tax.

2 Also 1 Freeman in BRADENHAM; always ½ c. of land; and 1 plough.
Under him 8 Freemen who hold ½ c. of land; always 1 plough.
Woodland for 20 pigs; meadow, 4 acres.

3 Also in PICKENHAM, 1 outlier, 2 ploughs in lordship.
Then and later 8 villagers, now 5. Now 2 smallholders.
Then and later 1 men's plough, now ½.
Also 6 Freemen on 20 acres; they have 1 plough.
Woodland for 20 pigs; meadow, 4 acres. When he acquired it he found 2 cobs, 18 pigs; 36 sheep; now (the same).
1 church at 17 acres;
value 17d.

4 Another outlier which they call (Great) CRESSINGHAM.
Then and always 5 villagers; 1 smallholder; 2 slaves.
1 plough in lordship.
Also 2 Freemen.
Between them all 2 ploughs.
Woodland, 8 pigs; meadow, 3 acres; 1 mill; 1 fishery. Always 1 cob; 2 head of cattle; 60 sheep less 2.
1 church at 15 acres;
value 15d.

5 In LITTLE CRESSINGHAM another outlier.
Always 20 villagers; 7 smallholders; 4 slaves.
Always 2 ploughs in lordship; 6 men's ploughs. Also 6 Freemen held 2 ploughs and they hold them (now).
Meadow, 10 acres; 1 mill. When he acquired it 2 cobs. Now 31 pigs; 32 sheep; 6 head of cattle.
It has 1 mile in length and ½ in width; it pays 3d in tax.

In caldachota ał beruita. ubi habet. rex fochā & fachā.
ı. car̄ t̄re. Semp. ıı. uiłł. ıı. bor̄. ı. ſer̄. 7 ııı. fochē. Tc̄ ī
dn̄io. ı. car̄. m̄. d. ı. car̄. hoūm. Qn̄. rec̄. ı. r̄. lx. oues.

235 b
m̄. xxıııı. oues. 7 hab̄. ī longo. d. ł. & ıııı. q̄r in lato. 7 rędd.
ī get. c̄ tentib. ī ea. v. d.
In culeſtorpa. ııı. foc̄. de qb3 tenebat rex focha & facha. & hab̄t.
ı. car̄ t̄ræ. 7 ı. car̄. 7 ı. bor̄.
In bodeneia. ııııı. fochēm̄. ı. carr̄ t̄re & ı. car̄. 7 ı. uiłł. ıı. ac̄r̄.
p̄ti. & fup eos hab̄ rex. focha & facha. 7 de. ı. moł. vııı. d. Hoc
totum fimul reddebat. h. vı. noc̄tes de firma. M̊ reddit. lx.
lib̄. ad penſū *H̄*. de Grimeſhou. In eſtereſtuna. ten̄. ı. lib̄ hō.
xxx. ac̄ t̄ræ. tc̄. dim̄ car̄. tc̄. uał. ıı. soł. m̄. xıı. d.
Wanelvnd. *H̄*. In cherebrœc. tenuit herold. t̄. r. e. ııı. car̄.
t̄re. bereuuita ī nechetuna. semp. ı. car̄ in dn̄io. tc̄. ı. uiłł.
sep. xııı. foc̄. 7. ı. ſ. xvı. ac̄. p̄ti. & ıı. car̄ hoūm filua. ccc.
por̄. tc̄. ı. r. & ııı. uac̄. 7 ıx. por̄. & ē in p̄tio deneketuna.
Lawendic. *H̄*. In Frouueſham. xvı. foc̄. heroldi. t̄. r. e.
ııı. car̄ t̄ræ. sēp. xıı. bor̄. 7 vı. ac̄. p̄ti. tc̄. ııı. car̄. m̄. ııııı. filū.
lx. por̄. femp. ı. moł. & ē in p̄tio de neketuna. Eudo filiꝰ clamahoc habuit. ı. car̄ t̄ræ. de iłł. ıııı. liberationem̄ quā diu uixit.
& eandē tenuit. Rad̄ de bella fago. m̄ eam h̄t. Rad̄ de toeni
ineketuna ubi jacuit t̄. r. e.
In dunham. ı. foc̄. heroldi. xxx. ac̄ t̄re. t̄. r. e. femp. bor̄.
ııııı. femp. ı. car̄. & hoc ē in p̄tio de neketuna.

6   In CALDECOTE another outlier where the King has the full jurisdiction, 1 c. of land.
    Always 2 villagers; 2 smallholders; 1 slave; 3 Freemen.
    Then in lordship 1 plough, now ½. 1 men's plough.
    When he acquired it 1 cob; 60 sheep. Now 24 sheep.   235 b
    It has ½ league in length and 4 furlongs in width; it pays in tax with those who hold on it, 5d.

7   In CUSTTHORPE 3 Freemen of whom the King held the full jurisdiction. They have 1 c. of land; 1 plough; 1 smallholder.

8   In BODNEY 4 Freemen; 1 c. of land; 1 plough.
    1 villager.
    Meadow, 2 acres.
    The King has the full jurisdiction over them.
    From 1 mill, 8d.
    All together this paid 6 nights' revenue to H(arold); now it pays £60 by weight.

The Hundred of GRIMSHOE
9   In STURSTON 1 free man holds 30 acres of land. Then ½ plough. Value then 2s; now 12d.

WAYLAND Hundred
10 In CARBROOKE, an outlier in Necton, Harold held 3 c. of land before 1066. Always 1 plough in lordship.
    Then 1 villager. Always 13 Freemen; 1 slave.
    Meadow, 16 acres; 2 men's ploughs; woodland, 300 pigs.
        Then 1 cob; 3 cows; 9 pigs.
    It is in the valuation of Necton.

LAUNDITCH Hundred
11 In FRANSHAM 16 Freemen of Harold's before 1066, 3 c. of land.
    Always 12 smallholders.
    Meadow, 6 acres. Then 3 ploughs, now 4. Woodland, 60 pigs; always 1 mill.
    It is in the valuation of Necton.
    Eudo son of Clamahoc had 1 c. of land of these 3 by livery as long as he lived. Ralph of Beaufour held the same; now Ralph of Tosny has it in (the lands of) Necton where it appertained before 1066.

12 In DUNHAM 1 Freeman of Harold's, 30½ acres of land before 1066.
    Always 4 smallholders.
    Always 1 plough.
    This is in the valuation of Necton.

In Goduic tenuit . I . lib̃ . regis . ẽ . hõ t̃ . r . e . I . cař . tr̃æ . semp.
vi . uiłł . 7 vii . bor . 7 . ix . ač . p̃ti . semp . ii . cař . silũ . cc . por.
& I . soč . IIII . ač tr̃æ . 7 ẽ in p̃tio de neketuna . & ht̃ . vi . q̃ř
in longo . 7 . IIII . in lato . 7 vi . d̃ . 7 . I . obulum de gelto . hañc tr̃am
tenet . Rad . inneketuna sed ñ jacuit in neketuna . t̃ . r . e.
nec tẽp̃ı . heroldi . & Rog̃ bigot eam reuocat de dono reg̃ . &
reuocat libatorem.

H̃ . DE CLAKESLOSA . In scingham . II . libi . h̃ . LXXX . ač tr̃æ .
t̃ . r . e . tč . I . cař m̃ . dim̃ . & jacent in naketuna.

H̃ . 7 dim̃ de fredrebruge . In Waltuna . II soč . in acre . xxx .
ač . 7 v . bor . 7 ẽ in p̃tio de nachetuna.
Acre tenuit herold . t . r . e . I . bereuuita ĩ nechetuna . III . cař
tr̃æ . semp . vi . uiłł . 7 viii . bor . 7 ii . ser . 7 IIII . ač p̃ti . semp.
ii . cař . in dñio . 7 I .   cař . hoũ silua . xl . por . 7 iii.
mol̃ . 7 dimus . 7 I . pisč .   7 v . sał . semp . v . ań . 7 xviii.
por . Tč . c . oũ . m̃ CLXV . Huic tr̃e jacent semp xvii . soč .
ccccv . ač tr̃æ . 7 xiiii . bor . 7 ii . ač p̃ti . semp . v . cař . In ead.
teñ tbn sub heroldo . ii . cař tr̃æ . t̃ . r . e . Tč xiii . bor . 7 m̃ ;
7 iiii . ač p̃ti . tč . ii . cař in d̃ . m̃ . i . 7 dim̃ . tč . i . p̃ cař hoũm
m̃ . ii . boues semp . i . mol̃ . huic tr̃e jacent . iiii . soč . xxx .
ač . sẽp dim̃ . cař . Et . i . lib̃ hõ in thorp . LX . tr̃æ . 7 iii . bor.
7 dim̃ . cař . Et in ketuna . iii . soč . LX . ač tr̃e . 7 i . bor . 7 iiii.
ač p̃ti . 7 i . cař . & in Lena . v . soč . LXXX . ač tr̃e . 7 iii . bor.
7 v . sał . 7 ii . cař . Et estuuinč . ii . soč . viii . ač tr̃e.
Tota ACRA . ht̃ . I . leug̃ . in long̃ 7 lat̃ . 7 lat̃ . 7 reddit xvi.
d̃ . de xx . soł . de gelto . Hóc totũ sup̃ı ẽ in p̃tio de naketuna.

13 In GODWICK 1 free (man) of King Edward's held 1 c. of land before 1066.
Always 6 villagers; 7 smallholders.
Meadow, 9 acres. Always 2 ploughs; woodland, 200 pigs.
Also 1 Freeman, 4 acres of land.
It is in the valuation of Necton. 236 a
It has 6 furlongs in length and 4 in width, tax of 6½d.
Ralph holds this land in (the lands of) Necton but it did not appertain in Necton before 1066 or in the time of Harold. Roger Bigot claims it (as) of the King's gift and vouches (the King) his deliverer.

The Hundred of CLACKCLOSE
14 In SHINGHAM 2 free (men of Harold's), 80 acres of land before 1066. Then 1 plough, now ½. They appertain in Necton.

The Hundred and a Half of FREEBRIDGE
15 In (East) WALTON 2 Freemen in Acre, 30 acres; 5 smallholders. It is in the valuation of Necton.

16 Harold held ACRE, 1 outlier in Necton, before 1066, 3 c. of land.
Always 6 villagers; 8 smallholders; 2 slaves.
Meadow, 4 acres. Always 2 ploughs in lordship; 1 men's plough; woodland, 40 pigs; 3½ mills; 1 fishery; 5 salt-houses. Always 5 head of cattle; 18 pigs. Then 100 sheep, now 165.
17 Freemen have always appertained to this land, 405 acres of land. 14 smallholders; meadow, 2 acres; always 5 ploughs.
In the same Thorbern held 2 c. of land under Harold before 1066.
Then and now 13 smallholders.
Meadow, 4 acres. Then 2 ploughs in lordship, now 1½. Then and later 1 men's plough, now 2 oxen. Always 1 mill.
4 Freemen appertained to this land, 30 acres; always ½ plough.

17 Also 1 free man in (Gayton) THORPE, 60 [acres] of land; 3 smallholders. ½ plough.

18 Also in NECTON 3 Freemen, 60 acres of land.
1 smallholder.
Meadow, 3 acres; 1 plough.

19 Also in LYNN 5 Freemen, 80 acres of land.
3 smallholders.
5 salt-houses. 2 ploughs.

20 Also EAST WINCH 2 Freemen, 8 acres of land.

The whole of Acre has 1 league in length and in width, of a 20s tax it pays 16d.
All the above is in the valuation of Necton.

H̄. Grimeſhou . In icheburna . I . ſoc̄ . horoldi . xxx.

236 b
ac̄ tr̄e . & ē app̄tiatū in neketuna.

WANELVND . H̄ . In Breccles . I . heroldi . xL . ac̄ tr̄e . 7
dim̄ . car̄ . 7 I . uiłłs . & ē in p̄tio de neketuna.

H̄ . de SCREPHAM . Wretham tenuit . Herold t̄ . r . e . II.
ca̓ tr̄æ . ſemp . xII . uiłłi . vIII . bor . 7 III . ſer . 7 vIII . ac̓ p̄ti.
ſemp . II'. car̄ . in dn̄io . 7 IIII . car̄ . hoūm . ſilu . xxx . por . 7 I.
r . 7 xII . por . Lxxx . ou̓ . In alio Wertham . III . car̄ tr̄e . tenuit
idē . ſēp . xI . uiłłi . 7 Ix . bor . 7 IIII . s . 7 vI . ac̓ p̄ti . tc̄ . III . car̄
in dn̄io . p̓ . 7 m̄ . II . 7 ͬcia poſſet eē . ſemp . IIII . car̄ . hoūm.
7 . I . mol̄ . 7 . I . r . 7 xxI . por . 7 Lxxxi . ou̓ . In alio Were-
-tham . tenuit idē . IIII . car̄   tr̄e . t̄ . r . e . tc̄ 7 p̓.
★ vIII . uiłłi . p̓ . 7 m̄ . 7 III .   ſēp . IIII . por . 7 II.
. ſ . 7 . II . ac̄ . p̄ti . ſēp . II . car̄ in dn̄io . tc̄ 7 p̓ . III . car̄ hoūm.
7 m̄ . I . 7 III . poſſunt eē . 7 II . ſoc̄ unā car̄ tr̄æ . 7 . xII . ac̓.
vIII . ac̓ p̄ti . 7 . v . bor . 7 . Lvi . ac̄ tr̄e . 7 . I . car̄ . & dim̄ . Hec
tria ſunt bereuuite in neketuna . 7 . in p̄tio . Totum ht.
II . leuḡ . in lonḡ . 7 . II . in lato . & . xx . d̄ . de gelto.

237 a
H̄ . DE GRANAHOU . Tr̄æ . Hugo de munteforti . Budeneia   :XXIII:
ten̄ . Bond . Tc̄ . vIII . uiłł . 7 . p̓ . IIII . m̄ . vII . bor . Tc̄ . vI . ſer.
m̄ . III . tc̄ in dn̄io . III . car̄ . & p̓ . II . m̄ . I . Tc̄ łt hēs . III . car̄ . m̄
d . Silua ad c . por . v . ac̓ p̄ti . I . mol̄ . & q̄rta pars . de al.
Qn̄ rec̄ . I . r̄ . m̄ . II . tc̄ . xIII . an̄ . m̄ . III . tc̄ . xLI . p̄ . m̄ . Ix . tc̄
: LI . oues . m̄ xI . Tc̄ . xvI . cap̄ . m̄ . v . 7 hab . I longo . I . ł . II.
q̄r . minus . 7 . IIII . q̄r . in lato . 7 redd in gel̄ . vIII . d̄ . cum tenen-
-tib; I ea . Tc̄ uał . c . s̄ . m̄ . Lx . s̄.

GRIMSHOE Hundred

21 In ICKBURGH 1 Freeman of Harold's, 30 acres of land.
It is assessed in Necton.   236 b

WAYLAND Hundred

22 In BRECKLES 1 [man] of Harold's, 40 acres of land; ½ plough.
1 villager.
It is in the valuation of Necton.

The Hundred of SHROPHAM

23 Harold held WRETHAM before 1066, 2 c. of land.
Always 12 villagers; 8 smallholders; 3 slaves.
Meadow, 8 acres. Always 2 ploughs in lordship; 4 men's ploughs; woodland, 30 pigs; 1 cob, 12 pigs; 80 sheep.
In the other WRETHAM he also held 3 c. of land.
Always 11 villagers; 9 smallholders; 4 slaves.
Meadow, 6 acres. Then 3 ploughs in lordship, later and now 2 and there could be a third. Always 4 men's ploughs.
1 mill; 1 cob, 21 pigs; 81 sheep.
In the other WRETHAM he also held 4 c. of land before 1066.
Then and later 8 villagers; later and now 3. Always 4 smallholders and 2 slaves.
Meadow, 2 acres; always 2 ploughs in lordship. Then and later 3 men's ploughs, now 1 but there can be 3.
Also 2 Freemen, 1 c. of land and 12 acres; meadow, 8 acres.
5 smallholders; 56 acres of land; 1½ ploughs.

These three are outliers in Necton and (they are) in the valuation. The whole has 2 leagues in length and 2 in width, tax of 20d.

23 LANDS OF HUGH OF MONTFORT 237 a

The Hundred of (South) GREENHOE

1 Bondi held BODNEY.
Then 8 villagers, later 4. Now 7 smallholders. Then 6 slaves, now 3.
Then 3 ploughs in lordship, later 2, now 1. Then 3 ploughs between the men, now ½.
Woodland for 100 pigs; meadow, 5 acres; 1 mill and a ¼ of another. When he acquired it 1 cob, now 2. Then 13 head of cattle, now 3. Then 41 pigs, now 9. Then 51 sheep, now 11. Then 16 goats, now 5.
It has 1 league less 2 furlongs in length and 4 furlongs in width, it pays 8d in tax with those who hold in it.
Value then 100s; now 60s.

Langafordā tenꝰ Bund. t.r.e. Tc. 7; p̊. xxi. uiłł; m̄. xvii.
Tc. ix. borꝰ. & vi. ſer & m̄. Semp in dn̄io. ii. carꝰ. Tc hoūm
& p̊. iiii; m̄. ii. Silua ad. c. por. xxv. acꝰ pti. ii. moł. i.
piſc. Qn̄. rec. ii; m̄. nut. tc. iiii. an̄. m̄. i. Tc xvii. porꝰ.
m̄. ix. tc. lxxi. oues. m̄. xli. m̄. ii; uas apū. 7 hab. i longo:
i. m̄. & d. i lato. 7 reddit. i geł. iiii d; qn̄. h̄. redd. xx. s̄
Tc uał. vi; i.m̄. redd. c. s̄. & v. s̄.

H̄ de galgou; Suthcreich. ten hug; tenꝰ qᵐ. Bund. ii; carr
tr̄e. Semp. iiii. uiłł. 7 vi. bor. Tc. iiii. ſer. m̄. ii. Sep̄
in dn̄io. ii. carꝰ. Tc hoūm. iii. carꝰ. m̄. ii. ſ; ibi poſſunt
eē. tc. iiii; rꝰ. tc. xx. por. m̄. vii. tc. cc. ou. m̄. lxxx.
Tc uał. lx. ſoł. m̄. iiii; lib. 7 hab. i. ngꝰ i longꝰ. 7 ał i latꝰ.
7 redd i gełt. iiii. ſoł.

H̄. de Brodercros. In brunehā ten idē. qm ten
Bondꝰ. lib ho. t. r. e. ii. carr. tr̄æ. Semp. xiiii.
bor. Semp i dn̄io. ii; carꝰ; Tc. hoūm. i; carꝰ.

modo. d. Silua ad; viii; porꝰ ᵗ·ᵃᶜ' ᵖᵗⁱ. i. moł. Tc. i. ſał. Semp. ii. rꝰ.
Tc. vii; por. m̄. iii. Tc. c. ou. m̄. xx. 7. vii. ſoc. de. lx. acꝰ tr̄e.
Tc. i. carꝰ 7 d. m̄. i. tc uał. iiii. lib. m̄ ſimił. In hoc hundret
redd. iii; ſol. de geł. 7 in alio menſurata.
In reinehā ten. Bondꝰ. t. r. e. ii. carrꝰ. tr̄æ. Sep̄. iiii. uiłł.
7. xiiii. borꝰ. 7; iiii. ſer. 7 in dn̄io. ii. carꝰ. 7 hoūm. i. carꝰ.
Silua ad. c; xx; por. vi. acꝰ pti. ii. moł. i. ſalin̄. Sep̄. iii. rꝰ.
7 iiii. an̄; 7 vi. por. 7. c. ou; Tc. ii. uas ap. 7; xiiii. ſoc. dimidꝰ
carr tr̄æ. 7 xv. bor. Sep̄; i. carꝰ. 7 d. vii; acꝰ pti. Huic man̄.
; i. beruita. ſutreinehā de. i. carꝰ tr̄æ. Tc. v. bor. m̄. iiii. 7. ii.
ſer. Sep̄. i dn̄io. i. carꝰ. Tc hoūm. i. carꝰ. m̄. d. v. acꝰ pti. i. moł.
Tc. iii. rꝰ. Sep̄. vi. por.

2 Bondi held LANGFORD before 1066.
> Then and later 21 villagers, now 17. Then and now 9 smallholders; 6 slaves.
> Always 2 ploughs in lordship. Then and later 4 men's [ploughs], now 2.
> Woodland for 100 pigs; meadow, 25 acres; 2 mills; 1 fishery. When he acquired it 2 [cobs], now none. Then 4 head of cattle, now 1. Then 17 pigs, now 9. Then 71 sheep, now 41. Now 2 beehives.
> It has 1 mile in length and ½ in width, it pays 4d in tax when the Hundred pays 20s.
> Value then £6; now it pays 100s and 5s.

The Hundred of GALLOW

3 Hugh holds SOUTH CREAKE which Bondi held, 2 c. of land.
> Always 4 villagers; 6 smallholders. Then 4 slaves, now 2.
> Always 2 ploughs in lordship. Then 3 men's ploughs, now 2 but there can be (another).
> Then 4 cobs. Then 20 pigs, now 7. Then 200 sheep, now 80.
> Value then 60s; now £4.
> It has 1 league in length and another in width, it pays 4s in tax.

The Hundred of BROTHERCROSS

4 In BURNHAM he also holds what Bondi, a free man, held before 1066, 2 c. of land.
> Always 14 smallholders.
> Always 2 ploughs in lordship. Then 1 men's plough, now ½.   237 b
> Woodland for 8 pigs; meadow, 1 acre; 1 mill. Then 1 salt-house; always 2 cobs. Then 7 pigs, now 3. Then 100 sheep, now 20.
> Also 7 Freemen, at 60 acres of land. Then 1½ ploughs, now 1.
> Value then £4; now the same. In this Hundred it pays tax of 3s and it is measured in another.

5 In RAYNHAM Bondi held 2 c. of land before 1066.
> Always 4 villagers; 14 smallholders; 4 slaves.
> 2 ploughs in lordship; 1 men's plough.
> Woodland for 120 pigs; meadow, 6 acres; 2 mills; 1 salt-house. Always 3 cobs; 4 head of cattle; 6 pigs; 100 sheep. Then 2 beehives.
> Also 14 Freemen, ½ c. of land. 15 smallholders; always 1½ ploughs; meadow, 7 acres.

1 outlier, SOUTH RAYNHAM, (appertains) to this manor, at 1 c. of land.
> Then 5 smallholders, now 4. 2 slaves.
> Always 1 plough in lordship. Then 1 men's plough, now ½.
> Meadow, 5 acres; 1 mill. Then 3 cobs; always 6 pigs.

In helgettina . i . foć . de . đ . cařr tře . Tć . viii . bor . m̂ . xii . Sep̄ɉ
. i . caŕ . ii . aĉ p̃ti . Tć ual . viii . liƀ . 7 p̓ . lx . s̃ . m̂ . viii . liƀ.
7 . x . fot . cū magña peña . 7 totā fcutreinahā haƀ . vi . q̃r ĩ long̃
7 iii . ĩ lat . 7 . x . in gelt

ERPINGAHĀ NORTH H̃ . Iñ rugutuñe teñ Hugo.
q̃m teñ . Bundo . i . liƀ . hõ ŧ . r . e . i . caŕ tře . Sep̄ . xii . bor.
Sep̄ . i . caŕ . ĩ dñio . & dim̃ caŕ . hoū . Silua ad xii . por . i . aĉ.
& dim̃ . p̃ti . Semp̓ . i . ř . tĉ . v . aāl . 7 m̂ . iii . tĉ . v . por.
m̂ . vii . tĉ . xx . oū . m̂ . xv . 7 . viii . foĉ . đ xxiiii . aĉ tře.
Semp . i . caŕ . tĉ 7 p̓ . ual . xx . fot . m̂ . xxx.
In befetune teñ idē . Hugo . quam teñ . Bundo.
. i . liƀ hõ . ŧ . r . e . i . caŕ tře . Semp̓ . viii . bor.

238 a

Semp . i . caŕ . ĩ dñio . 7 dim̃ . caŕ hoū . Silua ad . v . por . i . aĉ p̃ti.
Semp . i . ř . tĉ . ii . aāl . m̂ . tĉ . v . por . 7 m̂ . xi . tĉ . xx . cap̃.
m̂ . xxx . & iii . foĉ . xii . aĉ tře 7 dim̃ bor . Semp̓ dim̃ caŕ.
tĉ . 7 p̓ . ual . xx . fot . m̂ . xxx.

H̃ 7 dim̃ de clacheflofa . In marham . xxvi . foĉ q̃s teñ . Walt
sĉa adeldræda ŧ . ř . e . ad focha . tĉ . viii . bor . m̂ . viiii . Tĉ . v .
caŕ . m̂ . iiii . 7 . vi . aĉ p̃ti . Tĉ ual . lxxx . fot . p̓ . lx . m̂ . xl.
Hanc ťrā recep̃ p̓ efcangio . & eft menfurata in breui Sĉe Adeldret.

Fredeburge . H̃ . 7 dim̃ . In ilfinghetuna . ii . caŕ tře . teñ.
Bundo . ŧ . ř . e . femp . viii . bor . 7 . xv . aĉ p̃ti . Tĉ . ii . caŕ . ind̃.
Sep̄ . dim̃ . caŕ . hoū . huic mañ jac . xi . foĉ sep̄ . i . caŕ . 7 . xxx.
aĉ . de . v . ħt Stigand focā . totū ual . c . fot . In eadē tenent
idē . đ . caŕ tře . sep̄ . iiii . bor . Tĉ . i . caŕ . sep̄ . xl . aĉ . p̃ti . & ē
app̃tiata in fupiorib̧ c . fot.

6 In HELHOUGHTON 1 Freeman, at ½ c. of land.
   Then 8 smallholders, now 12.
   Always 1 plough; meadow, 2 acres.
   Value then £8; later 60s; now £8 10s with great difficulty.
   The whole of South Raynham has 6 furlongs in length and 3 in width; 10[d] in tax.

NORTH ERPINGHAM Hundred

7 In ROUGHTON Hugh also holds what Bondi, 1 free man, held before 1066, 1 c. of land.
   Always 12 smallholders.
   Always 1 plough in lordship; ½ men's plough.
   Woodland for 12 pigs; meadow, 1½ acres. Always 1 cob. Then 5 head of cattle, now 3. Then 5 pigs, now 7. Then 20 sheep, now 15.
   Also 8 Freemen, at 24 acres of land; always 1 plough.
   Value then and later 20s; now 30.

8 In BEESTON (Regis) Hugh also holds what Bondi, 1 free man, held before 1066, 1 c. of land.
   Always 8 smallholders.
   Always 1 plough in lordship; ½ men's plough.   238 a
   Woodland for 5 pigs; meadow, 1 acre. Always 1 cob. Then and now 2 head of cattle. Then 5 pigs, now 11. Then 20 goats, now 30.
   Also 3 Freemen, 12 acres of land; half a smallholder; always ½ plough.
   Value then and later 20s; now 30.

The Hundred and a Half of CLACKCLOSE

9 In MARHAM 26 Freemen whom Walter holds; St. Etheldreda held before 1066 at jurisdiction.
   Then 8 smallholders, now 9.
   Then 5 ploughs, now 4. Meadow, 6 acres.
   Value then 80s; later 60; now 40.
   (Hugh) acquired this land by exchange and it is measured in the return of St. Etheldreda.

FREEBRIDGE Hundred and a Half

10 In ISLINGTON Bondi held 2 c. of land before 1066.
    Always 8 smallholders.
    Meadow, 15 acres. Then 2 ploughs in lordship; always ½ men's plough.
    11 Freemen appertain to this manor, always 1 c. [of land] and 30 acres. Stigand had the jurisdiction of 5.
   Value of the whole, 100s.
   In the same the (Freemen) also hold ½ c. of land;
    always 4 smallholders.
    Then 1 plough; always meadow, 40 acres.
   It is assessed in the above 100s.

Mideltuna teñ. Aelod. quã teñ Bundo. t̄. r̄. e̓. ⁊ıı. car̃.
tr̃æ. sẽp. xıı. uiłł. 7. xvıı. bor̃. silu̓. ıııı. por. Tc̃. ıııı. f. m̃. ı.
7. xxxıı. ac̓ p̃ti. Tc̃. ıı. car̃. in dn̄io. m̃. ı. sẽp. ııı. car̓ houm
7. ı. mol. 7. ı. pisc̃. Tc̃. x. sał. m̃. vııı. Tc̃. ııı. añ. m̃. v. m̃. ı.
. ı. Tc̃. x. por. m̃. vı. Tc̃. xl. oṷ. m̃. xxxv. tc̃ uał. c. soł.
m̃. vı. lib̃. Hic jacent. ıı. sochem̃. q̓s teñ. idẽ homo. lxxxıııı.
ac̓ tc̃. ı. car̃. m̃. dim̃. & uał. v. soł. 7 poťant uende tr̃a suã

Benelai tenuit. L. Bundo p maner̓. t̄. r̄ e.
. v. car̃.tr̃æ. sẽp. xx. uiłł. 7 xıııı. bor̃.

238 b

7. v. ser̓. xx. ac̓ p̃ti. sẽp. ıı. car̃. in d̄. 7. ııı. car̃. hou̓. 7. ııı.
mol. silua. cc. por. 7 dim̃. sał. sẽp. ı. r. 7. ııı. añ. 7. x. por.
7 lxxxı. oṷ. Tc̃ uał. vııı. ł. p̓. lx. soł. m̃. vı. lib̃. Tota
ħt. vııı. q̃r in long. 7. ıııı. in łat̃. 7 reddit. vı. d̃. de. xx.
soł de gelto.

In Gaituna teñ. Rogerus. ı. car̓ terræ. q̃m teñ. Bundo.
lib̃ hō. t̄. r. e. Tc̃. vı. bor̓. 7. m̃. ııı. bor̃. 7. ı. f. 7. xıı. ac̃ p̃ti
sẽp. ı. car̓. in dn̄io. & dim̃. car̃. hou̓ & dim̃. mol
Tc̃. ııı. por̓. 7. m̃. sẽp. lx. oṷ. 7 uał. xlv. hoc. est. ı. bere-
-uuita in bilenei.

H̃. de Grimeshou. In estanforda teñ. ı. lib̃ hō. ı. car̓ tr̃æ.
Sẽp in dn̄io. ı. car̓. 7. vıı. uiłł. 7. ı. bor. ıı. ac̓ p̃ti. Sẽp. dim̃
car̃. hou̓m. 7 uał. x. soł. s̃; ipse redd̓. xv. 7 sup hunc ñ
habuit antecessor ej̓ ñ c̃md̃. tantu̓. 7 rex socham.

In Buchenham. ı. lib̃ hō. t̄. r̄. e̓. ı. car̓ tr̃æ. sẽp. ıııı.
uiłł. 7 ı. bor. 7 ıııı. ac̓ p̃ti. 7. ı. car̃ in d̄. 7 dim̃. car̃ hou̓m.
dim̃ mol. 7. vııı. soł. 7 tota ħt. ı. leug̃ in long 7 dim̃ in łat̃.
7 reddit. vııı d̃. de xx. soł de gelto. Rex 7 comes ht̃ socã.

11 Aethelwold holds MIDDLETON which Bondi held before 1066, 2 c.
of land.
  Always 12 villagers; 17 smallholders.
  Woodland, 4 pigs. Then 4 slaves, now 1. Meadow, 32 acres.
  Then 2 ploughs in lordship, now 1. Always 3 men's ploughs;
    1 mill; 1 fishery. Then 10 salt-houses, now 8. Then 3 head
    of cattle, now 5. Now 1 cob. Then 10 pigs, now 6. Then 40
    sheep, now 35.
Value then 10s; now £6.
  2 Freemen appertain here whom he also holds, 84 acres. Then
    1 plough, now ½.
Value 5s. They could sell their land.

12 L. Bondi held (West) BILNEY as a manor before 1066, 5 c. of land.
  Always 20 villagers; 14 smallholders; 5 slaves.   238 b
  Meadow, 20 acres. Always 2 ploughs in lordship; 3 men's
    ploughs; 3 mills; woodland, 200 pigs; ½ salt-house. Always
    1 cob; 3 head of cattle; 10 pigs; 81 sheep.
Value then £8; later 60s; now £6.
  The whole has 8 furlongs in length and 4 in width, of a 20s
tax it pays 6d.

13 Roger holds 1 c. of land in GAYTON which Bondi, a free man, held
before 1066.
  Then 6 smallholders. Now 3 smallholders; 1 slave.
  Meadow, 12 acres. Always 1 plough in lordship; ½ men's plough;
    ½ mill. Then and now 3 pigs; always 60 sheep.
Value 45 [s]. This is 1 outlier in (the lands of) (West) Bilney.

  The Hundred of GRIMSHOE
14 In STANFORD 1 free man holds 1 c. of land. Always 1 plough in
lordship.
  7 villagers; 1 smallholder.
  Meadow, 2 acres; always ½ men's plough.
Value 10s, but he pays 15.
  (Hugh's) predecessor had the patronage only over this man and
the King (had) the jurisdiction.

15 In BUCKENHAM (Tofts) 1 free man, 1 c. of land before 1066.
  Always 4 villagers; 1 smallholder.
  Meadow, 4 acres; 1 plough in lordship; ½ men's plough; ½ mill.
[Value] 8s.
  The whole has 1 league in length and ½ in width, of a 20s tax
it pays 8d. The King and the Earl have the jurisdiction.

H̃. de Gildecros. In Wica. tenuit. Godmundꝰ. II. carꝰ
træ. t̃. r. e. ꝑ man̄. tc̄. VII. uillī. pꝰ. 7 m̊. IIII. sēp. IIII.
borꝰ tc̄. III. s. pꝰ. 7 m̊. II. 7. III. ac. pti. sēp. II. carꝰ. in đ.
7. I. carꝰ. hom̄. silū. XII. por. 7. VII. socꝰ. LXXXX
ac tr̄e. V. bor̄ 7. I. ac p̄ti. Tc̄ 7 pꝰ.

239 a

II. carꝰ. 7 dim̄. m̊. III. sēp. I. r. Tc̄. III. an̄. m̊. II. por. sēp. LXX.
ou. Tc̄ 7 pꝰ. LX. sol. m̊. VI. lib. totū ht. I. leug in longo. 7. I.
leug. in lato. 7. XXXIIII. đ. 7. I. obol. de gelto.

LAWENDIC. H̃. Radulfus Gatelea ten̄ quam ten̄
Bundo lib hō. t̃. r. e. ꝑ man. IIII. carꝰ terre. sēp. XXIII.
uillī. tc̄. I. s. XXX. ac p̄ti. sēp. II. carꝰ in dn̄io. tc̄ 7 pꝰ. VI. carꝰ
hom̄. m̊. IIII. tc̄ silua. CCC. porꝰ. m̊. LXXX. sēp. II. r. tc̄
VII. an̄. m̊. V. tc̄. XXIII. por. m̊. VII. m̊. XXVIII. ou. tc̄
. LX. cap. m̊. XVII. 7. V. sochem̄. XXX. ac træ. 7. IIII. ac
p̄ti. sēp. I. carꝰ. tc̄ 7 pꝰ ual. CX. sol. m̊. IIII. lib. totū ht.
dim. leug in long. 7 dim. in lato. 7. X. đ. de gelto.

H̃. DE HOLT. In Bodhā ten̄. RADULFUS quam ten̄
Bundo. lib hō. t̃. r. e. II. carꝰ. træ. ꝑ man̄. Tc̄. XVII. uillī.
m̊. IIII. 7 IIII. bor. Tc̄ in dn̄io. II. carꝰ. 7 pꝰ. I. m̊. I. Tc̄ hōum
. II. m̊ nullī. II. ac p̄ti. Sēp. I. r. 7. III. an. tc̄. V. por. Semp.
XVII. cap. 7. II. soc. de XXX. ac tr̄e. Sēp. đ. carꝰ. Tc̄ ual.
XX. s̄. m̊. X. s̄. 7 hab. X. qr in log. 7. V. ĩ lat. 7. XII. đ. ĩ gelto.

The Hundred of GUILTCROSS

16 In *WICK* Godmund held 2 c. of land before 1066 as a manor.
>Then 7 villagers, later and now 4. Always 4 smallholders.
>>Then 3 slaves, later and now 2.
>>Meadow, 3 acres. Always 2 ploughs in lordship; 1 men's plough.
>>Woodland, 12 pigs.
>Also 7 Freemen, 90 acres of land;
>>5 smallholders; meadow, 1 acre. Then and later 2½ ploughs, now 3. Always 1 cob. Then 3 head of cattle. Now 2 pigs; always 70 sheep. 239 a
>
>[Value] then and later 60s; now £6.
>The whole has 1 league in length and 1 league in width, tax of 34½d.

LAUNDITCH Hundred

17 Ralph holds GATELEY which Bondi, a free man, held before 1066 as a manor, 4 c. of land.
>Always 23 villagers. Then 1 slave.
>Meadow, 30 acres. Always 2 ploughs in lordship. Then and later 6 men's ploughs, now 4.
>Then woodland, 300 pigs, now 80. Always 2 cobs. Then 7 head of cattle, now 5. Then 23 pigs, now 7. Now 29 sheep. Then 60 goats, now 17.
>Also 5 Freemen, 30 acres of land; meadow, 4 acres; always 1 plough.

Value then and later 110s; now £4.
The whole has ½ league in length and ½ in width, tax of 10d.

The Hundred of HOLT

18 In BODHAM Ralph holds what Bondi, a free man, held as a manor before 1066, 2 c. of land.
>Then 17 villagers, now 4. 4 smallholders.
>Then 2 ploughs in lordship, later 1, now 1. Then 2 men's [ploughs], now none.
>Meadow, 2 acres. Always 1 cob; 3 head of cattle. Then 5 pigs; always 17 goats.
>Also 2 Freemen, at 30 acres of land; always ½ plough.

Value then 20s; now 10s.
It has 10 furlongs in length and 5 in width, 12d in tax.

.XXIIII. TERRE EVDONIS DAPIFERI.

Scerepeham . H̄ . In Rokelvnt . teñ . Rikard̑.
x . lib̃ hoēs . ɪ . car tr̃æ . sēp . ɪ . bor . 7 . ɪɪɪ ac p̃ti . filua . ɪɪɪɪ . por.
Tc̄ . ɪɪɪɪ . car̃ . p̃ . ɪɪ . m̃ . ɪɪɪ . vɪɪɪ . pars mol̃ . Tc̄ ual̃ . c . fol.
p̃ . 7 m̃ . xʟ . Soca jacuit . t̃ . r . e . in Buchā regis . & p̃ . donec
Lifius habuit tr̃a . 7 hoc teftat̃ hund.

∫ In Scereph̃a . vɪɪɪ . lib̃i hōes . ɪ . car tr̃æ . 7 dim̃ . teñ . Roland̑.
7 vɪ p̃ti . filu . vɪ . por . tc̄ . ɪɪɪ . car̃ . p̃ . 7 . m̃ . ɪɪ . Tc̄ ual̃ . ʟx.
fol . m̃ . xxxvɪɪ . Soca in Buchã . Regis fed Lifius retinuit
& eulo fimil.

∫ In Rudhã teñ Radulfus . vɪɪɪ . lib̃i hoēs . ɪ . car tr̃æ . 7 . x .
ac̃ . 7 . ɪ . ac̃ . 7 . ɪ . uirg̃ p̃ti . sep . ɪɪ . car̃ . Tc̄ ual̃ . xʟ . fol . p̃ . 7 m̃
. xxx . Soca in buchã . fed Lifius retinuit . & . E . fimil.

∫ In brethã teñ . Turgis . vɪɪ . lib̃i . hoēs . t̃ . r . e . ɪ . car̃ . & dim̃.
tr̃e . ɪɪ . ac̃ p̃ti . Tc̄ 7 p̃ . ɪ . 7 dim̃ . car̃ . m̃ . ɪ . car̃ . & dim̃ . poffet
eē . Tc̄ ual̃ . xxx . fol . p̃ . m̃ . xx . Soca hoȝ . vɪ . in buchã regis.
de feptimo Sc̃a Adeldret foca & cōmd̃ . Sed Lefius totū reti
nuit . 7 . E . retinet totū ht̃ . ɪ . leug̃ . in long̃ . 7 . v . q̃r . ī lat̃.
& . xɪɪɪ . d̃ . 7 . ɪ . obulū de gelto.

∫ WALESSAM. Hund. In tuneftall &.
teñ efcule hō heroldi . t̃ . r . e . ɪ . car tr̃e . Tc̄ . vɪ . bor.
p̃ . 7 modo . v . 7 . vɪɪɪ . ac̃ p̃ti . Semp dim̃ . car̃ ī dñio.
7 dim̃ . hoū . tc̄ . cc . oū . m̃ . cc . xʟ . ɪ . ecc̃la . vɪɪɪ . ac̃.
7 ual̃ . vɪɪɪ . d̃ . Tc̄ ual̃ . xʟ . fol . p̃ 7 m̃ ɪɪɪ . lib̃ & ht̃.

vɪɪ . q̃r . in long̃ 7 . vɪ . ī lato . & de gelto . vɪɪɪ . d̃.

LANDS OF EUDO THE STEWARD

SHROPHAM Hundred

1 In ROCKLAND Richard holds; 10 free men, 1 c. of land.
   Always 1 smallholder.
   Meadow, 3 acres; woodland, 4 pigs. Then 4 ploughs, later 2, now 3. One-eighth of a mill. Value then 100s; later and now 40.

   The jurisdiction lay in the King's (manor of) Buckenham before 1066 and later until Lisois had the land. The Hundred testifies to this.

2 In SHROPHAM 8 free men, 1½ c. of land. Roland holds.
   Meadow, 6 [acres]; woodland, 6 pigs. Then 3 ploughs, later and now 2.
   Value then 60s; now 37.
   The jurisdiction is in the King's (manor of) Buckenham, but Lisois kept it, and Eudo likewise.

3 In ROUDHAM Ralph holds 8 free men, 1 c. of land and 10 acres.
   Meadow, 1 acre and 1 rood. Always 2 ploughs.
   Value then 40s; later and now 30.
   The jurisdiction (is) in Buckenham, but Lisois kept it, and Eudo likewise.

4 In BRETTENHAM Turgis held; 7 free men before 1066, 1½ c. of land.
   Meadow, 2 acres. Then and later 1½ ploughs, now 1 plough; and there could be ½.
   Value then 30s; later and now 20.
   The jurisdiction of 6 of these (is) in the King's (manor of) Buckenham; St. Etheldreda (had) the jurisdiction and patronage of the seventh. But Lisois kept the whole and E(udo) keeps it. The whole has 1 league in length and 5 furlongs in width, tax of 13½d.

WALSHAM Hundred

5 In TUNSTALL Skuli, Harold's man, held 1 c. of land before 1066.
   Then 6 smallholders, later and now 5.
   Meadow, 8 acres. Always ½ plough in lordship; ½ men's plough.
   Then 200 sheep, now 240.
   1 church, 8 acres; value 8d.
   Value then 40s; later and now £3.
   It has 7 furlongs in length and 6 in width, tax of 8d.

BLAFELDA. H̄. In poſſuic tēn. eſcule. 1. lib̄ hō
t̄. r. e. 11. car̊. trē. tc̄. vi. uiɫɫi. p̊. 7 m̊. v. Sēp. 1x. bor
7. 11. ſer. tc̄. 1. car̊. 7 dim̄. ī dn̄io. P̊ & m̊. 1. Sēp. 111.
car̊ hoū. Siluā. xl. por. 7 xv. ac̊ p̊ti. m̊. 1. moɫ. Sēp 111. r.
7. xv. añ. tc̄. xl. por. m̊. xvi. 1. eccɫa. xx. ac̊. 7 uaɫ. 11. ſoɫ.
Iſti adjac&. 1. b̄vuita cattuna. de xxx. ac̊ trǣ. 7 111. bor.
tc̄ dim̄ car̊. int̄ totū. 7 m̊. v. boues. v. ac̊ p̊ti. tc̄ uaɫ. xl.
ſoɫ. p̊. 7 m̊. 1111. lib̄.

V̄ In eadē tēn. Ratho. 1. lib̄. hō t̄. r. e. 1. car̊. trē. Sēp. 111.
uiɫɫi 7 v. bor. 7. 1. ſer. Sēp. 1. car̊. ī dn̄io. 7 dim̄. hoū.
Siluā. xx. por. 7. viii. p̊ti. Sēp. 111. por. 7. 11. ſoc̄.
de 1111. ac̊ trē. Tc̄ uaɫ. xx. 7 p̊. 7 m̊. xl.

V̄ Adhuc in eadē tēn. calp̊. lib̄ hō. t̄. r. e. 1. car̊ trǣ.
Sēp. 111. uiɫɫi. tc̄ 1. car̊ ī dn̄io. 7 sēp. dim̄ car̊ hoū.
Silu. xv. por. viii. ac̊ p̊ti. Tc̄ uaɫ. xv. ſoɫ. 7 m̊. xl.
Totū ɫit. 1. leug̊. ī long̊. 7 dim̄. in lato. Et de gelto.
x111. d̄. 7 oboɫ. hoc totū tēn Liſius p̊. 1. man̊. m̊ ten&.
eudo ſucceſſor. iɫɫius. & in tp̄r. r. e. ſoca 7 ſaca. fuit
in hund. ſ; m̊ tenet eudo.

H̄. de Humiliart. In tewda tēn. Radulfus. quam
tēn Coleman̊. liber hō. Stigandi. 1. car̊. trē. 7 dim̄.

BLOFIELD Hundred

6 In POSTWICK Skuli, 1 free man, held before 1066 2 c. of land.
>Then 6 villagers, later and now 5. Always 9 smallholders; 2 slaves.
>Then 1½ ploughs in lordship, later and now 1. Always 3 men's ploughs; woodland, 40 pigs; meadow, 15 acres. Now 1 mill. Always 3 cobs; 15 head of cattle. Then 40 pigs, now 16.

1 church, 20 acres;
value 2s.
1 outlier, CATTON, is attached to this, at 30 acres of land.
>3 smallholders.
>Then ½ a plough between the whole; now 5 oxen. Meadow, 5 acres.

Value then 40s; later and now £4.
In the same Rathi, 1 free man, held 1 c. of land before 1066.
>Always 3 villagers; 5 smallholders; 1 slave.
>Always 1 plough in lordship; ½ men's plough; woodland, 20 pigs; meadow, 8 [acres]; always 3 pigs.

Also 2 Freemen, at 4 acres of land.
Value then 20[s]; later and now 40.
Further in the same, Skalp, a free man, held 1 c. of land before 1066.
>Always 3 villagers.
>Then 1 plough in lordship. Always ½ men's plough; woodland, 15 pigs; meadow, 8 acres.

Value then 15s; now 40.
>The whole has 1 league in length and ½ in width, tax of 13½d.

Lisois held all this as 1 manor, now Eudo his successor holds. Before 1066 the full jurisdiction was in the Hundred, but now Eudo holds.

The Hundred of HUMBLEYARD

7 Ralph holds INTWOOD which Coleman, a free man of Stigand's, held; 1½ c. of land.

sep̃.iii.uilłi.⁊ iii.bor.Tc̃.ii.ſ.m̃.iii.ſemp.ii.caŕ.
in dñio.⁊.i.caŕ.⁊ dim̃.hom̃.iii.ac̃ p̃ti.Siluͣ.viii.

240 b
por.& qͬta pars mol̃.Tc̃.iiii.r.m̃.iii.sep̃.iiii.añ.tc̃
xl.por.m̃.xxx.tc̃.lx ou.m̃.l.i.ecc̃l̃a.xiiii.ac̃ tr̃e
⁊.i.ac̃ & dim̃.p̃ti.⁊.i.ƀwita.torp.lx.ac̃.⁊ caŕ.in dñio.
⁊.i.ac̃.⁊ dim̃.p̃ti.⁊ xv.foc̃.xl.ac̃ tr̃e.ſemp.ii.caŕ.⁊.iiii.
ac̃ p̃ti.⁊ v.liƀi.hoēs.xx.ac̃.⁊.i.caŕ.ex ħ habuit ſuus
⁊ ant c̃m̃d.t̃.r.e.⁊.ii.libi hoēs.& dim̃.lxxv.ac̃.
c̃m̃dat̃.tant̃.t̃.r.e.⁊.i.bor.⁊ dim̃.ſep̃.ii.caŕ.& dim̃.
⁊.ii.ſer.& i.liƀ.hō.de dim̃.ac̃.Tc̃ ual̃.x.ſol̃.m̃.xvii.
⁊ in tewida ħt.i.leu in long̃ ⁊ dim̃ in lat̃.⁊.ix.d.⁊.i.
ferding.de.g̃.& hoc maneriū ual̃.t̃.r.e.lx.ſol̃.
m̃.lxxx.

.XXV. TERRE.WALTĨ.GIFFARDI.*H̃.DE ENS-*
FORDA.Binnetre.teñ.Edric̃.i.liƀ hō.t̃.r.e.
.i.caŕ.tr̃e.sep̃.iii.Vill̃.⁊.viiii.bor.tc̃.i.ſ.sep̃.ii.
caŕ.in dñio.⁊.ii.caŕ.hou.⁊ viii.ac̃ p̃ti.m̃.ix.por.
⁊ lx.ou.tc̃.ual̃.xx.ſol̃.p̃.m̃.lx.Et.iiii.liƀi hoēs.
i.car tr̃e.sep̃.ii.caŕ.⁊.i.bor.⁊.iii.ac̃ p̃ti.tc̃
ual̃.xx.ſol̃.m̃.xii.ſol̃.Soca iſti tr̃e.t̃.r.e.jacuit
in folſa regis.m̃ ħt.Wal̃.⁊ ħt.v.quaŕ in longo.
⁊.iii.in lato.⁊ redd̃.xii.d.⁊ obl̃.de gelto regis.

241 a
 In Gegeſete.v.liberi hoēs.i.caŕ.tr̃e.⁊ dim̃.⁊.v.bor.
ſemp.iiii.caŕ.⁊ vi.ac̃ p̃ti.ſilua.viii.por.tc̃.ual̃.xx.
ſol̃.m̃.xl.⁊ Soca in folſa regis.t̃.r.e.m̃.ħt.Walt̃.⁊
ħt.dim̃.leug in long̃.⁊ in lat̃.⁊ redd̃.viii.d.⁊ obl̃.
de gelto.regis qͨq̃ ibi teneat.
 In Nortuna.iii.liƀi.hoēs.lxxii.ac̃ tr̃æ.sep̃.vi.bor.
sep̃.ii.caŕ.⁊.iiii.ac̃ p̃ti.ſilū.viii.por.tc̃.ual̃.xiii.ſol̃.
m̃.xx.⁊.i.de his hominiƀ; fuit c̃om̃d Almari ep̃i.

Always 3 villagers; 3 smallholders. Then 2 slaves, now 3.
Always 2 ploughs in lordship; 1½ men's ploughs; meadow, 3 acres; woodland, 8 pigs; ¼ of a mill. Then 4 cobs, now 3; always 4 head of cattle. Then 40 pigs, now 30. Then 60 sheep, now 50.

240 b

1 church, at 14 acres of land; meadow, 1½ acres.
1 outlier, SWAINSTHORPE, 60 acres.
A plough in lordship; meadow, 1½ acres.
Also 15 Freemen, 40 acres of land. Always 2 ploughs; meadow, 4 acres.
Also 5 free men, 20 acres; 1 plough.
His predecessor had the patronage of these before 1066.
Also 2 free men and a half, 75 acres, in patronage only before 1066.
1 smallholder and a half. Always 2½ ploughs. 2 slaves.
Also 1 free man, at ½ acre.
Value then 10s; now 17.
Intwood has 1 league in length and ½ in width; tax of 9¼d.
Value of this manor before 1066, 60s; now 80.

25   LAND OF WALTER GIFFARD

The Hundred of EYNSFORD

1 Edric, 1 free man, held BINTREE before 1066, 1 c. of land.
Always 3 villagers; 9 smallholders. Then 1 slave.
Always 2 ploughs in lordship; 2 men's ploughs; meadow, 8 acres. Now 9 pigs; 60 sheep.
Value then 20s; later and now 60.
Also 4 free men, 1 c. of land.
Always 2 ploughs; 1 smallholder; meadow, 3 acres.
Value then 20s; now 12s.
The jurisdiction of that land before 1066 lay in the King's (manor of) Foulsham; now Walter has it. It has 5 furlongs in length and 3 in width, it pays King's tax of 12½d.

2 In GUIST 5 free men, 1½ c. of land.

241 a

5 smallholders.
Always 4 ploughs; meadow, 6 acres; woodland, 8 pigs.
Value then 20s, now 40.
The jurisdiction (was) in the King's (manor of) Foulsham before 1066. Now Walter has it. It has ½ league in length and in width; it pays King's tax of 8½d, whoever holds there.

3 In (Wood) NORTON 3 free men, 72 acres of land.
Always 6 smallholders.
Always 2 ploughs; meadow, 4 acres; woodland, 8 pigs.
Value then 13s, now 20.
1 of these men was under the patronage of Bishop A(e)lmer.

⁋In Dallinga.v.libi hoēs.lxx.ac trae.tc̄ 7 p̃.ii.car.
& dim̄.m̂.i.& dim̄.7 dim̄.ac p̃ti.sēp.val.x.sol.Soca
in folsā regis.
⁋In Witcingehā.dim̄ car tre.ten.i.lib.hō.t̄.r.e.
sēp.i.vill.7 iii.bor.Et.ii.soc̄.iii.ac tre.7.iii.ac
p̃ti.silu.x.por.tc̄ Val.x sol.m̂.xx.sol.
⁋In Sueningatuna.vii.libi hoēs.i.car.tre.7 dim̄.
★ 7 xvi.ac tre.7.iii.ac p̃ti.7.i.bor.tc̄ 7 p̃.v.car.m̂.
★ m̂.Et.xii.soc̄.xl.ac tre.semp.ii.car.7 iii.ac.p̃ti
silu.vi.por.sēp.val.xl.sol.Soca.in folsā regis
t̄.r.e.m̂.tenet.W.7 ht dim̄.leug.in long.7 in
lato.7 redd.vii.d.de gelto regis.
⁋In Helmingehā ten.i.lib.hō.t̄.r.e.ii.car trae.
sēp.i.vill.7 iii.bor.7.iii.ser.tc̄.ii.car in dn̄io.
p̃.7.m̂.i.7.i.posset restaurari.semp.dim̄.car.
hou.7.iiii.ac p̃ti.7 i.mol.Et.xii.soc̄ xxx.ac tre.

semp.iii.car.7.ii.ac p̃ti.semp.val.xl.sol.
⁋In Remingaland.iii.libi.hoēs.lx.ac tre.semp
i.car.semp.i.car.7.ii.ac p̃ti.Val.x.sol.Soca in folsā
regis.t̄.r.e.m̂ tenet.W.

H̄.de Tauerham.In Atebruge.iii.libi hoēs.dim̄.
& v.ac terrae.sēp.ii.bor.Tc̄.ii.car.P̃.7 m̂.i.7.ii.ac
p̃ti.7 ual.x.sol.In felethorp.i.libi hoē.xxx.ac.Tc̄
.i.car.p̃.7 modo.dim̄.ii.ac p̃ti.7 ual.viii.sol.Rex.7
comes.de toto soca.t̄.r.e.7.m̂.ea ht.Galt.Tota At-
-tebruge.ht.i.leug in long.7.iii.qr in lat.7.viii.d.
7.iii.ferdingos.de gilto.

4   In (Wood) DALLING 5 free men, 70 acres of land.
        Then and later 2½ ploughs, now 1½. Meadow, ½ acre.
    Value always 10s.
        The jurisdiction (is) in the King's (manor of) Foulsham.

5   In WITCHINGHAM 1 free man held ½ c. of land before 1066.
        Always 1 villager; 3 smallholders.
        Also 2 freemen, 3 acres of land; meadow, 3 acres; woodland,
            10 pigs.
    Value then 10s; now 20s.

6   In SWANNINGTON 7 free men, 1½ c. of land and 16 acres of land;
    meadow, 3 acres.
        1 smallholder.
        Then and later 5 ploughs, now (3).
        Also 12 Freemen, 40 acres of land.
            Always 2 ploughs; meadow, 3 acres; woodland, 6 pigs.
    Value always 40s.
        The jurisdiction (was) in the King's (manor of) Foulsham
    before 1066. Now W(alter) holds. It has ½ league in length and
    in width, it pays King's tax of 7d.

7   In HELMINGHAM 1 free man held 2 c. of land before 1066.
        Always 1 villager; 3 smallholders; 3 slaves.
        Then 2 ploughs in lordship, later and now 1, and 1 could be
            restored. Always ½ men's plough; meadow, 4 acres; 1 mill.
        Also 12 Freemen, 30 acres of land.
            Always 3 ploughs; meadow, 2 acres.   241 b
    Value always 40s.

8   In RINGLAND 3 free men, 60 acres of land.
        Always 1 plough; meadow, 2 acres.
    Value 10s.
        The jurisdiction (was) in the King's (manor of) Foulsham
    before 1066. Now W(alter) holds.

   The Hundred of TAVERHAM
9   In ATTLEBRIDGE 3 free men and a half, 5 acres of land.
        Always 2 smallholders.
        Then 2 ploughs, later and now 1. Meadow, 2 acres.
    Value 10s.
        In FELTHORPE 1 free man, 30 acres.
        Then 1 plough, later and now ½. Meadow, 2 acres.
    Value 8s.
        The King and the Earl (had) the jurisdiction of the whole
    before 1066; now Walter has it. The whole of Attlebridge has 1
    league in length and 3 furlongs in width; tax of 8¾d.

*V*ÆRPINCHAM SVD . H̃ . In Stratuna . xviiii.
foc Heroldi in Marfã . fep̃ . ii . bor . Tc̃ . iiii . car . p̃ . 7 m̃.
iii . vi . ac p̃ti . Silũ . xxx . por . Tc̃ uat . xx . fot . m̃ . xl.
7 h̃t . i . leug̃ in long̃ . & dim̃ in lat̃ . 7 . xi . d̃ . de gelto.
In Euinchã . xxii . foc . Heroldi . ii . car . trã . 7 ii . bor.
femp . vi . car . 7 iiii . ac p̃ti . Silũ . x . por . Tc̃ uat . xxx.
fot . modo . l . 7 h̃t . ix . q̃r . 7 . i . perc̃ . i . in long̃ . 7 . v.
q̃r . 7 . ii . perc̃ . in lat̃ . 7 v . d̃ . 7 . obot de gelto . & Rip-
-petuna ẽ in adẽ m̃fura 7 redd̃ fimit . v . d̃ . 7 obot.
In Erminclanda . i . car . tr̃e . ten̄ . Edric lib̃ h̃õ . t . r . e.
fep̃ . i . uitts . 7 . iiii . bor . 7 . iii . foc . viii . ac tr̃e . fep̃ . i . car.
in dn̄io . 7 . i . car . h̃oum . 7 . iii . ac p̃ti . Silũ . xxx . por.

& ii . partes mot . Tc̃ . v . an̄ . m̃ . viii . 7 . i . r . 7 . viiii . por.
Tc̃ . uat . xx . fot . m̃ . xxx . 7 h̃t . vi . q̃r in long̃ . 7 . vi . in lat̃.
7 . iii . d̃ . de g̃ . *V*In Bechã . iii libi h̃oes . xxx . ac̃ . fep̃ . i.
car . Tc̃ uat . vi . fot . m̃ . xii.

H̃ de Greneho . In Phuldona . i . ca tr̃æ . t . r . e . Tc̃ . i . car.
p̃ . dim̃ . m̃ nulla . 7 uat . viii . fot.

*V*H̃ . de Grimefhou . In Lineforda 7 Iccheburc . xiiii . lib̃i
h̃oes . iiii . car tr̃e . 7 . xxxv . ac . Tc̃ . vi . car . p̃ . iii . m̃.
7 . iii . bor . ix . ac p̃ti . tc̃ uat . xx . fot . m̃ . x . hii fuer com̃dati.
anteceffori . Rad de Waer . p̃ libati . s̃t Bodin de uer ex
parte regis . Poftea de rationauit eos ad fuũ feudũ . Radut.
7 qm̃ forisfecit tenebat eos . Herueus de uer de illo . Hoc
teftat hundret . 7 totũ h̃t dim̃ . leug̃ in longo . 7 . iiii
q̃r in lat̃ . 7 redd̃ . iiii . d̃ . de xx . fot.

SOUTH ERPINGHAM Hundred

10 In STRATTON (Strawless) 19 Freemen of Harold's, in (the lands of) Marsham.
    Always 2 smallholders.
    Then 4 ploughs, later and now 3.
        Meadow, 6 acres; woodland, 30 pigs.
  Value then 20s; now 40.
    It has 1 league in length and ½ in width; tax of 11.d.

11 In HEVINGHAM 22 Freemen of Harold's, 2 c. of land.
    2 smallholders.
    Always 6 ploughs; meadow, 4 acres; woodland, 10 pigs.
  Value then 30s; now 50.
    It has 9 furlongs and 1 perch in length and 5 furlongs and 2 perches in width, tax of 5½d.
  RIPPON is in the same measurement and likewise pays 5½d.

12 In IRMINGLAND Edric, a free man, held 1 c. of land before 1066.
    Always 1 villager; 4 smallholders. Also 3 Freemen, 8 acres of land.
    Always 1 plough in lordship; 1 men's plough; meadow, 3 acres; woodland, 30 pigs; two-thirds of a mill. Then 5 head of cattle, now 8. 1 cob; 9 pigs.   242 a
  Value then 20s; now 30.
    It has 6 furlongs in length and 6 in width; tax of 3d.

13 In (West) BECKHAM 3 free men, 30 acres of land.
    Always 1 plough.
  Value then 6s; now 12.

The Hundred of (South) GREENHOE

14 In FOULDEN 1 c. of land before 1066.
    Then 1 plough, later ½, now none.
  Value 8s.

The Hundred of GRIMSHOE

15 In LYNFORD and ICKBURGH 14 free men, 4 c. of land and 35 acres.
    Then 6 ploughs, later 3, now (the same).
    3 smallholders.
    Meadow, 9 acres.
  Value then 20s; now 10.

These men were under patronage to the predecessor of Ralph Wader; later they were delivered on the King's behalf to Bodin de Vere. Afterwards Ralph proved them (to be) part of his Holding, and he held them when he forfeited, and Hervey de Vere (held them) from him. The Hundred testifies to this. The whole has ½ league in length and 4 furlongs in width, of a 20s [tax] it pays 4d.

⁊In Iccheburna. IIII. libi hoēs. t̄ r̄. e. I. car̄ tr̃e. 7 dim̃.
7 VIII. ac̄. Tc̄. p̧. III. car̄. m̃. II. III. ac̄ p̃ti. Tc̄. IIII.
por. m̃. I. Tc̄. c. ou. cc. Tc̄ 7 p̧. ual. xx. fol. m̃. xxx.
Totū ht dim̃. leug̃. in longo. 7 dim̃ in lat̃. 7 redd.
in gelto regis. de xx. fol. VIII. d.

⁊H̃. DE HOLT. In Leringafeta ten̄. Oftaç. lib hō. t̄. r. e.
. I. car̃ tr̃æ. Semp. VII. bor. 7 ī dn̄io. I. car̃ & dim̃. 7
hoūm. I. car̄. II. ac̄ p̃ti. I. mol. Tc̄. II. r. Semp. II.
an̄. 7 xx. por. 7 LXXX. ou. m̃. II. uafa ap̄. 7. I. foc

de. I. ac̄. Tc̄ ual. xx. fol. m̃. xxv. 7 hab. VIII. qr̃.
in long̃. 7 v. in lat̃. 7 XII. d. de gilt. q̃cumq̧. ibi teneat.
⁊In baiafelda. ten̄. Godric. lib hō. t̄. r. e. XL. ac̄ tr̃e.
Sep. III. bor. 7. I. car̃. 7 III. part. de. I. mol. 7. I. foc
de. x. ac̄. Tc̄ ual. x. fol. m̃. xx. fol.
⁊In glamforda. xxx. aç. ten̄. q̃dā lib. hō. t. r. e. Sep.
III. bor. 7. I. car̃. I. ac̄ p̃ti. Tc̄ ual. VIII. s̄. m̃. v. fol.
⁊& In efnuterlea. ten̄. Toka. fub heroldo. xxx. ac̄.
Tc̄. I. car̃ m̃. d. Tc̄ ual. v. s̄. m̃. x. fol.
⁊In bodenham. I. car̃. tr̃e. t. r. e. 7 p̃tinet ad Laringafeta
Semp. IX. bor. 7. II. fer̃. 7 in dn̄io. I. car̃ 7 hoūm. I. car̃.
Silua ad. v. por. II. ac̄ p̃ti. Tc̄ ual x. fol. m̃. xxx. fol.
⁊In Hunaworda. LX. aç. 7 p̃tinent ad Laringfeta. Tc̄. II.
car̃. m̃. I. I. ac̄ p̃ti. I. mol. & d. Tc̄ 7 femp ual. x. fol.

GRENEHOU. H. In Warham. ten̄ gert. II. libos
hōes. modo tenet. Walt Gifard. p̧ dim̃. car̃ tr̃e. sep.
. I. bor Tc̄. 7 p̧. II. car̃. m̃ ear & dim̃. tc̄ ual. XVI. fol
7 p̧. 7 m̃.

16 In ICKBURGH 4 free men before 1066, 1½ c. of land and 8 acres.
    Then and later 3 ploughs, now 2. Meadow, 3 acres. Then 4 pigs, now 1. Then 100 sheep, [now] 200.
    Value then and later 20s; now 30.
    The whole has ½ league in length and ½ in width, in the King's tax of 20s, it pays 8d.

The Hundred of HOLT

17 In LETHERINGSETT Oslac, a free man, held 1 c. of land before 1066.
    Always 7 smallholders.
    1½ ploughs in lordship; 1 men's plough; meadow, 2 acres; 1 mill. Then 2 cobs. Always 2 head of cattle; 20 pigs; 80 sheep. Now 2 beehives.
    Also 1 Freeman, at 1 acre.   242 b
    Value then 20s, now 25.
    It has 8 furlongs in length and 5 in width, tax of 12d, whoever holds there.

18 In BAYFIELD Godric, a free man, held 40 acres of land before 1066.
    Always 3 smallholders;
    1 plough; ¾ of 1 mill.
    Also 1 Freeman, at 10 acres.
    Value then 10s; now 20s.

19 In GLANDFORD a certain free man held 30 acres before 1066.
    Always 3 smallholders;
    1 plough; meadow, 1 acre.
    Value then 8s; now 5s.

20 In BLAKENEY Toki held 30 acres under Harold.
    Then 1 plough, now ½.
    Value then 5s; now 10s.

21 In BODHAM 1 c. of land before 1066. It belongs to Letheringsett.
    Always 9 smallholders; 2 slaves.
    1 plough in lordship; 1 men's plough; woodland for 5 pigs; meadow, 2 acres.
    Value then 10s; now 30s.

22 In HUNWORTH 60 acres. They belong to Letheringsett.
    Then 2 ploughs, now 1. Meadow, 1 acre; 1½ mills.
    Value then and always 10s.

(North) GREENHOE Hundred

23 In WARHAM Gyrth held 2 free men; now Walter Giffard holds, as ½ c. of land.
    Always 1 smallholder.
    Then and later 2 ploughs, now 1½ ploughs.
    Value then 16s; later and now (the same).

Erpingeham Nort. $\bar{H}$. In bningeham
teñ.i.lib hõ.Keē.xx.ac.tr̃e.t̃.r.e. Et.i.bor.
tc̃ uat.v.fol.m̃.ii. Et fuit liberata ad p̃ficiendũ.
Laringefere. *Heinestede*. $\bar{H}$.

In fcoteffam.iii.libi Hões.sc̃i.b.de holmo c̃om̃dat̃

243 a
7 v.foc.eũ õi c̃fuet̃.m̃ teñ Galtius ab odino anteceffore
fuo. 7 ht.int oẽs.lxxxx.ac tr̃e. 7 fub eis.iii.bor.
7.i.ac. 7 dim̃ p̃ti. Sẽp.ii.car̃. Tc̃ uat.x.fot.p̃.
7 m̃.xv.fot

In fafilingahã.ii.libi hoẽs.sc̃i.b.de holmo.c̃om̃dat.
de.l.ac tr̃e. 7.ii.ac p̃ti. 7.ii.bor. Sẽp.i.car̃. Tc̃ uat.
v.fot.m̃.redd.x.

Ifto kes.v.foc.sc̃i.b.de holmo.t̃.r.e.de.l.ac̃ terre.
7.ii.ac p̃ti. 7.i.bor. Sẽp.i.car̃. Tc̃ uat.v.fot. 7.iiii.
d̃ p̃. 7 m̃.x.fot

In fcotefsã.i.foc.sc̃i.b.de xiii.ac tr̃e 7.i.ac p̃ti. Sẽp
dim̃ car̃. Tc̃ uat.ii.oras. p̃ 7 m̃.v.fot

TERRE que fuer̃ Rog̃. pictauienfis. .XXVI.
$\bar{H}$.de Tauerhã. *F*Retham tenuit. Edricus lib hõ
t.r.e.p.iiii.car̃ terre. Sẽp.xviii.uitti. 7 xii.bor.
Tc̃ 7 p̃.ii.car̃.m̃.i.Tc̃.viii.car̃ hom̃.p̃.vi.m̃.v.
7.vi.ac p̃ti. Silu.lx.por. 7.iiii.hões.dim̃.car
terre.sẽp.i.car̃. 7.i.p̃ti. Tc̃.i.an.tc̃.xxvi.por.
m̃.xxiiii. Tc̃.cc.ou.m̃.ii.ou.Tc̃ uat.iiii.lib.

243 b
modo.viii. 7 ht.i.leug̃ iñ long̃. 7 dim̃.in lato. 7 xv.d̃.de gelto.

NORTH ERPINGHAM Hundred

24 In (North) BARNINGHAM 1 free man, Kene, held 20 acres of land before 1066.
    1 smallholder.
    Value then 5s; now 2.
    It was delivered to make up Letheringsett.

HENSTEAD Hundred

25 In SHOTESHAM 3 free men under the patronage of St. B(enedict) of Holme, and 5 Freemen with all customary dues. Now Walter holds them by (way of) his predecessor Bodin. They have between them all 90 acres of land.   243 a
    Under them 3 smallholders;
        meadow, 1½ acres; always 2 ploughs.
    Value then 10s; later and now 15s.

26 In SAXLINGHAM 2 free men under the patronage of St. B(enedict) of Holme, at 50 acres of land.
    Meadow, 2 acres;
    2 smallholders;
    always 1 plough.
    Value then 5s; now it pays 10.

27 In STOKE (Holy Cross) 5 Freemen of St. B(enedict's) of Holme before 1066, at 50 acres of land.
    Meadow, 2 acres.
    1 smallholder.
    Always 1 plough.
    Value then 5s 4d; later and now 10s.

28 In SHOTESHAM 1 Freeman of St. B(enedict's), at 13 acres of land.
    Meadow, 1 acre. Always 1 plough.
    Value then 2 *orae*; later and now 5s.

26   LANDS WHICH WERE OF ROGER OF POITOU

The Hundred of TAVERHAM

1 Edric, a free man, held FRETTENHAM before 1066, as 4 c. of land.
    Always 18 villagers; 12 smallholders.
    Then and later 2 ploughs, now 1. Then 8 men's ploughs, later 6, now 5. Meadow, 6 acres; woodland, 60 pigs.
    Also 4 men, ½ c. of land. Always 1 plough; meadow, 1 [acre]. Then 1 head of cattle. Then 26 pigs, now 24. Then 200 sheep, now 2 sheep.
    Value then £4, now 8.   243 b
    It has 1 league in length and ½ in width; tax of 15d.

Hamforda . teñ . Kitel ; fub ſtigando . t . r . e . 1 . car̃ . terre.
Tc̄ . vii . uiłłi . p̃ 7 m̃ . v . ſemp . iiii . bor . Tc̄ 7 p̃ . ii . car̃.
in dñio . m̃ . 1 . sẽp . 1 . car̃ hoūm . 7 . ii . ac̃ p̃ti . ſilũ . c . por̃.
7 . xiiii . hoēs . 1 . car̃ . tr̃e ; ſemp . iii . car̃ . ſilũ . lx . por.
7 . v . hoēs . xxx ; ac̃ tr̃e . in eſtratuna . Tc̄ . ii . car̃ . p̃.
7 m̃ . 1 . car̃ . & dim̃ . ſilũ . xii . por . In maideſtuna . teū
alƀt . 1 . car̃ . tr̃e ; ƀuuita huic manerio . ſemp . ii.
uiłłi . 7 . 1 . mol . 7 p̃ . 1 . car̃ . 7 ual . xxx . ſol m̃ . nichil.
In Croſtueit . vi . hoēs . 1 ; car̃ tr̃æ . Tc̄ 7 p̃ . ii . car̃.
m̃ dim̃ . De his hoĩƀȝ ħt . Stigandus ſocã . In dñio.
huj manerii . tc̄ . xx . por̃ . 7 . lx . oũ . 7 iiii an̄ . 7 m̃.
nichil . ſemp . xx . caþ . Tc̄ 7 p̃ . ual . c . ſol . m̃ . vii . liƀ.
7 tota hanforda ħt . 1 . leug̃ in long̃ . 7 dim̃ . in lat̃
7 . xxiii . đ . 7 . 1 . obolũ de gelto . 7 maideſtuna ħt . iii.
q̃r in long̃ 7 . iii . in lat̃ . 7 Croſtueit . dim̃ leug̃ in
long̃ . 7 . iiii . q̃r in lat̃ . 7 . x ; đ . de gelto.

¶Spikeſuurda . teñ . Alƀt . quam teñ . Suart . liƀ ho
ſub heroldo . t̃ . r . e . ii . car̃ . tr̃æ . Tc̄ . x . uiłłi . p̃ . 7 m̃
iiii . sẽp . iii . bor . Tc̄ 7 p̃ . ii . car̃ . in dñio . m̃ . nulla
Tc̄ . i . car̃ hoū . p̃ . 7 m̃ . dim̃ . 7 vi . ac̃ p̃ti . sẽp . i . mol.
Tc̄ . x . por . Tc̄ clxxxxiii . oũ . m̃ . xiii . oũ . In Spi
keſuurda . idē . vi . liƀi hoēs . i . car̃ . Stigandi . q̃ ſt
addidit Roƀ blancar tẽp̃r̃ . regis . W . ſemp . iiii . uiłłi.

Tc̄ . ii . car̃ . p̃ . 7 m̃ . 1 . 7 . iiii . ac̃ p̃ti . 7 totũ ul sẽp . iiii . liƀ.
7 ħt . 1 . leug̃ . 7 dim̃ . in long̃ . 7 . 1 . leug̃ in lat̃ . 7 . x . đ . de gelto.
Stigandus habuit ſocã . 7 Rog̃ eam teñ tr̃a.

¶Erpincham Svd . H̃ . In Coketeſhala teñ idē . iiii.
ſoc ſtigandi de fretã . xxx . ac̃ tr̃e . 7 . clxxx . ac̃ de dñio
de frethã . ſemp . iiii . bor . 7 . v . ac̃ p̃ti . 7 iiii . uiłłi . tc̄ . ii . car̃.
m̃ . 1 . 7 dim̃ . hoc ē in p̃tio de fretã.

¶Toneſteda . H̃ . Tuneſteda teñ idē . Alfere tegñ heroldi.
t̃ . r . e . v . car̃ & dim̃ . tr̃e . Semp xxiii . uiłłi . 7 . xvi . bor.

2 Ketel held HAINFORD under Stigand before 1066, 1 c. of land.
    Then 7 villagers, later and now 5. Always 4 smallholders.
    Then and later 2 ploughs in lordship, now 1. Always 1 men's plough; meadow, 2 acres; woodland, 100 pigs.
    Also 14 men, 1 c. of land. Always 3 ploughs; woodland, 60 pigs.
    Also 5 men, 30 acres of land, in STRATTON (Strawless). Then 2 ploughs, later and now 1½ ploughs; woodland, 12 pigs.
In MAYTON Albert holds 1 c. of land, an outlier to this manor. Always 2 villagers;
    1 mill. Later, 1 plough.
Value 30s, now nothing.
In CROSTWICK 6 men, 1 c. of land.
    Then and later 2 ploughs, now ½.
    Stigand had the jurisdiction of these men.
    In the lordship of this manor then 20 pigs; 60 sheep; 4 head of cattle; now nothing. Always 20 goats.
Value then and later 100s; now £7.
    The whole of Hainford has 1 league in length and ½ in width; tax of 23½d. Mayton has 3 furlongs in length and 3 in width, and Crostwick half a league in length and 4 furlongs in width; tax of 10d.

3 Albert holds SPIXWORTH which Swart, a free man, held under Harold before 1066, 2 c. of land.
    Then 10 villagers, later and now 4. Always 3 smallholders.
    Then and later 2 ploughs in lordship, now none. Then 1 men's plough, later and now ½. Meadow, 6 acres; always 1 mill.
    Then 10 pigs. Then 193 sheep, now 13 sheep.
In SPIXWORTH the same 6 free men, 1 c. [of land] of Stigand's, but Robert Blanchard added them (to this manor) after 1066.
    Always 4 villagers.
    Then 2 ploughs, later and now 1. Meadow, 4 acres.   244 a
Value of the whole, always £4.
    It has 1½ leagues in length and 1 league in width; tax of 10d.
Stigand had the jurisdiction, and Roger held it with the land.

  SOUTH ERPINGHAM Hundred
4 He also held in COLTISHALL, 4 Freemen of Stigand's belonging to Frettenham, 30 acres of land, and 180 acres from the lordship of Frettenham.
    Always 4 smallholders; meadow, 5 acres; 4 villagers.
    Then 2 ploughs, now 1½.
This is in the valuation of Frettenham.

  TUNSTEAD Hundred
5 He also held TUNSTEAD (which) Alfhere, a thane of Harold's, (held) before 1066, 5½ c. of land.
    Always 23 villagers; 16 smallholders.

Tc̄ 7 p̄ . ıı . car̄ . m̄ dım̄ . Tc̄ . xıı . car̄ hoū . Poſt 7 m̄ . vıı.
vııı . ac̄ p̃ti . ſilu . xıı . por . Tc̄ . ııı . añ . Tc̄ . ıııı . por . m̄ . ı . Tc̄
cxl . oū . m̄ . c . 7 xxıııı . ſoc̄ . ı . car̄ tr̄æ . Tc̄ . xıı . car̄ . p̄ . 7 m̄ .
v . 7 . ıı . ac̄ p̃ti . 7 idē ſt̄ additi . t̄ r . W . 7 R . comes . addid̄.
vı libī hōes . ı . car̄ tr̄e . 7 dım̄ . ex his h̄t ſc̄s benedictus
ſocā . 7 de uno cōmendatiōe 7 de xxıııı . tres forisfacturas
7 h̄t . vı . libi hōes ſub ſe . ıııı . bor . Tc̄ . ıııı . car̄ . p̄ . 7 m̄ . ııı.
7 . ıı . ac̄ p̃ti . Huic manero addidit Rob̄ arhal̄ . p̄ Rad̄.
comes forisfecit . ut dicit juſſu Godrici . ſ; ipſe negat . ı . car̄.

★ tr̄e que jacebat In Houetuna . t̄ r . e . quā . Rob̄ . comes dedit
ſc̄o benedicto cū vxore ſua . Tc̄ . vıı . uilli 7 q̄do Rob̄.
tulit . vıı . m̄ . vı . 7 ual̄ . x . ſol̄ . Tc̄ . ı . car̄ 7 dım̄ . 7 q̄do
Rob̄ tul̄ ſimil̄ . m̄ . ı . car̄ . 7 ıııı . ac̄ p̃ti . Tc̄ ual̄ . c . ſol̄ . 7.
q̄do Rotb̄ . arb̄ . eam ten̄ . in manu regis de Godrico . x . lib̄.
m̄ . xı . 7 h̄t . ı . leuḡ . in lonḡ . 7 . ı . qr̄ . 7 . ı . leuḡ in lat̄.

244 b

7 . xvııı . d . de . g . In Riſtuna . ı . lib̄ hō . vı . ac̄ tr̄æ . 7 . ı.
ac̄ p̃ti in eodē p̃tio . In Weſtuuic . ı . lib̄ . hō 7 dım̄ . xıı.
ac̄ . in odē p̃tio.

HERSam dım̄ . H̄ In ſcotoford ten̄ ulfriz . ı . lib̄ hō
t̄ . r . e . ı . car̄ tr̄e . 7 xv . ac̄ . Semp . x . uill̄ . 7 . ıııı . bor . Sep.
. ı . car̄ in dn̄io . 7 . ıı . car̄ . hoū . Silu . xl . por . 7 vıı . ac̄ p̃ti.
Tc̄ ual̄ . x . ſol̄ . m̄ . xx.

XXVII. **TERRE** Iuonis . Tailgeboſc . H̄ DE GRENEHOV.   ★

Noutuna ten̄ . odo . quo ten̄ . Ælfere lib̄ hō . Tc̄ . vı . uill̄
& m̄ . vııı . tc̄ . ııı . bor . m̄ . v . 7 . ı . ſer . tc̄ 7 m̄ in dn̄io . ı.
car̄ . Tc̄ hoūm . ıı . car̄ . m̄ . ı . Qm̄ rec̄ . ıııı . p̄ . m̄ . vı . Tc̄ 7 m̄.
v . añ . Tc̄ . xıı . joues . m̄ . xvı . 7 . ıı . libi hōes ibi man̄ . q̄s ten̄.
antecelſor ej . tenent̄ . ı . car̄ tr̄æ . 7 . ı . car̄ . 7 dım̄ . hab̄ . ıııı.
qr̄ . i longo . 7 . ııı in lato . 7 redd̄ i gelt̄ . vı . d̄ . Tc̄ ual̄ . xl.
ſ̄ . m̄ . ıııı . lib̄.

Then and later 2 ploughs, now ½. Then 12 men's ploughs,
later and now 7. Meadow, 8 acres; woodland, 12 pigs. Then
3 head of cattle. Then 4 pigs, now 1. Then 140 sheep,
now 100.
  Also 24 Freemen, 1 c. of land. Then 12 ploughs, later and
now 5. Meadow, 2 acres.
  They were added after 1066.
  And Earl R(alph) added 6 free men, 1½ c. of land.
  St. Benedict's has the jurisdiction of these, and the patronage
of one, and the 3 forfeitures of the 24.
  The 6 free men have under them 4 smallholders.
    Then 4 ploughs, later and now 3. Meadow, 2 acres.
To this manor Robert the Crossbowman added, after Ralph
forfeited — by order of Godric he says, but he himself denies it —
1 c. of land which lay in HOVETON before 1066, which Earl Ralph
gave to St. Benedict with his wife.
  Then 7 villagers, and when Robert took it 7, now 6.
Value 10s.
  Then 1½ ploughs, when Robert took it the same, now 1 plough.
    Meadow, 4 acres.
Value then 100s; when Robert the Crossbowman held it in the
King's hand from Godric £10; now 11.
  It has 1 league and 1 furlong in length and 1 league in width;
tax of 18d.

244 b

  In (Sco) RUSTON 1 free man, 6 acres of land; meadow, 1 acre.
In the same valuation.
  In WESTWICK 1 free man and a half, 12 acres.
In the same valuation.

  EARSHAM Half Hundred
6 In SHOTFORD Wulfric, 1 free man, held 1 c. of land and 15 acres
before 1066.
    Always 10 villagers; 4 smallholders.
    Always 1 plough in lordship; 2 men's ploughs; woodland, 40
      pigs; meadow, 7 acres.
  Value then 10s; now 20.

27   LANDS OF IVO TALLBOYS

  The Hundred of (South) GREENHOE
1 Odo holds NEWTON where Alfhere, a free man, held.
    Then 6 villagers, now 8. Then 3 smallholders, now 5. 1 slave.
    Then and now 1 plough in lordship. Then 2 men's ploughs,
      now 1. When he acquired it 4 [cobs], later and now 6.
    Then and now 5 head of cattle. Then 12 sheep, now 16.
    Also 2 free men dwell there whom his predecessor held,
      holding 1 c. of land. 1½ ploughs.
    It has 4 furlongs in length and 3 in width; it pays 6d in tax.
  Value then 40s; now £4.

H̃. de dochinga. In ferlebruna. xvi. libi hões. t. r. e.
quos ten̄. heroldus. tenentes. v. car 7 qdo recepit fimil.
m̃. iii. 7 idē m̃ ten̄ de iuone. Sēp. ii. uilti 7. i. ac 7 dim̄.
p̃ti. 7. i. mot. t̄c. 7 p. ual. xl. fol. m̃. iiii. lib hanc tr̃a
tenebat Rad̄. q̄n forisfecit. tota ht. i. leug in long.

245 a

7 dim̄. ĩ lato q̃cq. ibi teneat 7 reddit. xxvii. d. de. xx. fol.
de hac tr̃a tulit Rad̄. comes. i. car. tr̃e. uno anno anteq
foris faceret. Rogero filio Rainardi. tefte hund.

⋆ H̃. de Grenehou. TRE. Radulfi de Limefio. Oxenburh. .XXVIII.
ten̄. Turchill. Tc̄. xv. uilt. m̃. vii. Semp. ix. bor. 7 iii. fer.
Tc̄ ĩ dn̄io. 7 p. iii. car. m̃. iii. Tc̄ it hões. ii. m̃. i. Silua ad. xx.
por. xii. acr p̃ti. ii. mot. i. pifc. Qn̄ rec̄. i r. & m̃. Tc̄. xxxi.
por. m̃. xv. tc̄. cc. xx. oues. m̃. c. lxxx. 7 viii. libi hões.
ten̄. c. acr. &. vi. car. m̃. iii. car. xii. ac p̃ti Sēp. ii. uilt.
7 iiii. bor. 7 hab. in longo. i. m̃. 7 d. in lato. 7 redd. xi.
d. ĩ gelt. qn̄ h. redd. xx. s. Sēp ual. c. fol. 7. i. de illis hōibz
libis calumpniat. Radulfi de toenio. qa anteceffor ej. cum
foc̄ & fac̄. ten̄. ut. h. teftat.

Dudelingatuna ten̄ hardwin. Tc̄ & m̃. iii. bor. 7. i. fer.
7. i. car. Silua ad. xvi. por. ii. ac p̃ti. i. mot. i. pifc. Qn̄ rec̄.
7. m̃. i. r. Tc̄. xi. por. m̃. v. Tc̄. lx. oues. m̃. vi. Tc̄ ual. xx.
m̃. fimil.

245 b

.XXIX. TERRE. Eudonis filii Spiruwin. Fredrebruge. Hund ⋆
& dim̄. In idlinghetuna. ten̄ Gaufrid. ii. car. 7. xv. ac. ⋆
tr̃æ. quam ten̄ Godricus. fub heroldo lib hōc. t. r. e. sēp.
viii. uilti. 7 iiii. bor. 7. viii. ac p̃ti. 7. ii. car in dn̄io. 7. i. car.
houm. 7. i. mot. 7. dim̄. fal. Et. i. lib hō. ii. ac 7 dim̄. m̃. xvii.
por. 7 lx. ou. totum ual. iiii. lib.

The Hundred of DOCKING

2 In SHERNBORNE 16 free men before 1066, whom Harold held, holding 5 c. and when he received it the same, now 3. They now hold from Ivo.
Always 2 villagers.
Meadow, 1½ acres; 1 mill.
Value then and later 40s; now £4.
Ralph held this land when he forfeited. The whole has 1 league in length and ½ in width, whoever holds there, at 20s it pays 27d. From this land Earl Ralph took 1 c. of land one year before he forfeited for Roger son of Rainard, as the Hundred testify.

245 a

28   LANDS OF RALPH OF LIMÉSY

The Hundred of (South) GREENHOE
1 Thorkell held OXBOROUGH.
Then 15 villagers, now 7. Always 9 smallholders; 3 slaves.
Then and later 3 ploughs in lordship, now 3. Then 2 [ploughs] between the men, now 1. Woodland for 20 pigs; meadow, 12 acres; 2 mills; 1 fishery. When he acquired it and now 1 cob. Then 31 pigs, now 15. Then 220 sheep, now 180.
Also 8 free men hold 100 acres.
6 ploughs; now 3 ploughs. Meadow, 12 acres.
Always 2 villagers; 4 smallholders.
It has 1 mile in length and ½ in width, it pays 11d in tax when the Hundred pays 20s.
Value always 100s.
One of those free men is claimed (to be) Ralph of Tosny's because his predecessor held him with the full jurisdiction as the Hundred testifies.

2 Hardwin held DIDLINGTON.
Then and now 3 smallholders; 1 slave.
1 plough; woodland for 16 pigs; meadow, 2 acres; 1 mill; 1 fishery. When he acquired it and now 1 cob. Then 11 pigs, now 5. Then 60 sheep, now 6.
Value then 20s, now the same.

29   LANDS OF EUDO SON OF SPIRWIC   245 b

FREEBRIDGE Hundred and a Half
1 In HILLINGTON Geoffrey holds 2 c. and 5 acres of land which Godric, a free man, held under Harold before 1066.
Always 8 villagers; 4 smallholders.
Meadow, 8 acres; 2 ploughs in lordship; 1 men's plough; 1 mill; ½ salt-house.
Also 1 free man, 2½ acres. Now 17 pigs; 60 sheep.
Value of the whole £4.

Masincham tenet Buold quam tenuit. Scula. lib̃. homo.
t̃.r.e. sẽp. III. car̃ t̃re. Tc̃. VIII. uilli. m̃. VII. 7. I. s̃. Tc̃. II. car̃.
in dñio. 7 m̃. 7. I. car̃. hoũ. 7. III. car̃. poſſunt reſtaurari. sẽp. v.
por. 7 XL. oues. & ual. xx. ſol.

Babinghelea tenet Gaufrid. quam tenuit Scula. t̃ r.e. II. car̃.
t̃re. sẽp. IIII. uilli. 7. XXV. bor. 7. I. s̃. 7 XVI. ac̃ p̃ti. Tc̃. II. car̃
in dñio. p. m̃. I. sẽp. I. car̃. hoũ. Silua. LX. por. 7 ſemp. I. por.
7. LX. ou. hic jacent. LXII. ac̃. qđ teñ. VII. libi hões. 7. II. ac̃ p̃ti.
sẽp. I. car̃. 7. I. mol. Tc̃. IX. ſal. sẽp ual. LX. ſol.

Derſinchã tenet riuold. quam teñ. Schett. lib̃ hõ. t̃. r. e.
p mañ. sẽp. I. car̃. in dñio. 7. I. car̃. hoũ. sẽp. I. uills. 7. IIII. bor.
7. I. ſer. 7 VII. ac̃. 7 dim̃. p̃ti. tc̃. I. ſal. 7. IIII. libi hões. XLIIII. ac̃.
hos rec̃ ,p pſiciend ſuis maner̃. 7. I. lib̃. m. hõem de. XX. sẽp. dim̃.
car̃ 7. IIII. bor. Totũ ual. xx. ſol.

H̃. de Dochinge. Dochinghe teñ idẽ q̃ tenuit Aluric.
t̃.r.e. ſub ſtigando sẽp. I. car̃. in dñio. 7. V. uilli. 7 V. bor.
tc̃. II. s. tc̃. I. car̃. houm̃. m̃. I. car̃. 7 dim̃. sẽp. I. r. 7. I. uac̃.
7 XVII. por. LXXX. ou. 7. I. car̃. poſſet reſtaurari. & ual. xx. ſol.

totum ħt. I. leug̃ in long̃ & dim̃. in lato. & reddit v. ſol. 7. II. d.
7. I. obolũ. de gelto. q̃cq̃ ibi teneat.

Hersam. Dimid̃. H̃. In dentuna. teñ. tarmoht. I.
lib̃. homo. reg̃. e. II. car̃. terre. Tc̃. X. uilli. 7 VI. bor Tc̃ VIII.
m̃. Sẽp. III. ſer. Tc̃. II. car̃. in dñio. m̃. dim̃. Tc̃ VI. car̃. hoũ.
m̃. IIII. m̃. ſilũ. XXX. por. v. ac̃ p̃ti. 7 dim̃. mol. 7. IIII. de. XX. ac̃ t̃re.
Tc̃ ual. LX. ſol. m̃. IIII. lib̃.

2   Berold holds MASSINGHAM which Skuli, a free man, held before
    1066. Always 3 c. of land.
        Then 8 villagers, now 7. 1 slave.
        Then 2 ploughs in lordship, and now. 1 men's plough; 3
            ploughs could be restored. Always 5 pigs; 40 sheep.
    Value 20s.

3   Geoffrey holds BABINGLEY which Skuli held before 1066, 2 c. of
    land.
        Always 4 villagers; 25 smallholders; 1 slave.
        Meadow, 16 acres. Then 2 ploughs in lordship, later and now 1.
            Always 1 men's plough; woodland, 60 pigs. Always 1 pig;
            60 sheep.
        Here appertain 62 acres which 7 free men hold: meadow, 2
            acres. Always 1 plough; 1 mill. Then 9 salt-houses.
    Value always 60s.

4   Ricwold holds DERSINGHAM which Skeet, a free man, held before
    1066 as a manor.
        Always 1 plough in lordship; 1 men's plough.
        Always 1 villager; 4 smallholders; 1 slave.
        Meadow, 7½ acres. Then 1 salt-house.
        Also 4 free men, 44 acres. He acquired these to make up his
    manors, and 1 free man, at 20 [acres].
        Always ½ plough; 4 smallholders.
    Value of the whole 20s.

The Hundred of DOCKING

5   He also holds DOCKING where Aelfric held before 1066 under
    Stigand.
        Always 1 plough in lordship.
        5 villagers; 5 smallholders. Then 2 slaves.
        Then 1 men's plough; now 1½ ploughs. Always 1 cob; 1 cow;
            17 pigs; 80 sheep; 1 plough could be restored.
    Value 20s.
        The whole has 1 league in length and ½ in width, it pays   246 a
    tax of 5s 2½d, whoever holds there.

EARSHAM Half Hundred

6   In DENTON Thormoth, 1 free man of King Edward's, held 2 c. of
    land.
        Then 10 villagers. 6 smallholders then, 8 now. Always 3 slaves.
        Then 2 ploughs in lordship, now ½. Then 6 men's ploughs,
            now 4. Now woodland, 30 pigs; meadow, 5 acres; ½ mill.
        4 [?free men] at 20 acres of land.
    Value then 60s; now £4.

In eadem teñ. Alfriz. I. lib hō ſtigandi. t̄. r. e. II. car̄ tr̄æ. Tc̄. x. uiłłi. m̄. VIII. Tc̄. VIII. bor. m̄. VI. Sēp. III. ſer. Tc̄. II. car̄. i̇ dñio. m̄. dim̄. Tc̄. VI. car̄ hoūm. m̄. IIII. m̄ ſiłu. XXX. por. VI. acr̄ p̄ti. 7 dim̄. mol. 7. IIII. ſoc̄. de. XX. acr̄. tr̄e. Tc̄ ual. LX. ſol. m̄. IIII. lib. ħt. I. leuḡ. i̇ lonḡ. 7. IIII. q̄r. in lato. 7 de gelto. XVIII. d. Q̄c̄q̄ ibi teneat. Soca i̇ herſam.

In aldeb̄ga tenet. morua͂. q̄ tenuit alfriz. t̄. r. e. I. b̄wita͂. in tȳbenha͂. p̄tin̄r̄e. de. I. car̄. tr̄e. Tc̄ dim̄. car̄. m̄. nichil ap̄p̄tiata ⁒.

In ead̄ tenuit id̄e. I lib hō ſc̄e Aldride com̄d. q̄ nec dare nec. uend̄e pot̄at tr̄am. ext̄ eccła. Herfrind̄ hubuit ex lib̄atione ad p̄ſicienda. ma͂ſua. m̄ tenet. eudo. ſucceſſor ejus. ħt dim̄. car̄ tr̄e. Semp. I. bor. 7. I. ſer. Sēp. dim̄. car̄. 7. II. ac̄ p̄ti. Sēp. ual. x. ſol.

LOTHNINGA. H̄. Topecropt. teñ. Goduin⁹. lib hō gert com̄d. tantū. t̄. r. e. p̄ ma͂. III. car̄ tr̄e. Tc̄. XII. uiłłi. p̄ 7. m̄. II. Tc̄. XXX. bor. p̄. 7 m̄. XXXVI. Tc̄. VII. ſer. m̄. IIII. Tc̄. IIII. car̄. in dñio. m̄. II. Tc̄. VII. car̄. hou̇.

m̄. V. Silu͂. XX. por. 7. IIII ac̄ p̄ti. 7 ſub eod̄. IIII. lib̄i hōes. I. car̄. tr̄e. lib̄ati henfrido anteceſſore ſuo p̄ terra. 7 ſub. eis v. uiłłi. 7 XII. bor. Tc̄. v. car̄. int̄ oēs. m̄. IIII. 7. I. eq̄ i̇ aula. m̄. XL. por. 7 XX. cap̄. Tc̄ ual. totu͂. VI. lib. m̄. VIII.

In ead̄. teñ. Goduin⁹. lib hō dimidi. edrici. 7 dimidi ſc̄i edmundi com̄d. tantū. t̄. r. e. I. car̄. 7 dim̄. q̄ tenuit couinus. Sēp. VIII. uiłłi. 7. XI. bor. Sēp. IIII. ſer. Tc̄. II. car̄. m̄. nulla. Tc̄. VIII. car̄. 7. dim̄. hou̇. m̄. v. 7 dim̄. 7. III. ac̄ p̄ti Tc̄ totu͂ ual. XXX. ſol. m̄. XL. ħt. I. leuḡ. 7. I. q̄r. i̇ lonḡ. 7 IX. q̄r. i̇ lato. 7 de gelto. XX. d. q̄c̄q̄ ibi teneat.

In the same Aelfric, 1 free man of Stigand's, held 2 c. of land before 1066.
> Then 10 villagers, now 8. Then 8 smallholders, now 6. Always 3 slaves.
> Then 2 ploughs in lordship, now ½. Then 6 men's ploughs, now 4. Now woodland, 30 pigs; meadow, 6 acres; ½ mill.

Also 4 Freemen, at 20 acres of land.
Value then 60s, now £4.
> It has 1 league in length and 4 furlongs in width, tax of 18d, whoever holds there. The jurisdiction (is) in Earsham.

7 In ALBURGH Morvan holds, where Aelfric held before 1066, 1 outlier in Tibenham, at 1 c. of land.
> Then ½ plough, now nothing.

It has been assessed.
In the same he also holds; 1 free man under the patronage of St. Etheldreda, who could neither grant nor sell his land outside the church. Herfrith had him by livery to make up his manors, now Eudo, his successor, holds him. He has ½ c. of land.
> Always 1 smallholder; 1 slave.
> Always ½ plough; meadow, 2 acres.

Value always 10s.

LODDON Hundred

8 Godwin, a free man, under the patronage only of Gyrth before 1066, held TOPCROFT as a manor, 3 c. of land.
> Then 12 villagers, later and now 2. Then 30 smallholders, later and now 36. Then 7 slaves, now 4.
> Then 4 ploughs in lordship, now 2. Then 7 men's ploughs, now 5. Woodland, 20 pigs; meadow, 4 acres.

246 b

Under him 4 free men, 1 c. of land, delivered to Heinfrid his predecessor for land.
> Under these, 5 villagers; 12 smallholders.
> Then 5 ploughs between them all, now 4. 1 horse at the hall. Now 40 pigs; 20 goats.

Value of the whole then £6, now 8.
In the same Godwin, a free man, half Edric's and half St. Edmund's under patronage only before 1066, held 1½ c. [of land] where Godwin held.
> Always 8 villagers; 11 smallholders. Always 4 slaves.
> Then 2 ploughs, now none. Then 8½ men's ploughs, now 5½. Meadow, 3 acres.

Value of the whole then 30s, now 40.
> It has 1 league and 1 furlong in length, and 9 furlongs in width, tax of 20d, whoever holds there.

⁋ In Woderuna teñ idē . XI . libi hoēs . goduini . tokesone . 7 alt̄ goduini sub rege . e . 7 gert . dim̄ . car̛ . tr̄e . 7 . IIII . bor . Tc̄ III . car̛ . m̄ . II . 7 . I . ac̛ . 7 dim̄ . p̄ti . App̄tiatum ÷ Soca i hund̄.

⁋ H̄ . de depwada . Tibenham . teñ . Alric̛ teinn t̄ . r . e . III . car̛ . tr̄e . Sep̄ . II . ulli . 7 . XXI . bor . tc̄ . IIII . s . m̄ . II . sep̄ . II . car̛ . in dn̄io . tc̄ . VI . car̛ . hoū . m̄ . III . 7 XII . ac̛ . p̄ti . silu . XII . por . tc̄ . I . mol̄ . m̄ . XL . por . 7 XVII . oū . 7 IX . cap̄ . Et . XXVI . hoēs . soca . falde . 7 com̄d . 7 possent uēde tr̄a . s . p eā obtu lissent . dn̄o suo . Rex 7 comes socā . 7 h̄t . L . ac̄ . tc̄ . IIII . ca̛ . m̄ . II . 7 . I . ac̛ p̄ti .

⁋ In carletuna . I . lib̄ hō . VIII . ac̛ . Tc̄ val̄ . VII . lib̄ . m̄ . VIII . Istos libōs hoēs recepit hainfrid . ꝑ tr̄a . Tota . Carletuna . h̄t . I . leuḡ in lonḡ . 7 . IIII . q̄r̄ . 7 . X . q̄r̄ . in lat̄ . 7 . IIII . por . 7 . XXII . d̄ . 7 obolū . de gelto .

247 a

TERRA . DROGONIS DE BERARIA . H̄ . DE GRENEHOGA . Hindringahā . teñ . Vlf . 7 Osuuard . II . car̛ tr̄e . 7 . m̄ . tenet . drogo de beuraria . ꝑ . I . mañ . tc̄ . t̄ . r . e . VIII . vill̄ . 7 . VIII . bor . m̄ . II . vil̄ . 7 VIII . bor . semp . tc̄ . II . car̛ . dn̄io . m̄ . I . it̄ se . 7 illos . III . ac̛ p̄ti . tc̄ . val̄ . IIII . lib̄ . m̄ . XXX . sol̄ .

. XXX .

ERPINGEHAM . NORT H̄ .

Basingeham teñ . I . lib̄ . hō t̄ . r . e . com̄d . edrici . I . car̛ tr̄e . 7 in die q̄ pat̄ . R . malet iuit in seruitiū regis tenebat eum & hō drogoñ ꝓhibet . Semp . VIII . uilli . 7 VII . bor . Sep̄ . I . car̛ . i dn̄io 7 . II . hoū . I . ac̛ p̄ti . m̄ . II . por . tc̄ ual̄ . XX . m̄ . LX .

⁋ In b̄ningehā teñ Alwiñ . I . lib̄ . hō . I . ca̛ . tr̄e . tc̄ . V . bor . m̄ . III . Silua . ad . C . por . I . ac̛ . p̄ti . m̄ . IIII . p . m̄ . VIII . oū . tc̄ ual̄ . XX . sol̄ . 7 . m̄ . similit̄ .

9 He also holds in WOODTON 11 free men of Godwin Tokeson's and of another Godwin's under King Edward and Gyrth, ½ c. of land.
   4 smallholders. Then 3 ploughs, now 2. Meadow, 1½ acres.
   It has been assessed.
   The jurisdiction (is) in the Hundred.

The Hundred of DEPWADE
10 Alric, a thane, held TIBENHAM before 1066, 3 c. of land.
   Always 2 villagers; 21 smallholders. Then 4 slaves, now 2.
   Always 2 ploughs in lordship. Then 6 men's ploughs, now 3.
      Meadow, 12 acres; woodland, 12 pigs. Then 1 mill. Now
      40 pigs, 17 sheep, 9 goats.
   Also 26 men in fold-rights and patronage: they could sell their land, but after they had offered it to their lord. The King and the Earl (have) the jurisdiction. They have 50 acres.
   Then 4 ploughs, now 2. Meadow, 1 acre.

11 In CARLETON (Rode) 1 free man, 8 acres.
   Value then £7, now 8.
      Heinfrid acquired those free men for land.
      The whole of Carleton (Rode) has 1 league and 4 furlongs in length and 10 furlongs and 4 perches in width; tax of 22½d.

30   LAND OF DROGO OF BEUVRIÈRE   247 a

The Hundred of (North) GREENHOE
1 Ulf and Osward held HINDRINGHAM, 2 c. of land; now Drogo son of Beuvrière holds it as 1 manor.
   Then, before 1066, 8 villagers and 8 smallholders. Now 2 villagers; always 8 smallholders.
   Then 2 ploughs in lordship, now 1 between him and the men. Meadow, 3 acres.
   Value then £4, now 30s.

ERPINGHAM Hundred
2 1 free man held BESSINGHAM before 1066 under the patronage of Edric, 1 c. of land. On the day that R(obert) Malet's father went on the King's service he held him, but Drogo's man keeps him.
   Always 8 villagers; 7 smallholders.
   Always 1 plough in lordship; 2 men's [ploughs]; meadow, 1 acre. Now 2 pigs.
   Value then 20[s]; now 60.

3 In (North) BARNINGHAM A(i)lwin, 1 free man, holds 1 c. of land.
   Then 5 smallholders, now 3.
      Woodland for 100 pigs; meadow, 1 acre. Then 4 pigs. Now 8 sheep.
   Value then 20s, now the same.

ᚹHEINESTEDE. H̄. In saſilingaham. teñ. AILWARD.
. 1. lib hō. reḡ. e. 11. car. tr̃e. Tc̄. xii. bor. p̄. xii. m̄. ix. Tc̄
7 p̄. ii. car̊: in dn̄io. m̄. nulla. Sēp. 1. car̊. hoū. 7. 1. ac̊. 7 dim̄.
p̃ti. 7. v. ſoc̊. de xvii. ac̊ tr̃e. Sēp. 1. car̊. Tc̄ ual. xx. ſol. p̄. 7
m̄. ſimilit̃.

ᚹIn ead̃ teñ. ulnoht. 1. lib hō ſtigandi com̃d. de. xxx. ac̊ tr̃e.
Semp. v. bor. Tc̄. 1. car̊: in dn̄io. m̄ nulla. Tc̄ 7 p̄. 1. car̊ hoū.

247 b

m̄. 1. 7 dim̄. 7. iii. ac̊ p̃ti. 7. v. ſoc̊ d̃. xvii. ac̊ tr̃e. Tc̄. 1. car̊.
p̄. ſimilit m̄. dim̄. 7. 1. lib. de. vi. ac̊ tr̃e. Tc̄ ual. xx. ſol. p̄. 7 m̄.
xx. ſol.

ᚹErpinchā. ſud. H̄. Burc teñ. Maru en quedam liba femī.
t̃. r. e. iii. car tr̃æ. ſēp. viii. uiłłi. 7 ix. bor. 7. ii. car̊ in dn̄io. Tc̄
7 p̄. iiii. car̊. hom̃. m̄. iiii. 7 vii. ac̊ p̃ti. Sil. lx. por. ſēp. 1. mol. tc̄
xxiiii. por. m̄ xii. m̄. iii. an̄. 7 xvi. oū. 7 xx. cap̃. tc̄ ual. xl.
ſol. m̄. lx. 7 łt. 1. leuḡ in lon̄g. 7 v. q̄r̃. in lato. 7 v. d̃. de gelto.
Rex & comes. ſocā. In erpinchā. 1. car̊ tr̃e. 1. lib hō. t̃. r. e. ſēp.
ii. bor. 7. 1. car̊. 7. 1. ac̊ p̃ti. 7. ii. ſoc̊. iiii ac̊ tr̃e. 7. 1. ecc̃la de vi. ac̊
7 ual. vi. d̃. 7 ual. x. ſol. Rex 7 comes ſocā.

. XXXI. TERRE. RAD̃. BANIARDI. H̄. DE ENSFORD. In Kerdes-
tuna teñ. Tord. p̃ mañ. 1. lib hō. t̃. r. e. ii. car̊. tr̃e. m̄ tenet.
Gaosfridus. bainard. Tc̄. 7 p̄. xxx. uiłł. 7 m̄. xvi. 7 m̄. xiiii.
bor. tc̄. 7 p̄. ii. s. m̄. 1. ſēp. ii. car̊ in dn̄io. tc̄ 7 p̄. iiii. car̊.
hoūm. m̄. iii. 7 v. ac̊ p̃ti. filu. xx. por. q̄n. ii. r. m̄. iiii. Tc̄
iiii. an̄. m̄. x. ſemp. xl. por. m̄. l. oū. tc̄. lx. cap̃. m̄ xxviii.

★

HENSTEAD Hundred

4   In SAXLINGHAM Aelward, 1 free man of King Edward's, holds 2 c. of land.
   Then 12 smallholders, later 12, now 9.
   Then and later 2 ploughs in lordship, now none. Always 1 men's plough; meadow, 1½ acres.
   Also 5 Freemen, at 17 acres of land. Always 1 plough.
Value then 20s; later and now the same.
In the same Wulfnoth, 1 free man under the patronage of Stigand, holds, at 30 acres of land.
   Always 5 smallholders.
   Then 1 plough in lordship, now none. Then and later 1 men's plough, now 1½. Meadow, 3 acres.
   Also 5 Freemen, at 17 acres of land. Then 1 plough, later the same, now ½.
   Also 1 free (man) at 6 acres of land.
Value then 20s; later and now 20s.

247 b

SOUTH ERPINGHAM Hundred

5   Maerwynn, a certain free woman, held BURGH (Next Aylsham) before 1066, 3 c. of land.
   Always 8 villagers; 9 smallholders.
   2 ploughs in lordship. Then and later 3 men's ploughs, now 4. Meadow, 7 acres; woodland, 60 pigs; always 1 mill; then 24 pigs, now 12. Now 3 head of cattle; 16 sheep; 20 goats.
Value then 40s; now 60.
   It has 1 league in length and 5 furlongs in width, tax of 5d.
The King and the Earl (have) the jurisdiction.

6   In ERPINGHAM 1 c. of land, 1 free man (held) before 1066.
   Always 2 smallholders; 1 plough; meadow, 1 acre.
   Also 2 Freemen, 4 acres of land.
   1 church, at 6 acres;
value 6d.
Value 10s.
   The King and the Earl (have) the jurisdiction.

31   LANDS OF RALPH BAYNARD

The Hundred of EYNSFORD

1   In KERDISTON Thored, 1 free man, held as a manor, 2 c. of land, before 1066. Now Geoffrey Baynard holds.
   Then and later 30 villagers, now 16. Now 14 smallholders.
      Then and later 2 slaves, now 1.
   Always 2 ploughs in lordship. Then and later 4 men's ploughs, now 3. Meadow, 5 acres; woodland, 20 pigs. When [he acquired it] 2 cobs, now 4. Then 4 head of cattle, now 10. Always 40 pigs. Now 50 sheep. Then 60 goats, now 28.

7 . II . uasa . apū . 7 III . soć . 7 dim̄ . xxv . ać trǣ . semp . dim̄ . car̄.
semp . val . IIII . lib . 7 v . sol . Huic trē . jacent hões in Refham.
7 sŧ apṗtiati cum ipsa . tr̄a . 7 habet Refham . q́sq́s ibi teneat.
dim̄ . leug̃ . in long̃ . 7 . IIII . qr̃ . i lat . 7 . III . đ . de gelto.

248 a

V̄H DE ERPINGEHAM. Sut̄h. Scedgetuna ten̄ . Asgarus . I.
lib hō t̄ . r . e . II . car̄ . terre . 7 xxvII . ać . m̄ . tenet Gaosfridus . bainard
Tc̄ 7 ṗ . vII . uilt . m̄ . vi . semp . I . car̄ in dn̄io . tc̄ 7 ṗ . I . car̄ . houm̄.
m̄ . dim̄ . silu . lx . por . xx . ać ṗti . 7 . I . mol . qn̄ reć . II . r . m̄ . IIII.
7 m̄ . xvII . an̄ . Tc̄ . xII . por . m̄ . xx . Tc̄ . xxIIII . oũ . m̄ . xv . tc̄
xxIIII . caṗ . m̄ . xxxvII . Tc̄ 7 ṗ . Val . xx . sol . m̄ . xxx . 7 . III .
soć . lxxvIII ać . t . r . e . 7 . II . bor . tc̄ . I . car̄ m̄ . dim̄ . 7 vIII .
ać ṗti . silu . xv . por . 7 ual . vi . sol . Hoc totū ten̄ Sc̄s . bened.
t̄ . r . e . p̄t . IIII . ać . 7 ht . I . leug̃ in long̃ . 7 dim̄ . in lato . 7 . redd.
vIII . đ . in geldum regis.

Tonsteda . H̃ . In Crostwit . tenet Gaosfridus . xII . libi hões
cl . ać sep̄ . xII . bor . 7 . xvI . ać ṗti . 7 . III . car̄ . 7 dim̄ . Tc̄ ual . xxvII.
sol . m̄ . xxII . sol . 7 . IIII . đ . 7 totum . ht . I . leug̃ . in long̃ . 7 . vII . qr̃.
in lato . q́c̃q ibi teneat . 7 . x . đ . de g̃ . Sc̄s benedictus cōmdatio
nē de uno dimidio hōc 7 socā suṗ . om̄s

V̄ In btuna tenet Gaosfrid̃ . III . libi hōes . lxxx . ać . semp . xII . bor.
7 . II . car̄ & dim̄ . 7 . I . ać . & dim̄ ṗti . 7 ual . xxIIII . sol . 7 vIII . đ.
sc̄s . b . socā 7 totū ht . x . qr̃ . in longo . 7 . vi . in lato . 7 xvIII . đ.
de . g̃ . q́c̃q ibi teneat . Vn̄ illis trib; cum . xxx . ać erat ita soć
sc̄i benedicti ut nullo m̄ posset recede.

Hapinga . H̃ . In Ristuna tenet . Gaosfrid̃ . I . lib . hō.
qm̄ tenuit ansger̃ . sub angero stalra . II . car̄ tr̄e.
Tc̄ xv . uilt . m̄ . x . Tc̄ . v . ser . m̄ . I . sep̄ . II . car̄ . i dn̄o.
Tc̄ . II . car̄ . hom̄ . m̄ . I . silu . IIII . por . 7 . v . ać ṗti.

248 b

Tc̄ . v . r . 7 . x . an̄ . m̄ . II . Tc̄ . xl . por . m̄ . xIIII . Tc̄ . xII . oũ . m̄.

2 beehives.

Also 3 Freemen and a half, 25 acres of land; always ½ plough. Value always £4 5s.

Men in REEPHAM appertain to this land and they are assessed with this land. Whoever holds there, Reepham has ½ league in length and 4 furlongs in width; tax of 3d.

The Hundred of SOUTH ERPINGHAM

248 a

2 Asgar, 1 free man, held SKEYTON before 1066, 2 c. of land and 27 acres. Now Geoffrey Baynard holds.

Then and later 7 villagers, now 6.

Always 1 plough in lordship. Then and later 1 men's plough, now ½. Woodland, 60 pigs; meadow, 20 acres; 1 mill. When he acquired it 2 cobs, now 4. Now 17 head of cattle. Then 12 pigs, now 20. Then 24 sheep, now 15. Then 24 goats, now 37.

Value then and later 20s; now 30.

Also 3 Freemen, 78 acres, before 1066.

2 smallholders.

Then 1 plough, now ½. Meadow, 8 acres; woodland, 15 pigs.

Value 6s.

St. Benedict held all this before 1066 except 4 acres. It has 1 league in length and ½ in width; it pays 8d in the King's tax.

TUNSTEAD Hundred

3 In CROSTWIGHT Geoffrey holds 12 free men, 150 acres.

Always 12 smallholders.

Meadow, 16 acres; 3½ ploughs.

Value then 27s; now 22s 4d.

The whole has 1 league in length and 7 furlongs in width, whoever holds there; tax of 10d. St. Benedict (has) the patronage of one half-man, and the jurisdiction over all.

4 In BARTON (Turf) Geoffrey holds; 3 free men, 90 acres.

Always 12 smallholders.

2½ ploughs; meadow, 1½ acres.

Value 24s 8d.

St. B(enedict) (has) the jurisdiction. The whole has 10 furlongs in length and 6 in width; tax of 18d, whoever holds there. One of those three, with 30 acres, was a Freeman of St. Benedict's on such terms that he could not withdraw in any way.

HAPPING Hundred

5 In (East) RUSTON Geoffrey holds; 1 free man, 2 c. of land, which Asgar held under Asgar the Constable.

Then 15 villagers, now 10. Then 5 slaves, now 1.

Always 2 ploughs in lordship. Then 2 men's ploughs, now 1. Woodland, 4 pigs; meadow, 5 acres. Then 5 cobs; 10 head 248 b of cattle, now 2. Then 40 pigs, now 14. Then 12 sheep, now

xxvi. Tc̄. xl. cap̄. m̄. li. Semp. ual. lx. sol. 7 xli. libi hōes.
. i. car. tr̄e. Tc̄ 7 p̄. viii. car. m̄. iiii. 7. ii. ac. p̃ti sep ual. iiii. lib.
In eadē. i. lib hō. xxx ac. tr̄e. sep. ii. bor. tc̄ 7 p̄. i. ca. m̄. dim̄.
7 ual. vi. sol. In eadē. i. lib. hō. ii. ca. tr̄e. sub Stigando. Tc̄
xv. uilli. m̄. xi. tc̄. iii. s. m̄. i. Tc̄ 7 p̄. i. car 7 dim̄. in dr̄io. m̄.
. i. sep. i. car hou. 7. v. ac. p̃ti. silu. iiii. por. Sep ual. xl. sol.
7 iii. libi hōes. xii. ac. sep. dim̄. car. 7 ual. iiii. sol. In ead.
. i. lib homo. almari. epī. ii. car. ter. Tc̄. xv. uilli. m̄. xi. Tc̄
. iii. s. Tc̄ 7 p̄. i. car. m̄. nulla. semp. i. car. hōm. 7. v. ac.
p̃ti. silu. iiii. por. 7 ual. xx. sol. 7. iii. soc̄. v. ac. tc̄. i. mol.
7 ual. ii. sol. Inť totum. erant. x. lib. 7 xii. sol. m̄ totū redd.
xx. libras. Totum ht. i. leug̃. 7 dim̄. in long̃. 7. i. leug̃.
7 iiii. q̄r. in lato. 7 xviiii. d. 7 obolum de gelto.

⟨Depwade H̄. Hamehala tenuit Torn. ī r. e. p̄ man.
viii. car. tr̄e. tc̄. liiii. uilli. m̄. xxxiiii. tc̄. xli. bor. m̄.
lviii. 7 p̄r. ii. eccle. i. car tr̄e. 7. iiii; uilli. 7. iiii. bor. 7. ii.

26. Then 40 goats, now 51.
Value always 60s.
Also 41 free men, 1 c. of land.
Then and later 8 ploughs, now 4. Meadow, 2 acres.
Value always £4.
In the same 1 free man, 30 acres of land.
Always 2 smallholders.
Then and later 1 plough, now ½.
Value 6s.
In the same 1 free man, 2 c. of land, under Stigand.
Then 15 villagers, now 11. Then 3 slaves, now 1.
Then and later 1½ ploughs in lordship, now 1. Always 1 men's plough; meadow, 5 acres; woodland, 4 pigs.
Value always 40s.
Also 3 free men, 12 acres; always ½ plough.
Value 4s.
In the same 1 free man of Bishop A(e)lmer's, 2 c. of land.
Then 15 villagers, now 11. Then 3 slaves.
Then and later 1 plough, now none. Always 1 men's plough; meadow, 5 acres; woodland, 4 pigs.
Value 20s.
Also 3 Freemen, 5 acres; then 1 mill.
Value 2s.
In total they paid £10 12s; now the whole pays £20.
The whole has 1½ leagues in length and 1 league and 4 furlongs in width; tax of 19½d.

DEPWADE Hundred

6 Thorn held HEMPNALL as a manor before 1066, 8 c. of land and 16 acres.
Then 54 villagers, now 34. Then 41 smallholders, now 58.
A priest, 2 churches; 1 c. of land; 4 villagers; 4 smallholders, 2

car̅ . 7 ual̅ . xv . fot̅ . Tunc 7 p̄ . vii . m̅ . nullus . T̄c̄ 7 p̄ . iii car̅ .
in dn̄io . m̅ . iiii . T̄c̄ 7 p̄ . xxxv . car̅ . hom̅ . m̅ . xxiiii . xii ac̅ p̄ti .
Silu̅ . cc . por . parte ifti . filue calumpniat̅ sc̅s . b . qm̅ ten̅
t̅ . r . e . 7 uocat̅ . Schietefhaga . T̄c̄ . i . mot̅ . m̅ . ii . sēp . v .
r . T̄c̄ . ix . an̅ . m̅ . xii . T̄c̄ . c . por . m̅ . lx . t̄c̄ . iiiii . ou̅ .
m̅ . clxxxvi . T̄c̄ 7 p̄ . ual̅ . xv . lib̅ . m̅ . xxiiii .
lib̅ . 7 . v . fot̅ . 7 . iii . libi ho̅es . 7 qr̅ta pars

unius . liii . ac̅ . 7 . ii . ac̅ p̄ti . 7 viii . bor . T̄c̄ . i . car̅ . & dim̅ .
m̅ . i . 7 ual̅ . xv . fot̅ . Pt̄ hoc totum redd̅ hoc manerīu . vi .
uac . 7 . xx . por . 7 . xx . arietes . 7 ht̅ . ii . leug̅ . in long̅ . 7 . i .
leug̅ . 7 . dim̅ . in lato . 7 . xviii . d̅ . de g̅ . Bainard . foca̅ 7 faca̅ .
¶Boielvnd ten̅ . Randulfus q̊ tenuit . Torn . t̅ r . e . i .
car̅ . tr̅e . sēp . ii . uifti . 7 . v . bor . T̄c̄ . ii . s . sēp . i . car̅ . in dn̄io .
7 ii . car̅ . hou̅m . T̄c̄ 7 p̄ . ii . ac̅ p̄ti . m̅ . i . filu . iii por . m̅ . i . mot̅ .
7 xx ou̅ . 7 . iii . uafa ap̅ . 7 . i . foc 7 dim̅ . 7 . i . ac̅ 7 dim̅ . T̄c̄
ual̅ . xx . fot̅ . m̅ . xl . Bainard . focam . 7 fac̅ .
¶Hateftuna tenet Gaosfrid̅ . q̊ tenuit . Torn . t̅ . r . e . iiii .
car̅ tr̅e . 7 . i . ac̅ . T̄c̄ . ii . uifti m̅ . i . T̄c̄ . xxxiiii . bor . m̅ .
xxviii . t̄c̄ . iiii . fer . m̅ . i . t̄c̄ . ii . car̅ . in dn̄io . m̅ . iiii . t̄c̄
v . car̅ hou̅m . m̅ . ii . Silua . xx . por . xv . ac̅ p̄ti . T̄c̄ . iiii . r .
m̅ . i . T̄c̄ . viii . an̅ . m̅ . xi . T̄c̄ . xl . por . m̅ xxxiii . T̄c̄ . i . ou̅ .
m̅ . cxc . 7 . i . uas ap̅ . T̄c̄ 7 p̄ . ual̅ . c . fot̅ . m̅ . x . lib̅ . 7 . xii .
fot̅ . 7 huic manerio jacebunt xviii libi ho̅es . com̅d tant
m̅ . xii . i . car̅ tr̅e . 7 xx ac̅ . 7 . v . ac̅ p̄ti . t̄c̄ 7 p̄ . iiii . car̅
m̅ . ii . T̄c̄ ual̅ . xx fot̅ . m̅ . xxviii . Ifti libi ho̅es s̅t efcangio .
Totu̅ ht̅ . ii . leug̅ . in long̅ 7 . i . in lati . q̊r̅ . 7 . i . leug̅ . in lat̅ .
7 xv . pert̅ . 7 ix . d̅ . de gelto .
¶In Frietuna . & in herduic . x . ac̅ . ten̅ lib̅ . ho̅ t̅ . r . e
7 ual̅ . xx . d̅ . hoc ē additum huic . manerio . hoc ē in hamehala .

ploughs.
Value 15s.
> Then and later 7 [?slaves], now none.
> Then and later 3 ploughs in lordship, now 4. Then and later 35 men's ploughs, now 24. Meadow, 12 acres; woodland, 200 pigs. In part of this woodland St. B(enedict) claims what (the abbey) held before 1066, called *Schieteshaga*. Then 1 mill, now 2. Always 5 cobs. Then 9 head of cattle, now 12. Then 100 pigs, now 60. Then 5 sheep, now 186.

Value then and later £15; now £24 5s.
Also 3 free men and a fourth part of one, 53 acres.   249 a
> Meadow, 2 acres;
> 8 smallholders.
> Then 1½ ploughs, now 1.

Value 15s.
> Besides all this the manor pays 6 cows, 20 pigs, and 20 rams.

It has 2 leagues in length and 1½ in width; tax of 18d. Baynard (has) the full jurisdiction.

7 Randolph holds BOYLAND where Thorn held before 1066, 1 c. of land.
> Always 2 villagers; 5 smallholders. Then 2 slaves.
> Always 1 plough in lordship; 2 men's ploughs. Meadow, then and later 2 acres, now 1. Woodland, 3 pigs; 1 mill; 20 sheep; 3 beehives.

Also 1 Freeman and a half, 1½ acres.
Value then 20s; now 40.
> Baynard (has) the full jurisdiction.

8 Geoffrey holds HUDESTON where Thorn held before 1066, 4 c. and 1 acre of land.
> Then 2 villagers, now 1. Then 34 smallholders, now 28. Then 4 slaves, now 1.
> Then 2 ploughs in lordship, now 4. Then 5 men's ploughs, now 2. Woodland, 20 pigs; meadow, 15 acres. Then 4 cobs, now 1. Then 8 head of cattle, now 11. Then 40 pigs, now 33. Then 1 sheep, now 190. 1 beehive.

Value then and later 100s; now £10 12s.
18 free men appertained to this manor in patronage only, now 12; 1 c. and 20 acres of land.
> Meadow, 5 acres. Then and later 4 ploughs, now 2.

Value then 20s; now 28.
> These free men are by exchange. The whole has 2 leagues and 1 furlong in length and 1 league and 15 perches in width; tax of 9d.

9 In FRITTON and in HARDWICK a free man held 10 acres before 1066. Value 20d. This has been added to this manor; this is in Hempnall.

⁊Clauelinga. H̄. Rauenicham tenet Einbold. q̃ tenuit.
Torn. t̄. r. ē. ii. car t̄re. semp. iii. uilli. 7. vi. bor̃.

249 b

tc̄. ii ꝟ ser. Tc̄. 7 p̄. i. car̃ in dn̄io. m̄. i. car̃ & dim̄i. semp. dim̄ car̃.
hoūm. Silu̅. v. por. viii. ac̃ p̃ti. m̄. i. r. 7. viii. por. 7. xv. soc̃. lvi.
ac̃. semp. iii. car̃ 7. i. ac̃ p̃ti. Tc̄ ual. xxx. sol. m̄. l. 7 ht. i. leug̃
in long̃. 7. ix. q̃r 7 dim̄. in lat̃. 7. xii. d̃. de g̃.

⁊In Sudwda. tenet Wimund. i. lib̃ hō lx. ac̃. de q̃ antec̃. Godrici.
habuit co̅md. t̄ r. e. semp. ii. bor. tc̄ 7 p̄. i. car̃. 7 iii. ac̃. p̃ti. 7. xxvi.
libi hōes. sub illo co̅md. lxxxiii. 7 dim̄. ac̃. Tc̄ 7 p̄. vi. car̃. m̄. ii.
Tc̄ ual. xx. sol. m̄. xl ; hoc ē ꝑ escangio. hanc t̃ram reclamat. Rob̃.
fili. corbutionis de dono regis. 7 reuocat. libatore. sed sed hund
testat' qd baig. p̃ inde saisit fuit. Tota Sudwada ht. i. leug̃.
in long̃. 7. dim̄. in lat̃. 7. viii. d̃. de gelto.

In Kerkebey. i. lib̃. hō. Regis. e. xxx. ac̃ nomine Vlmarus hunc
calumpniant'. R. fili corbueun. 7 ht libatore. sep. ii. bor. tc̄. i. ser.
Tc̄. ii. car̃. p̄. 7 m̄. i. tc̄ dim̄. car̃ hom. m̄. ii. boues. Silu̅. ii. por.
iii. ac̃. p̃ti. 7. viii. libi hōes. soca. falde. 7 co̅md. xx. ac̃. sep. ii.
car̃ 7 dim̄. ac̃ p̃ti. Tc̄ ual. xx. sol. m̄. xl. hoc ē ꝑ escang̃.

⁊In Nortuna. i. lib̃. hō xxx. ac̃. 7. ii. libi hōes. ii. ac̃ 7 dim̄.
semp. i. car̃. 7. ii. ac̃ p̃ti. 7 ual. x. sol.

⁊In Lerpstuna. i. lib̃. hō. xxx. ac̃. medietas istius hominis.
fuit antecessoris. baing. co̅mdatione tantum. 7 alia medietas
sc̃i eadmundi c̄ dimidia. t̃ra. tc̄. 7 p̄. i. car̃. m̄. n̄. dimidia. ac̃ p̃ti.
7 ual. v. sol.

⁊In Rauincham. i. lib̃ hō. xxx. ac̃. 7. iii. bor. tc̄. 7 p̄. i. car̃.
m̄ dim̄. alia car̃ posset restaurari. iii. ac̃ p̃ti. hunc &iam

250 a

calumpniant'. Robb̃. 7 ht libatore.

CLAVERING Hundred

10 Einbold holds RAVENINGHAM where Thorn held before 1066, 2 c. of land.
    Always 3 villagers; 6 smallholders. Then 2 slaves.
    Then and later 1 plough in lordship, now 1½ ploughs. Always ½ men's plough; woodland, 5 pigs; meadow, 8 acres. Now 1 cob; 8 pigs.
    Also 15 Freemen, 56 acres. Always 3 ploughs; meadow, 1 acre.
Value then 30s; now 50.
It has 1 league in length and 9½ furlongs in width; tax of 12d.

249 b

11 In SOUTHWOOD Wimund, 1 free man of whom Godric's predecessor had the patronage before 1066, holds 60 acres.
    Always 2 smallholders.
    Then and later 1 plough; meadow, 2 acres.
    Also 26 free men in patronage under him, 83½ acres.
        Then and later 6 ploughs, now 2.
Value then 20s; now 40.
    This is by exchange. Robert son of Corbucion claims this land of the King's gift and vouches (the King) his deliverer, but the Hundred testifies that Baynard had possession of it before. The whole of Southwood has 1 league in length and ½ in width; tax of 8d.

12 In KIRBY (Cane) 1 free man of King Edward's, Wulfmer by name, 30 acres. R(obert) the son of Corbucion claims him and he has a deliverer.
    Always 2 smallholders. Then 1 slave.
    Then 2 ploughs, later and now 1. Then ½ men's plough, now 2 oxen. Woodland, 2 pigs; meadow, 3 acres.
    Also 8 free men in fold-rights and patronage, 20 acres.
        Always 2 ploughs; meadow, ½ acre.
Value then 20s; now 40.
This is by exchange.

13 In NORTON (Subcourse) 1 free man, 30 acres. Also 2 free men, 2½ acres.
    Always 1 plough; meadow, 2 acres.
    Value 10s.

14 In IERPSTUNA 1 free man, 30 acres. A moiety of this man (was) under the patronage only of Baynard's predecessor, the other moiety (was) St. Edmund's with half the land.
    Then and later 1 plough, now none. Meadow, ½ acre.
Value 5s.

15 In RAVENINGHAM 1 free man, 30 acres.
    3 smallholders.
    Then and later 1 plough, now ½, and another plough could be restored. Meadow, 3 acres.
This man also Robert claims, and he has a deliverer.

250 a

In eadem . IIII . libi hōies . xxx . ač . 7 . I . car . Tc ual . xx . fot . m̄ . xxx. ⸿In Hals . I . lib̄ hō Stigandi Toka francigine . xxx . ač tr̄e . tc III . uilt . m̄ . II . sēp . I . car . 7 III . ač p̄ti . m̄ . XII . por . 7 . LX . oū . 7 . XII . libi hoēs sub se . soca . falde . 7 cōmd . 7 m̄ . st̄ . x . 7 h̄t . XLI . ač tr̄æ . sēp . I . cař 7 dim̄ . 7 . III . ač p̄ti . Et . II. lib̄ homō cōmd tantū . XVIII ač tr̄e 7 dim̄ . 7 dim̄ . car. et . I . lib̄ hō cōmd tant . xxx . ač tr̄e . 7 . I . bor . 7 . I . cař. 7 . I . ač p̄ti . Totum ual . tc 7 p̄ . XVII . fot . m̄ . xxx . fot.
⸿In Hwateaker . I . lib̄ hō Heroldi . II car . terre . q̄ tenet fran kus . semp . x . villi . 7 . v . bor . tc . IIII . f . m̄ . II . sēp . II . cař . in dn̄io . 7 . II . cař . houm . silu . VIII . por . 7 . xxx . ač p̄ti . Hunc calumpniať . R . filī Corbucini . 7 h̄t libā torē . Partura . cc . oū . semp . II . r . tc . VII . añ . tc . XII . por . m̄ . XVII . tc . cc . oū . m̄ . c . tc . VI . uasa apū . Et . VII . libi hoēs soc faldæ cōmdatione . XVIII . ač . sēp . II . cař . 7 . I . ač . p̄ti . Tc ual . xxx . fot . m̄ . XLV . Totū p̄ escañ.
⸿Wateaker tenet . Gaosfridus q̄ tenuit Toreth . tenn̄ . t . r . e . II . cař . terre . semp . VI . uilli . 7 . XII . bor . Tc . II . ser . sēp . II . car in dn̄io . 7 . II . cař houm . Silu VIII . por . xxx . ač p̄ti . sēp . II . r . 7 . XI . añ . tc . xv . por . m̄ . xxx . Tc . CLX oū . m̄ . CLXXVI . 7 VI . libi hoēs soca falde . 7 cm̄d . t . r . e . XVIII . ač . sēp . I . cař 7 . dim̄ . 7 . I . ač . p̄ti . 7 . II . ecclæ . LX . ač . in elemosina . 7 ual . v . fot . Tc manerium ual . xxx . fot.

250 b

m̄ . L . 7 . h̄t . I . leuḡ . in lonḡ . 7 dim̄ . in laī . 7 . XVI . đ . de gelto. ⸿In hadefcov . I . lib̄ hō . Stigandi . xv . ač . sēp dim̄ . cař . 7 . I . ač p̄ti . 7 ual . II . fot . hoc . ē . p̄ escanḡ . Stigand̄ . socā. In Thuruertuna . I . lib̄ . hō cōm̄d . XII . ač 7 ual . XII . đ.

In the same 4 free men, 30 acres; 1 plough.
Value then 20s; now 30.

16 In HALES 1 free man of Stigand's, Toki; Frenchmen (now hold him), 30 acres of land.
    Then 3 villagers, now 2.
    Always 1 plough; meadow, 3 acres.
      Now 12 pigs; 60 sheep.
    Also 12 free men under him in fold-rights and patronage; now there are 10; they have 41 acres of land. Always 1½ ploughs; meadow, 3 acres.
    Also 2 free men in patronage only, 18½ acres of land. ½ plough.
    Also 1 free man in patronage only, 30 acres.
      1 smallholder; 1 plough; meadow, 1 acre.
Value of the whole then and later 17s, now 30s.

17 In WHEATACRE 1 free man of Harold's, 2 c. of land, where a Frenchman holds.
    Always 10 villagers; 5 smallholders. Then 4 slaves, now 2.
    Always 2 ploughs in lordship; 2 men's ploughs; woodland,
      8 pigs; meadow, 30 acres.
R(obert) son of Corbucion claims him, and he has a deliverer.
    Pasture, 200 sheep; always 2 cobs. Then 7 head of cattle.
      Then 12 pigs, now 17. Then 200 sheep, now 100. Then 6 beehives.
    Also 7 free men in fold-rights (and) patronage, 18 acres.
      Always 2 ploughs; meadow, 1 acre.
Value then 30s; now 45. The whole (is) by exchange.
Geoffrey holds WHEATACRE where Thored, a thane, held before 1066, 2 c. of land.
    Always 6 villagers; 12 smallholders. Then 2 slaves.
    Always 2 ploughs in lordship; 2 men's ploughs; woodland,
      8 pigs; meadow, 30 acres. Always 2 cobs, 11 head of cattle.
    Then 15 pigs, now 30. Then 160 sheep, now 176.
    Also 6 free men in fold-rights and patronage before 1066, 18 acres. Always 1½ ploughs; meadow, 1 acre.
    Also 2 churches, 60 acres in alms;
value 5s.
Value of the manor then 30s; now 50.   250 b
    It has 1 league in length and ½ in width, tax of 16d.

18 In HADDISCOE 1 free man of Stigand's, 15 acres.
    Always ½ plough; meadow, 1 acre.
Value 2s.
    This is by exchange. Stigand (had) the jurisdiction.

19 In THURLTON 1 free man in patronage, 12 acres.
Value 12d.

H̃. de clacheslosa. In phincham tenuit. Alid libᵃ fem̃. I. car̃.
tr̃e. Sep̃. IIII. bor. Tc̃. III. s. Sep̃. I. car̃. XII. ac̃. p̃ti. Quando
recepit. II. r. m̃. I. Tc̃. VIII. por. Tc̃. XL. oũ. m̃. XVIII. Tc̃ ual.
L. sol. p̃. LX. m̃. XL. Hanc tr̃am. calumpniant̃ sc̃a. adeldret.
& ĥt testatur. In eadẽ uilla. VI. libĩ hõ͞es. 7 dim̃. tep̃r.
r. e. m̃. VII. 7 dim̃. q̃ tenent. I. car̃. ter̃æ. Sep̃. II. bor. 7. I. cã.
VIIII. ac̃ p̃ti.

⁌ In b̃tuna ten̄. Ailid. I. libᵃ fem̃. t̃. r. e. II. car̃ tr̃e. 7. II. car̃.
Sep̃. IIII. uilt̃. 7. VII. bor. Tc̃. IIII. s. XX. ac̃ p̃ti. Qñ. Rad̃. II.
r. m̃. III. Tc̃. II. an̄. Tc̃. LX. por. m̃. XV. Tc̃. CXL. b̃. m̃. XL.
Tc̃ 7 p̃. ual. LXXX. sol. m̃. LX. sol. I. eccl̃a. XXIIII. ac̃. 7
II. sol. Huic manerio adjacent. semp̃. IIII. hõ͞es. de om̃i
consuetudine. 7 alii. IIII. ad sochã tantum. 7 hab̃. I. car̃.
7. VI. ac̃ p̃ti. Tc̃ ual. XX. sol. m̃. XXX.

⁌ Sculdeham ten̄ Ailid. t̃. r. e. semp̃. II. car̃ in d̃nio. Tc̃. II.
car̃ hoũ. m̃. I. 7 dim̃. Tc̃. XIIII. uilt̃i. m̃. XV. II. b. m̃. XII.
Tc̃. IIII. s. semp̃. 7. X. ac̃ p̃ti. 7 tres part̃. mol. 7. I. pisc̃.
Tc̃. II. r. m̃. I. Tc̃. VI. an̄. tc̃. XVI. por. m̃. VIIII. tc̃. LX. oũ.
m̃. L. II. eccl̃æ. LXXIII. ac̃. 7 VI. sol. 7. I. d̃. Tc̃ ual. VII. lib̃.
7. m̃. In alio sculdeham ten̄ ailid. II. car̃ in d̃nio Tc̃. VIII.

uilt̃. m̃. VI. Tc̃ VII. bor. m̃. VI. tc̃. IIII. s. X. ac̃ p̃ti. 7. I. salina.
sep̃. I. car̃. hoũm. tc̃. II. r. 7 XV. por. 7 LX. oues m̃. nichil. tc̃
ual. C. sol. m̃. VIII. lib̃. huic mañ. jacent. XV. sochem̃ de XXIII.
ac̃. sep̃. dim̃. car̃. 7 sunt in sup̃ior censu. Totum scuddeham.
ĥt. I. leug̃ in long̃. 7 dim̃. in lato. 7 reddit. XII. d̃ de XX. sol. de
gelto. regis.

The Hundred of CLACKCLOSE
20 In FINCHAM Aethelgyth, a free woman, held 1 c. of land.
Always 4 smallholders. Then 3 slaves.
Always 1 plough; meadow, 12 acres. When he acquired it 2 cobs, now 1. Then 8 pigs. Then 40 sheep, now 18.
Value then 50s; later 60; now 40.
St. Etheldreda claims this land and the Hundred testifies (to it). In the same village 6 free men and a half before 1066; now 7 and a half, who hold 1 c. of land.
Always 2 smallholders;
1 plough; meadow, 9 acres.

21 In BARTON (Bendish) Aethelgyth, 1 free woman, held before 1066 2 c. of land.
2 ploughs.
Always 4 villagers; 7 smallholders. Then 4 slaves.
Meadow, 20 acres. When Ralph [acquired it] 2 cobs, now 3.
Then 2 head of cattle. Then 60 pigs, now 15. Then 140 sheep, now 40.
Value then and later 80s; now 60s.
1 church, 24 acres;
[value] 2s.
4 men have always appertained to this manor with all customary dues, and another 4 at jurisdiction only.
They have 1 plough; meadow, 6 acres.
Value then 20s; now 30.

22 Aethelgyth held SHOULDAM before 1066.
Always 2 ploughs in lordship. Then 2 men's ploughs, now 1½.
Then 14 villagers, now 15. [Then] 2 smallholders, now 12.
Then and always 4 slaves;
meadow, 10 acres; ¾ of a mill; 1 fishery. Then 2 cobs, now 1.
Then 6 head of cattle. Then 16 pigs, now 9. Then 60 sheep, now 50.
2 churches, 73 acres;
[value] 6s 1d.
Value then and now £7.
Aethelgyth held in the other SHOULDAM.
2 ploughs in lordship.
Then 8 villagers, now 6. Then 7 smallholders, now 6. Then 4 slaves.

251 a

Meadow, 10 acres; 1 salt-house; always 1 men's plough. Then 2 cobs; 15 pigs; 60 sheep; now nothing.
Value then 100s; now £8.
15 Freemen appertain to this manor, at 23 acres. Always ½ plough. They are in the above tribute.
The whole of Shouldham has 1 league in length and ½ in width, it pays 12d in the King's tax of 20s.

In carboiſtorp . 7 in tottenhella . xxii . libi hões
7 dim̃ . de . cx . ac̃ tenẽt . Ailid . t̃ . r . e . ſẽp . i . cãr . 7 ual . xl . ſol.
tota ht̃ . iiii . q̃r in long̃ 7 iii . in lat̃o 7 redd . vi . d . de gelto . Hanc
reclam̃ . p̃ eſcangio.

Wigghenham tẽn Ailid . ii . cãr tr̃e . ſẽp . xiii . uilli . 7 xi . bor.
Tc̃ . v . ſ . ſemp . ii . cãr . in dñio . 7 . i . cãr . hoũm . 7 dim̃ . 7 dim̃.
moli . 7 . i . piſc̃ . 7 xx . ac̃ p̃ti . Tc̃ . ii . r . 7 m̃ . Tc̃ . v . añ . m̃ . iiii.
ſẽp . xx . pọr . Tc̃ cccc . oũ . m̃ . clx . Tc̃ ual . vi . lib̃ . m̃ . xii.

Buchetuna tẽn . ailid . i . cãr tr̃e . Tc̃ . v . bor . m̃ . vii . tc̃
i . s . ſẽp . i . cãr in dñio . Tc̃ . i . cãr . hoũ m̃ dim̃ . 7 . vi . ac̃ p̃ti
ſẽp . i . r . 7 . i . uac̃ . Tc̃ . xi . por . ſẽp . c . oues . 7 . i . eccla . xx.
ac̃ . 7 . xx . d̃ . 7 ual . xl . ſol . Huic maner̃ . jacent ad ſocã . vii.
toc̃ d̃ . xxx . ac̃ tr̃æ . 7 . iiii . ac̃ p̃ti . 7 . i . cãr . 7 ual . x . ſol.

In ſtoches . xiii . libi hões ad ſocã . ſemp . vi . bor . 7 . i . piſc̃ . 7
. ii . cãr . 7 ual . lx . ſol . Quart pars . ecclē . v . ac̃ 7 ual . v . d̃.
7 alia eccla . xxvii . ac̃ . xxvii . d̃ . hoc reclam̃ . p̃ eſcangio.

In phordham . xxx . ac̃ . tẽn . iii : i . bor . libi hões . app̃tiati
ſunt ſup̃i.

In dereham tẽne . Luuell̃ . i . cãr tr̃æ : 7 . i . cãr . ſemp . i . uill.
De hoc hab̃ . ſc̃s . b . xx . ſol . t̃ . r . e . teſte . hund̃ . Adjacent

251 b

huic manerio . l . ac̃ . q̃d tẽn . libi hões . t̃ . r . e . Tc̃ . i . cãr . 7 dim̃.
m̃ . i . cãr . 7 ual . x . ſol . de iſtis . ht̃ ſc̃s . b̃ . ſocã . Tota . Stokes ht̃
vi . q̃r . in long̃ . 7 . iiii . in lat̃ . 7 redd . vi . d̃ . 7 . i . obolum . q̃cq̃ ibi teneat.

23 In (Shouldham) THORPE and in TOTTENHILL 22 free men and a half hold, at 110 acres. Aethelgyth (held) before 1066.
    Always 1 plough.
    Value 40s.
    The whole has 4 furlongs in length and 3 in width, it pays tax of 6d. This (Ralph) claims by exchange.

24 Aethelgyth held WIGGENHALL, 2 c. of land.
    Always 13 villagers; 11 smallholders. Then 5 slaves.
    Always 2 ploughs in lordship; 1½ men's ploughs; ½ mill;
      1 fishery; meadow, 20 acres. Then and now 2 cobs. Then
      5 head of cattle, now 4. Always 20 pigs. Then 400 sheep,
      now 160.
    Value then £6; now 12.

25 Aethelgyth held BOUGHTON, 1 c. of land.
    Then 5 smallholders, now 7. Then 1 slave.
    Always 1 plough in lordship. Then 1 men's plough, now ½.
      Meadow, 6 acres. Always 1 cob; 1 cow. Then 11 pigs;
      always 100 sheep.
    Also 1 church, 20 acres;
    [value] 20d.
    Value 40s.
    7 Freemen appertain to this manor at jurisdiction, at 30 acres of land. Meadow, 4 acres; 1 plough.
    Value 10s.

26 In STOKE (Ferry) 13 free men at jurisdiction.
        Always 6 smallholders;
        1 fishery; 2 ploughs.
    Value 60s.
    ¼ of a church, 5 acres;
    value 5d.
        Also another church, 27 acres;
    [value] 27d.
        (Ralph) claims this by exchange.

27 In FORDHAM 3 free man (with) 1 smallholder hold 30 acres.
    They are assessed above.

28 In (West) DEREHAM Lovel holds 1 c. of land.
    1 plough.
    Always 1 villager.
    Of this St. Benedict had 20s before 1066, as the Hundred testifies.
    50 acres are attached to this manor which free men held before   251 b
    1066. Then 1½ ploughs, now 1 plough.
    Value 10s.
        St. B(enedict) has the jurisdiction of these. The whole of Stoke (Ferry) has 6 furlongs in length and 4 in width, it pays 6½d, whoever holds there.

251 a, b

҉ In hekefuuella . xii . libi hões de . i . cař . tře . 7 . iiii . uilti . Tc . iii . ca.
p . m̃ . ii . x . ac . p̃ti filua . xx . por . sẽp . ual . xl . fol . unum ex his rect.
W . de Wař . de . xxx ac 7 reuocat libatorẽ . Hoc reclamat . p efcang.
Tota becheſwella . ht dim̃ . leug̃ in lon . 7 lat . 7 redd . viii . d . de . xx.
fol . de gelto . In dereham . ii . libi hões . vi . ac . 7 st . p̃tiate.

҉ H . 7 dim̃ . De Fredrebruga . i . cař třé . Tilinghetuna
teñ Gaosfrid . i . cař . třé . quo tenuit Tort . t . r . e . femp . v . uilti.
7 iiii . bor . 7 xxiiii . ac p̃ti . sep . i . cař . in dñio . 7 . i . cař hõum . 7 . v.
faline . 7 dim̃ . m̃ . i . r . 7 . v . añ . 7 . vii . p . tc . xv . ou . m̃ . cc . Tc ual.
xl . fol . p . x . m̃ . lx.

҉ In Lun . lviii . ac p̃ti . 7 . iii . ac . třé . 7 . ii . faline . 7 . i libu . hẽm de
iii . ac 7 viii . ac p̃ti . 7 d . falin . p efcañ . 7 sup hunc hab ſtigand.
focã.

҉ H̃ . de Grimeſh'u . In Stertuna teñ Lvuellus . vi . cař.
třé . q̃ tenet torp . Tc . ix . uilt . 7 p . m̃ . ii . Semp . ii . b . x . ac
p̃ti . Sep . ii . cař . in dñio . 7 tcia poteſt eſſe . Tc . iii . cař . hõum
m̃ . ii . bou . Tc . ii . r . m̃ . iii . tc . viii . añ . m̃ . xi . tc . xx . por . m̃
xl . tc . iii . ou . m̃ . cc . tc xi . eque m̃ . n̄ . Semp ual . lx . fol.

҉ 7 in ead . xvi . libi hõs teñ . ii . cař . třé . 7 . i . ac . tc . vi . cař . int
eos 7 p m̃ . iii . tc ual . xx . fol . q̃s hab p efcang . tota ht
i . leug̃ . in long . 7 d . in lat 7 xi . d . de gelto.

29 In BEECHAMWELL 12 free men, at 1 c. of land.
4 villagers.
Then 3 ploughs, later and now 2. Meadow, 10 acres; woodland, 20 pigs.
Value always 40s.
W(illiam) of Warenne claims 1 of these, at 30 acres, and vouches his deliverer. (Ralph) claims this by exchange. The whole of Beechamwell has half a league in length and in width, at 20s it pays tax of 8d.

30 In (West) DEREHAM 2 free men, 6 acres. They have been assessed.

The Hundred and a Half of FREEBRIDGE. 1 c. of land.
31 Geoffrey holds TERRINGTON, 1 c. of land, where Thored held before 1066.
Always 5 villagers; 4 smallholders.
Meadow, 24 acres. Always 1 plough in lordship; 1 men's plough; 5½ salt-houses. Now 1 cob; 5 head of cattle; 7 pigs. Then 15 sheep, now 200.
Value then 40s, later 10; now 60.

32 In LYNN, meadow, 58 acres; 3 acres of land; 2 salt-houses.
1 free man, at 3 acres; meadow, 8 acres; ½ salt-house.
By exchange. Stigand had the jurisdiction over him.

The Hundred of GRIMSHOE
33 In STURSTON Lovell holds 6 c. of land where Thorp held.
Then 9 villagers and later, now 2; always 2 smallholders.
Meadow, 10 acres; always 2 ploughs in lordship and there could be a third. Then 3 men's ploughs, now 2 oxen. Then 2 cobs, now 3. Then 8 head of cattle, now 11. Then 20 pigs, now 11. Then 3 sheep, now 200. Then 11 mares, now none.
Value always 60s.
Also in the same 16 free men hold 2 c. of land and 1 acre.
Then 6 ploughs between them and later, now 3.
Value then 20s.
(Ralph) has them by exchange. The whole has 1 league in length and ½ in width, tax of 11d.

H̃ DE GRNEHOU. BRADEHÁ tenuit. Ailid.

quædam liba femina. t̃. r. e. m̃. B. p̃ mañ. Tc̃ 7 p̃. xii. uitt.
m̃. xv. Tc̃ 7 p̃. vi. bor. m̃. viii. Tc̃ iiii. fer. m̃. nutt. Tc̃ in dñio
ii. car. m̃. fimit. Sep. houm. iii. car. viii. acr. p̃ti. Silua ad
cc. por. 7 d. Quand rece. ii. r. m̃. i. Tc̃ & m̃. i. Tc̃ 7 m̃. ix.
an. 7 xviii. por. 7 lxxv. ou. Tc̃. lxxx. cap. m̃. xxvi. 7 hb
dim̃. lingã. in longo 7. ii. q̃r 7 iii. q̃r. in lato. 7 redd in gelto.
xviii. d. 7 viii. foche ptinent. huic. mañ. 7 hab. i. car. & dim̃.
7 sep. Tc̃ ual. vi lib. 7 p̃. m̃ xii. i. eccla xv. ac. 7 ual. xv. d.

H̃. WANELUND. Meretuna teñ. Ailid.

t̃. r. e. iii. car. t̃re. 7. i. uirgata. Tc̃ 7 p̃. xvii. uitt.
m̃. vi. tc̃ 7 p̃. iii. bor. m̃. i. tc̃ 7 p̃. vi. fer. m̃. nult. filua
ccxl. por. xxxvi. ac p̃ti. femp. iii. car. in dñio tc̃. iiii.
car. houm. p̃. ii. m̃. ñ. tc̃. v. r; iiii. Tc̃. xviii. an. m̃.
xx. ii. sep. xxiiii. por. tc̃. cl. ou. m̃. lxxxx. Sep. xxviiii.
foc. ii. car. t̃re. c̃ om̃i c̃fuetud. p̃t. vi. Tc̃. vii. car. p̃. m̃. vi.
7 In Greftuna. i. fochem. xx. ac. Tc̃ ual. c. fot. m̃. vi.
lib. f. reddidit. viii. lib. Totum ht. i. leug. in long
7 dim̃. in lat. 7 xv. d. de gelto.

H̃. SCREPHAM. Willebeih tenuit. Ailid.

i. car ter. t̃. r. e. m̃ tene. Solidarius.. femp. ii. uitti.
7. ii. bor. tc̃. i. f. 7. vi. ac p̃ti. filu. v. por. sep. i. car in dñio.
7 dim̃. car. houm. sep. i. r. tc̃. iii an. m̃. v. m̃. por tc̃
cxx. ou. m̃. cix. Tc̃ 7 p̃ ual. xl. fot. m̃. lx.

The Hundred of (South) GREENHOE   252 a

34 Aethelgyth, a certain free woman, held BRADENHAM before 1066, now B(aynard) (has it) as a manor.
    Then and later 12 villagers, now 15. Then and later 6 smallholders, now 8. Then 4 slaves, now none.
    Then 2 ploughs in lordship, now the same. Always 3 men's ploughs; meadow, 8 acres; woodland for 250 pigs. When he acquired it 2 cobs, now 1. Then and now 1 [ ]. Then and now 9 head of cattle; 18 pigs; 75 sheep. Then 80 goats, now 26.
    It has half a league and 2 furlongs in length and 3 furlongs in width, it pays 18d in tax.
    Also 8 Freemen belong to this manor. They have 1½ ploughs and always (had).
    Value then and later £6; now 12.
    1 church, 15 acres of land; value 15d.

WAYLAND Hundred

35 Aethelgyth held MERTON before 1066, 3 c. of land and 1 virgate.
    Then and later 17 villagers, now 6. Then and later 3 smallholders, now 1. Then and later 6 slaves, now none.
    Woodland, 240 pigs; meadow, 36 acres; always 3 ploughs in lordship. Then 4 men's ploughs, later 2, now none. Then 5 cobs, now 4. Then 18 head of cattle, now 22. Always 24 pigs. Then 150 sheep, now 90.
    Always 29 Freemen, 2 c. of land with all customary dues except the 6. Then 7 ploughs, later and now 6.

36 In GRISTON 1 Freeman, 20 acres.
    Value then 100s; now £6; but it has paid £8.
    The whole has 1 league in length and ½ in width, tax of 15d.

SHROPHAM Hundred

37 Aethelgyth held WILBY, 1 c. of land, before 1066. Now a soldier holds it.
    Always 2 villagers; 2 smallholders. Then 1 slave.
    Meadow, 6 acres; woodland, 5 pigs. Always 1 plough in lordship; ½ men's plough. Always 1 cob. Then 3 head of cattle, now 5. Now [ ] pigs. Then 120 sheep, now 109.
    Value then and later 40s; now 60.

H. LAWEDIC. Titeshala tenuit norman lib hō
t̄.r.e.m̄ tenet. Radulfus turmit.IIII.car tr̄e. Tc̄ 7 p̄.xII.
uilli.m̄.vIII.Tc̄ 7 p̄.IIII.bor.m̄.xIIII.Tc̄ 7 p̄.vI.f.m̄.II.x.
ac̄ p̄ti.semp.II.car in dn̄io.tc̄ 7 post.IIII.car houm.m̄.
II.7.silu.c.por.sēp.I.mol.Tc̄.vI.an̄.Tc̄.xxx.por.m̄.
.xvIIII.Tc̄.c.ou.m̄.Lxxx.Tc̄.xL.cap̄.m̄.LxxIII.7 IIII.
uasa.apū.7 I.soc̄.vI.ac̄.Tc̄ ual.Lxx.sol.7 m̄.simil.
7.I.eccla.vI.ac̄ 7 ual.v.d̄.Totum ht.Ix.q̄r.in long.7
dim̄.leug.in lato.7.v.d̄.de gelto.

¶Walnccham tenet idem. Radulfus, q̄ tenuit Herold
t̄.r.e.p̄ man̄.II.car terae.semp.Ix.uilli.Tc̄.III.bor.p̄ 7
m̄.II.xIIII.ac̄.p̄ti Tc̄.I.car.in dn̄io.7 posset restaurari.
semp.II.car.houm.silu.Lx.por.7 vII.soc̄.xx.ac̄ tr̄ae.Tc̄
7 p̄.dim̄.car.m̄ nichil.7 III.soc̄.Stigandi ē t̄o jacebant
in muleham.regis com̄ om̄i.consuetudine.sed uiuente
Stigando libatū.ē baignardo p̄ escangio.ut dic̄t sui hōs
7 ht.xL.ac̄ tr̄ae.Tc̄.7 p̄.I.car.m̄.nulla.Manerium
ual t̄.r.e.xx.sol.7.m̄.x.7 III.soc̄.ual.t̄.r.e.IIII.
sol.m̄.xL.d̄.Totum.ht.I.leug in long.7 vIIII.q̄r.
in lato.7.x.d̄.de gelto.q̄cq̄ ibi tr̄a habet.

¶IN SCHerninga sunt.Lxxx.ac̄ tr̄e.Hoc jacet
in brehendam.7 in p̄ti.7.II.soc̄.xII.ac̄ tr̄e.Soca ē sēp
juste in muleham.

¶FEORHOU.H̄.Wiclurde tenuit.Olfus.

lib hō t̄.r.e.I.car.tr̄ae.m̄ ten̄.Radulfus.sturm̄.sēp
xI.uilli.7 vIII.bor.tc̄.III.s.m̄.I.sēp.II.car.in dn̄io.7.I.
car houm.vI.ac̄.p̄ti:sēp.I.mol.7.vIII.soc̄.xxIIII.ac̄ tr̄e.
socā in Hincham.7 hūt.I.car.Tc̄ I.r.Tc̄.vII.por.m̄.
xxx.Tc̄ vI.ou.m̄.IIII uasa.apū.Tc̄ 7 p̄.ual.xL.sol.
m̄.Lx.7 ht I.leug.in longo.7 vII.q̄r.7.I.perca in lato.
q̄cq̄ ibi habeat.7 xvII.d̄.7 III.ferdingos de gelto.

LAUNDITCH Hundred

38 Norman, a free man, held TITTLESHALL before 1066, now Ralph Sturmy holds, 4 c. of land.
  Then and later 12 villagers, now 8. Then and later 4 smallholders, now 14. Then and later 6 slaves, now 2.
  Meadow, 10 acres; always 2 ploughs in lordship. Then and later 4 men's ploughs, now 2. Woodland, 100 pigs; always 1 mill. Then 6 head of cattle. Then 30 pigs, now 19. Then 100 sheep, now 80. Then 40 goats, now 73. 4 beehives.
  Also 1 Freeman, 6 acres.
Value then 70s, now the same.
  Also 1 church, 6 acres,
value 5d.
  The whole has 9 furlongs in length and ½ league in width, tax of 5d.

39 Ralph also holds WELLINGHAM where Harold held before 1066 as a manor, 2 c. of land.
  Always 9 villagers. Then 3 smallholders, later and now 2.
  Meadow, 14 acres. Then 1 plough in lordship and it could be restored. Always 2 men's ploughs; woodland, 60 pigs.
  Also 7 Freemen, 20 acres of land. Then and later ½ plough, now nothing.
  Also 3 Freemen of Stigand's who(se land) then lay in the King's (manor of) Mileham, with all customary dues; but during Stigand's lifetime it was delivered to Baynard by exchange, as his men say. They have 40 acres of land. Then and later 1 plough, now none.
Value of the manor before 1066 20s; now 10. And the value of the 3 Freemen before 1066 4s; now 40d.
  The whole has 1 league in length and 9 furlongs in width, tax of 10d, whoever has the land there.

40 In SCARNING there are 80 acres of land. This appertains in BRADENHAM, and (it is) in the valuation.
  Also 2 Freemen, 12 acres of land. The jurisdiction has always been lawfully in Mileham.

FOREHOE Hundred

41 Ulf, a free man, held WICKLEWOOD before 1066, 1 c. of land, now Ralph Sturmy holds.
  Always 11 villagers; 8 smallholders. Then 3 slaves, now 1.
  Always 2 ploughs in lordship; 1 men's plough; meadow, 6 acres; always 1 mill.
  Also 8 Freemen, 24 acres of land. The jurisdiction is in Hingham. They have 1 plough. Then 1 cob. Then 7 pigs, now 30. Then 6 sheep. Now 4 beehives.
Value then and later 40s; now 60.
  It has 1 league in length and 7 furlongs and 1 perch in width, whoever has it, tax of 17¾d.

İN DIKETHORP. tenuit Norman lib hō f. r. e. 1. tr̄e.
semp. 1. uil̄s. 7. tc̄. 1. bor. m̄ iiii tc̄ iii. fer. femp. 11. car
in dn̄io. 7. iiii. ac̄ p̄ti. m̄. 1. r. sēp. iiii. an̄. m̄. xxii. por.
Tc̄. v. oū. m̄. xl. Tc̄ ual̄. xl. fol. m̄. lxxx. quarta pars
v. ac̄. 7 ual. v. d̄. 7 hr̄. iiii. q̄r in longo 7 iiii in lato. 7
xi. d̄. 7. i. obolū. de gelto.

H LOTHNINGA. In fcatagraua tenuit. Toret.
ii. car̄. teræ. m̄. tenet Einbold p 1. man̄. Sēp. ii.
uil̄i 7 xviiii. bor. 7. iiii. fer. Sēp. ii. car in dn̄io 7. i.
car̄. 7 dim̄. hōum. Silū. xv. por. 7 xii. ac̄ p̄ti. 7. i. mol.
Tc̄. ii. r. Tc̄. iiii. an̄. m̄. iii. Tc̄. vii. por. Tc̄. cc. oū.
m̄. clx. Sēp. ual̄. xl. fol. 7 hr̄. ix. q̄r. in lonḡ. 7
viii. in lato. 7 de gelto. ii. d̄. 7 xiii. foc. libi hōes 7 dim̄.
toret. lxxxix. ac̄. Sēp. iiii. car tr̄e. 7 dim̄. int hōes
7. v ac̄ p̄ti. 7 ual. x. fol. 7 hos reclamat p efcangio.
İN fcatagraua. ten̄. Leuric. 1. lib. hō heroldi. cōmd.
m̄ tenet Gaosfridus p man̄. ii car terre. Sēp. iiii.

253 b
uil̄i. 7. vi. bor. Tc̄. 1. fer. m̄ nul̄l Tc̄. ii. car. in dn̄io.
p. dim̄. m̄. i. Tc̄. ii. car. Hou. p 7 m̄. i. 7 dim̄. Silū
xv. por. 7 xii. ac̄ p̄ti 7. i. mol. Tc̄. ii. an̄. m̄. i. Tc̄. v.
por. m̄ nul̄l. i. eccl̄a. l. ac̄. i. p̄ti ual. ii. oras. 7 vi. foc.
7 dim̄. de xxiii. ac̄. 7. i. lib̄ hō Lefrici cōmd de. xvii. foc
7 dim̄. tc̄. i. car m̄. i. 7 dim̄. Sēp. dim̄. car. 7 dim̄. ac̄
p̄ti. Tc̄ 7 p ual. xxx. fol m̄. xl. Rotb̄tus. filius cor
butionis calumpniat̄ hanc tr̄am. ex libatione fed bainard.
pmū fuit faifit. 7 p. Rotb̄tus & hund. nefcit. q̄m.
Soca in hund.
İN Karlentona ten̄. i. lib hō fub toret. xxx. ac̄. tr̄e.
t. r. e. m̄. tenet. Nigell. Semp. iii. uil̄i. Tc̄. ii. bor.
m̄. iiii. Sēp int hōes. i. car̄. 7. iii. ac̄ p̄ti. 7. iii. foc. de
xxiiii. ac̄. Semp. i. car. Tc̄ ual. x fol. m̄. xx. Soca in
hund. hoc ē p efcangio.

42 Norman, a free man, held DYKEBECK before 1066, 1 [c.] of land.
Always 1 villager. Then 1 smallholder, now 4. Then 3 slaves.
Always 2 ploughs in lordship; meadow, 4 acres. Now 1 cob;
   always 4 head of cattle. Now 22 pigs. Then 5 sheep, now 40.
Value then 40s; now 80.
¼ [of a church], 5 acres;
value 5d.
It has 4 furlongs in length and 4 in width; tax of 11½d.

LODDON Hundred

43 Thored held in CHEDGRAVE, 2 c. of land; now Einbold holds as 1 manor.
Always 2 villagers; 19 smallholders; 4 slaves.
Always 2 ploughs in lordship; 1½ men's ploughs; woodland,
   15 pigs; meadow, 12 acres; 1 mill. Then 2 cobs. Then 4
   head of cattle, now 3. Then 7 pigs. Then 200 sheep, now 160.
Value always 40s.
It has 9 furlongs in length and 8 in width; tax of 2d.
Also 13 Freemen and a half, free men of Thored's, 99 acres.
Always 4½ c. of land among the men; meadow, 5 acres.
Value 10s.
He claims these by exchange.

44 Leofric, 1 free man under the patronage of Harold, held in
CHEDGRAVE, now Geoffrey holds as a manor, 2 c. of land.
Always 4 villagers; 6 smallholders. Then 1 slave, now none.   253 b
Then 2 ploughs in lordship; later ½, now 1. Then 2 men's
   ploughs, later and now 1½. Woodland, 15 pigs; meadow,
   12 acres; 1 mill. Then 2 head of cattle, now 1. Then 5 pigs,
   now none.
1 church, 50 acres; meadow, 1 [acre];
value 2 *orae*.
Also 6 Freemen and a half, at 23 acres; 1 free man under the
patronage of Leofric with 17 Freemen and a half.
   Then 1 plough, now 1½. Always ½ plough; meadow, ½ acre.
Value then and later 30s; now 40.
   This is by exchange. Robert son of Corbucion claims (to hold)
this land by livery, but Baynard had possession first, Robert later,
and the Hundred does not know by what means. The jurisdiction
(is) in the Hundred.

45 In CARLETON (St. Peter) 1 free man under Thored held 30 acres'
before 1066, now Nigel holds.
Always 3 villagers. Then 2 smallholders, now 4.
Always 1 plough between the men; meadow, 3 acres.
Also 3 Freemen, at 24 acres; always 1 plough.
Value then 10s; now 20.
   The jurisdiction (is) in the Hundred. This is by exchange.

Terre Rannulfi Peverelli.

H̄. DE ENSFORDA. Billingeforda. ten̄. Tord.
I. lib̄ hō. t̄. r. e. III. car̄. terre. m̄ tenet. Humfridus.
Semp. VII. uilti. 7 VIII. bor. 7. II. Ser̄. Tc̄. III. car̄. in dn̄io
p̄. I. 7 dim̄. m̄. II. tc̄ 7 p̄. VIII. car̄. hou͞. m̄. v. 7 III car̄.
poſſent fieri. ſilu̇. XII por. 7. I. mol̄. 7. VI. ac̄ p̄ti. Hic p̄ti
nebant. t̄. r. e. VI. ſoc̄. XLVIII. ac̄. 7 Rad̄. comes abſtulit
7 m̄. tenet comes. Alamus. ſemp. I. r. 7. X. an̄. 7 XVI. por.
LXX. ou͞. m̄. IIII. uaſa apū. ſemp. Val̄. IIII. lib̄. 7 h̄t
I. leuḡ. in lonḡ. 7 dim̄. in lato. 7 redd. VIII. d̄. 7 obolū.
q̄cq̄. ibi teneat. Soca in folſā regis.

H̄. HUMILIART. WALSINCHAM ten̄. Garinus
quo tenuit Ketel teinn̄. Stigandi. t̄. r. e. p. I. car̄. 7 dim̄.
tr̄e. ſemp. II. uilti. 7. III. ſer̄. 7. II. car̄. in dn̄io. 7 dim̄. car̄. hou͞m
IIII. ac̄ p̄ti. Silu̇. XII. por. Tc̄. IIII. r̄. Tc̄. IIII. an̄. tc̄.
XXXV. por. m̄. XX. Tc̄. XXV. ou͞. m̄. LX. II. uaſa ap̄. 7
XIII. libi hōes ſoca falde. 7 c̄omd̄ tant̄. t̄. r. e. XXX.
ac̄. Tc̄. I. car̄. p̄. m̄. dim̄. II. ac̄ p̄ti. I. ecc̄la. LX. ac̄. in p̄tio manerii.
V̄In Carletuna tenet idem Garinus. q̄ ten̄. Godric̄ lib̄
hō. kitel. LXXV. ac̄. Tc̄. I. car̄. p̄. I. m̄. nichil. II. bor. 7 dim̄.
7 IX. lib̄ hōes ſoca falde 7 c̄omd̄. tantū. Rex 7 comes ſoc̄a.
7 h̄t. XXXIII. ac̄. Tc̄ 7 p̄. II. car̄. m̄. I. 7. II. ac̄ p̄ti. 7. I. lib̄ hō.
c̄omd̄ tant̄. XXIIII. ac̄. ſep̄ dim̄. car̄. 7. II. ac̄. p̄ti. Tc̄ 7 p̄.
ual̄. LX. ſol̄. m̄. CX. 7 carletuna ual̄. XX. ſol̄. 7 Lib̄ hō

ual̄. II ſol ſed ē in numero de. CX. ſol̄. 7 Walſincham h̄t. VI.
q̄r̄. in lonḡ 7. V. in lat̄. 7. VI. d̄. 7. III. ferdinḡ. de. ḡ.
V̄Meltuna tenet. Garin. quo tenuit Ketel. t̄. r. e. II. car̄. terræ.

LANDS OF RANULF PEVEREL

The Hundred of EYNSFORD

1 Thored, 1 free man, held BILLINGFORD before 1066, 3 c. of land. Now Humphrey holds.
    Always 7 villagers; 8 smallholders; 2 slaves.
    Then 3 ploughs in lordship, later 1½, now 2. Then and later 8 men's ploughs, now 5, and there could be 3. Woodland, 12 pigs; 1 mill; meadow, 6 acres.
    6 Freemen belonged here before 1066, 48 acres. Earl Ralph took them away and now Count Alan holds.
    Always 1 cob; 10 head of cattle; 16 pigs; 70 sheep. Now 4 beehives.
    Value always £4.
    It has 1 league in length and a half in width, it pays 8½d, whoever holds there. The jurisdiction (is) in the King's (manor of) Foulsham.

HUMBLEYARD Hundred

2 Warin(g) holds WALSINGHAM where Ketel, a thane of Stigand's, held before 1066, as 1½ c. of land.
    Always 2 villagers; 3 slaves.
    2 ploughs in lordship; ½ men's plough; meadow, 4 acres; woodland, 12 pigs. Then 4 cobs. Then 4 head of cattle. Then 35 pigs, now 20. Then 25 sheep, now 60. 2 beehives.
    Also 13 free men, in fold-rights and patronage only before 1066, 30 acres. Then 1 plough, later and now ½. Meadow, 2 acres.
    1 church, 60 acres;
in the valuation of the manor.

3 In (East) CARLETON Warin(g) also holds where Godric, a free man of Ketel's held, 75 acres.
    Then 1 plough, later 1, now nothing.
    2 smallholders and a half.
    Also 9 free men in fold-rights and patronage only. The King and the Earl (have) the jurisdiction. They have 33 acres.
    Then and later 2 ploughs, now 1. Meadow, 2 acres.
    Also 1 free man in patronage only, with 24 acres. Always ½ plough; meadow, 2 acres.
Value then and later 60s; now 110. Value of (East) Carleton 20s. Value of the free man 2s, but he is included in the 110s.
    Walsingham has 6 furlongs in length and 5 in width, tax of 6¾d.

4 Warin(g) also holds (Great) MELTON, where Ketel held before 1066, 2 c. of land.

semp. II. uilli. 7 XVII. bor. 7. II. ser. 7. II. car. in dnio. Tc v. car.
houm. p. 7 m. IIII. xx. ac pti. silu. c. por. semp. I. mol. 7. II.
r. Tc. IIII. an. m. VI. Tc XXX. por. m. XLV. Tc. LX. ou. m.
CXIIII. II. uasa. apu. 7 VI. liberi hoes. de XVII. ac. soca falde.
t. r. e 7 comd. tant. sep. LXXVII. ac. I. eccla. III. ac in ptio.
manerii. 7 ual. II. sol. 7 st in ptio. de. VII. lib. Tc 7 p. ual.
VI. lib. m. VII. 7 ht. I. leug. in long 7. III. qr. 7 dim. leug
in lat. 7 de. gelto. XVI. d. 7 obolu. qcq, ibi habeat.

*K*eterincham. tenet ide Garinus q tenuit Ketel. t. r. e.
I. car teræ. 7 dim. sep. III. bor. 7. I. car. 7. dim. in dnio. 7 dim
car. houm. IIII. ac pti. sep. I. r. 7 VII. por. m. XL. ou. 7
IIII. libi hoes soca falde. 7 comd. tantum. XV. ac 7 dim.
car. 7. I. ac. pti. Tc ual. XXX. sol. p. XL. m. LX. 7 libi hoes.
ual. II. sol. 7 st in ode. ptio. I

*I*n. Meltunana tenet ide Garin. I. lib ho. VI. ac. pti.
7 ual. VI. d. Hoc inuasit. R. peurel.

H̄. *H*ersa. *D*Ī*M*. Riuessala tenet Warincus. q ten
Henric. asco eadmundo omnino it ecclam. t. r. e. p. I. car
7 dim. tre. Semp. VII. uill. 7 III. bor. Sep. II. car. in dnio
7. I. car. hou. Silu. XL. por. 7. V. ac pti m. I. eq. 7. III. an.
Tc. L. por. m. XVII. Tc. XIX. ou. m. XVIII. m. XII. cap

Tc. III. uasa. apu. m. I. Tc 7 p ual. XL. sol. m. LX. ht dim
leug. in long 7. V. in lato. 7. de gelto. VIII. d. S ; plures ibi.
tenent. m tenet. hac tera. Ranul. ad feudu reg.

Always 2 villagers; 17 smallholders; 2 slaves.
2 ploughs in lordship. Then 5 men's ploughs, later and now 4.
   Meadow, 20 acres; woodland, 100 pigs. Always 1 mill;
   2 cobs. Then 4 head of cattle, now 6. Then 30 pigs, now 45.
   Then 60 sheep, now 114. 2 beehives.
Also 6 free men, at 17 acres in fold-rights before 1066 and in
   patronage only, always 77 acres.
   1 church, 3 acres;
in the valuation of the manor.
Value (of the free men) 2s. They are in the valuation of £7.
Value then and later £6; now 8.
   It has 1 league and 3 furlongs in length and ½ league in width,
tax of 16½d, whoever has it.

5 Warin(g) also holds KETTERINGHAM, where Ketel held before 1066,
1½ c. of land.
   Always 3 smallholders;
   1½ ploughs in lordship; ½ men's plough; meadow, 4 acres.
      Always 1 cob; 7 pigs. Now 40 sheep.
   Also 4 free men in fold-rights and in patronage only, 15 acres;
      ½ plough; meadow, 1 acre.
Value then 30s; later 40; now 60. Value of the free men 2s; they
are in the same valuation.

6 Warin(g) also holds in (Great) MELTON, 1 free man, 6 acres of
meadow.
   Value 6d. R(anulf) Peverel annexed this.

EARSHAM Half Hundred
7 Warin(g) holds RUSHALL, where Henry held from St. Edmund
entirely within the church before 1066, as 1½ c. of land.
   Always 7 villagers; 3 smallholders.
   Always 2 ploughs in lordship; 1 men's plough; woodland, 40
      pigs; meadow, 5 acres. Now 1 horse; 3 head of cattle. Then
      50 pigs, now 17. Then 19 sheep, now 18. Now 12 goats.
      Then 3 beehives, now 1.

255 a

Value then and later 40s; now 60.
   It has half a league in length and 5 [furlongs] in width, tax of
8d. But more hold there. Ranulf now holds this land as part of
the King's Holding.

Terra Rodḃti. **Grenonis** H̃. .XXXIII.

De ensford. Sparham tenet osḃtus q̃ teñ. Ulric⁹
. ı . liƀ hõ . t̃ . r . e . p mañ . ııı . car̃ træ . ſemp . vı uiłłi . 7 . v .
bor. Tc̃ . ıı . ſ . m̃ . nuł . ſẽp . ıı . car̃ . in dñio . 7 . ıı . car̃ . hoũm
7 . vı . ac̃ . p̃ti . 7 dim̃ . moł . ſił . c . por . q̃ñ rec̃ . ıx . por .
m̃ . vı . oũ . 7 . xxv . cap̃ . Et . ııı . ſoc̃ . xx . ac̃ t̃re . ſẽp . d̃ .
car̃. Tc̃ 7 p̃⁹. uał . lx . ſoł . 7 m̃ . ıııı . liƀ .

Erpincham Svd. H̃. Torp tenet osḃtus
q̃⁹ tenuit Vluric̃ . liƀ hõ Guerd . ıı car̃ . tere . t̃ . r . e .
Semp . ııı . uiłłi . 7 . x . bor. Tc̃ . ıı . ſ . m̃ . ı . Tc̃ . ııı . car̃ . in
dñio . m̃ . ıı . ſep . ı . car̃ . 7 dim̃ . hoũm . 7 . ı . eccła

255 b
de xxx . ac̃ . in elemoſina . Tc̃ ſiłu . xl . por . m̃ . xxx . ſemp . ıı .
. t̃ . 7 xvıı . por. Tc̃ . c . oũ . m̃ . lxxx . 7 . xl . cap̃ . 7 . ı . ſoc̃ . vııı .
ac̃ . ſẽp . dim̃ . car̃ . ſẽp . uał . xxx . ſoł . 7 h̃t . vı . q̃r̃ . in lõg̃ . 7 . v .
in lato . 7 vı . d̃ . 7 . ııı . ferding̃ . de . g̃ .

▽ H̃ . *Clavdinga.* In Nortuna . tenet idem . xıı . ac̃ .
de dñio . de Lodues . 7 uał . xıı . d̃ .

▽ In Narueſtuna . ıııı . ac̃ . t̃re . 7 . ı . liƀ . hõ Vluric̃⁹ . noẽ . t̃ . r . e .
7 uał . ıııı . d̃ .

H̃ . *Erpingehã. North.* In torp . tenet .
Osḃt⁹ . vıı . liƀi hoẽs de . xl . ac̃ . t̃re . ı . ac̃ . p̃ti . Semp . ı . car̃ .
& uał . xıı . ſoł .

H̃ . *Lothninga.* In Lothna tenet . Osḃt⁹ . q̃ teñ .
Vluric̃⁹ . liƀ hõ ſub gert . t̃ . r . e . ı . car̃ . terre . 7 dim̃ . Sẽp .
. ıı . uiłłi . 7 . xıı . bor. Tc̃ . ı . ſer. Semp . ıı . car̃ . in dñio . Tc̃ 7 p̃⁹.
ıı . car̃ . hoũm . m̃ . ı . 7 dim̃ . Siłu . xx . por . 7 . ıııı . ac̃ . p̃ti . 7 dim̃ .
moł . m̃ . ııı . eq̃ . in aula . 7 . ıııı . añ . Tc̃ . c . oũ . m̃ . lx . Tc̃ . x .
por . m̃ . xxı . 7 . ı . ſoc̃ . de . x . ac̃ . Sẽp . ı . car̃ . int oẽs . Tc̃
7 p̃⁹. uał . xx . ſoł . m̃ . xl . R . comes . ſocã .

▽ In Lathaham . ıııı . ac̃ . t̃re . in p̃tio . ÷ . xl . ſoł .

LAND OF ROBERT GERNON

The Hundred of EYNSFORD

1 Osbert holds SPARHAM where Wulfric, 1 free man, held before 1066, as a manor, 3 c. of land.
  Always 6 villagers; 5 smallholders. Then 2 slaves, now none.
  Always 2 ploughs in lordship; 2 men's ploughs; meadow, 6 acres; ½ mill; woodland, 100 pigs. When he acquired it 9 pigs. Now 6 sheep; 25 goats.
  Also 3 Freemen, 20 acres of land, always ½ plough.
  Value then and later 60s; now £4.

SOUTH ERPINGHAM Hundred

2 Osbert holds (Bacons)THORPE where Wulfric, a free man of Gyrth's, held 2 c. of land before 1066.
  Always 3 villagers; 10 smallholders. Then 2 slaves, now 1.
  Then 3 ploughs in lordship, now 2; always 1½ men's ploughs.
  Also 1 church, at 30 acres in alms. Then woodland, 40 pigs, now 30. Always 2 cobs; 17 pigs. Then 100 sheep, now 80. 40 goats.   255 b
  Also 1 Freeman, 8 acres; always ½ plough.
  Value always 30s.
  It has 6 furlongs in length and 5 in width, tax of 6¾d.

CLAVERING Hundred

3 In NORTON (Subcourse) he also holds 12 acres of the lordship of Loddon.
  Value 12d.

4 In *NARUESTUNA* 4 acres of land, and 1 free man, Wulfric by name, before 1066.
  Value 4d.

NORTH ERPINGHAM Hundred

5 In THORPE (Market) Osbert holds; 7 free men, at 40 acres of land; meadow, 1 acre. Always 1 plough.
  Value 12s.

LODDON Hundred

6 In LODDON Osbert holds where Wulfric, a free man under Gyrth, held before 1066, 1½ c. of land.
  Always 2 villagers; 12 smallholders. Then 1 slave.
  Always 2 ploughs in lordship. Then and later 2 men's ploughs, now 1½. Woodland, 20 pigs; meadow, 4 acres; ½ mill. Now 3 horses at the hall; 4 head of cattle. Then 100 sheep, now 60. Then 10 pigs, now 21.
  Also 1 Freeman, at 10 acres. Always 1 plough between them all.
  Value then and later 20s; now 40.
  Earl R(alph) (had) the jurisdiction.
In LODDON 4 acres of land.
It is in the valuation of 40s.

TERRÆ PETRI VALONIENSIS H̄. 7 dim̃.   .XXXIIII.

de fredrebruge. Babinkeleia tenet. Willī q̃m ten̄.

Tort. lib hō. t̄. r. e. p man̄. 1. car̄. tēr. IIII. uilli. 7 xv. bor
7. v. ser. 7 xvi. ac̄ p̃ti. silu. LX. por. Tc̃. II. car̄ in dn̄io p̄. 7. m̄
1. Tc̃. III. car̄ hōum. p̄ 7. m̄. II. 7 medietatē duoꝫ molinoꝫ.
7. v. sal. Quāndo. cec̄. I. r. Tc̃. x. an̄. m̄. vIII. Tc̃. xII. por.
m̄. xIII. Tc̃ CLx. ou. m̄. CLxxvII. Hic jacent. vII. soc̄. vi.
ac̄ tr̄e. semp. I. car̄. tam̄. ex h̄ t̄ habuit. Stigandus socam
Totū ual. xL. sol. Totum fit II. leug̃. in long̃. 7. I. leug̃. in
lat̄. q̃c̃q̃ ibi teneat 7 redd̄. II. sol. d̄. xx. sol. de gelto.

⸿Dersincham ten̄ t̄. r. e. I. lib hō. p man̄. semp. II. car̄
in dn̄io. 7 vII. uilli. 7. IIII. bor. tc̃ 7 p̄. IIII. s. m̄. II. 7 vII. ac̄.
7 dim̃. p̃ti. 7. I. car̄. hōum. 7. I. sal. Tc̃. v. r. m̄. I. Tc̃. III. an̄.
7 xvIII. por. 7. ccc. ou. m̄. nichil.
In eadem. ten. anant lib hō. II. car̄. teræ. in dn̄io p man̄.
semp. I. car̄. 7 dim̃. 7 xxx. uilli. 7 vI. bor. 7 vII. ser.
7 xvIII. ac̄ p̃ti. 7. I. mol. 7. I. pisc̄. 7. I. sal. Tc̃. vI. r. m̄. v.
Tc̃. IIII. an̄. 7. m̄. Tc̃ xL. por. m̄. xxI. Tc̃. DLx. ou. m̄.
de. cxLvi.

⸿In appletuna. tenet. Turgis. I. brewita que semp
jacet. huic manerio. I. car̄. tr̄e. 7. I. car̄. in dn̄io. Tc̃
7 p̄. III. bor. m̄. v. 7. vII. ac̄. p̃ti. 7 dim̃. Tc̃ 7 p̄. I. ser.
Tc̃. c. ou. m̄. II. ou. Totum. ual. xv. lib.
sed tm̃ redd̄. xvII. lib. 7. xIII. sol.

Totum dersincham fit. I. leug̃. in longo. 7 dim̃. in lat̄.
q̃c̃q̃ ibi teneat 7 redd̄. xvI. d̄. d̄. xx. de gelto.

LANDS OF PETER OF VALOGNES

The Hundred and a Half of FREEBRIDGE

1 William holds BABLINGLEY which Thored, a free man, held as a manor before 1066, 1 c. of land.
    4 villagers; 15 smallholders; 5 slaves.
    Meadow, 16 acres; woodland, 60 pigs. Then 2 ploughs in lordship, later and now 1. Then 3 men's ploughs, later and now 2. A moiety of 2 mills; 5 salt-houses. When he acquired it 1 cob. Then 10 head of cattle, now 8. Then 12 pigs, now 13. Then 160 sheep, now 177.
    7 Freemen appertain here, 6 acres of land; always 1 plough.
    Yet of these Stigand had the jurisdiction.
Value of the whole 40s.
The whole has 2 leagues in length and 1 league in width; whoever holds there, of a 20s tax, it pays 2s.

2 1 free man held DERSINGHAM as a manor before 1066.
    Always 2 ploughs in lordship.
    7 villagers; 4 smallholders. Then and later 4 slaves, now 2.
    Meadow, 7½ acres; 1 men's plough; 1 salt-house. Then 5 cobs, now 1. Then 3 head of cattle; 18 pigs; 300 sheep; now nothing.
In the same Anand, a free man, holds 2 c. of land in lordship as a manor.
    Always 1½ ploughs.
    30 villagers; 6 smallholders; 7 slaves.
    Meadow, 18 acres; 1 mill; 1 fishery; 1 salt-house. Then 6 cobs, now 5. Then 4 head of cattle and now. Then 40 pigs, now 21. Then 560 sheep, now 646.

3 In APPLETON Thorgils holds 1 outlier which has always appertained to this manor, 1 c. of land.
    1 plough in lordship.
    Then and later 3 smallholders, now 5.
    Meadow, 7½ acres.
    Then and later 1 slave.
    Then 100 sheep, now 2 sheep.
Value of the whole £15; but yet it pays £17 13s.
The whole of Dersingham has 1 league in length and ½ in width, whoever holds there, of a 20s tax, it pays 16d.

H. de Smetheduna. In evlveſtorp. tenuit tp̄r.
r.e. Toruert lib̃ hō. III. car̜. in dn̄io. Tc̃. 7 p̚. x. uiffi.
m̃. VII. ſemp. xv. bor. Tc̃ 7 p̚. II. ſer̜. m̃. v. 7. L. ac̃ p̃ti.
Tc̃. III. car̜. hoũm. p̚. 7 m̃. II. ſēp. II. moł. 7. I. ſał. tē. I.
piſc̃. Tc̃. VIII. r. m̃. IIII. Tc̃ xIIII. equæ. Tc̃. v. an̄. tc̃
LX. por. m̃. xv. Tc̃. cccxL. ou. m̃. cccxx. 7. III. lib̃i.
hoēs. xxxVIII. ac̃ tr̃e. I. car̜ de his habuit. ſuus. anteceſ.
ſocā. falde. 7 c̃ōmd̃. Stigandus ſocā aliam. Tc̃ 7 p̚. uał.
IX. lib̃. 7. m̃. x. ſed reddit. xII. lib̃. Totum ħt dim̃. leug̃.
in long̃. 7. v. qr̃. in lato. qc̃q̨ ibi teneat 7 redd̃. xII. d̃.
de xx. ſoł. de gelto.

$\bar{H}$. LAWENDIC. Pateſleia. tenet Rogerus.
q̃m tēn. Aleſtan̄. lib̃ hō. t̄. r. e. p̚ man̄. II. car̜ tr̃e.
in dn̄io. Tc̃ 7 p̚. I. car̜ hoũm m̃ nulla. ſed poſſet eē. ſitu
x. por. 7 dim̃. piſcē. m̃. I. r. 7 xv. an̄. Tc̃. IIII. por. m̃.
xIII. an̄. m̃. LVIIII. ou. ſēp. uał. xx. ſoł. 7 ħt. IIII. qr̃.
in long̃. 7 II. in lato. 7. III. d̃. de gelto. Soca in mełē.
maneriũ regis.

Et In gatelea tenet Radulfus. II. ſoc̃. xxx. IIII.
ac̃ tr̃e. de his habuit anteceſſorē Hugonis.
de monte forti ſocā falde. 7 c̃ōmdationē.
7. alia ſoca in muleham. regis.

m̃ eos tenet petrus. de lib̃ationē ſemp̚. I. 7. I. ac̃. 7 dim̃. p̃ti.
ſemp. uał. xx. ſoł.

$\bar{H}$. DE GALGOU. In eſnaringa tenet. Radulfus. q̃m
tēn. Manna. I. lib̃ hō t̄. r. e. I. car̜ terre. Semp. xxIIII. bor
Sēp̚. I. ſer̜. Tc̃. I. car̜ in dn̄io. 7. p̚. m̃. II. Semp̚ hoũm. I. car̜.
IIII. ac̃ p̃ti. Tc̃. I. moł. Semp. vI. an̄. 7 m̃. Lx. por. Tc̃. Lxxx. ou.
m̃. L. 7 vI. ſoc̃ de. xL. ac̃ tr̃e. 7. II. bor. 7. I. car̜. v. ac̃ p̃ti. Huic
manerio p̃tin. I. ſoc̃. de. III. ac̃. in halgetuna. Tc̃ uał. xL. ſoł.
m̃. ſimilit̃. 7 hab̃. dim̃. leug̃. in long̃. 7. III. qr̃ in lato. 7 xII.
d̃. in gelto.

The Hundred of SMETHDON

4 In INGOLDISTHORPE Thorbert, a free man, held 3 ploughs in lordship before 1066.
    Then and later 10 villagers, now 7. Always 15 smallholders. Then and later 2 slaves, now 5.
    Meadow, 50 acres. Then 3 men's ploughs, later and now 2. Always 2 mills; 1 salt-house. Then 1 fishery. Then 8 cobs, now 4. Then 14 mares. Then 5 head of cattle. Then 60 pigs, now 15. Then 340 sheep, now 420.
    Also 3 free men, 38 acres of land; 1 plough. His predecessor had the fold-rights and patronage of these, and Stigand the other jurisdiction.
    Value then £9; now 10; but it pays £12.
The whole has ½ league in length and 5 furlongs in width, whoever holds there, of a 20s tax, it pays 12d.

LAUNDITCH Hundred

5 Roger holds PATTESLEY which Alstan, a free man, held before 1066 as a manor, 2 c. of land in lordship.
    Then and later 1 men's plough, now none, but there could be. Woodland, 10 pigs; ½ fishery. Now 1 cob; 15 head of cattle. Then 4 pigs. Now 13 head of cattle. Now 59 sheep.
    Value always 20s.
It has 4 furlongs in length and 2 in width, tax of 3d. The jurisdiction is in Mileham, the King's manor.

6 Also in GATELEY Ralph holds; 2 Freemen, 34 acres of land. Of these the predecessor of Hugh of Montfort had the fold-rights and patronage. The other jurisdiction (is) in the King's (manor of) Mileham. Now Peter holds them by livery.   257 a
    Always 1 [?plough]; meadow, 1½ acres.
    Value always 20s.

The Hundred of GALLOW

7 In (Little) SNORING Ralph holds what Mann, 1 free man, held before 1066, 1 c. of land.
    Always 24 smallholders; always 1 slave.
    Then and later 1 plough in lordship, now 2. Always 1 men's plough; meadow, 4 acres. Then 1 mill; always 6 head of cattle. Now 60 pigs. Then 80 sheep, now 50.
    Also 6 Freemen, at 40 acres of land. 2 smallholders; meadow, 5 acres.
To this manor belongs 1 Freeman, at 3 acres, in HELHOUGHTON.
Value then 40s; now the same.
It has ½ league in length and 3 furlongs in width, 12d in tax.

⁊In *PARVA REIENBVRH*. tenet Tirus q̃m tẽn . 1 . lib̃ hõ
t . r . e . 1 . car̃ . tere . Tc̃ . ɪx . bor . m̃ . vɪ . Tc̃ . ɪɪ . ſer . Semp . in
dn̄io . 1 . car̃ . Tc̃ hoũm . 1 . car̃ . m̃ . đ . Silu . vɪ . por . ɪɪɪɪ . ac̃ p̃ti
1 . mot . Tc̃ . ɪɪ . r . m̃ . 1 . Sep̃ . vɪɪɪ . an . Tc̃ . ɪɪɪɪ . por . m̃ . xɪ . Tc̃
xxx pu . m̃ . xx . ou . ſemp . uat . xʟ . ſ̃ . ⁊ hb̃ . ɪɪɪ . q̃r̃ in long̃ .
⁊ . ɪɪ . in lat̃ . ⁊ . xɪɪ . đ . in gl̃to.

⁊H̃ *DE BRODERCROS* . In reienburh . tenet
Radulfus faeto . quam tẽn . Goerth . t̃ . r . e . ɪɪ . car̃ . terre.
Sep̃ . 1 . uitti . ⁊ . xɪ . bor . ⁊ . ɪɪɪɪ . ſer . ⁊ in dn̄io . ɪɪ . car̃ . ⁊ hoũm
1 . car̃ . Silva ad . xʟ . por . vɪ . ac̃ . p̃ti . 1 . mot . Sep̃ . ɪɪ . r . m̃
ɪx . an . Sep̃ . xʟ . por . Tc vɪɪ . ou . m̃ . ʟx . Huic man̄ . ptin̄
. 1 . beruita toftes . de . xxx . ac̃ . t̃re . Semp . ɪɪɪɪ . bor . Sep̃
in dn̄io . 1 . car̃ . Tc̃ ⁊ ſemp . dim̃ . car̃ . hoũm . Tc̃ uat . ɪɪɪɪ .
lib̃ . ⁊ m̃ . v . lib̃ . Reienburh . hab̃ . vɪɪ . q̃r̃ . in long̃ . ⁊ v .

in lato . ⁊ vɪɪɪɪ . đ . ⁊ 1 . ferting . in gelto . ⁊ totes hab̃ . ɪɪɪɪ . q̃r̃ . in
long̃ . ⁊ ɪɪɪ . in lato . ⁊ xv . đ . in gelto

⁊In eſtretona tenet Ricard q̃m tẽn . Toka . lib̃ hõ t̃ . r . e . dim̃ .
car̃ t̃ræ . Sep̃ . vɪɪ . bor . ⁊ . 1 . ſer . Sep̃ . in dn̄io . 1 . car̃ . Tc̃ hoũm
1 . ⁊ . p̃ m̃ . đ . car dim̃ ac̃ p̃ti . Tc̃ uat . x . ſot . m̃ ſimit.

⁊In rudehã tenet . Turgis . 1 . lib̃ . hõ de dim̃ . car̃ t̃re . Sep̃ . ɪɪɪ .
bor . ⁊ . 1 . ſer . Tc̃ . 1 . car̃ . p̃ . ⁊ dim̃ . m̃ . 1 . ⁊ . 1 . ac̃ p̃ti . ⁊ . ɪɪɪɪ . ſoc̃ . de
vɪ . ac̃ . Sep̃ . dim̃ . car̃ . Sep̃ . uat . x . ſot.

★ H̃ *DE GALGOV* . In ſaxelinghã tenet Theodric̃ . 1 .
lib̃ hõ de . dim̃ . car̃ . terre . Tc̃ . 1 . car̃ . m̃ . ſimit . Sep̃ . ɪɪ . bor
ɪɪ . ac̃ . p̃ti . Tc̃ uat . ɪɪ . ſ̃ m̃ . v . ſ̃.

H̃ . *DE HOLT* . In gunatorp . 1 . lib̃ hõ heroldi . de đ . car̃ .
t̃re . Sep̃ . vɪ . bor . ⁊ . 1 . ſer . Sep̃ . ɪɪ . car̃ . Silua . ad . ɪɪɪɪ . por .
1 . ac̃ p̃ti . ⁊ uat . x . ſot . Hec̃ fuit ſibi libata ad p̃ficiendum.
. 1 . manerium . berneia.

8   In LITTLE RYBURGH Thyri holds 1 c. of land which 1 free man held before 1066.
    Then 9 smallholders, now 6. Then 2 slaves.
    Always 1 plough in lordship. Then 1 men's plough, now ½. Woodland, 6 pigs; meadow, 4 acres; 1 mill. Then 2 cobs, now 1. Always 8 head of cattle. Then 4 pigs, now 11. Then 30 sheep, now 20 sheep.
    Value always 40s.
    It has 3 furlongs in length and 2 in width, 12d in tax.

The Hundred of BROTHERCROSS

9   In (Great) RYBURGH Ralph Fat holds what Gyrth held before 1066, 2 c. of land.
    Always 1 villager; 11 smallholders; 4 slaves.
    2 ploughs in lordship; 1 men's plough; woodland for 40 pigs; meadow, 6 acres; 1 mill; always 2 cobs. Now 9 head of cattle; always 40 pigs. Then 7 sheep, now 60.
    To this manor belongs 1 outlier, TOFTREES, at 30 acres of land.
    Always 4 smallholders.
    Always 1 plough in lordship. Then and always ½ men's plough.
    Value then £4; now £5.
    (Great) Ryburgh has 7 furlongs in length and 5 in width, 257 b
    9¼d in tax. Toftrees has 4 furlongs in length and 3 in width, 15d in tax.

10 In TESTERTON Richard holds what Toki, a free man, held before 1066, ½ c. of land.
    Always 7 smallholders; 1 slave.
    Always 1 plough in lordship. Then and later 1 men's plough, now ½ plough. Meadow, ½ acre.
    Value then 10s; now the same.

11 In RUDHAM Thorgils, 1 free man, holds, at ½ c. of land.
    Always 3 smallholders; 1 slave.
    Then 1 plough, later also ½, now 1. Meadow, 1 acre.
    Also 4 Freemen, at 6 acres. Always 1 plough.
    Value always 10s.

The Hundred of GALLOW

12 In SAXLINGHAM Theodoric, 1 free man, holds, at ½ c. of land.
    Then 1 plough, now the same.
    Always 2 smallholders.
    Meadow, 2 acres.
    Value then 2s; now 5s.

The Hundred of HOLT

13 In GUNTHORPE 1 free man of Harold's, at ½ c. of land.
    Always 6 smallholders; 1 slave.
    Always 2 ploughs; woodland for 4 pigs; meadow, 1 acre.
    Value 10s.
    This land was delivered to him to make up 1 manor, BARNEY.

In edisfelda teñ. Scet lib hō t̄.r.e.LX.7.xx.ac̝.Sep.v.
uill̃.7.I.bor.7.I.car̝.Silua ad.c.por.II.ac̄ p̃ti.7.II.foc̄.
de XII.ac̄.tr̃e.7 jacet ad bineham.

H̃. DE GRENEHOGA. Binneham. teñ. Efket.
t̄.r.e.III.car̝.tr̃e.III.villi.femp.sẽp.XIII.bor.II.s.7
Tc̄.II.car̝.7 p̃.7 m̃.VI.i dñio.Tc̄ 7 p̃.hoūm.II.ca.7 m̃.
.I.7.d.XI.ac̄.p̃ti.Tc̄.I.mol.7.XVI.fol.s ptinentes ad hanc.
uill̃a.xxx.ac̝.tr̃e.tc̄.II.ca.m̃.car̝ 7.dim̃.II.ac̝.p̃ti.
in aula dñica.tc̄.VIII.eq̃.m̃.v.tc̄.III.añ.m̃.I.tc̄.XVI.

258 a
poft.m̃.x.tc̄ cxx.m̃.d.c.ou̇.

Eduella jacet huic mañ.d.car̝.terre.I.bor.Tc̄ val.IIII.
L.7 p̃.m̃.ual.xx.lib.7 ht.I.leug̃.longi.7 d.lati.7 redd.
II.fol.de gelto.

Berlei tenet.Will.q̃m teñ.Turketel.t.r.e.II.car̝.
tr̃e.tc̄ 7 p̃.XIIII.bor.m̃.XIII.sẽp.II.car̝ in dñio.7.I.car̝
hoūm.Tc̄ 7 p̃.II.fer̝.m̃.I.Silua.ad.LX.por.XIIII.ac̝ p̃ti.
sẽp.I.r.Tc̄ XIIII.equæ filuatice.Tc̄ 7 p̃.x.añt.m̃.XIIII.Tc̄
xx.por.m̃.xxvIII.Tc̄.LX.ou.m̃.c.Tc̄ XL.cap̃.m̃.xxxvIII.
m̃.II.uafa.ap̄ 7 xvII.libos hoẽs.LXXX.ac̝ tr̃e.hos reclamat
ex delibatioñe ad pficiendum.hoc maneriũ Sẽp.II.car̝.VI.ac̝
p̃ti.Tc̄ 7 femp.ual.IIII.lib.7 ht d.leug̃.in long̃.7 dim̃.in lato.
7 de gelto.VI.d.7 de iftis calumpniat̝.I.feruiens reḡ.ad feudū
rad comitis.XIII.7 dim̃.q̃s tenebat q̃ndo se foris fecit q̃cumq̝.
judicio judicat̝ 7 hoc hund.teftat̝.7 tenent.LXXX.ac̝ tr̃e.
7.II.ac̝ p̃ti.7 redd.in fnaringa.xvII.fol.7 IIII.d.

14 In EDGEFIELD Skeet, a free man, held 60 and 20 acres before 1066.
    Always 5 villagers; 1 smallholder.
    1 plough; woodland for 100 pigs; meadow, 2 acres.
    Also 2 Freemen, at 12 acres of land.
    It appertains to Binham.

The Hundred of (North) GREENHOE

15 Skeet held BINHAM before 1066, 3 c. of land.
    Always 3 villagers. Always 13 smallholders; 2 slaves.
    Then 2 ploughs, later and now 6 in lordship. Then and later 2 men's ploughs, now 1½. Meadow, 11 acres. Then 1 mill.
    Also there are 16 Freemen belonging to this village, 30 acres of land. Then 2 ploughs, now 1½ ploughs. Meadow, 2 acres.
    Then 8 horses at the manor hall, now 5. Then 3 head of cattle, now 1. Then 16 pigs, now 10. Then 120 sheep, now half a hundred.   258 a

16 WELLS (Next the Sea) appertains to this manor, ½ c. of land.
    1 smallholder.
    Value (of Binham) then and later £4; now £20.
    It has 1 league in length and ½ in width, it pays tax of 2s.

17 William holds BARNEY which Thorketel held before 1066, 2 c. of land.
    Then and later 14 smallholders, now 13.
    Always 2 ploughs in lordship; 1 men's plough.
    Then and later 2 slaves, now 1.
    Woodland for 60 pigs; meadow, 14 acres; always 1 cob. Then 14 wild mares. Then and later 10 head of cattle, now 14. Then 20 pigs, now 28. Then 60 sheep, now 100. Then 40 goats, now 38. Now 2 beehives.
    Also 17 free men, 80 acres of land. He claims (to hold) these by livery to make up this manor.
    Always 2 ploughs; meadow, 6 acres.
Value then and always £4.
    It has half a league in length and a half in width, tax of 6d.
    One of the King's servants claims, by whatever mode of trial it be adjudged, 13 and a half of these (free men) as part of the Holding of Earl Ralph who held them when he forfeited, and this the Hundred testifies. They hold 80 acres of land; meadow, 2 acres. They pay 17s 4d in (Great) Snoring.

᚛In Walsingeham magno . tenet . Hunfrid quā teñ . bund̯.
1 . teñ . 1 . car tr̃e . 7 dim̃ . semp . 111 . uilli . 7 v11 . bor . 7 . 11 . car̯.
in dñio . 1111 . ac̯ p̃ti . tc̃ 7 p̃ . 1 . car̯ . 7 dim̃ . hoūm . 7 . m̃ . 1 . p̯.
111 ser . m̃ . 1111 . tc̃ . v . añ . m̃ . 1 . tc̃ xx . por . m̃ . xxv . semp . cLxxx.
ou̯ . Tc̃ 1x . uasa . apū . m̃ . v . 7 . 1 . soc̃ 1111 . ac̯ . tr̃æ . Tc̃ 7 p̯ . ual.
xxx sol . 7 . m̃ . xL . Hec tr̃a fuit libata ad p̃ficiendum.
hões sui . nesciunt qd . maneriū.

᚛In Hochahā . teñ . tocho . 1 . lib hō . xxx111 . ac̯ tr̃e . sep̃ . 11 . bor.
Sep̃ . ual . 11 . oras . 7 istam tenet sic̃ sup̃ dictam.

258 b
H̃ DE ENSFORD In Dallinga teñ 1 . lib hō . fisc . t . r . e.
1 . car terre . semp . v1111 . uilli 7 . xv1 . bor . 7 . 11 . s . semp . 1.
car̯ . in dñio . 7 . 111 . car̯ . hoūm 7 11 . ac̯ p̃ti . silu̯ . v1 . por . qn̄
cecep̃ . 1 . r . m̃ . 11 . tc̃ . v1 . añ . m̃ . xx . tc̃ . v1 . por . m̃ . xxx.
tc̃ . xv1 . ou̯ . m̃ . Lxxx . 7 xxx . cap̃ . 7 . v . soc̃ . xx . ac̯ tr̃æ.
sep̃ . 1 . car̯ . Soca in folsam . regis . 7 ual . xL . sol . 7 ħt 1.
leug̃ . in long̃ . 7 dim̃ . in lato . 7 redd . x1x . d̯ . in geldū regis.
q̃cq̧ ibi tenet.

. XXXV . TERRE Rob . filii corbutionis . S . H̃ . 7 dim̃. ★
de fredreb . Santdersincham . tenet . R̃anulfus.
quam teñ . 1 . lib hō sub heroldo t . r . e . Tc̃ 7 p̃ . 1 . car̯ . m̃.
n̄ . Tc̃ 7 p̃ . v . bor . m̃ . null̯ . Tc̃ 7 p̊ . 111 . s . m̃ . 1 . 7 . 111 . ac̯.
7 dim̃ . p̃ti . tc̃ 7 p̊ . car̯ . hoūm . Tc̃ 7 p̃ . 1 . sal . semp . ual . xx.
sol.

18 In GREAT WALSINGHAM Humphrey holds 1½ c. of land which Bondi, a thane, held.
>Always 3 villagers; 7 smallholders.
>2 ploughs in lordship; meadow, 4 acres. Then and later 1½ men's ploughs, now 1.
>Later 3 slaves, now 4.
>Then 5 head of cattle, now 1. Then 20 pigs, now 25. Always 180 sheep. Then 9 beehives, now 5.
>Also 1 Freeman, 4 acres of land.
>Value then and later 30s; now 40.
>This land was delivered to make up a manor, his men do not know which.

19 In HOLKHAM Toki, 1 free man, held 33 acres of land.
>Always 2 smallholders.
>Value always 2 *orae*.
>He holds this in the same way as that one mentioned above.

The Hundred of EYNSFORD

20 In (Wood) DALLING 1 free man, Fish, held 1 c. of land before 1066.
>Always 9 villagers; 16 smallholders; 2 slaves.
>Always 1 plough in lordship; 3 men's ploughs; meadow, 2 acres; woodland, 6 pigs. When he acquired it 1 cob, now 2. Then 6 head of cattle, now 20. Then 6 pigs, now 30. Then 16 sheep, now 80. 30 goats.
>Also 5 Freemen, 20 acres of land. Always 1 plough.
>The jurisdiction (is) in the King's (manor of) Foulsham.
>Value 40s.
>It has 1 league in length and ½ in width, it pays 19d in the King's tax, whoever holds there.

35   LANDS OF ROBERT SON OF CORBUCION

The Hundred and a Half of FREEBRIDGE

1 Ranulf holds SANDRINGHAM which 1 free man under Harold held before 1066.
>Then and later 1 plough, now none.
>Then and later 5 smallholders, now none. Then and later 3 slaves, now 1.
>Meadow, 3½ acres. Then and later 1 men's plough. Then and later 1 salt-house.
>Value always 20s.

H̄. *HEINESTEDE*. In Safilingahā tenet. Gunfrid.
quam ten̄. Lefolt. ɪ. lib̃ hō. Heroldi cōm̃d. de xxx. ac̃ t̃re.
Sep̃. v. bor. Tc̄. ɪɪ. fer. Tc̄ 7 p̃. ɪ. car̃. in dn̄io. 7. ɪ. car̃. hoūm
7. ɪɪ. libi hōes de. ɪɪɪ. ac̃. t̃re. 7. ɪɪ. ac̃ p̃ti. Tc̄ ual. xvɪ. fol.
m̃. xxɪɪ. fol.

V̄In ftokes tenet gifart. ɪɪɪ libi hōes ftigandi cōm̃d. ɪ.
car̃ t̃re. Semp. x. bor. 7. ɪɪ. fer. Sep̃. ɪ. car̃ 7 dim̃. in dn̄io.

259 a

7 dim̃. hoūm 7. ɪɪɪ. ac̃. p̃ti. Tc̄ ɪ. eq̃. Sep̃. ual. xxx. fol.

H̄. dim̃. Herfam. In riueffala tenet Gunfrid. quam
ten̄. Brictric. ɪ. lib̃. hō ftigandi. cōm̃d. fed nec dare nec uende
pot̃at t̃ram fuā fine licentia ej. ɪ. car̃. 7 dim̃. t̃re. Tc̄. vɪ. uilli.
p̃. 7 m̃. ɪɪɪ. Tc̄. ɪ. car̃ 7 dim̃. m̃. dim̃. Sep̃. dim̃. car̃ hoūm. Silũ
xl. por. 7. vɪ. ac̃ p̃ti. Tc̄ 7 p̃. ual. xx. fol. m̃. x.

V̄In ftereftuna tenet idē. quam. ten̄. Leuftan. ɪ. lib̃ hō ulfi cōm̃d.
tantū t̃. r. e. ɪ. car̃ terre. Sep̃. ɪ. car̃ in dn̄io. 7. ɪɪɪ. ac̃ p̃ti Tc̄ 7 p̃.
ual. xx. fol. m̃. xv.

H̄. *LOTHNINGA*. In Lothna. tenet Humfrid. quam ten̄
Aluric. ɪ. lib̃ hō t̃. r. e. fub ftigando. ɪ. car̃. terræ. 7 dim̃. 7 sep̃.
ɪ. uills. 7. ɪɪɪ. bor. 7. ɪ. fer. Tc̄. ɪ. car̃ 7 dim̃. p̃. ɪ. m̃. ɪ. 7 dim̃. in dn̄io.
Tc̄. ɪ. car̃ 7 dim̃. hoūm. p̃. 7 m̃. ɪ. Silũ. ad. xɪɪ. por. 7. dim̃. mol.
7 ɪɪɪɪ. ac̃ p̃ti. Tc̄. l. ou. m̃. lv. Tc̄. xɪɪɪ. m̃. xɪɪɪɪ. por. 7 ɪɪɪɪ.
foc̃. de. xɪɪ. ac̃. terre. Tc̄ int oms. ɪ. car̃. 7 dim̃. p̃. 7 m̃. ɪ. Tc̄ ual.
xx. fol. p̃. 7 m̃. xxx.

V̄In golofa. ten̄. idem. quam tenuit uluric. ɪ. car̃ t̃re. fub ftigando
Sep̃. ɪɪɪ uills 7 vɪɪ. bor. Sep̃ i dn̄io. ɪ. car̃. Tc̄. ɪ. car̃. hoūm. p̃. 7
m̃. ɪ. 7 dim̃. Silũ ɪɪɪɪ. por. Sep̃. ɪ. eq̃. Sep̃. ual. xx. fol. 7 ɪx. foc̃
fub. eo. de xx ac̃. Tc̄. ɪɪɪ. car̃ p̃. 7 m̃. ɪɪ. tc̄ ual. vɪɪ. fol. m̃. x. fol.
R. 7 c. focā.

HENSTEAD Hundred

2 In SAXLINGHAM Gunfrid holds what Leofwold, 1 free man under the patronage of Harold, held, at 30 acres of land.
Always 5 smallholders. Then 2 slaves.
Then and later 1 plough in lordship; 1 men's plough.
Also 2 free men, at 3 acres of land; meadow, 2 acres.
Value then 16s; now 22s.

3 In STOKE (Holy Cross) Gifard holds (what) 5 free men (held) under the patronage of Stigand, 1 c. of land.
Always 10 smallholders; 2 slaves.
Always 1½ ploughs in lordship; ½ men's [plough]; meadow, 3 acres. Then 1 horse.
Value always 30s.

259 a

EARSHAM Half Hundred

4 In RUSHALL Gunfrid holds what Brictric, 1 free man under the patronage of Stigand, held, but he could neither grant nor sell his land without his permission, 1½ c. of land.
Then 6 villagers, later and now 3.
Then 1½ ploughs, now ½. Always ½ men's plough; woodland, 40 pigs; meadow, 6 acres.
Value then and later 20s, now 10.

5 He also holds in STARSTON what Leofstan, 1 free man under the patronage only of Ulf, held before 1066, 1 c. of land.
Always 1 plough in lordship; meadow, 3 acres.
Value then and later 20s, now 15.

LODDON Hundred

6 In LODDON Humphrey holds what Aelfric, 1 free man under Stigand, held before 1066, 1½ c. of land.
Always 1 villager; 3 smallholders; 1 slave.
Then 1½ ploughs, later 1, now 1½ in lordship. Then 1½ men's ploughs, later and now 1. Woodland for 12 pigs; ½ mill; meadow, 4 acres. Then 50 sheep, now 55. Then 13 pigs, now 14.
Also 4 Freemen, at 12 acres of land. Then 1½ ploughs between them all, later and now 1.
Value then 20s; later and now 30.

7 He also holds what Wulfric held under Stigand in INGLOSS, 1 c. of land.
Always 3 villagers; 7 smallholders.
Always 1 plough in lordship. Then 1 men's plough, later and now 1½. Woodland, 4 pigs; always 1 horse.
Value always 20s.
Also 9 Freemen under him, at 20 acres. Then 3 ploughs, later and now 2.
Value then 7s; now 10s.
The King and the Earl (have) the jurisdiction.

H̄. LOTNINGA. In mundaham . tenet . Nigell . quam
ten̄ . Goduin̅⁹ . t . r . e . ɪ . lib̅ . hō . eduini . cōm̄d . anteces . Godrici
dapiferi . xxx . ac̄ tr̄e . Sep̄ . ɪ . car̊ . in dn̄io . Silu . ad . ɪɪ . por . 7 ɪɪɪɪ . ac̄ p̊ti.

259 b

7 . xɪ . lib̅i hōes etgari . xxx . ac̄ . Sep̄ . ɪ . car̊ . 7 dim̄ . Tc̄ ual . x . m̊
xx . Rex 7 comes . focā.

¶In mundahā tenet . Anger⁹ . quam ten̄ . ealgar⁹ . lib̅ hō . fub ftigando
ɪ . car̊ . tr̄æ . p man̄ . t̄ . r . e . Sep̄ . ɪɪɪɪ . uilli . Tc̄ 7 p̊⁹ . ɪɪ . car̊ . in dn̄io .
m̊ . dim̄ . car̊ . Sep̄ . dim̄ . car̊ . hōum . 7 dim̄ . ac̄ p̊ti . Sep̄ . ɪ . eq̊ .
in aula . Tc̄ . ɪɪ . an̄ . m̊ null̊ . Tc̄ vɪɪɪ . por . m̊ . ɪɪɪɪ . Tc̄ . xx . ou . m̊
v . 7 . ɪɪɪɪ . foc̊ 7 dim̄ . d . ɪɪɪɪ ac̊ tr̄e . 7 dim̄ . 7 . ɪ . lib̅ hō algari cōm̄d .
tantū . vɪ . ac̄ tr̄e . Int oēs . ɪ . cā . . Sep̄ . ual . x . fol.

¶In brom tenet Hunfrid⁹ . ɪɪ . car̊ tr̄e . quam tenuit anant tein⁹ .
t̄ . r . e . Tc̄ 7 p̊⁹ . ɪɪ . bor . m̊ . null̊ . Sep̄ . ɪ . fer . Sep̄ . ɪɪ . car̊ . in dn̄io .
Tc̄ . ɪɪ . boues . m̊ . ɪ . Silu . xx . por . 7 . xx . ac̊ p̊ti . 7 . ɪ . mol . 7 dim̄
pifcin̄ . 7 . ɪɪɪ . an̄ . m̊ . L . ou . Tc̄ xL . por . m̊ . xx . 7 . ɪɪ . uafa . apū .
7 v . lib̅i hōes cōm̄d . fub eo . x . ac̊ tr̄e . Sep̄ . dim̄ . car̊ . ht̄ . ōs .
Tc̄ 7 p̊⁹ . ual . xL . fol . m̊ . L . 7 ht̄ . ɪ . leug̃ . in long̃ . 7 . v . qr̊ . in lato .
7 de gelto . vɪɪɪ . d . ht̄ mundahā . xx . qr̊ . in longo . 7 . x . in lato .
7 de gelto . ɪɪ . folidos.

¶In Lotna . tenet . Hunfrid⁹ . fub . R . dim̊ . ac̊ tr̄e quam calū
niat̊ . scs . be . de holmo . 7 hund̊ . teftat̊ . qd̊ fuit . sci bē . in dn̄io.

H̄. DE SVD ERPINCHĀ. In Bernincham ; ɪ . lib̅ ^(ten Brant . d̊e . R.)
hō . Lxxxɪɪ . ac̊ tr̄e . femp . v . bor . 7 . ɪ . car̊ . in dn̄io . 7 dim̄ . hoūm .
7 ɪɪ . ac̊ p̊ti . Silu . xv . por . 7 ual . x . fol . 7 ht̄ . vɪɪ . qr̊ . in long 7 . ɪɪɪɪ .
in lat̄ . 7 . ɪɪɪ . d . 7 . ɪɪɪ . ferding̃ de gelto.

LODDON Hundred

8 In MUNDHAM Nigel holds what Godwin, 1 free man under the patronage of Edwin, Godric the Steward's predecessor, held before 1066, 30 acres of land.
   Always 1 plough in lordship; woodland for 2 pigs; meadow, 4 acres.
   Also 11 free men of Edgar's, 30 acres. Always 1½ ploughs.   259 b
   Value then 10[s]; now 20.
   The King and the Earl (have) the jurisdiction.

9 In MUNDHAM Ansger holds what Algar, a free man under Stigand, held as a manor before 1066, 1 c. of land.
   Always 4 villagers.
   Then and later 2 ploughs in lordship, now ½ plough. Always ½ men's plough; meadow, ½ acre. Always 1 horse at the hall. Then 2 head of cattle, now none. Then 8 pigs, now 4. Then 20 sheep, now 5.
   Also 4 Freemen and a half at 4½ acres of land. Also 1 free man under the patronage only of Algar, 6 acres of land. 1 plough between them all.
   Value always 10s.

10 In BROOME Humphrey holds 2 c. of land which Anand the thane held before 1066.
   Then and later 2 smallholders, now none; always 1 slave.
   Always 2 ploughs in lordship. Then 2 oxen, now 1. Woodland, 20 pigs; meadow, 20 acres; 1 mill; ½ fishery; 3 head of cattle. Now 50 sheep. Then 40 pigs, now 20; 2 beehives.
   Also 5 free man in patronage under him, 10 acres of land. They have all always had ½ plough.
   Value then and later 40s; now 50.
   It has 1 league in length and 5 furlongs in width, tax of 8d.
   Mundham has 20 furlongs in length and 10 in width, tax of 2s.

11 In LODDON Humphrey holds under R(obert) ½ acre of land which St. Benedict of Holme claims. The Hundred testifies that it was in the lordship of St. Benedict's.

The Hundred of SOUTH ERPINGHAM

12 In (Little) BARNINGHAM Brant holds from R(obert), 1 free man, 82 acres of land.
   Always 5 smallholders;
   1 plough in lordship; ½ men's [plough]; meadow, 2 acres; woodland, 15 pigs.
   Value 10s.
   It has 7 furlongs in length and 4 in width, tax of 3¾d.

H. DEPWADE. Sceltuna tenet. Nigell. quam ten.
Alduinus lib hō. Stigandi. xxx. ac. sep. 1. uills. 7. ix. bor. 7 dim.
260 a
7. 1. car. in dnio. 7. 1. car houm. 7. 11. ac. 7 dim pti. Tc. ual. x.
sol. m. xx.

In Sterstuna tenet idē. 1. car tre. ten. 1. lib. hō sep. 1. uill.
7. v. bor. 7. 1. car. in dnio 7 dim. car houm. 111. ac pti. Silu. 1111.
por. 7. 1. mol. 7. 1. lib. hō. 11. ac. 7. 1. r. 7. 111 an. Tc ual. x. sol.
m. xx.

Stratuna tenet. Hunfrid. quam ten. 1. ten. t. r. e. 11. car.
tre. semp xvii. bor. 7. 11. car. in dnio 7 tc. 111. car. houm.
p. 11. m. 1. vi. ac pti. Silu. vi. por. semp. t. r. 7. ct. v. por.
m. xi. tc x. ou. m. xxvi. 7 vi. cap. 7 vii. libi. hōes. xvii. ac
de qbȝ suus. antec habuit. comd. t. r. e. 7 ht eos p tra. Tc. 1. car
1. ac pti. Tc ual. xxx. sol. m. xl.

Fridetuna tenet Gifart quam ten. Olketel. lib hō edrici
de laxefelda. antecessoris Robti malet. xxx. ac. 7. 111. bor. Tc 7 p.
11. car. tc xvi. por. m. viii. tc. vi. an. 7 lx. ou m nichil. sep. dim.
car houm. 1. ac 7 dim. pti. soca falde. 7. vii. hōes qui possent.
uende terram suā si eā pus obtulissent dño suo. 7 ht. xiiii ac.
7 1. lib. hō. 1111. ac. sep. dim. car. sep. ual. xxv. sol. 7 ht. 1. leug
in long 7 dim. in lato. 7 ix. d. de gelto. Ex hac tra erat saisitus
W. malet. qdo iuit in maresc.

Gnaueringa H. In Hatescou tenet idem. 1. soc stigandi
xxx. ac. 7. 111. bor. 7 tc. 1. car. 7. 1111. ac. pti. 7 sub isto. 11. soc
1111. ac 7 dim. car. Tc ual. v. sol. m. xi.

In Larpestuna. 1. soc sci. eadmundi. xlvi. ac. 7. 11. bor.
260 b
Tc 1. car. m. 11. boues Tc ual. xx. sol. m. x.

DEPWADE Hundred

13 Nigel holds SHELTON which Aldwin, a free man of Stigand's, held, 30 acres.
    Always 1 villager; 9 smallholders and a half.
    1 plough in lordship; 1 men's plough; meadow, 2½ acres.   260 a
    Value then 10s; now 20.

14 In THARSTON he also holds 1 c. of land (which) 1 free man held.
    Always 1 villager; 5 smallholders.
    1 plough in lordship; ½ men's plough; meadow, 3 acres; woodland, 4 pigs; 1 mill.
    Also 1 free man, 2 acres. 1 cob; 3 head of cattle.
    Value then 10s; now 20.

15 Humphrey holds STRATTON which 1 thane held before 1066, 2 c. of land.
    Always 17 smallholders; 2 ploughs in lordship. Then 3 men's ploughs, later 2, now 1. Meadow, 6 acres; woodland, 6 pigs; always 1 cob. Then 5 pigs, now 11. Then 10 sheep, now 26; 6 goats.
    Also 7 free men, 17 acres, of whom his predecessor had the patronage before 1066 and he has them for land. Then 1 plough; meadow, 1 acre.
    Value then 30s; now 40.

16 Gifard holds FRITTON which Ulfketel, a free man of Edric of Laxfield the predecessor of Robert Malet, held, 30 acres.
    3 smallholders.
    Then and later 2 ploughs. Then 16 pigs, now 8. Then 6 head of cattle and 60 sheep, now nothing. Always ½ men's plough; meadow, 1½ acres; fold-rights.
    Also 7 free men who could sell their land if they had first offered it to their lord. They have 14 acres.
    Also 1 free man, 4 acres. Always ½ plough.
    Value always 25s.
    It has 1 league in length and ½ in width; tax of 9d. W(illiam) Malet had possession of this land when he went into the marsh.

17 He also holds in HADDISCOE; 1 Freeman of Stigand's, 30 acres.
    3 smallholders.
    Then 1 plough; meadow, 4 acres.
    And under him 2 Freemen, 4 acres; ½ plough.
    Value then 5s; now 11.

18 In IARPESTUNA 1 Freeman of St. Edmund's, 46 acres.
    2 smallholders.   260 b
    Then 1 plough, now 2 oxen.
    Value then 20s; now 10.

.XXXVI. TERRE RANVLFI FRIS ILGERI. H̃. de
SVDERPINCHĀ. In Erpinchā. tenet. hunfrid̉. 1. car̂
terre. quā teñ. Bund̉. lib̃. hō Heroldi. sēp. III. uilli᷃. 7 IX. bor.
7.1.car̂. in dñio. 7.1. houm̃. 7.11. ac̄ p̃ti. 7. tc̄. 1. r. 7. III. añ.
Tc̄ ual. x. sol̃. m̂. xx.

H̃. Consteda. In haninga tenet. idḛ̄. 1. car̂. tr̃e. 1. lib̃
hō t̄. r. e. sēp. VIII. uilli᷃. 7.1. bor. 7.1. car̂. in dñio. 7.1. car̂. houm̃
7 VIIII. ac̄ p̃ti. silu. IIII. por. sēp. 1. mol̃. 7. III. añ. 7. III. por. 7
II. soc̄. XIIIII · ac̄ tr̃e. 7.1. car̂. 7 II. ac̄ p̃ti. sēp. ual. xx. sol̃. Sc̄s
.b. socā. Suafelda. XVIII. ac̄. II. lib̃. hō. semp dim̃. car̂. 7
7 dimi ac̄ p̃ti. 7 ual. XVI. d̃.
In Ridlinketuna. XVI. soc̄. c. xx. ac̄ tr̃e. sēp. V. car̂. 7.1.
ac̄. p̃ti. 7 ual. xx. sol.

H̃. de Hapinga. Walecota tenet. idem. quam teñ.
Edric̉. tegn̉. t̄. r. e. IIII. car̂. tr̃æ. 7. VI. ac̄. semp. VIII. uilli᷃. 7 XVI.
bor. Tc̄ 7 p̃. II. car̂. in dñio. m̂. III. sēp. II. car̂ houm̃. VIII. ac̄ p̃ti 7. 1.
mol̃. m̂. II. r̂. tc̄. III. añ. m̂. XVI. tc̄. IIII. por. m̂. XXIIII. tc̄. LXXX.
oũ. m̂. LXX. 7. IIII. uasa. ap̃. 1. eccla. xx. ac̄. 7 ual. xx. d̃. 7 VII.

libi hoēs. 7 dim̃. cōmd̄. tantum̃. LXX. ac̄ tenet idḛ̄. tc̄ 7 p̃. II. car̂.
m̂. II. 7 dim̃. 7 IIII. libi hoēs tenet idḛ̄. q̃ s̄t additi. huic manerio.
t. r. W. xc. ac̄. quos addidit. Ran̂. fr̄. ilgeri. 7 Humfridus.
eos ten̄. Tc̄. III. car̂. m̂. II. 7 dim̃. 7 ual. xv. sol̃. De duob; habuit
suus antec̄. cōmd̄. tantum. 7 antec̄. Rob̃. malet. de uno similit̃
Rex. 7 comes. socam. 7. M. ual. tc̄. XL. sol̃. m̂. LX. 7 h̄t. 1.
leug̃. in long̃. 7 dim̃. in lat̃. 7 xv. d̃. de g̃. quicq; ibi teneat.

LANDS OF RANULF BROTHER OF ILGER

The Hundred of SOUTH ERPINGHAM

1 Humphrey holds 1 c. of land in ERPINGHAM which Bondi, a free man of Harold's, held.
   Always 3 villagers; 9 smallholders.
   1 plough in lordship; 1 men's [plough]; meadow, 2 acres.
      Then 1 cob; 3 head of cattle.
   Value then 10s; now 20.

TUNSTEAD Hundred

2 He also holds in HONING 1 c. of land, (which) 1 free man (held) before 1066.
   Always 8 villagers; 1 smallholder.
   1 plough in lordship; 1 men's plough; meadow, 9 acres; woodland, 4 pigs. Always 1 mill; 3 head of cattle; 3 pigs.
   Also 2 Freemen, 15 acres of land; 1 plough; meadow, 2 acres.
   Value always 20s.
   St. B(enedict has) the jurisdiction.

3 SWAFIELD, 18 acres. 2 free men.
   Always ½ plough; meadow, ½ acre.
   Value 16d.

4 In RIDLINGTON 16 Freemen, 120 acres of land.
   Always 5 ploughs; meadow, 1 acre.
   Value 20s.

The Hundred of HAPPING

5 He also holds WALCOTT which Edric, a thane, held before 1066. 4 c. of land and 6 acres.
   Always 8 villagers; 16 smallholders.
   Then and later 2 ploughs in lordship, now 3. Always 2 men's ploughs; meadow, 8 acres; 1 mill. Now 2 cobs. Then 3 head of cattle, now 16. Then 4 pigs, now 24. Then 80 sheep, now 70; 4 beehives.
   1 church, 20 acres;
   value 20d.
He also holds 7 free men and a half in patronage only, 70 acres.
   Then and later 2 ploughs, now 2½.
He also holds 4 free men who were added to this manor after 1066, 90 acres. Ranulf brother of Ilger added them and Humphrey holds them.
   Then 3 ploughs, now 2½.
   Value 15s.
   Of 2 of these his predecessor had the patronage only, and of one the predecessor of Robert Malet (had) likewise. The King and the Earl (have) the jurisdiction.
   Value of the manor then 40s; now 60.
   It has 1 league in length and ½ in width, tax of 15d, whoever holds there.

261 a

260 b, 261 a

H̃. DE HOLT. In edisfeldam . tenet . Hunfrid . q̃m
ten̄ . Bond . lib̃ hō . t̃ . r . e . 11 . car t̃re . Heroldi . Sep̃ . 11 . uilli
7 vII . bor . 7 . II . ser . Sep̃ . in dn̄io . II . car 7 hōum . II . car . Silua
ad . c . por . v . ac̃ p̃ti . 1 . mol . m̃ . 11 . r̃ . Tc̃ vII . por . m̃ . xxIII .
Tc̃ . vII . ou . m̃ . LXXX . Tc̃ . xIII . cap̃ . m̃ . xxI . Tc̃ uas ap̃ . m̃
II . 7 xvII . soc̃ . de xx . IIII . ac̃ t̃re isti sunt in sup̃i car . Tc̃ ual
xxx sol . m̃ . xL . 7 hab̃ . I . leug̃ . in long̃ . 7 d̃ . in lato . 7 . Ix . d̃ in g̃
In estodeia . tenet idẽ . I . lib̃ hō . de . II . car t̃re . Heroldi . m̃
Ro . p mañ . Sep̃ . vIII . uill . 7 vII . bor . 7 . I . ser . 7 in dn̄io . II . car
7 hōum . I . car . 7 dim̃ . Silua ad . xL . por . vI . ac̃ . p̃ti . III . Mol . Tc̃ . II . r̃ .
m̃ . I . m̃ . Ix . an̄ . Tc̃ v . por . m̃ . xII . m̃ . xL . ou Tc̃ . Lx . cap̃ . m̃ . xxv .
7 . III uas ap̃ . 7 IIII . soc̃ . de xvI . ac̃ . 7 dim̃ . car . Tc̃ ual . xxx . sol
m̃ . xL . huic mañ . p̃tin̄ . xxv . ac̃ . 7 dim̃ . car . in laringa seta ap
p̃tiata ÷ cum mañ.

XXXVII. TERRE TEHELI H̃. DE ENSFORD.

GUTHEKETVNA tenet . Osb̃tus quam tenuit . Lestanus
I . lib̃ . homo . t̃ . r . e . IIII . car t̃ræ . Tc̃ 7 p̃ . Ix . uilli . m̃ . IIII . tc̃
7 p̃ . xvII . bor . m̃ . xv . 7 II . s . tc̃ 7 p̃ . II . car in dn̄io m̃ . III . semp
IIII . car . hōum . 7 xxx . ac̃ p̃ti . silu Lx . por . 7 I . mol . sep̃ . IIII .
r . tc̃ . vIII . an̄ . m̃ . xIIII . tc̃ 7 xIIII . uasa ap̃u . 7 xvIII . soc̃ .
tenet idẽ . cxIII . ac̃ t̃re . 7 . I . bor . tc̃ 7 p̃ . IIII . cã . m̃ . III . 7 . III .
ac̃ 7 dim̃ . p̃ti . sup̃ totum rex 7 comes socā . Tc̃ 7 . p̃ . ual . IIII .
lib̃ . m̃ . vI . lib̃ . 7 h̃t I . leug̃ . in long̃ . 7 dim̃ . in lato . 7 reddit ; vII .
d̃ . in geltũ . regis.

The Hundred of HOLT

6 In EDGEFIELD Humphrey holds 2 c. of land which Bondi, a free man of Harold's, held before 1066.
   Always 2 villagers; 7 smallholders; 2 slaves.
   Always 2 ploughs in lordship; 2 men's ploughs; woodland for 100 pigs; meadow, 5 acres; 1 mill. Now 2 cobs. Then 7 pigs, now 23. Then 7 sheep, now 80. Then 13 goats, now 21. Then 1 beehive, now 2.
   Also 17 Freemen, at 24 acres of land. Their ploughs are included above.
   Value then 30s; now 40.
   It has 1 league in length and ½ in width, 9d in tax.

7 He also holds in STODY; 1 free man of Harold's, now R(obert's), at 2 c. of land, as a manor.
   Always 8 villagers; 7 smallholders; 1 slave.
   2 ploughs in lordship; 1½ men's ploughs; woodland for 40 pigs; meadow, 6 acres; 3 mills. Then 2 cobs, now 1. Now 9 head of cattle. Then 5 pigs, now 12. Now 40 sheep. Then 60 goats, now 25; 3 beehives.
   Also 4 Freemen, at 16 acres; ½ plough.
   Value then 30s; now 40.
   To this manor belong 25 acres and ½ plough in LETHERINGSETT. It has been valued with the manor.

37   LANDS OF TIHEL

The Hundred of EYNSFORD

1 Osbert holds GUTON which Leofstan, 1 free man, held before 1066, 4 c. of land.
   Then and later 9 villagers, now 4. Then and later 17 smallholders, now 15. 2 slaves.
   Then and later 2 ploughs in lordship, now 3. Always 4 men's ploughs; meadow, 30 acres; woodland, 60 pigs; 1 mill. Always 4 cobs. Then 8 head of cattle, now 14. Then also 14 beehives.
   He also holds 18 Freemen, 113 acres of land; 1 smallholder.
   Then and later 4 ploughs, now 3; meadow, 3½ acres.
   The King and the Earl (have) the jurisdiction over the whole.
   Value then and later £4; now £6.
   It has 1 league in length and ½ in width, it pays 7d towards the King's tax.

H̃. DE SVD ERPINCHAM. In Caletorp. tenent. Gueric.
7 Osbt. 1. car. tře. quam teñ. 1. lib hō. Lestanus. semp.. III. uilli
7 VIII. bor. 7. 1. car. in dñio. 7. 1. car. 7 dim̃. hoũm. vI. ac̃. p̃ti.
silũ. xv. por. T̃cia pars mol. T̃c. III. r. t̃c. III. r. T̃c. xIII. añ.
m̃. 1. t̃c. xxx. por. m̃. x. T̃c. vII. uasa. ap̃. m̃. II. t̃c ual. xx.
sol. xx. sol. m̃. xxx.

Botuna tenēt. idē. hões. 1. car. tře. 1. soc̃. heroldi. t̃. r. e. sep.
1. uills. 7. IIII. bor. 7. 1. s. 7. 1. car in dñio 7 dim̃ hoũm. 7. II.
ac̃. p̃ti. silũ. xvI. por. t̃c ual. x. sol. 7. m̃. Soca in caustuna.
hoc totũ fuit libatum. p uno manerio.

262 a

TERRE ROBTI DE UERLI. H̃ DE GILDECROS.   XXXVIII.
Herlinga teñ. Auti. t̃. r. e. 1. car tře. Semp. III. uilli. 7 III.
bor. 7. II. ser. IIII. ac̃. p̃ti. T̃c in dñio. 1. car. 7 p. II. boũ m̃. 1. car
T̃c. 1. car hoũm. 7. p. d. m̃. 1. car. Silũ. xII. por. t̃c vIII. añ.
m̃. III. 7 vIII. por. T̃c. xIIII. oũ. m̃. cxx. 7. v. soc̃. xxx ac̃ tře.
7 III. ac̃ p̃ti. sep. 1. car. 7 ual. xxx. sol. 7 vII. ac̃. 7 dim̃. tře.

H̃ DE GALGOV. In bruneham torp. teñ.. Goduinus. t̃. r. e
7 p. Radulfus. qñ se foris fecit. 1. car tře. Sep. vIII. bor. T̃c
1. ser. t̃c in dñio. 1. car. m̃. dim̃. T̃c hoũm. 1. car. m̃ dim̃. T̃c
II. r. m̃. 1. T̃c. c. Lxxx. oũ. m̃. xxi. 7. II. libi hões manent in
hanc car. tře. T̃c ual. xL. sol. m̃. xxx.

H̃. DE GRENEHOGA. In Dallinga. teñ. G. auun
culus radulsi. t̃. r. e. xI. libi hões. 1. car tře. m̃ tenet. R. de uer
lei. dicens. qd eam. tenet p mutuo de rochinges. Altius tře. t̃c
t̃c II. car. m̃. 1. 7. III. ac̃. p̃ti. sep. ual. xx. sol. 7 inde reuocat.
rotbtum. blondum. libatorē.

The Hundred of SOUTH ERPINGHAM

2 In CALTHORPE Guerri and Osbert hold 1 c. of land which 1 free man, Leofstan, held.
  Always 3 villagers, 8 smallholders.
  1 plough in lordship; 1½ men's ploughs; meadow, 6 acres; woodland, 15 pigs; one-third of a mill. Then 3 cobs. Then 13 head of cattle, now 1. Then 30 pigs, now 10. Then 7 beehives, now 2.
  Value then 20s; now 30.

3 They also hold BOOTON, 1 c. of land. 1 Freeman of Harold's (held) before 1066.
  Always 1 villager; 4 smallholders; 1 slave.
  1 plough in lordship; ½ men's (plough); meadow, 2 acres; woodland, 16 pigs.
  Value then, and now 10s.
  The jurisdiction (is) in Cawston. All this was delivered as 1 manor.

38   LANDS OF ROBERT OF VERLY

The Hundred of GUILTCROSS

1 Auti held (East) HARLING before 1066, 1 c. of land.
  Always 3 villagers; 3 smallholders; 2 slaves.
  Meadow, 4 acres. Then 1 plough in lordship, later 2 oxen, now 1 plough. Then 1 men's plough, later ½, now 1 plough. Woodland, 12 pigs. Then 8 head of cattle, now 3. 8 pigs. Then 14 sheep, now 120.
  Also 5 Freemen, 30 acres of land; meadow, 3 acres; always 1 plough.
  Value 30s. Also 7½ acres of land.

The Hundred of GALLOW

2 In BURNHAM THORPE Godwin held 1 c. of land before 1066, later Ralph when he forfeited, 1 c. of land.
  Always 8 smallholders. Then 1 slave.
  Then 1 plough in lordship, now ½. Then 1 men's plough, now ½. Then 2 cobs, now 1. Then 180 sheep, now 21.
  2 free men dwell on this c. of land.
  Value then 40s; now 30.

The Hundred of (North) GREENHOE

3 In (Field) DALLING G(odwin), the uncle of Ralph, held before 1066; 11 free men, 1 c. of land. Now R(obert) of Verly holds them, saying that he holds it by exchange for Roding in another county.
  Then 2 ploughs, now 1. Meadow, 3 acres.
  Value always 20s.
  In this he vouches Robert Blunt as the deliverer.

⩗H̃.*WALESSĀ*. In tuneſtalle tenet Calp̊.t̃.r.e.LXXX.
ac̃ tr̃e.Sep̃.VI.bor.Sep̃.I.car̊.in dño.I.car̊.hõum.X.ac̃ p̊ti.
Tc̃ LX.m̃.L.oũ.I.ſoł.Sep̃.uał.XX.ſoł.

TERRE HVMFRIDI FILII ALBI.H̃.Gildegros.   .XXXVIIII.
Redelefuuorda.I.car̊.tr̃e tenuit.Orgarus.lib hõ.t̃.r̊.c̊.

262 b

tunc 7 p̊.II.bor.m̃.null̊.ſemp.I.s.7 VIIII.ac̃.p̊ti.tc̃ 7 p̊.II.car̊
in dño.m̃.I.car̊.7 dim̃.7.IIII.libi hõēs XXVII.ac̃ tr̃e.7.III.bor.7 II.
ac̃ p̊ti.ſep̃.I.car̊.ſep̃.I.r.Tc̃.IX.por.modo.XIII.Tc̃.XXVI.oũ.
m̃.XXI.ſep̃.uał.XXX.ſoł.de.IIII.hoib; ſoca.in Keninghehala.
Totũ hr̃ dim̃.leug̃.in long̃.7 dim̃.in lato.7 XI.d̊.7.I.obolum.
de gelto.

H̃.*DE ENSFORD*.In Billingeforda.I.car̊ tr̃e.ten̄
I.liba ſem̃.p man̄.t̃.r.e.Sep̃.I.Vilł̃s 7 VII.bor.ſep̃.I.car̊.
in dño.7.I.car̊.hõum.7.II.ac̃.p̊ti.7.I.mol.qn̄.rec̃.I.r.
m̃.null̊.Sep̃.V.an̄.7 LX.oũ.ſemp.Vał.XX.ſoł.Soca in
folsā regis.t̃.r.e.modo tenet Humfrid.

.XL. TERRA HUMFRIDI DE BOHUM.H̃.*DEBRO*
DERCROS.In taterforda ten̄.Vlnoth.t̃.r.e.de ſtig.
ep̃i.I.car̊ tr̃e.Sep̃.III.uilłi.7.XI.bor.7.II.ſer.Semp.in dño
I.car̊.Tc̃ II.car̊.hõum m̃.I.7.d̊.III.ac̃ p̊ti.I.mol.Sep̃.II.an̄
Tc̃ X.por.m̃.XIIII 7.c.oũ.7.I.buita huic man̄.de dim̃.car̊.
tere.Semp.III.bor.7.I.car̊.II.ac̃ p̊ti.I.mol.Tc̃ uał.XL.ſoł.7
ſep̃.7 hab.d̊.leug̃.in long̃.7 III.qr̃ in lato.7.III.d̊.in gelto.7 III.ſer̊
De hoc manerio ſt ablati IIII.ſoc̃.XL.acr̃.7 tenet W.de War̄.

WALSHAM Hundred
4 In TUNSTALL Skalp held, before 1066, 80 acres of land.
Always 6 smallholders.
Always 1 plough in lordship; 1 men's plough; meadow, 10 acres.
Then 60 pigs, now 50. 1 salt-house.
Value always 20s.

39   LANDS OF HUMPHREY SON OF AUBREY

GUILTCROSS Hundred
1 Ordgar, a free man, held RIDDLESWORTH before 1066, 1 c. of land.
Then and later 2 smallholders, now none; always 1 slave.   262 b
Meadow, 9 acres. Then and later 2 ploughs in lordship, now 1½.
Also 4 free men, 27 acres of land. 3 smallholders. Meadow, 2 acres. Always 1 plough; always 1 cob. Then 9 pigs, now 13. Then 26 sheep, now 21.
Value always 30s.
The jurisdiction of the 4 men is in Kenninghall. The whole has half a league in length and half in width; tax of 11½d.

The Hundred of EYNSFORD
2 In BILLINGFORD 1 free woman held 1 c. of land as a manor before 1066.
Always 1 villager; 7 smallholders.
Always 1 plough in lordship; 1 men's plough; meadow, 2 acres; 1 mill. When he acquired it 1 cob, now none. Always 5 head of cattle, 60 sheep.
Value always 20s.
The jurisdiction was in the King's (manor of) Foulsham before 1066, now Humphrey holds it.

40   LAND OF HUMPHREY OF BOHUN

The Hundred of BROTHERCROSS
1 In TATTERFORD Wulfnoth held 1 c. of land from Bishop Stigand before 1066.
Always 3 villagers; 11 smallholders; 2 slaves.
Always 1 plough in lordship. Then 2 men's ploughs, now 1½. Meadow, 3 acres; 1 mill. Always 2 head of cattle. Then 10 pigs, now 14; 100 sheep.
Also 1 outlier to this manor, at ½ c. of land.
Always 3 smallholders;
1 plough; meadow, 2 acres; 1 mill.
Value then and always 40s.
It has ½ league in length and 3 furlongs in width; 3¾d in tax.
4 Freemen have been taken from this manor, 40 acres, and W(illiam) of Warenne holds them.

Terre Radvlfi de Felgeres. .XLI.

Dice Dimid Hund. Osmundestuna tenet algarus sub heroldo. t̄.r.e..p dim̄ car̄.tr̄e. Sēp.ii.uilli.Semp.vi.bor. Tc̄.ii.ser̄.m̄.i.Sēp.i.car̄.i dn̄io sed due.post c̄c̄.Semp.ii. car̄.hoūm Silu̅: x.por.vi.ac̄ p̄ti.Sep.i.eq̊.i aula.7.ii.an̄.7 x.por.7.iiii.lib̄i hōes.de xl.ac̄.terre.Tc̄.i.car̄.7 dim̄.p̊. 7 m̄.i.7.iiii.ac̄ p̄ti.Tc̄ ual.xl.sol̊.p.l.7.m̄.h̄t v.q̄r̄ in long 7.iiii.in lato.7 de gelto.ii.d̄.

Terre Gislebti. Filii Richeri. H̄.de clakes— .XLII.

Iosa.Midelhale ten̄.Ailict.t̄r.e.Tc̄.ii.car̄.m̄.i.sēp.xv. uilli.7 v.bor.tc̄ iiii.s.modo.ii.tc̄.ii.car̄ hoūm.m̄.i.tc̄.i.r. tc̄ xvi.por.m̄.viii.7.ii.an̄.sēp.xxviiii.oues.7 x.ac̄ p̄ti.tc̄ ual v.lib̄.m̄.iiii.

Terre Rogeri de Ramis. H̄.Winelvnd. .XLIII.

Totintuna tenet Waregius.quam ten̄.Aluuinus.lib̄ hō t̄.r.e.iii.car̄ terre.Tc̄ 7 p̊.ix.uilli.m̄.vii.tc̄.i.bor.tc̄ 7 p̊. ii.s.m̄.null̊.xii.ac̄ p̄ti.Tc̄ 7 p̊.i.car̄ in dn̄io.m̄.i.7.dim̄.tc̄ 7 p̊.ii.car̄.hoūm m̄.dim̄.sep.ii.r.7 xv.an̄.tc̄.xx.por.m̄.v.tc̄ lxxx.m̄.xiiii.vi.cap̄r Tc̄ 7 p̊.ual.xl.sol̊.m̄.xx.

H̄.Dim̄.Hersa. In plestuna tenet ide.xxiiii.ac̄ tr̄e.sed fuer̄ in aula sc̄i eadmundi 7 xii.lib̄i hōes sc̄i eadmundi q̊.nec dare nec uende.pot̄at tr̄am suam sine licentia sc̄i 7 stigandi q̊ habuit socam 7 sacā in ersam.h̄t hōes.lx.ac̄.7.ii.bor.Tc̄ 7 p̊. ii.car̄.m̄.i.7 dim̄.Tc̄ 7 p̊.ual.x.sol̊.m̄.v.

In eade tenet adhuc.xl.ac̄.tr̄e q̄s tenet sc̄s.ead.t̄ r.e.teste hund m̄.Warengerus sed hund nescit q̄m̄.

41 LANDS OF RALPH OF FOUGÈRES

DISS Half Hundred

1. Algar held OSMONDISTON under Harold before 1066, as ½ c. of land.
   Always 2 villagers; always 6 smallholders. Then 2 slaves, now 1.
   Always 1 plough in lordship, but there could be 2. Always 2 men's ploughs; woodland, 10 pigs; meadow, 6 acres. Always 1 horse at the hall; 2 head of cattle; 10 pigs.
   Also 4 free men, at 40 acres of land.
   Then 1½ ploughs, later and now 1. Meadow, 4 acres.
   Value then 40s; later and now 50.
   It has 5 furlongs in length and 4 in width, tax of 2d.

42 LANDS OF GILBERT SON OF RICHERE

The Hundred of CLACKCLOSE

1. Aethelgyth held MILDENHALL before 1066.
   Then 2 ploughs, now 1.
   Always 15 villagers; 5 smallholders. Then 4 slaves, now 2.
   Then 2 men's ploughs, now 1. Then 1 cob. Then 16 pigs, now 8. 2 head of cattle. Always 29 sheep; meadow, 10 acres.
   Value then £5; now 4.

43 LANDS OF ROGER OF RAISMES

WAYLAND Hundred

1. Warenger holds TOTTINGTON which A(i)lwin, a free man, held before 1066, 3 c. of land.
   Then and later 9 villagers, now 7. Then 1 smallholder. Then and later 2 slaves, now none.
   Meadow, 12 acres. Then and later 1 plough in lordship, now 1½. Then and later 2 men's ploughs, now ½. Always 2 cobs; 15 head of cattle. Then 20 pigs, now 5. Then 80 [?sheep], now 14. 6 goats.
   Value then and later 40s; now 20.

EARSHAM Hundred

2. He also holds in BILLINGFORD, 24 acres of land, but they were in the lordship of St. Edmund's.
   Also 12 free men of St. Edmund's who could neither grant nor sell their land without the permission of the Saint and of Stigand who had the full jurisdiction in Earsham. The men have 60 acres.
   2 smallholders.
   Then and later 2 ploughs, now 1½.
   Value then and later 10s; now 5.
   In the same he also holds a further 40 acres of land, which St. Edmund held before 1066 as the Hundred testifies; now Warenger (holds) but the Hundred does not know how.

In ſtereſtuna tenet idē II. libi hōēs ſtigandi . t̄ . e . r . p̄tinentes
in herſam quos tenet Warengarus ſub . R . de ramis.
de . XVI . ac̄ t̄re . Sēp . I . car̄ . t̄c 7 p̄ . ual . IIII . ſol . m̄ . XXXII . d̄.

H̄ de Humiliart Rainiltorp . tenuit Aluuinus I . lib hō
LX . ac̄ t̄re . modo tenet Wills . Semp . I . car̄ . 7 VII . ac̄ p̄ti . 7 II.
mol . 7 q̄nta pars mol . 7 VI . libi hōes VII . ac̄ . ſemp . dim̄ . car̄ . 7 . I .
lib . homo . cōm̄d . XXX . ac̄ . Tc̄ . II . uilli . m̄ . I . Sēp . dim̄ . car̄ . 7 . I . ac̄.
p̄ti . t̄c ual . XXX . ſol . m̄ . XLIII.

.XLIIII. TERRA IVIKELIS PRESBITERI . H̄ . de Humiliart ★
In Hethella . dim̄ . car̄ . t̄ræ . ten̄ . Algerus ſub . Edrico antec̄.
Rob . malet cōm̄d tantū . t̄ . r . e . ſēp . II . uill . 7 . II . bor . 7 . I . car̄ . in dn̄io
7 dim̄ . car̄ . hoūm III . ac̄ p̄ti . Silu . IIII . por . Tc̄ ual . XX . ſol . m̄ . XXX.

.XLV. TERRA . Colebni . p̄rbi . In H̄ . de Humiliart . Fecit
Colebnus q̄dā ecclam ſc̄i nicholai . conceſſu regis 7 ſi rex concedit ★
dabit . XX . ac̄ . 7 ideo . cantat . miſſā una quaq̄ ebdomada . 7 pſaltiū.
p̄ rege . 7 II . ſol . ual.

264 a
★ TERRE . EADMUNDI . FILII . PAGANI IN Dnham . .XLVI.
tenuit paganus . t̄ . r . e . IIII . car̄ . t̄re . ſemp . XII . uilli . t̄c 7 p̄.
IIII . bor . m̄ . XIII . t̄c . IIII . ſer . p̄ 7 . m̄ . II . XIIII . ac̄ p̄ti . ſēp . I . car̄
in dn̄io . Tc̄ 7 p̄ . V . car̄ hoūm . m̄ . IIII 7 . I . car̄ poteſt reſtaurari.

3   He also holds in STARSTON; 2 free men, of Stigand's before 1066, belonging in Earsham, whom Warenger holds under R(oger) of Raismes, at 16 acres of land.
   Always 1 plough.
   Value then and later 4s; now 32d.

   The Hundred of HUMBLEYARD
4   A(i)lwin, 1 free man, held RAINTHORPE, 60 acres of land. Now William holds.
   Always 1 plough; meadow, 7 acres; 2 mills and one-fifth of a mill.
   Also 6 free men, 7 acres; always ½ plough.
   Also 1 free man in patronage, 30 acres. Then 2 villagers, now 1.
   Always ½ plough; meadow, 1 acre.
   Value then 30s; now 43.

44   LAND OF JUDICAEL THE PRIEST

   The Hundred of HUMBLEYARD
1   In HETHEL Algar held ½ c. of land under Edric the predecessor of Robert Malet in patronage only before 1066.
   Always 2 villagers; 2 smallholders.
   1 plough in lordship; ½ men's plough; meadow, 3 acres; woodland, 4 pigs.
   Value then 20s; now 30.

45   LAND OF COLBERN THE PRIEST

1   In the Hundred of HUMBLEYARD Colebern built a certain church of St. Nicholas with the King's assent. If the King consents, he will give 20 acres of land. Therefore he sings Mass and the Psalms each week for the King.
   Value 2s.

46   LANDS OF EDMUND SON OF PAYNE

   [LAUNDITCH Hundred]
1   In DUNHAM Payne held 4 c. of land before 1066.
   Always 12 villagers. Then and later 4 smallholders, now 13.
   Then 4 slaves, later and now 2.
   Meadow, 14 acres; always 1 plough in lordship. Then and later 5 men's ploughs, now 4, and 1 plough could be restored.

silua . c . por . sep . 1 . mol . tc 1 . r . m . 11 . tc . 1111 . an . m . 1x . tc
1111 . por . m . xvii . m . c . ou . 7 111 . uasa apu . 7 111 . soc . xliii . ac
terræ . sep . 1 . car . Tc 7 p . ual . c . sol . m . viii . lib hoc tenet
Rainald pr . c filia . pagani 7 . habet . 1 . leug . in long . 7 . 111 . qr .
7 . 1 . leug . in lato . 7 v . d . de gelto.

TERRE . ISAC . H. WANELVND . In tomestuna . 1. .XLVII.
lib ho . 1 . car tre . sep . 1 . car 7 ual . xx . sol . Hoc est de feudo Ra
dulf comitis de Stou . Rob blundus libau.

Walessam H. Begetona ten . 1 . lib ho Hofward . t r . e
1 . car . terre . Sep . 111 . uill . 7 vii . bor . int oms . 1 . car vii . ac pti . Sep
ual . xl . sol . 7 e de soca . R . comitis.

H. LOTHNINGA . In tudetuna . 11 . libi hoes goduuini comd
tantu . t r . e . libati p . lx . ac . Tc . 11 . car . 7 p . m . 1 . 7 dim ac pti .
Tc 7 p ual . x . sol . m . v . Rex . 7 . comes soca.

⁋ In Langahala . 1 . lib ho . toli . uicecomitis . comd . t . r . e . 1 . car tre .
Sep . 1 . car . in dnio sed posset alia restaurari . 7 . v . sub eo . libi hoes
viii ac tre . 7 111 . bor . 7 dim . car . Tc ual . vii . sol . m . x.

⁋ In silinga t . r . e . 111 libi hoes godduuini . comd . lxxx . ac tre .
7 sub eis . 11 . uill . Tc 111 . car . p . 1 . car . 7 dimi . m n . . Tc ual . xx .
sol . m . xxx . In mundaha . 1 . lib ho goduuini comd . de x . ac tre .

7 . 1 . bor . apptiat ÷ supi.

Woodland, 100 pigs; always 1 mill. Then 1 cob, now 2. Then 4 head of cattle, now 9. Then 4 pigs, now 17. Now 100 sheep; 3 beehives.

Also 3 Freemen, 43 acres of land; always 1 plough.

Value then and later 100s; now £8.

Reynold the priest holds this, with the daughter of Payne. It has 1 league and 3 furlongs in length and 1 league in width, tax of 5d.

47 LANDS OF ISAAC

WAYLAND Hundred

1 In THOMPSON 1 free man, 1 c. of land. Always 1 plough.
Value 20s.
This is of Earl Ralph's Holding of Stow (Bedon). Robert Blunt delivered it.

WALSHAM Hundred

2 1 free man, Hofward, held BEIGHTON before 1066, 1 c. of land.
Always 3 villagers; 7 smallholders.
1 plough between them all; meadow, 7 acres.
Value always 40s.
It is of the jurisdiction of Earl R(alph).

LODDON Hundred

3 In WOODTON 2 free men under the patronage only of Godwin before 1066 were delivered for 60 acres.
Then 2 ploughs and later, now 1. Meadow, ½ acre.
Value then and later 10s; now 5.
The King and the Earl (have) the jurisdiction.

4 In LANGHALE 1 free man under the patronage only of Toli the Sheriff before 1066, 1 c. of land.
Always 1 plough in lordship, but another could be restored.
Also 5 free men under him, 8 acres of land. 3 smallholders; ½ plough.
Value then 7s; now 10.

5 In SEETHING 3 free men under the patronage of Godwin before 1066, 80 acres of land.
Under them 2 villagers.
Then 3 ploughs, later 1½ ploughs, now none.
Value then 20s; now 30.

6 In MUNDHAM 1 free man under Godwin's patronage at 10 acres of land
and 1 smallholder.
He is assessed above.

In sinthinga. calumpniat' quedam paup moniał IIII. ac tře q̃s illa teñ sub Radulfo tam ante 7 p̃q. se forefecisse 7 ita testat' hd̃. 7 isac reuocat ex dono reḡ. ad feudum suum.

XLVIII. TERRA TOUI. H̃. FEORHOV. Hakeforda. tenuit Ketel. lib̃ hō t̃.r.e.LX.ac̃ tr̃e. 7.VI. bor. 7.I.ac̃. silua. X. por. 7 ual x.sol. 7.III.q̃r. in lonḡ. 7.II. in lato. 7 VII. d̃. 7. I. ferding. de ḡ.

H̃. GRENEOV. Holchã. teñ. Ketel. I. lib̃ hō. III. car̃ tr̃e. sep̃. II. uilt̃. 7 VIII. bor. tc̃. V. ser. sep̃. II. car̃ in dñio. tc̃. I. car̃ 7 dim̃. houm̃. p̃. 7 m̃. I. 7 I. uirga p̃ti. sep̃. I. mol̃. tc̃ IIII añ. m̃. I. tc̃ XXI. por. m̃. V. sep̃. CCC. ou. 7 XVIII. soc̃ cũ om̃i. c̃suet sed h̃t sacã LVI. ac̃ tr̃e. sep̃. II. car̃. Huic mañ s̃t additi. III. lib̃i hões duo c̃om̃d. heral. 7. I. gert. I. car̃. 7 dim̃. tr̃e hos teñ. antecessor ejus sub eis. IX. bor. sep̃. VII. soc̃. XVI. ac̃. terre. tc̃. IIII. car̃. it̃ eos 7 p̃. 7. m̃. I. tc̃ ual. VI. lib̃ p̃. 7 m̃. VIII. h̃t. I. leug̃ in lonḡ. 7 in lato 7 de gelto. II. sol.

H̃. De Humiliart. Stokes teñ. In Galt̃i tenñ. t.r.e. LX. ac̃ tr̃e. Tc̃ VII. uilt̃. m̃. I. sep̃. VIII. bor. 7 II. car̃. 7 II. car̃ houm̃. 7 VI. ac̃ p̃ti. de hoc p̃to calumpniat' scs. benedictus. IIII. ac̃ qd tenuit. t̃ r.e. silua. V. por̃. 7 sep̃. I. mol.

In eadem tenuit ketel lib̃ hō Stigandi. XXX. ac̃. sep̃. I. uill̃s.

7 V. bor. Tc̃. I. car̃. Tc̃. dim̃. car̃ houm̃. IIII. ac̃. p̃ti. In ead̃e. I. lib̃. homo. Stigandi. XXX. Tc̃. I. car̃. hec tria maneria tenet. Touius p̃ uno. Sep̃. I. r. tc̃. I. añ. m̃. III. tc̃. III. por. m̃. XX. Tc̃. XL. ou. m̃. XXV. 7. I. uas ap̃. 7. V. lib̃i hões c̃om̃d 7 soca falde. t̃. r.e. XXV. ac̃. sep̃. I. car̃. Sep̃. ual. IIII. lib̃. 7 XVII. d̃. 7. I. eccl̃a. 7 dim̃. XXIII. ac̃.

7 In SEETHING a certain poor nun claims 4 acres of land which she held under Ralph both before and after he forfeited, and the Hundred testifies to this. Isaac claims it as part of his Holding from the King's gift.

48   LAND OF TOVI

FOREHOE Hundred

1 Ketel, a free man, held HACKFORD before 1066, 60 acres of land.
     6 smallholders. [Meadow,] 1 acre; woodland, 10 pigs.
    Value 10s.
     (It has) 3 furlongs in length and 2 in width, tax of 7¼d.

(North) GREENHOE Hundred

2 Ketel, 1 free man, held HOLKHAM, 3 c. of land.
     Always 2 villagers; 8 smallholders. Then 5 slaves.
     Always 2 ploughs in lordship. Then 1½ men's ploughs, later and now 1. Meadow, 1 rod; always 1 mill. Then 4 head of cattle, now 1. Then 21 pigs, now 5; always 300 sheep.
     Also 18 Freemen with all customary dues, but he has the jurisdiction, 56 acres of land; always 2 ploughs.
  3 free men have been added to this manor, 2 under the patronage of Harold, 1 of Gyrth. 1½ c. of land. His predecessor held these.
     Under them 9 smallholders.
     Always 7 Freemen, 16 acres of land. Then 4 ploughs between them, later and now 1.
    Value then £6; later and now 8.
     It has 1 league in length and in width, tax of 2s.

The Hundred of HUMBLEYARD

3 Ingold, a thane, held STOKE (Holy Cross) before 1066, 60 acres of land.
     Then 7 villagers, now 1; always 8 smallholders.
     2 ploughs; 2 men's ploughs; meadow, 6 acres. Of this meadow St. Benedict claims 4 acres which (the Saint) held before 1066. Woodland, 5 pigs; always 1 mill.
   In the same Ketel, a free man of Stigand's, held 30 acres.
     Always 1 villager; 5 smallholders.
     Then 1 plough. Then ½ men's plough; meadow, 4 acres.
   In the same 1 free man of Stigand's 30 [acres]. Then 1 plough.
   Tovi holds these 3 manors as 1.
     Always 1 cob. Then 1 head of cattle, now 3. Then 3 pigs, now 20. Then 40 sheep, now 25. 1 beehive.
   Also 5 free men in patronage and fold-rights before 1066, 25 acres.
     Always 1 plough.
    Value always £4 17d.
     Also 1½ churches, 23 acres.

265 a

In Torp . xv . libi . hoes . CLV . ac 7 de xi . 7 dimidio habuit Rad.
Stalra . comd . t . r . e . 7 de III . Stigandi similit 7 de dimidio antec
Godrici . dapiferi similit . Tc . vi . car . m . vii : 7 dim . 7 xi . ac pti.
7 dim mol . 7 xii . bor 7 ual . xxviiii . sol . I . eccla . xxiii . ac . 7 . I.
bor . 7 dim . 7 Stokes ht I . leug . in long . 7 IIII . qr . in lato . 7 . xi.
de . gelto . 7 Torp . ht dim . leug . in long . 7 dim leug . in lat . 7
xi . d . de gilto.

⟨In Niwetuna . II . libi . hoes . xxx . ac . de uno 7 dem . habuit
antecessor Rogi . bigot . comd . t . r . e . 7 de dimidio . antecessor . Radulfi
de bella fago . Sep . v . bor . 7 . I . ca . 7 III . ac pti . 7 : IIII . libi hoes . de . xii.
ac . 7 dim . Tc ual . x . sol . m . xiii . sol . 7 IIII . d.

⟨In KENINCHA . III . libi . de duobz ex h habuit antec . Roge bigot.
comd . t . r . e . de uno . antec . R . de bellafago . 7 ht . LXXV . ac.
7 v . libi hoes . sub . ill . de xviii . ac . 7 dim . 7 II bor . 7 II . car . tc . x.
sol . m . xiii . 7 . III . d . In ead . dim . lib ho . vii . ac 7 dim . 7 . II . bou
7 ual . xvi . d . 7 ht dim . leug . in long . 7 v . qr . in lato . 7 xi . d . de . g

⟨In Kenincha . I . lib ho . II . ac . 7 ual . xvi . d.

H . de Henesteda . I . lib ho . sci . ben . t . r . e . v . ac . 7 II . bor . 7 dim . 7 dim . car
7 ual . viii . sol . Oms eccle st in ptio c maneriis.

.XLIX. TERRE . Iohis . nepotes W . H . de Smethetuna . Rinc
teda tenuit . Bou . lib ho t . r . e . Tc . IIII . car in dnio . p . I . m . III
Tc 7 p . viii . bor . m . xvi . tc . vi . s . p . IIII . m . v . x . ac pti . sep.
I . car . houm . 7 . I . mol . sep . I . r . Tc . I . por . m . xx . tc . III . ou.
m . c . Tc ual . IIII . lib . p . xL . sol m . vi . lib.

4 In SWAINSTHORPE 15 free men, 155 acres. Ralph the Constable had the patronage of 11 and a half before 1066, Stigand likewise of 3, and the predecessor of Godric the Steward likewise of a half.
   Then 6 ploughs, now 7½. Meadow, 11 acres; ½ mill; 12 smallholders.
Value 29s.
   1 church, 23 acres; 1 and a half smallholders.
   Stoke (Holy Cross) has 1 league in length and 4 furlongs in width, tax of 11d. Swainsthorpe has ½ league in length and ½ league in width, tax of 11d.

5 In NEWTON (Flotman) 2 free men, 30 acres. Roger Bigot's predecessor had the patronage of 1 and a half before 1066, and the predecessor of Ralph of Beaufour of a half.
   Always 5 smallholders;
   1 plough; meadow, 3 acres.
   Also 4 free men, at 12½ acres.
Value then 10s; now 13s 4d.

6 In KENNINGHAM 3 free (men). Of 2 of these the predecessor of Roger Bigot had the patronage before 1066, of 1 the predecessor of R(alph) of Beaufour. They have 75 acres.
   Also 5 free men under these, at 18½ acres.
      2 smallholders;
      2 ploughs.
[Value] then 10s; now 13s 3d.
In the same a half-freeman, 7½ acres; 2 oxen.
Value 16d.
   It has half a league in length and 5 furlongs in width; tax of 11d.

7 In KENNINGHAM 1 free man, 2 acres.
Value 16d.

The Hundred of HENSTEAD

8 1 free man of St. Benedict's before 1066, 5 acres.
      2 smallholders and a half;
         ½ plough.
Value 8s.
   All the churches are in the valuation with the manors.

49   LANDS OF JOHN, NEPHEW OF W(ALERAN)   265 b

The Hundred of SMETHDON

1 Bovi, a free man, held RINGSTEAD, before 1066.
   Then 4 ploughs in lordship, later 1, now 3.
   Then and later 8 smallholders, now 16. Then 6 slaves, later 4, now 5.
   Meadow, 10 acres. Always 1 men's plough; 1 mill. Always 1 cob. Then 1 pig, now 20. Then 3 sheep, now 100.
Value then £4; later 40s; now £6.

Hunesta nestuna . teñ . iohannes idem . t̄ . r . e Tc̄ . ii . car̛.
p̊ . i . m̂ . ii . sēp . iiii . Tc̄ 7 p̊ . v . bor . m̂ . vii . Tc̄ 7 p̊ . iii . ser̄ . m̂ . iiii.
7 . ii . ac̄ p̃ti sēp . hōum . Tc̄ . i . uac̄ . m̂ . viii . an̄ . m̂ . xl . por . tc̄ i.
où . m̂ xl . 7 iii . uasa . apū . 7 . i . soc̄ . v . ac̄ . tc̄ 7 p̊ . uaɫ . xx . soɫ.
m̂ . xl . i . eccɫa . sine tr̄a . Tota Rincsteda . h̄t . i . leug̃ . in long̃
7 dim̄ . in lat̄ 7 redd . viii . đ . de . xx . soɫ.

H̃ . WANELVNT. Cherebroc . tenuit . Alfere lib hō t̄ . r . e.
iiii . car̛ 7 dim . Tc̄ 7 p̊ . x . uilli . m̂ . vi . sēp . xviii . bor . xxiiii . ac̄.
p̃ti . Tc̄ iii . car̛ in d̄nio . p̊ . i . m̂ . iii . sēp . vi . car̛ hōum . silu . cccc.
por . m̂ . i . moɫ . dim̄ . pisc̄ . Hic jacent sēp . xxiiii . soc̄ . i . car̛ tr̄æ.
ad omnē consuetudinē.

In grestuna teñ Osbt̛ . i . bereuita . i . car̛ tr̄e . que jacet semp̃
huic mañ . 7 ii . uilɫ . 7 . ii . ser̛ . 7 ii . ac̄ p̃ti . tc̄ . i . car̛ . 7 p̊ . m̂ . i . car̛
7 dim̄ . In d̄nio . iiii . r . 7 m̂ . 7 m̂ . x . an̄ . Tc̄ xx . por . m̂ . xxx . tc̄
xl . où . m̂ . xliiii . m̂ . x . uasa apū . Totū uaɫ . vii . lib . i . eccɫa
xxiiii . ac̄ . 7 uaɫ . ii . soɫ.

In Weskerebroc teñ idē . i . lib hō . xl . ac̄ tr̄e semp . i . bor . 7 . i . ser̛.
Tc̄ 7 p̊ . i . car̛ . 7 uaɫ . x . soɫ . Soca . n Sahā regis . Antecec̄ . Rog̃
bigot . cōnd tantū . Totū Cherebroc habet . viii . q̄r . in long̃ & dim̄
leug̃ . 7 in lat̄ . 7 xv . đ . de g̃ . i . eccɫa xx ac̄ uaɫ xii . đ.

2   John holds HUNSTANTON, (Bovi) also held before 1066.
    Then 2 ploughs, later 1, now 2.
    Always 4 [villagers]. Then and later 5 smallholders, now 7.
    Then and later 3 slaves, now 4.
    Meadow, 2 acres, always of the men. Then 1 cow. Now 8 head
       of cattle. Now 40 pigs. Then 1 sheep, now 40. 3 beehives.
    Also 1 Freeman, 5 acres.
  Value then and later 20s; now 40.
    1 church without land.
    The whole of Ringstead has 1 league in length and ½ in width,
    at 20s it pays 8d.

  WAYLAND Hundred
3   Alfhere, a free man, held CARBROOKE before 1066, 4½ c. [of
    land].
    Then and later 10 villagers, now 6. Always 18 smallholders.
    Meadow, 24 acres. Then 3 ploughs in lordship, later 1, now 3.
       Always 6 men's ploughs; woodland, 400 pigs. Now 1 mill;
       ½ fishery.
    Here 24 Freemen have always appertained, 1 c. of land, with
       all customary dues.

4   In GRISTON Osbert holds 1 outlier, 1 c. of land, which has always
    appertained to this manor.
    2 villagers; 2 slaves.
    Meadow, 2 acres. Then 1 plough and later, now 1½ ploughs, in
       lordship. Then 4 cobs and now. Now 10 head of cattle.
       Then 20 pigs, now 30. Then 40 sheep, now 44. Now 10
       beehives.
  Value of the whole £7.
    1 church, 24 acres;
  value 2s.

5   He also holds in WEST CARBROOKE; 1 free man, 40 acres of land.
    Always 1 smallholder; 1 slave.   266 a
    Then and later 1 plough.
  Value 10s.
    The jurisdiction (is) in the King's (manor of) Saham (Toney).
  Roger Bigot's predecessor (had) the patronage only. The whole
  of Carbrooke has 8 furlongs in length and half a league in width;
  tax of 15d.
    1 church, 20 acres;
  value 12d.

H̄. Screphā. Brethā tenet. Witt. ɪɪ. car�. tr̄e. q̃m tn̄. lib
hono t̄. r. e. sēp. ɪɪɪɪ. uitti. 7. ɪ. bor. 7. ɪ. ſer. xɪɪ. ac̄ p̄ti. Tc̄. ɪɪ. car̉
in dn̄io p̄. 7 m̂. ɪ. sēp. ɪ. car̄. hoūm. 7 ɪ. mot. Sēp. ʟx. oū. 7. ɪɪ.
lib u. xvɪɪɪɪ. ac̄. tr̄e. q̃s. habuit c̄m̄d. tantū. Socā in buchā.
7. ɪ. lib hō xxx. ac̄ tr̄e. ſoca in sc̄a. adet. totū uat. ʟx. ſot.
In eadē. ɪ. lib. hō. ɪɪ. car̉. tr̄e. t̄. r. e. Tc̄. xɪɪ. uitti. p̄. 7 m̂. ɪɪɪ. sēp.
ɪɪɪ. bor. 7. vɪɪɪ. ac̄ p̄ti. sēp. ɪɪ. car̄ in dn̄io. Tc̄. ɪɪɪ. car̉ hoūm. p̄.
7. m̂. ɪɪ. sēp. ɪ. mot. sēp. ɪɪ. an̄. m̂. xɪɪɪɪ. por. 7 ʟxx. oū. 7. v. uaſa.
apu. Tc̄ uat. ʟx. ſot. m̂. xʟ. Soca in buchā.

H̄. Hcinestede In ſaſilingahā ten̄. ſtergar huſcarla.
reḡ. e. xxx. ac̄ tr̄e. Sēp. dim̄. bor. Tc̄ ɪɪ. ſer. m̂. ɪ. 7 dim̄ mot.
ɪ. ac̄. 7 dim̄. p̄ti. tc̄. ɪ. car̉. m̂ nulla 7   Tc̄ 7 p̄. uat. xx. ſot.
m̂. xɪɪɪ. ɪ. eccta x. ac̄. 7 uat. xvɪ. d̄.

V̄ In Tmentuna ten̄. ɪ. lib hō t. e. r. Ketel ſub ſtigando. vɪɪɪ. ac̄
7 dim̄. ac̄ p̄ti. tc̄. ɪɪ. bou. Tc̄ uat. ɪɪ. ſot. m̂. xɪɪ. d̄.

H̄. 7 dim̄. DE FREDrebruge. Walpola ten̄. lib hō t̄. e r.
dim̄. car̉ tr̄e. sēp. vɪ. bor. 7 dim̄ car̉ 7 uat. v. ſot

SHROPHAM Hundred

6 William holds BRETTENHAM, 2 c. of land, which a free man held before 1066.
>Always 4 villagers; 1 smallholder; 1 slave.
>Meadow, 12 acres. Then 2 ploughs in lordship, later and now 1. Always 1 men's plough; 1 mill. Always 60 sheep.
>Also 2 free (men), 19 acres of land whom he had in patronage only. The jurisdiction (is) in Buckenham.
>Also 1 free man, 30 acres of land. The jurisdiction is St. Etheldreda's.

Value of the whole 60s.
>In the same 1 free man, 2 c. of land, before 1066.
>Then 12 villagers, later and now 3. Always 3 smallholders.
>Meadow, 8 acres; always 2 ploughs in lordship. Then 3 men's ploughs, later and now 2. Always 1 mill; always 2 head of cattle. Now 14 pigs; 70 sheep; 5 beehives.

Value then 60s; now 40.
>The jurisdiction (is) in Buckenham.

HENSTEAD Hundred

7 In SAXLINGHAM Stergar, King Edward's Guard, held 30 acres of land.
>Always half a smallholder. Then 2 slaves, now 1.
>½ mill; meadow, 1½ acres. Then 1 plough, now none; and [ ].

Value then and later 20s; now 13.
>1 church, 10 acres;

value 16d.

8 In THURTON 1 free man Ketel, held under Stigand, 8 acres.
>Meadow, ½ acre. Then 2 oxen.

Value then 2s; now 12d.

The Hundred and a Half of FREEBRIDGE

9 A free man held WALPOLE before 1066, ½ c. of land.
>Always 6 smallholders; ½ plough.

Value 5s.

.I.. **TERRE ROGERII FILII RENARDI.** *H̃*.De grimes
hou . Stanforda teñ . Alſtan̅ . t . e . r . 11 . car̄ . terre . Sep̃ . v.
uilł . 7 11 . bor. Tc̄ . v . ſer . 7 p̊ . m̊ . 11. viii . ac̄ p̊ti. Sep̃ . in dn̄io . 11 . car̄
tc̄ 7 p̊ . 1 . car̄ hoūm . m̊ . 11 . bou. Sep̃ . 1 . mol̄ . 7 dim̃ . Tc̄ 7 m̊ . 11 . r. Tc̄
viii . an̄ . m̊ . xii . Tc̄. viii . por . m̊ . x . Tc̄ . cc . ou . m̊ . iiii . uigin̄. Tc̄
ual . 7 m̊ . xl . ſoł . In eadē uilla ſt viii . libi hōes . de . 11 . car̄ tr̃e .
7 xxxvi . ac̄ . 7 . 1 . bor . 7 . 1 . ſer̊ . iiii . ac̄ p̊ti . Tc̄ iii . car̄ m̊ . 11 . Sep̃ .
ual . xx . ſoł . hos reclamat de dono regis. Totū habt̃ . 1 . leug̃ . in
long̃ . 7 dim̃ . in lato . 7 redd̃ . de gelto . xv . d̃ . de xx . ſoł . 7 ſup hos
rex ſochā 7 comes ht̃

In Buckenham . vii . libi . hōes . 1 . car̄ tr̃e . 7 xx . ac̄ . 7 vi . uilł .
ſep̃ . 11 . cā 7 ual . xi . ſoł . Rex 7 comes ſocā

*V*In Icheburc . 1 . lib̃ . hō xl . ac̄ . ſep̃ . dim̃ car̄ . 7 11 . ac̄ p̊ti . 7 ual
xvi . d̃.

H̃. Smetheduna Torp teñ . Turchetel . lib̃ hō t . e . r .
1 . car̄ tr̃e . 7 dim̃ . 7 . v . bor . Tc̄ . 11 . s . m̊ . 1 . 7 . iii . ac̄ . p̊ti . tc̄ . 11 .
car̄ . in dn̄io . p̊ . vi . bou . m̊ . 1 . car̄ . dim̃ . ſep̃ . dim̃ . car̄ . hoūm .
7 dim̃ . mol̄ . 7 . 1 . piſc̄ . ſep̃ . 1 . r . m̊ . xii . por . tc̄ xvi . ou . m̊ . c .
Tc̄ ual . xx . ſoł . m̊ . xxx . Stigandi ſocā

V WANELVND . Sculetuna . 11 . car̄ . tr̃æ . ten . 1 . lib̃ hō
t̃ . e . r . Tc̄ 7 p̊ . v uilti . m̊ . vi . Tc̄ 7 p̊ . 1 . bor . m̊ . iii . Tc̄ 7 p̊ .
11 . s . m̊ . 1 . xvi . ac̄ . p̊ti . ſep̃ . 11 . car̄ in dn̄io . Tc̄ . 11 . car̄ . 7 dim̃ .
hoūm . m̊ . 11 . filu . ccc . por . Tc̄ . x . an̄ . Tc̄ xxx . por . m̊ .
xv . Tc̄ lxv . ou . m̊ xviii . 7 . iiii . ſoc̄ . xii . ac̄ tr̃e . 7 ual . xl . ſoł .

LAND OF ROGER SON OF RAINARD

The Hundred of GRIMSHOE

1 Alstan held STANFORD before 1066, 2 c. of land.
Always 5 villagers; 2 smallholders. Then 5 slaves and later, now 2.
Meadow, 8 acres; always 2 ploughs in lordship. Then and later 1 men's plough, now 2 oxen; always 1½ mills. Then and now 2 cobs. Then 8 head of cattle, now 12. Then 8 pigs, now 10. Then 200 sheep, now 4 score.
Value then and now 40s.
In the same village are 8 free men, at 2 c. of land and 36 acres. 1 smallholder; 1 slave.
Meadow, 4 acres. Then 3 ploughs, now 2.
Value always 20s.
He claims this of the King's gift. The whole has 1 league in length and ½ in width, of a 20s tax it pays 15d. The King and the Earl have the jurisdiction over these.

2 In BUCKENHAM (Tofts) 7 free men, 1 c. of land and 20 acres.
6 villagers;
always 2 ploughs.
Value 11s.
The King and the Earl (have) the jurisdiction.

3 In ICKBURGH 1 free man, 40 acres.
Always ½ plough; meadow, 2 acres.
Value 16d.

SMETHDON Hundred

4 Thorketel, a free man, held (Ingoldis) THORPE before 1066, 1½ c. of land.
5 smallholders. Then 2 slaves, now 1.
Meadow, 3 acres. Then 2 ploughs in lordship, later 6 oxen, now 1½ ploughs. Always ½ men's plough; ½ mill; 1 fishery. Always 1 cob. Now 12 pigs. Then 16 sheep, now 100.
Value then 20s; now 30.
Stigand's jurisdiction.

WAYLAND [Hundred]

5 1 free man held SCOULTON before 1066, 2 c. of land.
Then and later 5 villagers, now 6. Then and later 1 smallholder, now 3. Then and later 2 slaves, now 1.
Meadow, 16 acres; always 2 ploughs in lordship. Then 2½ men's ploughs, now 2. Woodland, 300 pigs. Then 10 head of cattle. Then 30 pigs, now 15. Then 65 sheep, now 18.
Also 4 Freemen, 12 acres of land.
Value 40s.

H̄. DE SCREPHĀ. Atlebur. teñ. Toradre. t. r. e. ii. cā.
7 iii. ac̄.

Sēp. vi. uilli. 7. v. bor. Tc̄. i. s. m̄. iii. xxiii. ac̄ p̃ti. sēp. i. car. in dñio
7 ii. car. houm̄. silu. lx. por. 7 due part mol. dim̄. pisc̄. Tc̄. ii. r. m̄.
m̄. i. sēp. i. ua. tc̄. vi. por. m̄. v. 7. viii. oũ. 7. xxi. soc̄. lxxx. ac̄ tr̄e
7 xii. ac̄ p̃ti. silu. viii. por. tc̄ 7 p̃. ii. car. m̄. iii. tc̄ 7 p̃. ual. xl. sol.
m̄. lx.

In alio atlebure. tenuit turchill. t. r. e. ii. car tēre. semp. vi.
uilli. 7. v. bor. xxiiii. ac̄ p̃ti. silu. lx. por. sēp. i. car in dñio. 7. ii.
car houm̄. 7. i. car. posset. eē. m̄. dim̄. mol. 7 dim̄. pisc̄. 7 xvii. soc̄
xlvii. ac̄ tr̄e. viii. ac̄ p̃ti. silua. xii. por. sēp iii. car. tc̄. i. r. Sēp
ii. añ. tc̄ vi. por. m̄. iiii. Tc̄ 7 p̃. ual. xl. sol. m̄. lx. Totũ ht. ii.
leug̃. in long. 7. i. leug̃. in lato. q̃c̃q̃ ibi teneat. 7. xxxiiii. d. 7. i.
obolũ de gelto.

In Rokelund. i. car tr̄e. teñ. Ringul. lib̄ hō t. r. e. sēp. i.
uills. 7 viii. bor. Tc̄. ii. ser. m̄. i. 7. viii. ac̄ p̃ti. silu. viii. por. tc̄. ii.
car. in dñio. p̃. 7 m̄. i. tc̄ 7. p̃. i. car houm̄ m̄. dim̄. 7. i. car. posset
eē. m̄. i. añ. 7 v. por. 7 xxiiii. oũ. sēp ual. xx. sol.

H̄. DE. HOLT. In Kellinga. teñ. Wester lib̄ hō Guert. t. r. e.
ii. car. tr̄æ. m̄. Radulfus. sili. Hagana. Sēp. vi. uill. 7 xx. bor.
tc̄. ii. car in dñio. 7 p̃. i. m̄. ii. Sēp. ii. houm̄. i. acr p̃ti. Sēp. i. r
tc̄ xvi. p̃. m̄. xx. Sēp. xl. oũ. 7. xxiiii. cap̃. Tc̄ ual. xx. sol. m̄.
xl. sol.

H̄. LOTHNINGA. In mundaham teñ sc̄a Aldreda. t. r. e.

in dñio. xx. arc. m̄. tenet. Ro. Semp. ii. bor. 7 ual. iii. sol.

The Hundred of SHROPHAM

6 Thorold held ATTLEBOROUGH before 1066, 2 c. [of land] and 3 acres.
Always 6 villagers; and 5 smallholders. Then 1 slave, now 3.
Meadow, 23 acres. Always 1 plough in lordship; 2 men's ploughs; woodland, 60 pigs; two-thirds of a mill; ½ fishery. Then 2 cobs, now 1; always 1 cow. Then 6 pigs, now 5; 8 sheep.
Also 21 Freemen, 80 acres of land; meadow, 12 acres; woodland, 8 pigs. Then and later 2 ploughs, now 3.
Value then and later 40s; now 60.

7 In the other ATTLEBOROUGH Thorkell held 2 c. of land before 1066.
Always 6 villagers; and 5 smallholders.
Meadow, 24 acres; woodland, 60 pigs. Always 1 plough in lordship; 2 men's ploughs; there could be 1 plough. Now ½ mill; ½ fishery.
Also 17 Freemen, 47 acres of land; meadow, 8 acres; woodland, 12 pigs; always 3 ploughs. Then 1 cob; always 2 head of cattle. Then 6 pigs, now 4.
Value then and later 40s, now 60.
The whole has 2 leagues in length and 1 league in width, whoever holds there, tax of 34½d.

8 In ROCKLAND Ringwulf, a free man, held 1 c. of land before 1066.
Always 1 villager; and 8 smallholders. Then 2 slaves, now 1.
Meadow, 8 acres; woodland, 8 pigs.
Then 2 ploughs in lordship, later and now 1. Then and later 1 men's plough, now ½, and there could be 1 plough.
Now 1 head of cattle, 5 pigs; 24 sheep.
Value always 20s.

The Hundred of HOLT

9 *In KELLING Wester, a free man of Gyrth's, held 2 c. of land before 1066, now Ralph son of Hagan (holds).*
Always 6 villagers; 20 smallholders.
Then 2 ploughs in lordship, later 1, now 2. Always 2 men's [ploughs]; meadow, 1 acre. Always 1 cob. Then 16 pigs, now 20. Always 40 sheep; 24 goats.
Value then 20s, now 40s.

LODDON Hundred

10 *In MUNDHAM St. Etheldreda held 20 acres of land in lordship before 1066; now Roger holds.*
Always 2 smallholders.
Value 3s.

H̄. *DĒPWADE*. Hateſtuna . t̄n . Oſbnus . teinn̊ . t̄ . r . e . i.
car̄ tr̄æ . ſemp . III . uiłłi . 7 . xx . bor . tc̄ . I . car̄ . in dn̄io . m̄ . I . 7 dim̄.
Sēp . III . car̄ . houm̄ . vi . ac̄ p̃ti Tc̄ xxIIII . por . m̄ . xII . 7 . xx . ou . tc̄ uał
xx . ſoł . m̄ . xL.

H̄. Clauelinga . Rauelincham ten̄ . Oſbnus teinn̊ . t̄ . r . e . II . c̄a.
t̄eræ . 7 II . ac̄ 7 dim̄ . Tc̄ II . uiłłi . m̄ . III . Tc̄ II . ſer . Sēp . I . car̄ . in dn̄io .
7 I . car̄ . poſſet fieri . 7 . I . car̄ . houm̄ . vIII . ac̄ p̃ti . ſiłu . v . por . Tc̄ . IIII.
an̄ . m̄ . xII . por . 7 v . ſoc̄ . xIII . ac̄ . 7 . I . eccła . Lx . ac̄ . Tc̄ uał . xx.
ſoł . m̄ . xL.

In Turuertuna . xx . ac̄ . I . liƀ . hō ſub antec̄ . R . de bellafago com̄d.
tantum . 7 . II . ac̄ . p̃ti . 7 dim̄ . car̄ . 7 uał . vIII . ſoł.

.LI.

TERRE . BERNERI . ARƀ . *FRIDEBRUGE* *H̄*.

& dim̄ . In Grimeſtuna . I . car̄ tr̄æ . ten̄ . Vluerū . liƀa fem̄.
t̄ . r . e . Sēp vi . bor . 7 . I . ſer . 7 x . ac̄ p̃ti . Tc̄ . I . car̄ . p̃ . nichil . m̄ . I.
Sēp . I . moł . Hic jacent . II . ſoc̄ . III . ac̄ . 7 . III . liƀi . hōes . IIII . ac̄ . Totū
uał xx . ſoł.

In concham . I . liƀ . hō . Lx . ac̄ tr̄e 7 . I . bor 7 . III . ac̄ p̃ti . Tc̄ dim̄ .
car̄ . In ead̄e . IIII . liƀi hōes . III . ac̄ . Totum uał . x . ſoł . Iſtos om̄s . liƀos
hōes reuocat de dono regis

In Helingetuna . II . car̄ tr̄e . 7 xv . ac̄ . ten̄ . ead̄e Vluerun . t̄ . r . e.
ſēp vII . uiłłi . 7 vIII . bor . 7 . II . ſer . x . ac̄ p̃ti . Tc̄ . II . car̄ in dn̄io p̃ . I.
m̄ . II . ſēp . I . car̄ . houm̄ . I . moł . 7 . I . ſał . Tc̄ . c . ou . m̄ . Lxxx . tc̄
xII . por . m̄ . vII . Tc̄ 7 p̃ . uał . IIII . liƀ . m̄ . c . ſoł . Totum ħt . I.
leuḡ . 7 dim̄ . in lonḡ . 7 dim̄ . in lat̄ . qc̄q̃ ibi teneat 7 redd̄ . vIII . d̄.
de ḡ . de . xx . ſoł.

DEPWADE Hundred
11 Osbern the thane held HUDESTON before 1066, 1 c. of land.
   Always 3 villagers; 20 smallholders.
   Then 1 plough in lordship, now 1½. Always 3 men's ploughs; meadow, 6 acres. Then 24 pigs, now 12; 20 sheep.
   Value then 20s; now 40.

CLAVERING Hundred
12 Osbern the thane held RAVENINGHAM before 1066, 2 c. of land and 2½ acres.
   Then 2 villagers, now 3. Then 2 slaves.
   Always 1 plough in lordship and 1 plough could be there; 1 men's plough; meadow, 8 acres; woodland, 5 pigs. Then 4 head of cattle. Now 12 pigs.
   Also 5 Freemen, 13 acres.
   Also 1 church, 60 acres.
   Value then 20s; now 40.

13 In THURLTON, 20 acres, 1 free man in patronage only under R(alph) of Beaufour's predecessor.
   Meadow, 2 acres; ½ plough.
   Value 8s.

51 LANDS OF BERNER THE CROSSBOWMAN

FREEBRIDGE Hundred and a Half
1 In GRIMSTON Wulfrun, a free woman, held 1 c. of land before 1066.
   Always 6 smallholders; 1 slave.
   Meadow, 10 acres. Then 1 plough, later nothing, now 1.
   Always 1 mill.
   Here appertain 2 Freemen, 3 acres; also 3 free men, 4 acres.
   Value of the whole 20s.

2 In CONGHAM 1 free man, 60 acres of land.
   1 smallholder.
   Meadow, 3 acres. Then ½ plough.
   In the same 4 free men, 3 acres.
   Value of the whole 10s.
   He claims all these free men of the King's gift.

3 In HILLINGTON the same Wulfrun held 2 c. of land and 15 acres before 1066.
   Always 7 villagers, 8 smallholders; 2 slaves.
   Meadow, 10 acres. Then 2 ploughs in lordship, later 1, now 2.
   Always 1 men's plough; 1 mill; 1 salt-house. Then 100 sheep, now 80. Then 12 pigs, now 7.
   Value then and later £4; now 100s.
   The whole has 1½ leagues in length and ½ in width, whoever holds there, of a 20s tax it pays 8d.

H̄. DECHINGA. SCERNEBRUNE tēn . t̄ . e . r . 1 . lib̄ . hō . 1 . car̛
tr̄e . Tc̄ . 1 . in dn̄io . p̊ . n̄ . m̂ . 1 . v . bor . 1 . mot̂ . duodecim pars . 1 . sat̂
7 xii . pars 1 . mot̂ . ii . ac̄ p̊ti . 7 dim̄ . Tc 7 p̊ . xvi . s; m̂ . xx .

H̄. Wanelund . Asscelea tēn . Aluric̊ . tegn̊ . Heroldi . t̄ r . e . ii .
car̛ . tr̄e . Tc̄ . x . uitt̂ . P̊ . 7 m̂ . vii . sēp . xi . bor . xiii . ac̄ p̊ti . Tc̄ . 1 . car̛
in dn̄io . p̊ . 1 m̂ . . ii . Tc̄ v car̄ hoūm . p̊ . iii . m̂ . ii . silů . cxx . por . 7 . 1 .
pisc̄ . m̂ . 1 . an̄ . Tc̄ . x . por . m̂ . viii . 7 xxiiii . cap̊ . 7 lx . oū . m̂ . lxvii .
sēp . uat̂ . l . sot̂ . In eadē . vi . lib̄i hōēs . dim̄ . car̄ tr̄e . 7 vii . ac̄ tr̄e . tc̄
iiii . car̛ . p̊ 7 . m̂ . ii . ac̄ p̊ti . 7 uat̂ . x . sot̂ . hoc ē . p esc . 7 fuit d̂ maneriis
Rad̂ . comitis .

⁊ In Sculetuna tēn . 1 . lib̄ hō sub heroldo . t . e . r . iii . car̛ tr̄e . Tc̄ 7 p̊ .
vi . uitti m̂ . v . sēp . v . bor . xxvi . ac̄ p̊ti . 7 . ii . car̛ in dn̄io sēp . 1 . car̄
hoūm . silua̅ . ccc . por . sēp . ii . r̄ . 7 . iiii . an̄ . m̂ . x . 7 xxiiii . por . m̂
x . 7 xv . oū . m̂ . cx . 7 sēp . xxx . cap̊ . sēp . uat̂ . l . sot̂ . Totū ĥt . 1 . leug̃
7 dim̄ . in long̃ . 7 . 1 . leug̃ . in lat̂ . q̊cq̛ ibi teneat 7 de gelto xv . d̂ .
hoc ē de maneriis . Radulf .

⁊ In Tomestuna . 1 . car̛ tr̄e . tēn . t . r . e . tc̄ . 1 . car̛ . p̊ . 7 m̂ . dim̄ .
1 . bor . 7 uat̂ . xvi . sot̂ . Hoc etiam de feudo . Rad̂ .

H̄. ERPINGEHĀ NORT. In othestranda . tēn eschet . t . r . e .
p̊ . ii . car̛ tr̄e . Sēp . vi . uitti . 7 xviii . bor . 7 . ii . ser . tc̄ . ii . car̛ in
dn̄io . p̊ . 7 . m̂ . 1 . 7 . ii . car̛ hoūm . 1 . mot̂ . Silů . iii . por . Tc̄ . 1 . r̂ .

m̂ ii . Tc̄ ii . an̄ . m̂ . vi . Tc̄ iiii . m̂ . v . por . m̂ . xviiii . oū . Tc̄ xviii .
cap̊ . 7 . v . soc̄ d̂ . xxxii . ac̄ tr̄æ . 7 rex ĥt socam . 1 . ac̄ p̊ti . Sēp . 1 . car̛
tc̄ uat̂ . xl . sot̂ . 7 sēp . 7 ĥt . vii . q̄r . in long̃ . 7 . iiii . in lato . 7 de gelto .
vi . d̂ . 7 iii . ferd̂ .

DOCKING Hundred
4 1 free man held SHERNBORNE before 1066, 1 c. of land. Then 1 [plough] in lordship, later none, now 1.
    5 smallholders.
    1 mill; one-twelfth of a salt-house; one-twelfth of 1 mill; meadow, 2½ acres.
[Value] then and later 16[s]; but now 20.

WAYLAND Hundred
5 Aelfric, a thane of Harold's, held ASHILL before 1066, 2 c. of land. Then 10 villagers, later and now 7; always 11 smallholders.
    Meadow, 13 acres. Then 1 plough in lordship, later 1, now 2. Then 5 men's ploughs, later 3, now 2. Woodland, 120 pigs; 1 fishery. Now 1 head of cattle. Then 10 pigs, now 8; 24 goats. 60 sheep, now 67.
Value always 50s.
In the same 6 free men, ½ c. of land and 7 acres of land.
    Then 4 ploughs, later and now 2; meadow [?2] acres.
Value 10s.
    This is by exchange; it was one of Earl Ralph's manors.

6 In SCOULTON 1 free man under Harold held 3 c. of land before 1066.
    Then and later 6 villagers, now 5; always 5 smallholders.
    Meadow, 26 acres, 2 ploughs in lordship. Always 1 men's plough; woodland, 300 pigs. Always 2 cobs. 4 head of cattle, now 10. 24 pigs, now 10; 15 sheep, now 110. Always 30 goats.
Value always 50s.
    The whole has 1½ leagues in length and 1 league in width, whoever holds there, tax of 15d. This is one of Ralph's manors.

7 In THOMPSON 1 c. of land was held before 1066. Then 1 plough, later and now ½.
    1 smallholder.
Value 16s. This also (is) of Ralph's Holding.

NORTH ERPINGHAM Hundred
8 In OVERSTRAND Skeet held before 1066, at 2 c. of land.
    Always 6 villagers, 18 smallholders; 2 slaves.
    Then 2 ploughs in lordship, later and now 1. 2 men's ploughs; 1 mill; woodland, 3 pigs. Then 1 cob, now 2. Then 2 head 268 b of cattle, now 6. Then 4, now 5 pigs. Now 19 sheep. Then 18 goats.
    Also 5 Freemen, at 32 acres of land. The King has the jurisdiction. Meadow, 1 acre; always 1 plough.
Value then and always 40s.
    It has 7 furlongs in length and 4 in width, tax of 6¾d.

H̃. DE GRREHOV. In pikeham tñ. I. lib hō XII. ac̄ 7 I. domũ de feudo. R. comitis. 7 ē in socā hd. Sēp. I. mol̄. 7 ual. VII. sol̄. hoc libauit. R. blundus.

H̃. DE ENSFORDA. In Hacforda. teñ. I. lib hō. t̄. r. e. I. car̄ tr̄e. Semp. III. uill. 7. III. bor. sēp. I. car̄. in dñio. 7 dim̄. car̄ houm. 7. II. ac̄. p̄ti. silu. xxx. por. sēp. I. r. 7. v por. 7. XII. ou. 7 Val xx. sol̄.

.LII. TERRE. Gisleb̄ti. arbal. H̃. Scerepham. t̄ r. e. tñ. ★
Aluric. I. car̄. tr̄e. p. I. mañ. sēp. III. bor. Tc̄. 7 p̄. II. s. m̄. I. 7 x. ac̄ p̄ti. Tc̄. II. car̄ P̄ 7 m̄. I. sēp. I. mol̄. 7. I. lib hō addit. ē. hic p̄ escang̃ de. xxx. ac̄. IIII. ac̄ p̄ti. 7. I. bor. 7. sēp. dim̄. car̄. m̄. I. r. 7. II. añ Tc̄. III. por. m̄. VIII. Tc̄ LXXX. m̄. XL. 7. III. uasa ap̄. Totum. ual xxx. sol̄. Soca de lib̄o hōe in bucham.

H̃. WALESSA. In tunestalle teñ. I. lib homo. Ratho dim̄. car̄ terre. Sēp. VI. bor. VIII. ac̄ p̄ti. Tc̄ dim̄. car̄. m̄. I. car̄ in dñio. Sēp. dim̄. car̄ houm. III. añ tc̄. LII. ou. m̄. XXVIII. tc̄ ual. x. sol̄. m̄. XXII. sol̄.

H̃. BLAFELDA. In brundala. teñ. I. lib hō. p. I. car̄. tr̄æ goduuin. cōmd. gerti. p̄q rex ueñ. accep̄. R. comes. m̄. teñ. Gis. arb̄. p. II. car̄. tr̄e. Tc̄. v. 7 m̄. IIII. bor. tc̄ 7 p̄. I. car̄. in dñio. m̄. II. Sēp. cũ. II. bouib; ar̄ hōes. Silu v. por. 7 xxv. ac̄ p̄ti. 7 ibi. XII. lib hōes. 7 dim̄. de. LXXX. ac̄. 7 x. tr̄e. Sēp. I. car̄ 7 dim̄. Tc̄ ual. xxv. sol̄. m̄. XL. ht. I. leug̃. in long̃. 7 dim̄. in lato. 7 VII. d dgel.

The Hundred of (South) GREENHOE

9 In PICKENHAM 1 free man holds 12 acres and a house of Earl Ralph's Holding. It is in the Hundred's jurisdiction.
Always 1 mill.
Value 7s. R(obert) Blunt delivered this.

The Hundred of EYNSFORD

10 In HACKFORD 1 free man held 1 c. of land before 1066.
Always 3 villagers and 3 smallholders.
Always 1 plough in lordship; ½ men's plough; meadow, 2 acres; woodland, 30 pigs. Always 1 cob; 5 pigs; 12 sheep.
Value 20s.

52   LANDS OF GILBERT THE CROSSBOWMAN

SHROPHAM Hundred

1 Aelfric held [in SHROPHAM] 1 c. of land before 1066 as 1 manor.
Always 3 smallholders. Then and later 2 slaves, now 1.
Meadow, 10 acres. Then 2 ploughs, later and now 1; always 1 mill.
1 free man has been added here by exchange, at 30 acres.
Meadow, 4 acres.
1 smallholder,
always ½ plough. Now 1 cob; 2 head of cattle. Then 3 pigs, now 8. Then 80 [?sheep], now 40; 3 beehives.
Value of the whole 30s.
The jurisdiction of the free man (is) in Buckenham.

WALSHAM Hundred

2 In TUNSTALL 1 free man, Rathi, held ½ c. of land.
Always 6 smallholders.
Meadow, 8 acres. Then ½ plough, now 1 plough in lordship. Always ½ men's plough; 3 head of cattle. Then 52 sheep, now 28.
Value then 10s, now 22s.

BLOFIELD Hundred

3 In BRUNDALL 1 free man, Godwin, under the patronage of Gyrth held, as 1 c. of land. After the King came Earl R(alph) acquired it, now Gilbert the Crossbowman holds, as 2 c. of land.
Then 5, now 4 smallholders.
Then and later 1 plough in lordship, now 2. The men have always ploughed with 2 oxen.
Woodland, 5 pigs; meadow, 25 acres.
There also 12 free men and a half, at 80 acres and 10 (acres) of land; always 1½ ploughs.
Value then 25s, now 40.
It has 1 league in length and ½ in width, tax of 7d.

H̃.DICE DIMID̃. In teluentuna ten̄ Alfi fub rege.e.p.ıı.car̊
tr̄e.Sēp.ıııı.uilł.7.ıı.bor.Tc̄ 7 p̊.ıı.car.in dn̄io.m̊.ı.Sēp.ı.
car.houm.Silua xxx.por.7.ıııı.ac̄.p̊ti m̊.ı.eq̊.in aula.Tc̄
ıx an̄.m̊.vııı.Tc̄.vııı.por.m̊.xı.m̊.xx.ou.7.ı.uas.ap̊.7 vı.
libi.hões.ejdem com̄d.de.lx.ac̄ tr̄æ.Sēp.ıı.car int oēs.7 ıı.ac̄
p̊ti.Tc̄ 7 p̊.ual.xl.fol.m̊ xx.

TERRE.RADUL ARB̃.H̃.BLAFELDA.In plumes   .LIII.
tede ten̄.Toui.ı.lib̃ hõ gerti.t.e.r.ı.car̊ tr̄æ.Sēp.ı.uills
Tc̄ dim car̊ p̊ nichil.m̊ dim.7.ıı.ac̄.p̊ti.Tc̄.xı.ou.In ifto man̄
manebant.vı.libi hoēs.7 dim.xx.ac̄ tr̄e.ıı.ac̄ p̊ti.Sēp.ı.car.hos
reclamat ex libatione.Hoc qd̊.ē in dn̄io.tc̄ ual.v.fol.m̊.x.fol.7 libi
hões.v.fol.7 ht.ı.leug̃.in lat.7 dim.lati.7 de gelto.xıııı.d.q̊eq̊
ibi teneat.

TERRE.Rob̃.ARBAL.H̃.FEORHOU.In appethorp.ı.   .LIIII.
car tr̄e.tenuit Alfere lib̃ homo.t̄.r.e xxx.ac̄ tr̄æ.p̊ man̄.

269 b
Tc̄ ıı.uilł.m̊.ıııı.7.xv.foc̄.femp.ııı.car.filu.xv por.7.ıııı.ac p̊ti
m̊.vı.por.xx.ou.xx.cap̊.tc̄ ual.xx.fol.m̊.xxx.ıı.7 ht.ıııı.q̊r
in long̃.7.ıı.in lat.7 v.d̊.de gelto.

.LV. TERRE.RABELLI ARTIFICIS.H̃.BLAFELDA.
In mora.ten̄.firic̊.ı.lib̃ hõ.t̄.r.e.ıı.car̊ tr̄e.Tc̄ vııı.uilł.
p̊.7 m̊.v.tc̄.ıııı.fer̊.p̊.7.m̊.ıı.tc̄ ı.car̊ 7 dim.p̊.ı.7 m̊.ıı.in dn̄io
Semp dim car̊ houm.7.x.ac̄.p̊ti.m̊.ı.r.Sēp.ııı.an̄ tc̄ ııı.p̊.
7.m̊.xıı.m̊.c.ou.7.ı.fal.Tc̄ ual.xl.p̊.xxx.m̊.xl.7 ht.
vııı.q̊r.de leug̃.7.v.de lat.7 de gelto.xx.fol 7 foca.7 faca.
ē regis.7 com̄it̄

DISS Half Hundred
4 In THELVETON Alsi held under King Edward as 2 c. of land.
   Always 4 villagers; 2 smallholders.
   Then and later 2 ploughs in lordship, now 1. Always 1 men's
      plough; woodland, 30 pigs; meadow, 4 acres. Now 1 horse at
      the hall. Then 9 head of cattle, now 8. Then 8 pigs, now 11.
      Now 20 sheep; 1 beehive.
   Also 6 free men under the patronage of the same, at 60 acres of
      land. Always 2 ploughs between them all; meadow, 2 acres.
   Value then and later 40s; now 20.

53   LANDS OF RALPH THE CROSSBOWMAN

BLOFIELD Hundred
1 In PLUMSTEAD Tovi, 1 free man of Gyrth's, held 1 c. of land
   before 1066.
   Always 1 villager.
   Then ½ plough, later nothing, now ½. Meadow, 2 acres. Then
      11 sheep.
   6 free men and a half dwelt in this manor, 20 acres of land;
      meadow, 2 acres; always 1 plough. He claims these men by
      delivery.
   Value then of what is in lordship 5s, now 10s; of the free men, 5s.
   It has 1 league in length and ½ in width, tax of 14d, whoever
      holds there.

54   LANDS OF ROBERT THE CROSSBOWMAN

FOREHOE Hundred
1 In *APPETHORP* Alfhere a free man held 1 c. of land and 30 acres of
   land as a manor before 1066.
   Then 2 villagers, now 4.
   15 Freemen; 3 ploughs; woodland, 15 pigs; meadow, 4 acres.
   Now 6 pigs, 20 sheep, 20 goats.
   Value then 20s; now 32.
   It has 4 furlongs in length and 2 in width, tax of 5d.

55   LANDS OF RABEL THE ENGINEER

BLOFIELD Hundred
1 In MOOR Sigeric, 1 free man, held 2 c. of land before 1066.
   Then 8 villagers, later and now 5. Then 4 slaves, later and now 2.
   Then 1½ ploughs, later 1, now 2, in lordship. Always ½ men's
      plough;
   meadow, 10 acres. Now 1 cob; always 3 head of cattle. Then 3
      pigs, now 12. Now 100 sheep; 1 salt-house.
   Value then 40[s]; later 30; now 40.
   It has 8 furlongs in length and 5 in width, tax of 20s. The full
jurisdiction is the King's and the Earl's.

H̃. *EAST DE FLEG*. In Philebeỹ. II. car̃ tr̃e 7 xlvii. ac̃. ten̄
R. Stalara. t̃ r. e. p̃ man̄. Tc̃ viii. uilł. p̊. 7 m̃. vi. 7. ii. bor. femp.
I. car̃. in dn̄io. 7. i. car̃. houm̃. 7. xiiii. ac̃ p̃ti. sẽp. ii. r̃. 7. i. an̄. Tc̃
vii. por. m̃. x. 7. iii. foc̃. xv. ac̃. sẽp. i. car̃. 7 dim̃. 7. i. ac̃ p̃ti.
7. xiiii. libi. hões dim̃. car̃. tr̃e. 7 vi. ac̃ sẽp. ii. car̃. 7 dim̃. 7. i.
ac̃ p̃ti. Tc̃ uał. xl. foł. p̊. 7 m̃. l. Rex 7 comes. focā. de libis hōib;
7. ħt. i. leug̃. 7. iii. q̃r̃. 7 dim̃. in long̃. 7 dim̃. leug̃. in lat̃. 7. xxv.
perc̃. 7. ii. foł. de. g̃. q̃cq; ibi teneat.

.LVI. TERRE. HAGONIS. H̃. *DE ENSFORD*. In Binne
tre ten̄. Hagon̄. ppofitus regis. c. ac̃ tr̃e. sẽp. x. foc̃. sẽp. iiii.
car̃. int̃ fe hões. 7. vii. ac̃ p̃ti. sẽp. vał. xx. foł.

⁋ In Gegefete. c. ac̃. tr̃e. sẽp. ii. vilł. 7 v. bor. sẽp. ii. car̃. int̃ fe
hões. 7. iiii. ac̃ p̃ti. filỹ. viii. por. sẽp. Vał. xx. foł.

In Nortuna. l. ac̃ tr̃æ. 7 v. foc̃ in ipfa. tr̃a. manentes. sẽp.
ii. car̃. int̃ fe hões. 7 ii. ac̃ p̃ti. filũ. v. por. sẽp. vał. x. foł.
In Gegeftueit. l. ac̃. tr̃æ. femp. ii. foc̃. 7. i. bor. in ipfa.
tr̃a. sẽp. i. car̃. 7 dim̃. int̃ fe hões; 7 v. ac̃. p̃ti filũ. x. por.
sẽp. vał. x. foł. Et in Weftuna. i. foc̃. xvi. ac̃ tr̃e. sẽp. dim̃.
car̃. 7 vał. ii. foł.

⁋ Et in Sparham. i. lib̃ hom̃o. xxx. ac̃ tr̃æ. 7. i. bor. fup.
quem habuit fuus anteceffor com̃d̃ tantũ femp dim̃. car̃. 7. ii.
ac̃ p̃ti. 7 vał. iiii. foł.

The Hundred of EAST FLEGG

2 In FILBY R(alph) the Constable held 2 c. of land and 47 acres as a manor before 1066.
   Then 8 villagers, later and now 6; 2 smallholders.
   Always 1 plough in lordship; 1 men's plough;
   meadow, 14 acres. Always 2 cobs; 1 head of cattle. Then 7 pigs, now 10.
   Also 3 Freemen, 15 acres. Always 1½ ploughs; meadow, 1 acre.
   Also 14 free men, ½ c. of land and 6 acres. Always 2½ ploughs; meadow, 1 acre.
   Value then 40s; later and now 50.
   The King and the Earl (have) the jurisdiction of the free men. It has 1 league and 3½ furlongs in length and ½ league and 25 perches in width, tax of 2s, whoever holds there.

56 LAND OF HAGNI

The Hundred of EYNSFORD

1 In BINTREE Hagni the King's reeve holds 100 acres of land.
   Always 10 Freemen;
   always 4 ploughs between the men; meadow, 7 acres.
   Value always 20s.

2 In GUIST 100 acres of land.
   Always 2 villagers; 5 smallholders.
   Always 2 ploughs between the men; meadow, 4 acres; woodland, 8 pigs.
   Value always 20s.

3 In (Wood) NORTON 50 acres of land;
   5 Freemen dwelling on this land.
   Always 2 ploughs between the men; meadow, 2 acres; woodland, 5 pigs.
   Value always 10s.

4 In GUESTWICK 50 acres of land.
   Always 2 Freemen and 1 smallholder (dwelling) on this land.
   Always 1½ ploughs between the men; meadow, 5 acres; woodland, 10 pigs.
   Value always 10s.

5 Also in WESTON (Longville) 1 Freeman, 16 acres of land; always ½ plough.
   Value 2s.

6 Also in SPARHAM 1 free man, 30 acres of land.
   1 smallholder. His predecessor had the patronage only over him.
   Always ½ plough; meadow, 2 acres.
   Value 4s.

Et In Tytheby . 1 . lib homo . xv .
ac̄ . 7 . 11 . bor . sēp . dim̄ car̊ . 7 dim̄ . ac̄ p̃ti . filu̇ . 111 . por . semp
val̊ . 111 . fol̊ . Et in falla . 1 . foc̄ . Et i Tirninga . 1 . xx . ac̄
trǣ . sēp . 1 . car̊ . 7 . val̊ . 1111 . fol̊ .

TERRE . Rad̄ HAGONIS FILII . H̄ . DE HOLT . In Kel- .LVII.
linga . ten̄ . Wefter . lib homo . Guert . t̄ . r . e . 11 . car trē .
m̃ . Radulfus . filius hagana . Semp . vi uilt̄ . 7 xx . bor̊ . 7 p̊ .
1 . m̃ . 11 . Sēp . houm̄ . 11 . car̊ . 1 . ac̄ p̃ti . Sēp . 1 . r . Tc̄ . xvi . p̊ .
m̃ . xx . Semp . xl . oů . 7 xxiiii . caps̄ . Tc̄ ual̊ . xx . s̄ m̃ . xl .

H̄ . LOTHNINGA . In mundaham ten̄ sc̄a aldreda . in dn̄io
t̄ . r . e . xx . ac̄ . m̃ tenet . R . Sēp . 11 . bor̊ . 7 ual̊ . 111 . fol̊ .

H̄ . DE ENSFORDA . In Salla . ten̄ . Wefter . 1 . lib ho
t̄ . r . e . 1 . car̊ . trǣ . sēp . . 1 . Villīs . 7 . x . bor̊ . sēp . 1 . cā . in dn̄io . 7 . 11 .
cā . houm̄ . 7 . 1 . ac̄ p̃ti . filu̇ . vi . por . 7 dim̄ . mol̊ . 7 1111 . an̄ . 7 vi .
por 7 Val̊ . xx . fol̊ .

270 b

.LVIII. TERRE . VLCHETELLI . H̄ . DE SCERPHĀ . ★
In LVRINGA . 11 . car̊ trǣ . ten̄ id̄e Vlchetell . t . e r . tc̄
7 p̊ . vi uilt̄ . m̃ . 1111 . femp . 1 . bor . tc̄ 7 . s . viii . ac̄ . sēp . 11 . car̊ . in
dn̄io . Tc̄ . 11 . car̊ . houm̄ . m̃ . 1 . m̃ . 1 . mul̊ . 7 sēp . 11 . libī . hōes . xxvi .
ac̄ . trē . com̄d . tantum . 7 foca in buchā regis . sēp . 1 . car̊ 7 . 11 ★
ac̄ p̃ti . femp ual̊ . xl . s totum . h̄t dim̄ . leuḡ leuḡ 7 dim̄ . in
lato . q̃cumq̧ ibi teneat . 7 . viii . d̄ . 7 1 . obolū de gelto .

7 Also in TYBY 1 free man, 15 acres.
  2 smallholders.
  Always ½ plough; meadow, ½ acre; woodland, 3 pigs.
  Value always 3s.

8 Also in SALL 1 Freeman.

9 Also in THURNING 1, 20 acres of land; always 1 plough.
  Value 4s.

57 LANDS OF RALPH SON OF HAGNI

The Hundred of HOLT

1 In KELLING Wester, a free man of Gyrth's, held 2 c. of land before 1066; now Ralph son of Hagni holds.
  Always 6 villagers; 20 smallholders.
  Later 1, now 2 [ploughs]. Always 2 men's ploughs;
  meadow, 1 acre. Always 1 cob. Then 16 pigs, now 20. Always 40 sheep; 24 goats.
  Value then 20s; now 40.

LODDON Hundred

2 In MUNDHAM St. Etheldreda held 20 acres in lordship before 1066, now R(alph) holds.
  Always 2 smallholders.
  Value 3s.

The Hundred of EYNSFORD

3 In SALL Wester, 1 free man, held 1 c. of land before 1066.
  Always 1 villager; 10 smallholders.
  Always 1 plough in lordship; 2 men's ploughs;
  meadow, 1 acre; woodland, 6 pigs; ½ mill; 4 head of cattle; 6 pigs.
  Value 20s.

58 LANDS OF ULFKETEL

The Hundred of SHROPHAM

1 In LARLING Ulfketel also held 2 c. of land before 1066.
  Then and later 6 villagers, now 4; always 1 smallholder.
  Meadow, then and always 8 acres. Always 2 ploughs in lordship. Then 2 men's ploughs, now 1. Now 1 mill.
  Always 2 free men, 26 acres of land in patronage only; the jurisdiction (is) in the King's (manor of) Buckenham.
  Always 1 plough; meadow, 2 acres.
  Value of the whole always 40s.
  It has ½ league in length and ½ in width, whoever holds there, tax of 8½d.

H̄.Gillecros. IN Rusceuuorda.ii.car̷.tr̃e.tenuit
Bundo lib̃ homo t̃ r.e.semp.vi.uilli.7.i.bor.7.i.ser.7
xii.ac̃.p̃ti.7.ii.car.in dr̃io.Tc̃.ii.car.car̷.houm.m̃.
i.7 alia posset restaurari.7.i.lib̃ hõ.xiiii.ac̃ tr̃e.quẽ
reuocat de dono regis.semp.i.car̷.m̃.c.oũ.7 lii.cap̷.
7 vii.por.7 totũ ual.xl.sol.7 l̃it.i.leug̃ 7 dim̃.in long̃
7.iiii.q̃r.in lato.q̃cumq̃ ibi teneat.7 xi.d̃.7.i.obol de g̃.
Soca de lib̃o hõe in Keninchala.

H̃.WALESSÃ. In Witona tñ.ii.libi hões gerti
t.r.e.de c.xl.ac̃ tr̃e Sẽp.vi.bor.7.x.ac̃ p̃ti.tc̃.i.car̷
in dr̃io.m̃.i.7 dim̃.Sẽp.i.car̷.hoũ.Semp.ual.xv.sol.
Quando. Rad̃ se forisfecit. teñ in manu sua.7 p̃.blond̃
7 p̃ p̃ breue regis fuit.resaitus.in manu regis.

.LIX. TERRA ALFREDI. H̃.SCERPHÃ.IN ATLEBURC
ii.car̷ tr̃æ.p̃ mañ.semp.viii.uilli 7 xvi.ac̃ p̃ti.7 semp
ii.car̷.in dr̃io.7 i.car̷.houm̃.silũ.xl.por.7 xx.soc̃ dim̃.
car̷ tr̃e.vi.ac̃ p̃ti.semp.iiii.car̷.7 v.libi hões.i.car̷ tr̃e.

271 a
7 dim̃.7.iii.bor.7.xii.ac̃.p̃ti.sẽp.iii.car.silũ.viii.por.
semp.ii.r.7 tc̃.vi.añ.m̃.viii.tc̃.xx.por.m̃.xxviii.tc̃
xx.oũ.m̃.xxxviii.sẽp.xxvi.cap̷.tc̃ ual.lx.sol.p̃.7 m̃.iiii
lib̃.Soca.de ist.q̃nq̃ ĩ buchã.

GUILTCROSS Hundred

2 In RUSHFORD Bondi, a free man, held 2 c. of land before 1066.
    Always 6 villagers, 1 smallholder; 1 slave.
    Meadow, 12 acres; 2 ploughs in lordship. Then 2 men's ploughs, now 1, and another could be restored.
    Also 1 free man, 14 acres of land whom he claims of the King's gift; always 1 plough.
    Now 100 sheep, 52 goats; 7 pigs.
    Value of the whole, 40s.
    It has 1½ leagues in length and 4 furlongs in width, whoever holds there, tax of 11½d. The jurisdiction of the free man (is) in Kenninghall.

WALSHAM Hundred

3 In WITTON 2 free men of Gyrth's, held, at 140 acres of land before 1066.
    Always 6 smallholders.
    Meadow, 10 acres. Then 1 plough in lordship, now 1½; always 1 men's plough.
    Value always 15s.
    When (Earl) Ralph forfeited he held it in his hand and later (Robert) Blunt; afterwards it was again taken possession of in the King's hand by the King's writ.

59   LAND OF ALFRED

SHROPHAM Hundred

1 In ATTLEBOROUGH 2 c. of land as a manor.
    Always 8 villagers.
    Meadow, 16 acres. Always 2 ploughs in lordship; 1 men's plough; woodland, 40 pigs.
    Also 20 Freemen, ½ c. of land; meadow, 6 acres; always 4 ploughs.
    Also 5 free men, 1½ c. of land.
    3 smallholders.
    Meadow, 12 acres. Always 3 ploughs; woodland, 8 pigs.
        Always 2 cobs. Then 6 head of cattle, now 8. Then 20 pigs, now 28. Then 20 sheep, now 38. Always 26 goats.
    Value then 60s, later and now £4.
    The jurisdiction of these 5 (free men is) in Buckenham.

Terra Aldit H̃. de Grenehov. .LX.

Guella.ten̄.Ketel.t̄ r.e.i.lib̄ hō.ii.car̊.tr̃e.m̂
tenet.aldit.Semp.v.uilli.sēp.vii.bor.sēp.ii.car̊.in dn̄io
sēp.i.car̊ houm.Pastura.ad.cc.ou.iiii.an̄.tc̄.iiii.p̃.m̂
xvi.qū rec̄.lx.ou.m̂.cc..i.mol.xviiii.soc̄.ii.car̊ tr̃e
đ.mol.7 hij hoēs manent in Warham 7 ptinent in guella
tc̄.Val.c.sol.m̂.iiii.lib̄.7 ħt in leug̃.long̃.7 lat alia
s; plures habūt ubi tr̃am.7 xxiiii.đ.de gelto.int̄ guella
7 Warham.

Terre. Goduini. Ha.ldein H̃ de Tauer
ham. In Hailesduna.ii.car̊ tr̃e.ten̄.Stigand̊.
t̄.r.e.semp.xii.uilli.7 xi.bor.Tc̄.i.car̊.
in dn̄io.m̂.ii.Tc̄.i.car̊ houm.m̂.i.car̊.
7 dim̄.Silu.lx.por.xii.ac̄ p̃ti.semp.ii.
mol.7 i.psec̄.sēp.i.an̄.7 x.por.tc̄
x.ou.m̂.xxviiii.m̂.lx.cap̃.

.LXI.

271 b

7.vi.soc̄.i.ac̄.tr̃e.semp.i car̊ 7 dim̄.7.iiii.ac̄ p̃ti.semp
iiii.lib̄ 7 xii.sol.7.viii.đ.ual.una.eccla sine tr̃a.7 ħt.
i.leug̃.7 dim̄.7.xx.perc̄.in lato.7 i.leug̃ in lat̄.7 iii.qr̃.
7 viii.đ.7.i.ferding.7.i.obolū de g̃.

H̃. de Sud Herpingeham. Oxenedes ten̄.

Aildeig.i.lib̄ hō Sub.Guert.t̄.r.e.i.car̊ tr̃e.sēp.v.uill.
7 vii.bor.tc̄.i.car̊ in dn̄io.p̃.i.bos.m̂.ii.sēp.i.car̊.houm
7 xii.ac̄.p̃ti.silu.xxx.por.7.i.mol.m̂.xx.por.7 vi.uasa
apū.7.iii.soc̄.lx.ac̄ tr̃e.sēp.dim̄.car̊ 7.iiii.ac̄ p̃ti.
i.eccla.xxiiii.ac̄.7 ual.ii.sol.Tc̄ ual.xx.sol.p̃.x.sol.
m̂.xxx.sol.7 ħt.vii.qr̃.in long̃ 7 vi.in lato.7 redđ.v.
đ.in geltū regis rex & comes soca.

60 LAND OF ALDITH

The Hundred of (North) GREENHOE

1 Ketel, 1 free man, held WELLS (next the Sea) before 1066, 2 c. of land; now Aldith holds.

Always 5 villagers; always 7 smallholders.
Always 2 ploughs in lordship; always 1 men's plough;
pasture for 200 sheep; 4 head of cattle. Then 4 pigs, now 16. When she acquired it 60 sheep, now 200. 1 mill.
19 Freemen, 2 c. of land; ½ mill. These men dwell in Warham and belong in Wells (next the Sea).
Value then 100s; now £4.
It has a league in length and another in width but more have land there, tax of 24d between Wells (next the Sea) and Warham.

61 LANDS OF GODWIN HALDANE

The Hundred of TAVERHAM

1 In HELLESDON Stigand held 2 c. of land before 1066.

Always 12 villagers; 11 smallholders.
Then 1 plough in lordship, now 2. Then 1 men's plough, now 1½ ploughs.
Woodland, 60 pigs; meadow, 12 acres. Always 2 mills; 1 fishery. Always 1 head of cattle; 10 pigs. Then 10 sheep, now 29. Now 60 goats.
Also 6 Freemen, 1 acre of land; always 1½ ploughs; meadow, 4 acres.   271 b
Value always £4 12s 8d.
One church without land.
It has 1½ leagues and 20 perches in width and 1 league and 3 furlongs in width, 8¾d in tax.

The Hundred of SOUTH ERPINGHAM

2 Aildag, 1 free man under Gyrth, held OXNEAD before 1066, 1 c. of land.

Always 5 villagers; 7 smallholders.
Then 1 plough in lordship; later 1 ox, now 2. Always 1 men's plough; meadow, 12 acres; woodland, 30 pigs; 1 mill. Now 20 pigs; 6 beehives.
Also 3 Freemen, 60 acres of land. Always ½ plough; meadow, 4 acres.
1 church, 24 acres;
value 2s.
Value then 20s, later 10s; now 30s.
It has 7 furlongs in length and 6 in width, it pays 5d towards the King's tax. The King and the Earl (have) the jurisdiction.

$\tilde{H}$. Smetheduna. Nettinghetuna teñ idē. G. lib hō. t̄ r.e. I. car̄. t̄re. sub Guert. 7 sub. Rad. 7 m̃. de rege. sēp II. bor. 7. I. foc̄ I. ac̄. Tc̄ ual. x. sol. m̃. xx.

$\tilde{H}$. Feorhou. Bernham teñ. I. lib hō t̄. r.e. I. car̄ t̄re. sēp. II. uill. 7 III. bor. sēp. I. cā 7. III ac̄ p̃ti. sēp. I. mol. 7 ual. xx. sol.

.LXII.

TERRE. Starcolfi. $\tilde{H}$. FEORHOU.
Bernham tenuit idē. t. r. e. LX. ac̄ t̄re.
7. III. bor. 7. I. car̄. 7. II. ac̄. 7 ual. x. sol.

$\tilde{H}$. Mitteford. 7 dim̃. In toddenhā
XL. ac̄. t̄ræ. semp. III. bor. 7. I. car̄

7. III. ac̄ p̃ti. 7. ual. x. sol.

TERRE EDRICI. ACCIPITARI. $\tilde{H}$. DICE. DIM̃. .LXIII.
In Scelnangrā teñ edricus. xv. ac̄. sēp. II. bor 7 dim̃. car̄. Silu. III. por. 7. I. ac̄ p̃ti. Sēp. ual. II. sol.

SMETHDON Hundred

3 G(odwin), a free man, also held GNATINGDON before 1066 under Gyrth, 1 c. of land; (then) under Ralph and now from the King.
    Always 2 smallholders. Also 1 Freeman, 1 acre.
    Value then 10s; now 20.

FOREHOE Hundred

4 1 free man held BARNHAM (Broom) before 1066, 1 c. of land.
    Always 2 villagers; 3 smallholders.
    Always 1 plough; meadow, 3 acres; always 1 mill.
    Value 20s.

62   LANDS OF STARCULF

FOREHOE Hundred

1 He also held BARNHAM (Broom) before 1066, 60 acres of land.
    3 smallholders.
    1 plough; meadow, 2 acres.
    Value 10s.

MITFORD Hundred and a Half

2 In (North) TUDDENHAM, 40 acres of land.
    Always 3 smallholders.
    1 plough; meadow, 3 acres.   272 a
    Value 10s.

63   LANDS OF EDRIC THE FALCONER

DISS Half Hundred

1 In SHELFANGER Edric holds 15 acres.
    Always 2 smallholders.
    ½ plough; woodland, 3 pigs; meadow, 1 acre.
    Value always 2s.

Isti st libi hões t.e.r. ad nullā firma ptinentes. quos Almar custodit. qui additi st ad firmā t.r.W.

H. FLEC WEST. In burc tēn. iste guert libe. t r.e. LX. ac tre. 7 VIII. ac pti. 7 I. uilt. 7 VIII. libos hões. sub eo de XXVII. ac. tre. 7 VI. ac pti. 7 sep. II. car. int oēs. 7 II. sat. Tc ual. x. sot. m. xx. sot. in firma caluestune cui n ptinebant. 7 roger fecit ppositū. 7 burc ht. x qr in long. 7 VIII. d in lato. 7 de gelto II. sot. 7. I. d. 7. III ferding. S; plures ibi tenent.

Et in rothbfuesbei tēn. idē Almar. VIII. lib hões. 7 dim. sub gerto. LV. ac tre. in soca. 7 VI. ac pti. Sep. I. car. 7 dim. Tc ual IIII. sot. m. VIII. in sup dicta firma. Sed t r. e n ptinuerunt 7 ibi st additi.

In repes. tēn. id. xx. ac tre. 7 VII. libos hões. d. xxx. ac tre. 7. III. ac pti. Sep. I. cā. Tc ual. III. sot. m. IIII.

In clepebei. tēn id. v. libos hōs. de XLVI. ac tre. 7 v. ac pti. 7 qr pars. I. sat. Sep. I. car. Tc ual. III. sot. m. IIII.

272 b

In bastuic. tēn idē. II. libos. hões de xxv. ac tre. 7. III. ac pti Sep dim. car. Tc ual XII. d. m. XVI.

In bitlakebei tēn. idē IIII. libos hões. de. xxx ac tre. 7 sep dim. car. Tc ual. XVI. d. m. xx.

In somertuna tēn. idē in dnio. xx. ac tre. 7. v. libos hões de xv. ac 7. sep. dim. cā. Sep ual. II. sot.

In Wintretuna tēn. idē. VIII. libos. d. LIIII. ac tre. 7. I. ac pti. Sep. car & dim. Tc ual. IIII. sot. m. VI.

In martham tēn. adhuc. I. libū d. x. ac. tre. Sep ar cum duobz bouib. 7 sep ual. VIII. d. 7 hoc totū e in firma supdicta.

64 THESE ARE THE FREE MEN APPERTAINING TO NO REVENUE BEFORE 1066 OF WHOM A(E)LMER HAS CHARGE, WHO WERE ADDED TO THE REVENUE AFTER 1066.

WEST FLEGG Hundred

1. In BURGH (St. Margaret) Gyrth held freely 60 acres of land before 1066;
   meadow, 8 acres.
   1 villager.
   Also 8 free men under him, at 27 acres of land;
      meadow, 6 acres.
   Always 2 ploughs between them all. 2 salt-houses.
   Value then 10s; now 20s in the revenue of Cawston to which they did not belong.
   Roger appointed a reeve. Burgh (St. Margaret) has 10 furlongs in length and 8½ in width, tax of 2s 1¾d. But more hold there. A(e)lmer also holds.

2. In ROLLESBY 8 free men and a half under Gyrth, 55 acres of land in jurisdiction; meadow, 6 acres; always 1½ ploughs.
   Value then 4s, now 8 in the above mentioned revenue, but before 1066 they did not belong there and have been added there.

3. in REPPS 20 acres of land; 7 free men, at 30 acres of land; meadow, 3 acres; always 1 plough.
   Value then 3s; now 4.

4. in CLIPPESBY 5 free men, at 46 acres of land; meadow, 5 acres; ¼ of 1 salt-house; always 1 plough.
   Value then 3s; now 4.

5. in BASTWICK 2 free men, at 25 acres of land; meadow, 3 acres; always ½ plough.   272 b
   Value then 12d; now 16.

6. in BILLOCKBY 4 free men, at 30 acres of land; always ½ plough.
   Value then 16d; now 20.

7. in SOMERTON 20 acres of land in lordship; 5 free men, at 15 acres; always ½ plough.
   Value always 2s.

8. in WINTERTON 8 free (men), at 54 acres of land; meadow, 1 acre; always 1½ ploughs.
   Value then 4s; now 6.

9. Further he holds in MARTHAM 1 free (man), at 10 acres of land; he has always ploughed with 2 oxen.
   Value always 8d.
   All this is in the above-mentioned revenue.

,LXV. I...sṭ hōes libi regis   H̄.de Hapinga. In Horſeia.
Rolf.xxxi.ac̄.7 dim̄.sep̄.iii.bor.7 dim̄ car̄.7.iiii.ac̄ 7
dim̄.p̄ti.

∥ In Stalham ħt. Ailmar filius.Goduini.vii.libos hōes.de
l.ac̄.7 i.bor 7.dim̄.car̄.7.i.ac̄ p̄ti.7 ual.ii.ſol.

∥ In Lvdham tenet idē.iiii.libos hōes xii.ac̄.7.dim̄.car̄.7
ual xvi.d. Et in Eccles.iiii.libos hōes.xx.ac̄.7 dim̄ car̄
7 ual iii.ſol.   In Wactaneſhā.iii.libos.hōes.x.ac̄ 7 dim̄.
car̄.7 ual.xvi.d. In horſeia.iiii.xx.ac̄ 7 dim̄.car̄.7 ual
ii.ſol.

∥ In Echam.ii.libi.ii.ac̄.7 ual.ii.d.hos tenet.Godricus.de
273 a   ⟨Hecham.

H̄. EAST DE FLEC. In Haringebei.c.ac̄.i.lib hō
Almari ep̄i t̄.r.e.ſemp.xii.uiłł.7.ii.bor.7.i.car in dn̄io.7
.i.car 7 dim̄.houm̄.iiii.ac̄ p̄ti 7.iiii.ſał.7 dim̄.Huic t̄re jacent
viii.libi.hōes.xliii.ac̄ 7 dim̄.7.i.cā 7 dim̄.7 iii.ac̄ p̄ti.7.i.
ſał.Paſtura.c.ou.sēp.ual.xx.ſol hanc tenet.Rainbald
aurifaber 7 fuit de feudo.R.comitis.

∥ In Ronham.iiii.libi hōes.xvii.ac̄ sēp.i.car̄.7.ii ac̄ p̄ti.7
dim̄.ſał.In eadē.i.lib.hō.xxx.ac̄.7 ar̄ duobʒ bou.7.ii.ac̄ p̄ti.
7 i.ſał.7 ual.ii.ſol.7 iiii.d. Hos tenet.Ailmarus filius.Goduini.

∥ In Scrovtebey.i.lib.homo.x.ac̄ ſemp.dim̄ car̄.7.i.ac̄ p̄ti.7
ual.x.d.Hoc addidit Ailuin.de tedfort ad cenſum de ormeſbey
t.r.Wiłł.

THESE ARE THE KING'S FREE MEN

The Hundred of HAPPING

1. In HORSEY Ralph (holds) 31½ acres.
    Always 3 smallholders.
    ½ plough; meadow, 4½ acres.

2. In STALHAM A(e)lmer son of Godwin has 7 free men, at 50 acres; 1 smallholder.
    ½ plough; meadow, 1 acre.
    Value 2s.

3. In LUDHAM he also holds 4 free men, 12 acres; ½ plough.
    Value 16d.

4. Also in ECCLES (he has) 4 free men, 20 acres; ½ plough.
    Value 3s.

5. In WAXHAM (he has) 3 free men, 10 acres; ½ plough.
    Value 16d.

6. In HORSEY (he has) 4 score acres; ½ plough.
    Value 2s.

7. In (Potter) HEIGHAM 2 free (men), 2 acres.
    Value 2d.
    Godric of Heigham holds these.

The Hundred of EAST FLEGG

8. In HERRINGBY 100 acres, 1 free man of Bishop A(e)lmer's before 1066.
    Always 12 villagers; 2 smallholders.
    1 plough in lordship; 1½ men's ploughs; meadow, 4 acres; 4½ salt-houses.
    8 free men appertained to this land, 43½ acres; 1½ ploughs; meadow, 3 acres; 1 salt-house; pasture, 100 sheep.
    Value always 20s.
    Reinbald the Goldsmith holds this. It was of Earl R(alph's) Holding.

9. In RUNHAM 4 free men, 17 acres.
    Always 1 plough; meadow, 2 acres; ½ salt-house.
    In the same 1 free man, 30 acres.
    He ploughs with 2 oxen. Meadow, 2 acres; 1 salt-house.
    Value 2s 4d.
    Aelmer son of Godwin holds these.

10. In SCRATBY 1 free man, 10 acres. Always ½ plough; meadow, 1 acre.
    Value 10d.
    A(i)lwin of Thetford added this to the tribute of Ormesby after 1066.

H̄. de Humiliart In Carletuna . 1 . lib̄ hō . xxxii . ac̄ . sēp . dim̄
car̄ . 7 . 1 . ac̄ p̄ti . 7 ual . iii . sol . In dustuna . 1 . lib̄ hō . xiii . ac̄ . 7 ual
xii . d.

H̄. DEPWADE. In Mvletuna . Gouta 7 osketel . ii . libi hōes
ii . ac̄ 7 dim̄ . 7 ual . ii . d . 7 obolū . Asci . pr eos tenuit . hō abbis . de
holmo . & dedit . uadē . In Herduwic . 1 . lib̄ hō . nōē . Wistret . xxx .
ac̄ sēp . iiii . uill . 7 v . bor . 7 . ii . car . 7 ii . ac̄ p̄ti ; 7 ual . x . sol . Tota
Herduwic ht . 1 . leuḡ . in lonḡ ; 7 dim̄ in lato . 7 ix . d . de ḡ.

H̄. Gnaueringa . In Nortuna . 1 . lib̄ hō . sc̄i benedicti .
xxx . ac̄ . 7 . ii . bor . 7 dim̄ car . 7 dim̄ ac̄ p̄ti . 7 iiii . sol . hoc
tenet Goscelinus . de norwic .

In Turuertuna . viii . ac̄ . 1 . lib̄ hō antecessoris . Radulfi .

273 b

de belsao . 7 ual . xii . d . Hoc tenuit . H . Males man . teste
hund . sed ipse celat .
In Ruverincham . 1 . lib̄ hō Chetel friedai . vii . ac̄ . 7 . 1 . bor .
7 . 1 . maresc 7 ual . xii . d . hoc ē de feudo comitis . R . 7 erat inensa
ejusdē manerii . qn̄ . R . foris fecit . P ea tenuit tram suam .
ita qd nullū seruitium redidit regi . 7 ex hoc dedit uadem .

. LXVI . INVASIONES IN NORDFVLC . Invasio Hermeri de ferrariis .
Hund de Clacheslosa . In Phincham . xx . libi hōes . tenentes t . r . e . ii . car .
træ . s; tam̄ . viii . ex ill erant consuetudinarii ad faldā antecessoris sui alii erant
libi . pt comdone . In tra eoz . st sēp . ii . car . x . ac̄ . p̄ti . tc ual . xl . sol . m̄ . lviii .
7 . iiii . d . In Ead uill . xvi . ac̄ . tre . ual . xvi . d .

The Hundred of HUMBLEYARD

11　In (East) CARLETON 1 free man, 32 acres. Always ½ plough; meadow, 1 acre.
　　Value 3s.

12　In DUNSTON 1 free man, 13 acres.
　　Value 12d.

DEPWADE Hundred

13　In MOULTON (St. Michael) Gauti and Askell, 2 free men, 2½ acres.
　　Value 2½d.
　　Aski the priest, the Abbot of Holme's man, held them and has given pledge.

14　In HARDWICK 1 free man, Wihtred by name, 30 acres.
　　Always 4 villagers; 5 smallholders.
　　2 ploughs; meadow, 2 acres.
　　Value 10s.
　　The whole of Hardwick has 1 league in length and ½ in width, tax of 9d.

CLAVERING Hundred

15　In NORTON (Subcourse) 1 free man of St. Benedict's, 30 acres.
　　2 smallholders.
　　½ plough; meadow, ½ acre.
　　[Value] 4s.
　　Jocelyn of Norwich holds this.

16　In THURLTON 1 free man of Ralph of Beaufour's predecessor, 8 acres.
　　Value 12d.
　　H. Malemayns held this as the Hundred testify but he conceals it.　273 b

17　In RAVENINGHAM 1 free man, Ketel Friday, 7 acres.
　　1 smallholder. 1 marsh.
　　Value 12d.
　　This is of Earl R(alph's) Holding. It was board-land of the same manor when R(alph) forfeited. Later he held his land so that he rendered no service to the King. He has given pledge of this.

ANNEXATIONS IN NORFOLK

The annexation of Hermer of Ferrers

The Hundred of CLACKCLOSE

1　In FINCHAM 20 free men who held 2 c. of land before 1066.
　　However 8 of them were subject to customary dues at the fold of his predecessor; the others were free except for patronage.
　　On their land there have always been 2 ploughs; meadow, 10 acres.
　　Value then 40s, now 58(s) 4d.
　　In the same 16 acres of land. Value 16d.

273 a, b

⁊ In b̄tuna . I . lib hō . xii . ac.

que ten& . W . de hemero . sep̄ . dim̄ . car . val . iii . sot . De hoc n̄ habuit
antec n c̄m̄doem . ⁊ In Ead . I . lib hō c̄m̄dat tantū antecessori suo . lx . ac . Sēp . I . bor
dim̄ . car . viii . ac . p̄ti . val . ii . sol . 7 . viii . d.

⁊ In Wermegai . ii . libi hōes . tenentes . iiii . ac . s; suū ant . habuit totā 9suet.

⁊ In Wesbruge . iii . libi . hōes . dim̄ . car . ual . v . sol . h de his habuit suus
ant . c̄m̄d . tant . 7 . scs benedict socā . In Ead . viii . libi . c̄om̄d 7 . soca falde .
de . x . ac . val . ix . sol . ⁊ In Torpelanda . viii . 7 . dim . de . xx . ac . 7 . ii . ac . p̄ti .
val . xii . sol . In Ead . viii . consuetudinarii . ad faldā sui antecessoris . val . x . sol

274 a

7 . adhuc . iii . de . xxviii . ac . 7 . ual . ii . sol . 7 . viii . d . 7 adhuc
. xxx . ac trae . qd̄ tenuit Goduin lib hō . q p utlagauit . 7 ht . iii . ac . p̄ti .
7 . i . car . 7 . ii . runc . vi . porc . xl . oū . 7 . iiii . carrucatas de blato . &
inde dedit uadē 7 . de aliis reb𝔷 .

⁊ In Stou . xxxiiii . ac . trae . qd̄ tenuit lib hō . t . r . e . tc . i . car . m̄ . n . In
Hidlingheia . vi . ac . trae . qd̄ ten . Scs Eadmund . c̄m̄d tant . 7 . ual . viii . d.
In Ead uill . ii . libi . de . ii . ac . val . viii . d . Istos habuit antecessor
Hermeri c̄m̄daōc tant . 7 . m̄ tenebat Hermer .

⁊ In Winebotesham ten . iii . libi . hōes . xl . ac . t . r . e . 7 . iiii . libi hōes in Stou .
de . xl . ac . Isti om̄s h̄nt . ii . car . In his non habuit antec Hermeri p̄t c̄om̄datione . 7
dim soca . c̄ sco benedicto . 7 . ual . xx . sol . In bekesuuella . vii . libi hōes . de . i . car
trae . Sēp . iii . bor . tc . iii . car . Post 7 . m̄ . ii . v . ac . p̄ti . dim pisc . val . xii . sol . de
his habuit antec c̄om̄d tant .

2 In BARTON (Bendish) 1 free man, 12 acres, whom W holds from Hermer.
   Always ½ plough.
   Value 3s. Of this his predecessor had nothing except the patronage. In the same 1 free man in patronage only to his predecessor, 60 acres.
   Always 1 smallholder. ½ plough; meadow, 8 acres.
   Value 2s 8d.
3 In WORMEGAY 2 free men who hold 4 acres but his predecessor had all the customary dues.
4 In WEST BRIGGS 3 free men. ½ plough.
   Value 5s. His predecessor had the patronage only of these and St. Benedict the jurisdiction.
   In the same 8 free (men) in patronage and fold-rights, at 10 acres.
   Value 9s.
5 In THORPLAND 8½ [free men], at 20 acres; meadow, 2 acres.
   Value 12s.
   In the same 8 subject to customary dues at the fold of his predecessor.
   Value 10s.
   Further 3, at 28 acres. Value 2s 8d. 274 a
   Further 30 acres of land which Godwin, a free man who was later outlawed, held. Hermer also has 3 acres of meadow; 1 plough; 2 cobs, 6 pigs; 40 sheep; 4 c. under corn. He has given pledge of this and other things.
6 In STOW (Bardolph) 34 acres of land which a free man held before 1066.
   Then 1 plough, now none.
7 In HILGAY 6 acres of land which St. Edmund held in patronage only.
   Value 8d.
   In the same village 2 free (men), at 2 acres.
   Value 8d. Hermer's predecessor had these in patronage only, now Hermer holds them.
8 In WIMBOTSHAM 3 free men held 40 acres before 1066, and in STOW (Bardolph) 4 free men, at 40 acres. All these have 2 ploughs. In these Hermer's predecessor had nothing except for patronage and half the jurisdiction with St. Benedict.
   Value 20s.
9 In BEXWELL 7 free men, at 1 c. of land.
   Always 3 smallholders.
   Then 3 ploughs; later and now 2. Meadow, 5 acres; ½ fishery.
   (Belonging) to the church, 24 acres;
   value 16d.
   Value 12s. His predecessor had the patronage only of these.

In Ristuna . III . libi hões . comd tant LXXXX . ac . Sep . II . car.
val . v . fol . In Fordeham . III . libi . XXIIII . ac . cmd . tm . Sep . dim . car . val . II . fol.
de his n habuit suus ant . pt cmd . In Dereham . XXXII . libi . hões de . cxx . ac . t . r . e.
de xxv . ex istis habuit ant . hermeri comd . sep . II . car . val . xxxv . fol . Bordin ten&
de hermero . III . de oi medietate . 7 . VII . fuer cmdati antecessori . Rogi bigot . 7
in his nichil habuit antec hermeri . 7 . val . v . fol . hos . VII . inuasit hermer.

In Duneham . XIII . libi hões . XL . ac . sep . I . car . val . X . fol . In his n habuit ant ej
n . cmdoem . In Carboistorp . XI . libi hões . 7 . dim . LXXX . ac . 7 . v . ac . pti . I . bor . tc . III.
car . m . II . val . xvII . fol . 7 In his n cõmd . Dim Ecclia . xvI . ac . val . xII . d.

In Fotestorp . vI . libi hões . XL . ac . I . car . III . ac pti . val . v . fol . 7 In his n cõmd ; 7
qa n posst carere sua pastura : reddt ei consuetudinẽ.

In Wallinghetuna tenuit Tstin lib hõ . t . r . c . c . ac . Sep . xI . bor . xv . ac pti.

274 b

. I . car . val xII . fol . 7 In hoc n cmd . Ecclia xxvI . ac . val . xvI . d . In Ead uill
. vII . libi hões . t . r . e . LX . ac . Tc . I . car . 7 dim . P 7 m . I . val . xIIII . fol . de . vI . habuit suus antec.
cõmd . 7 . de . vII. Guert . comes . 7 ual . xx . d . Istu inuasit hermer . Totu ht . IIII . qr.
in long . 7 . III . in lat . 7 . vI . d . de . g . In ill omib3 ht Scs benedict soca.

10 In RYSTON 3 free men in patronage only, 90 acres. Always 2 ploughs.
Value 5s.

11 In FORDHAM 3 free (men) in patronage only, 24 acres. Always ½ plough.
Value 2s. Of these his predecessor had nothing except for patronage.

12 In (West) DEREHAM 32 free men, at 120 acres before 1066. Hermer's predecessor had the patronage of 25 of these. Always 2 ploughs.
Value 35s.
   Bordin holds 3 from Hermer in full moiety. 7 were in patronage to Roger Bigot's predecessor. In them Hermer's predecessor had nothing.
Value 5s. Hermer annexed these 7.

13 In DOWNHAM (Market) 13 free men, 40 acres. Always 1 plough.
Value 10s. In these his predecessor had nothing except the patronage.

14 In (Shouldham) THORPE 11 free men and a half, 80 acres; meadow, 5 acres.
   1 smallholder.
   Then 3 ploughs, now 2.
Value 17s. In these (his predecessor had nothing) except the patronage.
   ½ church, 16 acres;
value 12d.

15 In FODDERSTONE 6 free men, 40 acres. 1 plough and 3 acres of meadow.
Value 5s. In these (his predecessor had nothing) except the patronage. Because they cannot do without their pasture they pay him customary dues.

16 In WALLINGTON Thurstan, a free man, held 100 acres before 1066.
   Always 11 smallholders.   274 b
   Meadow, 15 acres; 1 plough.
Value 12s. In this (his predecessor had nothing) except the patronage.
   Belonging to the church, 26 acres;
value 16d.
In the same village 7 free men before 1066, 60 acres.
   Then 1½ ploughs; later and now 1.
Value 14s.
   His predecessor had the patronage of 6 and Earl Gyrth of the seventh.
Value 20d. Hermer annexed him.
   The whole has 4 furlongs in length and 3 in width, tax of 6d.
   In all these St. Benedict has the jurisdiction.

⁊ hund ⁊ dim.
de fredebruge

In Lena. ten& Hermer̅. ii. libos hōes q̃s habuit suus antec̅ co̅mdoe tantū. de. xxv.
ac̃. ⁊. i. sal. val. iiii. sol. ⁊. vi. d. In Wesuuenic. i. lib̃ hō. i. car̃. tr̃æ. ⁊. xii. bor. val
vi. sol ⁊. viii. d. ⁊. in hoc n̅ c̄m̅d. In Wigrehala. dim̃ car̃. tr̃æ. tenuit lib̃ hō
t. r. e. ⁊. ual. iii. sol. ⁊. in h̄ n̅ c̄m̅d. In Estuunic. ii. libi hōes. xxx. ac̃. qd̃ ten&. bordin̅.
Sēp. dim̃. car̃. ii. ac̃. p̃ti. val. xv. d. ⁊ in his n̅ c̄m̅d. Stigand̃ socã. In Waltuna. iii.
libi hōes. lxxxxi. ac̃. qd̃ ten& bordin̅. Sēp. ix. bor. xii. ac̃. p̃ti. Tc̄. i. car̃. ⁊. dim̃. m̃. i.
val. ix. sol. ⁊. iiii. d. ⁊. in h̄ n̅ c̄m̅d. Dim̃ ecclia. xv. ac̃. ual. ii. sol.
In Torp. i. car̃ tr̃æ. qd̃ tenuit Tchill lib̃ hō. sēp. ix. uill. viii. bor. i. car in dio.
. i. car̃. hom̃. vi. ac̃. p̃ti. ⁊. iiii. pars pisc̃. Val. xx. sol. ⁊ in hoc c̄m̅d tantū.
⁊. Stigand̃ socã. Dim̃ Ecclia. xxx. ac̃. val. xii. sol. In Gaituna. lib̃ hō
lx. ac̃. qd̃ ten& bordin̅. ii. bor. vi. ac̃. p̃ti. dim̃. car̃. val. iii. sol ⁊ in hoc n̅ c̄m̅d.
Stigand̃ socã

The Hundred and a Half of FREEBRIDGE

17 In LYNN Hermer holds 2 free men whom his predecessor had in patronage only, at 25 acres. 1 salt-house.
Value 4s 6d.

18 In WEST WINCH 1 free man, 1 c. of land.
    12 smallholders.
Value 6s 8d. In this (his predecessor had nothing) except the patronage.

19 In WIGGENHALL ½ c. of land. A free man held before 1066.
Value 3s. In this (his predecessor had nothing) except the patronage.

20 In EAST WINCH 2 free men, 30 acres which Bordin holds.
    Always ½ plough; meadow, 2 acres.
Value 15d. In these (his predecessor had nothing) except the patronage and Stigand the jurisdiction.

21 In (West) WALTON 3 free men, 91 acres which Bordin holds.
    Always 9 smallholders.
    Meadow, 12 acres. Then 1½ ploughs, now 1.
Value 9s 4d. In these (his predecessor had nothing) except the patronage.
    ½ church, 15 acres;
value 2s.

22 In (Gayton) THORPE 1 c. of land which Thorkel, a free man, held.
    Always 9 villagers; 8 smallholders.
    1 plough in lordship; 1 men's plough.
    Meadow, 6 acres; ¼ of a fishery.
Value 20s. In this (his predecessor had) the patronage only and Stigand the jurisdiction.
    ½ church, 30 acres;
value 12s.

23 In GAYTON a free man, 60 acres which Bordin holds.
    2 smallholders.
    Meadow, 6 acres. ½ plough.
Value 3s. In this (his predecessor had nothing) except the patronage and Stigand the jurisdiction.

/ Serepham Hund. In helingham. III. libi hões. cx. ac. qd ten& Wari-
bold. 7. v. ac. pti. sep. II. car. Silu. XII. por. val. xv. sol. 7. in his comd tantu.
Soca in bucham regis.

/ Lawendic Hund. In La Wingham. I. lib hõ. dim. car. træ. Sep. I. uill.
7. I. bor. 7. dim. car. II. ac pti. Silu. x. por. val. v. sol. 7 in hoc n cmd.
Soca in muleham reg.

/ Mittefort Hund. In Toruestuna. VII. libi hões. c. ac. Tc. IIII. car.
m. III. v. ac. pti. tc ual. xx. sol. m. xxvi. 7. VIII. d. 7 in h n comdatione.

275 a

In Raimerestuna. v. libi hões. xxx. ac. t. r. e. Tc. I. car. m. dim. II. ac. pti.
Tc ual. x. sol. m. vi. 7. In h n cmd.

In Jachesham. x. libi hões. LIIII. ac. træ. qd ten& Adeledm. de hermero. IIII. ac. pti.
Tc. I. car. 7. dim. m. I. Tc ual. xx. sol. m. x. 7 in h n cmd. In Mateshala. xx. libi hões
comd tantu. I. car. træ. xxxix. ac. Sep. III. uill. II. bor. xII. ac. pti. 7. di mol. Tc
. IIII. car. m. III. Tc ual. xxx. sol. m. xlII. 7 in h n cmd. In Toteha. vi. libi
hões. comd tantu. c. ac. xv. bor. II. fer. Silu. vi. porc. III. ac. pti. Sep. III. car.
Tc ual. xxvi. sol. 7. vIII. d. m. xxIIII. sol. In bicherstuna. I. lib. vIII. ac.
cmd tant. val. vi. d. In Nordtudenham. III. libi. hões. cmd tantu. xxxII. ac.
Sep. I. car. I. ac. pti. val. v. sol. In Letuna. II. libi hões cmd tantu. xxI. ac.
t. r. e. m. ten&. I. lib hõ. 7 IIII. ac. pti. Silu. IIII. por. val. v. sol. 7. IIII. d.
In Bc dim lib hõ. cmd tant. II. ac. val. vi. d.

SHROPHAM Hundred

24 In (Great) ELLINGHAM 3 free men, 110 acres which Warenbold holds. Meadow, 5 acres. Always 2 ploughs; woodland, 12 pigs. Value 15s. In these (his predecessor had) the patronage only. The jurisdiction (is) in the King's (manor of) Buckenham.

LAUNDITCH Hundred

25 In LONGHAM, 1 free man, ½ c. of land.
    Always 1 villager; 1 smallholder.
    ½ plough; meadow, 2 acres; woodland, 10 pigs.
Value 5s. In this (his predecessor had nothing) except the patronage. The jurisdiction (is) in the King's (manor of) Mileham.

MITFORD Hundred

26 In (?) THUXTON 7 free men, 100 acres. Then 4 ploughs, now 3.
    Meadow, 5 acres.
Value then 20s; now 26(s) 8d. In these (his predecessor had nothing) except the patronage.

27 In REYMERSTON 5 free men, 30 acres before 1066.   275 a
    Then 1 plough, now ½. Meadow, 2 acres.
Value then 10s; now 6. In these (his predecessor had nothing) except the patronage.

28 In YAXHAM 10 free men, 53 acres of land which Adelhelm holds from Hermer. Meadow, 4 acres. Then 1½ ploughs, now 1.
Value then 20s; now 10. In these (his predecessor had nothing) except the patronage.

29 In MATTISHALL 20 free men in patronage only, 1 c. of land and 39 acres.
    Always 3 villagers and 2 smallholders.
    Meadow, 12 acres; ½ mill. Then 4 ploughs, now 3.
Value then 30s; now 42. In these (his predecessor had nothing) except the patronage.

30 In (North) TUDDENHAM 6 free men in patronage only, 100 acres.
    15 smallholders; 2 slaves.
    Woodland, 6 pigs; meadow, 3 acres. Always 3 ploughs.
    Value then 26s 8d, now 24s.

31 In BICKERSTON 1 free (man) in patronage only, 8 acres.
    Value 6d.

32 In NORTH TUDDENHAM 3 free men in patronage only, 32 acres.
    Always 1 plough; meadow, 1 acre.
    Value 5s.

33 In LETTON 2 free men in patronage only before 1066, 21 acres; now 1 free man holds. Meadow, 4 acres; woodland, 4 pigs.
    Value 3s 4d.

34 In (South) BURGH a half-freeman in patronage only, 2 acres.
    Value 6d.

ℹInuasio baignardi In Phincham inuasit baignard̃.i.car̃ tr̃æ.qd̃ tenuer̃
vi.lib̃i hões.t.r̃.e.m̃.vii.7.dim̃.Sep̃.ii.bor.7.i.car̃.viii.ac̃.p̃ti.Tc̃ ual
.xx.fol.m̃.xl.hanc tr̃a reclamant sui hões ꝓ escangio.s; ñ bñt libatorẽ.
In b̃tuna xxx.ac̃.qd̃ tenuit lib̃ hõ.t.r̃.e.ex ill̃r dedit.iiii.ac̃.in
uadimonio.7.viii.tulit Wihenoc de burli.In Stoches.c.ac̃.ten.Vlchetel.
t.r̃.e.Sep̃.iiii.uill.7.iiii.bor.i.car̃.x.ac̃ p̃ti.val.xl.sol.hoc reclamat ꝓ esc.In Scerninga.
lib̃ hõ.xxiiii.ac̃ c̃m̃d tantũ.ii.bor.ii.ac̃.p̃ti.dim̃.car̃.val.v.sol.Soca in muleh̃a reg̃.
ℹFeorhou Hund.In hidichetorp.xxiiii.lib̃i hões.cxx.ac̃.qd̃
ten& baignard̃.de q̃b; suus antecessor.nec c̃õmdatione habuit.De q̃b;
fuer̃.iii.in Wimundeb̃a.& un in episcopatu.7.iii.de Kiburnelai.
7.xvii.in Hinch̃a.Int totũ hñt.iiii.car̃.v.ac̃ p̃ti.val.xxx.sol.

275 b

Abbas S̃ci Edmundi.ten& In Runghetuna.cl.ac̃.qd̃ tenuer̃.v.lib̃i hões
t.r̃.e.Tc̃.ii.car̃.7.dim̃.m̃.ii.iiii.bor.val.xx.sol.hanc tr̃a reclamat ex
dono reg̃ In Ead̃ uill ten lib̃ hõ.dim̃ car̃ tr̃æ.iiii.bor.ii.lib̃i hões de.vi.ac̃.
val.x.sol.In Ead̃.xlvi.ac̃.qd̃ ten.iii.lib̃i hões.7.dim̃.Sep̃.i.bor.iii.car̃.
vi.ac̃.p̃ti.Val.x.sol.
ℹIn Sceluagrauã.i.lib̃ hõ.Algari c̃õm̃d tantũ.t.r̃.e.xii.ac̃.de Wineferthinc.
q̃ fuit occis ad bellũ haftinges.p̃ea tenuit abbas in maneriũ suũ

The annexation of Baynard
[CLACKCLOSE Hundred]

35 In FINCHAM Baynard annexed 1 c. of land which 6 free men and a half held before 1066; now 7 and a half (hold).
   Always 2 smallholders.
   1 plough; meadow, 8 acres.
   Value then 20s, now 40.
   His men claim this land by exchange but they do not have a deliverer.

36 In BARTON (Bendish) 30 acres which a free man held before 1066. He gave 4 of these acres in pledge and Wihenoc of Burley took 8.

37 In STOKE (Ferry) Wulfketel held 100 acres before 1066.
   Always 4 villagers; 4 smallholders.
   1 plough; meadow, 10 acres.
   Value 40s. He claims this by exchange.

[LAUNDITCH Hundred]

38 In SCARNING a free man in patronage only, 24 acres.
   2 smallholders.
   Meadow, 2 acres; ½ plough.
   Value 5s. The jurisdiction is in the King's (manor of) Mileham.

FOREHOE Hundred

39 In DYKEBECK 24 free men, 120 acres which Baynard holds. His predecessor did not even have patronage of these. 4 of them were in Wymondham, 1 in the bishopric, 3 of Kimberley and 17 in Hingham.
   In total they have 4 ploughs; meadow, 5 acres.
   Value 30s.

[CLACKCLOSE Hundred]

40 In RUNCTON the Abbot of St. Edmund's holds 150 acres which 5 free men held before 1066.
   Then 2½ ploughs, now 2.
   4 smallholders.
   Value 20s. He claims this land from the King's gift.
   In the same village a free man holds ½ c. of land.
     4 smallholders; 2 free men at 6 acres.
   In the same 46 acres which 3 free men and a half hold.
     Always 1 smallholder.
     3 ploughs; meadow, 6 acres.
   Value 10s.

[DISS Hay Hundred]

41 In SHELFANGER 1 free man under the patronage only of Algar before 1066, 12 acres of Winfarthing. He was killed at the battle of Hastings. Later the Abbot held it as part of his manor of

brasincham Sep ual xvi. d. ſ; ſuus dapifer offert ſe neſciſſe ſicut
juditiū p portat. In Wineferthinc. i. lib hō. de. ii. ac. quē tenuit
. R. comes qn̄ ſe forisfecit. 7. poſt Godric in manu reḡ. Poſt Godricū
tenuit herolf in tr̄a ſc̄i Edmundi licentia p̄poſiti abbis teſte hundret.

In Scerephā. i. lib. xxx. ac. iii. ac. p̄ti. i. bor. dim. car. ual. iiii. ſol.

In Dereham ten& Rainald fili Iuonis. vi. libos hōes de. xxxii. ac.
q̄s inuaſit Wihenoc cōmdatos tantū ſuo anteceſſori. In Rocheſham. i. lib
hō. cm̄dat tantū de. ix. ac. ual. viii. ſol. 7. i. d. In Fordehā. iii. libi cm̄d.
7. ſc̄s ben̄. ſocī. de. xxv. ac. 7. i. lib hō de. v. ac. de iſto habuit Sc̄s Edm.
cm̄d. t. r. e. hoc ten& Rainald ual. v. ſol. In Duneham. iii. libi hōes
de. ii. ac. 7. dim. cōm̄d tant. ual. x. d. In ead. i. lib hō. de. vii. ac. cm̄dat
antec. Willi. de uuar. m̄ ten& Rainald. 7 ual. xii. d. In becheſuuella.
. ii. libi hōes. i. de. xv. ac. de q̄ habuit antec hermeri cm̄d. 7 ual. ii. ſol. 7
. viii. d. 7 ali habuit. iii. ac. 7. ual. vi. d. hos m̄ ten& Rainald.
In Wella tenuer̄. vi. libi hōes. ii. car. tr̄e. 7 xv. ac. ſep. ii. car. 7. ix. bord.
ual. xxvi. ſol. 7. viii. d. 7. iii. ex h̄ fuer̄ cōmdati anteceſſori hermeri. 7 hos
om̄s occupauit. Wihenoc.
In Weſuuenic addidit Wihenoc. i. libm hōem de. xxx. ac. ſep. iiii. uill
. vi. ac. p̄ti. ual. v. ſol.

Bressingham.
Value always 16d.
> But his steward offers to prove as judicial ordeal demands, that he did not know.

42 In WINFARTHING 1 free man, at 2 acres whom Earl R(alph) held when he forfeited; later Godric (held) in the King's hand; after Godric Herewulf held him in St. Edmund's land by permission of the Abbot's reeve as the Hundred testify.

[SHROPHAM Hundred]

43 In SHROPHAM 1 free man, 30 acres. Meadow, 3 acres.
> 1 smallholder.
> ½ plough.
> Value 4s.

[CLACKCLOSE Hundred]

44 In (West) DEREHAM Reynold son of Ivo holds 6 free men, at 32 acres; Wihenoc annexed them (although they were) in patronage only to his predecessor.

45 In ROXHAM 1 free man in patronage only, at 9 acres.
Value 8s 1d.

46 In FORDHAM 3 free (men) in patronage and St. Benedict (has) the jurisdiction, at 25 acres. Also 1 free man, at 5 acres, of whom St. Edmund had the patronage before 1066. Reynold holds this.
Value 5s.

47 In DOWNHAM (Market) 3 free men in patronage only, at 2½ acres. 276 a
Value 10d.
In the same 1 free man, at 7 acres under the patronage of the predecessor of William of Warenne; now Reynold holds.
Value 12d.

48 In BEXWELL 2 free men; 1 at 15 acres, of whom Hermer's predecessor had the patronage.
Value 2s 8d. The other had 3 acres;
value 6d.
Now Reynold holds these men.

49 In UPWELL 6 free men held 2 c. of land and 15 acres.
> Always 2 ploughs.
> 9 smallholders.
> Value 26s 8d.
> 3 of these were in patronage to Hermer's predecessor. Wihenoc appropriated all these.

[FREEBRIDGE Hundred and a Half]

50 In WEST WINCH Wihenoc added 1 free man, at 30 acres.
> Always 4 villagers.
> Meadow, 6 acres.
> Value 5s.

⌠Herluin hō . Iuonis . inuaſit In phinchā . 1 . libm hōm . de . xv . ac̃ . 7 vat . xvi . d̃ . 7 . 1 . ac̃ . 7 . dim̃ q̃m Mainard inuaſit . 7 uat . ix . d̃ .
⌠In Pichenham . 1 . lib hō . x . ac̃ . hoc inuaſit Wihenoc . 7 uat . xx . d̃ .

⌠In Fordham ten& Abbas de eli . de Sc̃a . A . xxx . ac̃ . q̃d tenuit lib hō . Sēp . 111 . bor . 7 . dim̃ . car̃ . vat . 1111 . ſot . de hoc ñ habuit ñ cōm̃datione . In Riſtuna . 111 . libi hōes ; vi . ac̃ . vat . xvi . d̃ . In h̃ ñ habuit ñ cōm̃datione . 7 . Sc̃s . bened ſocā .
⌠Hund 7 . dim̃ de Fredebruge . In Lena . 1 . lib hō . xiii . ac̃ . 7 . 1 . ſat . vat . 1111 . ſot . hoc tenuit abb de eli 7 . erat in Soca Stigandi.
⌠In Ilſinghatuna tenuit . Witt . de ſcohies . 11 . libos hōes de . vi . ac̃ . vat xii . d̃ .

276 b
⌠Scerephā ~~Hund~~ In Culuerteſtuna . 1 . lib hō cōm̃d tant . xi . ac̃ . Val . viii . d̃ . hoc
⌠In Leſiet tenuit Rob malet . 11 . libos hōes de . lx . ac̃ . 1111 . ac̃ . pti . tc̃ . 1 . car̃ . (ten& . Galf de Gadomo de Roſtro.)
. 1 . bor . 1 . mot . vat . v . ſot . de h̃ habuit anteceſſor Rōgi bigot cōm̃datione tantū .
In Geſſinga inuaſit Drogo hō Robti malet . x . ac̃ . de dnīca tr̃a Sc̃i Edmundi .
7 uat . xx . d̃ . In Frietuna . 1 . lib hō reg̃ . E . de . xv . ac̃ . quē tenuit Witt malet m̃ tenebat . R . 7 q̃a m̃ tandē cognouit eū ñ eſſe de feudo patris ſui ; dimiſit eū in manu reg̃ . 7 . ħt dim̃ . car̃ . 7 . 11 . bor . vat . xl . d̃ .

[CLACKCLOSE Hundred]

51 In FINCHAM Herlwin son of Ivo annexed 1 free man, at 15 acres.
Value 16d.
1½ acres which Maynard annexed.
Value 9d.

[South GREENHOE Hundred]

52 In PICKENHAM 1 free man, 10 acres. Wihenoc annexed this.
Value 20d.

[CLACKCLOSE Hundred]

53 In FORDHAM the Abbot of Ely holds from St. E(theldreda) 30 acres which a free man held.
Always 3 smallholders.
½ plough.
Value 4s. Of this he had nothing except the patronage.

54 In RYSTON 3 free men, 6 acres.
Value 16d. In these he had nothing except the patronage and St. Benedict the jurisdiction.

The Hundred and a Half of FREEBRIDGE

55 In LYNN 1 free man, 13 acres; 1 salt-house.
Value 4s. The Abbot of Ely held this and it was in Stigand's jurisdiction.

56 In ISLINGTON William of Écouis held 2 free men, at 6 acres.
Value 12d.

SHROPHAM Hundred   276 b

57 In KILVERSTONE 1 free man in patronage only, 11 acres.
Value 8d. Walter of Caen holds this man from Robert.

[FREEBRIDGE Hundred and a Half]

58 In LEZIATE Robert Malet held 2 free men, at 60 acres; meadow, 4 acres.
Then 1 plough. 1 smallholder. 1 mill.
Value 5s. Roger Bigot's predecessor had the patronage only of these.

[DISS Half Hundred]

59 In GISSING Drogo, Robert Malet's man, annexed 10 acres from St. Edmund's land (held) in lordship.
Value 20d.

60 In FRITTON 1 free man of King Edward's, at 15 acres, whom William Malet held; R(obert) Malet has been holding him. Because he has now at last acknowledged that (this man) is not of the Holding of his father, he has made him over in the King's hand.
He has ½ plough; 2 smallholders.
Value 40d.

276 a, b

Witt grofs tenebat
de . Robto . In Ferueffella . I . lib hō Alfi . cōmd . c̄ . IIII . ac . quē ten . W . malet die
q̃ fuit uiuus 7 mortuus 7 . Galt m̄ de . R . f; Rob malet c̄tdic̄ fe nefciffe ufq; adduē
q̃ fuit inbreuiat . Tc̄ . ar . II . boū . m̄ . I . val . VIII . d . In Dice . v̄ . lib hō . v . ac de dn̄io
man̄ quē ten . W . malet f; n̄ ptinuit adfudū fuū . eod m̄ offert fe nefciffe . fēp II . bob , val . x . d
Germund hō Wlti gifart . inuafit . IIII . ac . de Suafhā manerio comitis
Alani.

Witt de uuarenna ten& In bradeham dim car trǣ qd tenuit . Go
dric . Sēp . v . uitt . 7 . II . bor . 7 . I . fer . I . car . in dn̄io . I . car hom . 7 . II . libi hōes tenentes
trā . II . boū . Silu . xx . por . IIII . ac . pti . Tc̄ ual . x . fot . 7 m̄ fimit . f; hōes . Witti .
dic̄t qd ipfe ex eo nichil habuit . Hanc trā tenebat . W . anteqm foriffac&
f; ut teftat hund tenebat eā . R . qn forifecit . 7 poftea . Rob blund ad
firmā reḡ . 7 Godric in thefauro reḡ in breui fuo p . xx . fot . 7 pq
fuit in manu regis :' n̄ uider hōes de hund breuē ł legatū q̃ libaff& eā W.
In Claia . II . libi hōes . XIIII . ac . val . VII . d .
In Wiltuna . I . lib hō . hō . t . r . e . xl . ac . II . bor . I . ac pti . tc̄ 7 p dim . car .
val . xx . d . In hoc n̄ habuit n̄ cōmd fuus anteceffor .
In Scipedeham tenent : Witti de . War . XLIIII . ac . qd tenuit Brodo . 7
Aluuin de rege . t . r . e . I . bor . dim . car . tc̄ filu . XL . por . m̄ . xx . IIII . ac . pti .
val . VIII . fot . 7 . III . obot . hoc fuit fēp de manerio reḡ de Saham . 7 . n̄
habuit libatorē . ut hund teftat .

61   In FERSFIELD, William Gross held from Robert (Malet) 1 free man under the patronage of Alsi, with 4 acres, whom W(illiam) Malet held on the day he died. Walter now holds him from Robert (Malet) but Robert Malet counters that he did not know of it until the day when it was put in writing.
   Then he ploughed with 2 oxen, now with 1.
   Value 8d.

62   In DISS 1 free man, 5 acres of the lordship of the manor, whom W(illiam) Malet held but he did not belong to his Holding. In the same way he asserts that he did not know.
   Always 2 oxen.
   Value 10d.

[South GREENHOE Hundred]

63   Germund, Walter Giffard's man, annexed 4 acres of SWAFFHAM, from Count Alan's manor.

64   In BRADENHAM William of Warenne holds ½ c. of land which Godric held.
   Always 5 villagers, 2 smallholders; 1 slave.
   1 plough in lordship and 1 men's plough. Also 2 free men who hold land (ploughed) by 2 oxen.
   Woodland, 20 pigs; meadow, 4 acres.
Value then 10s; now the same, but William's men say that he had nothing from it. William held this land before (Ralph) forfeited but as the Hundred testify R(alph) held it when he forfeited. Afterwards Robert Blunt (held it) at revenue from the King and Godric (answered for it) in the King's treasury in his return for 20s. Later it was in the King's hand. The men of the Hundred did not see the writ or the commissioner who delivered it to W(illiam).

65   In (Cockley) CLEY 2 free men, 14 acres.
   Value 7d.

[GRIMSHOE Hundred]

66   In WILTON 1 free man before 1066, 40 acres.
   2 smallholders.
   Meadow, 1 acre. Then and later ½ plough.
   Value 20d. In this his predecessor had nothing except the patronage.

277 a

[MITFORD Hundred and a Half]

67   In SHIPDAM William of Warenne's men hold 44 acres which Brodo and A(i)lwin held from the King before 1066.
   1 smallholder.
   ½ plough. Then woodland, 40 pigs, now 20. Meadow, 4 acres.
   Value 8s and 3 half pence.
   This was always of the King's manor of Saham (Toney). They did not have a deliverer so the Hundred testify.

In Toddenham . IIII . libi hōes . dim̃ . car̃.
tr̃æ de feudo fedrici cõmdati ſuo antec̃ . ſep̃ . I . bor . II . car̃ . II . ac̃ . p̃ti . val . x.
ſot . Winemer tenẽ de . W.

¶ In Paruo Creſingham . ht̃ Rex in dn̄io . II . libos hoẽs . de . I . car tr̃æ . 7 . ĥt.
. II . car̃ . 7 . II . uilt . 7 . I . bor . 7 At . III . uilt . 7 . I . bor . IIII . ac̃ . p̃ti . 7 . reddit . XII . ſot.
q̃s Rad de todeneio huc uſq̃ habuit . In Holma . tenuit . I . lib̃ hõ . dim̃ . car̃ tr̃æ.
ſep̃ . dim̃ . car̃ . 7 . IIII . pars mol . II . ac̃ p̃ti . val . v . ſot . hoc &ĩa habuit . R . ſimit.

¶ Hund 7 . dim̃ de Fredebruge . Rog̃ bigot tenẽ In Plicham . x . libos
hoẽs . de LXXX . ac̃ . qd tenẽ Ranulf fili Galti . VI . ac̃ . 7 . dim̃ . p̃ti . II . car̃ . val
XII . ſot . De ĥ habuit ſuus antec̃ cõm̃d tantũ . 7 . Stigand ſup unũ ſocã.
7 . cõmdatione . 7 . ſup . alios ſocã.

¶ . H̃ . de Wanelunt . In Greſtuna . IIII . libi . hoẽs . XXVI . ac̃ . qd tenet Idẽ
. R . de R . 7 . ual . IIII . ſot . 7 In hoc n̄ habuit Anteceſſor Rog̃i n̄ cõm̃d . Rex.
7 . Comes ſocã . In Tumeſteda . I . lib̃ hõ . xv . ac̃ . 7 . I . ac̃ . p̃ti . tc̃ . dim̃ . car̃.
m̃ . II . bou . val . II . ſot . Idẽ R . tenẽ . Rex . 7 . Comes ſocã.
In Hocham . I . lib̃ hõ cõm̃d tantũ . VIII . ac̃ . val . VIII . d . Soca in bucham.
In Snetretuna . lib̃ hõ . v . ac̃ . 7 . III . uirg̃ 7 . II . bou . 7 . ual . XVI . d . de hoc
cõm̃d tantũ . Soca ĩ buchã . Rad fili herluini tenẽ de . R.

¶ Hund de Gildecros . In Snareſhul . I . lib̃ hõ . xv . ac̃ . ad feudũ Turſtini.
de Tedfort . 7 inde ſuus antec̃ habuit cõm̃d tantũ . Soca in Keninchala.
. reg̃ . val . xv . d . In Snareſhella . III . libi hoẽs cõm̃d . 7 ſoca faldæ Tota
alia ſoca in Keninchala . 7 . ſint . xx . ac̃ . Sep̃ . dim̃ . car̃ . val . xx . d.
hoc tenẽ Turſtin.

68 In (East) TUDDENHAM 4 free men, ½ c. of land from Frederick's Holding. (They were) in patronage to his predecessor.
Always 1 smallholder.
2 ploughs; meadow, 2 acres.
Value 10s. Winemer holds from W(illiam).

[South GREENHOE Hundred]

69 In LITTLE CRESSINGHAM the King has 2 free men in lordship, at 1 c. of land. [1] has 2 ploughs, 2 villagers and 1 smallholder; the other 3 villagers, 1 smallholder; meadow, 4 acres.
He pays 12s which Ralph of Tosny had hitherto.

70 In HOLME (Hale) 1 free man held ½ c. of land. Always ½ plough; ¼ of a mill; meadow, 2 acres.
Value 5s. R(alph) likewise had this too.

The Hundred and a Half of FREEBRIDGE

71 In FLITCHAM Roger Bigot holds 10 free men, at 80 acres which Ranulf son of Walter holds. Meadow, 6½ acres; 2 ploughs.
Value 12s. His predecessor had the patronage only of these and Stigand the jurisdiction and patronage over 1 and the jurisdiction over the others.

The Hundred of WAYLAND

72 In GRISTON 4 free men, 26 acres which R(anulf) also holds from R(oger).
Value 4s. In this Roger's predecessor had nothing except the patronage, the King and the Earl the jurisdiction.

73 In THOMPSON 1 free man, 15 acres. Meadow, 1 acre. Then ½ plough, now 2 oxen.   277 b
Value 2s. The same R(anulf) also holds. The King and the Earl (have) the jurisdiction.

[SHROPHAM Hundred]

74 In HOCKHAM 1 free man in patronage only, 8 acres.
Value 8d. The jurisdiction is in Buckenham.

75 In SNETTERTON a free man, 5 acres and 3 roods. 2 oxen.
Value 16d. Of this (Roger's predecessor had) the patronage only. The jurisdiction is in Buckenham. Ralph son of Herlwin holds from R(oger).

The Hundred of GUILTCROSS

76 In (Great) SNAREHILL 1 free man, 15 acres, as part of the Holding of Thurstan of Thetford. His predecessor had the patronage only there the jurisdiction (is) in the King's (manor of) Kenninghall.
Value 15d.

77 In (Great) SNAREHILL 3 free men in patronage and fold-rights. All other jurisdiction (is) in Kenninghall. They have 20 acres.
Always ½ plough.
Value 20d. Thurstan holds this.

ꝼIn Ṯna. I. lib hō. sc̄i benedicti c̄m̄d tant. XLIII. ac̄. 7 fuit ex lex. 7
q̇a Aluui fecit illegē ħt dim̄. trǣ. in feudo Rog̃i bigot. IX ac̄ p̃ti. Sēp. I. caȓ.
tc̄ ual. III. sot. m̂. IIII. In Som̄tuna. I. lib hō haroldi. XXX. ac̄. 7. I. bor.
7. I. car̃ 7. dim̄. 7. dim̄. car̄. hoc ten& p̃posuit Rog̃i 7. reddit uno q̇q̇
anno p̃posito reg̃ sub Rog̃o bigot. II. oras. s; n̄ ptinebat. 7. Rog̃ nesciuit.
ꝼHeinesteda Hund̄ In brābretuna ten& Aitard de Rūgo. XVI. ac̄. q̇d
tenuit liḃa femina c̄m̄d Edrici. 7. R. comes tenebat q̇n forisfec̄. teste hund̄.
7. Roḃ blund p̄ea in manu reg̃. 7 M ten& Aitard hō Rog̃i bigot c̄m̄d
pq̇. R. forisfec̄. Ita hund̄ esse testat. 7. illa femina offert judiciū q̇d uerū
est teste hund̄. 7 Aitard ꝯdicit. 7 sub ea s̄t. II. integri libi hōes. 7. dim̄.
de. VI. ac̄. 7. I. ac̄. 7. dim̄. p̃ti. Int om̄s sēp. dim̄. car̃. tc̄ ual. II. sot. m̂. IIII.
In bichesle. I. lib hō Anslec c̄m̄d. cū dim̄ liḃo. t. r. e. de. XVII. ac̄. Sēp
dim̄. car̄. I. uill. I. bor. Istū seruauit Rog̃ bigot in manu reg̃ sic̄ dicit
7. reddit censū in Hund̄. s; hund̄ testat. q̇d Godric dapifer tenuit
sub rege. ad feudū. R. comitis ante q̇ forisfacer&. I. anno. 7 p̃. p. II. annos
ex dono regis. 7 Contra: hō Rog̃i bigot contẽdicit juditio ĩ bello.
Godric reclamat ist̄ ī c̄ medietate trǣ que est in breue Rōg̃i bigot. hanc

recep̄ Godric dapifer p̄ dim̄ carrucat trǣ.
In Porringhelanda. I. lib hō Eduini c̄m̄d. t. r. e. Post Godric. 7 p̃
p̄pt̃ forisfactura Alured. 7. de illa forisfactura q̇etū se fecerat teste
hund̄. s; p̄ p̄ceptū ep̄i baiocensis seruauit Rog̃ bigot in manu reg̃
7 adhuc seruat. ten&. XV. ac̄. Tc̄. dim̄. car̃. m̂. II. bou. Sēp ual. XVI. d̃.
ꝼDice dim̄ Hund̄. In Osmundestuna Inuasit Hugo de Corbun
sub. Rog̃o. bigot medietate uni libi hominis c̄. X. ac̄. trǣ. 7 partehege.

[WEST FLEGG Hundred]

78   In THURNE 1 free man under the patronage only of St. Benedict, 43 acres. He was an outlaw. Because A(i)lwy made him an outlaw, he has half the land in Roger Bigot's Holding.
Meadow, 9 acres. Always 1 plough.
Value then 3s, now 4.

79   In SOMERTON 1 free man of Harold's, 30 acres.
1 smallholder.
[Meadow], 1½ acres; ½ plough.
Roger's reeve holds this and pays 2 *orae* every year to the King's reeve under Roger Bigot. But it did not belong to Roger and Roger did not know.

HENSTEAD Hundred

80   In BRAMERTON Aitard holds from Roger 16 acres which a free woman under the patronage of Edric held. Earl R(alph) held when he forfeited so the Hundred testify, and later Robert Blunt in the King's hand, and now Aitard, a man under the patronage of Roger Bigot, holds it since R(alph) forfeited. The Hundred testifies that it is so and the woman herself offers judicial ordeal that it is true as the Hundred testifies. Aitard counters this. Under her there are two whole free men and a half, at 6 acres.
Meadow, 1½ acres. Between them all always ½ plough.
Value then 2s; now 4.

81   In BIXLEY 1 free man under the patronage of Aslac with a half-freeman before 1066, at 17 acres.
Always ½ plough.
1 villager; 1 smallholder.
Roger Bigot had custody of him in the King's hand so he says and he pays tribute in the Hundred. But the Hundred testify that Godric the Steward held under the King as part of Earl R(alph's) Holding for 1 year before he forfeited and later for 2 years of the King's gift. Against this Roger Bigot offers to prove the contrary by judicial ordeal or by battle. Godric claims this (land) with half of the land which is in Roger Bigot's return. Godric the Steward acquired this for ½ c. of land.

82   In PORINGLAND 1 free man under the patronage of Edwin before 1066. Later Godric (held) and afterwards Alfred on account of a forfeiture. He had quit himself of that forfeiture as the Hundred testifies but by order of the Bishop of Bayeux Roger Bigot kept (the land) in the King's hand and still does so. He holds 15 acres.
Then ½ plough, now 2 oxen.
Value always 16d.

DISS Half Hundred

83   In OSMONDISTON Hugh of Corbon under Roger Bigot annexed a moiety of 1 free man, with 10 acres of land and part of a close.

hoc tenuit. R. comes qñ forisfec̄. 7. p̄ cū fuit in manu reḡ inuafit eū hugo
de Corbun q̊ m̄ ten&. Rađ de felgeris ten& Maneriū f; ñ h̄t hanc parte
Sep ual. ii. fol.

↯ Est hund de flec. In Phileby. li. ac̄. i. lib̄ hō. t. r. e. de uxore illi9 habebat
tc̄ Aluuin cōmdonē tantū. 7 ead uxor nichil habebat ex hac tr̄a. 7. Comes
. R. ex hac tr̄a faifit erat qñ forifecit. 7. Rob̄ blund eā tenuit ad cenfū in manu
reḡ Poft eū fub Godrico inuafit Idē Aluuin. antec̄. R. bigot. 7 Stanart fili9
ej eā tenebat. 7. ex hoc dedit uadē Roḡ bigot ñ reuocat hanc tr̄a ad fuū
feudū. M̄ feruat Godric9 in manu reḡ. 7 ē in illa tr̄a. i. car̄. 7. i. ac̄. 7. dim̄
p̄ti. Val. v. fol.

↯ Hund de Humiliart. In Suerdeftuna dim̄ lib̄ hō. de q̊ anteceffor
Godrici habuit cōmd tantū. t. r. e. 7 idē Godric erat inde faifit qñ
. R. comes forisfec̄. M̄ eū tenebat Rađ de Norun. 7. h̄t. xv. ac̄. 7. dim̄
bor. 7. dim̄. car̄. 7. dim̄ ac̄. p̄ti. 7. reddebat. Gođ. x. fol. m̄ reddebat
Rađ. xii. fol. 7 hunc hominē detinuit ađus Godricū. 7 aliū dim̄
hom̄ fimilit̄ de. v. ac̄. ual. xii. đ.

↯ Depuuade Hund. In Appetuna. i. lib̄. xv. ac̄. Val. xxxii. đ
hunc tenebat herb̄ camerari Roḡi bigot. 7 hōes comitis Euftachii eū
calūpniniant ad fuū feudū. 7 ē de fuo feudo; m̄ ē in manu reḡ.

278 b

De hoc dedit Herb̄t uadē de. xvi. đ. q̊s habuit

↯ hund 7 dim̄ de fedebruge
↯ In Derfincham. i. lib̄ hō. xii. ac̄. ual. xii. đ. hoc ten& Petr9 ualonienfis.
de hoc habuit fuus antec̄ cōmdatione tantū 7. Stigand focā. In Eadē. ten xxi.
libi hōs ii. car̄. tr̄æ. 7. xxxv. ac̄. v. bor. Sep. iii. car̄. vii. ac̄. p̄ti. Totū ual
xl. fol De h̄ omibȝ habuit fuus antec̄ cmd tant. 7 hoȝ. xviii. fi uellent recede
dar& q̊q̊ iii fol. Stigand de omibȝ focā. In Ead. ii. libi hōes. ii. car̄ tr̄e

Earl R(alph) held this land when he forfeited. Later when it was in the King's hand, Hugh of Corbon who now holds, annexed it. Ralph of Fougères holds the manor but he does not have this part. Value always 2s.

This is the Hundred of EAST FLEGG

84 In FILBY 51 acres; 1 free man before 1066. Then A(i)lwin had the patronage only of this man's wife and the wife had nothing out of this land. Earl R(alph) had possession of this land when he forfeited. Robert Blunt held it at tribute in the King's hand. Later the same A(i)lwin R(oger) Bigot's predecessor annexed it under Godric, and his son Stanard held it. Whereof Roger Bigot has given pledge and does not claim this land as part of his Holding. Now Godric has custody of it in the King's hand. There is on that land 1 plough; meadow, 1½ acres.
Value 5s.

The Hundred of HUMBLEYARD

85 In SWARDESTON a half-freeman of whom Godric's predecessor had the patronage only before 1066. The same Godric had possession when Earl R(alph) forfeited. Lately Ralph of Noron held him. He has 15 acres.
   Half a smallholder.
   ½ plough; meadow, ½ acre.
He paid 10s to Godric and lately he paid 12s to Ralph. (Ralph) kept back this man from Godric, and another half-man likewise, at 5 acres.
Value 12d.

DEPWADE Hundred

86 In HAPTON 1 free (man), 15 acres.
   Value 32d.
   Herbert, Roger Bigot's chamberlain, held this man. Count Eustace's men claim to him as part of his Holding and he is not of his Holding; now he is in the King's hand. Herbert has given pledge of this at 16d which he had.

278 b

The Hundred and a Half of FREEBRIDGE

87 In DERSINGHAM 1 free man, 12 acres.
   Value 12d.
   Peter of Valognes holds this man. His predecessor had the patronage only of him and Stigand the jurisdiction.
In the same 21 free men hold 2 c. of land and 35 acres.
   5 smallholders.
   Always 3 ploughs; meadow, 7 acres.
Value of the whole, 40s.
   His predecessor had the patronage only of all these; 18 of them were to give 2s each if they wished to withdraw. Stigand (had) the jurisdiction of them all.
In the same 2 free men, 2 c. of land.

Tc̃ 7 . p̃ . 11 . car̃ . in dñio . m̃ . 1 . Vn͡ ex ħ . habuit . vi . libos hōes . 7 . v . bor.
7 . aliͩ . 1111 . bor . sep̃ . 1 . car̃ . hom̃ . xi . ac̃ . 7 . dim̃ . p̃ti . Tc̃ . 7 p̃ ual̃ . xl . fot . m̃
. xxv.

╱ Hund̃ de Dochinga In Scernebruna . 1 . soc̃ heroldi . lx . ac̃ . q̃ jacebat
ad sexsordā . t̃ . r̃ . e . M ten& . W . de p̃tenai de . eo . 7 reclamat libatorē . val.
vi . fot . 7 . viii . d̃ . In Ead . 1 . lib c̄m̃d . tantū . vi . ac̃ . val . vi . d̃ . ╱ Grenehou . ħ.
╱ In Benincham ten& Petr͡ . ix . libos hōes . c̄m̃d Gu q̃ fuer̃ hōes reg̃ . 7 . Guerti
v . car̃ . trǣ . 7 . xxii . bor . Tc̃ . ix . car̃ int̃ ōes m̃ . vi . 7 . dim̃ . viii . ac̃ . p̃ti.
tc̃ . 1 . mot . Tc̃ . uat . 1111 . lib . m̃ . vii . de . xx . lib que st̃ in benincham.

╱ Scerepham Hund̃ . In Hercham ten& Rad̃ de bellafago . 11 . libos
hōes . de . xx . ac̃ . q̃s ten& Garin͡ de eo . 11 . ac̃ . p̃ti . tc̃ . 1 . car̃ . p̃ . dim̃ . m̃ . 11 . bou͡.
val . xx . d̃ . De ħ habuit suus antec̄ c̄m̃d tantū t̃ . r̃ . e . 7 Eudo eos tenuit.
Soca in buchcham
╱ Walesham Hund̃ . In bastuuic ten͡ Godric͡ lib ħo . c̄m̃d t̃ . r̃ . e xxx . ac̃.

7 fuit ho͡ Godrici de Roffa ; m̃ ten& Rad̃ de bellafago . 1111 . ac̃ ; p̃ti . semp
. 1 . car̃ int̃ se 7 hōes . sep̃ ual . 1111 . fot . 7 . 1111 . d̃ . min͡.
In optuna . 1111 . libos hōes Godrici . t̃ . r . e . c̄m̃d tañtū . de xxvi.
ac̃ trǣ . vi . ac̃ p̃ti . sep dim̃ . car̃ . 7 ual . 111 . fot . 7 viii . d̃.

Then and later 2 ploughs in lordship, now 1.
One of these had 6 free men and 5 smallholders, the other 4 smallholders.
Always 1 men's plough; meadow, 11½ acres.
Value then and later 40s; now 25.

The Hundred of DOCKING

88 In SHERNBORNE 1 Freeman of Harold's, 60 acres, who appertained to Sedgeford before 1066; now W(illiam) of Parthenay holds from him and vouches (him as) deliverer.
Value 6s 8d.
In the same 1 free (man) in patronage only, 6 acres.
Value 6d.

(North) GREENHOE Hundred

89 In BINHAM Peter holds 9 free men who were the King's men and Gyrth's; 5 c. of land.
22 smallholders.
Then 9 ploughs between them all, now 6½. Meadow, 8 acres.
Then 1 mill.
Value then £4; now 7 of the £20 which are in Binham.

SHROPHAM Hundred

90 In HARGHAM Ralph of Beaufour holds 2 free men, at 20 acres, whom Warin holds from him.
Meadow, 2 acres. Then 1 plough, later ½, now 2 oxen.
Value 20d.
His predecessor had the patronage only of these before 1066 and Eudo held them. The jurisdiction is in Buckenham.

WALSHAM Hundred

91 In (Wood) BASTWICK Godric, a free man in patronage, held 30 acres before 1066. He was Godric Ross's man; now Ralph of Beaufour holds. 279 a
Meadow, 4 acres; always 1 plough between him and the men.
Value always 4s less 4d.

92 In UPTON (Ralph has) 4 free men under the patronage only of Godric before 1066, at 26 acres of land.
Meadow, 6 acres; always ½ plough.
Value 3s 8d.

in baftuic ten ulchetel . IIII . libos hoēs cm̃d Heraldi . de xxx.
ac̃ træ . fep . dim . car . IIII . ac̃ p̃ti . tñc ual . II . fol . m̃ . III . fol.
7 VI . d . 7 adhuc ten ide Vlchetel . IIII . lib hoēs . de ; IIII . ac̃
træ . dim ac̃ p̃ti . fep . ar c̃ duobʒ boũ . 7 ual . XII . d.

BLASFEVDA. H̃. In torp . I . foc̃ . VIII . ac̃ træ omĩ c̃fuetud.
ab antec̃ fuo eudone clamahoc 7 ual . XVII . d.

V H̃ . de CHILLEGROS . In Wicha . I . libm hominem ten& hugo
de monte forti . de xxx . ac̃ træ cm̃d tañtũ . I . uill . III . bord.
fep . I . car in dñio . 7 dim car homũ . 7 ual . III . fol . 7 . IIII . d.
Soca in Kenin . In binelai ten& hugo . VIII . libos . cm̃d tañtũ . I . car . træ . I . car.
. VIII . ac̃ . p̃ti . III . bor . val . x . fol.

H̃ . DE HOLT. In Wabrune . xII . libos hoēs 7 dim ten& Rannulfi
de hugone Comite . cm̃d Heroldi . manentes in Wabrune . in falt
hus . & in challinga . & in botha ten . III . car træ . xv . acr . fep
. I . uill . xxv . bord . Tñc . VII . car & dim 7 m̃ . VI . filũ . xxx . pors.
. IIII . ac̃ . p̃ti . VII . mol . Tñc ual . VII . lib . m̃ . VI.

Clauelinga . H̃ . In rauingeha . I . libm hoem . de . III . ac̃ . 7 erat
in cenfu de rauingeha . qm̃o Rad forisfec̃ . hunc detinuit nicho
laus aurifab comitis hugon . 7 ual . VI . d . m̃ . e in manu regis.

Erpingeha Nort H̃ . In bningeha . VII . libi hoēs . vluurici.
t . r . e . m̃ ten& Robt gern . de xL . ac̃ træ . 7 . I . ac̃ p̃ti . tñc . I . car.
7 . dim . P 7 . m̃ . I . Tẽ ual . V . fol . 7 . IIII . d . m̃ . VIII . fol.

93　Further, in (Wood) BASTWICK Ulfketel holds 4 free men under the patronage of Harold, at 30 acres of land.
　　Always ½ plough; meadow, 4 acres.
Value then 2s, now 3s 6d.
Further, the same Ulfketel also holds 4 free men, at 4 acres of land.
　　Meadow, ½ acre. They have always ploughed with 2 oxen.
Value 12d.

BLOFIELD Hundred

94　In THORPE (St. Andrew) 1 Freeman, 8 acres of land with every customary due by his predecessor Eudo Clamahoc.
Value 17d.

The Hundred of GUILTCROSS

95　In WICK Hugh of Montfort holds 1 free man in patronage only, at 30 acres of land.
　　1 villager; 3 smallholders.
　　Always 1 plough in lordship; ½ men's plough.
Value 3s 4d. The jurisdiction is in Kenninghall.

96　In (West) BILNEY Hugh Holds 8 free (men) in patronage only, 1 c. of land.
　　1 plough; meadow, 8 acres.
　　3 smallholders.
Value 10s.

The Hundred of HOLT

97　In WEYBOURNE Ranulf holds 12 free men and a half from Earl Hugh (who were) under the patronage of Harold. They dwell in Weybourne, in Salthouse, in Kelling and in Bodham and hold 3 c. of land and 15 acres.
　　Always 1 villager; 25 smallholders.
　　Then 7½ ploughs, now 6. Woodland, 3 pigs; meadow, 4 acres; 7 mills.
Value then £7; now 6.

CLAVERING Hundred

98　In RAVENINGHAM (Earl Hugh holds) 1 free man at 3 acres. It was in the tribute of Raveningham when Ralph forfeited. Nicholas Earl Hugh's goldsmith kept him back.
Value 6d. Now he is in the King's hand.

NORTH ERPINGHAM Hundred

99　In (North) BARNINGHAM 7 free men of Wulfric's before 1066; now Robert Gernon holds, at 40 acres of land.
　　Meadow, 1 acre. Then 1½ ploughs, later and now 1.　　　279 b
Value then 5s 4d, now 8s.

¶ In Ead uill . II . libi comdati . t . r . e . 7 m̃ tenẽt Anschetel filĩ uspaci . de xxvIII . ac . tc̃ . dim̃ . car̃ . m̃ . II . bou . dim . ac . p̃ti . val . III . sol . idõ st in manu reg̃ q̃a nemo fuit q̃ redd& copotũ.

¶ Blasfelda . Hund . In Possuic . II . libi hoẽs . esculæ comd de . LX . ac . m̃ tenẽt Eudo dapifer ab antecessore suo . Lisuio . vIII . ac . p̃ti . Sep . I . car̃ . tc̃ . ual . v . sol . m̃ reddit . II . sol . cũ seruitio.

¶ In Torp 7 Lipehou tenẽt Rabell' carpentari' . xx . libos hoẽs sinci comdoe de . I . car . træ . 7 . xx . ac . 7 . vII . ac . p̃ti . Tc̃ . 7 . p . II . car . m̃ . III . Tc̃ ual . x . sol . m̃ . xI . 7 . vI . d̃. In Sutunde . ten . I . lib hõ Alsi cmd . t . r . e . qñ . R . forisfecit fuit in censu man reg . m̃ tenẽt . Rab carpent . IIII . ac . træ . val . vIII . d.

¶ Sud Herpincham Hund . In Herpincham . I . lib hõ . IIII . ac . 7 ual . xvI . d . hoc tenẽt Humfrid sub Ranulfo fr̃e Ilgeri.
¶ Hund de Hapinga . I Walcheta III . libi hoẽs . xc . ac . Tc̃ . III . car̃ . m̃ . II . 7 . dim . val . xx . sol.

¶ In Meltuna . I . lib hõ quẽ inuasit Ranulf pipereli 7 h̃t . vI . ac . 7 . dim . ac . p̃ti . val . vI . d.

280 a

¶ In Fornesseta tenuit Scula lib hõ . xIII . ac . de q̃ habuit antecessor Hermeri comdatione . t . r . e . m̃ e in manu reg̃ val . x . d . In hac tr̃a erat dom . t . r . e . quam Oschetel p̃posit . regis transtulit . 7 ex hoc dedit uade.

¶ In Tibham . I . lib hõ . xv . ac . de q̃ antecessor Rob̃ti malet habuit comdoem . t . r . e . sep . I . bor . val . II . sol . hanc tr̃a tenuit Galf canud p̃pt hoc qd suus antecessor habuit in uadimonio p . xvI . sol . t . r . e .

¶ In Est Wnic ten . t . r . e . Rainer . I . lib̃m hom . de . I . ac.

In the same village 2 free (men) in patronage before 1066; now Ansketel son of Ospak holds, at 28 acres.

Then ½ plough, now 2 oxen. Meadow, ½ acre.

Value 3s. They are in the King's hand because there was no-one to render account.

BLOFIELD Hundred

100 In POSTWICK 2 free men under the patronage of Skuli, at 60 acres. Now Eudo the Steward holds from his predecessor Lisois.

Meadow, 8 acres; always 1 plough.

Value then 5s, now he pays 2s with service.

101 In (Free) THORPE and LIMPENHOE Rabel the Carpenter holds 20 free men under the patronage of Finch, at 1 c. of land and 20 acres. Meadow, 7 acres. Then and later 2 ploughs, now 3.

Value then 10s; now 11(s) 6d.

102 In SOUTHWOOD 1 free man under the patronage of Alsi held before 1066. When R(alph) forfeited it was in the tribute of the King's manor; now Rabel the Carpenter holds, 4 acres of land.

Value 8d.

SOUTH ERPINGHAM Hundred

103 In ERPINGHAM 1 free man, 4 acres.

Value 16d. Humphrey holds this under Ranulf brother of Ilger.

The Hundred of HAPPING

104 In WALCOTT 3 free men, 90 acres. Then 3 ploughs, now 2½.

Value 20s.

[HUMBLEYARD Hundred]

105 In (Great) MELTON 1 free man whom Ranulf Peverel annexed. He has 6 acres; meadow, ½ acre.

Value 6d.

[DEPWADE Hundred]

106 In FORNCETT Skuli, a free man of whom Hermer's predecessor had the patronage, held 13 acres; now it is in the King's hand.

Value 10d.

280 a

There was a house on this land before 1066 which Ulfketel the King's reeve removed; of this he has given pledge.

107 In TIBBENHAM 1 free man of whom Robert Malet's predecessor had the patronage before 1066, 15 acres.

Always 1 smallholder.

Value 2s.

Walter Canute held this land for the reason that his predecessor had it in pledge before 1066 for 16s.

[FREEBRIDGE Hundred]

108 In EAST WINCH Rainer held 1 free man before 1066, at 1 acre.

E

NORFOLK HOLDINGS ENTERED ELSEWHERE IN THE SURVEY
The Latin text of these entries is given in the county concerned

In Suffolk

| 1 | LAND OF THE KING | 281 b |

ESf 1   HARTISMERE Hundred   282 a
    4 King Edward held DISS before 1066, 4 c. of land as a manor before 1066. Always 14 villagers; 24 smallholders; 2 slaves. 1 plough in lordship; 18 men's ploughs; meadow, 10 acres. A church, 24 acres. ½ plough; always 7 head of cattle. Then 5 pigs. Then 9 sheep, now 11. Always 5 goats.
Value then £15, with the jurisdiction of one Hundred and a half, and half a day's honey, with the customary dues; now £30 by weight.
It has 1 league in length and ½ in width, tax of 4d.

ESf 2   The half-hundred of LOTHINGLAND   283 a
    31 Gyrth held GORLESTON before 1066, 5 c. of land as 1 manor. Then 20 villagers, now 12. Always 5 smallholders. Then 5 slaves, now 4. Then 2 ploughs in lordship, now 1. Then 5 men's ploughs, now 3. Woodland for 5 pigs; meadow, 10 acres; 3 salt-houses. Then 2 cobs, now none. Then 5 head of cattle, now none. Always 300 sheep.

ESf 3   32 In YARMOUTH 24 fishermen belong to this manor.

ESf 4   38 In Norfolk, in GILLINGHAM, 30 acres. 1 villager. ½ plough.   283 b

ESf 5   42 In GORLESTON 20 free men, at 90 acres, who belong to the manor as to all customary dues. In the valuation of the manor. Then 7 ploughs, now 5.

ESf 6   54 In GORLESTON 4 free men, 1 c. of land. Then 2½ ploughs, now 2.   284 b
Value then 20s; now 16s.

ESf 7   56   LAND OF HUMPHREY SON OF AUBREY   436 a
    6 ... From the mill of BILLINGFORD 7s 4d.
In Eynsford Hundred in Norfolk.

NOTES

ABBREVIATIONS used in the Notes:
Bjorkmann NP ... E. Bjorkmann, *Nordische personennamen in England in alt- und frumittel-englischer Zeit* (Halle, 1910). Dauzat ... A. Dauzat, *Dictionnaire étymologique des noms de famille et prénoms de France* (rev. ed. by M-T. Morlet, Larousse, Paris 1951). DB ... Domesday Book. DBS ... see Reaney. Ellis ... Sir H. Ellis, *A general introduction to Domesday Book* (2 vols. 1883; reprinted 1971). EYC ... *Early Yorkshire charters* (vols. IV, V, Yorkshire Archaeological Society 1935-36) ed. C. T. Clay. Farrer ... W. Farrer, *Honors and Knights' fees* (3 vols. London and Manchester 1923-1925). FB ... for this text see above, *The Feudal Book of Abbot Baldwin of Bury St. Edmunds*; references are to pages in *Feudal documents from the Abbey of Bury St. Edmunds*, ed. D. C. Douglas (London 1932). Fellows-Jensen ... G. Fellows-Jensen, *Scandinavian personal names in Lincolnshire and Yorkshire* (Copenhagen 1968). Forssner ... T. Forssner, *Continental-Germanic personal names in England in Old and Middle English times* (Uppsala 1916). Förstemann ... E. Förstemann, *Altdeutsches Namenbuch*, Band 1, *Personennamen* (2nd ed. Bonn 1900). Freeman ... E. A. Freeman, *The History of the Norman conquest of England* (6 vols. Oxford 1867-79). Harmer ... F. E. Harmer, *Anglo-Saxon Writs* (Manchester 1952). IE, IEBrev, IENV ... for these texts see above, The Ely Inquiry; references are to pages in *Inquisitio Comitatus Cantabrigiensis*, ed. N. E. S. A. Hamilton (1876). LDB ... Little Domesday Book. Loyd ... *The origins of some Anglo-Norman families* (Harleian Society 1951). MS ... Manuscript. OE ... Old English. OEB ... G. Tengvik, *Old English Bynames* (*Nomina Germanica* IV, Uppsala 1938). OFr ... Old French. OWScand ... Old West Scandinavian. PNDB ... O. von Feilitzen, *The pre-conquest personal names of Domesday Book* (*Nomina Germanica* III, Uppsala 1937). Reaney ... P. H. Reaney, *A dictionary of British surnames* (2nd ed. by R. M. Wilson 1977), sometimes DBS. RyghGP ... O. Rygh, *Gamle Personnavne i Norske Stedsnavne* (Kristiana, 1901). VCH ... *The Victoria History of the county of Norfolk* (vol. ii 1906; *Domesday Survey*, i seq, introduction by C. Johnson, translation by C. Johnson and E. Salisbury). WD ... *Winchester Studies*, I, ed. M. Biddle *et al.* (Winchester 1976).

Notes on the MS

The Editor is indebted to Mr. John McN. Dodgson for his advice on various matters.

The text of the DB Survey for Norfolk is contained in Little Domesday Book (now preserved, with the larger volume, at the Public Record Office, London). The manuscript was written, by more than one scribe, on either side of leaves, or folios, of parchment (sheep-skin) measuring about 11 by 8 inches (28 by 20 cms). On each side, or page, is a single column, making two to each folio. The folios were numbered in the 17th century, and the two columns of each are here lettered a, b. Red ink was used to distinguish chapter and Hundred headings. Deletion was marked by putting a line (in the ink of the text) through incorrect words. The running title on the recto of folios was usually an abbreviated form of the name of the Landholder whom the chapter concerned; the running title on the verso was an abbreviation of the county name.

NORFOLK. *NORFULC* fol. 109a at the head of the list of landholders. *NORDFOLC* (fol. 109b) abbreviated as *NORDF̄* (fol. 110b) and *NORF̄*; and *NORFOLC* abbreviated as *NORF̄*. At the top of the page, to the left of centre.

References to other DB counties are to the Chapter and Section of the editions in this series.

LDB 182a,b are in a larger hand than their neighbours.

Notes on the translation

LIST OF LANDHOLDERS
- L 2   BISHOP OF BAYEUX. See 1,105 note.
- L 4   COUNT ALAN. See 1,1 note.
- L 6   EARL HUGH. See 1,19 note.
- L 7   ROBERT MALET. See 1,197 note.
- L 8   WILLIAM OF WARENNE. See 1,1 note.
- L 9   ROGER BIGOT. See 1,1 note.
- L 10   BISHOP WILLIAM. See 1,57 note.
- L 11   BISHOP OSBERN. MS. *Osbertus* in error, *cf.* heading to chapter 11; see 11 note.
- L 13   HERMER OF FERRERS. See 8,18 note.
- L 14   THE ABBOT OF ST. EDMUND. See 1,51 note.
- L 15   THE ABBOT OF ELY. The Benedictine Abbey of St. Etheldreda, Ely. See 1,226 note.
- L 16   THE ABBOT OF ST. BENEDICT OF RAMSEY. See 1,134 note.
- L 17   THE ABBOT OF HOLME. See 1,194 note.
- L 19   WILLIAM OF ÉCOUIS. See 1,1 note.
- L 20   RALPH OF BEAUFOUR. See 1,11 note.
- L 22   RALPH OF TOSNY. See 1,211 note.
- L 23   HUGH OF MONTFORT. Named from Montfort-sur-Risle (Eure), OEB 100-101. See also 10,53. He was a tenant-in-chief also in Kent, Essex and Suffolk; and, as Hugh Beard (*barbatus, alabarbe*), in Hants. (see Hants. 68,1 note and L 68). He acted with Odo of Bayeux and Earl William Fitz Osbern as regent in 1067. Cf. Essex 27 note.
- L 24   EUDO THE STEWARD. See 9,184 note.
- L 25   WALTER GIFFARD. See 1,19 note.
- L 26   ROGER OF POITOU. Son of Roger, Earl of Shrewsbury. He had been a tenant-in-chief also in Lancs., Derbys., Notts., Yorks., Lincs., Essex and Suffolk, but he had forfeited his lands in 1086. The forfeiture happened when the commissioners had almost finished their returns, so it is noticed in Norfolk and Derbyshire, but in other counties Roger is still recorded in possession.
- L 27   IVO TALLBOYS. Brother of Ralph Tallboys, Sheriff of Bedfordshire. The by-name is OFr *tailgebosc* 'cut-bush', OEB 388. Ivo held in Beds., Norfolk, Suffolk and Lincs. An important man; he commanded the siege of Hereward the Wake at Ely in 1069; he married Lucia sister and heiress of the Saxon earls Edwin of Warwick and Morcar of York; he was lord of Holland in Lincs.; he became Steward to King William Rufus; he died about 1115.
- L 28   RALPH OF LIMÉSY. Named from Limésy (Seine-Inf.), Loyd 54, OEB 95. The sister's-son to King William, he was tenant-in-chief in 10 counties, with 41 lordships, and received the lands of Christina sister of Prince Edgar.
- L 30   DROGO OF BEUVRIÈRE. See 10,61 note.
- L 32   RANULF PEVEREL. See 9,184 note.
- L 34   PETER OF VALOGNES. See 8,106 note.
- L 35   ROBERT SON OF CORBUCION. His patronym is perhaps OFr *Corbucion*, from Vulgar Latin **Corbutio* an extended form of Lat. *corvus* 'raven'.
- L 36   RANULPH BROTHER OF ILGER. Ranulph appears constantly in the DB Survey as 'the brother of Ilger', although in IE 149 he is called 'son of Ilger'. *Ilger* is from OG *Hilger*, OEB 187.
- L 37   TIHEL THE BRETON. See 2,11 note.
- L 43   ROGER OF RAISMES. See 1.226 note.
- L 45   COLBERN. MS. *Colebertus*. Alias Colbern, see 45 note.
- L 55   RABEL THE ENGINEER. The same person as Rabel the carpenter 66,101-102.
- L 56   HAGNI. See 1,81 note.

1,1   HAROLD, King Harold Godwinson. Died at the Battle of Hastings.
C., Carucate. See Technical Terms. The abbreviation 'c.' is used throughout.
FREEMEN. See Technical Terms and F. W. Maitland, *Domesday Book and Beyond* (Cambridge, 1897), 66-79.
40s. Old English currency lasted for a thousand years until 1971. The pound contained 20 shillings, each of 12 pence, abbreviated £(ibrae) s(olidi) and d(enarii). LDB often expresses sums above a shilling in pence and above a pound in shillings as here.
ROGER BIGOT. Sheriff of Norfolk and Suffolk. From Bigot (Calvados), Loyd 14. Ancestor of the Bigot earls of Norfolk.
WILLIAM OF ÉCOUIS. From Écouis (Eure) Loyd 39, OEB 114. He also held in Dorset, Herefords., Essex and Suffolk.
GUY OF ANJOU. *Wido angevinus*. See also Cambs. 15,2.

1,1	WILLIAM OF WARENNE. From Varenne near Bellencombre (Seine-Inf.), Loyd 111. A great landowner, holding in 13 counties. Created Earl of Surrey shortly after 16 April 1088, died 24 June 1088.
1,3	KING EDWARD. The Confessor. Died 5 January 1066.
	REYNOLD SON OF IVO. *Rainaldus*, see 10,35 note.
1,5	JURISDICTION. See Technical Terms and F. W. Maitland, *Domesday Book and Beyond* (Cambridge 1897) 80–107.
1,6	LEAGUE. Generally reckoned as a mile and a half.
	OF A 20s TAX. The liability of an East Anglian village was measured by the number of pence it was required to contribute when the Hundred where it lay paid 20s.
1,7	RALPH. Earl Ralph Wader. Son of Earl Ralph the Constable. Earl of East Anglia. Forfeited his lands and ended his life in exile after his revolt in 1075 in conspiracy with Roger of Breteuil, Earl of Hereford 1071-76, who was also disgraced, see DB Glos. S1 note. The name 'Wader' may be a place-name, see OEB 119.
	ROBERT BLUNT. Sheriff of Norfolk and King's officer. He is called *Albus*, *Blancardus*, 'white', as well as *Flavus*, 'yellow, fair', and *Blundus*, 'blonde', the origin of the modern surname. See OEB 293.
1,11	COUNT ALAN. Count of Brittany and lord of Richmond. Son of Count Eudo and son-in-law of King William.
	RALPH OF BEAUFOUR, named from Beaufour, Calvados, OEB 71. The same surname as Bishop William's, see 1,57 note; perhaps he was a relation.
	SESTERS. Usually 4, but sometimes 5 to 6 gallons, see R. E. Zupko, *A dictionary of English Weights and Measures from Anglo-Saxon times to the nineteenth century* (Univ. of Wisconsin Press, 1968), 155.
	EUDO SON OF CLAMAHOC. cf. 66,94. See OEB 178, *Clamahoc* is an OIrish personal-name.
1,19	WALTER GIFFARD. The first Walter Giffard, cousin of King William, came to England with the Conqueror in 1066. His son, another Walter, succeeded his father before 1085 and was later created Earl of Buckingham, probably after 1093.
	EARL HUGH. Hugh of Avranches, created Earl of Chester in 1071.
1,24	ORAE. An ora, literally an ounce, in Scandinavia a monetary unit and coin still in use; was reckoned at 16 (assayed) or 20 (unassayed) pence, see S. Harvey, 'Royal revenue and Domesday terminology', *Economic History Review*, 2nd series, xx (1967), 221-228.
1,28	A(I)LWIN. Since *Aethelwig* of Thetford, usually called *Alwi* (see *A(i)lwy*) is sometimes also called *A(i)lwin* of Thetford (see 9,72 note); it is likely that the personal names *Aluuin(us)*, *Aeluinus*, *Ailuuinus* could represent OE *Alwine* PNDB 158, or *Aethelwine* PNDB 190 as well as the *A(i)lwy* series; so they have been presented as *A(i)lwin*. See index.
	BISHOP A(E)LMER. The personal-name appears as LDB *Agelmarus* 10,20; *Almerus* here; *Almarus* and *Ailmarus* freq.; *Helmerus* 13,9; for OE *Aethelmaer*. See PNDB 154-5 and 147. This A(e)lmer was Bishop of Elmham from after August 1047 until his deposition c. 11 April 1070. Brother of Stigand, Archbishop of Canterbury, whom he succeeded as Bishop of Elmham when Stigand was translated to Winchester in 1047. Aelmer was deprived of office on the deposition of Stigand from Canterbury, 1070. Harmer, p. 553, notes, 'The fact that Aethelmaer had a wife (see 10,28) may, as Freeman suggests, have contributed to his deposition!' In Chapter 10, the See is named from Thetford, to which it was translated from Elmham in 1078.
1,29	GYRTH. Earl of East Anglia from 1057. Brother of King Harold. He died at the Battle of Hastings. In LDB *comes* is infrequently used to denote Earl Godwin's children, therefore some instances mentioning 'Harold' or 'Gyrth' may not refer to the last English royal house.
1,32	WIGHTON. The entry seems muddled about 'now' and 'then' and pigs and mills.
1,42	OSPAK. *Unspac*, Anglicised archaic form of the OScand personal-name *Óspakr* from *úspakr* 'unrestrained'. Compare 10,58 DB Notts. 2,1 and 9,103, and Ralph son of Ospak DB K. See OEB 202, PNDB 340.
1,51	THIS APPERTAINS TO DISS IN SUFFOLK. Diss is now in Norfolk. It gave its name to a Norfolk Hundred but it appears in the Suffolk text under Hartismere Hundred, see ESf 1, although Burston, its outlier, is here surveyed under Norfolk.
	ST. EDMUND'S LAND. Land of the Benedictine abbey of Bury St. Edmund's, Suffolk.
	STIGAND. Consecrated Bishop of Winchester in 1047, he held that See with the Archbishopric of Canterbury from 1052 until he was deposed in 1070. Died 1072.
1,52	1 ACRE OF LAND AND 10 ACRES. In the MS *ać*, possibly in error for *cať*.
	£11 10s BLANCHED. Or white pounds. A sample of coin was melted as a test for the

	presence of alloy or baser metal. Money could also be said to be blanched when, without a test by fire, a standard deduction was made to allow for alloying or clipping.
1,57	BISHOP WILLIAM HOLDS AND ERFAST HELD. Erfast was consecrated Bishop of Elmham in 1070. He moved the See from North Elmham to Thetford in 1071 or early in 1072. Bishop William de Bello Fago (Beaufour, Calvados; cf. 1,215 note), a royal clerk, was nominated Bishop 25 December 1085. There is no date for his consecration. He died or resigned before 27 January 1091. In 1094 or 1095 the See was moved to Norwich by Bishop Herbert Losinga.
	DRODO of BEUVRIÈRE. See OEB 73. *Drodo* may represent a mistake for *Drogo*.
1,58	ASFORD. LDB *Osfort* for OScand *Ásfrøthr*, PNDB 165; Fellows-Jensen 20; DB Notts. 9,34. LDB *Osfordus* 8,97 and *Osfort* 9,174 for OScand *Ásfrøthr*, but see PNDB 339, s.n. *Osfrith*, cf. Osferth 9,154.
1,59	THEN (AND) NOW 381 SHEEP. In the MS m̊.ccc.lxxxi, possibly in error for *m.ccc.lxxxi*, and 'then 1,381 sheep' is meant.
	RICHARD. Richard son of Alan see 10,43 and 44.
1,61	BELONGED TO KING EDWARD, HIS LORD. In the MS *regis E.*; Farley omits *E*.
	A WOMAN, STIGAND'S SISTER. Latin *mulier*; but on fol. 117a Latin *femina* is used, perhaps 'female'.
	WIHENOC. A Breton personal-name, found also in DB Devon and Glos.
	REYNOLD, ROGER BIGOT'S MAN. *Rainaldus*, see 10,35 note.
	ANSCULF UNLIKE. The OG personal-name *Ansculf*, PNDB 161, with a by-name not in OEB, *Unglicus*, representing an anglicised form of ON *úglíkr* 'unlike, different'.
	WALA. An OG fem. personal-name, Förstemann 1515; cf. Forssner 242; PNDB 409 s.v. *Walo*. Cf. *Wala*?, under Waleran 1,66.
	HERVEY DE VERE. In the MS *deb'* in error for *de v'*, 'de Ver'. This by-name has been identified with Ver (La Manche) or Ver (Calvados), OEB 118.
	EVERWIN. LDB *Euerwin(us)* for OG *Eburwin*, Forssner 85.
	RICHARD OF SAINT-CLAIR. In the MS *de Sentebor*, an odd form for *de Sentcler*, cf. 1,63; various place-name identifications have been suggested, OEB 112.
	G(ODWIN?). His 20s premium is associated with Earl Ralph's dues, so the *G.* in the MS could stand for the earl's uncle who appears in 1,144;184.
	PENSIONERS. Latin *Prebendarius*, one who receives an allowance of provisions. Cf. 1,70, a similar charge on the Borough of Thetford, and Essex B6, Colchester. Whether these were ecclesiastical Prebends or lay pensioners is not clear.
1,63	OF THE BURGESSES. Farley has *De bursensib'* for *De burgensib'* in the MS.
	BECCLES. In Suffolk.
	WALERAN. A royal officer, cf. 17,18.
1,64	ALWARD. OE *Alweard* for either *Aelfweard* or *Aethelweard*. Cf. 9,146.
1,66	RALPH VISDELOUP. 'Wolf's face', from the Latin *visus*, 'face' and *lupus*, 'wolf'; OEB 340.
	WYMER. *Wimerus*; also at 8,6;62;69;95. Probably the OE man's name *Wigmaer*. But *Wimerus* 1,66 may be a Frenchman with the OG personal-name *Wigmar*. See PNDB 413, DBS s.n. *Wymer*.
	WALERAN. *Wal(er)a* for *Wal(er)ā* for the OG man's name *Waleran*; cf. 1,63 note and Wala 1,61 note.
1,69	½ BOVATE. A bovate is a measure of land generally regarded as an eighth of a carucate.
1,70	IN THETFORD BEYOND THE WATER TOWARDS NORFOLK. The town of Thetford included land in both Norfolk and Suffolk.
	HERIOT. A payment due at the time of his death from a warrior to his lord, representing the return of his military equipment (OE *heregeatu*).
	THE ABBOT OF ELY (HAS) 3 CHURCHES AND 1 HOUSE (WHICH ARE) FREE.
	IE (130), 'St. Etheldreda holds 1 house (which is) free and 3 churches'.
1,71	OF 14 LEETS. The leet was a more ancient fiscal and administrative division than the Domesday Hundred. Each Domesday Hundred was composed of a number of leets. LDB also gives the number of leets in Clackclose Hundred, see 15,1. For a convenient summary of opinion regarding the origin and structure of the leet see R. Welldon Finn, *Domesday studies. The eastern counties* (London, 1967), 105–108.
	5 FURLONGS. A furlong is 220 yards or an eighth of a mile.
	PAID 20s SCOT-TAX. Note the use of the verb *scotare* here. For the assessment of an East Anglian village see Technical Terms.
1,72	6 FREE MEN DWELT THERE. *Libi* in the MS in error for *ibi*.
1,78	ALWAYS 3 SLAVES. *sol'* in the MS in error for *ser*.
1,80	THEN GODRIC PAYS. *tc̃* in the MS, possibly in error for *tñ* = *tamen* 'and yet'.

1,81 HAGNI. ODan *Hag(h)ni*, PNDB 282, Fellows-Jensen 122, a Scandinavian form of OG *Hagana, -ena, Haguna* whence the *Hagen* of epic poetry. In DB the spellings vary widely, *Haken(-a,-e), Hagan(-a,-e), Hagonus, -is*.
ALWAYS 4 SLAVES. In the MS *sol'* in error for *ser*.
1,86 OTHERS COULD BE RESTORED. In the MS *possñt* possibly in error for *posset*, 'the other could be restored'.
4 IN *THUSTUNA*, AND IN THUXTON 4. *In thustuna. iiii. & in turstanestuna. iiii.* DG regards both spellings as THUXTON; formally, this is improbable. Compare 66,26 note. *Turstanestuna* 1,86 and 8,81 represents 'Thurstan's farm', THUXTON. (Thurston, in Hawkedon, Suffolk, has the same name.) The unintelligible *Thustuna* is not the same name. It may be a mistake for *Thurstuna* (*r* and *s* in insular minuscule can look alike), a name also appearing as *Turestuna* 8.84, *Thurstuna* 9,134, *Turstuna* 15,21: representing 'Thurir's farm' unidentified but the same name as Thurston, near Bury St. Edmunds, Suffolk. However, the two names are geographically involved. In White's *History, Gazetteer and Directory of Norfolk*, 3rd edn., Sheffield, 1864, the parish is called 'Thuxton, or Thurston'. So it can be supposed that Thurstan's and Thurir's estates were adjacent, in Thuxton.
1,94 ALSI. This represents the OE personal-name *Alsige* PNDB 151, probably like *Aelsi*, 9,86, representing OE *Aethelsige* PNDB 187; but OE *Aelfsige* is also possible, cf. 15,25 note.
R(ALPH) THE CONSTABLE. Earl Ralph the Elder, Father of Earl Ralph Wader, Minister of King Edward. Earl of East Anglia from before March 1068. Died 1069/70.
1,97 R(ALPH THE CONSTABLE) and (EARL) R(ALPH). See 1,94 note.
1,99 THE JURISDICTION OVER 1. In the MS *semp'* in error for *super*.
1,100 UNDER THEM 18 FREEMEN. Under the two free men, that is.
1,101 THE THIRD PENNY. Here presumably the Earl's share in the profits of jurisdiction in the Hundred.
1,103 OUTLYING JURISDICTION OF (South) WALSHAM. An OE legal term *ut-socn*, Latinised *ut-soca*, here with a Norman French article in *de l'ut soca*, cf. 1,204 note.
1,105 THE BISHOP OF BAYEUX. Odo, half-brother of King William and elder brother of Robert, Count of Mortain. Earl of Kent 1066-7 to 1082, then 1087 to 1088. He was regent during some of King William's absences abroad. In spite of his imprisonment in 1082, DB records him as an extensive landowner in several counties.
1,106 EARL R(ALPH) HELD 3 WHOLE. Earl Ralph had the whole of their patronage. Shares of a man's patronage between lords are also frequently noted. The number of occasions when men are said to be *dimidü* is large, and smaller divisions were possible.
1,111 YELVERTON. MS *ailuertuna*; similarly 9,36;161;165., 12,10, also *aluertuna* 2,7. The forms *alinituna* 8,88, *ailumtuna* 9,166 are misreadings of some badly written exemplar of *a(i)luer-* in an insular minuscule. The place-name is probably OE 'Aegelfrith's farm'.
1,115 WHO SEEK ... FOLD. They had a duty to pen their sheep in their lord's fold so that he might have the benefit of the manure. See also 'fold-rights' in Technical Terms.
1,122 WHEN GODRIC TOOK OFFICE. When Godric became Steward.
1,128 RADA HELD REDENHALL. The line might be construed as 'Rada, 1 free man under the patronage of Edric, held Redenhall before 1066, 2 c. of land'. But this would give Rada the status of *liber homo*, whereas he is a patron of free men in 1,129-131; so the present reading is preferred.
PERCHES. A measure of length, usually reckoned as 5½ yards, though a 20-foot perch was in use for measuring woodland until last century. See Ellis i, 158.
TO 10 OF THESE THE HUNDRED ALSO TESTIFIES. To 10 of the 20 claimed, the Hundred testifies in the Bishop's favour.
AGNELI. Grammar prevents *Agnellus*, so the provenance of this personal-name cannot be specified.
1,130 WIHTRED. LDB *Wastret* perhaps a mistake for *Wistret*, see PNDB 409.
1,133 THEN 20 SALT-HOUSES. In the MS *sal'*; Farley reads *sol'* in error.
1,134 ST. BENEDICT. The Benedictine abbey of St. Benedict of Ramsey, Huntingdonshire.
1,135 THEN AND LATER 17 VILLAGERS. In the MS *xvii* corrected from *xii*. Farley prints *xv* and superscript *iv*.
1,139 THEN AND LATER 9 VILLAGERS. THEN 24, NOW 15, NOW 28 SMALLHOLDERS. Possibly this is in error for 'Then and later 9 villagers, now 15. Then 24 smallholders, now 28'.
1,144 THE SAME GODRIC. *Idem Godricus*. The Godric of 1,71 et seq.; or perhaps a mistake for *idem Godingus*, 'the same Goding'.
1,147 ANOTHER (FEMALE) FREE MAN, OIA. There is an OG personal-name *Oio*, Förstemann

1178. See also O. von Feilitzen *Stud. Neophil.* 40 (1968), 10. However, LDB reads *alia liber homo Oia* as if this person were a woman with the status of a free man, with a feminine form of the personal-name.
1,149 BECKHAM. MS *betheam* for *becheam*.
SIWARD BAIRN. From the OWScand *barn* 'child' (cf. OE *bearn*). The by-name might have a more specialised meaning, 'young person of a prominent family', OEB 237. See DB Wa. 19,1-3 and note.
1,150 ALFLAED. LDB *Elflet* here, and *Alflet* 8,29; an OE woman's name, *Alflaed* PNDB 144, for *Aethel-* or *Aelf-flaed*.
1,151 EARL RALPH THE ELDER. See 1,94 note.
1,168 THIS ENTRY. Not in VCH.
1,194 ST. BENEDICT'S. The Benedictine abbey of St. Benedict of Holme.
1,195 TIHEL. Of Hellean. See 2,11 note.
1,197 ROBERT MALET. Domesday lord of Eye, Suffolk. The Malets came from Graville-Ste-Honorine (Seine-Inf.), Loyd 56. He was the son of William Malet. Edric of Laxfield was predecessor of William and Robert Malet.
WHEN HE WENT INTO THE MARSH. See also 35,16. Freeman deduced that William Malet was killed during the invasion and rebellion in the Fenland of 1070-1, see Freeman IV, 473; but Round suggested *maresc* might be a mistranscription of *Eurvic*, York, see J. H. Round, 'The death of William Malet', *Academy* (26 August 1884).
1,198 (£)4. In the MS *lib'i ho'es*, probably in error for *lib'*.
1,201 ABBOT OF ST. BENEDICT'S. Of Holme.
LAND IN CORNWALL. DB Co. does not mention this.
1,203 2 FREE MEN HELD RUNHAM. There is no gallows mark in the MS before this entry as in Farley.
EDRIC OF LAXFIELD. Of Laxfield, Suffolk, OEB 45. Predecessor of Robert Malet. Exiled in both King Edward's and King William's reigns. Most of his extensive lands became first William Malet's and then Robert Malet's.
1,204 OUTLYING JURISDICTION OF (South) WALSHAM. Cf. 1,103.
1,208 FOLD-RIGHTS. See Technical Terms.
IN THE SAME ... The remainder of this entry is repeated, see 65,17.
1,209 WILLIAM OF NOYERS. Probably named from Noyers (Calvados) rather than Noyers (Eure), OEB 103.
1,210; THESE ENTRIES. IE 195 states that Stigand held Methwold and Croxton from the monks
211 of Ely for a food rent.
5 SMALLHOLDERS BEFORE 1066. IE 138, '5 smallholders, at 5 acres of land then'. Also IE 184.
1 CHURCH. ALSO 1 CHURCH OF ST. HELEN. IE 138, '1 church of St. Helen'. Also IE 184. In LDB '1 church' twice, probably in error.
1,210 WITH 1 C. OF LAND. IE 138 as LDB. IE 184, 'with 1 acre of land'.
IN UPWELL 3 SMALLHOLDERS. IE 138 as LDB. IE 184, 'in UPWELL 3 and 4 Freemen'.
4 FREE MEN. IE 138, '4 Freemen'.
1,211 EARL RALPH TOOK AFTER 1066. IE 138 adds 'Then 1 plough, and now'.
MEADOW, 3 ACRES. IE 138, 'Meadow, 4 acres'.
19 PIGS. IE 138, '18 pigs'.
RALPH OF TOSNY [1]. IE 138, 'Ralph of Tosny 1'. Of Tosny (Eure), OEB 116; important in Hertfordshire (at Flamstead) and Herefordshire (at Clifford).
1½ LEAGUES IN LENGTH AND 1 LEAGUE IN WIDTH. IE 138, '1 league in length and ½ in width'. In LDB *lat* in error for *long*.
AT THE END OF THIS ENTRY. IE 138 adds, 'Claim of St. Etheldreda. Methwold was for the monks' supplies before 1066. The abbot leased it to Archbishop Stigand on condition that after his death it would return to the abbey. The Hundred testifies that (it belonged) to the abbey and Croxton likewise. Stigand held the manors in 1066'.
VALUE OF THIS MANOR. Latin *cum tota soca* and *cum soca* appear tautologous. Perhaps a money figure has been omitted after 't.r.e.' and we should translate 'Value of this manor with all jurisdiction before 1066 [£?] with (the) jursidiction (worth) £20; now 60'.
TAKEN AWAY. Reading *ablati* for MS *abbati*, since 'Freemen who are the abbot's' seems irrelevant here.
1,215 RALPH OF BEAUFOUR. See 1,11 note.
1,217 ARCHBISHOP STIGAND. In the MS *archisti*, in error for *archiepiscopus Stigandus*.
1,218 EUDO CLAMAHOC. Or Eudo son of Clamahoc. His death is mentioned in 22,11. Predecessor of Ralph of Beaufour.

1,225   In the MS *C ač*; the number is not reproduced by Farley.
1,226   ST. ETHELDREDA. The Benedictine abbey of Ely, see L 15 note, 15 note.
        RAYMOND GERALD. Perhaps for *Fitzgerald* or *son of Gerald*. See DB Essex, 1,19 note.
        ROGER OF POITOU. See L 26.
        BILLINGFORD. Near Diss; *Billingford alias Pyrleston* down to 1864 at least (W. White, *History, Gazetteer and Directory of Norfolk*, 3rd edn., Sheffield, 1864). See also DG. The spellings *prelestuna* here, *plestuna* 15,25 and 43,2 are the result of mishandling an *er* abbreviation at the stage when LDB was being written. The first element of the place-name *Perlestuna* was probably OE **pyrl* 'a bubbling spring', found only as a place-name element.
        ROGER OF RAISMES. From Rames (Seine-Inf.), Loyd 84. Tengvik however believed he was of Raismes (Nord), OEB 109. Cf. Essex 39 note.
1,229   TOLI THE SHERIFF. Sheriff of Norfolk and Suffolk under Edward the Confessor *c.* 1055–1066. See Harmer 575. MS *To\ʰh′li*, an inaccurate 'correction' to *Tholi*, a Norman spelling. See PNDB 386.
1,230   TOFT (Monks). MS *sto\ʼs′tes*, inaccurate correction for *estoftes*, a Norman-French form for the place-name *Toft*, with prosthetic *(e)s-* (PNDB §§ 51, 112) and nominative *-es* suffix (PNDB § 158).
1,232   2 MILLS. In the MS *n.ii.mol'*. The *n* is probably the beginning of *mol'* begun in error before *ii*.
1,239   *IERPSTUNA*. Unidentified. *Ierp(e)stuna* 1,239 and 31,14, *Iarpestuna* 35,18. Thus DG etc. But the MS might well be read *Ierp(e)s-, larpes-* as Farley does. Neither reading yields an intelligible first element for the place-name.
        A(I)LWY OF THETFORD. Predecessor of Roger Bigot. His personal-name is often reported as *Alwi*, for Old English *Alwig* PNDB 157, occasionally as *Aelwius* (see 9,70), and *A(i)lwin(us)* etc., see 9,100 note. His name was *Aethelwig* of Thetford. PNDB observes, p. 189, n. 11: '... one of the wealthiest predecessors of Roger Bigod in Nf, and probably sheriff of the county. In several places he was succeeded by his son *Stanheard*, who held in 1086 and later. He appears as *Egelwy pater Stannardi* in the Reg. of St. Benet, 1101-07 Holme 169, as *AEgelwini* or *Egelwini* (gen.) *alderman* in a spurious charter (ostensible date *c.*1044-47) Holme 2f. = KCD 785, and is presumably the *AEgelwino* (dat.) *et omnibus burgensibus de Tedford* to whom Hardacnut addresses a writ (KCD 1331). See further Stenton EHR 37.227 n. 6,233, VCH Nf ii, 19'. For Stanheard, cf. Stannard, 9,10 etc.
2   THE BISHOP OF BAYEUX. See 1,105 note.
2,3   HUGH OF PORT. Named from Port-en-Bessin (Calvados), OEB 108. Sheriff of Hampshire.
2,4   (WEST) NEWTON. Farley has *in vetuna* for *niuetuna* in the MS.
2,11   TIHEL OF HELLEAN. Of Hellean (Morbihan), OEB 91. Otherwise Tihel the Breton, see 37; cf. 1,195.
3   LANDS OF COUNT R(OBERT) OF MORTAIN. A half-brother of King William, and younger brother of Odo Bishop of Bayeux; an extensive landholder, second only to the King, especially in Cornwall and the south-west.
        IN THE MARGIN of the MS *f*. In LDB, against the openings of a number of landholders' holdings, there are varying contractions in the margin, as here, which are not reproduced by Farley: *fr* or *r* for *fecit retornam*; *n, nf* or *nfr* for *non fecit retornam*, or *nichil*, to indicate whether or not a landholder has made a return. See further R. Welldon Finn, *Domesday studies. The eastern counties* (London, 1967), 61–62, and V. H. Galbraith, *The making of Domesday Book* (Oxford, 1961), 82, where it is thought these were *post factum* additions.
4   COUNT ALAN. See 1,11 note.
4,2   PHANCEON. This and *Faeicon* 4,16 (read as **Faēicon*) look like scribal variants of a name form **Fanceon, -cion*. But the themes **Fan-, *-ceon* are not known, so scribal or phonetic disaster is supposed. By Anglo-Norman phonetic and scribal process (*ph* for *f*; *n* for *r* by assimilation; *c* for *t* for *th*; *eo, io* for some dipthong with unstressed second element) one can reconstruct a form **Farteon, -tien, -tein*, representing ON *Farthegn* (PNDB 250; Fellows-Jensen 80; Rygh, *Gamle Personnavne* 67) as in *Farthin* (DB *Fardein*) DB Northants. 18,15. (JMD)
4,3   RIBALD. Brother of Count Alan. Probably an illegitimate son of Count Eudo.
4,7   WITH THE LAND OF W(ILLIAM) OF WA(RENNE). See 8.90.
        1 VILLAGER. Farley has *1. ll'* omitting *ui*.
4,14   *TOKETORP*. Also *TOCHESTORP* 8,74, *TOKESTORP* 8,76. Unidentified place. The name meaning 'Toki's outlying farm', an OScand place-name.
        ENISANT MUSARD. *Enisant* is a Breton personal-name, Forssner 75; for *musardus*, 'stupid', see OEB 352. It is possible that Enisant was Constable of Richmond, see EYC v, 84.

4,15 IN YAXHAM. Cf. IE 140, 'In YAXHAM 1 Freeman of St. Etheldreda's, 12 acres of land, whom Earl Ralph held when he forfeited. Now Alan holds him'.
4,16 PHANCEON *Faeicon*, perhaps ON *Farthegn*, see 4,2 note.
PHANCEON HOLDS. Cf. IE 194 which states that Walter son of Bloc (see OEB, 174) holds from the lordship.
WHICH ST. ETHELDREDA HELD BEFORE 1066. IE 140 adds 'Earl Ralph held it when he forfeited'.
4,26 WYMARC. Steward of Count Alan, see DB Cambs., 14,71 note. *Wymarc* is a Breton personal-name.
4,30 WIGWIN. *Gingom(us)* in the MS looks like a scribal error for *Guigoinus*, a Latinized French form for either OG *Wigwin* (see *Guiguin* Förstemann 1588) or an OE *Wigwine*.
4,31 THIS ENTRY. In the MS there is a cross in the margin. This is not reproduced in Farley.
GODRIC. Godric the Steward, see EYC iv, 4.
4,32 ANSKETEL. Ansketel of Fourneaux, see EYC v, 180. Of Fourneaux (Calvados or La Manche), OEB 89.
4,37 ST. BENEDICT. At Holme.
4,38 WYMARC. See 4,26 note.
4,39 EDRIC. Of Laxfield.
4,41 G. OF LAXFIELD'S. In the MS *G*, presumably in error for *E*, 'Edric'.
4,45 MIDDLETON. Near King's Lynn.
1 C. [OF LAND]. An alternative reading is '1 plough', *caruca*.
4,47 ANSKETEL. See 4,32 note.
4,48 RUMBURGH. In Suffolk.
4,49 ASGAR. ON *Ásgeirr*, ODan *Esger* are reflected interchangeably in the various spellings *As-, Es-, -ger, -gar*; and OG *Anger* influences spellings in *Ans-*; see PNDB 166.
HERVEY. LDB 149b and Farley read *herucus*, probably a scribal error for *Herueus*, OF *Hervi*, see Forssner 150 s.n. *Herewig* OG, Reaney s.n. *Harvey*.
4,51 ST. BENEDICT'S. At Holme.
4,53 EDRIC'S. Edric of Laxfield.
5 COUNT EUSTACE. Of Boulogne, brother-in-law of King Edward.
5,2 ALWAYS 4 PLOUGHS IN LORDSHIP. In the MS *iiii* altered from *ii*. Farley prints *ii*.
ALSO 3 FREEMEN. In the MS *in soc*, in error for *iii.soc*. Cf. 8,9 note.
6 EARL HUGH. See 1,19 note.
6,1 RICHARD OF VERNON. Of Vernon (Eure), OEB 119.
WALTER OF DOL. Of Dol or Dol-de-Bretagne (Ille-et-Villaine), OEB 86. Exiled in 1075.
6,4 WARING. The OG personal-name *Warin* (Forssner 246, 247) and its variant *Waring*, appear interchangeable in WARIN(G) 32,2-7 (*Garinus, Warincus*, fol. 254a); *Warin* also appears in *Garinus Cocus* 7,20 (fol. 156a), *Garinus* 66,90 (fol. 278b); *Waring* also in *Warincus* 6,7 (fol. 153a), *Caurincus* 20,6 (fol. 226a) see note. In DB Sussex *Warin* and *Waring* were indexed separately in case the latter turned out to be an OE personal-name. See DBS s.n. *Waring*.
6,7 WARING. See 6,4 note.
7 ROBERT MALET. See 1,197 note.
7,3 WALTER OF CAEN. Of Caen (Calvados), OEB 79.
7,10 MORCAR. LDB *Moithar*, a scribal error for *Morchar*, PNDB 328, 329.
7,14 LEOFRIC OF THORNDON. Of Thorndon, Suffolk, OEB 52.
7,16 THE 6 FORFEITURES. These, like the 3 forfeitures, were reserved pleas of the crown, although they might be bestowed on another. See Harmer 79.
7,20 HIS PREDECESSOR. Robert Malet's.
WARIN COOK. Cf. WARING 6,4 note.
7,21 EYE. In Suffolk.
8 WILLIAM OF WARENNE. See 1,1 note.
8,1 RANDOLPH. LDB *Rardulfus*, a scribal error for *Randulfus*, i.e. *Ranulf* Forssner 211, *Randolph* Reaney s.n. (ON *Rannulfr*, OG *Rannulf*). Named of Quesnay (Seine-Inf., see Loyd 27) in DB Sussex 6,1, he occurs elsewhere in LDB Norfolk as *Radulfus, Ralph* see 8,15;24;107;108;122. See also Farrer iii, 314.
WITHER. This and *Widder* Beds. 55,9 for DB *Widrus*, represent ODan *Withar*, ON *Vitharr* PNDB 406; also as *Wider, Wither* in Lincs.
8,2 BY EXCHANGE FOR 2 MANORS OF LEWES. There are constant references in Ch. 8 to the exchanges of William of Warenne. There are references to the exchange of Lewes, to the castellany or castle of Lewes, to Lewes alone, to the 'new land' and to unspecified exchanges. It seems that William acquired these lands in Norfolk, and others in Suffolk and Essex also, to compensate for estates he had lost in Sussex from his Rape or castlery

	of Lewes. See L. F. Salzman, 'The Rapes of Sussex', *Sussex Archaeological Collections* lxxii (1931), 25-26, and J. F. A. Mason, 'The Rapes of Sussex and the Norman Conquest', *Sussex Archaeological Collections* cii (1964), 80-87.
8,6	LOKKI. DB *Loca*; a Scandinavian personal-name, PNDB 321.
	ROD. The term *virgata* is used here as a yard measure.
	FREDERIC. It is virtually certain that Frederic was the brother-in-law, not brother, of William of Warenne, see L. C. Loyd, 'The origin of the family of Warenne', *Yorkshire Archaeological Journal* xxxi (1934), 111-113. He was killed in 1070.
8,7	TOKI. DB *Toca*; a Scandinavian personal-name, PNDB 385.
8,8	WITH HIS WIFE TO ST. BENEDICT. Of Holme. The meaning here is uncertain. The formula is generally used of lands given with a woman when she entered a nunnery. However Holme was a house of monks not nuns. Perhaps Ralph's wife joined with him in the grant, though she is not known to have held land in Norfolk.
	GYRTH. MS *Gued* lacking the feminine inflexion -*e* is not taken to represent the OE fem. personal-name *Gytha*; see PNDB 280-281.
8,9	3 (IN) CAWSTON. Or possibly *iii* in the MS is an error for *in*, and '(the jurisdiction is) in Cawston' is meant. Cf. 5,2 note.
8,10-12	ST. BENEDICT('S). At Holme.
8,13	ESTGAR. Perhaps OE **Eastgar* or ON *Ásgeirr*, see PNDB 248, cf. Asgar 4,49 note.
	THEN 3 SALT-HOUSES. In the MS *sal'*; Farley prints *sol'*.
8,16	A FREEMAN HELD AT THE JURISDICTION OF THE ABBOT OF RAMSEY, 2 C. OF LAND. IE 139, 'St. Etheldreda had the full jurisdiction and patronage over Anand, 2 c. of land; over his men St. Benedict of Ramsey had the jurisdiction'.
	HUGH. Of Wanchy (Seine-Inf.), Loyd 111, cf. OEB 119. Warenne tenant in Norfolk in Denver, West Dereham, Fordham, Dunham, Larling, Barsham and Fincham and in Suffolk, see Farrer iii, 380-381.
8,17	FOR THE SUPPLIES OF THE MONKS OF ST. BENEDICT. Of Ramsey. The monks were provided from the revenue with a certain amount of food.
8,18	WILLIAM. Of Cailli (Seine-Inf.), Loyd 22. Warenne tenant in Norfolk, see Farrer iii, 382.
	HERMER. Of Ferrers. From Ferrières-St.-Hillaire (Eure), OEB 88.
8,19	FINCHAM. The reading of this place-name is uncertain, possibly *Futham*. Farley read *Forham*.
8,21	ST. PETER. The abbey of St. Peter and St. Paul, Cluny in Burgundy.
8,22	FREDERIC. MS *fedrici* (gen.) with dissimilatory loss of first *r*. Cf. 8,113. See PNDB 254, s.n. *Frideric*.
8,24	AELFEVA. LDB *Alueua*. The OE woman's name *Aelfgifu*, PNDB 173.
8,29	ALFLAED. See 1,150 note.
	WIHENOC. Farley *Wihewoc* represents *-uuoc* for *-nnoc*.
8,30	WALTER. Of Grandcourt (Seine-Inf.), Loyd 47. Warenne tenant in Norfolk, see Farrer iii, 389.
8,31	1 FREE MAN. Or possibly '1 free woman'.
	GUY. Of Anjou.
8,33	SIMON. Warenne tenant in Norfolk and ancestor of the family of Rosei, see Farrer iii, 371.
8,34	THEN 10 SLAVES, NOW 8. In the MS *sol'*, probably in error for *ser*.
8,37-54	THESE ENTRIES are also represented in IE.
8,37	40 FREEMEN. IE 139 and 184, '41 Freemen'. IE 194, 'William of Warenne holds 45 Freemen' who perform certain services.
	7 VILLAGERS. IE 139, '8 villagers'.
	VALUE 20s. IE 139, 'value always 20s'.
	THIS ENTRY. IE 194 states that Gerard, man-at-arms of William de Warenne, was holding ½ c. of land in Feltwell in lordship.
8,39	34 FREEMEN. IE 194, '35 Freemen' who perform certain services at Feltwell.
8,40	7 FREEMEN. IE 194-195, '5 Freemen' who perform certain services at Feltwell.
8,44	WASCELIN AND OSWARD HOLD 2 C., A THIRD OF THE WHOLE. Cf. IE 194, 'Gerard, man-at-arms of William of Warenne, holds land of 3 c. in Weeting'.
	ALWAYS 6 PLOUGHS. IE 138, 'Always 8 ploughs'.
	VALUE ALWAYS 60s. IE 138, 'Value then 60s'.
8,46	WILLIAM ALSO HOLDS 1 FREE MAN; ST. ETHELDREDA (HAS THE) JURISDICTION AND PATRONAGE. Cf. IE 138, 'St. Etheldreda held Anand, 1 free man, with the full jurisdiction and the patronage before 1066'.
	2 C. OF LAND. IE 184, '5½ c.'.
	9 VILLAGERS. IE 138, '11 villagers'.

8,46 MEADOW, 4 ACRES. IE 138-139, 'Meadow, 2 acres'.
THEN AND LATER 4½ MEN'S PLOUGHS, NOW 3. IE 139, 'Then and later 4 men's ploughs, now 3½'.
½ MILL. IE 139 and 184, '1 mill'.
4 COBS; 6 HEAD OF CATTLE; 14 PIGS. IE 139, 'Always 4 cobs. Then 6 head of cattle; 14 pigs'.
7 FURLONGS. IE 139, '8 furlongs'.
OF A 20s TAX IT PAYS 9½d. IE 139, 'It pays 8d in tax'.
OF THE CASTELLANY OF LEWES. In the MS *de castellatione de Lauues*; Farley prints *de castellatione Lauues*.
8,50 HUGH. Son of Golda. Warenne tenant in Norfolk in Threxton and Barsham, and in Suffolk and Sussex, see Farrer iii, 334.
8,54 THIS ENTRY. Cf. IE 140, 'In LARLING 1 free man, 1½ c. of land. St. Etheldreda had the full jurisdiction over him, and of annual customary due he paid 2 sesters of honey before 1066'.
8,62 WIMER. Of Gressenhall. Warenne tenant in Norfolk and Suffolk, see Farrer iii, 395-396.
8,64 OF THE EXCHANGE OF THE NEW LAND. Land William held of the exchange of Lewes as opposed to the estates he held by inheritance from Frederic. The latter were described temp. Henry II as the earl of Warenne's 'old land'.
8,80 OF THE LAND OF THE SAINTS. Perhaps a reference to the Cluniac priory of St. Pancras, Lewes, which William of Warenne and his wife founded.
8,81-84 THESE ENTRIES. Cf. IE 140, 'In LETTON, (South)BURGH, SHIPDAM AND THUXTON 13 Freemen whom William of Warenne holds', and IE 195, 'W(illiam) holds in SHIPDAM the land of 7 men from the lordship'.
8,88 YELVERTON. *alinituna*. See 1,111 note.
8,89 THIS ENTRY. Cf. IE 140, 'In DIDLINGTON the land of 1 Freeman, named Thurstan, where the abbot of Ely has the full jurisdiction and the patronage'.
8,90 WILLIAM. Son of Reginald of Poynings, Sussex. Warenne tenant in Foulden and in Sussex and Suffolk, see Farrer iii, 327.
8,93 THIS SAME FREE MAN. William of Cailli.
8,94 ST. RIQUIER. A Benedictine abbey in Normandy (Somme).
8,97 ASFORD. See 1,58 note.
8,99 200 SHEEP AND A HALF. Perhaps for 2½ hundred sheep, 250.
8,102 LAMBERT. Of Rosay (Seine-Inf.), Loyd 86. Warenne tenant in Norfolk.
8,103 TOKI HELD. MS *tenet* for *tenuit*.
8,106 PETER OF VALOGNES. Of Valognes (La Manche), OEB 117. Sheriff of Essex and Hertfordshire 1086. Brother-in-law of Eudo the Steward. Founder of Binham Priory. Warenne tenant in Norfolk, see Farrer iii, 393.
8,113 1 VILLAGER. MS repeats the number, *i.villi*.
8,117 ALWOLD. OE *Alweald* for *Aethel-* or *Aelf-weald*, PNDB 154.
8,119 RATHI. See PNDB 293 s.n. *Hrathi* ON, *Rathi* ODan.
8,128 ABBOT ALFWOLD. Abbot of St. Benedict of Holme 1064-89.
8,129 G. This makes no sense. Perhaps it is an uncancelled anticipation of the initial letter of the next entry.
3 IN PATRONAGE. A query has been crossed out here.
8,131 ROOD. Generally reckoned at a quarter of an acre. A loose term for a small piece of land.
8,132 WIGULF. *Viulfus*; representing ON *Vigolfr*, ODan *Wighulf*; rather than OG *Wigulf*; PNDB 404.
8,133 A(I)LWIN. *Aluuin cil* for *Alwine cild*. On the name *A(i)lwin* see 1,28 note.
9 ROGER BIGOT. See 1,1 note.
9,3 GYRTH. MS *Gurert* with the first *r* expunged, see PNDB 280, note 2.
9,5 A(I)LWY. Of Thetford. See 1,239 note.
HUMPHREY OF CULEY. From Culey-le-Patray (Calvados), Loyd 36, OEB 84.
9,8 TOVI. MS *tou&* for *Tovet* a Normanised form of ODan *Tovi*, see PNDB § 149 and p. 385.
RALPH OF TOURLEVILLE. Of Tourleville (La Manche), OEB 116.
9,9 5 ACRES, NOW 5½. Perhaps the word *prati* 'of meadow' was omitted here.
9,10 STANARD. OE *Stanheard*. Name of the son of A(i)lwy of Thetford. See 1,239 note.
9,12 IN LENGTH. In the MS *lat*, in error for *long*.
9,18 WITHRI. An otherwise unrecorded name, probably Scandinavian, see PNDB 416.
9,25 W(ILLIAM) PETCH. *Peccatum* equivalent to OFr *peche*, 'sin', OEB 353.
9,26 OF THE EXCHANGE OF ISAAC'S LAND. See also 9,86 and 9,32. Possibly these lands were to compensate for unallotted lands taken out of Roger Bigot's custody as Sheriff.

9,29	THIRD ... FOURTH ... FIFTH. Thus the MS, probably in error for fourth, fifth, and sixth. ROBERT OF COURSON. From Courson (Calvados), OEB 85.
9,30	2 SMALLHOLDERS [DWELL]. *manent* crossed out.
9,33	EARL ALGAR. Of East Anglia 1051-52, 1053-57; of Mercia 1057-62. He was probably dead by 1066, see Harmer 546-547.
9,45	WALTER HOLDS, 3 FREE MEN. *Liberi ...... homines* cannot be the object of the verb *tenere*.
9,48	ALGAR TREC. AN rendering of OE *thraec* 'force, courage, violence'. The nickname probably means 'the vigorous, violent one', OEB 357.
	HUGH OF CORBON. Of Corbon (Calvados), Loyd 32, OEB 83.
9,49	RUMBURGH. In Suffolk.
9,52	*ALGAMUNDESTUNA*. Unidentified in DG; but DEPN puts Alpington (in Yelverton, Loddon Hundred), cf. 9,68 note. The form represents an OE place-name *Alhmundestune* 'at Ealhmund's estate'. An alternative version of the place-name (? perhaps the same place, being in the same Hundred) is *ALCMUNTONA* 12,25, representing OE *Alhmundtune* 'the Ealhmund estate'.
9,59	60s. Here the words *ibi tenent* have been crossed out.
9,64	A(E)LMER. MS *algari* for Algar, altered to *almari*.
9,68	ALPINGTON. MS *appletona*; also *Appletuna* 12,17; OE for 'apple(tree) farm', the same name as Appleton in Freebridge Hundred; identified by DG as Alpington, but DEPN identifies Alpington with *Alcmuntona, Algamundestuna*, see 9,52 note.
9,71	THANE. See Technical Terms.
	7 SLAVES, NOW 3. In the MS *sol'*, probably in error for *servi*.
	THEN 220 WILD MARES. The large number of mares may have been confused with the number of sheep.
9,72	A(I)LWIN. i.e. A(i)lwy, of Thetford. Cf. notes on 1,28;239; and 9,100. See index.
9,75	CARRYING-SERVICE. *Summagium*, the service of carriage by pack-animals, often commuted, as here, to a money payment. Parallel to the *avera* of other counties.
9,76	THEN 1 COB ... NOW 2. There is presumably an error here.
9,78	LOPHAM ... OUTLIER AFTER 1066. A blank space is left for the name of the tenant before 1066.
9,79	BERARD. See 11,3 note.
9,82	ALDWY. PNDB 242 s.n. *Ealdwig*.
9,83	COCK HAGNI. See PNDB 306. MS *Kochagana, Kochaga* for the ODan personal-name *Haghni* with a prefixed epithet.
9,84	1 C. OF LAND WHICH. Latin plural *quas* for *quam* singular.
9,86	ALSI. LDB *Aelsi* for OE *Alsige* or *Aethelsige*. See 1,94 note.
	[LATER] GOD' ... AND ROBERT. The names are interlined, probably signifying later tenants. *God'* is an abbreviation for OE *Godric, Godwin, Godhelm*, etc., men's names, or *Godgifu*, woman's name.
	R(OGER) THE SHERIFF. Roger Bigot was Sheriff of Norfolk and Suffolk at the time of the Inquest.
	BY EXCHANGE ... TO ISAAC. See 9,26 note.
9,87	GODWIN OF SCOTTOW. MS *quod uuinus* for *goduuinus*. Was this error calligraphic or phonetic?
9,88	THIS WAS OF THE. MS erroneously repeats *hoc* 'this'.
	APULIA. The Norman Dukedom of Apulia in Southern Italy.
9,98	HALAS. See also 9,206. Location unidentified. The name is the OE plural of *halh* 'nook, corner' and would have become '*HALES*'.
9,100	A(I)LWIN OF THETFORD. This is the same man as A(i)lwy of Thetford, see 1,239 note, cf. index. The DB and LDB scribes often confused the OE personal-names *Alwig* PNDB and *Alwine* PNDB (for *Aethel-, Aelf-, -wig, -wine*); see PNDB § 148.
	RALPH BERLANG'. The expansion *Rad blang'* to Ralph Berlang (or Berlanger) may represent, with *a* for *u*, a contraction of the Nf place-name Burlingham, as a surname without preposition, OEB 30, 125 (but cf. Feilitzen *NoB* 27 (1939), 120). But the *-er* derivative would be unlikely at this date (see G. Fransson, *Middle English Surnames of Occupation, 1100-1350* (Lund, 1935), 193) and the abbreviation too drastic to be readily recognizable as the Nf place-name unless this were a well-known, often-mentioned Ralph, or this entry were clearly connected with Burlingham. Perhaps the original was *Radb lang'* for *Radb lang'* 'Radbod Long', from the OG personal-name *Radbod* (Forssner 203) and a by-name from OE *lang* 'tall' (OEB 320). Compare Radbod 20,31.
9,102	HARDEKIN. MS *Hardekinc*, see PNDB 286.

9,111 ROGER HOLDS HIM AS PART OF. In the MS *Roḡ Sad*, in error for *Roḡs ad*.
9,116 GRIMSTONE. In the MS *Erimestuna*; Farley prints *Ernnestuna*.
9,131 WILLIAM OF BOURNEVILLE. Of Bourneville (Eure), OEB 78.
9,133 IN KENNINGHALL. At the end of this entry in the MS, *Mitte*, in error. The next Hundred heading was begun on the wrong line.
9,146 TAX OF 5d. MS *de delto* for *de gelto*.
ALWARD. See 1,64 note.
1 FREE MAN. MS has *hōi* for *homini*, instead of *hō* for *homo*.
9,148 BUT ... THE MEN. Or perhaps 'Robert Malet's men claim him' is meant.
9,150 ALWOLD. Cf. 8,117 note.
9,152 YLFING. An OScand man's name, see PNDB 429 s.n. *Ylfingr*. Translated *Ilving* Staffs. 1,42, Derbys. 6,77.
9,153 SHIPDEN. Lost in the sea near Cromer; VCH.
9,154 OSFERTH. OE *Osfrith*: this personal-name may lie behind the *Asford* forms, see 1,58 note.
9,155 BECKHAM. Farley *betham* for *becham*, through confusion of *c* and *t*.
9,158 AELWARD. LDB *Ailwardus*, for OE *Aethelweard*; see PNDB s.nn. *Aethel-*, *Al-weard*. Cf. 30,4 note.
9,160 ROGER BIGOT. In the MS *Ro baiḡ*, which looks like Roger Baynard, presumably in error for *Ro biḡ*, Roger Bigot.
9,166 YELVERTON. *ailumtuna*. See 1,111 note. *Hunt* before this place-name in the MS is taken by VCH, p. 109 note, to be an error which should have been deleted. Alternatively, this may be a place-name with affix; say, OE *hunte* 'hunting-ground', indicating a sporting estate at Yelverton.
9,167 WITHOUT THE PERMISSION OF ST. ETHELDREDA AND OF STIGAND. IE 141, 'Outside the church'.
3 SMALLHOLDERS. IE 142, 'always 3 smallholders'.
9,169 HE ALSO HOLDS 6 FREE MEN. MS *liberi homines* nominative for *liberos homines* accusative.
ONE VILLAGER. MS *i.uillani* plural for *i.uillanus* singular.
9,174 ASFORD. See 1,58 note.
9,180 ST. BENEDICT. Of Holme.
9,182 HUGH OF HOUDAIN. From either Houdain (Pas-de-Calais) or perhaps Houdeng-au-Bosc (Seine-Inf.), or possibly even Houdain (Nord), OEB 92.
9,183 HIS PREDECESSOR ALWIN. Alfwy of Thetford, see 1,239 note.
9,184 HE HAS 1½ C. OF LAND AND 10 ACRES. MS *et habet i. car' terre et dediṁ. et x. ac'*. Dr. Morris read *dediṁ* as an error for *diṁ* 'a half'. If we read it as *de diṁ* 'as to the half', the text could be translated 'He (or it?) has 1 c. of land, and from the half (of a free man) an additional 10 acres'.
RANULF PEVEREL. The by-name is from the OFr *peurel* 'pepper', Latin *piperellus*, OEB 326. Ranulph held in Berks., Oxfords., Essex, Norfolk and Suffolk. He had married a former mistress of King William before the Conquest, and was step-father of William Peverel the King's child by her.
EUDO THE STEWARD. Steward of King William. The youngest of the four sons of Hubert of Ryes (Calvados), Loyd 40, hence also named Eudo son of Hubert. Tenant-in-chief in eleven counties.
9,187 HERMER. Of Ferrers.
9,199 WARENGER. OG, Forssner 246.
9 FREEMEN. *x* changed to *ix* with *i* prefixed above the line.
9,206 HALAS. MS. *halsa* for *halas*. See 9,98 note.
9,219 BERARD. See 11,3 note.
9,227 HERMER. Of Ferrers.
ON THE DAY THAT KING EDWARD WAS ALIVE AND DEAD. 5 January 1066.
9,228 ALWIN. Alfwy of Thetford, see 1,239 note.
10 THETFORD. The East Anglian see of Elmham was translated to Thetford in 1078. See 1,28 note.
BISHOP WILLIAM. See 1,57 note.
10,2 BISHOP A(E)LMER. See 1,28 note.
10,4 ELI. *Heli(us)*, also 10,28;73;79;81. *Helius*; latinized OFr *(H)Eli* for Biblical *Eli*, see Reaney 117 s.nn. *Hely*, *Ely*, Dauzat 234, 323 s.nn. *(H)Elie*; cf. PNDB 247 (Welsh *Eli* at Chesh. 2,22 would still be Biblical). *Helio*, nom., Staffs. 11,26;47 is probably a scribal error for *Helius*.
10,16 GUNFRID THE ARCHDEACON. Of Norfolk. Since he occurs without a territorial title

he cannot be assigned to a particular archdeaconry. Cf. Gunfrid 10,18. 35,2;4-5. The personal-name is the OScand man's name *Gunnfrithr*, variant of *Gunnfrøthr*, see Fellows-Jensen 114, cf. PNDB 277.
10,20 LAND OF THE HOLDING OF THE SAME. Lands acquired by Bishop Aelmer, distinct from the ancient lands of the See.
10,21 EARL RALPH ... EARL RALPH HIS SON. See 1,94 note and 1,7 note.
BISHOP ERFAST. See 1,57 note.
10,25 SEEKING THE FOLD. See 1,114 note and 'fold-rights' in Technical Terms.
10,27 1 FREE MAN. *i liberum hominem*, accusative case, object of the suspended verb, *tenere*. The subject, or his name, is omitted.
10,28 BLOFIELD Hundred. *HUNDRET.BLAFELDA*. $\bar{H}$. in the MS repeats the word *Hundred*.
REYNOLD. See 10,35 note.
10,30-33 A(E)LMER STIGAND'S BROTHER. See 1,28 note.
10,30 RICHARD AGAINST 30s. *Ricardus super xxx solidos* above the line. See MLWL s.v. *super* 'at a charge or cost of'.
AT 6 ACRES. MS repeats *de*.
10,32 MENDHAM. In Suffolk. There are also six entries in LDB Suffolk relating to Mendham. At the time of LDB Mendham straddled both sides of the county boundary.
10,33 ANAND ... HELD. MS *tenent* for *tenuit*.
7 HORSES, NOW 6. In MS, after *modo, do* has been cancelled.
10,35 REYNOLD. *Rainaldus* 10,28, *Renoldus* 10,35;72, *Reinald(us)* 10,78, *Raenoldus* 10,79: OG *Rainald, Raginald, Reginald* Forssner 208. Thus also Reynold of Pierrepoint 10,93, Reynold, Roger Bigot's man 1,61, Reynold son of Ivo 1,3 etc., Renold the Priest 46,1 in Nf, and *Raynoldus* Notts. 11,25, *Rainaldus* Chesh. 22. 27,3. But the names translated *Reginald* Notts. 9,127. 14,2. 17,2 represent *Ragenald* (for ON *Regnaldr* PNDB 346) as in Chesh. 1,35.
10,40 IN WIDTH. In the MS *longo*, in error for *lato*.
10,44 GYRTH. MS *Guend* for *Guerd*, minuscule *n* and *r* being similar.
10,50 HIS PREDECESSOR HAD. Or possibly 'his predecessors had' is meant.
10,53 HUGH OF MONTFORT. See L 23 note.
10,58 ANSKETEL SON OF OSPAK. *Unspac*, see 1,42 note.
10,61 DROGO OF BEUVRIÈRE. Of La Beuvrière (Pas-de-Calais), OEB 73. In line 1 of the entry, after this name, the cancellation of *et an* indicates the anticipation of '*et antecessor*' which appears in the following line.
SAEWULF. MS *Seolf*; see PNDB 355.
10,72 LETHA. Unidentified. The form may represent OE *hlete* locative of *hlet* 'a share or portion of an estate; a division; an allotment'.
10,73 10 FURLONGS. After the numeral, a cancelled *g*, a mistake for *q*.
10,74 WILLIAM OF NOYERS. *Eps* ('bishop') cancelled after *William*.
10,75 LETA. See *Letha* 10,72 note.
10,76 E(DRIC'S) PREDECESSOR. In the MS *antecessor e*, so possibly 'his (*eius*) predecessor', i.e. the Bishop's.
10,77 BRADESTON. In the MS *Breiestuna*; Farley prints *Brerestuna*.
10,81 HELOISE. LDB *Helewis*, OG, Forssner 145, cf. Devon 17,92 note s.v. *Elous*.
FROM BISHOP W(ILLIAM). In the MS *a . W. ep̄o*; Farley misprints *A.W. ēpō*.
10,83 BERARD. See 11,3 note. The name is written above the line.
10,87 ABBOT ALFWOLD. See 8,128 note.
10,90 FOR SUPPLIES. See 8,17 note.
BERNARD. MS *b(er)nar*. For loss of final *d* see PNDB 99, §103.
10,93 REYNOLD OF PIERREPONT. *Reinaldus*, see 10,93 note. Of Pierrepont (Calvados) or perhaps Saint-Nicholas-de-Pierrepont (La Manche) or Saint-Sauveur-de-Pierrepont (La Manche), OEB 106.
VALUE THEN 5s; NOW 20. IE 141, 'Value then 5s; now 10s'.
10a ST. MICHAEL OF NORWICH. In Tombland. In the margin of the MS *f*, see 3 note.
11 BISHOP OSBERN. Of Exeter. Consecrated 27 May 1072. Died 1103. Also a tenant in Surrey, Sussex, Wilts. and Cornwall.
11,3 3 FREEMEN ... BEFORE 1066. MS repeats *iii liberi homines tempore regis Edwardi*.
BERARD. OG masc. personal-name, Forssner 282 and 44 n.5. Cf. 9,219. 10,83. 9,79;219.
DROGO. Of Beuvrière. See 10,61 note.
12,1 EARL R(ALPH). MS *Ro* in error.
12,5 *TOKETORP*. See 4,14 note.
12,6 TOFA. ODan fem. personal-name; the MS *Touu* may represent the OScand fem. acc. sg. inflexion, see PNDB 384. She was the 'free man'.

12,6 THE THIRD. *Tercius*. Perhaps a mistake for quartus, the fourth.
REDGER. OG, masc., PNDB 348.
12,17 EDWIN HELD ALPINGTON. IE 141 adds, 'a certain free man'.
ALPINGTON. *Appletuna*. See 9,68 note.
12 PIGS. IE 141, '6 pigs'.
1 HORSE. IE 141, '1 cob'.
ALSO 8 FREEMEN AND A HALF ... ALWAYS 1 PLOUGH. IE 141, 'To this manor belong 8 Freemen and a half and 2 free men, at 40 acres of land; meadow, 1 acre, 1 plough'.
THE PREDECESSOR OF GODRIC. MS *ante* for *antecessoris*. Cf. 12,34.
MEADOW, 1 ACRE. After '1 acre' MS deletes an *&*.
VALUE THEN 40s; NOW £3 10s. IE 141, 'Value then 30s; now £3', and adds, 'It has 1 league in length and 1 in width. It pays tax of 13d. St. Etheldreda ought to have this land by exchange of Bergh (Apton)'.
12,19 HALF ASHBY (ST. MARY). This is probably what is meant here unless *d'* is in error.
12,20 SIX HALVES OF A FREE MAN. That is, half a free man, six times.
12,24 OF THE SAME MAN'S, HALF OF 30 ACRES. In the MS *ej'dē. dim̃* is possibly in error for *ej'dē Eduini*. If so 'of Edwin's also, 30 acres' is meant.
12,25-26 *ALCMUNTONA*. See 9,52 note. (12,26. MS reads *Alt-* through confusion of *c* and *t* in minuscule script.)
12,30 THE KING AND EARL. Repeated in MS.
12,32 FORFEITED. In the MS *fecit*, in error for *forisfecit*.
12,34 PREDECESSOR. In the MS *ante*, in error for *antecessore*; cf. 12,17.
12,37 7 [FREE MEN]. MS gives the number, but omits the category. VCH p. 127 reads the MS *Suerdest. vii* as an error for the place-name *Suerdestun*, whence an alternative translation 'In SWARDESTON 42 acres; 2 free men ...'.
12,42 17 FREE MEN, 1 C. OF LAND. MS *i. cař. i. car'. terrae* as if intending '1 plough, 1 c. of land'. Presumably *i.cař* is an error.
12,45 ROGER SON OF RAINARD. *Rainard* an OG personal-name, see OEB 195, Forssner 208.
13 HERMER. Of Ferrers. See 8,18 note.
13,6 BORDIN. MS *Bordinus*. Probably the Norman variant, with *o* for *u* (PNDB §§17–18) of the OFr by-name *Burdin* from Med Lat *burdinus* 'little donkey'. See WD 208, cf. Förstemann PN 346, DBS s.n. *Burden*.
13,7 BOUND TO THE FOLD. See 'Fold-rights' in Technical Terms.
13,9 AELMER. MS *helmerus* for *elmerus*, *Elmer* for OE *Aelmer*. See PNDB 148–9 s.n. *Almaer*, and 119, §138.
13,15 WARENBOLD. MS *Warinboldus*; OG masc. personal-name, Forssner 246.
13,16 ROOD. *virgata*. Here a small piece of land is meant.
13,19 THIS ENTRY. Cf. IE 140, 'In REYMERSTON St. Etheldreda held 14 acres of land in lordship. Value 14d. Hermer holds these but his predecessor did not have any customary dues on these'.
13,24 WAGEN. LDB *Vaganus*, for ODan *Vagn* PNDB 402 and n.4. The same personal-name appears as *Waga* DB Staffs., Warwicks., — a nom. form derived presumably from taking *Wagan*, *Wagen* as oblique case weak masculine forms.
14 ST. EDMUND'S. See 1,51 note.
14,1 IN ANOTHER HUNDRED. Freebridge.
14,3 ST. BENEDICT. At Holme.
14,4 26 ACRES OF LAND. FB i 12, '20 acres of land'.
14,7 JOCELYN. Of Loddon, see FD lxxxiv and 109. Tenant of the abbey in Norfolk.
½ C. OF LAND. FB ii 23, '60 acres'.
14,10 FULCHER HOLDS ... FB i 21, 'at (Great) Livermere (in Suffolk) and at (Great) Snarehill, Fulcher the Breton holds 1 c. of land; 3 smallholders'. Cf. LDB Suffolk 14,22.
14,13 MARLINGFORD. FB i 12 adds, '1 c. of land'.
14,14 FOR SUPPLIES. See 8,17 note.
FROM ST. EDMUND. FB i 12 adds, 'and from Abbot Baldwin'.
10 FREE MEN. FB ii 16, '9 free (men)'.
14,16 BERENGER. OG, Forssner 44.
BERENGER HOLDS 20 ACRES. FB ii 16 adds, 'and 3 smallholders'.
KING WILLIAM ... TO ST. EDMUNDS. FB i 13 states that this was on the first occasion when William sought the Saint's support. And adds, 'When he made the grant with bowed head and a ready heart he placed a small sheathed knife on the Saint's altar in the presence of many of the best of his men. Furthermore he gave his letters with his seal, which (the monks) still have, in which he fully granted to the Saint this manor and its appurtenances'.
14,17 THE FULL JURISDICTION. FB i 13 adds, 'and all other customary dues as fully and as

14,19 well as Gyrth the very powerful earl had it in the time of good King Edward'.
MENDHAM. In Suffolk. In FB ii 23 the number of Freemen, villagers and smallholders Frodo was holding in Mendham are totalled together. In LDB there are two entries, one in Suffolk, see LDB Suffolk 14,106.
FRODO. Abbot Baldwin's brother. He held in chief in Essex and Suffolk.
14,21a FROM THE ABBOT. FB i 13, 'from St. Edmund and Abbot Baldwin'.
14,23 FULCHER. In Norfolk a tenant of the abbey at Gissing, Roydon, Semere and Shimpling, FB ii 18. This is Roydon in Diss Hundred.
FULCHER HOLDS ... ALWAYS 3 SMALLHOLDERS. Take this with '40 ACRES ... 2 SMALLHOLDERS' and 14,30. 20 ACRES ... 2 SMALLHOLDERS. For these three entries, cf. FB ii 18, 'At SEMERE, and at SHIMPLING, and at GISSING, [Fulchere] holds 70 acres of land and 4 smallholders'.
14,25 FROM THE SAINT. FB i 14 adds, 'and from Abbot Baldwin'.
14,26 21 ACRES OF MEADOW. FB i 14 and ii 18, '21 acres of land'.
14,27 ½ C. OF LAND AND 6 ACRES. FB i 14, '½ c. of land'.
UNDER HIM. *Sub eo*. Perhaps for *sub eis* 'under them'.
14,29 12 SMALLHOLDERS. FB i 14, '7 smallholders'.
14,35 FRODO. FB ii 22, 'Jocelyn'. Jocelyn was Frodo's tenant, see FD lxxxiv and note.
14,35 FROM THE ABBOT. FB i 14, 'from St. Edmund and Abbot Baldwin'. And adds, 'in exchange for one of the manors of Brictwulf for the reason already mentioned above'. Abbot Baldwin gave Frodo Mendham in Suffolk and Loddon in exchange for 2 manors nearer the abbey, see FB i 14.
3 C. OF LAND AND 10 ACRES. FB i 14, '2 c. of land'; FB ii 22, '3 c. of land'.
11 FREEMEN. FB i 14, '9 Freemen'.
HE ALSO HOLDS. In LDB Frodo is meant. Cf. FB ii 22, 'Jocelyn'. See above.
DAY'S ALLOWANCE. Of food, etc.
14,37 2 PRIESTS ... BEFORE 1066. These are also recorded in FB i 14.
14,38 27 FREEMEN. FB i 14, '24 Freemen'.
11 SMALLHOLDERS. FB i 14, '10 smallholders'.
THEY ARE ASSESSED IN. FB i 14, 'They belong in'.
14,39 5 VILLAGERS. FB ii 15, '6 villagers'.
14,40 7 VILLAGERS. FB i 15, '2 villagers'.
9 FREE MEN AND A HALF. FB i 15, '9 free men'.
IN FRITTON HE ALSO HOLDS. In the MS *Frithetuna*; Farley prints *Frichetuna*.
14,41 1 VILLAGER. FB i 15, '7 villagers'.
11 SMALLHOLDERS. FB i 15, '41 smallholders'.
3 FREE MEN, 3 C. OF LAND. FB i 15, '3 (free men), at 90 acres of land', and adds, '2 smallholders'. FB ii 17, '57 Freemen, at 2 c. of land and 55 acres'.
14,42 64 ACRES. FB i 15, '60 acres'. Note that in LDB *iiii* has been interlined over *lx* to correct to *lxiiii*.
5 FREE MEN, 6 ACRES. FB i 15, '7 free (men), at 7 acres'.
IN NORTON (SUBCOURSE) ... Cf. FB ii 22, 'At NORTON (Subcourse) [Jocelyn] holds 1 c. of land. 5 villagers; 5 smallholders'.
15 ST. ETHELDREDA. See 1,226 note.
LEETS. See 1,71 note.
15,1 THEN 4 PLOUGHS IN LORDSHIP, NOW 3. IE 130, '4 c. of land; always 3 ploughs in lordship'.
THEN 1 COW, NOW 6. IE 130, 'Then 1 head of cattle, now 6'.
1 FREEMAN, AT 6 ACRES FROM THE CHURCH. IE 130, '1 Freeman with 1 c. of land and 6 acres from the church'.
15,2 IN BEXWELL ... VALUE 20s. IE 130, 'Value always 20s'.
IN FINCHAM ... 1 PLOUGH. IEBrev 171, '1 men's plough'.
IN HILGAY 4 SMALLHOLDERS. IEBrev 171, '3 smallholders'.
IN FODDERSTONE ... VALUE 20s. IE 131, 'Value always 20s'.
ON THE DAY KING EDWARD DIED. IE 131 adds here 'and both gave their pledge'.
15,3 TAX OF 4d. IE 131, 'Of a 20s tax it pays 4d'.
15,4 THEN 17 SLAVES. IE 131, 'Then 18 slaves'.
THEN 18 HEAD OF CATTLE, NOW 16. IE 131, 'Then 18 head of cattle, now 11'.
THEN 22 PIGS. IE 131, 'Then 31 pigs'.
47 ACRES OF LAND. IE 131, '40 acres of land in lordship'.
VALUE ALWAYS £15. IE 131, 'Value then £9; now £15'.
15,5 ½ PLOUGH. IEBrev 171, '½ men's plough'.
VALUE 3s. IE 131, 'Value always 3s'.

15,6 THEN 1 PLOUGH. IE 131 adds here, 'in lordship'.
AT 17½ ACRES. IE 131, 'at 17 acres of land and ½ plough'.
15,7 THEN 5 PLOUGHS IN LORDSHIP, NOW 4. IE 132, 'Then 4 ploughs in lordship, now 5' and IEBrev 171 also '5 ploughs in lordship'.
NOW 28. IEBrev 171, '18 villagers'.
NOW 7. IEBrev 171, '8 men's ploughs', and IENV 175, '6 men's ploughs'.
IT HAS 1½ LEAGUES IN LENGTH AND 1 LEAGUE IN WIDTH. IE 132, 'It has 1 league in length and ½ in width'.
34 FREEMEN. IE 132, '34 men'.
AND 6 FREE MEN IN JURISDICTION AND PATRONAGE ONLY. IE 132, 'And 7 others were free men who could sell their lands, but the jurisdiction and patronage remained St. Etheldreda's'.
15,8 NOW 3. IEBrev 171 and IENV 175, '5 men's ploughs'.
3 FREEMEN. IE 132, '30 Freemen'.
IN JURISDICTION AND PATRONAGE ONLY. IE 132, 'who could sell their lands but the jurisdiction and patronage remained St. Etheldreda's'.
THEN 2 SLAVES, NOW 3. IE 132, 'Then 2 pigs, now 3'.
15,9 NOW 2. IEBrev 171 and IENV 175, '3 men's ploughs'.
VALUE 40s. IE 132, 'Value always £2'.
IT HAS 1 LEAGUE IN LENGTH. IE 132, 'It has ½ league in length'.
15,10 3 PLOUGHS IN LORDSHIP. IEBrev 171, '2 ploughs in lordship'.
2 COBS. IE 132, 'Always 2 cobs'.
25 PIGS. IE 132, 'Always 15 pigs'.
3 FURLONGS. IE 132, '4 furlongs'.
12d. IE 132, '11d'.
PRIEST ... VALUE 2s. IE 133, 'Priest ... at 10 acres; he pays 2s'.
ALSO 1 FREEMAN. Before this IE 133 adds, 'In Guiltcross Hundred'.
15,11 2 C. OF LAND. IE 180, '2 c. of thaneland'. For 'thaneland' see 15,13 note.
THEN 2 PLOUGHS IN LORDSHIP, LATER ½. IE 133, 'Then 2 ploughs in lordship, later 3 oxen'.
15,12 ST. E(THELDREDA) HELD. IE 133 adds, 'before 1066'.
JOHN NEPHEW OF WALERAN HOLDS THIS. IE 133, 'John nephew of W(aleran) held this land from the Abbot'.
IN KENNINGHALL. IE 133 adds, 'the King's (manor)'.
15,13 80 ACRES. IE 178 adds, 'and 1 acre of thaneland'. Thaneland, land leased to a tenant which was to remain inalienable.
VALUE 15s. IE 133, 'Value always 15s'.
15,14 THIS ENTRY. Cf. IE 194, 'Wihenoc, a man-at-arms, holds half the village called Oxwick lordship'.
THEN 2 MEN'S PLOUGHS, NOW ½. IE 134, 'Then 2 men's ploughs, later and now ½'.
VALUE 20s. IE 134, 'Value always 20s'.
15,15 3 PLOUGHS. IE 134, 'Always 3 ploughs'. IEBrev 171, '3 men's ploughs'.
½ PLOUGH. IE 134, 'Always ½ plough'.
THE ABBOT HAD THE PATRONAGE. IE 134, 'The Abbot had the patronage only before 1066'.
15,16 NOW 7. IEBrev 171 and IENV 175, '8 men's ploughs'.
15,17 7½ MEN'S PLOUGHS. IENV 175, '7 men's ploughs'.
15d. IE 134 adds, 'of tax'.
15,18 BERNER. IE 134 and 181, 'Berner the Crossbowman'.
1 PLOUGH IN LORDSHIP. IE 134, 'Always 1 plough in lordship'.
15,19 2 C. OF LAND. IE 135, '1 c. of land'.
VALUE THEN 20s. IE 135, 'Value then and later 20s'.
15,20 THIS ENTRY. IE 135 adds, 'R(alph) of Beaufour holds this from the Abbot'. In IE this statement is omitted in 15,19.
15,21 THIS ENTRY. IE 135 adds, 'Robert the Crossbowman holds this from the Abbot'.
15,22 90 ACRES. IE 178, '94 acres'.
ROGER BIGOT HOLDS FROM THE ABBOT, BUT FORMERLY HE HELD FROM THE KING. IE 135 adds, 'the Abbot proved (his claim to) them before the Bishop of Coutances'.
15,23 [ ] C. OF LAND. IE 135, '½ c. of land'. In LDB something has been erased but nothing put in its place.
VALUE OF THE HALF, 10s. In LDB *val'.d.x.sol*'; Farley prints *val'.LX.sol*'. IE 135, 'Value always 20s'.

15,24 HENSTEAD HALF HUNDRED. IE 135, 'Earsham Half Hundred'. LDB is in error.
3 COBS. IE 135, 'Always 3 cobs'.
VALUE THEN £8; NOW 15. IE 135, 'Value then £8; now 20'.
15,25 A FREE MAN HELD. IE 135 adds, 'Alfsi'. See PNDB s.n. *Aelfsige*.
BILLINGFORD. See 1,226 note.
THEN AND LATER 2 PLOUGHS IN LORDSHIP, NOW 3. IE 135, 'Then and later 2 ploughs in lordship, now 1'.
15,26 2 C. OF LAND. IE 136, '2 v(irgates) of land'.
VALUE 20s. IE 136, 'Value always 20s'.
½ IN WIDTH. IE 136, '5 furlongs in width'.
15,27 2 VILLAGERS AND A HALF. IE 136, 'Always 2 villagers and a half'.
1 PLOUGH. IE 136, 'Always 1 plough between him and the men'.
VALUE 10s. IE 136, 'Value always 10s', and adds, 'These appertain in Pulham'.
15,28 THIS ENTRY. IE 136 has the following: 'In HENSTEAD Hundred. St. Etheldreda held BERGH (Apton) before 1066, 4 c. of land. Always 10 villagers; 5 smallholders. Now 2 villagers; 5 smallholders. Now 2 slaves. Always 2 ploughs in lordship; 1 plough (belonging) to the men; meadow, 30 acres. Now 1 mill; woodland for 16 pigs. Then 4 head of cattle; always 2 cobs. 12 Freemen belong to this manor who are in Loddon Hundred. They have 30 acres of land; 11 smallholders; meadow, 1 acre; 2½ ploughs. Also 8 Freemen who are in Henstead Hundred. They have 40 acres of land; always 1 plough. Also 1 free man, at 30 acres of land; always ½ plough. 1 smallholder. [Value] then £2; now £4. Now Godric the Steward holds under St. Etheldreda from his predecessor'.
15,29 1 FREEMAN HELD 12 ACRES BEFORE 1066. IE 136, '1 Freeman, at 12 acres of land', and adds, 'He belongs in Pulham'.
½ PLOUGH. IE 136, 'always ½ plough'.
VALUE 2s. IE 136 adds, 'He also belongs to Pulham'.
AT THE END OF THE NORFOLK SECTION. IE 136 adds, 'Of the whole which we have in Norfolk, £100 8s'; and then 136-137 records certain churches not mentioned in the returns of LDB 'In (East) DEREHAM 1 church, at 30 acres of free land; 1 plough; value 4s. In *TORP* 1 church, at 12 acres of free land; ½ plough; value 18d. In PULHAM 2 churches, at 2 acres; value 3d; in BRIDGHAM 1 church, at 12 acres of free land; value 2s.
In FELTWELL 1 church, at 30 acres of free land; value 4s. In NORTHWOLD 1 church, at 12 acres of free land; value 18d. In (West) WALTON ½ church, at 7 acres of free land; value 2d'.
16 ST. BENEDICT OF RAMSEY. See 1,134 note. In the margin of the MS *fr*, see 3 note.
17 ST. BENEDICT OF HOLME. See 1,194 note.
FOR THE SUPPLIES OF THE MONKS. See 8,17 note.
17,3 WHO SOUGHT THE FOLD. See 1,114 note and 'Fold-rights' in Technical Terms.
17,18 WALERAN. A royal officer, cf. 1,63 note.
17,21 HOVETON (ST. JOHN). The Abbot held here in 1346, *Inquisitions and assessments relating to Feudal Aids with other analogous documents preserved in the Public Records Office AD 1284-1431* (6 vols. London, 1890-1920) III, 484.
17,23 NORTH ERPINGHAM HUNDRED. An error for 'South Erpingham Hundred'.
17,24 WITH HIS WIFE TO THE ABBEY. See 8,8 note.
17,35 THE SITE OF THE ABBEY. The abbey was in Horning.
1 LEAGUE *AND A HALF*. MS *et dim*'; underlined for cancellation?
17,44 SUPPLIES OF THE MONKS. See 8,17 note.
17,51 ROBERT OF GLANVILLE. Of Glanville (Calvados), OEB 89-90.
17,56 *1 MEN'S PLOUGH*. Underlined in MS. For deletion?
17,63 *UNDER THE ABBOT ... ONLY*. Underlined in MS. For deletion?
18 ST. STEPHEN OF CAEN. Benedictine abbey at Caen, Normandy, founded by King William as Duke of Normandy. In the margin of the MS *f*, see 3 note.
19 WILLIAM OF ÉCOUIS. See 1,1 note.
19,1 SKULI. See PNDB 366, ODan *Skuli*. Also as *Escul* incorrectly translated *Aswulf* at DB Notts. 10,23;52. 30,28.
19,2 *RICHARD ... W(ILLIAM)*. Underlined in MS. For deletion?
WULFWY. PNDB 426; LDB *Vruoius* for *Vluoius* (Cf. 19,7) represents *Ulvwius*; with Anglo-Norman *l/r* interchange and *o* for *w*.
19,9 R(OGER) OF EVREUX. Of Evreux (Eure), Loyd 41, OEB 87.
BRUNARD. OG, Förstemann 340.
19,10 ROGER. Of Evreux.
19,11 FATHIR. MS *Fader* for the OScand masc. personal-name, see PNDB 250.

19,12 ROGER. Of Evreux.
19,13 ODER. MS *Odarus* for *Oderus*, OG *Odher*; less likely ON *Authr*; see Forssner 196, Bjorkman *Namenkunde* 64.
19,21 THORKELL HAKO. The by-name is from OWScand *haki*, 'hook, crook', OEB 221.
19,24 REEDHAM. The reading of this place-name is uncertain. Farley read *Redtchā*. The letters '*tc*' are blurred. The original form may well have been *Redāhā*, the abbreviation macron placed too low across open *a* could produce the semblance of *tc*. DG 285 and DEPN s.n. Reedham are unsatisfactory here.
19,35 ST. BENEDICT. Of Holme.
20 R(ALPH) OF BEAUFOUR. See 1,215 note.
20,1 EUDO. Son of Clamahoc. See 1,218 note.
20,2 FATHIR. MS *Fradre*, see PNDB 250, and 19,11 note.
20,3 ST. BENEDICT. Of Ramsey.
20,6 WARING. LDB *Caurincus* for *Guarincus* = *Waringus* from OG *Warin*, OFr *Guarin* whence the forms *Warin* and *Waring*. See 6,4 note.
LATER 2 OXEN. In the MS *hoū*, in error for *boū*.
20,8 ANOTHER COULD BE RESTORED. In the MS *post*, in error for *potest*.
20,18 THIS ENTRY. Cf. IE 195, 'In MATTISHALL Eudo son of Clamahoc holds the land of 7 men who could neither grant nor sell, nor do anything else without the permission of the Abbot (of Ely)'.
20,23 BOSE. Probably the OScand man's name *Bosi*, but OE *Bosa* is possible, see PNDB 207.
20,24 1 PLOUGH. At the end of a line in MS. First half of next line is blank.
20,29 MALET. It is not stated whether this is Robert or William Malet, both of whom held in Norfolk; see OEB 350.
20,31 RADBOD. OG, PNDB 344, Forssner 205. Cf. 9,100 note.
20,32 THOROLD ... HELD. MS *tenet* for *tenuit*.
20,36 *THURKETELIART*. DG, a lost place in Aldeby. The name appears to be an Anglicized form of an OScand 'Thorketel's garth', from ON *garthr* 'enclosure, yard'.
NOW 1 ... MEADOW, 15 ACRES. MS *modo.i.x.i.xv.acrae prati.* The extra figures 10,1, must represent some sort of error, not corrected.
21,2 VALUE THEN 40s. In the MS *val'.xl.sol'*; Farley prints *val'.lx.sol'*.
21,3 ANOTHER FREE WOMAN. Farley *alia*. Dr. von Feilitzen read the MS as *alid* (this also fol. 250b, see 31,20), for the OE fem. personal-name *Aethelgyth*. See PNDB 183, note 6. *Aethelgyth* also appears at 21,20 and 31,20-25.
21,6 IN LENGTH. In the MS *lat'*, in error for *long*.
21,7 10 FREE MEN ... APPERTAINED. MS *jacent*, present-tense, in error.
21,12 STANFORD. MS *estarforda* for *estanforda*, OE *stan-ford* 'stone ford', with Norman prosthetic *e*, and confusion of minuscule *n* and *r*.
21,14 ARNOLD. See Forssner 33; OG *Arnald, -old*, OFr *Arn-, Ernaut*, ME *Arn-, Ernald, -old*.
A CERTAIN FREE MAN. These words should probably have been deleted.
21,19 OLOVA. LDB *O(l)ova*; for ODan *Qlof*, fem., see PNDB 335.
21,20 YAXHAM. Farley *liachesham* for *I iachesham*, i.e. In Yaxham.
21,22 HAROLD'S MAN. In the MS *hēm Heroldi* the 'm' is squeezed in; Farley omits it.
21,24 15 PIGS. In the MS *p'(ost)*, in error for *por*.
ALWAYS 5 [...]. The item is omitted; perhaps 'head of cattle'.
21,25 ALWAYS ½ C. OF LAND. 'Always ½ plough' is possibly meant here.
21,26 AELFRIC. MS *alficus* omits an *(e)r* abbreviation.
21,36 SKEET. LDB *Scheit*; *Schett* 29,4; *Scet*, *Esket* 34,14-15; for ON *skiótr* (from *skjótr* adj., 'swift, fleet') see PNDB 366, Reaney s.n. Skeat. Compare 31,6 note.
22 RALPH OF TOSNY. See 1,211 note.
22,1 THIS ENTRY. Cf. IE 139, 'In NECTON the monks of Ely claim 1 c. of land in lordship against Ralph of Tosny, and the Hundred testifies (to this). In Caldecote ½ c. of land in the same way'.
PAYS 20s SCOT-TAX. See 1,71 note.
22,3 1 CHURCH AT 17 ACRES: VALUE 17d. In the MS *silva ad*, a scribal error for *val'*, see 22,4 note.
22,4 1 CHURCH AT 15 ACRES: VALUE 15d. In the MS *val'* written over *silva ad* which has been erased, cf. 22,3 note.
22,6 THIS ENTRY. See 22,1 note.
22,8 ALL TOGETHER THIS. That is all the land in South Greenhoe.
22,22 1 [MAN] OF HAROLD'S. MS *I.heroldi*. Perhaps for 1 Freeman as in 22,21.
22,23 LATER AND NOW 3. MS *post et modo et iii.* The second *et* superfluous.

22,23 4 SMALLHOLDERS. In the MS *por* in error for *bor*.
23   HUGH OF MONTFORT. See L 23 note.
23,3 1 LEAGUE IN LENGTH. MS *i..ng'* in *long'* probably for *i.leug'* in *long'*.
23,9 WALTER HOLDS. IE 195, 'Walter holds and with him Durand, men of Hugh of Montfort'.
      THIS ENTRY. Cf. IE 186, 'In MARHAM 26 acres, 5 c. of land'.
23,11 AETHELWOLD. LDB *Aelod* for *Aelold* for *Aethel(w)old*, see PNDB s.n. *Aethelweald*.
23,12 L.BONDI. The significance of the capital L has not been discovered.
23,16 THIS ENTRY. Cf. IE 140, 'In GARBOLDISHAM 1 Freeman of St. Etheldreda's, at ½ c.
      of land, whom Hugh of Montfort held and his predecessor Godmund before 1066. The
      Hundred testifies that it has always appertained to the abbey'. Wick is lost in Garboldisham.
24   EUDO THE STEWARD. See 9,184 note.
24,1 RICHARD. Of Sackville. From Secqueville-en-Bessin (Calvados), Loyd 88. However, cf.
      OEB 111, where Sacquenville (Eure) is preferred.
      LISOIS. Of Moutiers. The predecessor of Eudo the Steward. Cf. 66,100.
24,4 THIS ENTRY. Cf. IE 140, 'In BRETTENHAM Eudo the Steward holds 1 freeman, named
      Unban, where the Abbot had the full jurisdiction and patronage. The Hundred testifies
      to this'.
24,6 SKALP. LDB *Calpus*; also 38,4; see PNDB 365 s.n. *Skalpr* ON. The personal-name in LDB
      Essex and Suffolk is in the weak declension, *Skalpi*.
25   WALTER GIFFARD. See 1,19 note.
25,6 NOW (3). In the MS $\overset{o}{m}$ $\overset{}{m}$, probably in error for $\overset{}{m}$ *iii*.
25,15 BODIN OF VERE. Of Ver (La Manche) or possibly Ver (Calvados), OEB 118.
25,23 The Hundred heading is rubricated in the MS.
25,24 The Hundred heading is rubricated in the MS.
      KENE? LDB *Keē*; PNDB 302 rejects as corrupt; but cf. Reaney s.n. *Keen*, for which this
      may be an earlier instance.
25,25 BODIN. Of Vere. Farley prints *ab odino*; in the MS *abodino*.
26   ROGER OF POITOU. See 1,226 note.
26,3 ROBERT BLANCHARD. See 1,7 note.
26,5 EARL RALPH. In the MS *Rob'. comes*, in error for *Rad'. comes*.
      GAVE TO ST. BENEDICT WITH HIS WIFE. See 8,8 note.
27   IVO TALLBOYS. See L 27 note. In the margin of the MS *ñ f'r*, see 3 note.
27,1 12 SHEEP. Unaccountable letter *t* added initially to *oues*.
28   RALPH OF LIMÉSY. See L 28 note. In the margin of the MS *r ñ f*, see 3 note.
29   EUDO SON OF SPIRWIC. Landholder in Lincs., Norfolk and Suffolk. On *Spirwic*, taken
      to be an OG personal-name in OEB 198, see Feilitzen *NoB* 27 (1939) 126, where a
      Breton origin is suggested. In the margin of the MS *ñ*, see 3 above.
29,1 GODRIC, A FREE MAN ... UNDER HAROLD. MS *liber hōc* for *liber homo*.
29,2 BEROLD. LDB *B(er)uoldus*; OG *Berold*, Forssner 282 s.v. *Berardus*, Förstemann 265.
29,4 RICWOLD. LDB *Riuoldus* for *Ricwoldus*, *Rucowaldus* for OG *Ric(h)old* etc., Forssner 215
      s.n. *Ricwald*.
29,6 4 [?FREE MEN]. The category is omitted.
29,7 COULD NEITHER GRANT NOR SELL HIS LAND OUTSIDE THE CHURCH. IE 140,
      'could not sell his land without the Abbot's permission'.
      HERFRITH. LDB *Herfrindus* perhaps a mistake for *Henfridus* 29,8; but it could represent
      OG *Herfrid* Förstemann 769, Feilitzen *PN & BN Winchester* 162.
29,8 HEINFRID. LDB *Henfridus*; also *Hainfridus* 29,11; OG *Heim-*, *Heinfrid*, Forssner 144;
      cf. *Herfrith* 29,7 note.
      GODWIN. *Covinus*, see PNDB 273.
29,9 AND GYRTH. Or possibly 'and of Gyrth's'.
29,11 HEINFRID. See 29,8.
30   DROGO OF BEUVRIÈRE. See 10,61 note. In the margin of the MS *fr*, see 3 note.
30,4 AELWARD. LDB *Ailward*, for OE *Aethelweard*, cf. 9,158 note.
30,5 MARWEN. LDB *Maru(u)en*, for the OE fem. personal-name *Maerwynn* PNDB 326.
31   RALPH BAYNARD. In the margin of the MS *ñ*, see 3 note.
31,6 *SCHIETESHAGA*. In Hempnall. The place-name is 'Skeet's enclosure', from OE *haga* and
      the OScand personal-name *Skiotr*, see 21,36 note and PNDB 366.
31,10 EINBOLD. OG *Einbald*, *Aginbold*, Förstemann 38.
31,11 WIMUND. *Wimundus*, for OE *Wigmund* or OScand *Vigmundr*, PNDB 413.
31,14 *IERPSTUNA*. Farley *Lerpstuna*. See 1,239 note.
31,20 THEN 3 SLAVES. ALWAYS 1 PLOUGH. IE 137, 'Always 3 slaves; 1 plough'.
      2 COBS. IE 137, '2 horses'.

31,20 THEN 40 SHEEP, NOW 18. IE 137, 'Then 40 sheep, now 24'.
ST. ETHELDREDA CLAIMS THIS LAND. IE 137 adds, 'in lordship'.
31,21 SHEEP. In the MS *b'* but sheep are probably meant.
31,23 (SHOULDHAM) THORPE. MS *Carboistorp* here and 66,14. *Thorp* 21,8. It is not yet ascertained whether *Carbois—* represents an OFrench by-name *Gardebois* (see DBS s.n. *Warboys*, perhaps also Dauzat s.n. *Guerbois*), or the Norman French version of a place-name like Warboys Hunts. (see EP-N Soc. III 226).
31,35 VIRGATE. A quarter-carucate is probably meant here, but possibly a quarter-acre or rood.
THE 6. The 6 Forfeitures, see 7,16 note.
31,37 SOLDIER. *Solidarius*, a mercenary soldier.
31,43 13 FREEMEN. Note that here the 'sokemen' are also 'free men'.
4½ C. OF LAND. Possibly '4½ ploughs' is meant (*c.* for *caruca* rather than *carucata*).
32 RANULF PEVEREL. See 9,184 note. In the margin of the MS what appears to be *f* altered to *n*. See 3 note.
32,2-7 WARIN(G). See 6,4 note.
33 LAND OF ROBERT GERNON. THE HUNDRED. In the MS *TERRA RODB'TI GRENONIS H.* has been written on one line and not two as printed by Farley. In the margin of the MS *fr*, see 3 note.
ROBERT GERNON. The by-name is from OFr *grenon* 'moustache', OEB 314-315.
33,4 *NARUESTUNA*. Location unidentified. The etymology of the name is not obvious; the final element is OE *tun*.
34 PETER OF VALOGNES. See 8,106 note. In the margin of the MS *ñ*, see 3 note. Also in the margin numbered XXXIIII; the number is not printed by Farley.
34,2 NOW 646. In the MS *de.CXLVI.*, probably in error for *DCXLVI*.
34,8 THYRI. LDB *Tirus*; cf. *Terius* Suffolk 41,11, PNDB 383; these appear to be masculine inflexions of the ODan fem. personal-name *Thyri*, PNDB 397, Bjorkmann NP 164, Fellows-Jensen 319.
34,9 RALPH FAT. LDB *Faetus* for OE *Faetta*, 'the fat', OEB 312.
34,12 THE HUNDRED OF GALLOW. In error for Holt.
34,15 FREEMEN. In the MS *sol'*, in error for *soć*.
PIGS. In the MS *post* in error for *por*.
34,15 HALF A HUNDRED. *d.c.*; or possibly 600 is meant, *D.C.*
34,20 FISH. LDB *Fisc* represents either OE *fisc*, FISH, or ON *fiskr*, FISKE, see PNDB 251; Reaney, DBS s.nn.
35 ROBERT SON OF CORBUCION. In the margin of the MS *ñ*, see 3 note.
35,2 GUNFRID. On the personal-name see 10,16 note.
35,3 GIFARD. OG personal-name, Forssner 220, not to be confused with the OFr by-name *Giffard*, OEB 219.
35,13 ALDWIN. PNDB 242 s.n. *Ealdwine*.
35,16-17 GIFARD. See 35,3 note.
35,16 WHEN HE WENT INTO THE MARSH. See 1,197 note.
35,18 *IARPESTUNA*. Farley *Larpestuna*. See 1,239 note.
36 RANULF BROTHER OF ILGER. Tenant-in-chief in eight counties. OEB 187 cites Ranulph *son* of Ilger from IE 149, 195. In the margin of the MS *fr*, see 3 note.
36,2 ST. B(ENEDICT). Of Holme.
36,7 THIS ENTRY. Below fol. 216a are the figures 65, 120, 90 in roman numerals. These, which are not reproduced by Farley, are written in a small script and were probably inscribed later. They are clearly connected with the number of carucates at which the holdings of the landholder, here Ranulf brother of Ilger, were assessed. Cf. also 48,8 note, and see further R. Welldon Finn, *Domesday studies. The eastern counties* (London, 1967), 77.
37 TIHEL. See 2,11 note. In the margin of the MS *f*, see 3 note.
37,2 GUERRI. LDB *Guericus*; also DB Middx. 3,16 *Gueri* (wrongly translated *Gyrth*); OFr *Guerri*, OG *Werric, Wericus*, Forssner 251.
38 ROBERT OF VERLY. Of Verly (Aisne), OEB 118. In the margin of the MS *f*, see 3 note.
38,1 (EAST) HARLING. A Verly held here in 1302, *Inquisitions and assessments relating to Feudal Aids with other analogous documents preserved in the Public Records Office AD 1284-1431* (6 vols., London, 1899-1920) III, 441.
38,3 RODING. In Essex. See DB Essex ENf.
38,4 SALT-HOUSE. In the MS *sol'*, in error for *sal'*.
39 HUMPHREY SON OF AUBREY. In the margin of the MS *f*, see 3 note.
40 HUMPHREY OF BOHUN. Of Bohon (La Manche), OEB 73. Ancestor of the Earls of Hereford, Ellis i 383n. In the margin of the MS *f*, see 3 note.

41	RALPH OF FOUGÈRES. Of Fougères (Ille-et-Vilaine), OEB 88. In the margin of the MS *f*, see 3 note.
42	GILBERT SON OF RICHERE. OEB 195. Also Gilbert son of Richere of Aigle, named from Laigle (Orne), France, OEB 66, in DB Surrey 24. In the margin of the MS *nich'* for 'nihil', see 3 note.
42,1	MILDENHALL. In Suffolk.
43	ROGER OF RAISMES. See 1,226 note.
43,2	BILLINGFORD. *Plestuna*. See 1,226 note.
44	JUDICAEL THE PRIEST. In the margin of the MS *f*, see 3 note. JUDICAEL. LDB *Iuikel* (*Iuikell* in list of Landholders), and *Iuichel* LDB Suffolk 64, represent an Anglo-Norman development (intervocalic *d* lost) of OBret *Judicael*, PNDB 301, Reaney s.n. *Jekyll*.
44,1	EDRIC. Of Laxfield.
45	COLBERN THE PRIEST. In the margin of the MS $\bar{n}$, see 3 note. COLBERN. Alias *Colbert*; here *Colebern(us)*, but *Colebertus* in list of landholders; a confusion of ON *Kolbjorn* (Bjorkmann NP 83; Rygh GP 164) which seems rare in England, and OFr *Colbert* (OG *Colobert*, Forssner 55), a name which appears in Devon, Hants., Chesh., Lincs. The confusion is probably due to ambiguous pronunciation of unstressed *-er(.)* ending. Perhaps the landholders list substitutes a better known name for the less known original in the returns?
45,1	CHURCH OF ST. NICHOLAS. Thought to be the church of St. Nicholas outside the gates of Norwich in Bracondale, cf. *Inquisitions and assessments relating to Feudal Aids with other analogous documents preserved in the Public Record Office AD 1284-1431* (6 vols., London, 1899-1920) III, 606.
46	EDMUND SON OF PAYNE. Also in Somerset 46,21-23, Hants. 69,51; see OEB 193. In the margin of the MS *f*, see 3 note.
46,1	REYNOLD THE PRIEST *Rainaldus*, see 10,35 note.
47,2	HOFWARD. See PNDB 291. This is probably an OE by-name from *hofweard* 'house guard', but could be an erroneous form of OG *Howard* PNDB 292, Forssner 154.
48	TOVI. In the margin of the MS $\bar{n}$ (?)$ac^{us}s$. Although the reading of the second word is uncertain it seems that Tovi did not make a return, see 3 note.
48,3	ST. BENEDICT. Of Holme.
48,8	THIS ENTRY. Below fol. 256a are the figures 5,75, 30, 2½, 155, 30, 30, 60, 60, 25, 18. See 36,7 note.
49	JOHN NEPHEW OF W(ALERAN). He is also named in Essex. John son of Waleran appears in Cambs., Essex and Suffolk. In the margin of the MS *f r*, see 3 note.
49,6	ALSO 1 FREE MAN, 30 ACRES OF LAND. THE JURISDICTION IS ST. ETHELDREDA'S. Cf. IE 140, 'In BRIDGHAM John nephew of Waleran holds 1 free man, where the abbot has the full jurisdiction only'. Cf. also IE 195. STERGAR. Anglicized form of an OScand man's name recorded in OSwedish, *Styrger*, but perhaps there was also an ON version *Styrgeirr*; see PNDB 377.
49,7	GUARD. Or housecarl. A descriptive term probably denoting a trained soldier.
49,8	THURTON? *Termentuna*. The identification is not certain. The names are not the same, compare Thurton Ey (*Tortuna* 19,34. 21,34) and Thurton Lo (*Tortuna* 9,64;68. 15,28).
50	ROGER SON OF RAINARD. In the margin of the MS *f r*, see 3 note.
50,6	THORODD. LDB *Toradre* for ON *Thoroddr*, see PNDB 386, 396; ON *Thoraldr* (i.e. *Thorold*) seems less likely.
50,9 & 10	THESE TWO ENTRIES. Underlined for cancellation because entered at 57,1;2, fol. 270, with slight difference. See VCH p. 189 note. They belong to the holding of Ralph son of Hagni (ODan personal-name *Haghni*, PNDB 282).
50,9	WESTER. ON *Vestarr*, man's name, PNDB 403. 16 PIGS. In the MS *p'(ost)*, in error for *por*.
50,12	COULD BE THERE. Lat. *fieri* for the usual *esse*.
51	BERNER THE CROSSBOWMAN. In the margin of the MS *f*, see 3 note.
52	GILBERT THE CROSSBOWMAN. In the margin of the MS *f.*, see 3 note.
53,1	IN LENGTH. In the MS *lat̄*, in error for *lonḡ*.
55	RABEL THE ENGINEER. Also Rabel the Carpenter. In the margin of the MS *f*, see 3 note.
55,1	3 PIGS. In the MS *p'(ost)*, in error for *por*. IN LENGTH. In the MS *leug*, in error for *lonḡ*.
56	HAGNI. See 1,81 note.
56,9	IN THURNING 1. Presumably '1 Freeman' as in 56,8.
57	SON OF HAGNI. Cf. 1,81 note.

57,1 & 2 THESE TWO ENTRIES. Cf. 50,9 & 10 note.
57,2 NOW R(ALPH) HOLDS. IE 141, 'now Roger son of Rainard holds', in error.
58 ULFKETEL. In the margin of the MS *f*, see 3 note.
58,1 IN LENGTH. In the MS *leuḡ*, in error for *lonḡ*.
60 ALDITH. LDB *Aldit*, for OE *Ealdgyth*, PNDB 240.
61 GODWIN HALDANE. The by-name means 'half-Dane', OEB 221. In the margin of the MS *f*, see 3 note.
61,1 IN WIDTH. In the MS *lato*, in error for *lonḡ*.
61,2 AILDAG. LDB *Aildeig* represents a partial Anglicization of OG *Aildag*, PNDB 141.
62 STARCULF. Probably OG *Starculf* Forssner 226, PNDB 373; but Fellows-Jensen 263 indicates that Anglo-Scand *Starkulfr* is possible.
65,16 H. MALEMAYNS. The by-name is OFr *Malesmains* 'bad hands', see OEB 350.
65,17 THIS ENTRY is repeated, see 1,208 note.
BOARD-LAND. Land appertaining to the table (*mensa*), i.e. the provision of food. Farley and facsimile read *inensa* for *mensa*.
66,4 OF THESE. MS has an unexplained *h* before *de his*.
66,5 4 C. OF CORN. Or possibly '4 loads of corn' is meant.
66,13 IN FULL MOIETY. i.e. Bordin and Hermer have equal rights over the 3 men.
66,16 ST. BENEDICT. At Holme.
66,26 (?)THUXTON. *Torvestuna*. This identification is not certain. *Torveston* does not represent the name Thuxton, see 1,86 note. It may be a mistake for *Torverton* representing THURLTON (*T(h)urvertuna* 1,241 etc., 'Thurferth's farm') or another place of that name.
66,28 ADELHELM. LDB *Adeledmus* for *Adelelmus*, representing OE *Aethelhelm* or more likely OG *Adel(h)eln*, see PNDB 184.
66,33 3s. Corrected from 5s.
66,36 WIHENOC OF BURLEY. See OEB 38; the place of origin is unidentified.
66,39 24 FREE MEN. 25 are accounted for.
66,53 30 ACRES WHICH A FREE MAN HELD. IE 137, '1 Freeman, at 30 acres'.
ALWAYS 3 SMALLHOLDERS. ½ PLOUGH. IE 137, '3 smallholders. Always ½ plough'.
66,54 ST. BENEDICT. Of Ramsey.
66,55 1 FREE MAN. IE 131, '1 Freeman'.
VALUE 4s. IE 131, 'Value always 4s'.
66,57 ROBERT. Malet.
66,60 R(OBERT). Malet.
HAS NOW BEEN HOLDING HIM. For *modo tenebat*.
66,61 WILLIAM GROSS. Latin *grossus* 'fat'.
66,62 1 FREE MAN. Corrected from 5.
66,78 ST. BENEDICT. Of Holme.
66,79 2 ORAE. See 1,24 note.
66,81 ASLAC. LDB *Anslec* indicates OScand *Ásleikr*, a variant of *Aslak*, PNDB 168.
66,85 RALPH OF NORON. Of Noron (Calvados), OEB 103.
66,88 W(ILLIAM) OF PARTHENAY. Of Parthenay (Deux-Sèvres) or possibly Parthenay-de-Bretagne (Ille-et-Vilaine), OEB 105.
66,89 THE £20 ... IN BINHAM. Binham was valued at £20, see 34,16.
66,90 WARIN. See WARING 6,4 note.
66,91 GODRIC OF ROSS. The place of origin of the surname *de Rossa* is unidentified, see OEB 49.
66,94 EUDO CLAMAHOC. Cf. Eudo son of Clamahoc, 1,11 note. See OEB 216.
66,100 LISOIS. Of Moutiers. Cf. 24,1.
66,101-102 RABEL THE CARPENTER. The same as Rabel the engineer, L 55 note.
66,101 FINCH. Latin *Fincus* for OE *Finc*, by-name from *finc* 'a finch'.
66,107 WALTER CANUTE. LDB *Canud*. See OEB 215, where the derivation is discussed—from the OScand personal-name *Knutr*, or from Med Lat *canutus* 'grey-haired'. Cf. DB Wilts. 28,9 note.

INDEX OF PERSONS

Familiar modern spellings are given where they exist. Unfamiliar names are usually given in an approximate late 11th century form, avoiding variants that were already obsolescent or pedantic. Spellings that mislead the modern eye are avoided where possible. Two, however, cannot be avoided; they are combined in the name 'Lèofgeat', pronounced 'Leffyet', or 'Levyet'. The definite article is used before bynames where there is a probability that they described the individual, rather than one of his ancestors. While an attempt has been made, with the aid of additional information supplied by IE and ICC, to differentiate individuals with the same name, there remain several individuals who cannot be so differentiated. Readers are therefore advised that a group of references given under a single name (e.g. Aelmer) do not necessarily refer to the same individual. *References are to persons named in the Text of LDB, to those identified in the notes from information supplied by IE or ICC, and to jurors named in the Appendix. All names or name-forms which are not contained in LDB itself are printed in italics, as are the chapter-numbers of listed landholders.*

A.	9,10;89. 10,81
Abba	1,61. 9,7
Acwulf	7,8
Adelhelm	13,20. 66,28
Aelfeva	8,24-25;34-35;87
Aelfric	1,2;77;136;145. 4,26. 6,6. 8,18. 9,49;114. 11,1. 21,26. 29,5-7. 35,6. 51,5. 52,1
A(elmer)	10,6-7;9;13
(Bishop) A(elmer)	10,12
Bishop A(e)lmer	1,28;61;68. 8,12. 9,20;30-31;178. 10,2-13; 16-17;19-21;25-26;28;35;42-43;45-47;60; 63;65-68. 25,3. 31,5. 65,8
(Bishop) A(e)lmer	10,10-11;23;28;70;72-75;79-81;85-92
A(e)lmer son of Godwin	65,2-6
A(e)lmer Stigand's brother	10,30;33
A(e)lmer	8,14;127. 9,64;150. 10,10-11. 13,9 and note. 14,25. 19,39.64
A(e)lmer's son	4,8
Aelward	30,4
Aelward of Felbrigg	9,158
Aethelgyth	21,3(?);20. 31,20-25;34-35;37. 42,1
Aethelsige	9,86
Aethelsige, see Alsi	
Aethelward, see Aelward	
Aethelwold	23,11
Aethelwold, see also Alwold	
Aildag	61,2
A(i)lwin of Thetford	9,100;104;105. 65,10
A(i)lwin (of Thetford)	9,72-73;75;81;89-93. 66,84
Young A(i)lwin	8,133
A(i)lwin	1,28;41;78. 9,145;183. 19,31. 30,3. 43,1;4. 66,67
A(i)lwin, see also A(i)lwy (of Thetford, etc.)	
A(i)lwy of Colchester, a reeve	17,22
A(i)lwy of Thetford	1,239. 9,14;25;29;60
A(i)lwy	9,5;12;16;19-20;23;62;70;100;101;108;157; 228. 10,30. 66,78
A(i)lwy, see also A(i)lwin	
Aitard of Vaux	1,120-122
Aitard, R. Bigot's man	1,105;111
Aitard	9,26;94;140;160;165;198. 66,80
Count Alan	1,11;57;197;215. 4.9;49. 10,19. 12,35. 32,1. 66,63
Count A(lan)	10,59
Alan, see Richard	

Albert	26,2-5
Aldith	*60*
Aldreda	9,11
Aldwin	35,13
Aldwulf	20,26
Aldwy the priest	9,82
Alfheah	4,2;17;29. 9,233
Alfhere	1,77;135. 26,5. 27,1. 49,3. 54,1
Alflaed	1,150. 8,29
Alfred the priest	2,12
Alfred	1,111;120-121. 2,8. 9,29;78. *59*. 66,82
Alfsi	1,94 note. 15,25 note
Abbot Alfwold	8,128. 10,87
Alfwold, see also Alwold	8,117. 9,150
Earl Algar	9,33. 10,25;30
Algar Trec	9,48
Algar (free man of Harold)	1,169-171
Algar	1,173;182;229. 4,50. 6,4-5. 9,6;63. 10,32. 35,9. 41,1. 44,1. 66,41
Alnoth	1,105-112. 8,47
Alric (thane)	29,10
Alsi, King Edward's thane	1,175
Alsi	1,94-95;177-179. 9,77-78;86. 10,71;91. *15.25 IE.* 52,4. 66,61;102
Alstan an Englishman	9,75
Alstan	4,3;21. 7,7. 9,8;104. 12,42. 34,5. 50,1
Alward of Newton	1,64
Alward	9,146
Alward, see Aelward	
Alwin, see A(i)lwin	
Alwold	8,11. 9,150
Alwold, see also Aethelwold, Alfwold	
Alwy, see A(i)lwy	
Anand	6,1.8,*16* note; *46 IE*. 10,33. 34,2. 35,10
Ansculf	12,39
Ansculf Unlike	1,61
Ansgar	9,26. 35,9
Ansgot	9,162
Ansketel the reeve	10,58
Ansketel son of Ospak	66,99
Ansketel	4,32;47
Arnold	21,14
Asford	1,58. 8,97. 9,174
Asgar the constable	4,49. 31,5
Asgar	31,2;5
Askell	65,13
Aski	65,13
Aslac	12,16;19-20. 66,81
Athelstan	4,35
Aubrey, see Humphrey	
Auti	38,1
Azelin	9,219
Baldwin the reeve	10,71
Baldwin	1,61. 10,28
Baynard	13,10. 31,6-7;11;14;34;39;44. 66,35
Baynard, see Ralph, Roger	
Beorhtflaed	14,21
Berard	9,219. 20,83. 11,3
Berenger	14,16;37
Bernard	10,90
Berner	15,18
Berner the crossbowman	1,3. 15,*18 note*. *51*
Berold	29,2

Bloc, see Walter	
Bodin de Vere	25,15
Bodin	1,57. 25,25
Bondi	1,83. 9,111;147. 10,53. 20,4. 21,22. 23,1-5;7-8; 10-13;17-18. 34,18. 36,1;6. 58,2
Bondi, see L. Bondi	
Bordin	13,6;19. 66,12;20-21;23
Bose, see Leofric	
Boteric	21,19;22;28
Bovi	49,1-2
Brant	35,12
Brictric	19,24. 35,4
Brictwulf	14,*35 note*
Brode	8,55
Brodo	66,67
Brown, Roger Bigot's reeve	1,2
Brunard	19,9
Burghard	1,61. 6,6
Clamahoc, see Eudo	
Cock Hagni	9,83-84
Cola	4,49
Colbern the priest	45, note
Colbert the priest	L45, note
Coleman	9,98. 20,13. 24,7
Corbucion, see Robert	
Drodo of Beuvrière	1,57 note
Drogo of Beuvrière	1,57 note. 8,134;137. 10,61. *30*
Drogo	8,82. 11,3. 66,59
Durand	9,216. 23,*9 IE*
Earlgyrth	14,16-17
Edmund son of Payne	*46*
Edric of Laxfield	1,203;205. 4,38;39;40;51;53. 7,4;5-8;9-13. 9,88;105. 35,16
Edric (Count Alan's man)	1,197. 4,51
Edric, Edric of Laxfield's man	4,39;41-42
Edric the falconer	*63*
Edric	1,104;114-120;128;131;172;188;197. 4,4;42; 51. 7,3;9;11;16-19. 8,123-125;127;132. 9,18; 21;48;71;148;166;181. 10,56;76. 12,5. 17,18; 51. 19,35. 21,29. 25,1;12. 26,1. 29,8. 30,2. 36,5. 44,1. 66,80
Edric, see Godwin	
Edwin	1,183;229. 9,30;139. 10,49. 12,4;7-18;22-25; 27;30;32. 19,23;36. 35,8. 66,82
Edwy the King's reeve	4,20
Einbold	31,10;43
Eli	10,4;28;73;79;81
Englishman, see Alstan	
Englishman, see William	
Enisant Musard	4,14
Bishop Erfast	1,59;61;69. 10,21;27;29;43;53-54;69;78;81; 90;93
Erfast	1,57
Estan	4,22
Estgar	8,13 note
Eudo Clamahoc	66,94
Eudo son of Clamahoc	1,11;218. 20,*18 note*. 22,11
Eudo son of Spirwic	1,221. 9,100. *29*
Eudo the steward	9,184. *24*. 66,100
Eudo, Earl Ralph's man	1,7
Eudo	20,1;7;31-32. 66,90
Count Eustace	*5*. 8,31. 66,86

Everwin	1,61
Ewicman	1,62. 21,37
Fathin	4,*2 note*
Fathir	19,11;13. 20,2;8
Finch	66,101
Fish	34,20
Frank	8,137
Frederic	8,6-7;22;33;47;62-63;66-67;94-95;98;111; 113;116-118;130;132;137. 66,68
Fredregis	8,67
Frenchman	31,16-17
Frodo	14,19;22;35;42-43
Fulbert (priest of Hermer's)	1,61
Fulbert	13,10;17
Fulcher, the Abbot's man	1,66
Fulcher the Breton	14,*10 note*
Fulcher	8,59. 14,10;23;30
G.	1,61, see note
G. of Laxfield	4,41
Gauti	65,13
Genred	9,29;32
Geoffrey of Baynard	31,1-5
Geoffrey Ridel	9,88
Geoffrey	4,18;44. 10,37. 29,1;3. 31,8;17;31;44
Gerard, William of Warenne's man-at-arms	8,*37 note*;*44 note*
Gerard the watchman	1,61
Germund	66,63
Gifard	35,3 note;16-17
Gilbert son of Richere	42
Gilbert the crossbowman	1,61. *52*
Gilbert the watchman	1,61
Gilbert	8,66
God ...	9,86
Goding	1,144
Godmund	23,16 note
Godram	4,26
Godric of Heigham	65,7
Godric of Ross	66,91
Godric the steward	1,7;127;142. 9,30;42;111;190. *12*. 15,28 note. 35,8. 48,4. 66,81
Godric	1,10;57;71-75;77-78;80;87;90-91;96;111; 120;122;124;131-132;133a;144;174;195; 201;209;213. 4,10;31. 6,1. 8,5;37;71. 9,193-194;196-198;200;204;232. 10,39;71;81. 12,38. 15,18. 17,55;63. 20,19-20. 25,18. 26,5. 29,1. 31,11. 32,3. 66,42;64;82;84-85; 91;92
Godwin, freeman of Edric's	29,8
Godwin, Gyrith's freeman	29,8-9
Godwin Haldane	*61*
Godwin Halden	1,216
Godwin of Scotton	9,87
Godwin the thane	1,198
Godwin Tokeson son of Toki	29,9
Godwin uncle of Earl Ralph	1,61?;144;184
Godwin	1,61?;133;193-194;198;200. 2,7. 4,6;38. 5,4 7,1. 8,1. 9,15;26;43-44;63;167;170;173. 10,67. 19,8;25. 20,7;22;35. 21,9;29;31. 35,8. 38,2-3. 47,3;5-6. 52,3. 66,5
Godwin, see A(e)lmer	
G(odwin?)	1,61
Grimketel	8,123
Guerri	37,2-3
Gunfrid the archdeacon	10,16

Gunfrid	10,18. 35,2;4-5
Gunni	4,23
Guy of Anjou	1,1. 5,1
Guy	8,31
Guy, see Osmund	
Guy, see Thurstan	
Earl Gyrth	14,*17 note*. 66,16
Gyrth	1,29;45-46;59-60;148;155;192;195. 4,9-10;15;34; 54. 6,6. 8,8. 9,3a;89;146;159-160;169-170; 182;234. 10,20;22;44;67;69;78;81. 12,6;18. 14,17. 19,20;36. 25,23. 29,8-9. 33,2;6. 34,9. 48,2. 50,9. 52,3. 53,1. 57,1. 58,3. 61,2-3. 64,1-2. 66,89. *ESf 2*
Gyrth, see Godwin	
H. Malemayns	65,16
Hagni	1,81-82;84;86-87;182. 6,2. 9,2. 12,42. *56*
Haimer	1,33
Hardekin	9,102
Hardwin	19,20;27-28;36. 28,2
H(arold)	10,43
Earl Harold	3,2. 4,26;35
Harold	1,1;2;4-6;15;45;53;55;57;61;141;169. 4,15; 18-20;22;53. 5,1. 8,8. 9,29;33;40;46;88;124; 138. 9,104;117;143;149;151;172;174;176; 178;231;233. 10,38;40;55-58. 20,9;19;24; 31. 21,16-17;22;33-34. 22,1;10-13;16;21-23. 24,5-6. 25,10-11;20. 26,3;5. 27,2. 29,1. 31,17; 44. 34,13. 35,1-2. 36,1;6-7. 37,3. 41,1. 48,2. 51,5-6. 66,79;88;93;97
Heinfrid	29,8;11
Helmer, see Aelmer	
Heloise	10,81
Henry	32,7
Herbert, Roger Bigot's chamberlain	66,86
Hereberd the ditcher	1,61
Herewulf	66,42
Herfrith	29,7-8;11
Herlwin son of Ivo	66,51
Herlwin	21,15;29;34
Herlwin, see Ralph	
Herman	21,8
Hermer of Ferrers	13. 66,1-34
Hermer	1,66. 8,18. 9,187;191;227. 15,2. 66,48-49;106
Hermer, see Fulbert, William	
Hervey de Vere	1,61. 25,15
Hervey	4,49
Hildebrand the lorimer	1,61
Hofward	47,2 note
Hubert	7,9;11
Earl Hugh	*6.* 66,97-98
Hugh de Montfort	10,53. 15,1. *23*. 23,*9 note*; *16 note*. 34,6. 66,95-96
Hugh of Corbon	9,48. 66,83
Hugh of Houdain	9,182
Hugh of Port	2,3
Hugh, William of Écouis's man	1,61
Hugh	1,61. 8,18;50;99;211;230;232. 10,15. 19,25; 28;37. 20,11;23. 21,4
Humphrey of Bohun	*40*
Humphrey of Culey	9,5;84
Humphrey of St. Omer	8,8

Humphrey nephew of Ranulf Ilger's brother	1,192
Humphrey son of Aubrey	39. *ESf* 7
Humphrey	1,57;192. 7,6. 8,137. 33,1. 34,18. 35,6-7;10-11; 15. 36,1-2;5-7. 66,103
Huscarl	1,192
Ilger, see Ranulf	
Ilving, see Ylfing	
Ingold	48,3
Ingulf	10,20. 19,15;21
Isaac	1,66. 9,26;32;86. 47
Ivo father of Reynold	8,29
Ivo Tallboys	1,131. 4,44;51. 27
Ivo, see Herlwin	
Jocelyn of Norwich	65,15
Jocelyn	14,7-8; 36;42 note
Jocelyn	*14,35 note*
John nephew of Waleran	8,51. 15,12. 17,18. *49*. 49,6 note
Judicael the priest	44
Judichael, the Earl's falconer	1,131
Kene	25,24
Ketelbern	4,46
Ketel Friday	1,208. 65,17
Ketel	1,29;92;147;183. 8,124;126;133. 9,146. 10,90. 13,9. 19,15. 21,2;24-25;27-28;32. 26,2. 32,2-5. 48,1-3. 49,8. 60,1
L. Bondi	23,12
Lambert	8,102;109
Leofric of Thorndon	7,14
Leofric son of Bose	20,23
Leofric	12,19-20. 21,10. 31,44
Leofsi	8,61
Leofstan	1,195. 9,86. 35,5. 37,1-2
Leofwin	20,10-11
Leofwold	13,24. 35,2
Lisois	24,1-4;6. 66,100
Lokki	8,6
Lord	4,31
Lovell	31,28;33
Malemayns, H.	65,16
Malet	20,29 note. See also Robert Malet, William Malet
Mann	34,7
Marwen	30,5
Mauger	9,212
Maynard the watchman	1,61
Maynard	1,61. 9,160. 66,51
Modgifu	4,50
Morcar	7,10
Morel	10,11
Mortain, the count of	3
Morvan	29,7
Nicholas, Earl Hugh's goldsmith	66,98
Nigel	31,45. 35,8;13-14
Norman	31,38;42
O.	10,13
Oder	19,13;27;31;40. 20,4;9;26;28
Odo	27,1
Offa	9,168
Oger	8,89
Oia	1,147 note
Oio?	*1,147 note*
Olova	21,19
Ordgar	5,1-3. 39,1
Ording	20,34
Bishop Osbern	L*11*

Osbern	9,153
Osbern the thane	50,11-12
Bishop Osbert	L11 *note*
Osbert	8,128. 9,225. 33,1-3;5-6. 37,1-3. 49,4-5
Osferth	9,154
Osgot	6,3. 12,1
Oslac	9,221-222. 25,17
Osmund uncle of Guy	8,31
Osmund	1,72. 5,2. 6,7. 8,18;91-93
Ospak	1,42. 9,150
Ospak, see Ansketel	
Osward	8,44. 12,2. 30,1
Payne's daughter	46,1
Payne	9,130. 46,1
Payne, see Edmund	
Petch, see William	
Peter of Valognes	8,106. 10,22. *34*. 66,87;89
Peter	1,61. 8,113
Phanceon	4,2 note;16
Quintin	19,20;32
Rabel the carpenter	66,101-102
Rabel the engineer	*55*
Rabel	1,61
Rada	1,128-131
Radbod	20,31
Radbod Lang?	9,*100 note*
Radfrid	14,41. 15,11. 16,5. 19,2;6;9
Rainard, see Roger	
Rainer	8,100;110. 66,108
Earl Ralph (junior)	10,21
Earl Ralph (senior)	1,151;153. 10,21
Earl Ralph	1,7;10;57;64;66;71;81;139;147;185;197;209; 211; 213. 4,*15-16 IE*; 28; 30;44-45. 8,10;56-57. 9,88. 10,8. 14,32. 17,50. 32,1. 34,17. 47,1-2. 51,5-7
Earl Ralph's wife	8,10
Earl R(alph)	1,63-64;75;95;111;131;152;172;201-222;216. 4,1;26;52;56. 8,5. 9,4;13;30;49;160. 10,59; 69;71. 12,1;42. 15,18; 17,1;30. 19,25. 21,14. 26,5. 38,2-3. 51,9. 52,3. 65,8;17. 66,42;80-81; 83-84
(Earl) Ralph	1,7;77-78;136;181-182;194-195. 4,42. 6,1. 19,20. 27,2. 47,7. 58,3. 66,98
(Earl) R(alph)	1,73;97;106;120-121;161. 4,51. 66,64;102
Ralph Baynard	1,1. 9,232. 20,13. *31*
Ralph Berlang?	9,100 note
Ralph Fat	34,9
Ralph of Beaufour	1,11;66;215;218;239;241. 6,7. 15,19;*20 note*. 19, 40. *20*. 22,11. 48,5-6. 50,13. 65,16. 66,90-91
Ralph of Fougères	*41*. 66,83
Ralph of Limésy	*28*
Ralph of Noron	66,85
Ralph of Tosny	1,211. 21,15. *22*. 22,*1 note*. 66,69-70
Ralph of Tourleville	9,8
Ralph son of Hagni	50,9. *57*
Ralph son of Herlwin	9,8-9;12;73;231. 19,8. 66,75
Ralph son of H(erlwin)	9,118
R(alph) son of H(erlwin)	9,120
Ralph Sturmy	31,38-39;41
Ralph Tallboys	1,52
Ralph the constable	1,202-204. 4,23;37. 8,8;10;124. 10,66. 17,21; 24;33;37. 20,31. 48,4
R(alph) the constable	1,94;96;98-99. 10,80. 55,2
R(alph the constable)	1,97

Ralph the crossbowman	1,61. *53*
Ralph Visdeloup	1,66
Ralph Wader	25,15
Ralph (Earl) Wader	1,215
Ralph	1,57;140. 8,15;24;37;107-108;122. 9,42. 12,4; 6;18;34. 21,11-12. 23,17-18. 24,3;7. 34,6-7. 61,3
R(alph)	9,196;198. 10,19. 12,45
Ralph, see Hagni	
Randolph	8,1-2 note. 31,7
Ranulf brother of Ilger	1,192. *36*. 66,103
Ranulf Peverel	9,184;189. *32*. 66,105
R(anulf) Peverel	9,194. 32,6
Ranulf son of Walter	1,64. 9,6;11;24;32;45;80;82;197. 66,71-73
R(anulf son of Walter)	66,73
Ranulf	6,2. 9,161. 10,19. 21,6-8;18;21;25;29. 35,1. 66,97
Rathi of Gimingham	8,128
Rathi	8,119. 24,6. 52,2
Raymond Gerald	1,226
Redger	12,6
Reynold of Pierrepont	10,93
Reynold, Roger Bigot's man	1,61
Reynold son of Ivo	1,3;57;61-62. 8,29. 15,14. *21*. 66,44
Reynold the priest	46,1
Reynold	10,28;35 note;72;78-79. 66,46-48
Reynold, see Ivo	
R(eynold son of Ivo)	21,13
Reinbald the goldsmith	65,8
Ribald	4,3;6-7;14;20-21;25;35;43;45;52
Richard of Saint-Clair	1,61;63
Richard of Vernon	6,1
Richard Poynant	1,217. 9,167
Richard son of Alan	10,43-44
Richard	10,4;30. 14,5;11-12;39. 19,24. 20,3;8;11;15; 26-27;34. 24,1. 34,10
Richere, see Gilbert	
Ricwold	29,4-5
Ringwulf	9,14;21. 50,8
Robert Baron	1,61
Robert Blanchard (= Blunt)	1,*7 note*;231. 26,3
Robert Blunt	1,7;66;87;136;206;209. 19,20. 38,3. 47,1. 66,64;80;84. See also Robert Blanchard
R(obert) Blunt	1,113;216. 8,5. 10,69. 51,9. 58,3
Robert Gernon	*33*. 66,99
Robert the lorimer	1,61
Robert (Malet)	66,60
Robert Malet	1,197;205;208. 4,39. 7. 9,211. 17,51. 20,*29 note*; 35,16. 36,5. 44,1. 66,58;61;107. See also Malet
R(obert) Malet	4,53. 8,129. 9,100;179-180. 14,31
R(obert Malet)	66,60-61
Robert Malet's father	30,2
Robert Malet's mother	7,14
Robert of Courson	9,29;100;178
Robert (of Courson)	9,31
Robert of Glanville	17,51
Count R(obert) of Mortain	3
Robert of Vaux	9,2-4;46;53;56;64-65;67;99;116;233-234. 14,40. 19,36
Robert of Verly	*38*
Robert son of Corbucion	1,229. 31,11-12;17;44. *35*
Robert the crossbowman	1.66. 15,*21 IE*. 17,43. 26,5. *54*
Robert	9,61;86;88;103;107-108;110;124;134. 31,15. 66,57

Roger Baynard?	9,*160 note*
Roger Bigot	1,1;57;61;63;66;215;220. 2,1;7;12. 4,39;56. 6,6. *9*. 9,?160. 12,34;38. 14,14;21;25. 15,10; 22. 16,5-6. 22,13. 48,5-6. 49,5. 65,12. 66,58-59;71-73;78-84;86
R(oger) Bigot	1,70;106;111;223;229. 4,55. 12,42. 15,13
Roger Longsword	10,57-59
Roger of Evreux	19,39
R(oger) of Evreux	19,9
Roger of Poitou	1,61;231. *26*
Roger of Raismes	9,200. 15,25. *43*
Roger, Roger Malet's man	14,31
Roger son of Rainard	12,45. 27,2. *50*. 57,*2 note*
Roger the sheriff	9,86
Roger	1,1;2. 8,41. 10,40;58. 14,14. 19,10;12. 21,4;10; 32;35-36. 23,13. 34,5. 64,1
Roland	24,2
Rolf	4,44. 65,1
Saewulf	10,61
Sigar	20,14
Sigeric	55,1
Simon	8,33;37-38;55;108
Siward Bairn	1,149. 19,18-19
Siward	1,209;213
Skalp	24,6. 38,4
Skeet	21,36. 29,4. 34,14-15. 51,8
Skuli	19,1. 21,21. 24,5-6. 29,2-3. 66,100;106
Spirwic, see Eudo	
Stanard	9,10;14-17;81;91;121;157. 66,84
Starculf	*62*
Stergar, King Edward's guard	49,7
Archbishop Stigand	1,105;121. 8,120. 9,6-8. 12,1
(Arch)Bishop Stigand	1,209-241
Bishop Stigand	9,31-32;139. 40,1
Stigand's sister	1,61
Stigand	1,51;60-62;77-79;81;123;142;182. 2,2-8;10; 12. 4,8;14;55. 5,5-6. 6,4-7. 8,8;12;14;38;48-49; 64-65;70. 9,24;26;28-29;43-44;46-47;49; 56-57;59;63-65;67;98;99;103;161;165;167-169;171;191;198-201;218;224;228-229. 10,5; 30;50-51;69. 10a,1. 11,5. 12,42. 13,13. 14,20. 17,18. 18,1. 19,6;9;31;39. 20,1;9-13;24;31; 34-36. 21,19;37. 23,10. 26,2-4. 29,5-6. 30,4. 31,5;16;18;32;39. 32,2. 34,4. 35,3-4;6-7;9; 13;17. 43,2-3. 48,3-4. 49,8. 50,4. 61,1. 66,20; 22-23;55;71;87
Swart	26,3
Swarting	13,10
Sweetman	9,56
Theobald	1,61
Theodoric	34,12
Thor	19,9
Thorald, William of Warenne's man	1,195
Thorbern	4,18;32. 22,16
Thorbert	4,33. 9,46. 34,4
Thored	31,1;17;31;43;45. 32,1. 34,1
Thorgils	24,4. 34,3;11
Thorgrim	8,115
Thorkell	4,45. 19,4-5;7;17. 21,2-3;6-7. 28,1. 50,7. 66,22
Thorkell Hako	19,21
Thorketel	13,1;3-7;12-17;19;23. 21,23. 34,17. 50,1
Thormoth	29,6

Thorn	9,9. 31,6-8;10
Thorodd	50,6
Thorold	8,3;8;13;133-136. 9,30;60;62;72;106;141;177; 228. 20,19;32. 50,6(?)
Thorp	31,33
Thorulf	11,4
Thurstan of Thetford	66,76-77
Thurstan son of Guy	9,83;85;135-138;150
Thurstan	4,46. 8,*89 IE*. 9,1;74;153. 19,17. 66,16
Thyri	34,8
Tihel	1,195
Tihel the Breton	L37 note. 2,*11 note*. 37
Tihel of Hellean	2,11 note
Tofa (fem.)	12,6
Toki of Winterton	9,87
Toki	1,89. 4,14. 8,7;21-22;30;47;62;68;98-100;103-105;107;110;116. 9,172. 25,20. 31,16. 34,10; 19
Toki, see Godwin Tokeson	
Toli the sheriff	1,229. 14,35. 47,4
Toli	21,2;4-5;14
Tosti	10,83
Tovi	9,8;117. 20,1. *48*. 53,1
Ulf	1,85;147;186;208. 4,52. 9,76;94-96;98;159; 161;163-164;184;186. 20,6;27. 30,1. 31,41. 35,5
Ulfketel, the King's reeve	9,49-50. 66,106
Ulfketel	1,120. 4,47. 7,5;15. 8,63;85. 9,18;26-29;33-42; 52-55;69-109;111. 15,2. 20,19. 21,29. 35,16. *58*. 66,37;93-94
Unban	24,*4 note*
W	8,91-92. 66,2
Wagen	13,24
Wala	1,61
Waleran, a certain priest	1,66
Waleran	1,63. 8,120. 17,18
Waleran, see John	
Walter Canute	66,107
Walter Giffard	1,19;52;55;57. *25*. 66,63
Walter of Caen	7,3. 66,57
Walter of Dol	6,1;5-6
Walter son of Bloc	4,*16 IE*
Walter the deacon	1,64. 10,19
Walter	1,61. 7,4;8;12-13;15. 8,30;38;42-43;105;118. 9,102. 12,5;34. 23,9. 66,61
Walter, see Ranulf	
Warin	6,*4 note*. 66,90
Warin Cook	6,*4 note*. 7,20
Warin(g)	6,*4 note*. 32,2-7
Waring	6,4 note;7. 20,6
Warenger	9,199;202. 43,1-3
Warenbold	13,15. 66,24
Wastret	1,130 note
Wazelin	8,44
Wester	50,9. 57,1;3
Wigulf	8,132. 10,64
Wigwin	4,30
Wihenoc of Burley	66,36
Wihenoc	1,61. 8,29. 9,233. 15,*14 IE*. 21,1;5;7-8;12-15; 32;35. 66,44;49-50;52
Wihtred	1,130 note. 65,14
William, an Englishman	1,61
William Brant	8,16
William Gross	66,60

William, Hervey de Vere's man	1,61
William, Hermer's man	1,61
William Malet	9,211. 20,29 note. 66,60-62. See also Malet
W(illiam) Malet	8,12. 17,52. 35,16. 66,62
William of Bourneville	9,131
William (of Cailli)	8,28
William of Écouis	1,1;61. 15,11. 16,5. *19*. 66,56
William of Noyers	1,61. 10,23;26;60;62-64
W(illiam) of Noyers	1,63;79;209-241. 9,167. 10,1;13;31-32;42;56; 68;73-74;77;165
W(illiam) of Parthenay	66,88
William of Warenne	1,11;57;195;215. *8*. 16,1. 19,8. 66,47;64;67
William (of Warenne)	*8*
W(illiam) of Warenne	1,1;211. 4,3. 15,1;7-8. 16,5. 31,29. 40,1
William of Warenne, see Gerard	
Bishop William	1,57;61;68;128. *10*
W(illiam) Petch	9,25
William	7,7. 8,18 etc. 9,88;98. 13,3. 34,1;17. 43,4. 49,6
W(illiam)	10,7;52. 15,9. 19,6
Wimerus, see Wymer	
Wimund	31,11
Winemer	66,68
Wistan	1,202
Wither	8,1;3
Withri	9,87;142-144;148-149. 20,19
Wulfgeat	1,51;88;206. 4,45
Wulflet	9,31
Wulfmer	1,129-130. 21,11. 31,12
Wulfnoth	3,1. 30,4. 40,1
Wulfric	9,99. 15,12. 26,6. 33,1-2;4;6. 35,7. 66,99
Wulfrun	51,1;3
Wulfsi	21,26
Wulfstan	8,130. 9,87;144
Wulfward	1,153
Wulfwy	19,2;7
Wymarc	4,26;38
Wymer	1,66. 8,6;62;69;95
Ylfing	9,152 note

CHURCHES AND CLERGY

ALL SAINTS, see NORWICH	
BRACONDALE, see St. Nicholas	
BURY ST. EDMUND'S, see EDMUND	
BAYEUX	Bishop 1,111;120-122. 2. 4,44. 66,82.
CAEN, see ST. STEPHEN	
CLUNY, see SS. PETER AND PAUL	
COUTANCES	Bishop 15,22 *IE*
ELY, see ST. ETHELDREDA	
HOLME, see ST. BENEDICT	
HOLY TRINITY, see NORWICH	
NORWICH CHURCHES	All Saints 1,61
	St. Laurence 1,61
	Holy Trinity 1,61
	St. Martin 1,61
	St. Michael 1,61
	SS. Simon and Jude 1,61
RAMSEY, see ST. BENEDICT	
ST. BENEDICT, HOLME	Abbey 1,59;194;209. 4,26;37;40;42;51. 8,8; 10-12. 9,13;16;20;?88;91;159;180. 10,82-84;90. 12,32;?44. 13,7. 14,3. 20,31-33. 21,32. 25,25-28. 26,5. 31,2-4;6;28. 35,11. 36,2. 48,3;8. 65,15. 66,16;78
	Abbot 1,61;201. 8,128. 10,43. 12,6;32. *17*. 19,24. 65,13
ST. BENEDICT, RAMSEY (Hunts.)	Abbey 1,134. 8,17-20. 9,8;?88. 12,?44. 20,3. 21,3. 66,4;8;46;54
	Abbot 8,16. *16*
ST. EDMUND, BURY ST. EDMUND'S (Suffolk)	Abbey 1,172;220-221;225-226. 9,28. 10,93. 21,30. 29,8. 31,14. 32,7. 35,18. 43,2. 66,7; 46;59
	Abbot 1,62;130;144;239. *14*. 66,40-42
ST. ETHELDREDA, Ely (Cambs.)	Abbey 4,*15 IE*;16. 8,15;*16 IE*;37;39-40;44. 9,79;167. 10,93. 12,*17 IE*. 13,1;*19 IE*. 22,*1 IE*. 23,9;*16 IE*. 24,4. 29,7. 49,6. 50,10. 57,2
	Abbot 1,61. 8,*89 IE*. 10,43. 12,6. *15*. 19,24. 65,13. 66,53
ST. HELEN, Thetford	1,210
ST. LAURENCE, see NORWICH	
ST. MARTIN, see NORWICH	
ST. MICHAEL, see NORWICH	
ST. NICHOLAS, Bracondale	45,1
SS. PETER AND PAUL, Cluny (Burgundy)	Abbey 8,21
ST. STEPHEN, Caen (Normandy)	Abbey *18*

Abbot:	see St. Benedict, Holme; St. Benedict, Ramsey; St. Edmund, Bury; St. Etheldreda, Ely
Abbot:	Alfwold (of Holme)
Archdeacon:	Gunfrid
Archbishop:	Stigand, William
Bishop:	A(e)lmer, Erfast, Osbern, Stigand
Deacon:	Walter
Priest:	Alfred, Aldwy, Colbern, Fulbert, Judicael, Reynold, Waleran

SECULAR TITLES AND OCCUPATIONAL NAMES

Carpenter — Rabel
Chamberlain, Roger Bigot's — Herbert
Constable — Asgar, Ralph
Cook — Warin
Count — Alan, Eustace, Robert, of Mortain
Crossbowman — Berner, Gilbert, Ralph, Robert
Ditcher — Hereberd
Earl — Algar, Gyrth, Harold, Hugh, Ralph junior, Ralph senior

Engineer — Rabel
Falconer — Edric
Falconer, the Earl's — Judichael
Goldsmith — Reinbald
Goldsmith, Earl Hugh's — Nicholas
Guard, King Edward's — Stergar
Lorimer — Hildebrand, Robert
Reeve — Brown, Baldwin, A(i)lwy, Ansketel
Reeve, the King's — Edwy, Ulfketel
Sheriff — Roger, Toli
Steward — Eudo, Godric
Thane — Godwin, Osbern
Thane, King Edward's — Alsi
Watchman — Gerard, Gilbert, Maynard

INDEX OF PLACES

The name of each place is followed by (i) the abbreviated name of its Hundred and its location on the Map in this volume; (ii) its National Grid reference; (iii) chapter and section references in DB, or a reference to a note on a particular DB section which identifies the place, or a reference to the Appendix. Bracketed chapter and section references denote mention in sections dealing with a different place. Unless otherwise stated, the identifications of EPNS and the spellings of the Ordnance Survey are followed for places in England; of OEB for places abroad. The National Grid reference system is explained on all Ordnance Survey maps, and in the Automobile Association Handbooks; the figures reading from left to right are given before those reading from bottom to top of the map. All places in the index are in the 100-km grid square lettered TF TG TL TM. Where DB does not differentiate between what are now two distinct settlements, e.g. Acre (Castle and West), both sets of Grid references are given. The Norfolk Hundreds are Blofield (Bl), Brothercross (Br), Clackclose (Cl), Clavering (C), Depwade (De), Diss (Di), Docking (Do), Earsham (E), North Erpingham (NE), South Erpingham (SE), Eynsford (Ey), East Flegg (EF), West Flegg (WF), Forehoe (Fo), Freebridge (Fr), Gallow (G), North Greenhoe (NG), South Greenhoe (SG), Grimshoe (Gr), Guiltcross (Gu), Happing (Ha), Henstead (He), Holt (Ho), Humbleyard (Hu), Launditch (La), Loddon (Lo), Mitford (Mi), Norwich (N), Shropham (Sh), Smethdon (Sm), Taverham (Ta), Thetford (Th), Tunstead (Tu), Walsham (W), Wayland (Wa).

	Map	Grid	Text
Acle	W 8	TG 40 10	1,151
Acre (Castle and West)	Fr 44 Fr 43	TF 80 15 TF 78 15	8,22;88. 15,5. 22,15;16;20
(South) Acre	SG 2	TF 80 14	1,71;75. 8,95. 12,2
Alburgh	E 3	TM 27 87	1,129;221. 4,48. 29,7
Alby	SE 6	TG 19 34	9,87;174
Alcmuntona	Lo	unidentified	9,68 *note*.12,25 *note*; 26
Aldborough	NE 25	TG 18 34	8,130. 9,87;146;151
Aldeby	C 11	TM 45 93	20,36
Alethorpe	G 14	TF 94 31	1,16
Algamundestuna	Lo	unidentified	9,52 *note*; 68 *note*
Alpington	He 18	TM 29 01	9,?52 *note*; ?68 *note*. 12,?17 *note*; ?25-26 *note*
Anmer	Fr 3	TF 73 29	5,2. 8,31
Antingham	NE 29	TG 25 32	9,149;150;180. 17,8
Appethorp	Fo	unidentified	4,15. 54,1
Appleton	Fr 6	TF 70 27	9,7. 34,3
Appletona, -tuna	Lo	unidentified	9,68 note. 12,*17 note*
Arminghall	He 5	TG 25 04	1,218
Ashby	Sh 17	TM 00 90	1,140
Ashby	WF 10	TG 41 15	10,84. 17,11. 19,30
Ashby (St. Mary)	Lo 4	TG 32 02	9,57;61;65;69. 12,19;22
Ashill	Wa 2	TF 88 04	21,17. 15,5
(Ashwell) Thorpe	De 1	TM 14 97	5,6
(Ash) Wicken	Fr 31	TF 69 18	4,45. 21,10
Aslacton	De 23	TM 15 91	4,56. 9,98;211;223
Attleborough (and Attleborough Minor)	Sh 5	TM 04 95	50,6;7. 59,1
Attlebridge	Ta 4	TG 12 16	4,34. 10,37. 19,33. 25,9
Aylmerton	NE 6	TG 18 40	8,132. 9,145;146
Aylsham	SE 23	TG 19 27	1,91;149;192;194;195. 8,8
Babingley	Fr 8	TF 66 26	29,3. 34,1
Baconsthorpe	Sh 2	TM 04 95	4,46
(Bacons) Thorpe	SE 2	TG 12 36	9,177. 33,12
Bacton	Tu 2	TG 33 33	7,18
Bagthorpe	Br 7	TF 79 32	8,108
Bale	Ho 13	TG 01 36	1,21. 4,19
Banham	Gu 2	TM 06 88	8,61. 9,79. 11,1. 15,11. 19,13
Banningham	SE 17	TG 21 29	8,136. 17,31. 21,35
Barford	Fo 13	TG 10 07	4,9. 17,4. 20,12

	Map	Grid	Text
Barmer	Br 6	TF 80 33	8,108
Barney	NG 18	TF 99 32	34,13;17
Barnham (Broom)	Fo 12	TG 08 07	8,72. 61,4. 62,1
(Little) Barningham	SE 4	TG 14 33	1,194. 8,8. 10,39. 35,12
(North) Barningham	NE 13	TG 15 37	8,133. 9,146;149;154;156. 10,64. 25,24. 30,3. 66,99
Barsham (East	G 9	TF 91 33	1,16. 8,99;117
and West)	G 8	TF 90 33	
North Barsham	G 7	TF 91 34	8,134
Barton (Bendish)	Cl 18	TF 71 05	13,3. 21,2. 31,21. 66,2;36
Barton (Turf)	Tu 18	TG 34 21	8,12. 17,42;46;50. 31,4
Barwick	Do 6	TF 80 35	8,33
Baskenea	Mi	unidentified	4,15
Bastwick	WF 4	TG 42 17	4,27. 9,21. 10,88. 17,15. 64,5
Bawburgh	Fo 9	TG 15 08	4,9
Bawdeswell	Ey 20	TG 04 20	4,29;31
Bawsey	Fr 25	TF 65 19	4,45. 7,2
Bayfield	Ho 9	TG 05 40	1,25. 25,18
Beccles (In Suffolk, Wangford Hundred)	Wg	TM 42 90	1,63
Beck	Ey 19	TG 02 20	4,30
(East) Beckham	NE 8	TG 15 39	1,149. 9,155. 10,8;65
(West) Beckham	SE 1	TG 14 39	25,13
Bedingham	Lo 19	TM 28 93	1,182;184. 9,168
Beechamwell	Cl 19	TF 75 05	4,43. 9,233. 21,8. 31,29
Beeston (Regis)	NE 3	TG 17 43	19,21;22. 23,18
Beeston (St. Andrew)	Ta 15	TG 25 13	1,189;191. 7,17. 12,29. 20,25
Beeston (St. Lawrence)	Tu 17	TG 32 21	17,44
Beetley	La 15	TF 97 18	10,5
Beighton	W 10	TG 38 08	10,25. 47,2
Belaugh	SE 43	TG 28 18	1,194;235. 17,33. 20,31
Bergh (Apton)	He 20	TM 31 99	12,*17 note*. 15,28 note
Bessingham	NE 14	TG 16 37	30,2
Besthorpe	Sh 3	TM 06 95	9,126;129
Bexwell	Cl 23	TF 63 03	9,231. 15,2. 66,9;48
Bickerston	Fo 6	TG 08 08	66,31
Billingford (near Diss)	E 14	TM 16 79	1,226 note. 15,25. 43,2
Billingford	Ey 18	TG 01 20	4,31. 32,1. 39,2. ESf 7
Billockby	WF 14	TG 42 13	9,19. 10,90. 17,14. 64,6
(West) Bilney	Fr 41	TF 71 15	23,12-13. 66,96
Binham	NG 8	TF 98 39	34,14;15. 66,89
Bintree	Ey 12	TG 01 23	12,28. 25,1. 56,1
(Great) Bircham	Do 10	TF 77 32	19,9;10. 20,2
(Bircham) Newton	Do 8	TF 76 33	20,1
(Bircham) Tofts	Do 11	TF 77 32	2,5
Bittering	La 19	TF 93 17	1,80;213
Bixley	He 6	TG 25 04	9,32;42;45;114. 66,81
Blakeney	Ho 2	TG 03 43	1,19. 10,56. 25,20
Blickling	SE 20	TG 17 28	1,57. 10,38;39;65
Blofield	Bl 5	TG 33 09	10,28. 20,21
(Blo) Morton	Gu 16	TM 01 79	8,59. 9,78. 14,8. 15,13
Bodham	Ho 12	TG 12 38	23,18. 25,21. 66,97
Bodney	SG 24	TL 83 93	8,96. 22,8. 23,1
Booton	SE 36	TG 12 22	37,3
Boughton	Cl 30	TF 70 02	21,6. 31,25
Bowthorpe	Fo 10	TG 17 09	1,82;206
Boyland	De 9	TM 22 94	31,7
Bracon Ash	Hu 23	TG 17 00	9,186;189
Bradenham (East	SG 10	TG 93 08	8,93. 22,2. 31,34;40. 66,64
and West)	SG 9	TG 91 09	

	Map	Grid	Text
Bradeston	Bl 8	TG 34 08	10,76;77
Bramerton	He 8	TG 29 04	1,120. 2,9. 9,28;45;161e. 12,13. 66,80
Brampton	SE 28	TG 21 24	8,8. 20,30;31
Brancaster	Do 2	TF 77 43	15,4
Brandiston	Ey 24	TG 14 21	1,54
Brandon (Parva)	Fo 11	TG 07 08	4,11
Brant	Lo	unidentified	19,31
Breckles	Wa 17	TL 95 94	1,5;7;9;10;137. 9,123. 22,22
Bressingham	Di 12	TM 07 80	1,179. 14,24;25;34. 66,41
Brettenham	Sh 22	TL 93 83	9,131. 15,10. 24,4 note. 49,6
Bridgham	Sh 20	TL 95 85	15,10;*29 note*. 49,6 note
Briningham	Ho 21	TG 03 34	4,18. 10,57;59
Brinton	Ho 17	TG 03 35	10,8
Briston	Ho 25	TG 06 32	1,22. 8,116
Brockdish	E 16	TM 21 79	1,226. 14,18
Brooke	He 19	TM 29 99	14,16;17;38
Broome	Lo 23	TM 35 91	9,172. 14,35. 35,10
Broomsthorpe	Br 16	TF 85 28	15,23
Brumstead	Ha 7	TG 36 26	9,88;183
Brundall	Bl 7	TG 32 08	1,192. 10,80. 52,3
Buckenham	Bl 14	TG 35 05	1,103. 10,79. 14,14
Buckenham	Sh 13	TM 06 91	1,139. 4,46. 6,1. 8,55;56;57;58. 9,126;127;129;130;131. 14,6. 19,12. 20,5. 24,1;2;3;4. 49,6. 52,1. 58,1. 59,1. 66,24;74;75; 90
Buckenham (Tofts)	Gr 7	TL 83 94	23,15. 50,2
Burgh (next Aylsham)	SE 25	TG 21 25	9,175. 30,5
Burgh (St. Margaret)	WF 15	TG 44 14	1,165. 9,18;157. 10,87. 17,14. 64,1
(South) Burgh	Mi 17	TG 00 04	8,81-84 note. 66,34
(North) Burlingham	Bl 3	TG 36 10	1,99. 10,68;73. 19,23;28
South Burlingham	Bl 9	TG 37 07	10,74;77
(Burnham) Deepdale	Br 1	TF 80 44	9,138
Burnham (Norton	Br 2	TF 82 43	
Sutton	Br 4	TF 83 41	8,118. 9,84;136. 16,6. 23,4
Ulph	Br 3		
and Westgate)	Br 5	TF 83 42	
Burnham (Overy)	G 1	TF 84 42	1,147
Burnham Thorpe	G 2	TF 85 41	8,105. 38,2
Burston	Di 7	TM 13 83	1,151;170;176;178;179. 7.8;10; 14. 14,32
Buxton	SE 38	TG 23 22	20,29;32
Bylaugh	Ey 27	TG 03 18	4,30
Caister	EF 7	TG 51 12	1,164;165;201. 17,63
Caistor (St. Edmunds)	He 10	TG 23 03	14,15. 20,22
Caldecote	SG 16	TF 74 03	21,13. 22,*1 note*;6
Calthorpe	SE 10	TG 18 31	9,87. 17,26. 37,2
Calvely	Mi 18	TG 01 05	15,18
Cantley	Bl 18	TG 38 04	1,94
Carbrooke	Wa 5	TF 94 02	22,10. 49,3;5
West Carbrooke	Wa 4	TF 95 01	49,5
(East) Carleton	Hu 14	TG 17 02	9,96;184. 20,34. 32,3. 65,11
Carleton (Forehoe)	Fo 15	TG 08 05	1,81. 4,11. 17,4
Carleton (Rode)	De 20	TM 11 92	1,207. 4,56. 8,14. 9,207;209;222. 29,11
Carleton (St. Peter)	Lo 5	TG 33 02	9,59;66;173. 12,23. 21,26. 31,45
(Castle) Rising	Fr 12	TF 66 24	2,4
Caston	Wa 13	TL 95 97	1,4;8;16;135. 8,51
Catfield	Ha 15	TG 38 21	4,51. 9,88
Catton	Bl 13	TG 29 07	10,78;79. 24,6

	Map	Grid	Text
Catton	Ta 16	TG 23 12	1,188;233
Cawston	SE 29	TG 13 23	1,30;53;54;55;57;195. 8,8;9. 10,17. 21,34;35. 37,3. 64,1
Chedgrave	Lo 12	TM 36 99	31,43;44
Clareia	Tu	unidentified	3,2
Claxton	Lo 3	TG 32 03	9,53;56;59. 12,20;22
Clenchwarton	Fr 20	TF 58 20	19,2
Cley (next the Sea)	Ho 3	TG 04 43	1,19
Cleythorpe	SG 17	TF 79 03	21,14
Clippesby	WF 13	TG 42 14	1,46-7;166. 9,16. 10,91. 17,15. 64,4
Clipstone	G 19	TF 97 30	8,101
(Cockley) Cley	SG 14	TF 79 04	1,73. 8,92. 66,65
(Cock) Thorpe	NG 6	TF 98 42	10,12;62
Colby	SE 12	TG 22 31	1,57
Colkirk	Br 21	TF 91 26	10,6;54
Colney	Hu 1	TG 18 07	9,199. 12,34. 19,38
Coltishall	SE 42	TG 27 19	8,8;12. 24,4
Colton	Fo 7	TG 10 09	8,73
Colveston	Gr 5	TL 79 95	8,40
Corgham	Fr 15	TF 71 23	8,26;27. 51,2
Corpusty	SE 15	TG 11 29	8,8. 10,17. 19,34
Costessy	Fo 2	TG 17 12	4,9;11;15;28;34;54;56
Crackford	SE 21	TG 22 29	1,195. 8,8
Cranwich	Gr 4	TL 78 94	8,46
Cranworth	Mi 15	TF 98 04	1,85;87
Creake (North	G 4	TF 85 38	1,16. 8,102. 9,83;85;135. 19,17. 23,3
and South)	G 5	TF 85 36	
(Great) Cressingham	SG 19	TF 85 01	4,7. 10,1;48-49. 22,4
(Little) Cressingham	SG 22	TF 87 00	22,5. 66,69
Crimplesham	Cl 24	TF 64 03	21,3
Cringleford	Hu 7	TG 19 05	2,9;12. 4,55. 9,201
Crostwick	Ta 12	TG 25 15	20,25. 26,26
Crostwight	Tu 8	TG 33 29	31,3
Crownthorpe	Fo 18	TG 08 03	1,83. 20,13
Croxton	G 15	TF 98 31	8,104
Croxton	Gr 19	TL 87 86	1,*210-211 note;*211 note
Custhorpe	SE 44	TF 78 13	22,7
Denton	E 1	TM 27 88	1,220. 29,6
Denver	Cl 26	TF 61 01	8,18
Deopham	Fo 22	TG 05 00	8,79. 20,10
(East) Dereham	Mi 1	TF 98 13	15,15;16;*29 note.* 20,9
(West) Dereham	Cl 28	TF 66 02	8,19. 9,232. 13,3. 16,2. 31,28-30. 66,12;44
Dersingham	Fr 2	TF 69 30	29,4. 34,2;13. 66,87
Dickleburgh	Di 10	TM 16 82	14,29
Didlington	SG 25	TL 77 96	8,89 note. 28,2
Dilham	Tu 12	TG 33 25	4,37. 7,19. 9,181. 17,47
Diss	Di 14	TM 11 80	1,51. 66,62
Diss (In Suffolk, Hartismere Hundred)	–	–	ESf 1
Ditchingham	Lo 21	TM 32 92	1,228
Docking	Do 4	TF 76 37	2,5. 29,5
Downham (Market)	Cl 22	TF 61 03	8,19. 9,231. 15,3. 66,13;47
Drayton	Ta 14	TG 18 13	20,26
Dunham (Great	La 26	TF 87 14	1,212. 22,12. 46,1
and Little)	La 27	TF 86 12	
Dunston	Hu 17	TG 22 02	4,53. 9,192. 12,36. 20,35. 65,12
Dunton	Br 9	TF 87 30	1,17
Dykebeck	Fo 23	TG 09 01	31,42. 66,39
Earlham	Hu 2	TG 19 08	1,206. 4,53

	Map	Grid	Text
Earsham	E 2	TM 31 88	1,219-220;223;225;226;228-229;239. 9,63;167. 14,20-21. 29,6. 43,2-3.
Earsham Half Hundred	—	—	15,24 note
Easton	Fo 4	TG 13 10	4,9
Easton	SE 35	TG 27 23	17,24;48
Eaton	Hu 8	TG 20 06	1,104;114;126;184;190;205
Eccles	Sh 18	TM 01 89	10,21
Eccles	Ha 6	TG 41 28	17,58. 65,4
Edgefield	Ho 22	TG 09 34	34,14. 36,6
Egmere	NG 10	TF 89 37	1,36. 8,117. 10,11
Ellingham	C 12	TM 35 92	1,239
(Great) Ellingham	Sh 1	TM 01 96	13,15. 20,5. 66,24
(Little) Ellingham	Wa 10	TM 00 99	1,7;136. 8,53
(North) Elmham, see under N			
Elsing	Ey 30	TG 05 16	8,6
Erpingham	SE 11	TG 19 31	9,176. 17,29. 30,6. 36,1. 66,103
Eye (In Suffolk, Hartismere Hundred)		TM 14 73	7,21
Fakenham	G 17	TF 91 29	1,2;15-18;29;40. 8,138. 10,54. 21,22
Felbrigg	NE 9	TG 20 39	9,146
Felmingham	Tu 6	TG 25 29	1,58. 9,179. 17,39
Felthorpe	Ta 5	TG 16 17	1,56. 4,34. 20,26. 21,31. 25,9
Feltwell	Gr 14	TL 71 90	1,210. 8,35;37 note; 39 note;40 note. 15,7; 29 note
Fersfield	Di 8	TM 06 82	1,175-177;179;181. 66,61
(Field) Dalling	NG 12	TG 00 39	1,42. 4,20. 9,86. 38,3
Filby	EF 4	TG 46 13	8,13. 9,91. 17,61. 19,37. 55,2. 66,84
Fincham	Cl 14	TF 68 06	8,16;19. 13,2. 14,1. 15,2. 21,1. 31,20. 66,1;35;51
Fishley	W 7	TG 39 11	1,153-154. 17,1. 19,26
Flitcham	Fr 7	TF 72 26	2,4. 8,32. 9,4;6. 66,71
Flockthorpe	Mi 21	TG 03 04	1,12-13;87. 4,15
Flordon	Hu 28	TM 18 97	2,12. 4,54. 9,97;186;190;200; 204. 12,38
Fodderstone	Cl 5	TF 65 09	15,2. 21,8. 66,15
Fordham	Cl 31	TL 61 99	15,3. 16,2. 31,27. 66,11;46;53
Forncett (St. Mary	De 14	TM 16 93	9,98;205;223. 11,5. 66,106
and St. Peter)	De 13	TM 16 92	
Foulden	SG 23	TL 76 99	4,3. 8,90. 25,14
Foulsham	Ey 8	TG 03 24	1,52;185-186. 4,28. 5,4. 17,20. 19,32. 25,1-2;4;6;8. 32,1. 34,20. 39,2
Foxley	Ey 15	TG 03 21	4,31
Framingham (Earl	He 12	TG 27 02	1,49. 2,7. 9,30;33;51;113;161. 12,9
and Pigot)	He 11	TG 27 03	
Fransham (Great	La 28	TF 89 13	8,66;68. 22,11
and Little)	La 30	TF 90 12	
Freethorpe	Bl 17	TG 40 05	1,97. 10,71. 66,101
Frenze	Di 15	TM 13 80	7,11. 14,28
Frettenham	Ta 6	TG 24 18	26,1;4
Fring	Do 7	TF 73 34	5,3. 8,49. 10,20
Fritton	De 16	TM 22 92	7,20-21. 9,98;161;208. 14,40. 31,9. 35,16. 66,60
Fulmodeston	G 16	TF 99 30	8,103
Fundenhall	De 2	TM 15 96	6,6. 9,220;225
Garboldisham	Gu 12	TM 00 81	1,145. 23,16 note
Garveston	Mi 11	TG 02 07	13,19
Gasthorpe	Gu 11	TL 98 81	1,146. 14,9
Gateley	La 3	TF 96 24	10,53. 23,17. 34,6

	Map	Grid	Text
Gayton	Fr 32	TF 73 19	8,23–24. 18,1. 19,7. 23,13. 66,23
(Gayton) Thorpe	Fr 33	TF 74 18	2,1. 9,3. 13,16. 22,17. 66,22
Gaywood	Fr 24	TF 65 20	10,2
Gillingham	C 13	TM 41 92	1,60;239. ESf 4
Gimingham	NE 19	TG 28 36	8,119–121
Gissing	Di 5	TM 14 85	1,171. 7,7;13. 9,47. 14,23 note; 31–32. 66,59
Glandford	Ho 7	TG 04 41	1,26. 25,19
Glosthorpe	Fr 30	TF 69 18	7,1
Gnatingdon	Sm 5	TF 71 39	61,3
Godwick	La 8	TF 90 22	22,13
Gooderstone	SG 18	TF 76 02	12,1;3
Gorleston	Lo 1	TG 52 04	1,60. ESf 2;5–6
(Great) Ryburgh	Br 23	TF 96 27	8,113. 34,9
(Great) Snarehill	Gu 6	TL 87 80	9,74. 14,10 note. 66,76–77
(Great) Snoring	NG 16	TF 94 34	1,92. 34,17
Grensvill	He 16	TG 26 00	17,17
Gresham	NE 12	TG 16 38	8,130. 9,146
Gressenhall	La 25	TF 95 15	8,62
Grimston	Fr 18	TF 72 21	2,2. 8,25;27. 9,116. 51,1
Griston	Wa 9	TL 94 99	1,4–5;138. 8,71. 9,122. 31,36. 49,4. 66,72
Guestwick	Ey 5	TG 06 27	10,15. 56,4
Guiltcross Hundred	—	—	15,10 note
Guist	Ey 7	TF 99 25	10,15;34. 25,2. 56,2
Gunthorpe	Ho 16	TG 01 35	1,28;30. 34,15
Gunton	NE 26	TG 22 34	4,24. 10,23;24
Guton	Ey 23	TG 13 20	37,1
Hackford	Fo 20	TG 05 02	48,1
Hackford	Ey 13	TG 07 22	8,3. 51,10
Haddiscoe	C 6	TM 43 96	1,238. 9,103;105;107;228. 31,18. 35,17
Hainford	Ta 3	TG 22 18	26,2
Halas	De	unidentified	9,98 note;206 note
Hales	C 4	TM 38 97	9,104. 12,43. 14,42;43. 31,16
Halvergate	W 12	TG 41 06	1,152
Hanworth	NE 22	TG 19 35	9,87;142
Happisburgh	Ha 2	TG 37 31	1,197. 4,51
Hapton	De 3	TM 17 96	6,6. 9,218. 66,86
Hardley	Lo 8	TG 38 00	17,19
Hardwick	De 24	TM 22 90	7,21. 9,98. 15,29. 31,9. 65,14
Hargham	Sh 12	TM 02 91	20,6. 66,90
Harleston	E 9	TM 24 83	14,20;22
Harling (East and West)	Gu 4 Gu 3	TL 99 86 TL 97 85	1,143. 4,47. 14,11. 19,15. 38,1
Harpley	Fr 10	TF 78 26	2,3. 8,30
Hassingham	Bl 15	TG 36 05	1,96
Hautbois (Great and Little)	SE 40 SE 39	TG 26 20 TG 25 21	8,10. 17,28. 20,32
Haveringland	Ey 25	TG 15 20	21,29;31
Heacham	Sm 6	TF 68 37	8,47
Heckingham	C 1	TM 38 98	9,106;111;229. 12,42. 14,43
Hedenham	Lo 20	TM 31 93	6,4;5
Heigham	Hu 3	TG 21 08	17,64
Helhoughton	Br 20	TF 86 27	1,88. 8,108;111;137. 23,6. 34,7
Hellesdon	Ta 18	TG 20 10	61,1
Hellington	Lo 2	TG 31 03	9,58. 12,18;20;21
Helmingham	Ey 31	TG 11 16	10,16;35. 25,7
Hemblington	W 6	TG 35 11	1,159. 10,14;66
Hempnall (see also *Schieteshaga*)	De 10	TM 24 94	9,101. 31,6;9
Hempstead	Ho 15	TG 10 37	1,20. 10,8

	Map	Grid	Text
Hempstead	Ha 5	TG 40 28	1,199
Hempton	Br 12	TF 91 29	8,114
Hemsby	WF 7	TG 49 17	10,30;43
Henstead Hundred	—	—	15,28 *note*
Herringby	EF 9	TG 44 10	65,8
Hethel	Hu 20	TG 17 00	9,94–95;97. 44,1
Hethersett	Hu 10	TG 16 04	4,52. 12,31;35
Hevingham	SE 37	TG 19 21	1,195. 10,38. 25,11
Hickling	Ha 12	TG 41 24	4,38
Hilborough	SG 21	TF 82 00	8,91
Hilgay	Cl 35	TL 62 98	1,210. 8,17. 9,230. 14,3. 15,2. 16,1. 66,7
Hillington	Fr 9	TF 72 25	8,28. 29,1. 51,3
Hindolveston	Ey 1	TG 02 29	10,9;15
Hindringham	NG 14	TF 98 36	1,39. 10,10;13;26;60;61. 11,3. 30,1
Hingham	Fo 19	TG 02 02	1,11;12;14. 8,79. 9,81. 20,10–12. 31,41. 66,39
Hockering	Mi 3	TG 07 13	20,14;15
Hockham	Sh 6	TL 95 92	9,71;126. 66,74
Little Hockham	Sh 10	TL 94 90	9,72
Hockwold	Gr 15	TL 72 88	8,35
Hoe	La 20	TF 99 16	15,15
Holkham	NG 1	TF 87 43	1,34;41. 4,20. 8,118. 10,13;26. 34,19. 48,2
Holme (Hale)	SG 12	TF 88 07	1,74. 66,70
Holme (next the Sea)	Sm 1	TF 70 43	1,134. 19,10
Holt	Ho 11	TG 07 38	1,19;29;31;42
Holverston	He 15	TG 30 03	1,122. 2,7;9. 9,35. 12,11
Honing	Tu 9	TG 32 27	17,51. 36,2
Honingham	Fo 1	TG 11 12	4,9;11
(Honingham) Thorpe	Fo 3	TG 11 11	4,9
Horning	Tu 22	TG 35 16	17,35
Horningtoft	La 7	TF 93 23	1,77
Horsey	Ha 14	TG 45 23	9,88;183. 10,42. 65,1;6
Horsford	Ta 9	TG 19 15	7,16
Horsham	Ta 10	TG 21 15	7,17
Horstead	Ta 2	TG 26 19	1,231–232;235
Hottune	NE	unidentified	10,63
Houghton	Br 13	TF 79 28	8,108
Houghton (on the Hill)	SG 13	TF 86 05	21,15
Houghton (St. Giles)	NG 15	TF 92 35	1,33
Hoveton (St. John and St. Peter)	Tu 21 Tu 20	TG 30 18 TG 31 19	8,10. 17,21;24;33;37. 20,31. 26,5
Howe	He 17	TM 27 99	1,105. 14,17
Hudeston	De 12	TM 11 93	9,100. 31,8. 50,11
Hunstanton	Sm 3	TF 68 41	1,209. 9,9;118. 10,51. 16,5. 49,2
'Hunt' Yelverton	—	—	9,166 note;cf. Yelverton
Hunworth	Ho 20	TG 06 35	1,23. 4,21. 25,22
Iarpestuna, see *Ierpes-*			
Ickburgh	Gr 6	TL 81 95	8,41. 22,21. 25,15;16. 50,2
Ierp(e)stuna?	C	unidentified	1,239 and note. 31,14. 35,18
Illington	Sh 14	TL 94 90	8,58
Ingham	Ha 8	TG 39 26	4,39;41. 17,57
Ingloss	Lo 15	TM 34 96	35,7
Ingoldisthorpe	Sm 8	TF 69 32	34,4
(Ingoldis) Thorpe	Sm 8		50,4
Ingworth	SE 16	TG 19 29	9,87. 21,33
Intwood	Hu 12	TG 19 04	24,7
Irmingland	SE 18	TG 12 29	8,8;9. 25,12
Islington	Fr 36	TF 57 16	4,44. 13,13. 14,1;4. 15,4;6. 19,1; 3. 23,10. 66,56

	Map	Grid	Text
Itteringham	SE 14	TG 14 30	1,195. 8,8
Kelling	Ho 8	TG 08 41	6,3. 50,9. 57,1. 66,97
Kempston	La 22	TF 88 16	8,65
Kenninghall	Gu 5	TM 04 85	1,76;143–144;146. 4,47. 8,59–60. 9,75;77;132–133. 11,2. 14,9. 15,11–12. 19,14. 39,1. 58,2. 66,76–77;95
Kenningham	Hu 24	TM 20 99	12,39. 48,6;7
Kerdiston	Ey 9	TG 08 24	8,2. 31,1
Keswick	Hu 11	TG 21 04	9,94;198. 12,41
Ketteringham	Hu 13	TG 16 02	9,95;197. 32,5
Kettlestone	G 13	TG 96 31	8,101
Kettleton	De 6	TM 14 94	4,56. 9,98;210;223
Kilverstone	Sh 21	TL 89 84	1,142. 7,3. 66,57
Kimberley	Fo 17	TG 07 04	1,81. 66,39
Kipton	La 4	TF 84 23	1,77
Kirby (Bedon)	He 7	TG 27 05	1,115;119;126. 2,7. 9,29;34. 12,15
Kirby (Cane)	C 9	TM 37 94	6,7. 14,41. 31,12
Kirstead	Lo 9	TM 27 98	14,38
Kirtling	La 24	TF 94 15	1,214
Knapton	NE 28	TG 30 34	8,121
Knettishall (in Suffolk)	Gu 10	TL 97 80	1,76
Lakenham	Hu 6	TG 23 07	1,236
Lamas	SE 33	TG 24 23	20,32
Langford	SG 26	TL 83 96	23,2
Langhale	Lo 13	TM 30 96	14,38. 47,4
Langham	Ho 6	TG 00 41	10,12;22;55
Langley	Lo 7	TG 35 00	10,31;33
Larling	Sh 15	TL 98 89	8,54 note. 58,1
Larpestuna? Lerp(e)stuna?			1,*239* note
Lessingham	Ha 4	TG 39 28	1,198
Let(h)a	Bl	unidentified	10,72 and note;75
Letheringsett	Ho 10	TG 06 38	25,17;21–22;24. 36,7
Letton	Mi 13	TF 97 05	8,81–84 note. 19,16. 66,33
Lexham (East	La 17	TF 85 17	8,63. 20,8
and West)	La 16	TF 84 17	
Leziate	Fr 26	TF 69 20	66,58
Limpenhoe	Bl 19	TG 39 03	1,95. 19,27. 66,101
Litcham	La 18	TF 88 17	1,212. 13,16;18
(Little) Snarehill	Gu 7	TL 88 81	9,75
(Little) Snoring	G 12	TF 95 32	1,16. 8,101. 34,7
(Great) Livermere (Suffolk)	—	—	14,*10* note
Loddon	Lo 16	TM 36 98	12,23. 14,35 note;42. 33,3;6. 35,6–11
Loddon Hundred	—	—	15,28 note
Longham	La 23	TF 94 15	66,25
Lopham (North	Gu 14	TM 03 82	9,76–78;132
and South)	Gu 15	TM 03 81	
Ludham	Ha 17	TG 38 18	4,38;51;53;59. 65,3
Lynford	Gr 11	TL 81 94	9,10. 25,15
Lyng	Ey 29	TG 06 17	4,29
Lynn (King's	Fr 23	TF 61 20	
North	Fr 22	TF 61 21	22,19. 31,32. 66,17;55
South	Fr 28	TF 61 20	
and West)	Fr 21	TF 61 19	
Mangreen	Hu 16	TG 21 03	9,193
Mannington	SE 7	TG 14 31	1,194. 8,8
Manson	Mi 20	TG 02 03	1,87
Marham	Cl 6	TF 70 09	8,15. 13,1. 15,1. 23,9 note
Markshall	Hu 9	TG 22 05	20,22;35

	Map	Grid	Text
Marlingford	Fo 8	TG 13 09	4,13
Marsham	SE 30	TG 19 23	1,57. 10,40-41. 20,30. 25,10
Martham	WF 6	TG 45 18	1,45;164. 4,27. 10,30;86. 17,15. 64,9
Massingham (Great and Little)	Fr 16 Fr 13	TF 79 22 TF 79 24	1,1. 5,1. 8,29. 9,5. 19,8. 21,11. 29,2
Matlask	SE 3	TG 15 34	1,57;193. 4,22;25
Mattishall	Mi 6	TG 05 11	8,81. 15,20. 20,16;18 note. 66,29
Mautby	EF 6	TG 48 12	1,202. 9,93. 19,37
Mayton	Ta 1	TG 24 21	26,2
(Great) Melton	Hu 4	TG 14 06	12,30;32-33. 32,4;6. 66,105
(Little) Melton	Hu 5	TG 15 06	12,32-33
Melton (Constable)	Ho 24	TG 03 31	10,58
Mendham (in Suffolk)	E 12	TM 27 82	10,32. 14,19;35 note
Merton	Wa 11	TL 91 98	31,35
Methwold	Gr 3	TL 73 94	1,210;*211 note*. 8,38
Metton	NE 16	TG 19 37	9,143;146
Middleton	De 17	TM 15 92	4,56
Middleton	Fr 39	TF 66 16	4,45. 14,5. 19,4;6. 23,11
Mildenhall (In Suffolk, Lackford Hundred)		TL 71 74	42,1
Mileham	La 13	TF 92 19	1,80;212;214;217;232. 4,8. 8,69-70. 9,80. 10,5;53. 13,17. 15,15. 20,7-9. 21,19. 31,39-40. 34,5-6. 66,25;38
Mintlyn	Fr 29	TF 65 19	10,50
Moor	Bl 12	TG 37 07	55,1
Morley (St. Botolph) (St. Peter)	Fo 25 Fo 26	TG 06 00 TM 06 98	8,78. 20,11
Morning Thorpe	De 19	TM 21 92	4,56. 14,40
Morston	Ho 1	TG 00 43	1,29;148. 9,141
Mortoft	SE 22	TG 11 28	8,8
Moulton (St. Mary)	W 11	TG 40 07	1,43;150;160;163
Moulton (St. Michael)	De 21	TM 16 90	4,56. 9,98;212;223. 65,13
Mulbarton	Hu 19	TG 19 01	9,196. 20,34
Mundesley	NE 20	TG 31 36	8,123;129
Mundford	Gr 10	TL 80 93	8,40. 9,119. 15,9
Mundham	Lo 10	TM 32 98	1,183;229. 9,49;50;55;60;67; 170. 14,36. 35,8-10. 47,6. 50,10. 57,2
Murlai	Ng	unidentified	10,11
Narborough	SG 3	TF 74 12	9,70
Narford	SG 4	TF 76 13	4,2
Naruestuna	C	unidentified	33,4
Nayland	Hu 25	TF 15 98	5,5. 6,6. 9,187;191
Neatishead	Tu 19	TG 34 20	17,36
Necton	SG 8	TF 87 09	22,1 note;10-16;18;20-23
Ness	WF 1	TG 48 21	9,92
Neutuna (Lost, nr. Holt)	Ho	unidentified	1,27
Newton	SG 1	TF 83 15	1,72. 27,1
Newton	He 1	TG 25 08	1,123
Newton (Flotman)	Hu 27	TM 21 98	9,97;203. 48,5
(West) Newton	Fr 5	TF 69 27	2,4
(North) Elmham	La 9	TF 98 21	10,5
Northrepps	NE 10	TG 24 39	See Repps
(North) Walsham	Tu 7	TG 28 30	8,12. 17,38;52
Northwold	Gr 1	TL 75 97	8,39. 15,8; *29 note*
Norton (Subcourse)	C 2	TM 40 98	9,55;109. 12,21;44. 14,42. 20,36. 31,13. 33,3. 65,15
Norwich	N 1	TG 23 08	1,61;63;66. 21,37
Oby	WF 12	TG 41 14	9,14;22. 17,13;15
Ocselea	Mi	unidentified	1,14

	Map	Grid	Text
Ormesby (St. Margaret	EF 2	TG 49 14	1,45–46;48;59. 9,16. 10,44. 65,10
and St. Michael)	EF 1	TG 48 14	
Osmondiston	Di 18	TM 15 79	9,48. 41,1. 66,83
Ottering Hithe	Gr 2	TL 71 94	8,43;45
Oulton	SE 19	TG 13 28	1,57
Outwell	Cl 21	TF 51 03	8,20. 16,2
Overstrand	NE 7	TG 24 40	51,8
Oxborough	SG 20	TF 73 00	12,3. 28,1
Oxhead	SE 32	TG 22 24	61,2
Oxwick	La 1	TF 91 25	15,14 note
Palgrave	SG 5	TF 83 11	1,71. 4,5. 8,94
Palling	Ha 9	TG 42 26	1,200. 4,51. 9,182
Panworth	Wa 1	TF 89 04	21,16
Panxworth	W 3	TG 34 13	1,156–157. 4,37. 19,25
Paston	Tu 1	TG 32 34	8,11. 17,40. 19,35
Pattesley	La 2	TF 89 24	34,5
Pensthorpe	G 18	TF 94 29	21,21
Pentney	Fr 49	TF 72 13	9,2
Pickenham (North	SG 11	TF 86 06	1,71;75. 4,6-7. 8,97. 21,14-15.
and South)	SG 15	TF 85 04	22,3. 51,9. 66,52
Pirnhow	Lo 22	TM 33 91	9,63
Plumstead	NE 24	TG 13 34	8,134
Plumstead (Great	Bl 2	TG 30 09	1,100;102;104. 10,29;67;69;70.
and Little)	Bl 1	TG 31 12	19,28. 20,20. 53,1
Poringland	He 13	TG 27 01	1,112. 2,8. 9,37;115–116. 12,8.
			14,17. 66,82
Postwick	Bl 10	TG 29 07	24,6. 66,100
(Potter) Heigham	Ha 16	TG 41 19	65,7
(Pudding) Norton	Br 19	TF 92 27	1,16;18
Pulham (St. Mary Magdalene	E 4	TM 19 86	
and St. Mary the Virgin)	E 5	TM 21 85	1,226. 15,24;27 note;29 note
Pyrleston, see Billingford (nr. Diss)	—	—	—
Quarles	NG 9	TF 88 38	1,35. 9,85
Quidenham	Gu 1	TM 02 87	1,144. 9,133. 14,7
Rackheath	Ta 17	TG 27 14	1,191. 17,22. 20,25
Rainthorpe	Hu 29	TM 20 97	9,202. 43,4
Ranworth	W 2	TG 35 14	1,157
Raveningham	C 5	TM 39 96	1,208;240. 6,7. 9,108. 10,47.
			20,36. 31,10;15. 50,12. 65,17.
			66,98
Raynham (East	Br 25	TF 87 25	1,88. 9,139. 21,22. 23,5
and West)	Br 24		
South Raynham	Br 26	TF 88 24	9,140. 23,5;6
Redenhall	E 8	TM 26 84	1,128;131;222;226
Reedham	W 14	TG 42 02	1,162. 17,3. 19,24
Reepham	Ey 14	TG 10 22	31,1
Repps	WF 8	TG 42 16	4,27. 9,13;20;23. 17,15. 19,30.
			64,3
Repps		—	8,125. 17,7. 19,20
(Northrepps)	NE 10	TG 24 39	8,126;128
(Southrepps)	NE 18	TG 25 36	8,128
Reymerston	Mi 14	TG 01 06	13,19 note. 66,27
Riddlesworth	Gu 9	TL 96 81	39,1
Ridlington	Tu 5	TG 34 31	36,4
Ringland	Ey 33	TG 13 14	25,8
Ringstead	Sm 4	TF 70 40	9,8. 16,5. 19,10. 20,3. 49,1;2
Rippon	SE 31	TG 21 22	25,11
Rising	Gr 13	TL 70 90	8,35-36
Rockland (All Saints	Sh 4	TL 99 96	
and St. Andrew)	Sh 4	TL 99 96	8,55. 9,130. 24,1. 50,8
Rockland (St. Mary)	He 9	TG 31 04	1,109;116;120. 9,27;41;44;
			161. 10,31. 12,12;16

	Map	Grid	Text
Rockland (St. Peter)	Wa 14	TL 99 97	8,52
Roding (Aythorpe, High, Leaden, Margaret and White; in Essex)	—	—	38,3
Rollesby	WF 11	TG 44 15	1,167. 9,13. 10,87. 17,10;15. 64,2
Roudham	Sh 19	TL 95 87	1,141. 8,57. 15,10. 24,3
Rougham	La 10	TF 83 20	1,78. 8,68. 13,17
Roughton	NE 17	TG 21 36	3,1. 9,87;148. 23,7
Roxham	Cl 32	TL 63 99	66,45
Roydon	Di 13	TM 09 80	7,12. 14,*23 note*; 26;34. 20,23
Roydon	Fr 14	TF 69 23	2,4. 14,*23 note*
Rudham (East	Br 15	TF 82 28	4,17. 8,107-109. 34,11
and West)	Br 14	TF 81 27	
Runcton (Holme	Cl 4	TF 61 09	14,1;3. 66,40
and South)	Cl 8	TF 63 08	
(North) Runcton	Fr 38	TF 64 15	13,14. 19,5
Runhall	Fo 14	TG 05 06	1,84. 4,11
Runham	EF 10	TG 45 10	1,59;203. 9,90. 65,9
Runton	NE 4	TG 17 42	9,147. 19,22
Rushall	E 10	TM 19 82	1,224. 32,7. 35,4
Rushford	Gu 8	TL 92 81	15,12. 58,2
(East) Ruston	Ha 18	TG 34 27	31,5
(Great) Ryburgh	Br 23	TF 96 27	8,113. 34,9
(Little) Ryburgh	G 20	TF 96 27	8,106. 34,8
Ryston	Cl 27	TF 62 01	13,9. 66,10;54
Saham (Toney)	Wa 3	TF 89 02	1,3;7;9-10;135-136. 9,124. 21,17. 49,5. 66,67
Sall	Ey 10	TG 11 24	1,185. 8,5. 20,28. 56,8. 57,3
Salthouse	NE 1	TG 07 43	8,130. 19,19. 66,97
Sandringham	Fr 4	TF 69 28	35,1
Santon	Gr 18	TL 82 87	8,42
Saxlingham	G 3	TG 02 39	10,7;8;55. 34,12
Saxlingham (Nethergate	He 25	TM 23 97	1,118;127. 7,4. 9,164. 17,18. 25,26. 30,4. 35,2. 49,7
and Thorpe)	He 24	TM 21 97	
Saxthorpe	SE 13	TG 11 30	1,193. 4,22;35
Searning	La 31	TF 95 12	8,62;67. 31,40. 66,38
Schieteshaga in Hempnall	—	—	31,6
Sco	WF 5	TG 45 18	10,30;89
(Sco) Ruston	Tu 16	TG 28 21	8,12. 17,45. 26,5
Scole, see Osmondiston			
Scottow	SE 34	TG 26 23	1,194. 4,36. 17,23;45. 20,31-32. 21,32;36
Scoulton	Wa 7	TF 97 00	8,53. 50,5. 51,6
Scratby	EF 3	TG 50 15	10,43. 17,62. 65,10
Sculthorpe	G 10	TF 89 31	4,4;98
Sedgeford	Sm 7	TF 70 36	10,20. 66,88
Seething	Lo 14	TM 31 97	1,230. 6,5. 9,25;51;62;69;169; 171. 47,5;7
Semere	E 6	TM 18 84	7,13. 14,*23 note*; 30
Sharrington	Ho 14	TG 03 36	1,29;31
Shelfhanger	Di 6	TM 10 83	1,174. 4,49;50. 14,27;32. 63,1. 66,41
Shelton	De 22	TM 22 91	9,98;216. 35,13
Shereford	Br 11	TF 88 29	8,112
Sheringham	NE 2	TG 15 43	19,18;19
Shernborne	Do 9	TF 71 32	2,4. 8,86. 27,2. 51,4. 66,88
Shimpling	Di 9	TM 15 82	1,172;180. 7,13. 9,46. 14,*23 note*; 33
Shingham	Cl 20	TF 76 05	22,14
Shipden (Lost)	NE 5	TG 22 42	9,153. 10,24. 17,6
Shipdham	Mi 10	TF 95 07	1,87;192. 8,*81-84 note*;84. 13,20. 66,67

	Map	Grid	Text
Shotesham (All Saints	He 22	TM 24 99	1,106;110;113;184. 2,8. 7,5. 9,24;
and St. Mary)	He 23	TM 23 98	38;159;163. 14,16. 17,16. 25,25;28
Shotford	E 11	TM 25 82	7,6. 26,6
Shouldham (All Saints	Cl 11	TF 68 08	
and St. Margaret)	Cl 9	TF 68 09	21,7. 31,32
(Shouldham) Thorpe	Cl 12	TF 66 07	21,8. 31,23 note. 66,14
Shropham	Sh 7	TL 98 92	6,1. 9,126–128. 24,2. 52,1. 66,43
Sidestrand	NE 11	TG 25 39	8,120;121. 8,127
Sisland	Lo 11	TM 34 98	1,183. 12,25
Skeyton	SE 26	TG 24 25	20,31. 31,2
Sloley	Tu 13	TG 29 24	17,48. 20,33. 21,36
Smallburgh	Tu 14	TG 33 23	9,180. 17,49
(Great) Snarehill	Gu 6	TL 87 80	9,74. 14,10 note. 66,76-77
(Little) Snarehill	Gu 7	TL 88 81	9,75
Snetterton	Sh 11	TL 99 91	6,1. 9,73. 66,75
Snettisham	Fr 1	TF 69 34	2,1;3–5;10. 8,48
Snore	Cl 34	TL 62 99	16,2
(Great) Snoring	NG 16	TF 94 34	1,92. 34,17
(Little) Snoring	G 12	TF 95 32	1,16. 8,101. 34,7
Somerton (East	WF 2	TG 48 19	1,217. 4,26-27. 9,23. 10,83.
and West)	WF 3	TG 47 19	64,7. 66,79
Southery	Cl 36	TL 62 94	14,2
Southmere	Do 3	TF 75 37	1,2
Southrepps	NE 18	TG 25 36	See Repps
Southwood	Bl 16	TG 39 05	12,45. 19,29. 31,11. 66,102
Sparham	Ey 26	TG 07 19	12,27. 33,1. 56,6
Spixworth	Ta 11	TG 24 15	26,3
Sporle	SG 6	TF 84 11	1,71;132;137–138;188;234. 7,17
Stalham	Ha 11	TG 37 25	4,38–39. 9,88;183. 17,56. 65,2
Stanfield	La 12	TF 93 20	4,8. 8,70
Stanford	Gr 8	TL 85 94	9,121. 10,52. 21,12. 23,14. 50,1
Stanhoe	Do 5	TF 80 36	1,2;16. 2,5. 8,85
Stanninghall	Ta 7	TG 25 17	1,232
Starston	E 7	TM 23 84	1,130;223. 9,167. 14,21. 35,5.
			43,3
Stibbard	G 21	TF 98 28	1,16. 8,106
Stiffkey	NG 5	TF 97 43	1,38;89;91;148. 21,25
Stinton	Ey 11	TG 11 25	8,1
Stockton	C 8	TM 38 94	1,239
Stody	Ho 19	TG 05 35	1,24. 36,7
Stoke (Ferry)	Cl 33	TL 70 99	4,43. 21,4. 31,26;28. 66,37
Stoke (Holy Cross)	Hu 22	TG 23 00	1,107;117;125;205. 9,25;39;160.
			12,7. 25,27. 35,3. 48,3–4
Stokesby	EF 8	TG 43 10	19,23;28;30;36
Stow (Bardolph)	Cl 16	TF 62 05	13,7–8. 66,6;8
Stow (Bedon)	Wa 15	TL 96 95	1,10;135–136. 8,71. 47,1
Stradsett	Cl 17	TF 66 05	9,232. 13,10
Stratton (St. Mary	De 18	TM 19 92	4,56. 9,98(5);215;223. 10,19;
and St. Michael)	De 15	TM 20 93	46. 14,40. 15,29. 35,15
Stratton (Strawless)	SE 41	TG 22 20	1,57. 10,41. 25,10. 26,2
Strumpshaw	Bl 11	TG 34 07	1,98
Sturston	Gr 9	TL 87 94	9,120. 22,9. 31,33
Suffield	NE 30	TG 23 31	4,23. 9,149;179;181
Surlingham	He 4	TG 30 06	1,108. 9,26;40;43;161. 10,31;92.
			12,14
Sustead	NE 15	TG 18 37	8,131. 9,87;144;146
Sutton	La 14	TF 92 18	21,19
Sutton	Ha 13	TG 38 23	9,13;88
Swaffham	SG 7	TF 82 08	4,1;3. 66,63
Swafield	Tu 3	TG 28 83	10,18. 19,35. 36,3
Swainsthorpe	Hu 21	TG 21 00	9,195. 12,40. 24,7. 48,4

	Map	Grid	Text
Swannington	Ey 28	TG 13 19	4,32. 25,6
Swanton	De 7	TM 16 94	4,56. 9,98;102;213;221;223
Swanton (Abbot)	SE 27	TG 26 26	17,25
Swanton (Morley)	La 21	TG 01 17	20,7
Swanton (Novers)	Ho 23	TG 01 32	10,9
Swardeston	Hu 15	TG 19 02	9,185;194. 12,37. 20,34. 66,85
Swathing	Mi 16	TF 98 04	1,84;86
Syderstone	Br 8	TF 83 32	4,17. 8,108;109
Tacolneston	De 4	TM 14 95	1,237. 9,224
Tasburgh	De 5	TM 20 95	4,56. 9,219;227. 11,4;5. 19,39
Tatterford	Br 17	TF 86 28	40,1
Tattersett	Br 10	TF 85 29	8,110
Taverham	Ta 13	TG 16 13	1,55. 4,33. 8,7. 10,36. 10a,1. 20,27
Termentuna	—	—	49,8 note
Terrington (St. Clement	Fr 19	TF 55 20	13,12. 31,31
and St. John)	Fr 35	TF 53 15	
Testerton	Br 22	TF 93 26	34,10
Tharston	De 8	TM 19 94	9,98(5);99. 35,14
Thelveton	Di 11	TM 16 81	7,9;13. 15,26. 52,4
Thetford	Th 1	TL 87 82	1,69;70;210;211. 9,1
Thompson	Wa 12	TL 92 96	8,53. 9,125. 47,1. 51,7. 66,73
Thornage	Ho 18	TG 04 36	10,7;8
Thornham	Sm 2	TF 73 43	10,3
Thorpe, in Shipdham	Mi 8	TF 97 08	15,17;21
Thorpe (Abbots)	E 15	TM 20 79	1,225;226. 14,18
Thorpe (Market)	NE 23	TG 24 35	8,122;128. 33,5
Thorpe (Parva)	Di 16	TM 16 79	7,9
Thorpe (St. Andrew)	Bl 6	TG 27 09	1,63;216;218;233–234;236. 66,94
Thorpland	Cl 7	TF 61 08	13,6. 14,3. 66,5
Thorpland	G 11	TF 93 32	1,16
Threxton	Wa 8	TF 88 00	8,50. 21,18
Thrigby	EF 5	TG 46 12	1,204. 9,89. 10,45. 19,37
Thur(e)stuna	—	—	1,86 note. 8,84. 9,134. 15,12
Thurgarton	NE 21	TG 18 35	9,87;152. 17,5
Thurketeliart, lost in Aldeby	C 14	unidentified	20,36
Thurlton	C 3	TM 41 98	1,241. 4,57. 9,110. 19,40. 31,19. 50,13. 65,16. 66,26 note
Thurne	WF 9	TG 40 15	9,17. 17,12. 66,78
Thurning	Ey 2	TG 08 29	1,186. 8,4. 10,34. 56,9
Thursford	NG 17	TF 98 33	1,93
Thurstuna, see *Thur(e)stuna*	—	—	—
Thurton	Ey 17	TG 10 21	19,34. 21,34
Thurton	Lo 6	TG 32 00	9,64;68. 15,28. 49,8 note
Thustuna, see *Thur(e)stuna*	—	—	—
Thuxton	Mi 12	TG 03 07	1,86 note. 8,81 note. 66,26 note
Thwaite	SE 9	TG 19 32	17,27
Tibenham	De 25	TM 13 89	4,56. 9,98;217;223;226. 14,39. 17,65. 29,7;10. 66,107
Titchwell	Do 1	TF 76 43	1,2. 9,117. 116,5
Tittleshall	La 11	TF 89 20	8,69. 31,38
Tivetshall (St. Margaret	Di 2	TM 16 87	1,173. 10,93. 14,23. 15,27
and St. Mary)	Di 3	TM 16 86	
Tochestorp, Toke(s)torp	Fo	unidentified	4,14. 8,74;76. 12,5
Toft (Monks)	C 7	TM 42 95	1,230;238;240. 20,36
Toftrees	Br 18	TF 89 27	8,98. 34,9
Toke(s)torp, see *Tochestorp*	—	—	—
Toombers	Cl 13	TF 65 06	21,3
Topcroft	Lo 18	TM 26 92	14,37. 29,8
Torp	Lo	unidentified	12,26. 15,28;29 note
Torvestuna	—	—	66,26 note

	Map	Grid	Text
Tottenhill	Cl 1	TF 64 11	31,23
Tottington	Wa 16	TL 89 95	9,12. 43,1
Trowse	He 2	TG 24 06	1,49;121;124. 9,162
Trunch	NE 27	TG 28 34	8,124;129
(East) Tuddenham	Mi 1	TG 08 11	4,15;29. 13,23. 20,17. 66,68
(North) Tuddenham	Mi 2	TG 05 12	15,19. 20,15. 62,2. 66,30;32
Tunstall	W 9	TG 41 08	20,19. 24,5. 38,4. 52,2
Tunstead	Tu 15	TG 30 22	26,5
Tuttington	SE 24	TG 22 27	8,8. 17,30
Tyby	Ey 3	TG 00 28	56,7
Upton	W 5	TG 39 12	1,154. 12,6. 17,1. 66,92
Upwell	Cl 25	TF 50 02	1,210. 13,11. 21,5;8. 66,49
Wacton	Di 1	TM 17 91	4,56. 9,98;214;216;223
Walcott	Ha 1	TG 36 31	36,5. 66,104
Wallington	Cl 10	TF 62 07	9,230. 66,16
Walpole	Fr 34	TF 50 16	49,9
(North) Walsham	Tu 7	TG 28 30	8,12. 17,38;52
(South) Walsham	W 4	TG 36 13	1,103;150;155;168;204. 10,27. 12,6. 17.1
Walsingham	Hu 18	TG 17 01	9,188. 32,2-3
Walsingham (Great and Little)	NG 11 NG 13	TF 93 37 TF 93 36	1,40. 21,24. 34,18
Walsoken	Fr 50	TF 47 10	16,3
(East) Walton	Fr 42	TF 74 16	4,45. 9,2. 22,15
(West) Walton	Fr 45	TF 47 13	8,21. 15,4;29 note. 20,4. 66,21
Warham (All Saints and St. Mary)	NG 4 NG 3	TF 94 41 TF 94 41	1,37;42. 2,6. 4,20. 10,10. 25,23. 60,1
Washingford	He 21	TG 31 01	12,24
Waterden	G 6	TF 88 35	8,102
Watlingeseta (lost in Diss)	Di 17	TM 12 79	1,50
Watton	Wa 6	TF 92 00	9,11
Waxham	Ha 10	TG 44 26	4,40;42. 9,182. 17,54. 65,5
Weasenham (All Saints and St. Peter)	La 33 La 32	TF 84 21 TF 85 22	1,79. 8,64
Weeting	Gr 17	TF 77 89	1,210. 8,44 note
Welborne	Fo 5	TF 06 10	8,75
Well	Fr 27	TF 72 20	18,1
Wellingham	La 5	TF 87 22	31,39
Wells (next the Sea)	NG 2	TF 91 43	1,37;90. 4,20. 10,10. 34,16. 60,1
Wendling	La 29	TF 93 13	14,12
Wereham	Cl 29	TF 68 01	21,4
West Briggs	Cl 2	TF 65 10	13,5. 66,4
Westfield	Mi 4	TF 99 09	4,16
Weston (Longville)	Ey 32	TG 11 15	2,10. 4,28. 19,32. 56,5
(West) Tofts	Gr 12	TL 83 92	10,4
Westwick	Tu 10	TG 28 25	26,5
Weybourne	Ho 5	TG 11 43	6,2. 66,97
Wheatacre	C 10	TM 46 93	31,17
Whimpwell	Ha 3	TG 38 29	17,55;60
Whinburgh	Mi 9	TG 00 08	13,19;21
Whissonsett	La 6	TF 91 23	9,80
Whitlingham	He 3	TG 27 07	1,114;120. 9,31
Whitwell	Ey 16	TG 10 22	1,53. 21,27
Wick	Gu 13	TM 01 82	8,60. 11,2. 23,16. 66,95
Wick (in Garboldisham)	Gu	unidentified	23,16 note
Wickhampton	W 13	TG 42 05	1,161;163
Wicklewood	Fo 21	TG 07 02	8,77. 31,41
Wickmere	SE 5	TG 17 33	1,57. 2,11. 8,8. 9,178. 17,34
Wiggenhall (St. Germans St. Mary Magdalen St. Mary the Virgin St. Peter)	Fr 47 Fr 51 Fr 46 Fr 48	TF 59 14 TF 59 11 TF 58 14 TF 60 13	31,24. 66,19

	Map	*Grid*	*Text*
Wighton	NG 7	TF 94 39	1,32;41–42
Wilby	Sh 16	TM 03 89	9,126. 19,11. 31,37
Wilton	Gr 16	TL 73 88	8,34. 66,66
Wimbotsham	Cl 15	TF 62 04	8,17. 13,8. 16,1. 66,8
(East) Winch	Fr 40	TF 69 16	1,132. 9,3;234. 22,20. 66,20;108
West Winch	Fr 37	TF 63 15	13,14. 21,9. 66,18;50
Winfarthing	Di 4	TM 10 85	1,169;174;181. 66,41;42
Winterton	WF 16	TG 49 19	1,48;168. 9,158. 10,30;82;85. 17,9. 19,30. 64,8
Witchingham Great	Ey 21	TG 10 20	1,187. 5,4. 17,20. 19,32–34.
and Little	Ey 22	TG 11 20	21,28. 25,5
Witton	Tu 4	TG 33 31	1,196. 8,12. 17,41
Witton	Bl 4	TG 31 09	1,101. 10,81. 58,3
Wiveton	Ho 4	TG 04 42	8,115. 21,23
Wolterton	SE 8	TG 16 32	8,135. 17,32. 20,32
(Wood) Bastwick	W 1	TG 33 15	1,44;158. 17,2;3. 20,19. 66,91;93
(Wood) Dalling	Ey 6	TG 08 27	8,4. 25,4. 34,20
(Wood) Norton	Ey 4	TG 01 27	10,15. 21,30. 25,3. 56,3
(Wood) Rising	Mi 19	TF 98 03	1,14. 8,87
Woodton	Lo 17	TM 28 94	1,182;184. 6,5. 7,15. 9,54. 29,9. 47,3
Wootton (North	Fr 11	TF 63 24	1,133
and South)	Fr 17	TF 64 22	
Wormegay	Cl 3	TF 66 11	13,4. 66,3
Worstead	Tu 11	TG 30 26	4,37. 17,43. 21,36
Wramplingham	Fo 16	TG 11 06	4,10;12. 12,4;5
Wreningham	Hu 26	TM 16 98	9,187. 13,24
Wretham (East	Sh 9	TL 91 90	22,23
and West)	Sh 8	TL 89 91	
Wroxham	Ta 8	TG 29 17	1,190. 17,21. 20,19–21;24–25
Wymondham	Fo 24	TG 11 01	1,215;237. 8,72;80. 66,39
Yarmouth	EF 11	TG 52 07	1,67. ESf 3
Yaxham	Mi 5	TG 00 10	4,15. 9,82. 13,22. 15,21–22. 21,20. 66,28
Yelverton	He 4	TG 29 02	1,111. 2,7. 8,88. 9,36;161;165; 166. 12,10
Yelverton, see 'Hunt'	—	—	—

Places not named, at present unlocated: 9,112. 48,8

Places outside Norfolk: Cornwall 1,201

Places outside Britain: Anjou ... Guy. Apulia ... 9,88. Bayeux ... Bishop of. Beaufour ... Ralph. Beuvrière ... Drogo. Bigot ... Roger. Bohun ... Humphrey. Bourneville ... William. Brittany ... Fulcher. Caen ... St. Stephen, Walter. Cailli ... William. Cluny ... SS. Peter and Paul. Corbon ... Hugh. Courson ... Robert. Coutances ... Bishop. Culey ... Humphrey. Denmark ... 10,77. Dol ... Walter. Écouis ... William. Evreux ... R(oger). Ferrers ... Hermer. Fougères ... Ralph. Fourneaux ... Ansketel. Glanville ... Robert. Grancourt ... Walter. Hellean ... Tihel. Houdain ... Hugh. Limésy ... Ralph. Montfort ... Hugh. Mortain ... Robert. Moutiers ... Lisois. Noron ... Ralph. Noyers ... William. Parthenay ... W(illiam). Pierrepont ... Reynold. Poitou ... Roger. Port(-en-Bessin) ... Hugh. Raismes ... Roger. Rosay ... Lambert. Sackville ... Tichard. Saint-Clair ... Richard. St. Omer ... Humphrey. Tosny ... Ralph. Tourleville ... Ralph. Valognes ... Peter. Vaux ... Robert. Ver, Vere ... Bodin, Hervey. Verly ... Robert. Vernon ... Richard. Wanchy ... Hugh. Warenne ... William.

MAPS AND MAP KEYS

The County Boundary is marked by thick lines, dotted for the modern boundary; Hundred boundaries by thin lines, broken where uncertain.

An open circle denotes a place in another county but referred to in this text, or in the Notes.

The letters of National Grid 10-kilometre squares are shown on the map border. Each four-figure square covers one square kilometre (5/8th of a square mile).

NORFOLK WESTERN HUNDREDS

Brothercross (Br)
7 Bagthorpe
6 Barmer
16 Broomsthorpe
1 (Burnham) Deepdale
2 Burnham (Norton)
4 Burnham (Sutton
3 Burnham (Ulph)
5 Burnham (Westgate)
21 Colkirk
9 Dunton
23 (Great) Ryburgh
20 Helhoughton
12 Hempton
13 Houghton
19 (Pudding) Norton
25 Raynham (East)
24 Raynham (West)
15 Rudham (East)
14 Rudham (West)
11 Shereford
26 South Raynham
8 Syderstone
17 Tatterford
10 Tattersett
22 Testerton
18 Toftrees

Clackclose (Cl)
18 Barton (Bendish)
19 Beechamwell
23 Bexwell
30 Boughton
24 Crimplesham
26 Denver
22 Downham Market
14 Fincham
5 Fodderstone
31 Fordham
35 Hilgay
6 Marham
21 Outwell
32 Roxham
4 Runcton (Holme)
8 Runcton (South)
27 Ryston
20 Shingham

11 Shouldham (All Saints)
9 Shouldham (St Margaret
12 (Shouldham) Thorpe
34 Snore
36 Southery
33 Stoke (Ferry)
16 Stow (Bardolph)
17 Stradsett
7 Thorpland
13 Toombers
1 Tottenhill
25 Upwell
10 Wallington
29 Wereham
2 West Briggs
28 (West) Dereham
15 Wimbotsham
3 Wormegay

Docking (Do)
6 Barwick
8 (Bircham) Newton
11 (Bircham) Tofts
2 Brancaster
4 Docking
7 Fring
10 (Great) Bircham
9 Shernborne
3 Southmere
5 Stanhoe
1 Titchwell

Freebridge (Fr)
44 Acre (Castle)
43 Acre (West)
3 Anmer
6 Appleton
31 (Ash) Wicken
8 Babingley
25 Bawsey
12 (Castle) Rising
20 Clenchwarton
15 Corgham
2 Dersingham
42 (East) Walton
40 East Winch

7 Flitcham
32 Gayton
33 (Gayton) Thorpe
24 Gaywood
30 Glosthorpe
18 Grimston
10 Harpley
9 Hillington
36 Islington
26 Leziate
23 Lynn (King's)
22 Lynn (North)
28 Lynn (South)
21 Lynn (West)
16 Massingham (Great)
13 Massingham (Little)
39 Middleton
29 Mintlyn
38 (North) Runcton
49 Pentney
14 Roydon
4 Sandringham
1 Snettisham
19 Terrington (St Clement)
35 Terrington (St John)
34 Walpole
50 Walsoken
27 Well
41 (West) Bilney
5 (West) Newton
45 (West) Walton
37 West Winch
47 Wiggenhall (St Germans)
51 Wiggenhall (St Mary Magdalen)
46 Wiggenhall (St Mary the Virgin)
48 Wiggenhall (St Peter)
11 Wootton (North)
17 Wootton (South)

Gallow (G)
14 Alethorpe
9 Barsham (East)
8 Barsham (West)

1 Burnham (Overy)
2 Burnham Thorpe
19 Clipstone
4 Creake (North)
5 Creake (South)
15 Croxton
17 Fakenham
16 Fulmodeston
13 Kettlestone
20 (Little) Ryburgh
12 (Little) Snoring
7 North Barsham
18 Pensthorpe
3 Saxlingham
10 Sculthorpe
21 Stibbard
11 Thorpland
6 Waterden

Greenhoe (North) (NG)
18 Barney
8 Binham
6 (Cock) Thorpe
10 Egmere
12 (Field) Dalling
16 (Great) Snoring
14 Hindringham
1 Holkham
15 Houghton (St Giles) *Murlai*
9 Quarles
5 Stiffkey
17 Thursford
11 Walsingham (Great)
13 Walsingham (Little)
4 Warham (All Saints)
3 Warham (St Mary)
2 Wells (next the Sea)
7 Wighton

Greenhoe (South) (SG)
24 Bodney
10 Bradenham (East)
9 Bradenham (West)
16 Caldecote
17 Cleythorpe
14 (Cockley) Cley
25 Didlington
23 Foulden
18 Gooderstone
19 (Great) Cressingham
21 Hilborough
12 Holme (Hale)
13 Houghton (on the Hill)
26 Langford
22 (Little) Cressingham
3 Narborough
4 Narford

8 Necton
1 Newton
20 Oxborough
5 Palgrave
11 Pickenham (North)
15 Pickenham (South)
2 (South) Acre
6 Sporle
7 Swaffham

Grimshoe (Gr)
7 Buckenham (Tofts)
5 Colveston
4 Cranwich
19 Croxton
14 Feltwell
15 Hockwold
6 Ickburgh
11 Lynford
3 Methwold
10 Mundford
1 Northwold
2 Ottering Hithe
13 Rising
18 Santon
8 Stanford
9 Sturston
17 Weeting
12 (West) Tofts
16 Wilton

Guiltcross (Gu)
2 Banham
16 (Blo) Morton
12 Garboldisham
11 Gasthorpe
6 (Great) Snarehill
4 Harling (East)
3 Harling (West)
5 Kenninghall
10 Knettishall (in Suffolk)
7 (Little) Snarehill
14 Lopham (North)
15 Lopham (South)
1 Quidenham
9 Riddlesworth
8 Rushford
13 Wick

Launditch (La)
15 Beetley
19 Bittering
26 Dunham (Great)
27 Dunham (Little)
28 Fransham (Great)
30 Fransham (Little)

3 Gateley
8 Godwick
25 Gressenhall
20 Hoe
7 Horningtoft
22 Kempston
4 Kipton
24 Kirtling
17 Lexham (East)
16 Lexham (West)
18 Litcham
23 Longham
13 Mileham
9 (North) Elmham
1 Oxwick
2 Pattesley
10 Rougham
31 Searning
12 Stanfield
14 Sutton
21 Swanton (Morley)
11 Tittleshall
32 Weasenham (All Saints)
33 Weasenham (St Peter)
5 Wellingham
29 Wendling
6 Whissonsett

Smethdon (Sm)
5 Gnatingdon
6 Heacham
1 Holme (next the Sea)
3 Hunstanton
8 Ingoldisthorpe (Ingoldis Thorpe)
4 Ringstead
7 Sedgeford
2 Thornham

Wayland (Wa)
2 Ashill
17 Breckles
5 Carbrooke
13 Caston
9 Griston
10 (Little) Ellingham
11 Merton
1 Panworth
14 Rockland (St Peter)
3 Saham (Toney)
7 Scoulton
15 Stow (Bedon)
12 Thompson
8 Threxton
16 Tottington
6 Watton
4 West Carbrooke

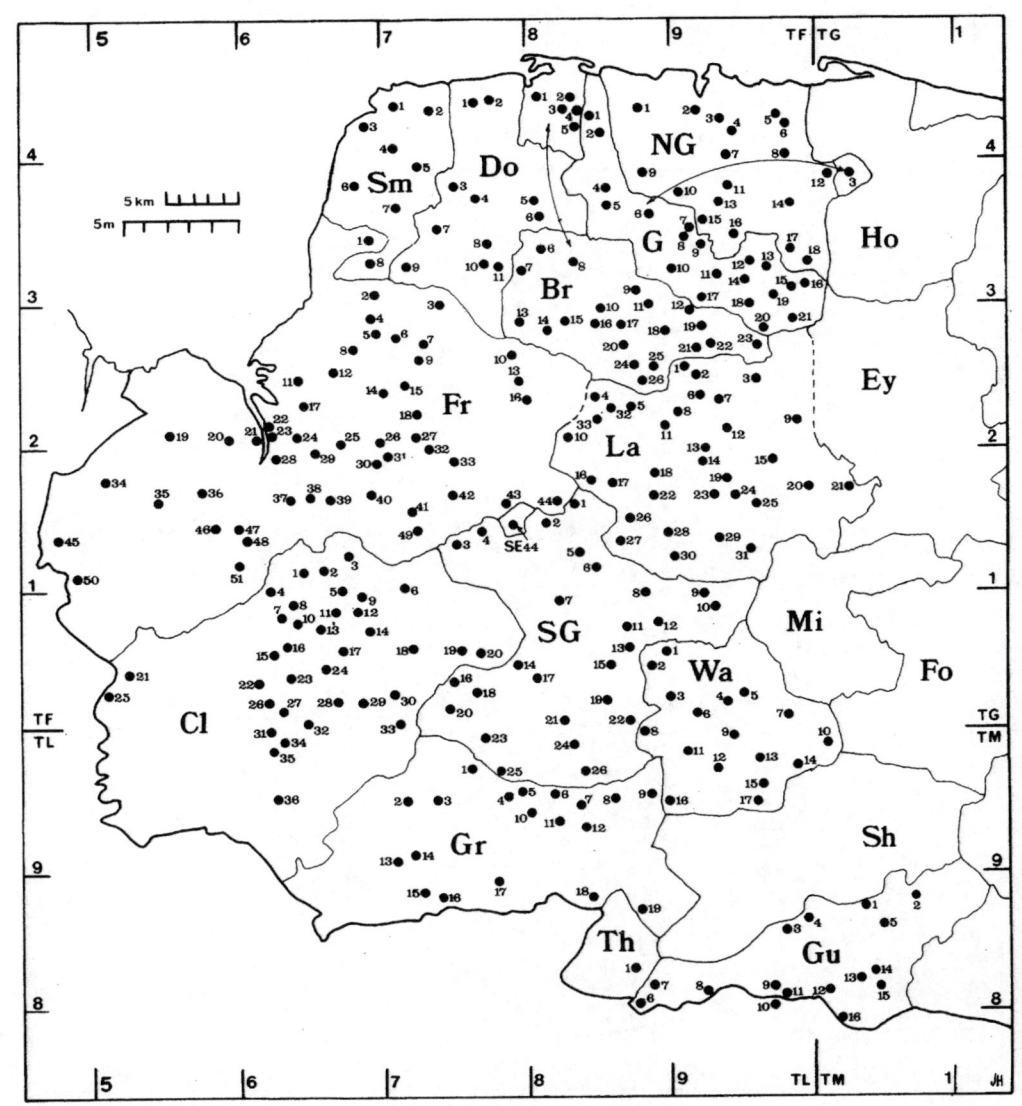

NORFOLK WESTERN HUNDREDS

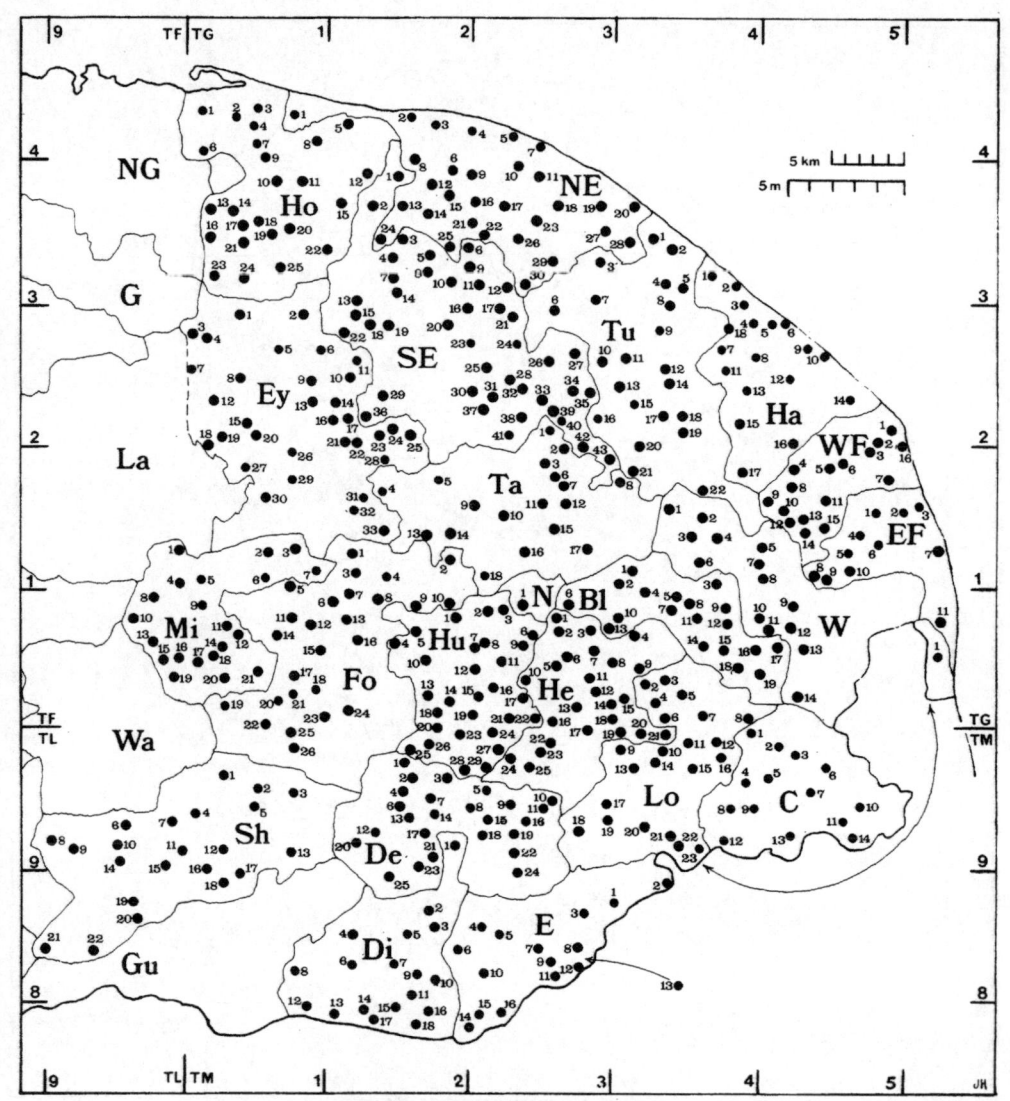

NORFOLK EASTERN HUNDREDS

NORFOLK EASTERN HUNDREDS

Blofield (Bl)
5 Blofield
8 Bradeston
7 Brundall
14 Buckenham
18 Cantley
13 Catton
17 Freethorpe
15 Hassingham
   Let(h)a
19 Limpenhoe
12 Moor
3 (North) Burlingham
2 Plumstead (Great)
1 Plumstead (Little)
10 Postwick
9 South Burlingham
16 Southwood
11 Strumpshaw
6 Thorpe (St Andrew)
4 Witton

Clavering (C)
11 Aldeby
12 Ellingham
13 Gillingham
6 Haddiscoe
4 Hales
1 Heckingham
   Ierpestuna
9 Kirby (Cane)
   Naruestuna
2 Norton (Subcourse)
5 Raveningham
8 Stockton
14 *Thurketeliart* (lost in Aldeby)
3 Thurlton
7 Toft (Monks)
10 Wheatacre

Depwade (De)
1 (Ashwell) Thorpe
23 Aslacton
9 Boyland
20 Carleton (Rode)
14 Forncett (St Mary)
13 Forncett (St Peter)
16 Fritton
2 Fundenhall
   Halas
3 Hapton
24 Hardwick
10 Hempnall
12 Hudeston
6 Kettleton
17 Middleton
19 Morning Thorpe
21 Moulton (St Michael)
11 *Schieteshagg*
22 Shelton
18 Stratton (St Mary)
15 Stratton (St Michael)
7 Swanton
4 Tacolneston
5 Tasburgh
8 Tharston
25 Tibenham

Diss (Di)
12 Bressingham
7 Burston
10 Dickleburgh
14 Diss
8 Fersfield
15 Frenze
5 Gissing
18 Osmondiston
13 Roydon
6 Shelfhanger
9 Shimpling
11 Thelveton
16 Thorpe (Parva)
2 Tivetshall (St Margaret)
3 Tivetshall (St Mary)
1 Wacton
17 *Watlingeseta* (lost in Diss)
4 Winfarthing

Earsham (E)
3 Alburgh
14 Billingford (near Diss)
16 Brockdish
1 Denton
2 Earsham
9 Harleston
12 Mendham (in Suffolk)
4 Pulham St Mary Magdalene
5 Pulham St Mary the Virgin
8 Redenhall
13 Rumburgh (in Suffolk)
10 Rushall
6 Semere
11 Shotford
7 Starston
15 Thorpe (Abbots)

North Erpingham (NE)
25 Aldborough
29 Antingham
6 Aylmerton
3 Beeston (Regis)
14 Bessingham
8 (East) Beckham
9 Felbrigg
19 Gimingham
12 Gresham
26 Gunton
22 Hanworth
   Hottune
28 Knapton
16 Metton
20 Mundesley
13 (North) Barningham
7 Overstrand
24 Plumstead
10 Repps (North Repps)
18 Repps (South Repps)
17 Roughton
4 Runton
1 Salthouse
2 Sheringham
5 Shipden (Lost)
11 Sidestrand
30 Suffield
15 Sustead
23 Thorpe (Market)
21 Thurgarton
27 Trunch

South Erpingham (SE)
6 Alby
23 Aylsham
2 (Bacons) Thorpe
17 Banningham
43 Belaugh
20 Blickling
36 Booton
28 Brampton
25 Burgh (next Aylsham)
38 Buxton
10 Calthorpe
29 Cawston
12 Colby

42 Coltishall
15 Corpusty
21 Crackford
44 Custhorpe
35 Easton
11 Erpingham
40 Hautbois (Great)
39 Hautbois (Little)
37 Hevingham
16 Ingworth
18 Irmingland
14 Itteringham
33 Lamas
 4 (Little) Barningham
 7 Mannington
30 Marsham
 3 Matlask
22 Mortoft
19 Oulton
32 Oxhead
31 Rippon
13 Saxthorpe
34 Scottow
26 Skeyton
41 Stratton (Strawless)
27 Swanton (Abbot)
 9 Thwaite
24 Tuttington
 1 (West) Beckham
 5 Wickmere
 8 Wolterton

Eynsford (Ey)
20 Bawdeswell
19 Beck
18 Billingford
12 Bintree
24 Brandiston
27 Bylaugh
30 Elsing
 8 Foulsham
15 Foxley
 5 Guestwick
 7 Guist
23 Guton
13 Hackford
25 Haveringland
31 Helmingham
 1 Hindolveston
 9 Kerdiston
29 Lyng
14 Reepham
33 Ringland
10 Sall
26 Sparham

11 Stinton
28 Swannington
 2 Thurning
17 Thurton
 3 Tyby
32 Weston (Longville)
16 Whitwell
21 Witchingham (Great)
22 Witchingham (Little)
 6 (Wood) Dalling
 4 (Wood) Norton

Flegg (East) (EF)
 7 Caister
 4 Filby
 9 Herringby
 6 Mautby
 2 Ormesby (St
    Margaret)
 1 Ormesby (St Michael)
10 Runham
 3 Scratby
 8 Stokesby
 5 Thrigby
11 Yarmouth

Flegg (West) (WF)
10 Ashby
 4 Bastwick
14 Billockby
15 Burgh (St Margaret)
13 Clippesby
 7 Hemsby
 6 Martham
 1 Ness
12 Oby
 8 Repps
11 Rollesby
 5 Sco
 2 Somerton (East)
 3 Somerton (West)
 9 Thurne
16 Winterton

Forehoe (Fo)
 Appethorp
13 Barford
12 Barnham (Broom)
 9 Bawburgh
 6 Bickerston
10 Bowthorpe
11 Brandon (Parva)
15 Carleton (Forehoe)
 7 Colton
 2 Costessy

18 Crownthorpe
22 Deopham
23 Dykebeck
 4 Easton
20 Hackford
19 Hingham
 1 Honingham
 3 (Honingham) Thorpe
17 Kimberley
 8 Marlingford
25 Morley (St Botolph)
26 Morley (St Peter)
14 Runhall
    Tochestorp,
    Toke(s)torp
 5 Welborne
21 Wicklewood
16 Wramplingham
24 Wymondham

Happing (Ha)
 7 Brumstead
15 Catfield
 6 Eccles
 2 Happisburgh
 5 Hempstead
12 Hickling
14 Horsey
 8 Ingham
 4 Lessingham
17 Ludham
 9 Palling
16 (Potter) Heigham
18 (East) Ruston
11 Stalham
13 Sutton
 1 Walcott
10 Waxham
 3 Whimpwell

Henstead (He)
18 Alpington
 5 Arminghall
20 Bergh (Apton)
 6 Bixley
 8 Bramerton
19 Brooke
10 Caistor (St Edmunds)
12 Framingham (Earl)
11 Framingham (Pigot)
16 Grensvill
15 Holverston
17 Howe
 7 Kirby (Bedon)
 1 Newton

13 Poringland
9 Rockland (St Mary)
25 Saxlingham (Nethergate)
24 Saxlingham (Thorpe)
22 Shotesham (All Saints)
23 Shotesham (St Mary)
4 Surlingham
2 Trowse
21 Washingford
3 Whitlingham
14 Yelverton

Holt (Ho)
13 Bale
9 Bayfield
2 Blakeney
12 Bodham
21 Briningham
17 Brinton
25 Briston
3 Cley (next the Sea)
22 Edgefield
7 Glandford
16 Gunthorpe
15 Hempstead
11 Holt
20 Hunworth
8 Kelling
6 Langham
10 Letheringsett
24 Melton (Constable)
1 Morston
Neutuna (lost near Holt)
14 Sharrington
19 Stody
23 Swanton (Novers)
18 Thornage
5 Weybourne
4 Wiveton

Humbleyard (Hu)
23 Bracon Ash
1 Colney
7 Cringleford
17 Dunston
2 Earlham
14 (East) Carleton
8 Eaton
28 Flordon
4 (Great) Melton
3 Heigham

20 Hethel
10 Hethersett
12 Intwood
24 Kenningham
11 Keswick
13 Ketteringham
6 Lakenham
5 Little Melton
16 Mangreen
9 Markshall
19 Mulbarton
25 Nayland
27 Newton (Flotman)
29 Rainthorpe
22 Stoke (Holy Cross)
21 Swainsthorpe
15 Swardeston
18 Walsingham
26 Wreningham

Loddon (Lo)
Alcmuntona
Algamundestuna
Appletona, -tuna
4 Ashby (St Mary)
19 Bedingham
Brant
23 Broome
5 Carleton (St Peter)
12 Chedgrave
3 Claxton
21 Ditchingham
1 Gorleston
8 Hardley
20 Hedenham
2 Hellington
15 Ingloss
9 Kirstead
13 Langhale
7 Langley
16 Loddon
10 Mundham
22 Pirnhow
14 Seething
11 Sisland
6 Thurton
18 Topcroft
Torp
17 Woodton

Mitford (Mi)
Baskenea
18 Calvely
15 Cranworth

1 (East) Dereham
7 East Tuddenham
21 Flockthorpe
11 Garveston
3 Hockering
13 Letton
20 Manson
6 Mattishall
2 (North) Tuddenham
Ocselea
14 Reymerston
10 Shipdham
17 (South) Burgh
16 Swathing
8 Thorpe, in Shipdham
12 Thuxton
4 Westfield
9 Whinburgh
19 (Wood) Rising
5 Yaxham

Norwich (N)
1 Norwich

Shropham (Sh)
17 Ashby
5 Attleborough (and minor)
2 Baconsthorpe
3 Besthorpe
22 Brettenham
20 Bridgham
13 Buckenham
18 Eccles
1 Great Ellingham
12 Hargham
6 Hockham
14 Illington
21 Kilverstone
15 Larling
10 Little Hockham
4 Rockland (All Saints and St Andrew)
19 Roudham
7 Shropham
11 Snetterton
16 Wilby
9 Wretham (East)
8 Wretham (West)

Taverham (Ta)
4 Attlebridge
15 Beeston (St Andrew)
16 Catton

12 Crostwick
14 Drayton
5 Felthorpe
6 Frettenham
3 Hainford
18 Hellesdon
9 Horsford
10 Horsham
2 Horstead
1 Mayton
17 Rackheath
11 Spixworth
7 Stanninghall
13 Taverham
8 Wroxham

Thetford (Th)
1 Thetford

Tunstead (Tu)
2 Bacton

18 Barton (Turf)
17 Beeston (St Lawrence) *Clareia*
8 Crostwight
12 Dilham
6 Felmingham
9 Honing
22 Horning
21 Hoveton (St John)
20 Hoveton (St Peter)
19 Neatishead
7 (North) Walsham
1 Paston
5 Ridlington
16 (Sco) Ruston
13 Sloley
14 Smallburgh
3 Swafield
15 Tunstead

10 Westwick
4 Witton
11 Worstead

Walsham (W)
8 Acle
10 Beighton
7 Fishley
12 Halvergate
6 Hemblington
11 Moulton (St Mary)
3 Panxworth
2 Ranworth
14 Reedham
4 (South) Walsham
9 Tunstall
5 Upton
13 Wickhampton
1 (Wood) Bastwick

SYSTEMS OF REFERENCE TO THE TWO VOLUMES OF DOMESDAY BOOK

The manuscript of the larger volume (here referred to as DB) is divided into numbered chapters, and the chapters into sections, usually marked by large initials and red ink. Farley did not number the sections and later historians, using his edition, have referred to the text of DB by folio numbers, which cannot be closer than an entire page or column. Moreover, several different ways of referring to the same column have been devised. In 1816 Ellis used three separate systems in his indices: (i) on pages i–cvii, 435-518, 537-570; (ii) on pages 1-144; (iii) on pages 145-433 and 519-535. Other systems have since come into use, notably that used by Vinogradoff, here followed. The present edition numbers the sections, the normal practicable form of close reference; but since all discussion of DB for two hundred years has been obliged to refer to folio or column, a comparative table will help to locate references given. The five columns below give Vinogradoff's notation, Ellis's three systems, and that used by Welldon Finn and others. Maitland, Stenton, Darby, and others have usually followed Ellis (i).

Vinogradoff	*Ellis (i)*	*Ellis (ii)*	*Ellis (iii)*	*Finn*
152 a	152	152 a	152	152 ai
152 b	152	152 a	152.2	152 a2
152 c	152 b	152 b	152 b	152 bi
152 d	152 b	152 b	152 b2	152 b2

The manuscript of Little Domesday Book (here referred to as LDB), in which the text of the Norfolk survey is preserved, has one column per page but it is again divided into numbered chapters and the chapters into sections, usually distinguished by paragraph-marks. Modern users of LDB have referred to its text by folio number, e.g. 152(a) 152b. Farley's edition presents both *recto* and *verso* of a folio on one printed page. In Norfolk, the relation between the column notation and the chapters and sections is:

109a	Landholders		123a	1,94 — 1,99	137a	1,212 — 1,214
109b	1,1 — 1,2	123b	1,99 — 1,106	137b	1,215 — 1,216
110a	1,2 — 1,6	124a	1,106 — 1,115	138a	1,216 — 1,218
110b	1,6 — 1,11	124b	1,116 — 1,121	138b	1,218 — 1,221
111a	1,11 — 1,16	125a	1,122 — 1,128	139a	1,221 — 1,226
111b	1,16 — 1,19	125b	1,128 — 1,132	139b	1,226 — 1,228
112a	1,19 — 1,26	126a	1,132 — 1,135	140a	1,228 — 1,231
112b	1,26 — 1,32	126b	1,135 — 1,139	140b	1,231 — 1,236
113a	1,32 — 1,41	127a	1,139 — 1,143	141a	1,237 — 1,239
113b	1,41 — 1,48	127b	1,143 — 1,146	141b	1,239 — 1,241
114a	1,48 — 1,52	128a	1,146 — 1,149	142a	2,1 — 2,4
114b	1,52 — 1,57	128b	1,150 — 1,152	142b	2,4 — 2,4
115a	1,57 — 1,57	129a	1,152 — 1,159	143a	2,5 — 2,8
115b	1,57 — 1,59	129b	1,159 — 1,169	143b	2,8 — 3,1
116a	1,59 — 1,61	130a	1,169 — 1,176	144a	3,1 — 4,2
116b	1,61 — 1,61	130b	1,176 — 1,182	144b	4,2 — 4,9
117a	1,61 — 1,61	131a	1,182 — 1,185	145a	4,9 — 4,11
117b	1,61 — 1,64	131b	1,185 — 1,188	145b	4,11 — 4,17
118a	1,65 — 1,67	132a	1,189 — 1,192	146a	4,17 — 4,22
118b	1,67 — 1,70	132b	1,192 — 1,194	146b	4,22 — 4,27
119a	1,70 — 1,70	133a	1,194 — 1,196	147a	4,27 — 4,31
119b	1,70 — 1,71	133b	1,196 — 1,198	147b	4,31 — 4,34
120a	1,71 — 1,75	134a	1,198 — 1,201	148a	4,34 — 4,39
120b	1,76 — 1,78	134b	1,201 — 1,203	148b	4,39 — 4,41
121a	1,78 — 1,82	135a	1,203 — 1,206	149a	4,41 — 4,45
121b	1,82 — 1,86	135b	1,206 — 1,209	149b	4,45 — 4,50
122a	1,87 — 1,88	136a	1,209 — 1,210	150a	4,50 — 4,53
122b	1,89 — 1,94	136b	1,210 — 1,212	150b	4,53 — 4,56

151a	4,56	–	5,2	179a	9,80	–	9,86	207a	13,12	– 13,15
151b	5,2	–	5,6	179b	9,86	–	9,88	207b	13,16	– 13,19
152a	5,6	–	6,3	180a	9,88	–	9,94	208a	13,19	– 13,24
152b	6,3	–	6,6	180b	9,94	–	9,98	208b	13,24	– 13,24
153a	6,6	–	6,7	181a	9,98	–	9,99	209a	14,1	– 14,6
153b	7,1	–	7,3	181b	9,100	–	9,104	209b	14,6	– 14,13
154a	7,3	–	7,8	182a	9,104	–	9,108	210a	14,14	– 14,17
154b	7,8	–	7,13	182b	9,109	–	9,115	210b	14,17	– 14,23
155a	7,13	–	7,16	183a	9,115	–	9,126	211a	14,23	– 14,29
155b	7,16	–	7,18	183b	9,126	–	9,136	211b	14,29	– 14,37
156a	7,18	–	7,21	184a	9,137	–	9,146	212a	14,37	– 14,42
156b	blank			184b	9,146	–	9,150	212b	14,42	– 15,2
157a	8,1	–	8,2	185a	9,150	–	9,157	213a	15,2	– 15,7
157b	8,3	–	8,7	185b	9,157	–	9,164	213b	15,7	– 15,11
158a	8,7	–	8,8	186a	9,164	–	9,169	214a	15,11	– 15,17
158b	8,8	–	8,11	186b	9,169	–	9,177	214b	15,17	– 15,25
159a	8,11	–	8,13	187a	9,177	–	9,182	215a	15,25	– 16,1
159b	8,14	–	8,17	187b	9,183	–	9,190	215b	16,1	– 16,6
160a	8,17	–	8,21	188a	9,190	–	9,196	216a	17,1	– 17,8
160b	8,21	–	8,24	188b	9,196	–	9,200	216b	17,8	– 17,13
161a	8,25	–	8,29	189a	9,200	–	9,212	217a	17,14	– 17,18
161b	8,29	–	8,34	189b	9,212	–	9,223	217b	17,18	– 17,24
162a	8,34	–	8,39	190a	9,223	–	9,232	218a	17,24	– 17,31
162b	8,39	–	8,45	190b	9,232	–	9,234	218b	17,32	– 17,38
163a	8,45	–	8,47	191a	10,1	–	10,3	219a	17,38	– 17,43
163b	8,47	–	8,52	191b	10,4	–	10,6	219b	17,44	– 17,52
164a	8,53	–	8,56	192a	10,7	–	10,10	220a	17,52	– 17,55
164b	8,57	–	8,61	192b	10,11	–	10,15	220b	17,56	– 17,62
165a	8,61	–	8,64	193a	10,15	–	10,19	221a	17,62	– 17,65
165b	8,64	–	8,69	193b	10,20	–	10,20	221b	18,1	– 19,2
166a	8,69	–	8,77	194a	10,21	–	10,23	222a	19,3	– 19,8
166b	8,78	–	8,84	194b	10,24	–	10,28	222b	19,9	– 19,11
167a	8,84	–	8,90	195a	10,28	–	10,30	223a	19,11	– 19,15
167b	8,90	–	8,95	195b	10,30	–	10,33	223b	19,16	– 19,20
168a	8,95	–	8,99	196a	10,33	–	10,37	224a	19,21	– 19,25
168b	8,99	–	8,103	196b	10,38	–	10,42	224b	19,26	– 19,32
169a	8,103	–	8,107	197a	10,42	–	10,47	225a	19,32	– 19,36
169b	8,108	–	8,110	197b	10,48	–	10,55	225b	19,36	– 20,1
170a	8,110	–	8,116	198a	10,55	–	10,59	226a	20,1	– 20,6
170b	8,117	–	8,121	198b	10,60	–	10,65	226b	20,6	– 20,8
171a	8,121	–	8,126	199a	10,66	–	10,71	227a	20,8	– 20,10
171b	8,127	–	8,132	199b	10,71	–	10,74	227b	20,10	– 20,14
172a	8,132	–	8,137	200a	10,74	–	10,80	228a	20,14	– 20,19
172b	8,137	–	8,138	200b	10,80	–	10,85	228b	20,19	– 20,24
173a	9,1	–	9,4	201a	10,86	–	10,90	229a	20,24	– 20,29
173b	9,6	–	9,9	201b	10,91	–	11,1	229b	20,29	– 20,34
174a	9,9	–	9,13	202a	11,1	–	12,1	230a	20,35	– 21,2
174b	9,13	–	9,23	202b	12,1	–	12,6	230b	21,2	– 21,5
175a	9,24	–	9,28	203a	12,7	–	12,17	231a	21,5	– 21,8
175b	9,28	–	9,31	203b	12,17	–	12,24	231b	21,8	– 21,12
176a	9,32	–	9,42	204a	12,25	–	12,30	232a	21,13	– 21,16
176b	9,42	–	9,49	204b	12,30	–	12,34	232b	21,17	– 21,21
177a	9,49	–	9,59	205a	12,34	–	12,42	233a	21,22	– 21,25
177b	9,59	–	9,70	205b	12,42	–	13,3	233b	21,25	– 21,27
178a	9,70	–	9,75	206a	13,3	–	13,7	234a	21,28	– 21,31
178b	9,75	–	9,80	206b	13,7	–	13,12	234b	21,32	– 21,37

235a 22,1 – 22,6	250a 31,15 – 31,17	265a 48,3 – 48,8
235b 22,6 – 22,13	250b 31,17 – 31,22	265b 49,1 – 49,5
236a 22,13 – 22,21	251a 31,22 – 31,28	266a 49,5 – 49,9
236b 22,21 – 22,23	251b 31,28 – 31,33	266b 50,1 – 50,5
237a 23,1 – 23,4	252a 31,34 – 31,37	267a 50,6 – 50,10
237b 23,4 – 23,8	252b 31,38 – 31,40	267b 50,10 – 51,3
238a 23,8 – 23,12	253a 31,41 – 31,44	268a 51,3 – 51,8
238b 23,12 – 23,16	253b 31,44 – 31,45	268b 51,8 – 52,2
239a 23,16 – 23,18	254a 32,1 – 32,3	269a 52,3 – 54,1
239b 24,1 – 24,5	254b 32,3 – 32,7	269b 54,1 – 56,2
240a 24,5 – 24,7	255a 32,7 – 33,2	270a 56,3 – 57,3
240b 24,7 – 25,1	255b 33,2 – 33,6	270b 58,1 – 59,1
241a 25,2 – 25,7	256a 34,1 – 34,3	271a 59,1 – 61,1
241b 25,7 – 25,12	256b 34,3 – 34,6	271b 61,1 – 62,2
242a 25,12 – 25,17	257a 34,6 – 34,9	272a 62,2 – 64,4
242b 25,17 – 25,25	257b 34,9 – 34,15	272b 64,5 – 65,7
243a 25,25 – 26,1	258a 34,15 – 34,19	273a 65,8 – 65,16
243b 26,1 – 26,3	258b 34,20 – 35,3	273b 65,16 – 66,5
244a 26,3 – 26,5	259a 35,3 – 35,8	274a 66,5 – 66,16
244b 26,5 – 27,2	259b 35,8 – 35,13	274b 66,16 – 66,26
245a 27,2 – 28,2	260a 35,13 – 35,18	275a 66,27 – 66,39
245b 29,1 – 29,5	260b 35,18 – 36,5	275b 66,40 – 66,46
246a 29,5 – 29,8	261a 36,5 – 36,7	276a 66,47 – 66,56
246b 29,8 – 29,11	261b 37,1 – 37,3	276b 66,57 – 66,66
247a 30,1 – 30,4	262a 38,1 – 39,1	277a 66,66 – 66,73
247b 30,4 – 31,1	262b 39,1 – 40,1	277b 66,73 – 66,81
248a 31,2 – 31,5	263a 41,1 – 43,2	278a 66,81 – 66,86
248b 31,5 – 31,6	263b 43,2 – 45,1	278b 66,86 – 66,91
249a 31,6 – 31,10	264a 46,1 – 47,6	279a 66,91 – 66,99
249b 31,10 – 31,15	264b 47,6 – 48,3	279b 66,99 – 66,105
		280a 66,106 – 66,108

TECHNICAL TERMS

Most of the words expressing measurements have to be transliterated. Translation may not, however, dodge other problems by the use of obsolete or made-up words which do not exist in modern English. The translations here used are given below in italics. They cannot be exact; they aim at the nearest modern equivalent.

ANTECESSOR. Person whom a tenant had followed in the rightful possession of his holding; also the previous holder of an office. *predecessor*

BORDARIUS. Cultivator of inferior status, usually with a little land. *smallholder*

CARUCA. A plough, with the oxen who pulled it, usually reckoned as 8. *plough*

CARUCATA. A unit of land measurement, and probably in East Anglia also, a fiscal measurement. It is likely that there were 120 acres to the carucate. *carucate* (abbreviated to c.)

COMMENDATIO. (adj. COMMENDATUS). The situation in which a free man gave up rights over his land to someone who could guarantee his protection. *patronage*

CONSUETUDO. A fixed rent or service payable at regular intervals. *customary due*

DOMINIUM. The mastery or dominion of a lord (*dominus*); including ploughs, land, men, villages, etc., reserved for the lord's use; often concentrated in a home farm or demesne. *lordship*

FEUDUM. Continental variant, not used in England before 1066, of *feuum* (the Latin form of Old English *feoh*, cattle, money, possessions in general); either a landholder's holding, or land held under the terms of a specific grant. *Holding*

FIRMA. Old English *feorm*, provisions due to the King or lord; a fixed sum paid in place of these and of other miscellaneous dues. *revenue*

GELDUM. The principal royal tax, originally levied during the Danish wars. An East Anglian village was assessed in terms of the number of pence it was expected to contribute when its Hundred paid 20s. *tax*

GERSUMA. Any kind of extraordinary payment. *premium*

HUNDREDUM and DIMIDIUM HUNDREDUM. Administrative districts within a shire, each of whose assemblies of notables and village representatives usually met once a month. *Hundred* and *Half Hundred*

LETA. A more ancient fiscal and administrative division than the Domesday Hundred (cf. 1,71 note). *leet*

MANERIUM. A territorial and jurisdictional holding. *manor*

PRAEPOSITUS. Old English *gerefa*, a local official of the King or lord. *reeve*

SACA and SOCA. 'Sake and Soke', the right to collect profits of justice, and probably also the right to hold a private court, granted away by the King to a subject. *full jurisdiction*. 'Sake', from the Old English *sacu*, dispute, accusation or prosecution for crime. 'Soke', from the Old English *socn*, seeking, obligation to come to court comparable with the Latin *quaestio*. Both terms are also found standing on their own, although 'soke' is used much more frequently. 'Sake' is found standing alone in LDB Norfolk twice, 11,3 and 20,3, and in LDB Suffolk five times, 14,75 (twice); 16,35; 25,30; 31,47. In practice either term on its own or the two together seem to have had much the same meaning, although 'soke' had a wider context than 'sake', since it also conveyed the sense of the territory in which *soca* was exercised. Both terms standing alone have been translated *jurisdiction*. See further F. E. Harmer, *Anglo-Saxon writs* (Manchester 1952), 73-74; F. W. Maitland, *Domesday Book and beyond* (Cambridge 1897), 84, 97.

SOCA FALDAE. The right of the lord to make his tenants pen their sheep in his fold so he might have the benefit of the manure. *fold-rights*

SOCHEMANNUS. 'Soke-man', liable to attend the court of a *soca* and serve its lord; before 1066 often with more land and higher status than villagers; bracketed in the Commissioners' brief with the *liber homo* (*free man*). In LDB the distinction between the sochemannus and *liber homo* is often drawn but what the distinction was is not clear although the latter is used to denote both peasants and men of obviously higher rank whilst the former was seldom if ever a man of wealth. Together they formed a very large proportion of the rural population of East Anglia; see further F. W. Maitland, *Domesday Book and beyond* (Cambridge 1897), 104-107. *Sochemannus* has been translated *Freeman*

TEINUS or TEIGNUS. Person of superior status; originally one of the King's military companions, later often in his service in an administrative capacity. *thane*

T.R.E. *tempore regis Edwardi*, in King Edward's time. *before 1066*

VILLA. Translating Old English *tun*, estate, town, village. The later distinction between a small *village* and large *town* was not yet in use in 1066. *village* or *town*

VILLANUS. Member of a *villa*, usually with more land than a *bordarius*. *villager*

VIRGATA. A quarter of a hide: 30 fiscal acres in DB. *virgate*